FOR DUMMIES
BESTSELLING BOOK SERIES

Office XP 9 in 1 Desk Reference For Dummies®

Cheat Sheet

A Typical Office Scene

Office consists of a number of applications, but they all look eerily similar. This figure shows the parts of the Office screen that are common to all Office applications.

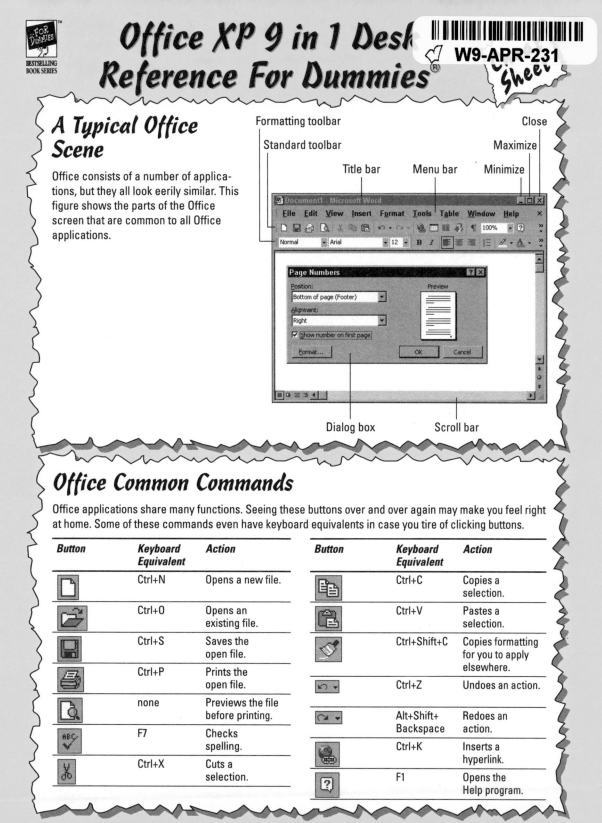

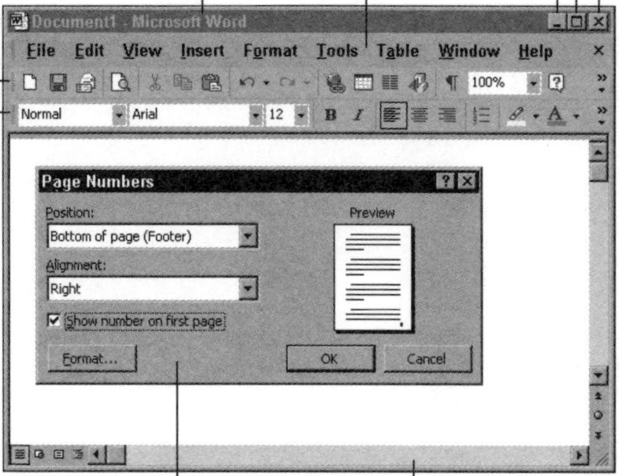

Office Common Commands

Office applications share many functions. Seeing these buttons over and over again may make you feel right at home. Some of these commands even have keyboard equivalents in case you tire of clicking buttons.

Button	Keyboard Equivalent	Action
	Ctrl+N	Opens a new file.
	Ctrl+O	Opens an existing file.
	Ctrl+S	Saves the open file.
	Ctrl+P	Prints the open file.
	none	Previews the file before printing.
	F7	Checks spelling.
	Ctrl+X	Cuts a selection.

Button	Keyboard Equivalent	Action
	Ctrl+C	Copies a selection.
	Ctrl+V	Pastes a selection.
	Ctrl+Shift+C	Copies formatting for you to apply elsewhere.
	Ctrl+Z	Undoes an action.
	Alt+Shift+Backspace	Redoes an action.
	Ctrl+K	Inserts a hyperlink.
	F1	Opens the Help program.

For Dummies: Bestselling Book Series for Beginners

Office XP 9 in 1 Desk Reference For Dummies®

Cheat Sheet

Office Survival Glossary

Being productive in Office isn't so hard, especially if you can figure out some of the lingo. The following brief glossary introduces some of the vocabulary that you may encounter and need to know:

application: A techie way of saying *program.* (Word is an application, for example.)

check box: A square box (next to an option) inside a dialog box. Click the box to place a check mark there and activate the option. Click again to remove the check mark.

click: To press the left mouse button once. If you need to click the right mouse button, you are asked to *right-click.*

Clipboard: The place in your system memory where the program stores items that you cut or copy from one place to another. The Clipboard can hold 24 items.

default: The built-in setting. In a dialog box, the default setting is the one that an application uses unless you tell it to do something else.

dialog box: A box that appears on-screen if the program you're working in needs more information to complete a task. Fill in the dialog box and click the OK button to give a command.

drop-down list: In a dialog box or on a toolbar, a control (marked by an upside-down triangle) that you can click to reveal more options.

formatting: The process of changing the appearance of something. In Word, for example, you may italicize text and thereby change its formatting. In Excel, you may add background color to a column.

shortcut menu: A menu that appears after you right-click something. Which shortcut menu you see depends on the item that you right-click.

toolbar: An assortment of buttons for performing tasks. Toolbars usually appear at the top of the screen, but you can drag them and reposition them elsewhere.

ToolTip: If you run your mouse pointer over a toolbar button, a little text box pops up displaying a reminder of what the button is or does.

Wizard: A series of dialog boxes that assist you in performing an operation.

The Three-Fingered Salute

Press Ctrl+Alt+Del when a program stops operating. With luck, you can get out of the frozen program without having to quit other open programs or reboot the computer. After you press Ctrl+Alt+Del, the Close Program dialog box appears. It lists all open programs, including the one that isn't responding. Click the name of the unresponsive program and click the End Task button.

Item 0819-9.
For more information about Wiley Publishing, call 1-800-762-2974.

For Dummies: Bestselling Book Series for Beginners

Office XP

9 IN 1 DESK REFERENCE

FOR DUMMIES®

Office XP
9 IN 1 DESK REFERENCE
FOR DUMMIES®

by Greg Harvey, Peter Weverka, John Walkenbach, Alison Barrows, Bill Dyszel, Camille McCue, Damon Dean, Jim McCarter

Edited by Peter Weverka

WILEY

Wiley Publishing, Inc.

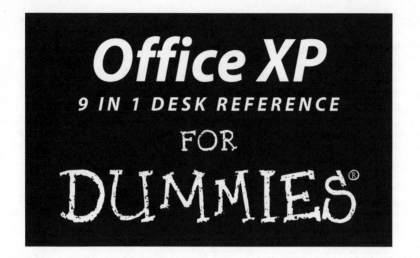

Office XP 9 in 1 Desk Reference For Dummies®

Published by
Wiley Publishing, Inc.
909 Third Avenue
New York, NY 10022
www.wiley.com

For general information on our other products and services or to obtain technical support, please contact our Customer Care Department within the U.S. at 800-762-2974, outside the U.S. at 317-572-3993, or fax 317-572-4002.

Wiley also publishes its books in a variety of electronic formats. Some content that appears in print may not be available in electronic books.

Library of Congress Cataloging-in-Publication Data:

Library of Congress Control Number: 2001086568

ISBN: 0-7645-0819-9

Manufactured in the United States of America

10 9 8 7 6 5 4

1B/RT/QS/QT/IN

Acknowledgments

Hungry Minds, Inc., gratefully acknowledges the contributions of these authors and contributing writers: Greg Harvey, Peter Weverka, John Walkenbach, Alison Barrows, Bill Dyszel, Camille McCue, Damon Dean, Jim McCarter, Colin Banfield, and Paul Sanna. Peter Weverka's developmental and editorial expertise and keen awareness of our readers served to make this book an invaluable resource. In addition, Hungry Minds gratefully acknowledges Bill Helling and Constance Carlisle for their editorial contributions to the first edition of this book.

Publisher's Acknowledgments

We're proud of this book; please send us your comments through our Online Registration Form located at www.dummies.com/register.

Some of the people who helped bring this book to market include the following:

Acquisitions, Editorial, and Media Development

Senior Project Editor: Jodi Jensen

(Previous Edition: Constance Carlisle)

Senior Acquisitions Editor: Steven H. Hayes

Copy Editor: Jeremy Zucker

Technical Editor: Lee Musick

Editorial Manager: Kyle Looper

Editorial Assistant: Jean Rogers

Production

Project Coordinator: Maridee Ennis

Layout and Graphics: Joe Bucki, Jill Piscitelli, Brian Torwelle, Erin Zeltner

Proofreaders: Jennifer Mahern, Nancy Price, Linda Quigley, Marianne Santy

Indexer: Ty Koontz

Special Help:

William A Barton

Publishing and Editorial for Technology Dummies

Richard Swadley, Vice President and Executive Group Publisher
Andy Cummings, Vice President and Publisher
Mary C. Corder, Editorial Director

Publishing for Consumer Dummies

Diane Graves Steele, Vice President and Publisher
Joyce Pepple, Acquisitions Director

Composition Services

Gerry Fahey, Vice President of Production Services
Debbie Stailey, Director of Composition Services

Contents at a Glance

Cartoons at a Glance

By Rich Tennant

page 69

page 307

page 513

page 769

page 673

page 429

page 7

page 211

page 723

page 601

Cartoon Information:
Fax: 978-546-7747
E-Mail: richtennant@the5thwave.com
World Wide Web: www.the5thwave.com

Table of Contents

Introduction

Microsoft just doesn't let up. For your computing convenience, Microsoft is again bundling some of its most useful software products into Microsoft Office. If you're finally getting familiar with Office 2000, the previous version of Office, don't despair. A lot of what you already know carries over to the new kid on the block. But what if you've never used a Microsoft Office product before and can't tell a Word document from an Excel worksheet? Well, you're still in the right place, because this book doesn't start over your head.

Microsoft Office is a powerful bundle of software, to be sure. You can write a report, make a spreadsheet, design a database, organize a presentation, create a Web page, and do much, much more. What's new in this edition of Office? Well, Microsoft has made a number of improvements here and there. The interface now includes something known as the *task pane,* a mini-window where you can search for files, import clip art, and perform other tasks as well. Collaboration is the keyword in this version of Office. You get many new tools for collaborating. You can use foreign-language text and even make translations. In keeping with trends from earlier versions, you can create Web pages much more easily. Most important of all, the programs are more integrated than ever. Trading data between Office programs now goes more smoothly. And you find common tools all across the board in the Office programs.

In case you didn't know, all the Office programs run under the Windows operating system. If you've never used a Windows operating system before, welcome aboard. I don't leave you behind, either. With just a little help, you can find out how to manage your files and folders within Windows. And as an added benefit, the knowledge and experience that you pick up in Windows — or in any of the Office XP products — applies to all the other Windows programs, too. What a deal!

About This Book

Office XP 9 in 1 Desk Reference For Dummies is intended to serve as a reference for all the great things (and maybe a few not-so-great things) that you may need to know when using Windows or any of the Microsoft Office programs: Word, Excel, Access, Outlook, PowerPoint, FrontPage, and Publisher. You can go out and buy one different book for Windows and one for each of the Office products, but who's going to carry them home for you? (And think of the shelf space you'd need!) *Office XP 9 in 1 Desk Reference For Dummies* doesn't pretend to be a comprehensive reference. It doesn't cover every nook and cranny of the Office programs. Instead, this book shows you how to get up and running fast so that you have more time to do the things that you really want to do.

Office XP 9 in 1 Desk Reference For Dummies strives to include in one book all the important details that you can probably locate in individual books but really want to find in one source. This book consists of several smaller books — or minibooks, so to speak. Whenever you make one big thing out of several smaller things, confusion is always a possibility, right? That's why *Office XP 9 in 1 Desk Reference For Dummies* gives you what I call *multiple access points* (or should I call them *MAPs?*) to help you find what you want. Each minibook presents its own parts page that includes a Contents at a Glance. Useful running heads (the text that you find at the very top of a page) abound. And who can overlook those handy thumb tabs with minibook and chapter information? Finally, a small index can be found at the end of each minibook — and that's in addition to the regular index at the end of the entire book.

Who Are You?

Although making too many assumptions about readers is a dangerous thing, you very possibly fit into more than one of the following categories:

- ✦ You've never used a Windows-based computer but you want to get a start in Windows and all those Office products.
- ✦ You've used a Windows-based computer before as well as some Office programs, but you never really got the hang of them before Windows 2000 or Windows Me and Office came on the scene.
- ✦ You have no idea what Microsoft Office really is, but someone told you that the software you need to use — Word, Excel, and so on — belongs to this package.
- ✦ You may have heard about all those power users who can take full advantage of the integrated products from Microsoft Office, and you want to join their ranks.
- ✦ You think that you know everything about Windows and Microsoft Office — and you probably know a lot — but you need a good reference in case your memory fails you (say, your boss asks you to design a new presentation by tomorrow morning or your kid's sixth-grade science project really needs a neat chart).

What this book doesn't assume is that you're a dummy. Unfortunately, the Microsoft products don't operate themselves (just yet), and the way to do things isn't always evident. You don't have time to hunt down a Microsoft

Certified System Engineer, and guessing which button to push isn't an option that you care for. If you want to help yourself quickly and easily, this book is the one for you.

How to Use This Book

You can probably find out a lot by reading this entire book in order from cover to cover as if it were a Tolstoy novel. Resist that urge. You can gain much more by simply going to the part that holds the information that you need. That's right; jump around, as necessary, according to your whims and desires. And just try reading a Tolstoy novel that way!

This book acts as a reference so that you can locate what you want to know, get in, and do something as quickly as possible. In this book, you can find concise descriptions introducing important concepts, task-oriented topics to help you realize what you need to do, and step-by-step instructions where necessary to show you the way.

At times, this book presents you with specific ways of performing certain actions. If you must use a menu command, for example, you may see something that looks like this:

File⇨Save

This phrase simply means to use the mouse to open the File menu and choose the Save command on that menu. You place the mouse pointer on the word File, click the left mouse button, move the pointer down to the word Save in the menu that appears, and click. If you look closely, you can see some underlined letters in the words *File* and *Save*. Those letters are the keyboard *hot keys* for the command. To use a keyboard hot key, first press the Alt key and then release it. Next press the actual letter to open that menu. (In the case of File, you press F.)

At other times, this book may ask you to use specific keyboard shortcuts. These shortcuts are key combinations, such as the following:

Ctrl+X

This shortcut means to press and hold the Ctrl key as you press the X key. Then release both keys together. (No, don't attempt to type a plus sign!)

When you're asked to click or double-click something, this book assumes that you haven't changed your mouse settings. In this case, if you're told to click something, use the left mouse button. Any time you need to use the right mouse button, you're specifically told to *right-click*.

How This Book Is Organized

Each of the minibooks in *Office XP 9 in 1 Desk Reference For Dummies* can stand alone. Remember that each offers a Contents at a Glance and an index. The first minibook covers Windows, the operating system under which all the Office products run. After that, the Office minibooks fall into a rough order of popularity among Office users until you come to Book 9, which covers a few common Office techniques that you can use in all or most of the programs. But you should be jumping around anyway, according to what you need to do. The order in which these minibooks appear is merely a publishing convenience, not a recommendation as to the order in which books should be read. The following sections, then, give you a brief description of what you can find in each minibook.

Windows

In this minibook, you get a brief overview of all the basic features in Windows 98 and Windows Me, from taskbars and toolbars to dialog boxes and menus. Find out how to manage your files and folders as well as manipulate your desktop.

Word 2002

Word is the most powerful word-processing program around! By using Word, you can create something as simple as a memo or as complex as a 1,000-page novel complete with a table of contents and an index.

Excel 2002

So you want to get something done with a spreadsheet and make some fancy charts to boot? Ask Excel to give you a hand. This minibook tells you what you need to know to get going fast.

Access 2002

Don't let the mention of databases scare you any longer. By using this minibook, you can uncover the fundamentals of a great database program that does everything for you except enter data. (That's your job.)

Outlook 2002

Who doesn't need e-mail, a time-managing calendar, a tasks list, a contacts organizer, and the like? Outlook helps you keep up in this fast-paced world, and this minibook is your entry pass.

PowerPoint 2002

PowerPoint enables you to create those great-looking presentations that impressed you in the past. This minibook helps you on your way toward slides and overheads — and why not throw in a graph and a chart while you're at it?

FrontPage 2002

In this minibook, you find out how easy and painless it is to make a Web page. FrontPage helps you every step of the way, from inserting hyperlinks to adding impressive graphics.

Publisher 2002

If you ever wanted to produce some of those nice publications that desktop-publishing programs turn out, you can take advantage of Publisher. By using this program, you, too, can become a desktop publisher.

Bringing It All Together

This minibook offers a handful of techniques that you can use in most, if not all, the Office programs. You find out how to search for files, trade data among different Office programs, use Microsoft Graph to create charts, use the Microsoft Clip Organizer to manage and insert media files, and draw lines and shapes by using the drawing tools.

Appendix A

Because so many tasks are similar among the Office products and the management of Windows stuff applies across the board, this appendix can save you time (and us paper) by showing you the basics, such as starting an Office application and using the mouse. You can also get some advice on how to use the various Help features in Office. By eliminating repeated information, we can reduce your déjà vu experiences.

Appendix B

If you compose that Word document or create that Excel spreadsheet (or any other Office product), you probably want to print it, too. Although some Office applications have very specific printing demands here and there, the general printing routine is pretty much the same for all of them. Appendix B gets you going in printing your creations.

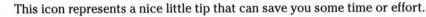

Icons Used in This Book

Icons are peppered throughout this book, but not in any haphazard manner! The following icons signal special information:

This icon represents a nice little tip that can save you some time or effort.

Heads up! This icon signals a potential problem or danger for you to avoid.

Just a reminder: This information may prove worth keeping in mind.

This icon points out something that may help you with common tasks — if you apply the advice to what you're doing.

The different Office programs work well together by design, and this icon helps to remind you of this capability!

This icon shows you a fast and efficient way to perform a task.

Book I

Windows

The 5th Wave — By Rich Tennant

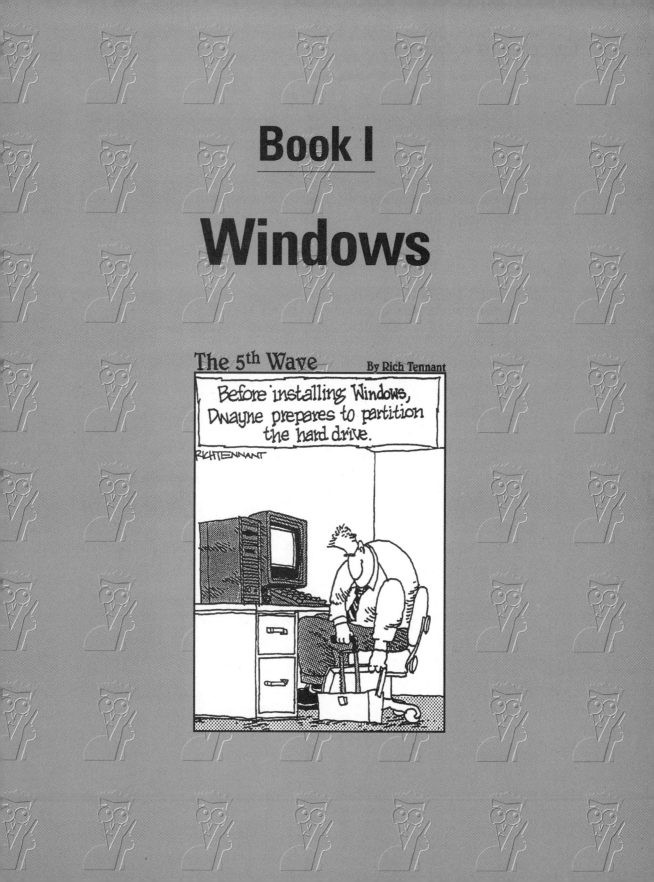

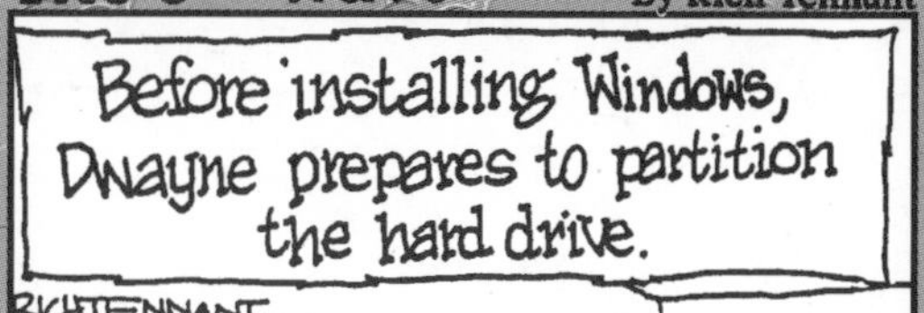

Before installing Windows,
Dwayne prepares to partition
the hard drive.
RICHTENNANT

Contents at a Glance

Chapter 1: Getting to Know the Windows Desktop

In This Chapter

- **Becoming comfortable with the Windows desktop**
- **Recognizing icons**
- **Clicking and opening icons**
- **Checking out some standard Windows icons**

If you've used an early version of Windows, such as Windows 95, welcome back to somewhat the same look and feel — with a few added features. If you're a complete novice, you're also in the right place. To get along in the world of Windows 98 or Windows Me, you need to feel comfortable with the Windows desktop — the screen where you eventually end up after you start your computer. And what's the most common element that populates the desktop? Those pretty little pictures called *icons*.

This chapter introduces you to desktop basics and gets you started on working with icons. By the way, it doesn't matter which version of Windows you use with Office. Office is on good terms with all of them.

Windows Desktop

The *Windows desktop* is the background against which all the action takes place. The desktop contains the standard Windows icons such as My Computer, Recycle Bin, and the like (which I explain later in this chapter). In addition, the desktop area holds all the shortcut icons that you may create. (See Chapter 6 for the lowdown on shortcuts.) Finally, the desktop also contains the Windows taskbar (which you can read about in Chapter 2). See Figure 1-1 for a typical desktop.

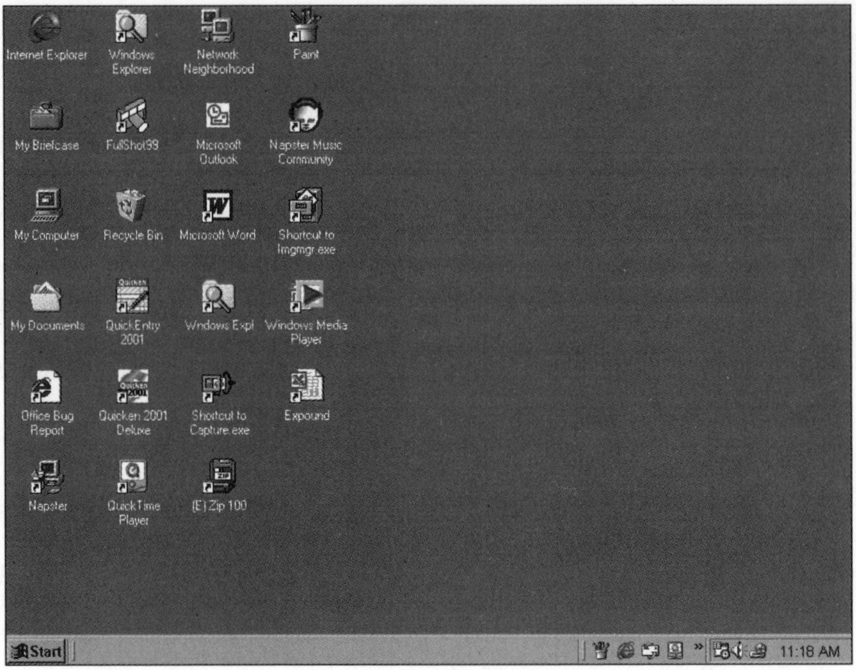

Figure 1-1: A typical Windows desktop in all its glory.

Although working with the Windows desktop isn't a high-maintenance routine, you should know how to manage your desktop and its icons to make your life a little easier. (You can find an explanation of icons later in this chapter.) The easiest way to manage your desktop is to use the desktop shortcut menu. You open this menu by right-clicking any open area of the desktop (off the taskbar and any icons), as shown in Figure 1-2. The shortcut menu contains the following commands, which enable you to customize the look and feel of the Windows desktop:

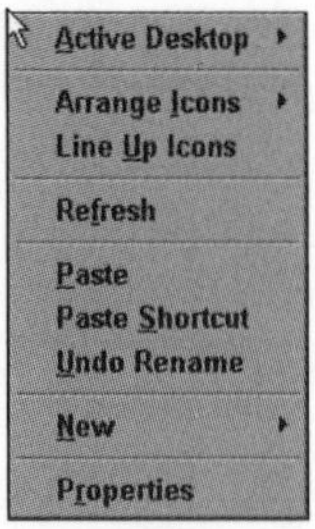

Figure 1-2: The desktop shortcut menu is only a right-click away.

✦ **Active Desktop:** Offers commands for making the desktop behave like a Web page (see Chapter 8); also opens the Display Properties dialog box so that you can change the look of the desktop (see Chapter 8).

- **Arrange Icons:** Enables you to arrange the desktop icons by Name, by Type, by Size, or by Date, or you can use Auto Arrange to have Windows arrange the icons into a tidy grid.
- **Line up Icons:** Also arranges the icons in a tidy grid. What's the difference between this command and Auto Arrange? With this one, you can slide the icons out of the gird, but when the Auto Arrange command holds sway, the icons stay in the grid no matter where you drag them.
- **Refresh:** Updates icons and Active Desktop items displayed on the desktop.
- **Paste:** Creates a shortcut to whatever document you're currently working on and pastes its icon onto the desktop. You can read about shortcuts in Chapter 6.
- **Paste Shortcut:** Pastes whatever shortcut you cut or copy to the Clipboard.
- **New:** Creates an empty folder, a file of a particular type (such as an Excel file or Word document), or a new shortcut. You can read about all this stuff in Chapter 6.
- **Properties:** Opens the Display Properties dialog box, where you can change display stuff, such as the video settings and windows color combinations.

Icons

Icons are the small pictures identifying the type of object (whether a disk drive, folder, file, or some other such thing) that you're dealing with in Windows. You run into icons everywhere you turn — they're all over the desktop, and the Internet Explorer 5 and My Computer windows are lousy with them.

TIP

Windows gives you a number of new ways to modify the appearance of the icons as well as to determine the order in which they appear on the desktop or within their window (a job that Windows usually does all by itself). See Chapter 3 for details.

It takes all types of icons

The icons that you encounter in Windows fall into one of the following types:

- **Disk icons:** Represent the various drives on your computer or drives that are currently connected to your computer.
- **File icons:** Represent the different types of documents that Windows uses and that the programs that you run on your computer produce.

✦ **Folder icons:** Represent the various directories that you have on your computer.

✦ **Windows component icons:** Represent the various modules that are running on your computer, such as the desktop, My Computer, Internet Explorer, and the Recycle Bin.

✦ **Program icons:** Represent the various executable programs that you've installed on your computer.

✦ **Shortcut icons:** Point to files, folders, Windows components, or executable programs located elsewhere on the computer.

Icons are made for clicking

All the icons that you meet in Windows are made for clicking with the mouse — you know, that little handheld gizmo that came with your computer. Table 1-1 shows the various mouse-click techniques that you employ on the icons you encounter in Windows.

Table 1-1 Clicking Icons

Name	*Mouse Action*
Click	Point the mouse pointer at the object and then press and quickly release the primary mouse button. The primary mouse button, whether you're right-or left-handed, is the one closest to your thumb.
Double-click	Press and release the primary mouse two times in rapid succession.
Right-click	Press and release the button that's not designated as your primary mouse button. This action often opens context menus and other goodies.
Drag-and-drop	First point to an object with the mouse pointer; then click and hold down the primary mouse button as you move the mouse to drag the object to a new position on-screen. Finally, let go of the mouse button to drop the object onto its new position. This action is quite useful if you're rearranging icons or moving files to the Recycle Bin.

Selecting and Opening Icons

One thing that you need to know as you handle icons is the difference between selecting an icon and opening an icon, as the following list describes:

✦ **Selecting:** Single-click the icon. You can tell that an icon's selected because it's highlighted.

✦ **Opening:** Double-click the icon to open its object. (See the section "It takes all types of icons," earlier in this chapter, for details on the different types of Windows objects.)

Pages on the World Wide Web, however, typically use a slightly different mouse-click scheme to differentiate between selecting and following (the equivalent of opening) *hyperlinks*, which attach to graphics or text on the Web page, as follows:

- **Selecting:** Move the mouse pointer over the hyperlink (which the mouse pointer's change to the hand icon indicates).
- **Opening:** Click (don't double-click) the hyperlink to follow the link. (Normally, following the link means to jump to another section of the page or to open a completely different Web page.)

With the addition of the Active Desktop to Windows (see Chapter 8 for full details) and its stated goal of marrying the Web to the Windows interface, you now can choose between selecting and opening Windows icons the normal way (single- and double-click) or the normal Web way (point at and click).

After Windows is first installed on your computer, the traditional, single- and double-click scheme is in effect. If you want to switch over and experiment with the Web point-and-click system, you can do so at any time by making a few simple modifications to the Folders Options. (See Chapter 8 for the fine points of putting this new system into effect.)

Selecting More Than One Icon at a Time

You may sometimes need to select more than one icon at a time, especially if these icons represent files and folders. You may want to drag a bunch of files from one folder to another, for example, or carry out a group delete without performing the same action for each icon.

First, you need to know which method you're using to select icons, as I explain in the preceding section. Next, you need to know whether the icons are *contiguous* or *noncontiguous,* which affects how you select more than one icon. So if you know which method you're using to select icons and whether these icons are contiguous or noncontiguous, the rest is simple! (The following sections provide the details.)

Selecting contiguous icons

Contiguous simply means that the icons appear next to each other. Actually seeing what icons lie next to each other is often a lot easier if you view the icons in a window in a list form (see Chapter 3). To select contiguous icons, follow these steps:

1. **Select the first icon in a group (either at the top or bottom of the list, which is a whole lot easier to see if the icons are in list form).**

2. **Press and hold the Shift key and then select the last icon in your group.**

   All the icons between the two files you select become your "selection," as shown in Figure 1-3.

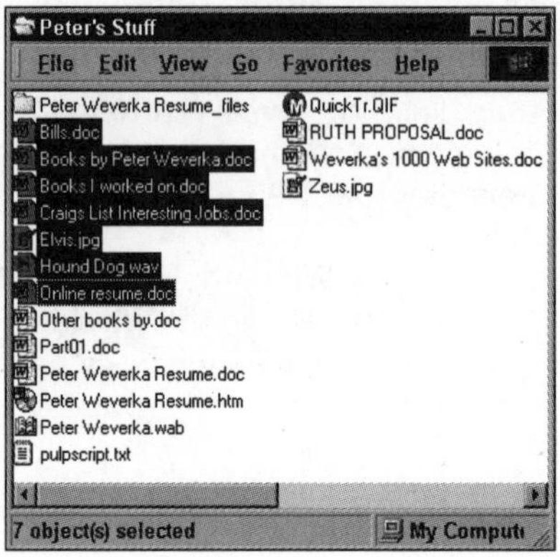

Figure 1-3: Selecting contiguous icons (if the ones you want are grouped together).

Selecting noncontiguous icons

Noncontiguous simply means that the icons are *not* all listed next to each other. Follow these steps to select noncontiguous icons.

1. **Select the first icon (select any icon; you need to start somewhere!).**
2. **Press and hold the Ctrl key and select each and every icon that you want.**

   All the icons that you select remain selected (as shown in Figure 1-4). If you slip up and select a file that you don't want, simply deselect it — which is simply a matter of reselecting it while still holding down the Ctrl key.

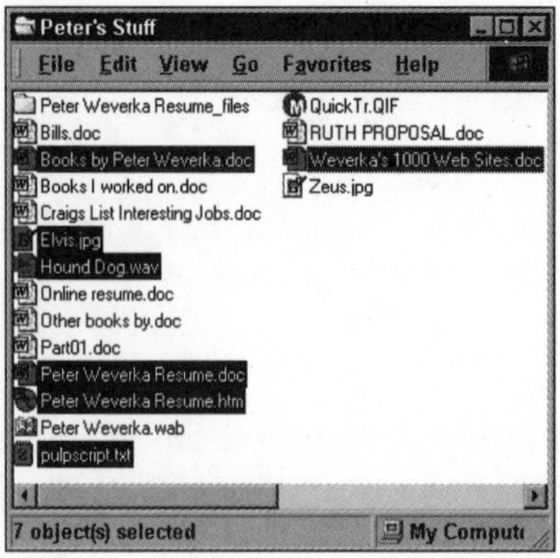

Figure 1-4: Selecting noncontiguous icons (if the ones you want are scattered here and there).

REAL WORLD

Lasso them icons

Have you ever seen how easily some of those cowboys and cowgirls in a rodeo can lasso a runaway steer? Well, you can do sort of the same thing with your icons without needing to whoop and holler — and your icons never try to run away from you. To select icons by lassoing, simply click outside the icons and, while holding down the mouse button, drag through the icons that you want to select. As you drag, you can see an ever-expanding rectangle that indicates your area of selection. The icons that you select become highlighted. After you let go of the mouse button, the icons remain selected. If you accidentally select an icon that you don't want, simply deselect it by clicking it with the Ctrl button held down or point to it with the Ctrl button held down (depending on whether your selection method is traditional or Web-based, as I explain in the section "Selecting and Opening Icons," earlier in this chapter).

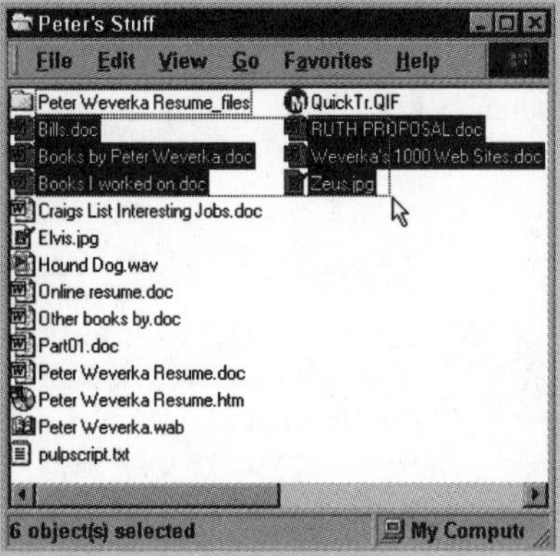

Standard Desktop Icons

After you install Windows, you notice that the desktop is littered with a few icons that enable you to perform some essential tasks. This section gives a brief overview of some standard desktop icons that every Windows user deals with at some time or another. Double-clicking an icon (or single-clicking, depending on your setup) opens the window, file, or folder (or whatever the icon represents!). You can also right-click an icon and select Open from the shortcut menu that appears.

My Computer

My Computer gives you quick access to all the major *local* components of your computer system. After you first open the My Computer window, it displays all the local drives attached to your computer, along with folders for your printers, Control Panel utilities, Dial-Up Networking connections, and regularly scheduled tasks (see Figure 1-5).

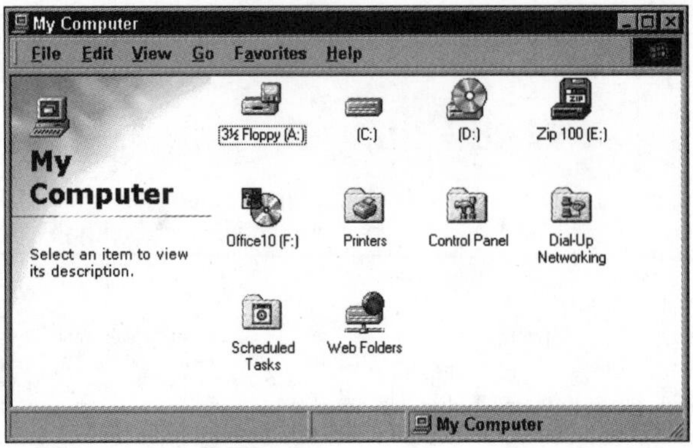

Figure 1-5: My Computer enables you to get to the innards of your computer.

Network Neighborhood (My Network Places)

The Network Neighborhood (it's called My Network Places in Windows Me) gives you an overview of all the workgroups, computers, and shared resources on your Local Area Network (LAN). It's a permanent resident on the desktop, whether you're on a LAN or not; you can open it to get a graphic view of the workgroups set up on your network and the resources that network together.

Recycle Bin

The Recycle Bin is the trashcan for Windows. Don't be confused by the "recycle" name; you're not going to put things in there for reuse. Anything that you delete in Windows goes into the Recycle Bin and stays there until you either retrieve the deleted item or empty the Recycle Bin. The only thing that you gain if you empty the Recycle Bin is the space that the deleted items took up. (See Chapter 7 for details about how to use the Recycle Bin.)

My Briefcase

My Briefcase enables you to synchronize versions of files from different computers or disks so that you don't drive yourself crazy trying to figure out which version of the file isn't as up-to-date as the other one.

Online Services

Microsoft's been kind enough to offer easy-access wizards for signing up with some of the largest Internet service providers (ISPs) in the country.

In the Online Services folder (which you open with the Online Services shortcut that appears on the desktop after you install Windows), you find icons that enable you to jump right online — assuming that you have a modem — and set up an account with any of several companies (including the Microsoft Network).

Chapter 2: Getting Started (And Stopped) in Windows

In This Chapter

- Using the taskbar
- Customizing the taskbar for your needs
- Launching and switching between programs
- Shutting down Windows

A journey of 1,000 miles begins with the first step, or so the saying goes, and you can usually find one of the best first steps in Windows at the bottom of the desktop screen. Customarily, this area is where the taskbar lurks, and from here you can begin your computer journey. This chapter shows you how to get things going and how to make the taskbar fit your computing needs. You also find out how to end any odyssey so that Windows continues to welcome you warmly on your future journeys.

Taskbar Basics

The taskbar forms the base of the Windows desktop. Running along the bottom — the complete width of the screen — the taskbar is divided into three sections: the *Start button* at the far left, with its accompanying Start menu that pops up when you click the button; buttons that display the names of open toolbars and windows in the center area; and, at the far right, the *system tray,* with icons that show the status of computer components, programs, and processes currently running in the background. Figure 2-1 shows you a typical taskbar.

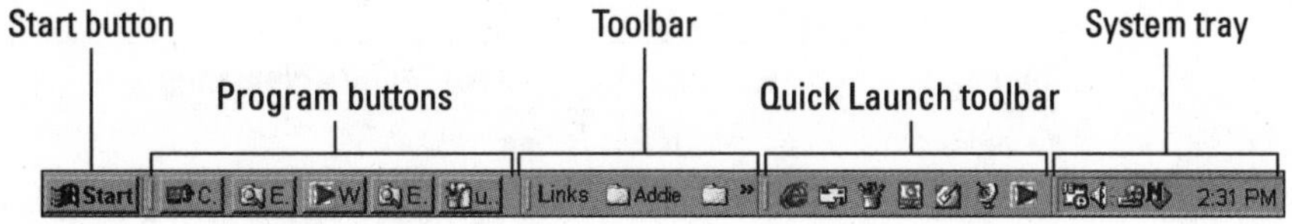

Figure 2-1: You'll spend many happy hours at the Windows taskbar.

Whenever you open a window or program on the Windows desktop, Windows adds a button representing that window or program to the center section of the taskbar. Clicking one of the window or program buttons on the taskbar brings its window, which is temporarily hidden behind others, to the front. So you can use the taskbar buttons to quickly switch between the programs you have running in open windows.

Starting off with the Start menu

The Start button that opens the Start menu always appears as the leftmost button on the taskbar. The Start menu is the most basic menu in Windows, containing almost all the commands you ever need to use. To open the Start menu (as shown in Figure 2-2), simply click the Start button in the corner of the taskbar or press Ctrl+Esc.

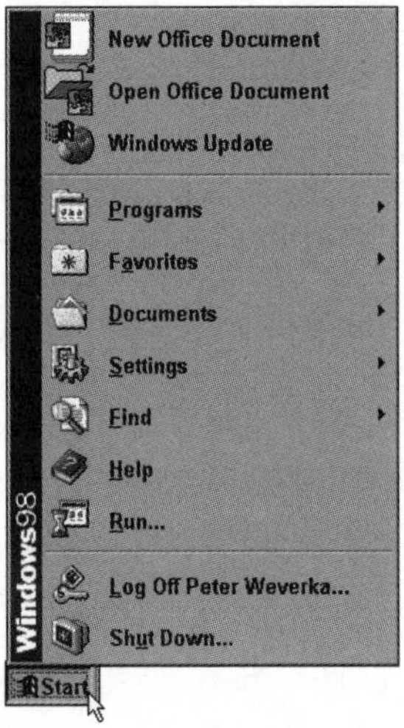

Figure 2-2: The Start menu gives you access to almost anything you want to do.

Table 2-1 lists the commands that you encounter on the Start menu (running from bottom to top). To select a command on the Start menu, just navigate to it with the mouse pointer and click.

Table 2-1 Start Menu Commands

Command	*What It Does*
Shut Down	Opens the Shut Down Windows dialog box, where you can either shut off the computer, restart the computer, restart the computer in MS-DOS mode (in Windows), or, in the case of some computers, put the computer on Standby, a kind of "sleep" mode that consumes less power if you leave your computer on for extended periods of time.

Command	*What It Does*
Log Off	On a Local Area Network (LAN), enables you to log off the current user so that you can then log on as yourself.
Run	Opens the Run dialog box, where you enter the pathname of the file, folder, program, or Internet resource that you want Windows to locate and open.
Help	Opens Windows Help, an online Help database that also includes Web elements so that you can jump to the Internet for even more help.
Search (Find)*	Opens a submenu with the following options: *Files or Folders,* to find particular files on local or networked disk drives; *Computer,* to find a particular computer on your network; *On the Internet,* to find a Web site on the Internet; *People,* to find a particular person or business in one of the online directories; or *Using Microsoft Outlook,* to open the Advanced Find dialog box and search for Office files (Word files, Excel files, and so on).
Settings	Opens a submenu with the following options: *Control Panel,* to open the Control Panel window; *Printers,* to open the Printers window; *Taskbar & Start Menu,* to open the Taskbar Properties dialog box, where you can modify the appearance of the Start menu and the taskbar. Windows 98 also offers options for displaying folder contents *(Folders Options);* for activating, customizing, and updating the Active Desktop *(Active Desktop);* and for updating Windows from a Web site *(Windows Update).* Windows Me also offers the *Dial Up Networking* option for connecting your computer to the Internet.
Documents	Opens a submenu containing shortcuts to the last 15 files you opened. You can purge this list from time to time by using the Taskbar Properties dialog box (choose Settings⇨Taskbar & Start Menu).
Favorites	Enables you to access the items designated as your favorite files, folders, Web channels, or Web pages (not found in Windows Me).
Programs	Opens a submenu containing all the programs installed on your computer at the time you installed Windows. You can control which programs appear on the Programs continuation menu by adding folders to or removing folders from the Programs folder.
Windows Update	Connects you to the Microsoft Web site, which then checks your computer system to see if your version of Windows needs updating, and, if you set it up to do so, automatically downloads and installs the new updated components.
Open Office Document	As long as Microsoft Office is installed on your computer, you can use this command to display the Open Office Document dialog box, where you can search the particular Office document (such as Word, Excel, PowerPoint, or Access) you want to open.
New Office Document	If Microsoft Office is installed on your computer, you can use this command to open a new Office document using one of many different types of templates available (Word, Web page, Excel, PowerPoint, Binder, or Access).

* This command is Find in Windows 98 and Search in Windows Me.

Taskbar toolbars for every taste

In case you feel as though you're suffering from a shortage of toolbars, Windows enables you to add such toolbars as the Address, Quick Launch, and Desktop toolbars to the center section of the taskbar. You can then use their buttons to accomplish routine tasks in Windows. See Chapter 4 for details on displaying and using these different toolbars.

System tray, anyone?

The system tray contains icons that indicate the current status of various physical components, such as a printer attached to a desktop computer, as well as the status of various programs or processes that run in the background, such as a virus-scanning program or the video display settings you're using. The system tray is a coveted piece of real estate. Sometimes when you install a new program on your computer, a new icon appears in the system tray.

To identify an icon that appears in the status area, position the mouse pointer over it until its *ToolTip* appears. A ToolTip is a word or two of explanation that sometimes appears in a bubble caption when you move the pointer over an icon. To change the status of an icon, right-click it to display its shortcut menu and then click the appropriate menu option.

Note: You can customize your taskbar so that it removes the clock, shows smaller icons, hides itself, and so on. You can also fool around with your Start menu. Click the Start button and choose Settings⇨Taskbar & Start Menu to get started. See the appropriate edition of *Windows For Dummies,* by Andy Rathbone (from IDG Books Worldwide, Inc.), for all the gory details.

Starting Your Programs

In Windows, you can open the programs that you've installed on your hard drive in any one of the following three ways:

- **Select the program on the Programs menu, which you open from the Start menu:** See the section "Starting off with the Start menu," earlier in this chapter, for information about the Start menu.
- **Open a shortcut to the program or to a document that you open regularly:** See Chapter 6 for information about creating shortcuts for opening a program or a file that in turn opens its associated program.
- **Open a file created with the program:** See Chapter 6 for information about opening a program by opening its file.

Alt+Tab your way between stuff on the taskbar

After you begin to open a few programs and folders, you may notice that your taskbar gets pretty full and you can't actually read much of the descriptive text on the buttons. If you like playing games, you can take a chance and guess which button belongs to which folder or which file is running under which program. If you want to greatly increase your odds of choosing the right button, however, press and hold the Alt key while you also press Tab. A dialog box appears and displays icons for each program and folder window you have open, along with text that describes the highlighted icon. Highlighted icons are indicated by a blue box surrounding the icon.

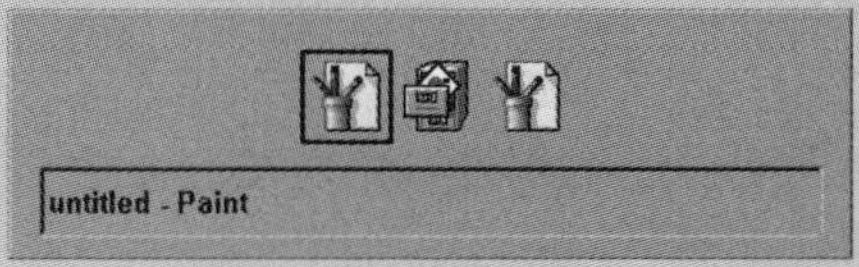

After you release both the Alt and Tab keys, Windows activates (brings onto your screen) whatever program or window was selected. To continue to switch among selections, press and hold down the Alt key again as you tap the Tab key.

Switching between Programs

The Windows taskbar makes switching between programs as easy as clicking the button representing the program's window. (Open folders are also represented on the taskbar.) To activate a program (or access an open folder) and bring its window to the top of your screen display, click the appropriate button on the taskbar.

Shutting Down Windows

Windows includes a shut-down procedure that you should follow before you turn off your machine. To shut down Windows so that you can safely shut off your computer and get on with your life, follow these steps:

1. **Click the Start button and then choose Shut Down from the Start menu to open the Shut Down Windows dialog box, as shown in Figure 2-3.**

2. **To completely shut down Windows and power down your computer, make sure that the Shut Down radio button is selected (in Windows 98) or the Shut Down option is chosen from the drop-down menu (in Windows Me); then click the OK button or press Enter.**

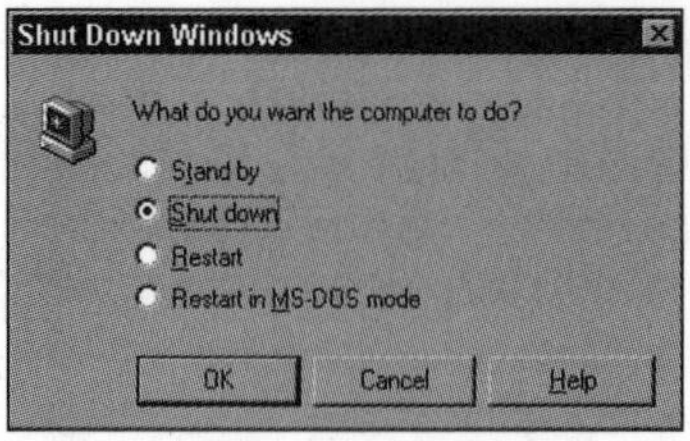

Figure 2-3: Shutting down Windows the correct way (in Windows 98).

In addition to the Shut Down option, you can select the following options in the Shut Down Windows dialog box:

- **Standby:** Choose this option if you want to put your computer into a deep sleep. (The option isn't available on all computers.) This mode powers down the computer but maintains the state of your desktop. In other words, the programs that were open when your computer started napping will be open when the nap is over.
- **Restart:** Choose this option if you need to restart the computer (which you often must do after installing a new piece of hardware or software, for example). You can also use this option in the unlikely event that Windows becomes so screwed up that you need to restart the whole shebang (if, for example, all the colors on the desktop get messed up and go all magenta and green on you).
- **Restart in MS-DOS mode:** Choose this options (available only in Windows 98) if you're inexplicably possessed by a need to type some DOS command or to take one last look at that ugly old DOS prompt.

Suppose you shut down Windows and nothing happens. In that case, give the three-fingered salute: Press Ctrl+Alt+Del. The Close Program dialog box appears. Click the Shut Down button.

Chapter 3: Working with Windows (Within Windows)

In This Chapter

- Working with those on-screen windows
- Manipulating windows
- Making Windows display icons the way you want
- Using My Computer and Windows Explorer
- Exploring Explorer bars

In this chapter, I dispense helpful information for the Windows newbie and the seasoned pro alike. If you're just starting out with the Windows operating system or need a refresher on its fundamentals, you've come to the right place. A lot of this information also applies to the programs that you use with Windows (and can read about in the rest of this book). This just may be your lucky day!

Windows (The On-Screen Type)

Windows — whether they're the windows that you see after you open a system window, such as My Computer, or a window from a program such as Word — contain various combinations of controls and features that you use to modify the window and, in the case of program windows, navigate a program. Figure 3-1 gives you an idea of a typical window.

The following list describes the features and controls you find on all your typical windows:

- **Title bar:** Identifies the program or file open in the window; it also houses the Control menu, which appears after you click the program's icon at the left end of the Title bar.
- **Menu bar:** Contains pull-down menus with commands specific to a program. (See Chapter 5 for more about menu bars.)

- **Minimize button:** Shrinks the window down to a button on the taskbar.

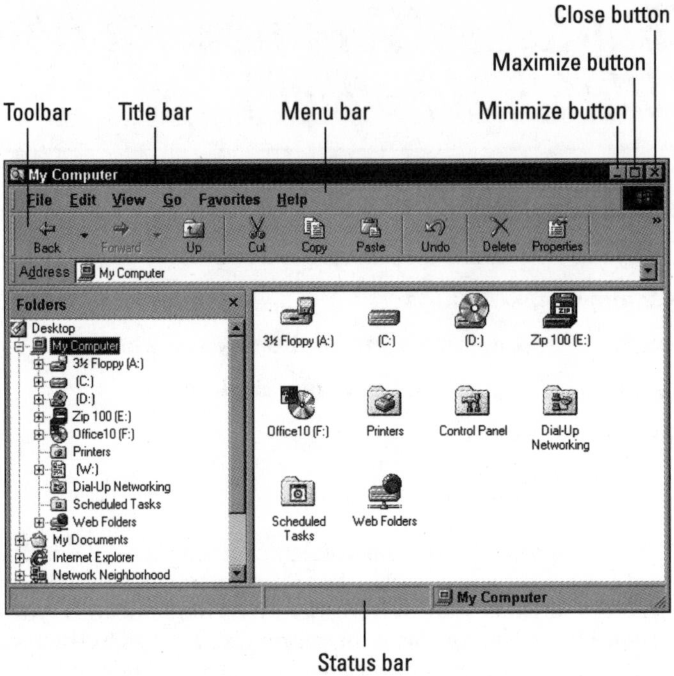

Figure 3-1: The anatomy of a window.

- **Maximize button:** Zooms the window up to full size; to restore a maximized window to its former size, click the Restore button that replaces the Maximize button.

- **Close button:** Closes the window and exits any program running in it.
- **Toolbars:** If the window is equipped with other toolbars, you usually find these extra toolbars below the menu bar.
- **Vertical scroll bar:** Enables you to vertically scroll new parts of the window into view by using the up and down arrows or by dragging the scroll button.
- **Horizontal scroll bar:** Lets you horizontally scroll new parts of the window into view by using the arrows or scroll button.
- **Status bar:** Gives you different sorts of information about the current state of the program.

Following are some basic tips on dealing with the windows that you encounter in Windows:

- A window must be active before you can select any of its commands or use any of its features. To activate a window, click it anywhere. The active window is immediately placed on top of the desktop and its title bar becomes highlighted.

- You can change the size of a window by dragging its borders with the mouse or by using the Size command. (See the section "Moving and Resizing Windows," later in this chapter.)
- To move a window on the desktop, position the mouse pointer somewhere on the window's title bar and click and drag the outline to the new location by using the mouse.
- If the window contains a toolbar button and you haven't a clue as to what the button does, point to the button with the mouse, and Windows displays a ToolTip containing the tool's name.

See Chapter 5 for the lowdown on this special type of window.

Moving and Resizing Windows

You can move windows around the desktop and resize them from full-screen (called *maximized*) all the way down to wee buttons on the taskbar (called *minimized*) at your convenience. To move a window, follow these steps:

1. **If necessary, restore the window to an in-between size, either by clicking the Restore Window button if the window is maximized or by clicking its taskbar button if the window is minimized.**
2. **Position the mouse pointer over the window's title bar.**
3. **Click and drag the outline of the window to its new location on the desktop.**
4. **Release the mouse button to drop the window in its new location on the desktop.**

To maximize a window, you can choose from the following two methods:

- Click the Maximize button on the window's title bar if the window appears at less than full size. (The Maximize button is the middle of the three buttons at the right side of the title bar.) Otherwise, click the window's taskbar button if the window is minimized.
- Choose Maximize from the window's Control menu (which you open by clicking the program's icon at the far left of the window's title bar).

Remember that, after you maximize a window, you can restore the window to its original size by taking one of the following two actions:

- Click the Restore button on the window's title bar. (The Restore button is the middle of the three buttons at the right side of the title bar.)
- Choose Restore from the window's Control menu (which you open by clicking the program's icon at the far left of the window's title bar).

To minimize a window to just a button on the taskbar, you can take either of the following actions:

- Click the Minimize button on the window's title bar. (The Minimize button is the one with the minus sign, the leftmost of the three buttons at the right side of the title bar.)
- Choose Minimize from the window's Control menu (which you open by clicking the program's icon at the far left of the window's title bar).

In addition to using the automatic sizing controls, you can manually size a window (assuming that it's not currently minimized or maximized) by dragging any of its sides or corners. You can always tell whether you can move one or more of the sides of a window by dragging, because the mouse pointer changes from the standard pointer to a double-headed arrow.

Arranging and Sizing Icons in a Window

If you're browsing local files in any browsing window, you can modify the size of the icons that represent files and folders, as well as determine how much (if any) information about them appears.

To change the way that icons appear in any of these windows, as shown in Figure 3-2, choose from the following commands in the window's View menu (and notice that the same menu options appear if you right-click the window to open its shortcut menu):

- **Large Icons (the default):** Displays the largest version of the folder and file icons, with their names appearing below the icons.
- **Small Icons:** Displays a smaller version of the folder and file icons, with their names appearing at the right side of the icons.
- **List:** Uses the same icons as the Small Icons option except that the icons with their folders and filenames are arranged in a single column along the left side of the window.
- **Details:** Adds columns of additional information (such as a description, or the file type, the file size, and so on) to the arrangement that appears if you select the List option.

TIP: Switch to the Small Icons viewing option if you need to see as much of the window's contents as possible. Switch to the Details viewing option if you need to get as much information as possible about the files and folders in a window.

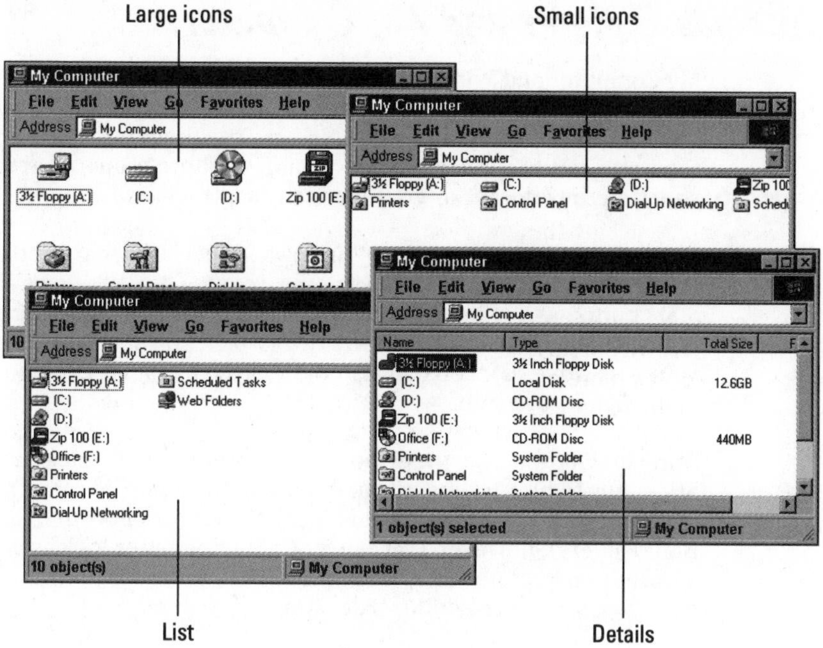

Figure 3-2: Different views of the same icons in a window.

After you decide how file and folder icons appear in a window, you can also choose their arrangement. Choose View➪Arrange Icons and choose among the following options on the Arrange Icons submenu:

- **By Name:** Sorts icons alphabetically by name.
- **By Type:** Sorts icons by file type.
- **By Size:** Sorts icons by size, from smallest to largest.
- **By Date:** Sorts icons by date, from oldest to most recent.
- **Auto Arrange:** Has Windows sort icons by the default setting (which happens to be By Type).

TIP

After you point to a menu command, the status bar at the bottom of the window displays a description of what that command does.

These methods of arranging icons in windows are pretty old hat to most Windows users. To give your window icons a complete makeover courtesy of Web integration in Windows, see Chapter 8.

Windows Explorer and My Computer

My Computer and Windows Explorer, the two file-handling utility programs that come with Windows, enable you to view the contents of any part of your computer system. You can also use the programs to open files (and their associated application programs), start programs, or even open Web pages on the Internet or your company's intranet.

To open Windows Explorer in Windows 98, click the Start button and then choose Programs⇨Windows Explorer. To open it in Windows Me, click the Start button and choose Programs⇨Accessories⇨Windows Explorer. Windows opens an Exploring window (which you see in the Figure 3-3) for your disk drive (C). You can also right-click any folder and choose Explore on the shortcut menu.

Note: In Windows Me, the Windows Explorer utility is relegated to secondary status (which is why you find it on the Accessories menu). By opening My Computer and clicking the Folders button (or choosing View⇨Explorer Bar⇨Folders), however, you can make My Computer look and work exactly as Windows Explorer does in Windows 98. To open My Computer, double-click its icon on the Windows desktop.

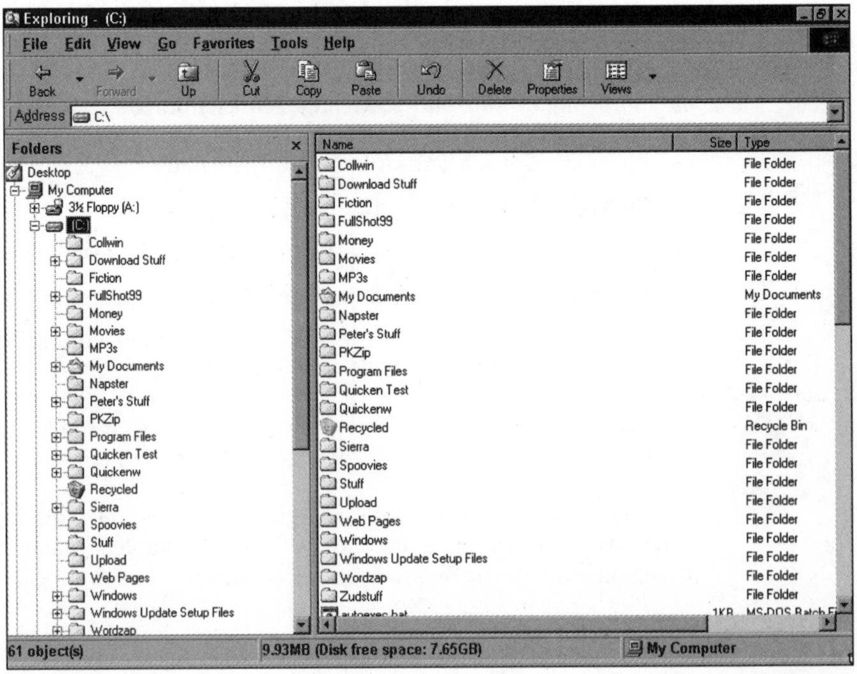

Figure 3-3: The Windows Explorer window in Windows 98 (and the My Computer window after you click the Folders button) enables you to see different parts of your computer.

Windows Explorer (and My Computer after you click the Folders button) is divided into the following two panes:

- The Folders pane on the left shows an outline view of all the components on your computer system.
- The Contents pane on the right displays the folders and files in whatever component is currently selected in the All Folders pane (also shown on the Address bar at the top of the window). In the figure, drive C is selected.

To select a new part of your system to view in the Contents area pane, simply click the icon for that component in the Folders pane. An icon in the Folders pane with a plus sign connected to it indicates a sublevel within that icon.

After you click a plus sign, Windows expands the outline, showing all the subfolders within the next level. Notice also that, after you click the plus sign, it turns into a minus sign, and the next level in the item's hierarchy appears. Clicking the minus sign collapses the sublevel to which it attaches, thus condensing the outline. Glance at Figure 3-4 for a quick demonstration.

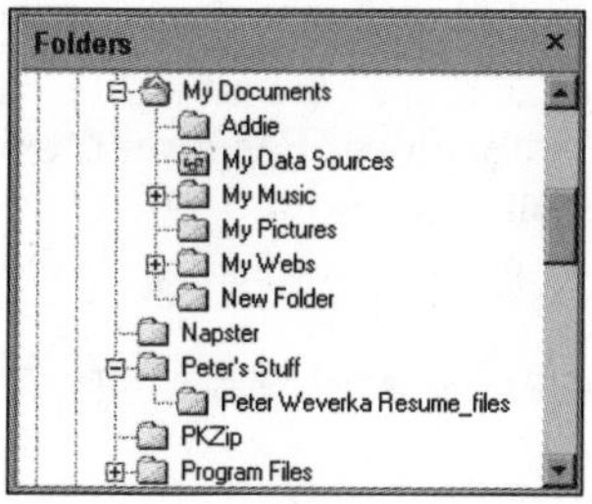

Figure 3-4: Expand an outline by clicking the plus sign next to an icon.

Sometimes, the expanded folder/subfolder outline in the Folders pane (or the icon arrangements in the Contents pane) becomes too large to view in its entirety given the current window size. If this situation occurs, vertical and horizontal scroll bars appear as needed to help you navigate your way through the lists of folders and system components.

Explorer Bars

If you open an *Explorer bar* in My Computer, Windows Explorer, or Internet Explorer, a new window pane appears, and you see one pane on the left and one on the right. The Explorer bar appears in the left pane, and the object or objects that you decide to explore appear in the pane on the right (as suitably shown in Figure 3-5). The Explorer bar offers tools for doing a task — finding out what's in a folder or searching the Internet, for example.

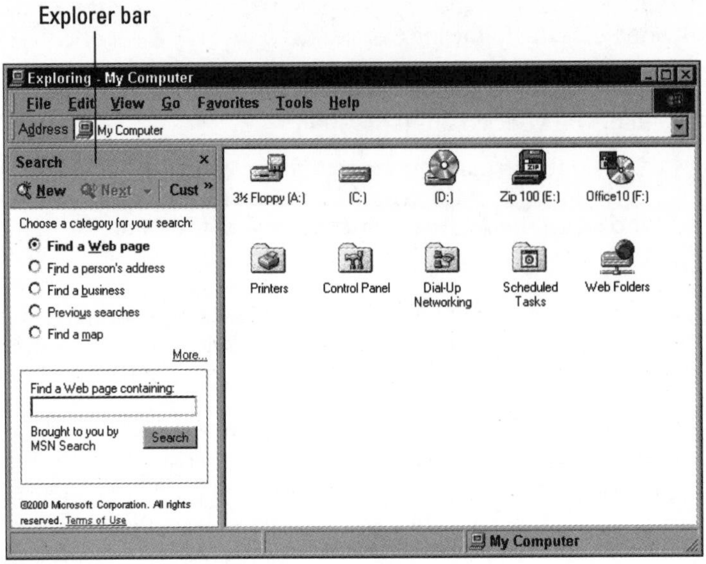

Figure 3-5: Explorer bars give you a new way to examine stuff.

Windows offers several different types of Explorer bars (most of which are Internet related). To display a particular Explorer bar, either click a toolbar button if it's available or choose View⇨Explorer Bar from the window's menu bar and then select one of the following commands from the submenu that appears:

- **Search:** Opens or closes the Search Explorer bar, where you can embark on a search of the Internet.
- **Favorites:** Opens or closes the Favorites Explorer bar, which contains a list of hyperlinks to your favorite Web sites, folders, and files.
- **History:** Opens or closes the History Explorer bar, which contains a chronological list of hyperlinks to Web sites you've recently visited and the folders and files that you've recently opened.
- **Folders:** Opens or closes the Folders pane. If the Folders pane is open (as it normally is), you can open any of the objects that make up your computer system.

Chapter 4: Dealing with Toolbars

In This Chapter

- Using toolbars
- Placing special toolbars on your taskbar
- Customizing your toolbars

Toolbars contain the buttons and menus that you love to click and pull in Windows. Different types of toolbars (each with its own group of buttons) can appear within the various windows, such as My Computer, Windows Explorer, and Internet Explorer, as well as on the taskbar on the Windows desktop. No matter where you place them, toolbars become a means to get things done *your* way.

Toolbars

After you display toolbars in a window, they appear docked one on top of the other in neat little rows at the top of the window. After you display toolbars on the taskbar, they appear one after the other on the taskbar, often scrunching up the buttons representing the various windows open on the desktop.

To display a certain type of toolbar in a window such as My Computer, Windows Explorer, or Internet Explorer, choose View⇨Toolbars and then select one of the following commands on the submenu that appears:

- **Standard Buttons:** Displays or hides the Standard Buttons toolbar. The particular buttons that appear on this toolbar depend on whether you're browsing local files and folders or Web pages on the Internet or the corporate intranet.
- **Address:** Displays or hides the Address bar. The Address bar contains a text box in which you can enter the URL of the Web page that you want to visit or the pathname of the folders that you want to browse.
- **Links:** Displays or hides the Links bar. The Links bar contains buttons with links to favorite Web pages.
- **Radio:** Displays or hides the Radio bar (if your edition of Windows includes the Media Player). Click the Radio Stations button and choose Radio Station Guide to choose the radio station that you want to hear.

- **Text Labels/Customize:** In Windows 98, choose Text Labels to display or hide text labels under the icons on the Standard Buttons bar. In Windows Me, choose Customize and, in the Customize Toolbar dialog box, open the Text Options drop-down list and choose Show Text Labels or No Text Labels.

Figure 4-1 shows you a window with all the toolbars displayed. By the way, you can right-click a toolbar and, from the shortcut menu, choose to hide or display toolbars.

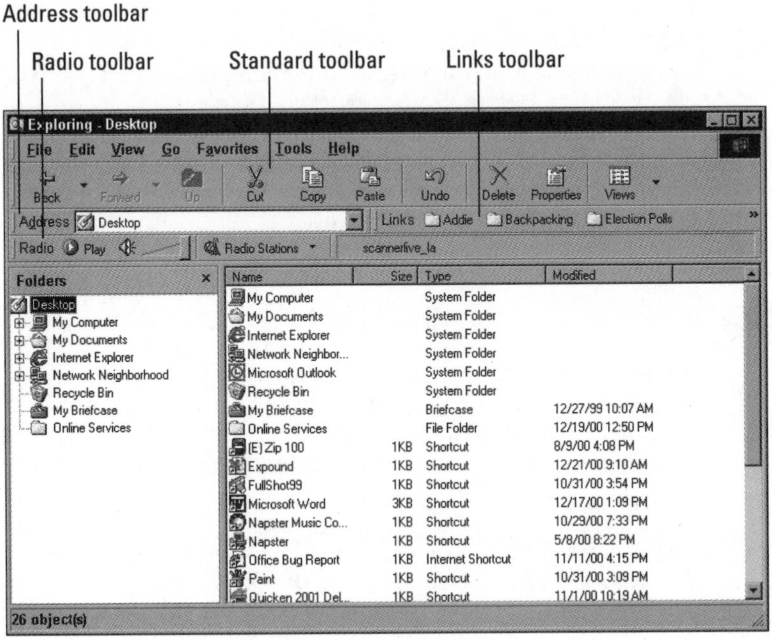

Figure 4-1: You can pick and choose among the different toolbars for a window.

Standing up to the Standard Buttons Toolbar

The Standard Buttons toolbar (also known simply as the *toolbar*) is the main toolbar that appears in the My Computer, Windows Explorer, and Internet Explorer windows (see Figure 4-2). It's also the most chameleonlike toolbar, because its buttons change to suit the particular type of browsing you're doing. If you browse local files and folders on your computer, the Standard Buttons toolbar contains the following buttons:

- **Back:** Returns to the previously browsed folder or Web page.
- **Forward:** Returns to the folder or Web page that you browsed right before using the Back button to return to the current page.

- **Up:** Moves up one level in the directory structure.
- **Cut:** Moves the currently selected files or folders to the Clipboard.
- **Copy:** Copies the currently selected files or folders to the Clipboard.
- **Paste:** Places files or folders you moved or copied to the Clipboard in the current folder.
- **Undo:** Eliminates your latest change (blunder?).
- **Delete:** Gets rid of the files or folders you selected (see Chapter 7 for more details).
- **Properties:** Gets properties information about the disks, files, or folders you selected (see Chapter 5 for more information).
- **Views:** Click repeatedly to rotate through the icon view options or use the attached menu to select a different icon view for the current window.

Figure 4-2: The Standard Buttons toolbar.

If you browse a Web page, whether a local HTML document on your hard drive or one located on a Web server somewhere in cyberspace, the Back and Forward buttons that you see while browsing local folders and files are then joined by the following new buttons (see Figure 4-3):

- **Stop:** Immediately halts the downloading of a Web page that's just taking far too long to come in.
- **Refresh:** Refreshes the display of the current Web page (which sometimes helps if the contents of the page appear jumbled or incomplete).
- **Home:** Displays the Web page designated as your start page. This Web page appears each time that you launch Internet Explorer 5 and connect to the Internet.
- **Search:** Displays the Search Explorer bar for searching the Internet.
- **Favorites:** Displays the Favorites Explorer bar for revisiting favorite Web pages that you've bookmarked.
- **History:** Displays the History Explorer bar for revisiting Web pages that you visited within the last few days or weeks.

- **Mail:** Displays a pop-up menu of e-mail options, including Read Mail, New Message, Send a Link, Send Page, and Read News.
- **Print:** Sends the current Web page to your printer.
- **Edit:** Opens a menu whereby you can open a program to edit the contents of the Web page you're looking at.

Figure 4-3: Standard Buttons toolbar when browsing a Web page.

Displaying Toolbars on Your Taskbar

In addition to using toolbars with windows, you can also place toolbars on your Windows taskbar to customize — or complicate — your computing style. (Read all about the taskbar in Chapter 2.) To display a certain type of toolbar on the taskbar, right-click on an empty area of the taskbar (be sure that you don't click the Start button or any of the other buttons that currently appear on the taskbar), select Toolbars from the shortcut menu, and choose Links, Address, Desktop, Quick Launch, or New Toolbar from the cascading menu that appears.

Latching onto the Links toolbar

The buttons on the Links toolbar (more often than not called simply the *Links bar*) are hyperlinks that open favorite Web pages. As you first start using Windows, the Links bar contains only buttons with links to Web pages on the Microsoft Web site, but you can, if you want, add to the Links toolbar. To add a button with a link to a preferred Web page, folder, or file, you simply drag its icon to the place on the Links bar where you want it to appear. (This icon appears on the Address bar in front of the Web page's URL, folder, or file pathname.)

TIP

To delete a button that you no longer want on the Links bar, right-click the button and then choose the Delete command on the button's shortcut menu.

Taking advantage of the Address bar

You can use the Address bar to search or browse Web pages on the Internet or your corporate intranet or to browse folders and files on local or networked disk drives. Just click the Address bar to insert the cursor into its text, type the URL of the Web page or the pathname of the folder that you want to browse (see Figure 4-4), and press the Enter key.

Figure 4-4: The Address bar.

Dealing with the Desktop toolbar

The Desktop toolbar contains buttons for all the icons that appear on the Windows desktop. These buttons include ones for the standard Desktop icons, such as My Computer, Internet Explorer, and Recycle Bin, as well as those for the program, folder, and file shortcuts that you create. (See Chapter 6 for more information on shortcuts.)

Calling on the Quick Launch toolbar

The Quick Launch toolbar is a collection of buttons that you can click to start the programs you use most frequently. These buttons, shown in Figure 4-5, include the following:

Figure 4-5: Quick Launch toolbar.

- **Launch Internet Explorer Browser:** Starts Internet Explorer for browsing Web pages.
- **Launch Outlook Express:** Starts Outlook Express for sending and receiving e-mail and messages from the newsgroups to which you have subscribed.
- **Show Desktop:** Minimizes all open windows to obtain immediate access to the Windows Desktop. This is a mighty nice little shortcut.
- **View Channels:** Starts the Active Channel viewer for subscribing to, updating, and browsing particular Web channels.
- **Windows Media Player:** Starts Windows Media Player so that you can play a CD, video file, or sound file, or listen to the Internet radio (if your edition of Windows includes the Media Player).

In addition to these standard buttons, you can add your own custom buttons to the Quick Launch toolbar by dragging the shortcuts to your favorite program or its executable file from the desktop to the Quick Launch toolbar. Follow these steps:

1. **Open the folder that contains the executable file that starts the program or that contains a shortcut to this executable file.**

   To find an executable (.exe) file, switch to Details view in My Computer or Windows Explorer and look for the word *Application* in the Type column.

2. **Select and drag the program's file icon or shortcut icon to the desired position on the Quick Launch toolbar and then release the mouse button.**

   A button for the program appears at the position of the I-beam in the Quick Launch toolbar.

You can delete any of the buttons from the Quick Launch toolbar by right-clicking the button, choosing the Delete command on the shortcut menu, and then choosing the Yes button in the alert box that asks you to confirm the deletion.

New Toolbar

You can use the New Toolbar option to create a custom toolbar of buttons made from the items in a particular folder. To do so, follow these steps:

1. **Right-click an empty area of the taskbar and choose New Toolbar from the shortcut menu.**

   The New Toolbar dialog box opens.

2. **Browse through the dialog box until you find the folder containing the items that you want to use as buttons on your custom toolbar.**

3. **Click to select the folder and then click OK to close the New Toolbar dialog box.**

   Windows adds the new toolbar to your taskbar and shows at least some of the items from the folder as buttons on the toolbar. (You may have to press the double arrow at the right end of the toolbar to be able to see the remaining elements in the folder.) Notice that Windows uses the name of the folder you selected as the name of the toolbar and places it at the left end of the custom toolbar.

All custom toolbars that you create last only for the duration of your current work session. In other words, whenever you close a custom toolbar or restart your computer, the toolbar is automatically erased and you must re-create it the next time that you want it.

Customizing the Appearance of a Toolbar

You can customize the appearance of each toolbar that you display in Windows by changing its position on the desktop or on the taskbar. In the case of the My Computer, Windows Explorer, and Internet Explorer windows, you can change the order in which toolbars appear in the window. You can also customize a toolbar by modifying its size and the amount of descriptive information that appears along with the icons.

In repositioning or resizing a toolbar, keep the following things in mind:

✦ To change the position or length of a toolbar, you drag the toolbar by its sizing handle (the double vertical bar that appears at the very beginning of the toolbar) as soon as the mouse pointer assumes the shape of a double-headed arrow, as shown in Figure 4-6.

Figure 4-6: Changing a toolbar's size.

✦ In repositioning a toolbar on the Windows taskbar, you can undock the toolbar and relocate it somewhere on the Windows desktop. Just drag its sizing handle up and off the taskbar, releasing the mouse button after the pointer reaches the desired position on the desktop. It then appears in its own toolbar window, complete with a Close box. You can also dock the toolbar at the top, far left, or far right of the screen by dragging it to the top edge, left edge, or right edge of the screen before you release the mouse button.

REAL WORLD

Button, button, who's got the button?

If you don't use a button regularly (or after you've created several new buttons), trying to remember what it's for can prove a difficult task. If you experience this problem, remember that you can identify each of the buttons on the toolbars that appear on the taskbar or at the top of the My Computer, Windows Explorer, or Internet Explorer windows by displaying the button's ToolTip. To display a button's ToolTip, you simply hover the mouse pointer over the button's icon until the comment box containing the button's text label appears, as the following figure shows.

Chapter 5: Dialog Boxes and Menus

In This Chapter

- **Working with dialog boxes**
- **Managing your pull-down menus**
- **Using context and Control menus**

If you enjoy checking off little boxes, filling in blanks, clicking buttons, tugging on sliders, and this sort of thing, you're certain to love dealing with the dialog boxes that Windows — and any Windows program — throws at you.

Dialog boxes give you some exercise in responsibility because *you* make the choices. And if you have a taste for reading little menus that precede even the most mundane action, you invested your money wisely. The Windows dialog boxes and menus are your gateway to getting productive.

Dialog Boxes

A *dialog box* is a special type of window that enables you to specify a bunch of settings at the same time. Most dialog boxes appear after you select a menu command from either a pull-down menu or a shortcut menu. You can always tell whether choosing a command opens a dialog box because an *ellipsis* (that's Greek for three dots in a row) follows the command's name.

At the top of each dialog box, you find a title bar that contains the name of the dialog box. You can reposition the dialog box on-screen by dragging it by its title bar (and nowhere else). You can't, however, resize a dialog box, which is the one of the major differences between a dialog box and a window.

Dialog boxes also contain any number of buttons and boxes that you use to make your selections known to Windows or the particular Windows program you have open. Figure 5-1 points out the various boxes and buttons you encounter in dialog boxes. Table 5-1 tells you how to use the boxes and buttons.

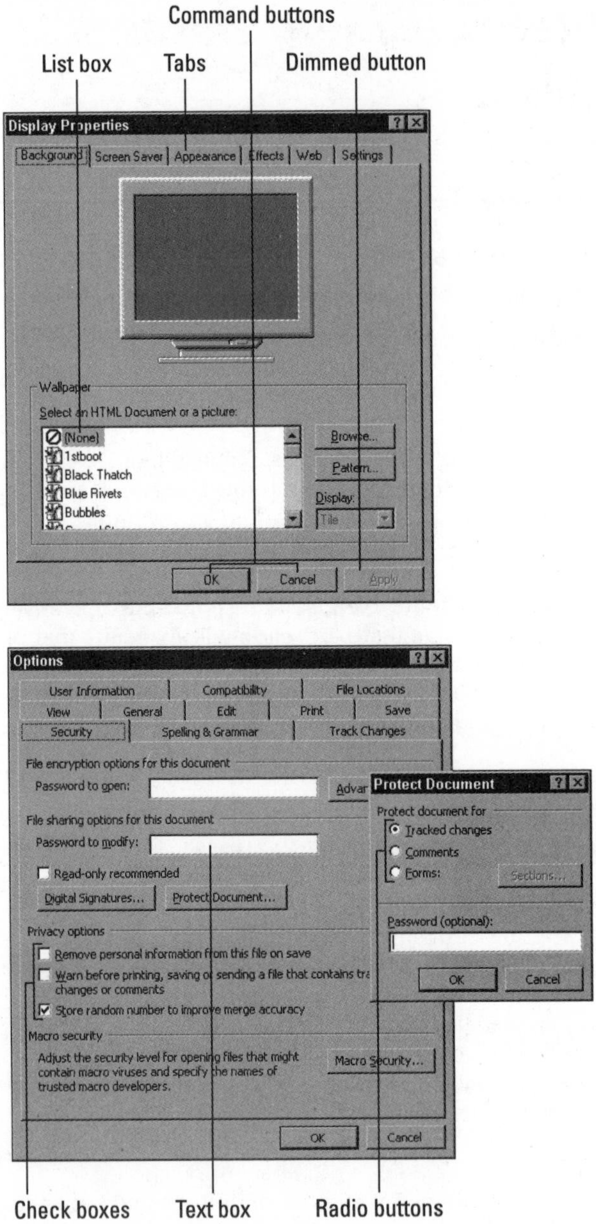

Figure 5-1: Dialog boxes in various programs share many features.

Table 5-1 Common Dialog Box Elements

Parts of a Dialog Box	*What You Do with Them*
Check box	Use with items in which you can choose more than one option. When a check box is selected, a check mark appears inside the box beside its name.
Command button	Use to initiate an action, such as putting the options you select into effect by clicking the OK button.
Dimmed button	If the command name appears dimmed, the button is temporarily out of commission — until you select another prerequisite option.
Drop-down list box	Looks like a text box with a down-arrow button right next door. Click the arrow button to open a list box of possible choices. If the list contains more choices than fit in the box, use the scroll bar on the right to display more choices.
List box	Displays an alphabetical list of all choices for an item. Use the scroll bar on the right to display new choices. The current choice is highlighted in the list.
Radio button	Use with items for which you can choose only one of several options. The selected option appears with a dot in the middle of the radio button and a faint, dotted line around the option name. Also known as an *option button.*
Slider	Enables you to change a value (such as the sound playback volume or mouse speed) by dragging the slider back and forth (usually between Low and High, marked at each end).
Spinner button	Enables you to select a new number in an accompanying text box without actually typing a value in that box. Clicking the up-arrow spinner button increases the value by one, and clicking the down-arrow spinner button decreases it by one.
Tab	Enables you to select a new page of options in the same dialog box, complete with its own buttons and boxes.
Text (edit) box	Shows you the current setting and enables you to edit it or type an entire new setting. If the text inside the box is selected, anything that you type replaces the highlighted text. You can also delete text by pressing the Delete or Backspace key.

Notice that if the name on a command button is followed by an ellipsis (. . .), clicking the button opens another dialog box. If two greater-than symbols (>) follow the name of a command button, however, choosing the button expands the current dialog box to display more choices.

After you use these various buttons and boxes to make changes to the current settings that the dialog box controls, you can close the dialog box and put the new settings into effect by choosing the OK button.

If you want to close the dialog box without making *any* changes to the current settings, press the Esc key, click the Cancel button, or click the Close button of the dialog box.

Menu Management

Menus provide the means for Windows to organize and display the command choices you have at any given time, as well as the means for you to indicate your particular command choice. Windows relies mainly on three types of command menus (each of which I describe in the following sections).

Following are a few general guidelines that apply when you use these types of menus:

- If you see a right-facing arrowhead (>) to the right of an option on a menu, another menu — known as a *submenu* — containing more options appears after you highlight (or select) that option.
- If you see an ellipsis (. . .) at the end of an option in a menu, a dialog box appears after you select that option. (See the section "Dialog Boxes," earlier in this chapter.)
- If you don't see any kind of symbol next to a menu option, the selected option is carried out immediately.

REAL WORLD

Your typical menu bar for a window

If you begin to notice some similarity between menu bars, you're not imagining things. The menu bar in Windows modules (such as My Computer, Windows Explorer, and Internet Explorer) contain the following menus that you use to perform all kinds of routine tasks:

- **File:** Does file-type stuff, such as renaming or deleting files and folders or creating shortcuts to them.
- **Edit:** Does editing-type stuff, such as cutting, copying, or pasting files or folders.
- **View:** Does show-and-tell stuff, such as displaying or hiding particular toolbars or parts of the window and changing the way that file and folder icons appear in their windows.
- **Go:** Does navigation-type stuff, such as going forward and backward through the folders or Web pages you just viewed (Windows 98 only).
- **Tools:** For doing a host of maintenance tasks, including opening the Options dialog box (Windows Me only).
- **Favorites:** Adds to, opens, or organizes the folders, files, and Web pages that you bookmark or subscribe to.
- **Help:** Enables you to consult particular Help topics that direct you in how to use Windows.

Tugging on the old pull-down menus

Pull-down menus are the primary way to make your wishes known in Windows. Although most commands on these menus live up to their name and appear below the menu, some (for example, the Start menu), actually display their options above the menu name after you open them. Within windows, the pull-down menus are located on their own menu bar right below the title bar (as shown in Figure 5-2).

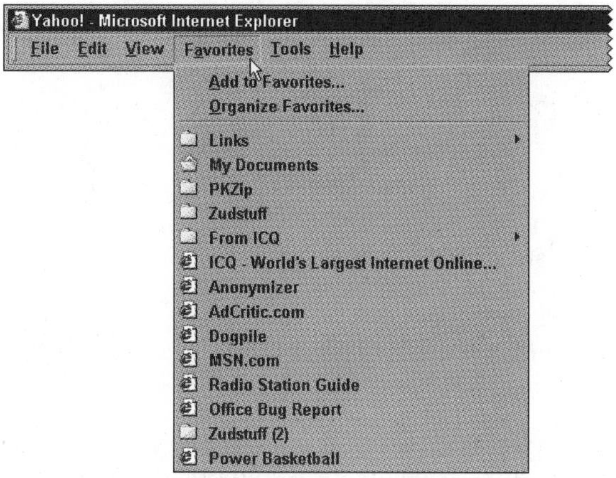

Figure 5-2: Opening the Favorites menu.

You can use the following two methods to open pull-down menus and select commands:

- **Use the mouse:** Point to the name of the menu on the menu bar (an "embossed" button appears) and then click it to open the menu. Move the mouse pointer down through the menu to highlight the desired command and then click to select the menu command.
- **Use the Alt key:** Press and hold the Alt key as you type the command letter in the menu name (that is, the underlined letter) to open the menu. Type the command letter of the menu item to select the command.

TIP

To open the Start menu on the Windows taskbar by using the keyboard, press Ctrl+Esc or click the Windows button on your keyboard.

Getting acclimated to shortcut menus

Shortcut menus are menus that attach to particular objects in Windows, such as the desktop icons or even the desktop itself. These menus contain commands directly related to the object to which they are attached. To open a shortcut menu, simply right-click the object with the mouse.

In Figure 5-3, you see the shortcut menu associated with the hard drive icon in the My Computer window. You can open this menu and gain access to these additional commands by right-clicking the hard drive icon (shown in the figure with `(C:)` underneath).

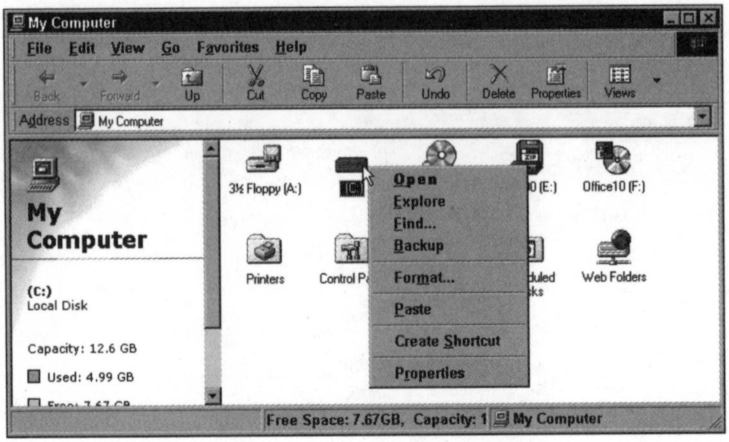

Figure 5-3: Right-clicking leads you to shortcut menus.

After you open a shortcut menu, you can use any of the menu methods that I describe in the section "Tugging on the old pull-down menus" to choose a command from the menu.

Shortcut menus attached to program, folder, and file icons on the desktop or in a window usually contain varying assortments of the following commands:

- **Open:** Opens the object.
- **Create Shortcut:** Creates a shortcut for the selected object.
- **Properties:** Gives the lowdown on the selected object. For example, you can find out when it was created, when it was last saved, and who created it.
- **View:** Changes the size of the icons in a window and the order in which the window's icons appear.
- **Explore:** Opens the selected object and shows its contents in the Windows Explorer.
- **Cut or Copy:** Cuts or copies the object to the Clipboard so that you can move or copy the object to another place on your system or network.
- **Delete:** Deletes the object by putting it into the Recycle Bin.
- **Rename:** Changes the name of the selected object.

✦ **Send To:** Sends a copy of the object to an e-mail recipient, a specific floppy drive, or the My Documents folder or creates a shortcut to it on the desktop.

Using the Control menu

The Control menu is a standard pull-down menu attached to all the windows that you'll ever open in Windows. To open the Control menu, click the little icon to the immediate left of the window's name in the upper-left corner of the window's title bar.

TIP

If you double-click this icon instead of single-clicking it, Windows closes the window and quits any application program that happens to be running in it. If you have an unsaved document open in the program whose window you just closed, Windows displays an alert dialog box that gives you a chance to save it before shutting down the shop.

Almost every Control menu that you run into contains the same old, tired commands, as Table 5-2 describes.

Table 5-2 Control Menu Commands

Common Control Menu Commands	*What They Do*
Restore	Restores a maximized or minimized window to an in-between size that you can easily change.
Move	Moves the window to a new location on the desktop.
Size	Enables you to resize the window by moving its left, right, top, or bottom side.
Minimize	Shrinks the window all the way down to a button on the taskbar at the bottom of the screen.
Maximize	Zooms the window to full size so that it fills up the entire screen.
Close (Alt+F4)	Closes the window, thus automatically exiting the program running in it.

A menu for keeping up-to-date

The Windows Update command on the Start menu provides an almost completely automated method for keeping your Windows operating system software up-to-date. As soon as you choose the Windows Update command on the Start menu, Windows puts you online and connects you to the Windows Update Web page on the Microsoft Web site. From there, you can find out about updating your edition of Windows and maybe even download software from the Web site to update it.

REAL WORLD

Owning up to properties dialog boxes

A *properties dialog box* appears when you select an object's icon and then choose the Properties command (either from the File pull-down menu or if you right-click an object and choose Properties from its shortcut menu).

After you open the Properties dialog box for a particular object (such as a program, folder, or file), the dialog box gives you information about that object's current settings. Most of the time, you can't do much with the properties for a particular Windows object — nor do you want to. Depending on the object, you may have zero chance of changing any of its settings. In those situations where Windows does enable you to fool around with the property settings, please be very careful not to screw up your computer by foolishly selecting some incompatible setting that you had no business changing.

Chapter 6: The Lowdown on Files and Folders

In This Chapter

- **Getting to know files**
- **Using folders**
- **Opening files and folders**
- **Creating shortcuts to files and folders**

If you work with any Windows-based program (such as Microsoft Word, Excel, and so on) for more than a few minutes, you're probably already starting a collection of files that you may soon begin to lose track of. Obviously, this isn't good. What if you need to finish your letter to the editor or redo the presentation that you're giving the next morning? Without a little organization and file-savvy, you can find yourself in trouble.

This chapter introduces you to files and folders in general and tells you how to deal with their basics. Chapter 7 then gives you some more ideas on how to manage them.

Files

Files contain all the precious data that you create with those sophisticated (and expensive) Windows-based programs. Files occupy a certain amount of space on a disk, whether it's your hard drive or a removable floppy disk. This file space is measured in *kilobytes* (K), which is Greek for *thousands of bytes.* If you write a letter to your brother in Microsoft Word, for example, and then save the document to your hard drive, you just created a file.

Naming files

Each filename in Windows consists of two parts: a main filename and a file extension. The file *extension,* which identifies the type of file and what program created it, consists of a maximum of three characters that the creating program automatically assigns. Typically, these file extensions don't appear in the lists of filenames that you see. (For information about how to display the file extensions, see Chapter 8.)

Whereas the creating program normally assigns the file extension, Windows enables you to call the main part of the filename whatever the heck you want, up to a maximum of 255 characters (including spaces).

Keep in mind, however, that all pre-Windows 95 programs — and even some that run on current versions of Windows — don't support long filenames. These programs enable you to use a maximum of only eight characters, with no spaces.

Identifying files with their icons

Windows assigns files special icons that correspond to the type of file and its underlying program. These icons help you quickly identify what program the file was created in. Table 6-1 shows some examples of these icons. (See Chapter 1 for more on the care and feeding of icons.)

Table 6-1 Icons Associated with Certain Files

File Icon	*File Type and Program That Opens It*
	Word document that opens in Microsoft Word
	Excel workbook that opens in Microsoft Excel
	HTML document that opens in Internet Explorer
	Text file that opens in the Notepad utility
	Unidentified generic file that opens the Open With dialog box and asks you to identify a program that can open the file

Folders

Folders are the data containers in Windows. You can recognize folder icons because they actually look like those nice manila folders that you never seem to have enough of. Well, don't worry. In Windows, you can access an endless supply of folders. (And to prevent any confusion while increasing your boredom, folders in Windows always have the little tab on the left side.) Folders can contain files, other folders, or a combination of files and folders (see Figure 6-1). Like files, folders occupy a certain amount of space on a particular disk (whether hard drive or floppy) and are also measured in kilobytes (K). The amount of kilobytes a folder takes up is actually an indication of the size of the data files within the folder.

REAL WORLD

Knowing all about your files

Keep in mind that you can get lots of good information on a file — such as which program created it, how big it is, when it was created and last revised, and so on. Choose the Properties command on the file's shortcut menu. (Right-click an icon to open the shortcut menu.) You can also press Alt+Enter when the icon is selected.

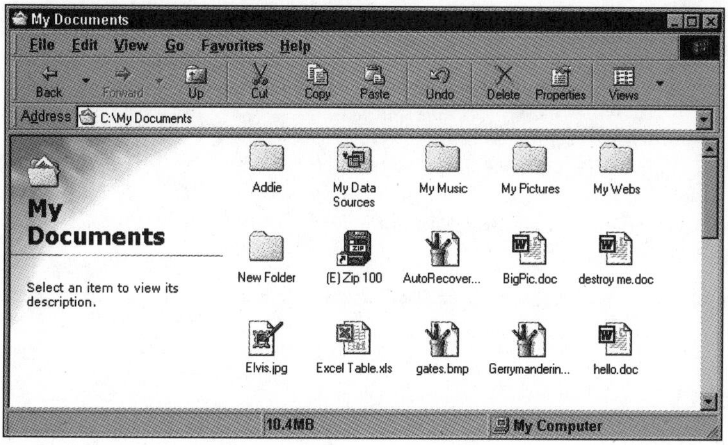

Figure 6-1: If you examine the icons in this figure, you can see that this folder contains both files and other folders.

Opening Files and Folders

The most common way to open a file or folder is to open its icon in one of the three browsing windows (My Computer, Windows Explorer, or Internet Explorer 5). How you open the file or folder icon after you display it in a browsing window depends on the Active Desktop setting that your computer uses, as follows:

✦ Double-click the icon if you set up the Active Desktop with the so-called "classic" setting.

✦ Single-click the icon if you set up the Active Desktop so that icons act and look the same as hyperlinks (so-called Web style). See Chapter 8 for information about changing between Web and classic styles.

TIP

Remember that you can also open a file or folder by right-clicking its icon and then choosing the Open command at the top of its shortcut menu.

REAL WORLD

The path to your files and folders

Sure, you can physically see your file or folder right there on-screen! Nevertheless, that file or folder has a unique path leading directly to it. If you're still enamored of the old DOS way of doing things and can type with more than just two fingers, you can often just as easily use a *path* (such as in an address bar) to get to something.

You identify the location of a folder (known in tech talk as the folder's *directory path*) by the letter of the drive that holds its disk, the other folder or folders within which it's embedded, and a unique name. The following is an example of a Workstuff folder's directory path, which indicates that Workstuff is a subfolder within the My Documents folder on drive C:

```
C:\My Documents\Workstuff
```

You Identify the location of a file (its *pathname*) by the letter of the drive that holds its disk, the folder or subfolders within which it's embedded, and a unique filename. A typical pathname could look as follows:

```
C:\MyDocuments\Workstuff\
    invoice15.xls
```

This pathname is shorthand to indicate that you can find a file by the name `invoice 15.xls` in a folder by the name Workstuff, which itself resides in the My Documents folder, which, in turn, you find on drive C (the hard drive) of your computer.

Shortcuts

Shortcuts enable you to open an object, such as a favorite document, folder, program, or Web page, directly from the desktop of the computer — even if you have absolutely no idea how deep the object is buried on your computer or where it may lie in cyberspace. The following list gives the basic lowdown on shortcuts:

- ✦ You can locate shortcuts anywhere on your computer, but you're best off keeping them right out in the open on the desktop so that you can get at them easily.
- ✦ If you create a shortcut for an object, Windows creates an icon for it with a name such as `Shortcut to such and such`. You can rename the shortcut to whatever name suits you, just as you can rename any file or folder in Windows (see Chapter 7).
- ✦ You can always tell a shortcut icon from the regular icon because the shortcut icon contains a little box with a curved arrow pointing up to the right.

To create a shortcut for a folder, file, or other type of local object on the Windows desktop, follow these steps:

1. **Select the icon for the object for which you want to create a shortcut.**
2. **Choose File ➪Create Shortcut from the menu bar or right-click the object and choose Create Shortcut from its shortcut menu.**
3. **If Windows displays the error message** `Unable to create a shortcut here. Do you want the shortcut placed on the desktop?`, **choose Yes.**

   If Windows doesn't give you this error message, it places the new shortcut in the currently open window. If you want the shortcut on the desktop, where you can always access it, drag the shortcut's icon to any place on the desktop and release the mouse button.

You mess up a shortcut if you move the object to which it refers to a new place on your computer, because Windows still looks for it (unsuccessfully) in the old location. If you do mess up a shortcut by moving the object it refers to, trash the shortcut and then re-create it, move the original file back to its location, or right-click and choose Properties on the shortcut menu to open the icon's Properties dialog box, where you can enter the correct path to the shortcut.

Chapter 7: File and Folder Management

In This Chapter

- Creating files and folders
- Copying and moving files and folders
- Finding files and folders
- Renaming files and folders
- Deleting unwanted files and folders

You don't need a degree from Harvard Business School to manage your files and folders in Windows. In fact, if you can click a mouse or punch a keyboard, you pretty much qualify as an expert file and folder manager. You don't even need to worry about filling out those mid-year performance reviews as most managers do. Your files and folders are simple to boss around because they do whatever you tell them to do. How much easier can managing be? This chapter shows you the best ways to create, select, move, copy, paste, find, rename, and delete files and folders.

Creating New Files and Folders

You create empty folders to hold your files and empty files to hold new documents of a particular type right within Windows. To create an empty folder, follow these steps:

1. **Open the folder inside a browsing window in which the new folder is to appear.**
2. **Choose File⇨New⇨Folder from the menu bar or right-click inside the window and choose New⇨Folder from the window's shortcut menu.**
3. **Replace the temporary folder name (New Folder) by typing a name of your choosing and pressing Enter.**

To create an empty file of a certain type, follow these steps:

1. **Open the window and the folder where you need the new file.**
2. **Choose File⇨New from the menu bar or right-click a blank space inside the window and choose New from the window's shortcut menu.**

3. **Choose the type of file that you want to create (such as Microsoft PowerPoint Presentation, Microsoft Excel Worksheet, Microsoft Word Document, Microsoft Access Database, Wave Sound, Text Document, or Briefcase, and so on) from the New submenu.**
4. **Replace the temporary file name (such as New Microsoft Word Document) by typing a name of your choosing and pressing Enter.**

Create a new folder if you need a new place to store your files and other folders. Create an empty file in a particular folder before you put something in it. (Create lots of empty files and folders with the name Income 1991-2001 to confuse the IRS long enough for you to get to the Bahamas.)

Copying (And Moving) Files and Folders

You copy and move files and folders in Windows by using the two universal methods that I describe in this section — drag-and-drop or copy/cut-and-paste.

Drag 'em up, drop 'em down

The art of drag-and-drop is simplicity itself. To copy files by using drag-and-drop, follow these steps:

1. **In My Computer or Windows Explorer, open the window that contains the items that you want to copy, as well as the window with the folder or disk to which you want to copy the items.**
2. **Select all the items that you want to copy (see Chapter 1 for details on selecting).**
3. **Press and hold the Ctrl key as you drag the selected items to the folder to which you want to copy them.**

   Notice the appearance of a plus sign next to the pointer as you drag the items. This symbol indicates that you are *copying* the items, rather than *moving* them, which means that the files will exist in both locations.
4. **When the destination folder is highlighted (selected), release the mouse button to drop the selected items into the folder.**

The flavors of copy-and-paste

You can perform the copy and paste operations, as you can many of the everyday tasks in Windows, either by selecting commands on the menu bar or by using keyboard combination shortcuts. To copy files by using copy-and-paste, using either menu commands or keyboard shortcuts, follow these steps:

1. **In My Computer or Windows Explorer, open a window that holds the items that you want to copy.**

2. **Select all the items that you want to copy (see Chapter 1 for the details about selecting) and then choose Edit⇨Copy or press Ctrl+C.**

   The items are copied to the Clipboard.

3. **In My Computer or Windows Explorer, open a window that holds the folder or disk where the copied items are to appear.**

4. **Open the folder or disk that you want to hold the copied items and then choose Edit⇨Paste or press Ctrl+V.**

Use drag-and-drop to copy when the folder with the items that you want to copy and the destination folder or disk appear on the desktop (as they are when you use the Windows Explorer or My Computer). Use copy-and-paste to copy if you can't easily display both the folder with the items that you want to copy and the destination folder or disk together on the desktop.

TIP

Suppose the folder to which you want to copy or move files is closed. You can open it in the course of copying or moving files. To do so, drag the files over the folder and let the mouse pointer hang there for a moment. The folder opens shortly after.

Move over folders and files

You can move files and folders in the Windows Explorer or My Computer by using either the drag-and-drop or the cut-and-paste method. To move an object by using drag-and-drop, follow these steps:

1. **In My Computer or Windows Explorer, open the window that contains the folders and files that you want to move.**

   If you're just moving some files in a folder, make sure that you open that folder in the window.

2. **Open a window that displays the icon for the folder or disk to which you intend to move the files and folders you're about to select in the first folder that I describe in Step 1.**

3. **Select in the first window all the files and folders that you want to move.**

4. **Drag the selected files and folders from the first window to the window that contains the destination folder or disk (the one to which you're moving the files).**

5. **As soon as you select the icon of the destination folder or disk (which now appears with its name highlighted), release the mouse button to move the files into that folder or disk.**

If you drag files or folders from one disk to another, Windows automatically copies the files and folders rather than moving them (meaning that you must still delete them from their original disk if you need the space).

Why copy and drag if you can send?

If all you want to do is back up some files from your hard drive to a floppy disk in drive A or B, you can do so by using the Send To command. After selecting the files to copy, just open the shortcut menu attached to one of the file icons by right-clicking the icon. Then choose the correct floppy drive, such as 3½ Floppy (A) on the Send To menu. One more thing: Don't forget to insert a disk in that drive — and preferably one that's already formatted and ready to go — before you start this little operation.

You can also send a file or folder to a folder by using the Send To command. Just place a shortcut to that folder in your SendTo folder (located itself in the Windows folder on your C: drive — just look in My Computer). After you right-click an icon for a file or folder, you can see the shortcut to your folder on the menu.

Using drag-and-drop to move files from folder to folder is great because it's really fast. This method does, however, have a major drawback: Dropping your file icons into the wrong folder is pretty easy to do. Instead of having a cow if you open up what you thought was the destination folder and find that your files are gone, you can locate them by using the Find Files or Folders command. (See the section "Finding Files and Folders," later in this chapter.)

Moving files and folders via the cut-and-paste method ensures that the lost-files scenario that I just described doesn't happen — although it's much clunkier than using the elegant drag-and-drop method. To move files and folders by using cut-and-paste, follow these steps:

1. **Open a window that displays all the files and folders that you want to move.**
2. **Select all the files and folders that you want to move (and see Chapter 1 for info on selecting).**
3. **Choose Edit⇨Cut from the menu bar or press Ctrl+X to cut the selected files and place them on the Clipboard.**

   Notice that the files become gray to show that they have been cut to the Clipboard.
4. **Open a window that contains the destination folder or disk (the one to which you want to move the selected files or folders).**
5. **Choose Edit⇨Paste in the window where you want to move the selected stuff or press Ctrl+V to insert the files into the folder or disk.**

Use the drag-and-drop method if both the files and folders that you want to move and the folder to which you are moving them are visible on the desktop. Switch to the cut-and-paste method if you can't see both on the desktop.

Windows automatically moves files as you drag their file icons from one folder to another on the same disk and copies files (which the appearance of a plus sign next to the pointer indicates) as you drag their icons from one disk to another.

If you use the cut and paste commands to move files or folders, you don't need to keep open the first window in which they originally resided after you cut them. Just make sure that you paste the cut files or folders in a location before you choose Edit⇨Copy or Edit⇨Cut again in Windows. If you choose the command again, the files or folders you originally cut are lost. They are replaced by whatever you recently copied to the Clipboard.

Finding Files and Folders

The Find feature enables you to quickly locate all those misplaced files and folders that you're just sure are hiding somewhere on your hard drive. To open the Find window to search for a file or folder, follow these steps:

1. **Click the Start button on the taskbar, choose Find in Windows 98 (or Search in Windows Me), and then choose Files or Folders (or For Files or Folders in Windows Me).**

   This action opens the Find: All Files window (in Windows 98) or the Search Results window (in Windows Me), as shown in Figure 7-1. In the Figure, the search is complete and you can see the search results.

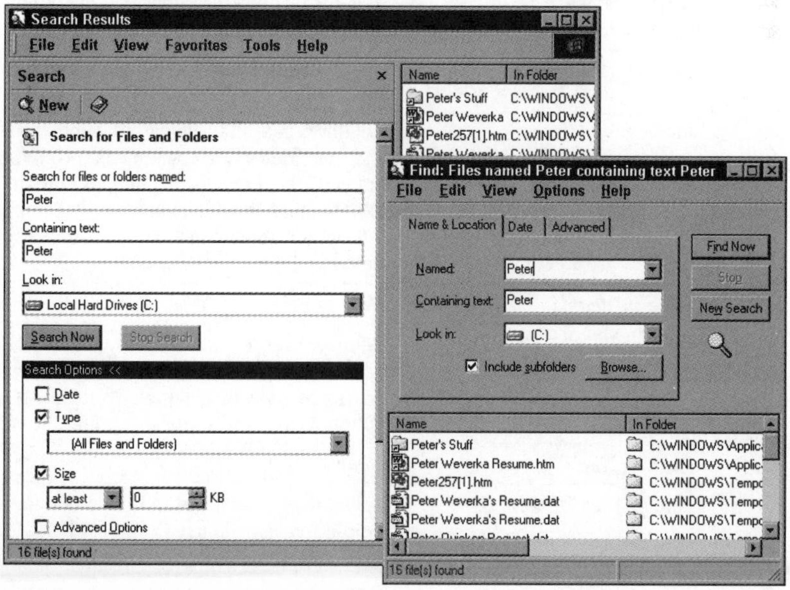

Figure 7-1: Finding files and folders in Windows Me (left) and Windows 98 (right).

2. **Enter the search conditions (see Table 7-1).**
3. **Click the Find Now (or the Search Now) button to start the search.**

After Windows completes a search, it expands the dialog box or window to display in a list box all the files that meet your search conditions (refer to Figure 7-1). This list box shows the name, location, size, type, and the date the file was last modified. (Scroll to the right to see everything.)

In Windows 98, the Find dialog box offers three tabs — Name & Location, Date, and Advanced — that offer various options for setting search conditions. In Windows Me, you can get different search options by clicking the check boxes at the bottom of the window. Click the Date check box, and you get options for searching for certain types of files. In both Windows 98 and Me, you use the search options in Table 7-1.

Keep in mind that you don't have to know the name of the file to use the Find/Search feature because Windows can search for specific text in a file if you use the Containing Text box.

Table 7-1 Find/Search Options

Name & Location Options	*How to Use*
Named	Enter all or part of the file or folder name you're looking for in this text box. Don't worry about capitalization. Windows remembers the stuff that you enter in this text box so that you can reselect search text in the drop-down list box.
Containing text	Use this text box to specify a string of characters, a word, or a phrase that the files you're looking for contain.
Look In	Use this drop-down box (or the Browse button in Windows 98) to select the drive you want to search.
Include Subfolders	Windows searches all folders within the folders on the disk specified in the Look In edit box. If the files and folders you want don't lie any deeper than the first level of folders, deselect this check box. In Windows Me, access this option (known as Search Subfolders) by clicking the Advanced Options check box.
Date Options	*How to Use*
All Files/Date	Windows searches all the files on your computer or in the area where you ask to search, but you can also ask it to search by date. In Windows 98, deselect the All Files button. In Windows Me, select the Date box.
Date Options	*How to Use*
Find All Files/Date Menu	Select the Find All Files button in Windows 98. From the drop-down list, choose Created, Modified, or Last Accessed to tell Windows which kind of date to target.

Date Options	*How to Use*
Between/And	Enter the two dates between which the files or folders must have been created, edited, or accessed. The two dates that you enter in the Between text boxes are included in the search.
During the Previous Days	Rather than enter dates, you can also simply tell Windows to look in a previous number of months or days.
During the Previous Months	Select this radio button and enter the number of months in the month(s) text box during which files and folders were created, modified, or accessed.
Advanced/Type/Size Options	***How to Use***
Of Type	Specify a particular type of file to search for (rather than All Files and Folders, which is the default).
Size Is	Select At Least or At Most in the drop-down list and enter the number of kilobytes (K) that the files must have attained or not exceeded.

Renaming Files and Folders

You can rename file and folder icons directly in Windows by typing over or editing the existing file or folder name as I outline in the following steps:

1. **In My Computer or Windows Explorer, right-click the icon of the file or folder that you want to rename and select Rename from its shortcut menu.**
2. **Type the new name directly over the old one.**

   Names can be up to 255 characters. You can also edit the old one by using the Delete key to remove characters.
3. **After you finish editing the file or folder name, press the Enter key to complete the renaming procedure.**

TIP

After the file or folder name is selected for editing, typing anything entirely replaces the current name. If you want to edit the file or folder name rather than replace it, you need to click the insertion point at the place in the name that needs editing before you begin typing. Of course, you can also press arrow keys, Home, or End.

Deleting Junk

Because the purpose of working on computers is to create junk, you need to know how to get rid of unneeded files and folders to free up space on your hard drive. To delete files or folders, follow these steps:

1. **In My Computer or Windows Explorer, open the folder that holds the files or folders that you want to delete.**

2. **Select all the files and folders that you want to delete (and see Chapter 1 for the lowdown on selecting items).**

3. **Choose File⇨Delete from the menu bar or press the Delete key.**

 You can also drag the selected items to the Recycle Bin.

4. **Click the Yes button in the Confirm File Delete dialog box that asks whether you want to send the selected file or files to the Recycle Bin.**

Windows puts all items that you delete in the Recycle Bin. To get rid of all the items in the Recycle Bin, you must open the Recycle Bin and choose File⇨Empty Recycle Bin. Click the Yes button or press Enter in the Confirm File Delete or Confirm Multiple File Delete dialog box that asks whether you want to delete the selected file or files. Be aware, however, that there's no turning back from this step. After you remove a folder or file from the Recycle Bin, you can't recover it. Figure 7-2 shows an open Recycle Bin.

Recycle Bin				
File Edit View Go Favorites Help				
Back Forward Up Cut Copy Paste Undo Delete Properties Views				
Address Recycle Bin				
Name	Original Location	Date Deleted	Type	
Pt04.doc	C:\PKZip	12/12/00 11:39 AM	Micro:	
Pt05.doc	C:\PKZip	12/12/00 2:54 PM	Micro:	
Pt06.doc	C:\PKZip	12/12/00 9:17 PM	Micro:	
Pt07.doc	C:\PKZip	12/13/00 2:14 PM	Micro:	
Pt08.doc	C:\PKZip	12/13/00 2:17 PM	Micro:	
Pt09.doc	C:\PKZip	12/13/00 11:23 PM	Micro:	
Pt10.doc	C:\PKZip	12/14/00 12:52 PM	Micro:	
Pt11.doc	C:\PKZip	12/14/00 1:00 PM	Micro:	
Revised Table of Contents (12-14-00).doc	C:\PKZip	12/17/00 1:42 PM	Micro:	
Template for Quick Reference Navigational Guide -- Word.doc	C:\PKZip	12/17/00 1:42 PM	Micro:	
TOC.doc	C:\PKZip	12/18/00 10:04 PM	Micro:	
Word Quick Ref TOC.doc	C:\PKZip	12/12/00 2:53 PM	Micro:	
(Soplame.Com) - Johnny Cash The_Rebel_(Johnny_Yuma).mp3	C:\MP3s	12/11/00 10:46 PM	MP3	
(Soplame.Com) - Lucha Reyes - Dos almas.mp3	C:\MP3s	12/11/00 10:46 PM	MP3	
(Soplame.Com) - Lucha Reyes - La Canción del Porvenir.mp3	C:\MP3s	12/11/00 10:52 PM	MP3	
113 object(s)	145MB			

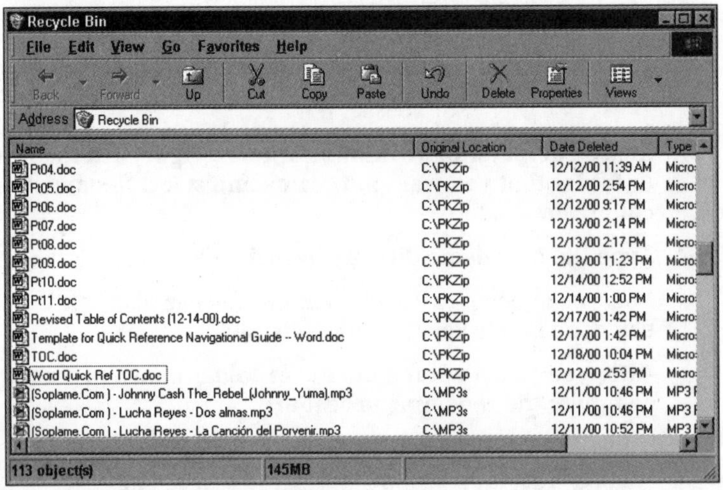

Figure 7-2: You can usually find one or two good things when you rummage in the trash.

Use the following tips to work efficiently with the Recycle Bin:

✦ **To retrieve stuff from the Recycle Bin:** Open the Recycle Bin and drag the files and folders that you want to save from the Recycle Bin to the desired location.

✦ **To empty the Recycle Bin:** Open the Recycle Bin and choose File⇨ Empty Recycle Bin from the Recycle Bin window's menu bar. Or right-click the Recycle Bin icon and choose Empty Recycle Bin.

Chapter 8: Getting a Better Look at Files and Folders

In This Chapter

- **Choosing how you view folders and files in windows**
- **Browsing folders the Windows way**
- **Changing the way you deal with folders**

If you're fooling around with files and folders or searching for a certain file or folder, it helps to know the different ways to view files. Windows offers a bunch of ways to work with files and folders. You can make a folder look and behave like a Web page. You can view files as *thumbnails* (small, preview-sized versions of graphics) — a handy technique when you're working with images.

Making Windows Work like a Web Browser

For fans of the World Wide Web and Web browsing, Windows gives you the opportunity to make the Windows desktop and all folders look and behave like Web pages. Rather than double-click to open a file or make use of a shortcut, you click just once. And instead of the pointer behaving like the pointer most people know and love, it behaves like a pointer behaves on a Web page. If you move it over anything that you can click — an icon, for example — the pointer turns into a gloved hand (see Figure 8-1).

Follow these steps for a Web-style Windows or if you have a Web-style Windows and you want to go back to the Classic style:

1. **Go to the Folder Options dialog box.**

   How you get there depends on your version of Windows:

   - **Windows 98:** Click the Start button and choose Settings⇨Folder Options.
   - **Windows Me:** Click the Start button and choose Settings⇨Control Panel; then double-click the Folder Options icon.

2. **Make your choices on the General tab of the Folder Options dialog box:**

   - **Windows 98:** Click the Web Style radio button.

- **Windows Me:** Under Web View, choose Enable Web Content in Folders. Then, under Click Items as Follows, choose Single-click to Open Item and choose an Underline option as well.

3. **Click OK.**

Figure 8-1: Is it Windows . . . or a Web browser?

Browsing Folders on a Local Disk

You can use any of the three Windows browsing windows (My Computer, Windows Explorer, or Internet Explorer) to browse the contents of the drives that attach to your computer. These disks can be in local drives, such as your floppy drive (A), hard drive (C), or CD-ROM drive (D). If your computer is on a Local Area Network (LAN), these disks can be disks on remote drives to which you have access, such as a network E, F, or G drive. Browsing folders by using My Computer and Windows Explorer is much more direct (because these windows both sport icons for the drives attached to your computer) and thus is the topic of this section.

Browsing folders with Web Page view turned on

Windows supports a folder view known as *Web Page view*. If you turn on this view in one of the browsing windows, vital statistics appear in an info panel in the window each time that you select a particular file or folder icon. These statistics include the folder name or filename, the last date modified, and, in the case of files, the file type and size in kilobytes. Moreover, if you select an application file, such as a Microsoft Word or Excel document, the name of the person who wrote the document also appears in the info panel. And if you select a graphics file of a format that Windows can decipher or an HTML document, a thumbnail of the image or page appears as well.

Figure 8-2 shows the Windows Explorer after you select a graphic image with the Web Page view turned on. Notice the third windowpane (in the middle). It offers information about the graphic and even shows a thumbnail depiction of it.

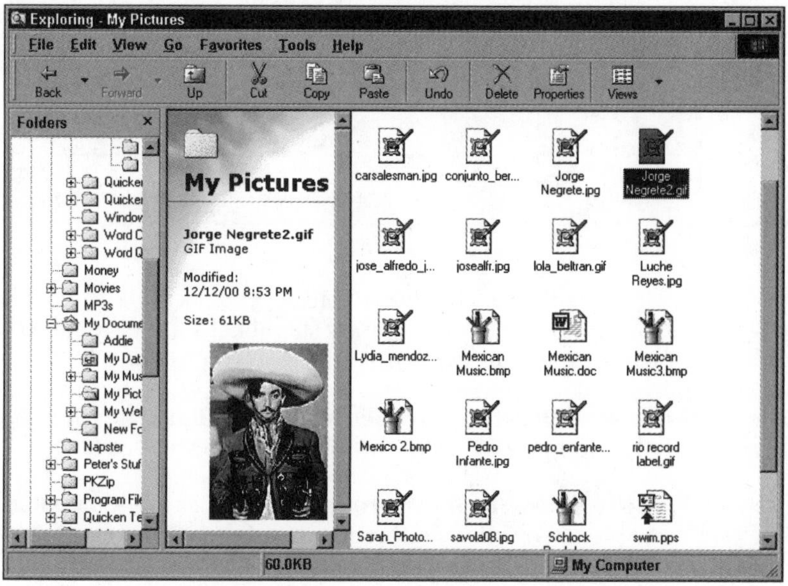

Figure 8-2: In Web Page view, you can view all sorts of stats about files on your computer.

To see files in Web Page view, follow these instructions:

- ✦ **In Windows 98:** Choose View⇨As Web Page from the menu bar of the browsing window or right-click on a blank area inside the window and choose View⇨As Web Page.
- ✦ **In Windows Me:** Enable Web content in folders. The section "Making Windows Work like a Web Browser," earlier in this chapter, explains how to do so.

Browsing folders with thumbnail view turned on

If you're browsing folders that contain numerous graphics or Web pages (for example, the pages that you're developing for your own Web site on the Internet), you can view thumbnail images of the graphic or Web-page files. As shown in Figure 8-3, each thumbnail gives you a fair image of the file in question.

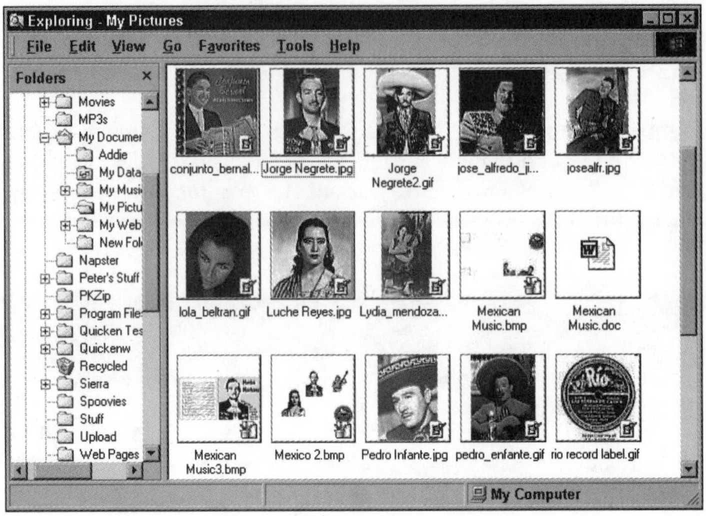

Figure 8-3: By using Thumbnail view, you can see actual images of the graphics and Web pages in your folder.

To view thumbnails in Windows Me, all you need to do is right-click the folder window and choose View⇨Thumbnails from the shortcut menu or choose View⇨Thumbnails from the menu bar.

Before you can use the Thumbnail view in Windows 98, however, you must add the Thumbnail view to the folder's properties, as follows:

1. **Open one of the three browsing windows (My Computer, Windows Explorer, or Internet Explorer) and then select the drive or folder whose contents you want to see in Thumbnail view.**
2. **Right-click the folder's icon and choose Properties from the shortcut menu to open the Properties dialog box for that folder.**
3. **Click to select the Enable Thumbnail View check box on the General tab of the folder's Properties dialog box and then click OK.**

After you enable the Thumbnail view for the folder, you can turn it on:

1. **Select the folder for which you enabled the Thumbnail view in the My Computer, Windows Explorer, or Internet Explorer window.**
2. **Choose View⇨Thumbnails or click the drop-down button attached to the Views button on the Standard toolbar; then choose Thumbnails.**

TIP

To turn off the Thumbnail view for a folder, just select another view (such as Large Icons or List) from the View menu. (You don't need to go to the trouble of disabling the Thumbnail view in the folder's Properties dialog box.)

Index

T

V

W

Z

Book II

Word 2002

The 5th Wave By Rich Tennant

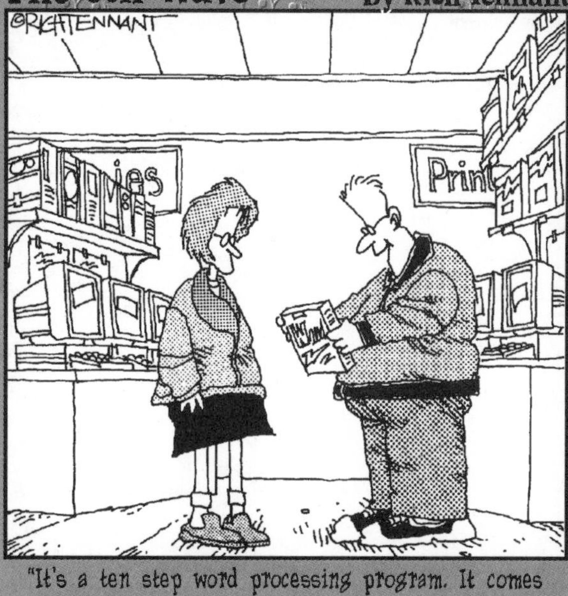

"It's a ten step word processing program. It comes with a spell-checker, grammar-checker, cliche-checker, whine-checker, passive/aggressive-checker, politically correct-checker, hissy-fit-checker, pretentious pontificating-checker, boring anecdote-checker and a Freudian reference-checker."

Contents at a Glance

Chapter 1: Word Basics

In This Chapter

- Discovering the Word screen
- Making a new document
- Opening an existing document
- Navigating in Word
- Getting familiar with paragraphs
- Working on more than one document at a time
- Working in more than one place in a document at a time
- Zooming in and zooming out

If you've been around word processors for a while, you probably know a lot of this stuff already. In case you need a refresher, however, don't jump ahead too soon. And in case you've never even touched a word processor before, you've come to the right place. This chapter gets you going by explaining some basic word-processing functions such as opening a document, moving about in a document, zooming in on a document, and the like. So what's a document you say? Well, you've come to the right place.

What All That Stuff On-Screen Is

Seeing the Word screen for the first time is sort of like trying to find your way through Tokyo's busy Ikebukuro subway station. It's intimidating, as Figure 1-1 shows. But after you start using Word, you quickly learn what everything is. In the meantime, Table 1-1 gives you some shorthand descriptions.

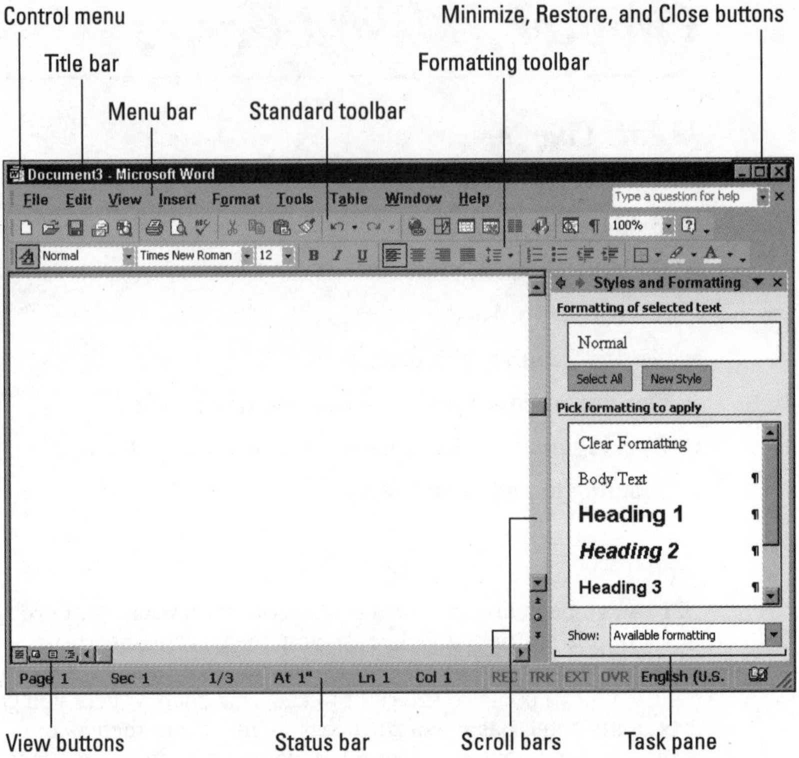

Figure 1-1: The Word screen — where the action is.

Table 1-1	**The Word Screen**
Part of Screen	***What It Is***
Title bar	At the top of the screen, the title bar tells you the name of the program you're working in and the document you're working on.
Control menu	Click here to open a menu with options for minimizing, maximizing, moving, and closing the window.
Minimize, Restore, Close buttons	These three magic buttons enable you to very easily shrink, enlarge, and close the window you're working in.
Menu bar	The menu options, from File to Help, from which you choose to give commands.
Standard toolbar	Offers buttons that you click to execute commands.
Formatting toolbar	Offers formatting buttons and drop-down lists for changing the appearance or layout of text.
Scroll bars	The scroll bars help you get from place to place in a document.
View buttons	Click one of these to change your view of a document.

Part of Screen	What It Is
Status bar	The status bar gives you basic information about where you are and what you're doing in a document. It tells you what page and what section you're in, the total number of pages in the document, and where the insertion point is on the page.
Task pane	Offers commands and links to make your work go faster.

REMEMBER

The task pane is new in Word 2002. When you choose certain Word commands, the task pane appears on the right side of the Word window (refer to Figure 1-1). It offers menus, buttons, and tools for completing tasks. To close the task pane, click its Close button. To switch task panes when a task pane is open, click the down arrow to open the task pane drop-down list, and choose the name of the task pane you want to see.

Creating a New Document

Document is just a fancy word for a letter, report, announcement, or proclamation that you create in Word. When you first start Word, you see a document with the generic name *Document1*. Apart from the new document that appears when you start Word, the program offers a bunch of ways to create a brand new document, as follows:

- **Starting from a blank document:** Click the New Blank Document button on the Standard toolbar, press Ctrl+N, or click the Blank Document hyperlink in the New Document task pane, as shown in Figure 1-2. (Choose File⇨New to open the New Document task pane.) Go this route and you make a blank document from the Normal template. For most occasions, the blank document is a fine place to start.
- **Starting with a sophisticated template:** In the New Document task pane, click the General Templates hyperlink (which you find under the New from Template heading; see Figure 1-2). The Templates dialog box appears. Click a tab, select a template or wizard, and click the OK button. Each template comes with its own sophisticated styles so that you don't need to create fancy layouts yourself. A template is a foundation for starting documents. Instead of creating formats yourself, the formats are created for you. A *wizard* is a series of dialog boxes in which you make choices about the kind of document that you want. If you're in the market for a fancy document, you can save a lot of time by creating it with a template or a wizard, because you don't need to do the formatting yourself.

✦ **Starting with a template from the Microsoft Web site:** Click the Templates on Microsoft.com hyperlink (which you find in the task pane under the New from Template heading). Your browser opens and you go to the Microsoft Web site, where you can choose a template. After you click the Edit in Microsoft Word link, the new document appears on your Word screen. (Make sure that you delete the copyright notices if you use templates from Microsoft! You find these notices at the end of the documents that you create.)

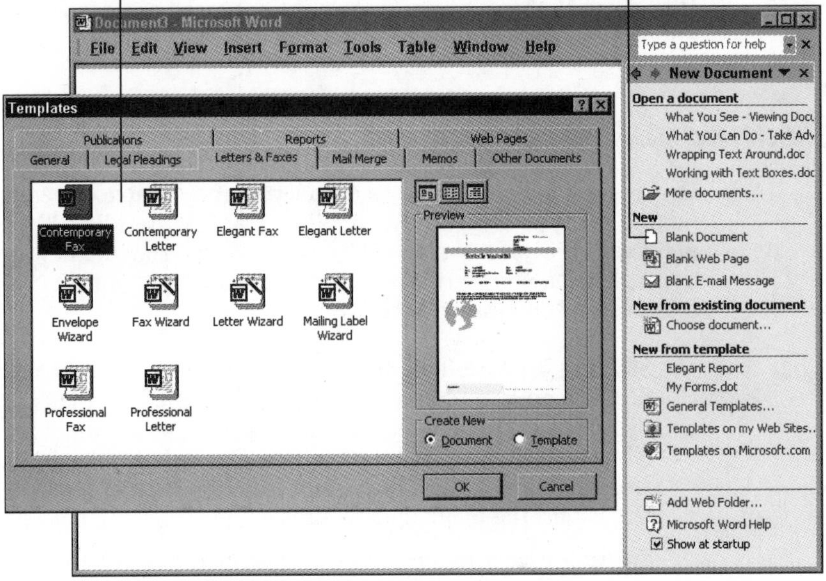

Figure 1-2: Creating a brand-new document in Word.

To see the New Document task pane again, choose File⇨New. You can also choose View⇨Task Pane to display the task pane, click the down arrow on the task pane to open a drop-down list of task panes, and select New Document.

Opening a Document You Already Created

Before you can start working on a document that you previously created and named, you must open it. And because finding the document that you want to open can sometimes prove difficult, Word offers several amenities to help you locate documents and quickly open them. The following sections provide instructions for opening and closing documents.

The conventional way to open a document

Following is the conventional method of opening a document:

1. **Choose File➪Open, press Ctrl+O, or click the Open button.**

   You see the Open dialog box, as shown in Figure 1-3.

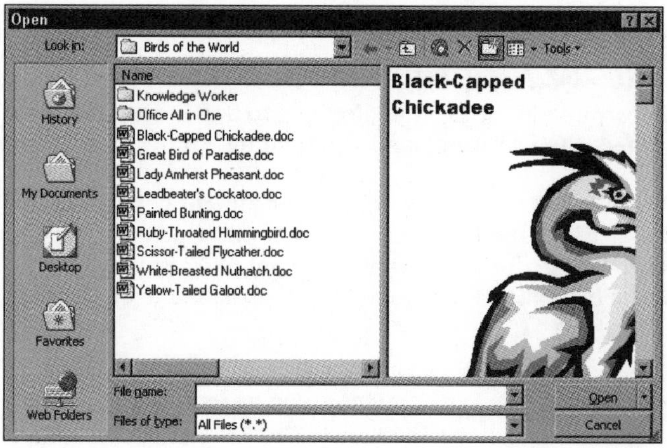

Figure 1-3: The Open dialog box is for opening documents that you created.

2. **Find the folder that holds the document that you want to open by using any of these nifty tools:**

   * **Look In drop-down list:** Open the Look In drop-down list and then click a drive letter or folder to see its contents.

   * **Back button:** If you stray too far in your search, click the Back button to see the folder that you looked at previously. In long, futile searches, click the down arrow beside the button and choose a folder from the list of folders you looked in.

   * **Up One Level button:** Click the Up One Level button to climb up the hierarchy of folders on your computer system.

   * **Views button and list:** Click the Views down arrow and choose an option from the drop-down list to examine the contents of a folder more closely. The List option lists filenames; the Details option tells how large files are and when they were last modified; the Properties option provides details about the file selected in the dialog box; and the Preview option shows you the file. You can also click the Views button to cycle through the choices on the list.
   * **Folders:** Double-click a folder in the Open dialog box to place its name in the Look In box and see its contents.

3. **After you find the right folder and it appears in the Look In box, you can either double-click the document's name in the Name list to open it or click once to select the name of the document and then click the Open button.**

You find out about using dialog boxes and making menu and list choices in the Windows portion of this book (Book 1). The basic concepts are the same!

Speedy ways to open documents

Rooting around in the Open dialog box to find a document is a bother, so Word offers the following handy techniques for opening documents:

- **File menu:** If you want to open a document you worked on recently, it may be on the File menu. Check it out. Open the File menu and see whether the document that you want to open is one of the four listed at the bottom of the menu. If so, click its name or press its number (1 through 4).
- **Document list in New Document task pane:** The same documents that are listed on the File menu can also be found at the top of the New Document task pane. Click a file there to open it.
- **History button in the Open dialog box:** Click the History button in the Open dialog box to see a list of the last three-dozen documents and folders that you opened. Double-click a document to reopen it; double-click a folder to see its contents.
- **My Documents button in the Open dialog box:** Click the My Documents button to see the contents of the My Documents folder. Double-click a document to open it. The My Documents folder is a good place to keep documents that you're currently working on. After you're done with a current document, you can move it to a different folder for safekeeping.
- **Favorites button in the Open dialog box:** Click the Favorites button to see the contents of the Favorites folder and then double-click a shortcut icon to open a document or folder.
- **Windows Documents menu:** Click the Start button and choose Documents to see a list of the last 15 files you opened (in Word and in other programs). Choose a Word document on the list to open it in Word.

To create a shortcut to a document and place it in the Favorites folder, find and select the document in the Open dialog box. Then open the Tools drop-down menu and choose Add to Favorites. (To remove a shortcut icon, select it and then click the Delete button. By doing so, you delete the shortcut but not the document or folder itself.)

TIP

To list more than four documents at the bottom of the File menu and the top of the New Document task pane, choose Tools⇨Options, click the General tab in the Options dialog box, and enter a number higher than 4 in the Recently Used File List box.

Moving Around in Documents

Word offers a couple of very speedy techniques for jumping around in documents: Scrolling by using the scroll bar and pressing shortcut keys. I describe these techniques in the following sections. (Check out Chapter 8 to discover other ways to get around in Word.)

Keys for getting around quickly

One of the fastest ways to go from place to place is to press the keys and key combinations in Table 1-2.

Table 1-2 Word Navigation Shortcuts

Key	*Where It Takes You*
PgUp	Up the length of one screen.
PgDn	Down the length of one screen.
Ctrl+PgUp	To the previous page in the document.
Ctrl+PgDn	To the next page in the document.
Ctrl+Home	To the top of the document.
Ctrl+End	To the bottom of the document.

TIP

If pressing Ctrl+PgUp or Ctrl+PgDn doesn't get you to the top or bottom of a page, you must have clicked the Select Browse Object button (the one that resembles a circle) near the bottom of the vertical scroll bar. When you click this button and make a choice (bookmark, comment, heading, or whatever) from the pop-up list, Word jumps to the next thing you chose each time you press Ctrl+PgUp or Ctrl+PgDn. Click the Select Browse Object button and choose Browse by Page to make these key combinations work again.

Zipping around with the scroll bar

You can also use the scroll bar to get around in documents. The *scroll bar* is the vertical stripe along the right side of the screen that resembles an elevator shaft. Here's how to move around by using the scroll bar:

- To move through a document quickly, grab the *elevator* (also known as the *scroll box*) and drag it up or down. As you scroll, a box appears with the page number and the names of headings on the pages that you scroll past (providing that you assigned Word styles to those headings, which are explained in Chapter 6).
- To move line by line up or down, click the up or down arrow at the top or bottom of the scroll bar.
- To move screen by screen, click anywhere on the scroll bar except on the arrows or the elevator.

By the way, the scroll bar on the bottom of the screen is for moving from side to side (horizontally).

Understanding How Paragraphs Work

Back in English class, your teacher taught you that a paragraph is a part of a longer composition that presents one idea or, in the case of dialogue, presents the words of one speaker. Your teacher was right, too, but for word-processing purposes, a paragraph is a lot less than that. In word processing, a paragraph is simply what you put on-screen before you press the Enter key.

A heading, for example, is a paragraph. So is a graphic. If you press Enter on a blank line to go to the next line, the blank line is considered a paragraph. If you type **Dear John** at the top of a letter and press Enter, "Dear John" is a paragraph.

Knowing this fact is important, because paragraphs have a lot to do with formatting. If you choose the Format⇨Paragraph command and monkey around with the paragraph formatting, all your changes affect everything in the paragraph that the cursor's in. To make format changes to an entire paragraph, all you need to do is place the cursor there. You don't need to select the paragraph. And if you want to make format changes to several paragraphs in a row, all you need to do is select those paragraphs first.

Working on Many Documents at Once

In Word, you can work on more than one document at the same time. You can even work in two different places in the same document (as you discover in the very next section).

After you open a new document, a new button appears on the taskbar. To go from one document to another, you can just click its taskbar button. You can also open the Window menu and click the name of a document to see it on-screen. And if you want to see all open documents at once, choose Window⇨Arrange All. To move from one document to the next, either click inside a new window pane or press Ctrl+F6.

To focus on one window if several are open, click the window's Maximize button. By doing so, you enlarge the window so that it fills the screen. Click the window's Restore button (the one in the middle with a square in it) to shrink it and see the other windows as well.

Working in Two Places in the Same Document

You can open a window on two different places at once in a document. Why do that? Suppose you're writing a long report and want the introduction to support the conclusion, and you also want the conclusion to fulfill all promises made by the introduction. That's difficult to do sometimes, but you can make the process easier by opening the document to both places and writing the conclusion and introduction at the same time.

You can use two methods to open the same document to two different places: Opening a second window on the document or splitting the screen. The following sections describe these two methods.

Opening a second window

To open a second window in a document, choose Window⇨New Window. Immediately, a second window opens and you see the start of your document. The following list describes what you can do with these two windows:

- Open the Window menu, and you see that it now lists two versions of your document, number 1 and number 2. (The numbers appear after the filename.) Choose number 1 to go back to where you were before. You can also click a taskbar button to go from window to window.
- You can move around in either window as you please. If you make changes in either window, you make them to the same document. Choose the File⇨Save command in either window and you save all the changes that you made in both windows. The important thing to remember here is that you're working on a single document, not two documents.

- When you want to close either window, just click its Close Window button. You go back to the other window, and only one version of your document appears in the Window menu.

Splitting the screen

Splitting a window means to divide it into top and bottom halves. To do so, choose Window➪Split. A gray line appears on-screen. Roll the mouse down until the gray line is where you want the split to be, and click. You get two screens split down the middle, as shown in Figure 1-4.

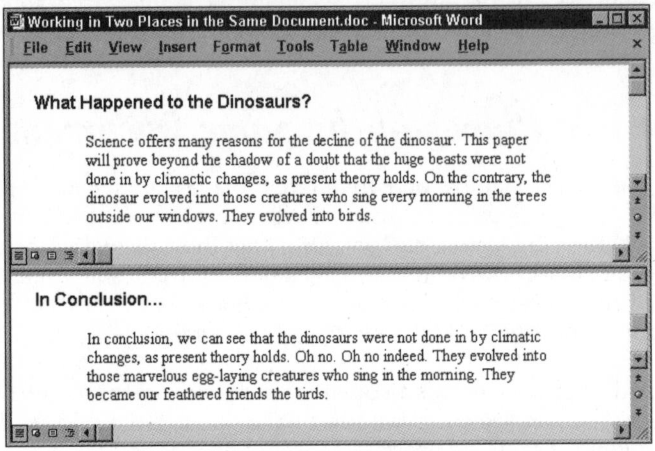

Figure 1-4: Work in two places in a document at one time by using Word's split-screen capability.

Now you have two windows and two sets of scroll bars along the right side of the screen. The following list describes what you can do next:

- ✦ Use the scroll bars to move up or down on either side of the split that divides the screen, or press PgUp or PgDn or press the arrow keys. Click the other side if you want to move the cursor there.
- ✦ When you tire of this schizophrenic arrangement, choose Window➪ Remove Split or drag the gray line to the top or bottom of the screen to return to a single document.

TIP

In a split screen, you can choose a different view for the different halves. Choose Outline view for one half, for example, and Normal view for the other to see the headings in a document while you write the introduction. To change views, click a View button in the lower-left corner of the screen or open the View menu and make a choice (refer to Figure 1-1 to see where the View buttons are located).

FAST TRACK

You can also split a screen by moving the mouse cursor to the *split box* at the top of the scroll bar on the right. Move the cursor just above the arrow. After the cursor turns into double-arrows, click and drag the gray line down the screen. After you release the mouse button, you have a split screen. To quickly "unsplit" a screen, double-click the line that splits the screen in two.

Zooming In, Zooming Out

Eyes weren't meant to stare at computer screens all day, which makes the Zoom command all the more valuable. Use this command freely and often to enlarge or shrink the text on-screen and preserve your eyes for important things, such as gazing at the horizon.

Give this command in one of two ways:

- ✦ Click the down arrow next to the Zoom drop-down list box and choose a magnification percentage from the drop-down list, as shown in Figure 1-5. You find the Zoom drop-down list box on the Standard toolbar.
- ✦ Click inside the Zoom text box, type a percentage of your own, and press the Enter key.

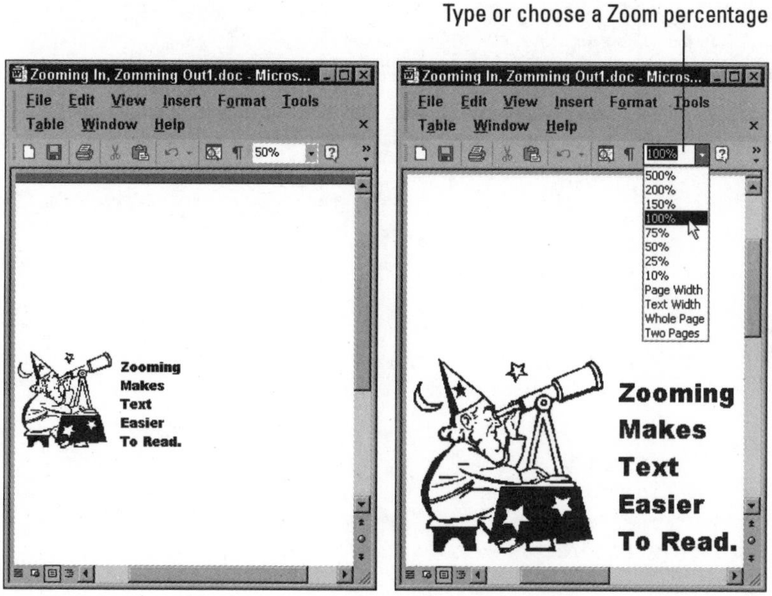

Figure 1-5: Now you can choose a size for any eyes.

Sometimes shrinking the text way down to see how pages are laid out pays off. After you lay out a table, for example, you can shrink it down to see how it looks from a bird's-eye view.

Going to a specific item in your document

Sure, you can move around a document by hitting some keys or using the scroll bar, but if you know exactly where you want to go, Word provides an easy way to get there.

1. **Choose Edit⇨Go To or simply double-click the page number box on the status bar in the lower left of the screen.**
2. **In the Go To tab of the Find and Replace dialog box that appears, select the type of item that you want to go directly to.**

   You can choose to go to a specific page, a section, a line, a bookmark, and many more things that you may never dream of putting into your Word document!

3. **To go to a specific item, type the name or number of the item (depending on what you selected) in the Enter Page Number box and then click Go To (or press Ctrl+G).**

   To zip along to the next or previous item of the same type, leave the Enter Page Number box empty and then click the Next or Previous button.

Chapter 2: Saving, Naming, Deleting, and Exiting

In This Chapter

- **Saving a document**
- **Renaming a document**
- **Closing a document**
- **Deleting a document**
- **Working in more than one place in a document at a time**
- **Exiting Word**
- **Sharing documents with other word processors**

So you're working right along on your word-processing document, spending precious time and effort composing and fine-tuning a document of inestimable value. Maybe you've been sitting there for hours, your thoughts so unique that you're sure that you can never repeat them. Thank goodness you're using Word to give your creativity some tangible form. Suddenly, however, your computer freezes. Have you saved your document? Oh, no! Well, your creativity's suddenly become very intangible again. That hurts.

This scenario can happen to you (as it's happened to many others before you). This chapter helps you avoid such losses by showing you how to save and name your documents so that you can keep them forever — or for at least a very long time. Along the way, you also find out how to delete a document just in case you really want to lose something forever.

Saving Documents

Make sure that you save your documents for a rainy day. The first time that you save, Word asks you to name your document. After that, you can just save and save and save.

Saving a document for the first time

After you open a new document and work on it, you need to save it. As part of saving a document for the first time, Word opens a dialog box and invites you to give the document a name and choose the folder to keep it in. So the first time that you save, you do three things at once — you save your work, choose which folder to save the document in, and name your document.

To save a document for the first time, follow these steps:

1. **Choose File⇨Save, press Ctrl+S, or click the Save button.**

   The Save As dialog box appears, as shown in Figure 2-1.

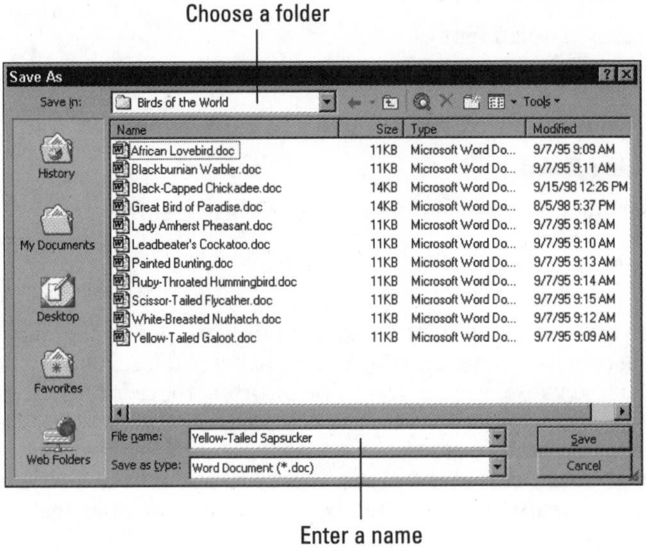

Figure 2-1: The Save As dialog box is your ticket to successful saving.

2. **Find and select the folder that you want to save document file in.**

   See Chapter 1 to find out more about opening a document. The same techniques for finding folders apply in the Open and Save As dialog boxes.

3. **Word suggests a name for the file in the File Name text box (which it takes from the first line in the document), but if that name isn't suitable, you can enter another.**

   Make sure that you enter one that you can remember later.

4. **Click the Save button.**

INTEGRATION

Document names can be 255 characters long and can include all characters and numbers except these: / ? : * " < > |. They can even include spaces. This limitation applies to all the Office applications, so getting into a consistent naming scheme for all your Office creations is a good habit. You no longer need to name your Sales Report document, for example, as **salesrpt** or something similarly cryptic. (Forget those old DOS restrictions!) Heck, you can now rear back and name it **Sales Report**.

Saving a document you've been working on

It behooves you to save your documents from time to time as you work on them. (No, *behooves* is not computer jargon. The word just means that you should.) When you save a document, Word takes the work that you've done since the last time you saved your document and stores the work safely on the hard disk.

You can save a document by using any of the following methods:

- ✦ Choose File➪Save from the menu bar.
- ✦ Click the Save button on the toolbar.
- ✦ Press Ctrl+S on the keyboard.

TIP

Save early and often. Make a habit of clicking the Save button whenever you leave your desk, take a phone call, or let the cat out. If you don't save your work and you experience a power outage or somebody trips over the computer's power cord, you lose all the work you did since the last time you saved your document.

Saving Versions of Documents

In a lengthy document such as a manual or a report that requires many drafts, saving different drafts can prove helpful. That way, if you want to retrieve something that you dropped from an earlier draft, you can do so. One way to save drafts of a document is to save drafts under different names, but why do that if you can rely on the Versions command on the File menu?

Follow these steps to save different versions of a document as it evolves into a masterpiece:

1. **Choose File➪Versions from the menu bar.**

   The Versions In dialog box appears. It lists past versions of the document that you saved, as shown in Figure 2-2.

2. **Click the Save Now button.**
3. **In the Save Version dialog box that appears (refer to Figure 2-2), write a descriptive comment about this version of the document and click OK.**

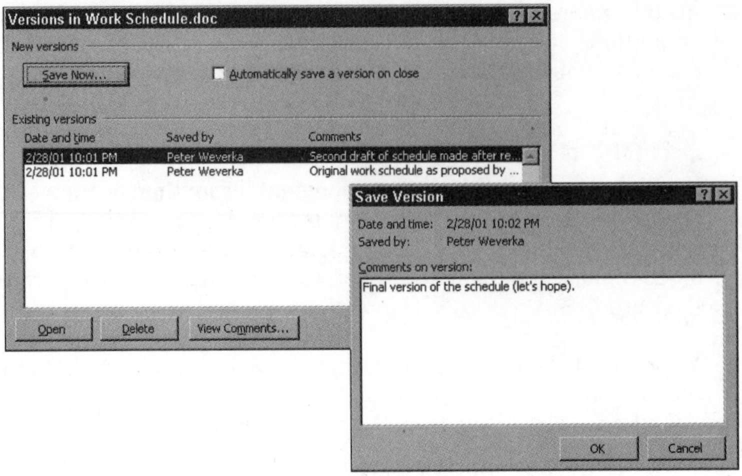

Figure 2-2: Keep track of versions of your documents in the Versions In and Save Version dialog boxes.

To review an earlier version of a document, choose File⇨Versions. In the Versions In dialog box, read comments to find the version that you want to open, select that version, and then click Open. The earlier version appears in its own window next to the up-to-date version. You can tell which version you're dealing with by glancing at the title bar, which lists the date that you saved the earlier version.

Select a version and click the Delete button in the Versions In dialog box to erase a version; click the View Comments button to read a comment in its entirety in the View Comments dialog box.

WARNING!

The Versions In dialog box also offers a check box for saving a version of the document each time that you close it, but I don't recommend saving versions automatically. If you do so, you don't get the opportunity to describe the document, which makes determining which draft is which very hard if you want to revisit a draft that you worked on before.

TIP

If a version of a document deserves to be a document in its own right, open it, choose File⇨Save As, and save it under its own name. That way, you can get at it more easily.

REAL WORLD

Renaming a document

If the name that you gave to a document suddenly seems inappropriate or downright meaningless, you can rename it. Here's how:

1. **Choose File⇨Open, press Ctrl+O, or click the Open button.**
2. **In the Open dialog box that appears, find and select the document that you want to rename.**

3. **Click the Tools button and choose Rena<u>m</u>e from the drop-down list.**

   The old name is highlighted.

4. **Enter a new name in place of the hold one.**
5. **Press the Enter key.**
6. **Either open the renamed file or click the Cancel button in the Open dialog box.**

Closing a Document

Choose File⇨Close to close a document after you're done working on it. You can also click the Close Window button, which is in the upper-right corner of the screen, right below its identical twin, the Close button.

If you try to close a document and you've made changes to it that you haven't saved yet, a dialog box appears and asks whether you want to save your changes. Click Yes, unless you're abandoning the document because you want to start all over again. In that case, click the No button.

Deleting a Word Document

Deleting documents is really the duty of the Windows operating system, but you can delete documents one at a time without leaving Word by following these steps:

1. **Choose File⇨Open as if you were opening a document and not deleting one.**
2. **In the Open dialog box, find the document that you want to delete and click to select it.**
3. **Either click the Delete button at the top of the dialog box or press the Delete key.**

   You can also right-click the document you want to delete and choose Delete on the shortcut menu.

4. **When Word asks whether you really want to go through with it and send the file to the Recycle Bin, click the Yes button.**
5. **Click Cancel or press Esc to close the Open dialog box.**

TIP

If you regret deleting a document, you can resuscitate it. On the Windows desktop, double-click the Recycle Bin icon. The Recycle Bin opens with a list of the files that you deleted. Click the one that you regret deleting and choose File⇨Restore.

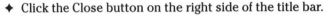

Exiting Word

When you're ready to say good-bye to Word, first save and close all your documents. Then do one of the following:

- Choose File⇨Exit.
- Click the Close button on the right side of the title bar.
- Press Alt+F4.

If, perchance, you forget to save and close a document, you see a dialog box that asks `Do you want to save the changes?` Click Yes.

Importing and Exporting Files

Word enables you to easily use files from other Microsoft Office applications, from other versions of Microsoft Word (including Macintosh versions), from Works, and from WordPerfect. Other files are a different story. Word isn't on speaking terms with WordPro, for example, not to mention antique word processors such as WordStar, XYWrite, and MultiMate (oh, the memories!).

Exporting files to and importing files from applications that Word recognizes and is friendly with is easy. Your coworkers who use WordPerfect, for example, can use your files, but your friends who use other word processors may well need to use stripped-down versions of your files with the text but none of the formats.

Even if you import or export a file successfully, some things can get lost. Special characters and symbols, for example, often don't translate well. Nor do certain fonts. Footers, endnotes, and comments are especially susceptible to problems. Carefully proofread files that you import or export to make sure that everything came out right.

Importing a file

To import a file, you open it and have Word turn it into a Word file by following these steps:

1. **Click the Open button, press Ctrl+O, or choose File⇨Open to access the Open dialog box.**
2. **Open the Files of Type drop-down list and see whether the kind of file you want to import is on the list and, if it is, select it; if it isn't (or if you can't find the file you're looking for in Step 3), choose All Files (*.*), the first option on the drop-down list.**

3. **Find the file that you want to import in the Open dialog box and select it.**
4. **Click the Open button.**

   With any luck, Word opens the file successfully.

TIP: Here's one way to get around file-importing impasses: If the application that you want to import the file from works in Windows, open the application, open the file that you want to copy, and copy the parts of the file that you need to the Clipboard. Then paste what's on the Clipboard into Word.

TIP: Another way to get around the problem is to see whether the other application can save files in Microsoft Word format. If it can, save the file as a Microsoft Word file in the other application and then open it in Word.

Exporting a Word document

To export a file so that someone with another kind of word processor can use it, you save the file in a new format by following these steps:

1. **Choose File⇨Save As.**
2. **Find the file that you want to export in the Save As dialog box and select it.**
3. **Open the Save as Type drop-down list and see whether the kind of file that you want to export is on the list and, if it is on the list, select it; if it isn't, select one of the following options from the drop-down list.**
   - **Rich Text Format (*.rft):** Retains the formatting of the text, but some word processors can't understand it. This option should be your first choice for exporting a file.
   - **Plain Text (*.txt):** Strips all the formatting but retains the text.
   - **Text with Layout (*.ans):** Strips most of the formatting and retains the text. It also retains line breaks and basic formats such as boldface and italics.
4. **Click the Save button.**

TIP: Most Windows-compatible applications can accept text from Word. Try copying the text to the Clipboard and then pasting it into the other application.

Chapter 3: Changing the Look of Your Document

In This Chapter

- **Customizing your screen**
- **Placing headers and footers**
- **Numbering pages**
- **Breaking a line or a page**
- **Hyphenating**
- **Spacing lines**
- **Inserting symbols**
- **Putting a border around a page**

Don't just sit down and start pounding away at the keyboard! You can do a number of things before you start to make your word-processing chores go a lot more smoothly. Start by getting the screen to look how you want it. Next, decide how to number your pages, whether you need footers, where you want a page to break, and so on. Have you even given a thought to automatic hyphenation? Probably not. This chapter helps you think of these things now rather than later — when you need to get down to some serious work.

Viewing Documents in Different Ways

In word processing, you want to focus sometimes on the writing, sometimes on the layout, and sometimes on the organization of your work. To help you stay in focus, Word offers the following different ways of viewing a document:

- **Normal view:** Choose View➪Normal or click the Normal View button (in the lower-left corner of the screen) when you want to focus on the words. Normal view is best for writing first drafts and proofreading.
- **Web Layout view:** Choose View➪Web Layout or click the Web Layout View button when you're creating a Web page.
- **Print Layout view:** Choose View➪Print Layout or click the Print Layout View button to see the big picture. You can see graphics, headers, and footers, and even page borders in Print Layout view.

- **Outline view:** Choose View⇨Outline or click the Outline View button to see how your work is organized. In Outline view, you see only the headings in a document and can easily move chunks of a document from place to place. (See Chapter 9 for more about Outline view.)
- **Full Screen view:** Choose View⇨Full Screen to display only the text that you're working on, as shown in Figure 3-1. When you choose Full Screen view, everything gets stripped away — buttons, menus, scroll bars, and all. Only a single button, Close Full Screen, remains. Click it or press Esc when you want the buttons, menus, and so on to come back. As the figure shows, however, you can also give commands from the menus on the menu bar in Full Screen view by moving the pointer to the top of the screen to make the menu bar appear.

Figure 3-1: You can see more of your creation by using Full Screen view.

Putting Headers and Footers on Pages

A *header* is a little description that appears along the top of a page so that the reader knows what's what. Usually, headers include the page number and a title. A *footer* is the same thing as a header, except that it appears along the bottom of the page, as befits its name.

To put a header or a footer in a document, follow these steps:

1. **Choose View⇨Header and Footer.**

   The Header box appears, as shown in Figure 3-2.

2. **Type your header in the box or, if you want a footer, click the Switch between Header and Footer button and type your footer.**
3. **Click the Close button.**

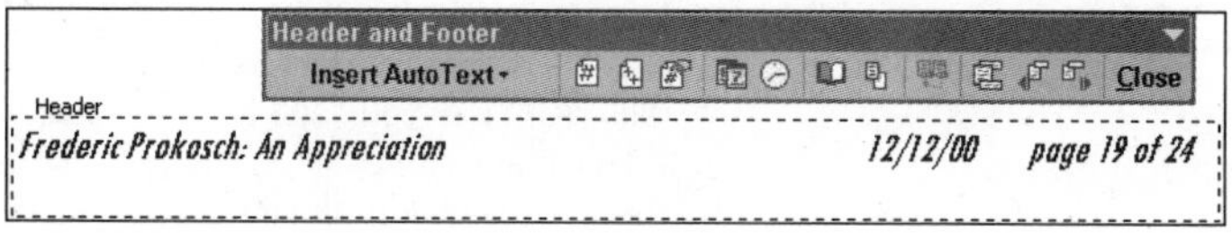

Figure 3-2: A header box and the Header and Footer toolbar.

TIP

While you're typing away in the Header or Footer box, you can call on most of the commands on the Standard and Formatting toolbars. You can change the text's font and font size, click an alignment button, and paste text from the Clipboard.

You can also take advantage of the buttons on the Header and Footer toolbar, as listed in Table 3-1.

Table 3-1 Header and Footer Buttons

Button	*What It Does*
Insert AutoText	Opens a drop-down list for making AutoText entries, including when it was last saved and printed and who created it.
	Inserts the page number.
	Inserts the number of pages in the entire document.
	Opens the Page Number Format dialog box so that you can choose a format for the page number in the header of footer.
 	These buttons insert the date and the time in the header or footer. The date and time are updated automatically.
	Opens the Layout tab of the Page Setup dialog box so that you can tell Word that you want a different header and footer on the first page of the document or that you want different headers and footers on odd and even pages. (You can use this feature if you're printing on both sides of the page.)
	Shows the text on the page so that you can see what the header or footer looks like in relation to the text.

(continued)

Table 3-1 *(continued)*

Button	*What It Does*
	Tells Word that you don't want this header or footer to be the same as the header or footer in the previous section of the document. When this button is selected, the header or footer is the same as the header or footer in the previous section of the document, and the Header or Footer box reads, Same as Previous. To enter a different header or footer for a section, click this button and enter the new header or footer. To change headers or footers, you must divide a document into sections.
	Switches between the header and the footer.
 	Shows the header or footer in the previous and next sections of a document that contains more than one section.

Removing headers and footers is easy; just follow these steps:

1. **Choose View⇨Header and Footer or double-click the header or footer in Print Layout view.**
2. **Select the header or footer.**
3. **Press the Delete key.**

To choose how much space the header and footer occupy on the page, choose File⇨Page Setup. Then, on the Layout tab of the Page Setup dialog box, enter measurements in the Header and Footer text boxes.

TIP

To remove a header or footer from the first page of a document, choose File⇨Page Setup (or click the Page Setup button on the Header and Footer toolbar). In the Page Setup dialog box, click the Layout tab, check the Different First Page check box, and click OK.

Numbering the Pages

Word numbers the pages of a document automatically, which is great, but if your document has a title page and table of contents and you want to start numbering pages on the fifth page, or if your document includes more than one section, page numbers can turn into a sticky business.

The first thing to ask yourself is whether you included headers or footers in your document. If so, go to the previous section in this part, "Putting Headers and Footers on Pages." It explains how to put page numbers in a header or footer.

Meantime, use the Insert➪Page Numbers command to put plain old page numbers on the pages of a document:

1. **Choose Insert➪Page Numbers to open the Page Numbers dialog box, as shown in Figure 3-3.**

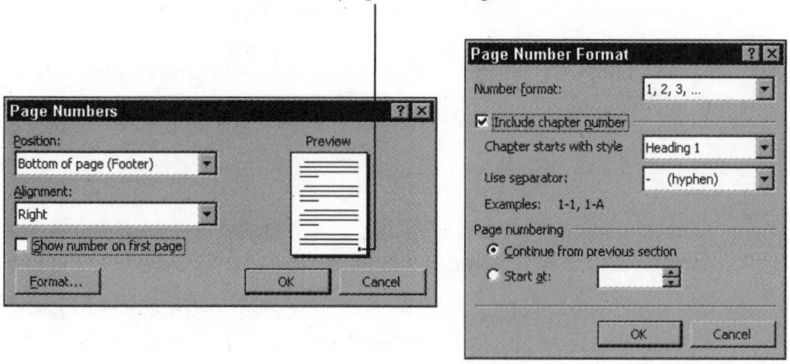

Figure 3-3: Enter a page number (left) and choose a format for page numbers (right).

2. **In the Position and Alignment drop-down list boxes, choose where you want the page number to appear.**

   The lovely Preview box on the right shows where your page number goes.

3. **Click to deselect the Show Number on First Page check box if you're working on a letter or other type of document that usually doesn't have a number on page 1.**

4. **Click OK.**

If you want to get fancy, I should warn you that doing so in headers and footers is easier than in the Page Numbers dialog box. Follow the first three steps in the preceding list and click the Format button. Then, in the Page Number Format dialog box that appears (refer to Figure 3-3), choose one of these options:

- **Number Format:** Choose a new way to number the pages if you want to. (Notice the *i, ii, iii* choice. That's how the title pages and tables of contents in a book, including this one, are usually numbered.)
- **Include Chapter Number:** Select this check box if you want to start numbering pages anew at the beginning of each chapter. Pages in Chapter 1, for example, get the numbers 1-1, 1-2, and so on, and pages in Chapter 2 get the numbers 2-1, 2-2, and so on.
- **Chapter Starts with Style:** If necessary, choose a heading style from the drop-down list to tell Word where new chapters begin. You usually tag chapter titles with the Heading 1 style, but if your chapters begin with another style, choose it from the list.

- **Use Separator:** From the list, tell Word how you want to separate the chapter number from the page number. Choose the hyphen (1-1), period (1.1), colon (1:1), or one of the dashes (1–1).
- **Page Numbering:** This option is the one that matters if you divide your document into sections. Either start numbering the pages anew and enter a new page number (probably 1) in the Start At text box or else number pages where the previous section left off by selecting the Continue From Previous Section option button.

After you finish, click OK twice to number the pages and get back to your document.

To get rid of the page numbers if you don't like them, follow these steps:

1. **Either choose View⇨Header and Footer or double-click the page number in Print Layout view.**

2. **On the Header and Footer toolbar that appears, click the Switch Between Header and Footer button, if necessary, to get to the footer.**
3. **Select the page number by clicking it and then press the Delete key.**

   You may need to click the number a couple of times to select it correctly. You know the number is selected when black squares appear around it.

Breaking a Line

You can break a line in the middle, before it reaches the right margin, without starting a new paragraph. To do so, press Shift+Enter or choose Insert⇨Break and select the Text Wrapping Break option in the Break dialog box. Breaking a line this way is a great way to keep ugly white spaces from appearing on the right sides of lines.

Figure 3-4 shows how you can press Shift+Enter to make lines break better. The paragraphs are identical, but I broke lines in the right-hand paragraph to make the text easier to read. The ↵ symbol marks line breaks. To erase line breaks, click the Show/Hide ¶ button to see these symbols and then backspace over them.

Figure 3-4: Break your lines for a nicer look.

"A·computer·in·every·home·and·a·chicken·in·every·pot·is·our·goal,"·stated·Rupert·T.·Verguenza,·President·and·CEO·of·the·New·Technics·Corporation·International·at·the·annual·shareholder·meeting·this·week.¶	"A·computer·in·every·home·and·a·chicken·↵ in·every·pot·is·our·goal,"·stated·Rupert·T.·Verguenza,·President·and·CEO·of·the·New·Technics·Corporation·International·at·the·↵ annual·shareholder·meeting·this·week.¶

Breaking a Page

Word gives you another page so that you can keep going after you fill up one page. But what if you're impatient and want to start a new page right away? Whatever you do, *don't* press Enter over and over until you fill up the page. If you do that, the blank lines will get pushed here and there as you edit your document, and you may end up with a lot of blank spaces where you least expect it. Instead, create a page break by taking either of the following actions:

- ✦ Press Ctrl+Enter.
- ✦ Choose Insert⇨Break and select the Page Break option in the Break dialog box.

In Normal view, you know where a page break is because you see the words `Page Break` and a dotted line appear on-screen. In Print Layout view, you can't tell where you inserted a page break. To delete a page break, switch to Normal view, click the words `Page Break`, and press the Delete key. Change views by clicking the View buttons in the lower-left corner of the screen.

Hyphenating a Document

The first thing that you should know about hyphenating the words in a document is that you may not need to do it. Text that isn't hyphenated is much easier to read, which is why the majority of text in this book, for example, isn't hyphenated. It has a *ragged right margin,* to borrow typesetter lingo. Hyphenate only if text is trapped in columns or in other narrow places or if you want a very formal-looking document.

TIP

You can hyphenate text as you enter it, but I think that you should wait until after you write everything so that you can concentrate on the words themselves. Then, after you're done with your writing, you can either tell Word to hyphenate the document automatically or you can do it yourself.

WARNING!

Don't insert a hyphen simply by pressing the hyphen key, because the hyphen stays there even if the word appears in the middle a line and doesn't need to be broken in half. Instead, if a big gap appears in the right margin and a word is crying out to be hyphenated, put the cursor where the hyphen needs to go and press Ctrl+hyphen.

Hyphenating a document automatically

To hyphenate a document automatically, follow these steps:

1. **Choose Tools⇨Language⇨Hyphenation.**

   The Hyphenation dialog box appears, as shown in Figure 3-5.

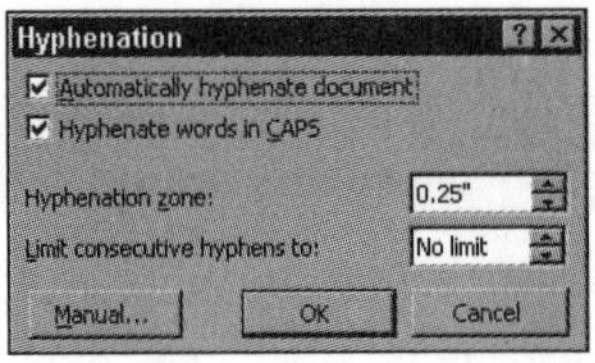

Figure 3-5: Use this dialog box to hyphenate a document automatically.

2. **Select the Automatically Hyphenate Document check box.**
3. **Click Hyphenate Words in CAPS to deselect the check box if you don't care to hyphenate words in uppercase.**

   If the text isn't justified — that is, if it's ragged right — you can play with the Hyphenation Zone setting (but I don't think that you should hyphenate ragged right text anyway). Words that fall in the Zone are hyphenated, so a large zone means a less ragged margin but more ugly hyphens, and a small zone means fewer ugly hyphens but a more ragged right margin.
4. **More than two consecutive hyphens on the right margin looks bad, so enter** 2 **in the Limit Consecutive Hyphens To text box.**
5. **Click OK.**

Hyphenating a document manually

The other way to hyphenate is to see where Word wants to put hyphens and "Yea" or "Nay" them one at a time:

1. **Select the part of the document that you want to hyphenate or place the cursor where you want hyphens to start appearing.**
2. **Choose Tools⇨Language⇨Hyphenation.**

   The Hyphenation dialog box appears (refer to Figure 3-5).

3. **Click the Manual button.**

   As shown in Figure 3-6, Word displays a dialog box with hyphenation choices. The cursor blinks on the spot where Word suggests putting a hyphen.

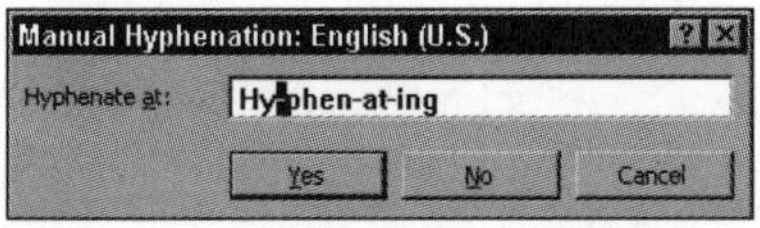

Figure 3-6: Manual hyphenation gives you control over where Word places hyphens.

4. **Click Yes or No to accept or reject Word's suggestion.**
5. **Keep accepting or rejecting Word's suggestions as it makes them.**

   A box appears to tell you that Word is finished hyphenating.
6. **Click the Cancel button in the Manual Hyphenation dialog box to quit hyphenating yourself.**

Unhyphenating and other hyphenation tasks

Here's some more hyphenation esoterica:

- To "unhyphenate" a document that you hyphenate automatically, choose Tools⇨Language⇨Hyphenation, deselect the Automatically Hyphenate Document check box, and click OK.
- To prevent Word from hyphenating a paragraph, choose Format⇨Paragraph, click the Line and Page Breaks tab, and select the Don't Hyphenate check box. (If you can't hyphenate a paragraph, it's probably because this box is selected unintentionally.)
- To hyphenate a single paragraph in the middle of a document — maybe because it's a long quotation or some other thing that needs to stand out — select the paragraph and hyphenate it manually by clicking the Manual button in the Hyphenation dialog box.

Spacing Lines

To change the spacing between lines, select the lines that you want to change or simply put the cursor in a paragraph if you're changing the line spacing in a single paragraph. (If you're just starting a document, you're ready to go.) Then click the down-arrow beside the Line Spacing button and choose an option from the drop-down list that appears.

To take advantage of more line-spacing options, choose Format➪Paragraph (or select More, the last option on the Line Spacing button list). Then, in the Paragraph dialog box that appears, select a Line Spacing option:

- **At Least:** Choose this option if you want Word to adjust for tall symbols or other unusual text. Word adjusts the lines but makes sure that, at minimum, the number of points that you enter in the At text box appears between each line.
- **Exactly:** Choose this option and enter a number in the At text box if you want a specific amount of space between lines.
- **Multiple:** Choose this option and put a number in the At text box to get triple-, quadruple-, quintuple-, or any other-spaced lines.

To quickly single-space text, click the paragraph or select the text if you want to change more than one paragraph and then press Ctrl+1. To quickly double-space text, select the text and press Ctrl+2. Press Ctrl+5 to put one and a half lines between lines of text.

Symbols and Special Characters

You can decorate your documents with all kinds of symbols and special characters — a death's head, a smiley face, the Yen symbol, and so on. To insert a symbol, click where you want it to go and follow these steps:

1. **Choose Insert➪Symbol.**

   The Symbol dialog box opens, as shown in Figure 3-7.

2. **Click the Font drop-down list to choose a symbol set.**

   When you choose some fonts, a Subset drop-down list appears.

3. **Choose a subset name from the list — Latin-1, for example — to help locate the symbol you're looking for.**
4. **Select a symbol.**
5. **Click the Insert button.**

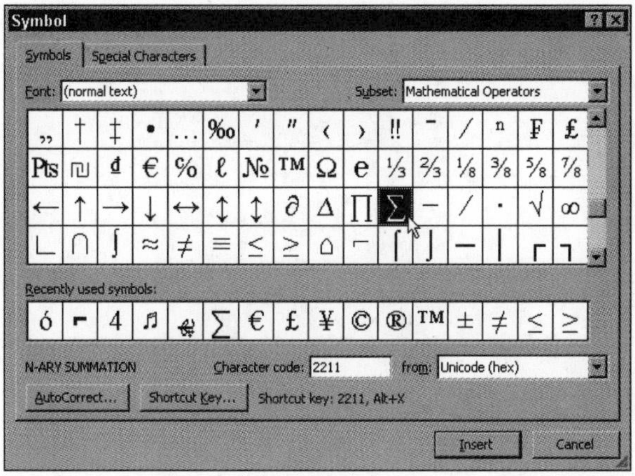

Figure 3-7: Use the Symbol dialog box to give your text symbolic meaning!

The symbol that you choose lands in your document, but the Symbol dialog box stays open so that you can select another symbol. Select another one or click Cancel (or press Esc) after you're done. You can choose special characters and unusual punctuation from the Special Characters tab of the Symbol dialog box.

Decorating a Page with a Border

Word offers a means of decorating title pages, certificates, menus, and similar documents with a page border. Besides lines, you can decorate the sides of a page with stars, pieces of cake, and other artwork. If you want to place a border around a page in the middle of the document, you must create a section break where the page is. Here's how to put borders around a page:

1. **Place the cursor on the first page of a document if you want to put a border around only the first page.**

   If your document is divided in sections and you want to put borders around certain pages in a section, place the cursor in the section — either on the first page, if you want the borders to go around it, or in a subsequent page.

2. **Choose Format➪Borders and Shading.**

3. **Click the Page Border tab in the Borders and Shading dialog box.**

   Figure 3-8 shows the Page Borders tab.

4. **In the Setting area of the Page Borders tab, choose a border.**

   The Custom setting is for putting borders on one, two, or three sides of the page, not four. Use the None setting to remove borders.

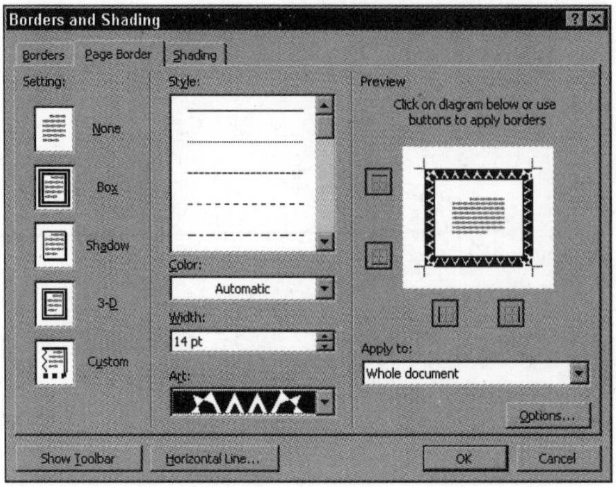

Figure 3-8: Why not use the Borders and Shading dialog box to add a border to your page.

5. **In the Apply To drop-down list box, tell Word which page or pages in the document get borders.**
6. **Select options to construct the border you want and then click OK.**

The Page Border tab offers a bunch of tools for fashioning a border:

- **Line for borders:** In the Style list, scroll down and choose a line for the borders. You will find interesting choices at the bottom of the menu. Look in the Preview window to see what your choices look like.
- **Color for borders:** Open the Color drop-down list and choose a color for the borderlines if you want a color border and you have a color printer.
- **Width of borders:** If you chose artwork for the borders, use the Width drop-down list to tell Word how wide to make the lines or artwork.
- **Artwork for borders:** Open the Art drop-down list and choose a symbol, illustration, star, piece of cake, or other artwork, if that's what you want for the borders. You will find some amusing choices on this long list, including ice cream cones, bats, and umbrellas.
- **Borders on different sides of the page:** Use the four buttons in the Preview window to tell Word on which sides of the page you want borders. Click these buttons to remove or add borders, as you wish.
- **Distance from edge of page:** Click the Options button and fill in the Border and Shading Options dialog box if you want to get specific about how close the borders can come to the edge of the page or pages.

Chapter 4: Editing Made Easy

In This Chapter

- Selecting text
- Deleting text and undoing mistakes
- Finding and replacing text
- Using the Thesaurus
- Spell-checking and grammar-checking
- Lowercasing and uppercasing

If you've always wanted to find, cut, paste, and replace text like those high-paid editors who helped to put this book together (ha!), this is the chapter for you. If you know a few simple routines, you can save yourself lots of time, especially if you never paid much attention in that high school typing class (who needs to know how to type?). As a bonus, this chapter reveals the secrets of spell-checking and grammar-checking documents. Who needs editors when you can do all this stuff yourself?

Selecting Text in Speedy Ways

To move text or copy it from one place to another, you have to select it first. You can also erase a great gob of text merely by selecting it and pressing the Delete key. So it pays to know how to select text. Table 4-1 lists some shortcuts for doing it.

Table 4-1 Selecting Shortcuts

To Select This	*Do This*
A word	Double-click the word.
A line	Click in the left margin next to the line.
Some lines	Drag the mouse over the lines or drag the mouse pointer down the left margin.
A paragraph	Double-click in the left margin next to the paragraph, or triple-click inside the paragraph.
A mess of text	Click at the start of the text, hold down the Shift key, and click at the end of the text.

(continued)

Table 4-1 *(continued)*	
To Select This	***Do This***
A gob of text	Put the cursor where you want to start selecting, press F8 or double-click EXT (it stands for Extend) on the status bar, and press an arrow key, drag the mouse, or click at the end of the selection.
Yet more text	If you select text and realize you want to select yet more text, double-click EXT on the status bar and start dragging the mouse or pressing arrow keys.
Text with the same formats	Right-click text that is formatted a certain way and choose Select Text with Similar Formatting.
A document	Hold down the Ctrl key and click in the left margin, or triple-click in the left margin, or choose Edit⇨Select All, or press Ctrl+A.

If you have a bunch of highlighted text on-screen and you want it to go away but it won't (because you pressed F8 or double-clicked EXT to select it), double-click EXT again.

TIP

After you press F8 or double-click EXT, all the keyboard shortcuts for moving the cursor also work for selecting text. For example, press F8 and press Ctrl+Home to select everything from the cursor to the top of the document. Double-click EXT and press End to select to the end of the line.

Deleting Text

To delete a bunch of text at once, select the text you want to delete and press the Delete key or choose Edit⇨Clear⇨Contents.

FAST TRACK

By the way, you can kill two birds with one stone by selecting text and then starting to type. The letters you type immediately take the place of and delete the text you selected.

Undoing a Mistake

Fortunately for you, all is not lost if you make a big blunder in Word, because the program has a marvelous little tool called the Undo command. This command "remembers" all the editorial changes you made since you opened your document. As long as you catch your error before you do five or six new things, you can "undo" your mistake. Try one of these undo techniques:

Too many errors to keep track of?

What if you commit a monstrous error but can't correct it with the Undo command? You can try closing your document without saving the changes you made to it. As long as you didn't save your document after you made the error, the error won't be in your document when you open it again — but neither will the changes you want to keep.

✦ **Choose Edit➪Undo (or press Ctrl+Z).** This command changes names, depending on what you did last. For example, if you just typed a sentence, it says `Undo Typing`.

✦ **Click the Undo button to undo your most recent change.** If you made your error and went on to do something else before you caught it, click the down arrow next to the Undo button. You see a menu of your last six actions, as shown in Figure 4-1. Click the one you want to undo or, if it isn't on the list, click the down-arrow on the scroll bar until you find the error, and then click it. If you do this, however, you also undo all the actions on the Undo menu above the one you're undoing. For example, if you undo the 98th action on the list, you also undo the 97 before it.

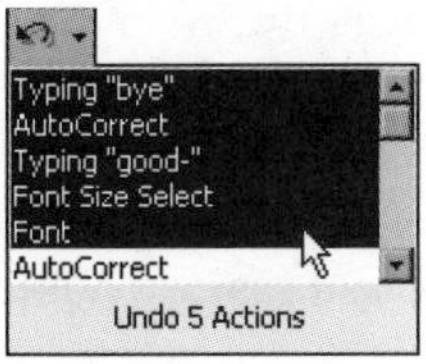

Figure 4-1: Select an action from the menu to undo.

Contrary to the Undo command is the Redo command. It "redoes" the commands you "undid." If you undo a bunch of commands and regret doing so, you can pull down the Redo menu by clicking its down arrow and choose the commands you thoughtlessly "undid" the first time around.

Searching for Text and Formatting

You can search for a word in a document, and even for fonts, special characters, and formats. Here's how:

1. **Choose Edit⇨Find, press Ctrl+F, or click the Select Browse Object button in the lower-right corner of the screen and choose Find.**

   The Find and Replace dialog box appears, as shown in Figure 4-2. (In this figure, the More button is clicked so that you can see all the Find options.)

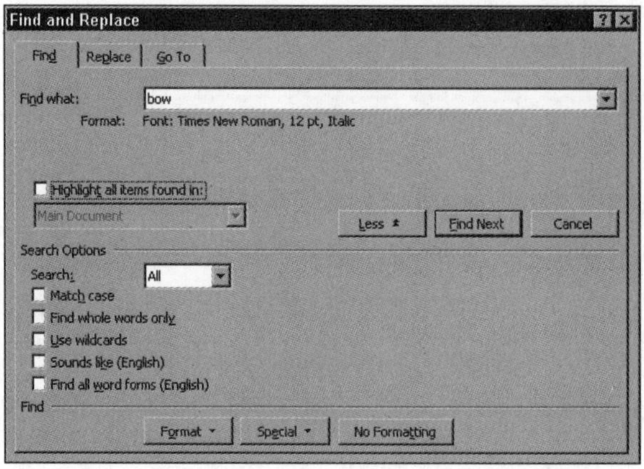

Figure 4-2: The Find and Replace options.

2. **Enter the word, phrase, or format that you're looking for in the Find What text box (I explain how to search for formats shortly).**

   The words and phrases you looked for recently are in the Find What drop-down list. If you want, you can click the down-arrow to open the Find What drop-down list and make a selection.

3. **To search for all instances of the thing you are looking for, select the Highlight All Items Found In check box and make a choice from the drop-down list below it.**

   If you go this route, Word highlights all instances of the thing you are looking for.

4. **Click the Find Next button if you are looking for a simple word or phrase, or the Find All button to highlight all instances of a word or phrase in your document.**

   To conduct a more sophisticated search, click the More button.

If Word finds what you're looking for, it highlights it — or all instances of it, if that is the way you chose to search — in the document. To find the next instance of the thing you are looking for, click Find Next again. You can also close the Find and Replace dialog box and click either the Previous Find/Go

To or Next Find/Go To button at the bottom of the scroll bar to the right of the screen (or press Ctrl+Page Up or Ctrl+Page Down) to go to the previous or next instance of the thing you're looking for.

By clicking the More button in the Find and Replace dialog box, you can get very selective about what to search for and how to search for it:

✦ **Search:** Click the down arrow and choose All, Up, or Down to search the whole document, search from the cursor position upward, or search from the cursor position downward, respectively.

✦ **Match Case:** Searches for words with upper- and lowercase letters that exactly match those in the Find What box. With this box selected, a search for *bow* finds that word, but not *Bow* or *BOW.*

✦ **Find Whole Words Only:** Normally, a search for *bow* yields *elbow, bowler, bow-wow,* and all other words with the letters *b-o-w* (in that order). Click this option and you only get *bow.*

✦ **Use Wildcards:** Click here if you intend to use wildcards in searches. A *wildcard* is a character that represents characters in a search expression. For example, the asterisk (*) represents zero or more characters; the question mark (?) represents a group of characters.

✦ **Sounds Like:** Looks for words that sound like the one in the Find What box. A search for *bow* with this option selected finds *beau,* for example.

✦ **Find All Word Forms:** Takes into account verb endings and plurals. With this option clicked, you get *bows, bowing,* and *bowed,* as well as *bow.*

To search for words, paragraphs, tab settings, and styles, among other things, that are formatted a certain way, click the Format button and choose an option from the menu. You see the familiar dialog box you used in the first place to format the text. In the Find dialog box shown in Figure 4-2, I chose Font from the Format menu and filled in the Font dialog box in order to search for the word *bow* in Times Roman, 12-point, italicized font.

Click the Special button to look for format characters, manual page breaks, and other unusual stuff.

That No Formatting button is there so you can clear all the formatting from the Find What box. After you've found something, you can give Word instructions for replacing it by clicking the Replace tab (see the next section).

After you click the More button to get at the sophisticated search options, the button changes its name to Less. In this instance, More is Less. Click the Less button to shrink the dialog box and get more room to work on-screen.

Replacing Text and Formats

The Edit⇨Replace command is a very powerful tool indeed. If you're writing a Russian novel, and you decide on page 816 to change the main character's last name from Oblonsky to Oblomov, you can change it on all 816 pages with the Edit⇨Replace command in about a half a minute.

To replace words, phrases, or formats throughout a document:

1. **Choose Edit⇨Replace, or press Ctrl+H.**

   You see the Replace tab of the Find and Replace dialog box, as shown in Figure 4-3. (In the figure, the More button has been pressed and you can see all the options.)

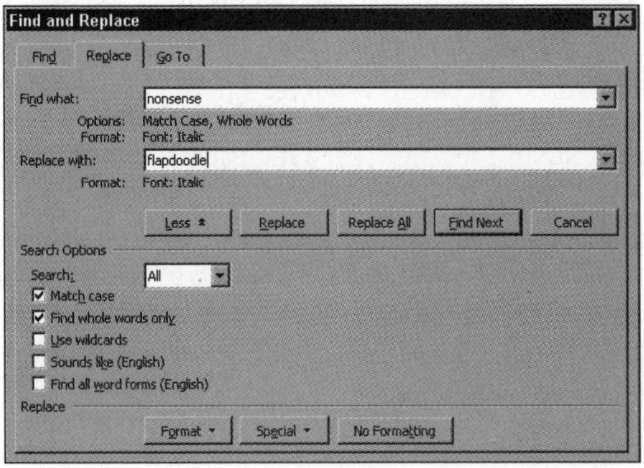

Figure 4-3: Word seeks and replaces per your instructions.

2. **Fill in the Find What box just as you would if you were searching for text or formats, and be sure to click the Find Whole Words Only check box if you want to replace one word with another.**

   Depending on which options appear in the dialog box, you may have to click the More button to see all of them. (See the preceding section to find out how to conduct a search.)

3. **In the Replace With box, enter the text that will replace what is in the Find What box. If you're replacing a format, click the Format button and then choose the format from the pop-up list.**

4. **Either replace everything at once or do it one at a time:**

   - Click Replace All to make all replacements in an instant.
   - Click Find Next and then either click Replace to make the replacement or Find Next to bypass it.

Word tells you when it has searched the entire document.

The Role of the Thesaurus in Finding the Right Word

If you can't seem to find the right word; if the word is on the tip of your tongue but you can't quite remember it; you can always give the Thesaurus a shot. To find synonyms (words that have the same or a similar meaning) for a word in your document, start by right-clicking the word and choosing Synonyms on the shortcut menu. With luck, the synonym you're looking for appears on the submenu and all you have to do is click to enter the synonym in your document. Usually, however, finding a good synonym is a journey, not a Sunday stroll. Follow these steps to search for a synonym:

1. **Place the cursor in the word.**
2. **Choose Tools➪Language➪Thesaurus, or press Shift+F7.**

   You see the Thesaurus dialog box, as shown in Figure 4-4.

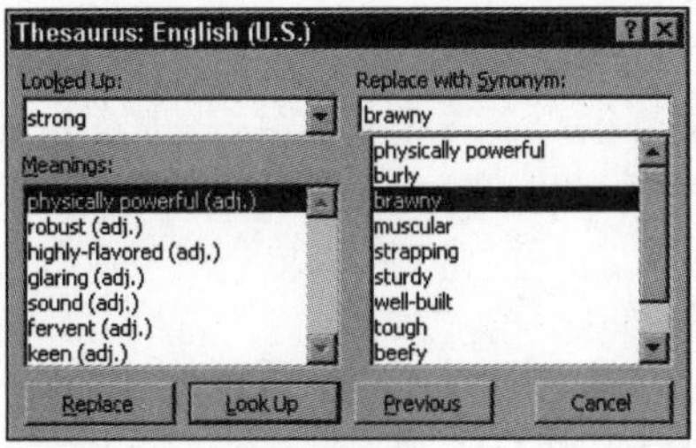

Figure 4-4: Using a thesaurus has never been easier.

3. **Begin your quest for the right word.**
4. **When you find it, click it in the list of words in the Replace with Synonym box and then click the Replace button.**

Finding the right words is nine-tenths of writing, so the Thesaurus dialog box tries to make it easier by offering these amenities:

- **Looked Up:** Provides a drop-down list with all the words you've investigated in your quest. To go back to a word you considered earlier, click it in this list, or click the Previous button.
- **Meanings:** Lists different ways the term can be used — as a verb or noun, for example. Click here to turn your search in a different direction.
- **Replace with Synonym:** If the Thesaurus isn't being helpful, type a word into this box and click the Look Up button.
- **Look Up:** Click the Look Up button to investigate the word highlighted in the Replace with Synonym box scroll list.

At worst, if you know the opposite of the word you want, you can look it up in the Thesaurus and perhaps see its antonym listed in the Replace with Synonym box.

Spell-Checking (And Grammar-Checking) a Document

As you must have noticed by now, red wiggly lines appear under words that are misspelled, and green wiggly lines appear under words and sentences that Word thinks are grammatically incorrect. Correct spelling and grammar errors by right-clicking them and choosing an option from the shortcut menu. If the red or green lines annoy you, you can remove them from the screen. Choose Tools⇨Options, click the Spelling & Grammar tab, and click to remove the check marks from the Check Spelling as You Type or Check Grammar as You Type options.

That's the one-at-a-time method for correcting misspelled words and grammatical errors. You can also go the whole hog and spell- or grammar-check an entire document or text selection by starting in one of these ways:

- ✦ Choose Tools⇨Spelling and Grammar
- ✦ Press F7
- ✦ Click the Spelling and Grammar button

The Spelling and Grammar dialog box appears, as shown in Figure 4-5. Spelling errors appear in red type in this dialog box. Grammatical errors are colored green.

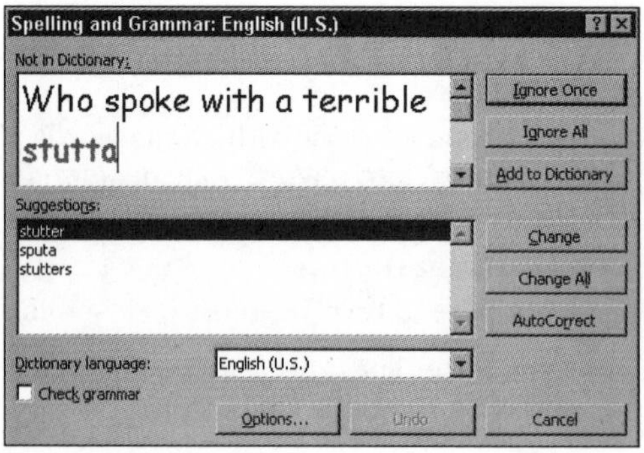

Figure 4-5: Now you have one less excuse for making a spelling mistake.

Correcting misspellings

Here are your options for handling red spelling errors:

- **Not in Dictionary:** Shows the word that is spelled incorrectly in context. You can click the scroll arrows in this box to see preceding or following text.
- **Suggestions:** Provides a list of words to use in place of the misspelling. Either double-click the word that you want to replace the misspelled one or click it and then click the Change button.
- **Ignore Once:** Ignores the misspelling, but stops on it again if it appears later in the document.
- **Ignore All:** Ignores the misspelling wherever it appears in the document. Not only that, it ignores it in all your other open documents.
- **Add to Dictionary:** Adds the word in the Not in Dictionary box to the words in the dictionary that Microsoft Word deems correct. Click this button the first time that the spell-checker stops on your last name to add your last name to the spelling dictionary.
- **Change:** Click this button to insert the word in the Suggestions box in your document in place of the misspelled word.
- **Delete:** The Delete button appears where the Change button is when the Spell-Checker finds two words in a row ("the the," for example). Click the Delete button to remove the second word.
- **Change All:** Changes not only this misspelling to the word in the Suggestions box, but all identical misspellings in the document.
- **AutoCorrect:** Adds the suggested spelling correction to the list of words that are corrected automatically as you type them (see Chapter 8).
- **Undo:** Goes back to the last misspelling you corrected and gives you a chance to repent and try again.

You can click outside the Spelling dialog box and fool around in your document, in which case the Ignore button changes names and becomes Resume. Click the Resume button to start the spell-check again.

WARNING!

You probably shouldn't trust your smell-checker, because it can't catch all misspelled words. If you mean to type **middle** but type **fiddle** instead, the spell-checker won't catch the error because *fiddle* is a legitimate word. The moral is: If you're working on an important document, proofread it carefully. Don't rely on the spell-checker to catch all your smelling errors.

But I know that my spelling is correct!

Suppose that you have a bunch of computer code or French language text that you want the spell-checker to either ignore or check against its French dictionary instead of its English dictionary. To tell the spell-checker how to handle text like that, select the text and choose Tools➪Language➪Set Language. In the Language dialog box, choose a new language for your words to be spell-checked against, or else click the Do Not Check Spelling or Grammar check box.

Fixing grammar errors

Word's Grammar Checker is theoretically able to correct grammatical mistakes in a document. Personally, I think the thing is of little use and don't recommend using it. And I'm not just saying that because I'm an editor and writer and I (supposedly) have mastered grammar. I just think that a machine can't tell what's good writing and what isn't. Period.

Anyhow, grammar errors appear in green in the top of the Spelling and Grammar dialog box, as shown in Figure 4-6.

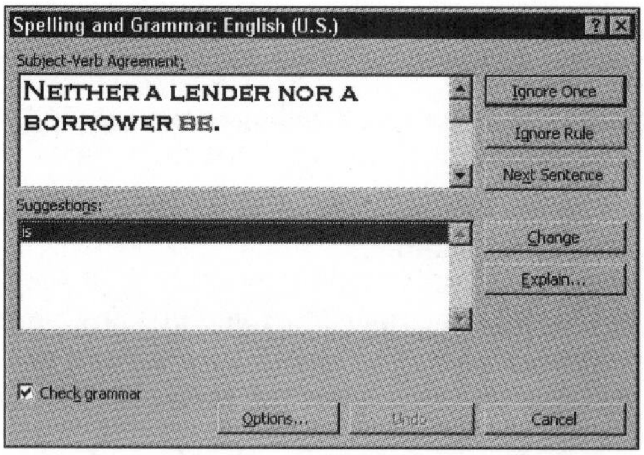

Figure 4-6: Shakespeare wouldn't make it beyond his first page in the Grammar Checker.

Click the following buttons to fix errors with the robo-grammarian:

- **Suggestions:** Lists ways to correct the error. Click the correction you want to make.
- **Ignore Once:** Lets the error stand in your document. Word will, however, flag the error the next time it occurs.

- **Ignore Rule:** Ignores this grammatical error and all other grammatical errors of this type in this document and all open documents.
- **Next Sentence:** Ignores the error and takes you to the grammatical error in the text.
- **Change:** Replaces the error with what is in the Suggestions box.
- **Explain:** Opens the Office Assistant so that you can read about your grammar error and receive a little grammar lesson.
- **Undo:** Reverses your most recent correction.

Changing lowercase to UPPERCASE and UPPERCASE to lowercase

What do you do if you look at your screen and discover to your dismay that you entered characters IN THE WRONG CASE! It happens. And sometimes Word does mysterious things to letters at the start of sentences and capital letters in the middle of words. What can you do about that? You can fix uppercase and lowercase problems in two ways.

The fastest way is to select the text you entered incorrectly and press Shift+F3. Keep pressing Shift+F3 until the text looks right. Shift+F3 changes the characters to all lowercase, to Initial Capitals, to ALL UPPERCASE, and then back to all lowercase again.

The other way is to select the text, choose Format➪Change Case, and select an option in the Change Case dialog box. The tOGGLE cASE option, incidentally, is for changing the case of letters when you accidentally entered them while the Caps Lock key was pressed down.

Microsoft Weird is very presumptuous about how it thinks capital letters should be used. You've probably noticed that already. You can't type a lowercase letter after a period without Word uppercasing it. You can't enter lowercase computer code at the start of a line without Word capitalizing the first letter. If Word capitalizes a letter against your will, move the pointer over the letter. You see the AutoCorrect Options button. At that point, you can click the button to open a drop-down menu and choose an option to undo the capitalization. For that matter, you can click the Control AutoCorrect Options command to open the AutoCorrect dialog box and choose for yourself what is "corrected" automatically. (See Chapter 8 for more information about making changes to your text.)

Chapter 5: Basic Formatting

In This Chapter

- Bolding, italicizing, and underlining
- Centering, justifying, and aligning
- Changing fonts and colors
- Copying formatting with the Format Painter
- Creating numbered and bulleted lists
- Indenting and setting margins
- Using tabs

So you be the judge:

```
Bob, I really need you to help me with the Henderson
contracts, the school board proposal, and the review of
Johnson's 2001 Fiduciary Returns. If you don't help, we'll
all be in big trouble when the boss gets back.
```

Bob, I *really* need you to help me with

- **the Henderson contracts**
- **the school board proposal**
- **the review of Johnson's 1999 *Fiduciary Returns***

If you don't help, we'll all be in B I G trouble when the boss gets back.

If you think that the first sample is easier to read, just go ahead and skip on to another chapter. If you like the idea of formatting your documents to make them more effective, you've turned to the right page. This chapter shows you how to squeeze some nice looking text out of any ordinary document.

Adding Bold, Italic, Underline, and Other Effects

Embellishing text with **boldface,** *italics,* underlines, and other font styles and text effects is easy. You can do it with the Formatting toolbar or by choosing Format➪FontFirst the Formatting toolbar:

- **Boldface:** Click the Bold button (or press Ctrl+B) and start typing. If you've already entered the text, select the text first and then click Bold or press Ctrl+B. Bold text is often used in headings.
- **Italics:** Click the Italic button (or press Ctrl+I). Select the text first if you've already entered it. Italics are used to show emphasis and also for foreign words such as *voilà, gung hay fat choy,* and *Que magnifico!*
- **Underline:** Click the Underline button (or press Ctrl+U). Select the text first and then click the button if you've already typed the text. You can also get double underlines with the Format➪Font command.

The second way to get boldface, italicized, and underline text is to choose Format➪Font or right-click text and choose Font from the shortcut menu. When the Font dialog box appears, choose options from the Font Style scroll list.

The Font dialog box offers many other options for embellishing text. By choosing combinations of font styles and text effects, you can create interesting but sometimes unreadable letters and words.

Centering, Justifying, and Aligning Text

All you have to do to align text in a new way is select the text and either click an Alignment button on the Formatting toolbar or press a keyboard shortcut, as shown in Table 5-1.

Table 5-1 Alignment Buttons

Button	*Button Name*	*Keyboard Shortcut*	*What It Does*
	Align Left	Ctrl+L	Lines up text along the left margin or left side of columns.
	Center	Ctrl+E	Centers text, leaving space on both sides.
	Align Right	Ctrl+R	Lines up text along the right margin or right side of columns.
	Justify	Ctrl+J	Lines up text on both the left and right margins or sides of columns.

Unless it is in columns, text is aligned with respect to the left and right *margins,* not the left and right sides of the page. Figure 5-1 may give you a clearer idea of the alignment options.

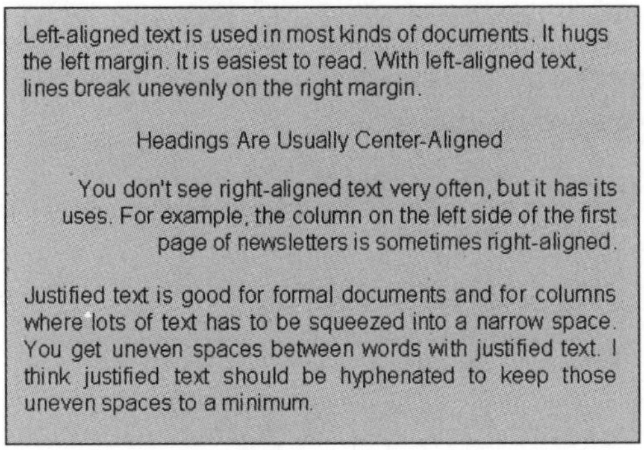
Left-aligned text is used in most kinds of documents. It hugs the left margin. It is easiest to read. With left-aligned text, lines break unevenly on the right margin.

Headings Are Usually Center-Aligned

You don't see right-aligned text very often, but it has its uses. For example, the column on the left side of the first page of newsletters is sometimes right-aligned.

Justified text is good for formal documents and for columns where lots of text has to be squeezed into a narrow space. You get uneven spaces between words with justified text. I think justified text should be hyphenated to keep those uneven spaces to a minimum.

Figure 5-1: Choosing different alignment options makes for interesting layouts.

Word offers a special feature called *click and type* for aligning text. Instead of choosing an alignment option, you can move the cursor to a part of the page whose text you want to align and then double-click on-screen when you see the click-and-type icon. This icon changes appearance, depending on where the cursor is on the page, to show lines that correspond to alignment commands. When you see lines that indicate the kind of alignment you want, you can double-click to give an alignment command.

Changing the Font and Size of Text

Font is the catchall name for type style and type size. When you change fonts, you choose another style of type or change the size of the letters. Word offers a whole bunch of different fonts. You can see their names by clicking the down arrow next to the Font drop-down list and scrolling down the list.

To change the font, follow these steps:

1. **Select the text or place the cursor where you want the font to change.**
2. **Click the down arrow on the Font drop-down list.**

   You see the names of fonts, each one dressed up and looking exactly like itself, as shown in Figure 5-2. Word puts all the fonts you've used so far in the document at the top of the Font drop-down list to make it easier for you to find the fonts you use most often.

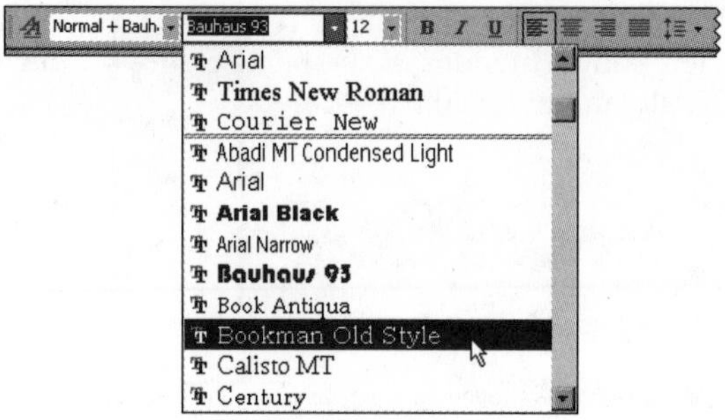

Figure 5-2: Pick a font, any font.

3. **Scroll down the list of fonts, if necessary.**
4. **Click a font name.**

Fonts with *TT* beside their names are *TrueType fonts.* These fonts look the same on-screen as they do when printed on paper.

Type is measured in *points.* A point is 1/72 of an inch. The larger the point size, the larger the letters. To change the size of letters, follow these steps:

1. **Select the letters or place the cursor where you want the larger or smaller letters to start appearing.**
2. **Click the down arrow on the Font Size drop-down list.**
3. **Scroll down the list if you want a large font.**
4. **Click a point size — 8, 12, 36, 48, and so on.**

You can also change font sizes quickly by selecting the text and pressing Ctrl+Shift+< or Ctrl+Shift+>, or by clicking in the Font Size drop-down list, entering a point size yourself, and pressing Enter. To change fonts and fonts sizes at the same time, choose Format⇨Font and make your choices in the Font dialog box.

Coloring Text

If you own or have access to a color printer, you can print text in different colors. And even if you don't own a color printer, you can change the color of text on-screen. You may do that to call attention to parts of a document or Web page, for example. To change the color of text, follow these steps:

1. **Select the text.**

2. **Click the down arrow beside the Font Color button and click a color, black, white, or one of the four gray shades (see Figure 5-3).**

Figure 5-3: If only this figure were in color, you could see your color choices.

After you choose a color, the Font Color button changes color and becomes the color you chose. To apply the same color again, click the Font Color button without having to open the drop-down list. You can also apply colors by way of the Font Color menu in the Font dialog box. To get there, choose Format➪Font.

To remove the color from text, select it, open the Font Color drop-down list, and choose Automatic.

Fast Formatting with the Format Painter

The fastest way — though not necessarily the most efficient way — to format a document is to use the Format Painter. You can use the Format Painter to make sure that the headings, lists, text paragraphs, and whatnot in your document are formatted the same way.

To use the Format Painter, follow these steps:

1. **Click the text whose formats you want to apply throughout your document.**

   For example, if you want to sprinkle 22-point, Helvetica text throughout your document, click some 22-point, Helvetica text.

2. **Double-click the Format Painter button. The mouse pointer changes into a paint brush icon.**

3. **Find the text you want to copy the format to, click the mouse button, and roll the mouse pointer over it as though you were selecting it.**

   When you're done, the text takes on the new formats.

4. **Keep going. Find every place in your document that you can copy this format to and baste it with the Format Painter. You can click the scroll bar and use keyboard commands to move through your document.**

5. **Click the Format Painter button or press Esc when you're done.**

Creating Numbered and Bulleted Lists

Numbered lists are invaluable in manuals and books like this one that present a lot of step-by-step procedures. Use bulleted lists when you want to present alternatives to the reader. A *bullet* is a black filled-in circle or other character.

Simple numbered and bulleted lists

The fastest, cleanest, and most honest way to create a numbered or bulleted list is to enter the text without any concern for numbers or bullets. Just press Enter at the end of each step or bulleted entry. After you're done, select the list and click the Numbering or Bullets button on the Formatting toolbar.

TIP

Another way to create a numbered list is to type the number 1, type a period, press the spacebar, type the first entry in the list, and press Enter to get to the next line and type the second entry. As soon as you press Enter, Word inserts the number 2 and formats the list for you. In the same manner, Word creates bulleted lists when you type an asterisk (*), press the spacebar, type the first entry in the list, and press Enter. (If this kind of stuff annoys you, click the AutoCorrect Options button — it appears automatically — and choose Stop Automatically Creating Lists; or choose Format⇨AutoCorrect Options, select the AutoFormat As You Type tab in the AutoCorrect dialog box, and uncheck the Automatic Numbered Lists and Automatic Bulleted Lists check boxes.)

Ending and continuing lists

To end a numbered or bulleted list and tell Word that you want to go back to writing normal paragraphs, press the Enter key twice. Pressing Enter twice stops the numbering, but it also puts in an extra paragraph. To stop the numbering, press Enter after the last numbered item; then, on the next numbered line, press the Backspace key. That stops the numbering and leaves you on the same line.

You can also choose Format⇨Bullets and Numbering or right-click the list and choose Bullets and Numbering to open the Bullets and Numbering dialog box (see Figure 5-4). From there, click the None option on the Numbered or Bulleted tab and click OK.

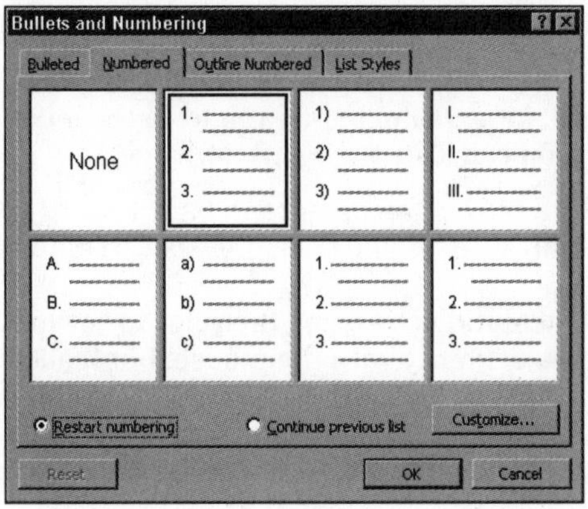

Figure 5-4: The Bullets and Numbering dialog box.

Suppose that you want a numbered list to pick up where a list you entered earlier ended. In other words, suppose that you ended a four-step list a couple of paragraphs back and now you want the list to resume at Step 5. In that case, click the Numbering button to start numbering again. The AutoCorrect Options button appears on-screen. Click it and choose Continue Numbering. You can also open the Bullets and Numbering dialog box and select the Continue Previous List option. The list will pick up where the previous numbered list in the document left off.

Also in the Bullets and Numbering dialog box is an option for starting a list anew. Choose Restart Numbering when Word insists on starting a list with a number other than 1 or when you want to break off one list and start another.

Indenting Paragraphs and First Lines

An *indent* is the distance between a margin and the text, not the left side of the page and the text. Word offers a handful of different ways to change the indentation of paragraphs.

The fastest way is to use the Increase Indent and Decrease Indent buttons on the Formatting toolbar to move the paragraph away from or toward the left margin:

1. **Click in the paragraph whose indentation you want to change. If you want to change more than one paragraph, select them.**

2. **Click one of these buttons as many times as necessary to indent the text:**

- **Increase Indent:** Indents the paragraph from the left margin by one tab stop. (You can also press Ctrl+M.)

- **Decrease Indent:** Moves the paragraph back toward the left margin by one tab stop. (You can also press Ctrl+Shift+M.)

You can also change indentations by using the ruler to "eyeball it." This technique requires some dexterity with the mouse, but it allows you to see precisely where paragraphs and the first lines of paragraphs are indented.

1. **Choose View⇨Ruler, if necessary, to put the ruler on-screen (see Figure 5-5).**
2. **Select the paragraph or paragraphs whose indentation you want to change.**
3. **Slide the indent markers with the mouse:**

- **First-line indent marker:** Drag the down-pointing arrow on the ruler to indent the first line of the paragraph only.

- **Left indent marker:** This one, on the bottom-left side of the ruler, comes in two parts. Drag the arrow that points up (called the hanging indent marker), but not the box underneath it, to move the left margin independently of the first-line indentation. To move the left indentation *and* the first-line indentation relative to the left margin, slide the box. Doing so moves everything on the left side of the ruler.

- **Right indent marker:** Drag this one to move the right side of the paragraph away from or toward the right margin.

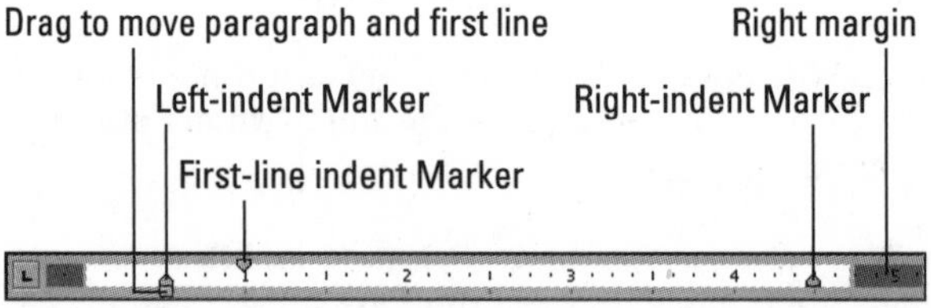

Figure 5-5: Indenting with the ruler.

If you're not one for "eyeballing it," you can use the Format⇨Paragraph command to indent paragraphs:

1. **Choose Format⇨Paragraph or double-click the Left or Right indent marker on the ruler.**

2. **Make your selections in the Indentation area.**
3. **Click OK.**

The Indentation options are self-explanatory. As you experiment, watch the Preview box — it shows exactly what your choices will do to the paragraph. In the Special drop-down list, you can choose First Line to indent the first line from the left margin or Hanging to create a *hanging indent,* an indent in which the second and subsequent lines in the paragraph are indented farther from the left margin than the first line. Enter a measurement in the By box to say how far you want these indents to travel. Did you notice that Alignment drop-down list in the upper-left corner? You can even align paragraphs from this dialog box.

Setting Up and Changing the Margins

Margins are the empty spaces along the left, right, top, and bottom sides of a page. Headers and footers are printed in the top and bottom margins, respectively.

WARNING!

Don't confuse margins with indents. Text is indented from the margin, not from the edge of the page. If you want to change how far a paragraph is indented, use the ruler or the Format⇨Paragraph command and change its indentation.

To change the margin settings for a simple document, follow these steps:

1. **Place the cursor where you want to change margins if you are changing margins in the middle of a document. Otherwise, to change the margins in the entire document, it doesn't matter where you place the cursor.**
2. **Choose File⇨Page Setup.**

   The Page Setup dialog box appears, as shown in Figure 5-6.
3. **Click the Margins tab and watch the Preview box to see what your choices do:**
   - **Top, Bottom, Left, Right:** Enter measurements for the top, bottom, left, and right margins.
   - **Apply To:** Choose Whole Document to apply your settings to the entire document, This Section to apply them to a section, or This Point Forward to change margins for the rest of a document. When you choose This Point Forward, Word creates a new section.
4. **Click OK.**

Working with the ruler

The ruler along the top of the screen is there to help you change and identify margins, tab settings, and indents, as well as place graphics and text boxes. (If you don't see it, choose View➪Ruler.) In Print Layout View, there is a similar ruler along the left side of the screen.

You can change the unit of measurement that is shown on the rulers. Choose Tools➪Options, click the General tab, and choose Inches, Centimeters, Millimeters, Points, or Picas on the Measurement Units drop-down list.

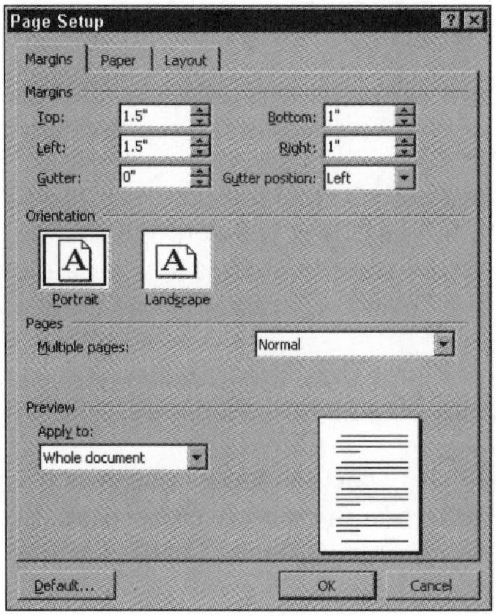

Figure 5-6: The Page Setup dialog box.

You can change the top and bottom margins with the horizontal ruler in Print Layout View. Simply drag the margin bar up or down.

Working with Tabs

A *tab stop* is a point on the ruler around which or against which text is formatted. When you press the Tab key, you advance the text cursor by one tab stop. Tab stops are set at half-inch intervals on the ruler, but you can change that if you want to. Figure 5-7 shows the different kinds of tabs.

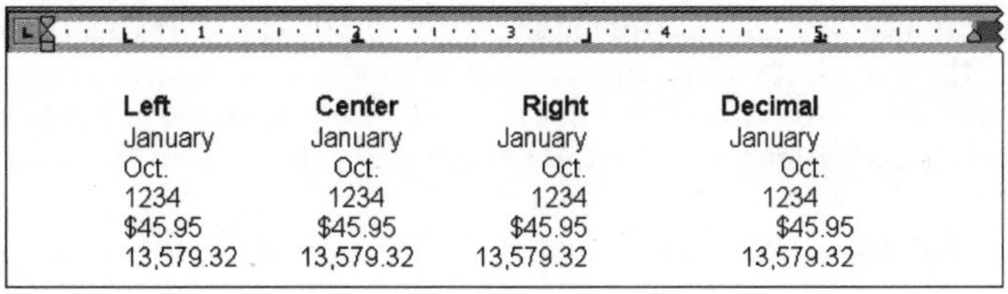

Left Center Right Decimal
January January January January
Oct. Oct. Oct. Oct.
1234 1234 1234 1234
$45.95 $45.95 $45.95 $45.95
13,579.32 13,579.32 13,579.32 13,579.32

Figure 5-7: Tabbing as it should be done.

You can also change the type of tab. By default, tabs are left-aligned, which means that when you enter letters after you press the Tab key, the letters move toward the right in the same way that they move toward the right when text is left-aligned. But Word also offers right, center, decimal, and bar tabs. The following illustration shows the differences between the tab settings. Notice the symbols on the ruler — they tell you what type of tab you're dealing with.

Tabs are a throwback to the days of the typewriter, when it was necessary to make tab stops in order to align next. Except for making leaders, everything you can do with tabs can also be done by creating a table — and it can be done far faster. All you have to do is align the text inside the table and then remove the table borders. See Chapter 10 for more information.

To change tabs or change where tabs appear on the ruler, follow these steps:

1. **Click in the box on the left side of the ruler to get different tab settings. As you click, the symbols change, as shown:**

Symbol	*Tab Type*
	Left-aligned tab
	Center-aligned tab
	Right-aligned tab
	Decimal tab
	Bar tab

2. **When you come to the symbol that represents the type of tab you want (keep clicking), click at the place on the ruler where you want to put a tab stop. You can click as many times as you want and enter more than one kind of tab.**

TIP

You can move a tab on the ruler simply by dragging it to a new location. Text that has been aligned with the tab moves as well, if you select it first. To remove a tab, drag it off the ruler. When you remove a tab, the text to which it was aligned is aligned to the next tab stop on the ruler.

You can also make tab settings with the Tabs dialog box. To do so, follow these steps:

1. **Place the cursor where you want your new tab settings to take effect. Or select the text to which you want to apply your new tabs.**
2. **Choose Format⇨Tabs.**

   You see the Tabs dialog box.
3. **Enter a position for the first new tab in the Tab Stop Position box.**
4. **Choose an Alignment option. The Bar option places a vertical bar, or straight line, at the tab stop position.**

   You can place numbers inside the bar tabs, for example, to help line them up, although doing so is utterly ridiculous when you can do that far more easily in a table. My personal opinion is that Microsoft invented this tab solely to be able to call it a "bar tab." Perhaps the inventor ran up a large bar tab somewhere and wanted to commemorate the event.
5. **Choose a leader, if you want one. For example, if you choose 2, Word places periods in the document whenever you press Tab at this setting.**

   A *leader* is a series of identical characters. Leaders are often found in tables of contents — they are the periods between the table of contents entry and the page number it refers to.
6. **Click the Set button.**
7. **Repeat Steps 3 through 6 for the next tab setting and all other tab settings. If you change your mind about a setting, select it in the Tab Stop Position scroll box and click Clear. Click Clear All if you change your mind in a big way and want to start all over.**
8. **Click OK.**

Sometimes it is hard to tell where tabs were put in the text. To find out, click the Show/Hide + button to see the formatting characters, including the arrows that show where the Tab key was pressed (see Figure 5-8).

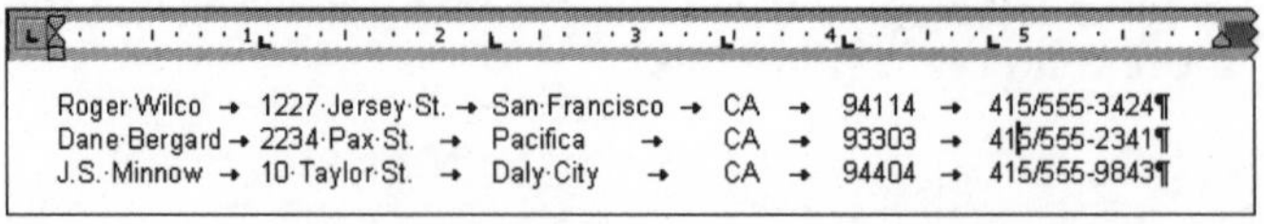

Roger·Wilco → 1227·Jersey·St. → San·Francisco → CA → 94114 → 415/555-3424¶
Dane·Bergard → 2234·Pax·St. → Pacifica → CA → 93303 → 415/555-2341¶
J.S.·Minnow → 10·Taylor·St. → Daly·City → CA → 94404 → 415/555-9843¶

Figure 5-8: Finding out where the tabs really are.

Chapter 6: Advanced Formatting

In This Chapter

- Applying styles
- Creating and modifying styles
- Using a drop cap
- Dividing a document into sections
- Making newspaper-like columns

Sometimes if you go that extra yard (.91 m), people will sit up and take notice. Why not find out how to give your documents that extra little push so that they stand out from the rest? If you know how to bold, italicize, underline, and all that other stuff explained in Chapter 5, you are qualified to undertake advanced formatting. But even if you haven't glanced at Chapter 5 and have no idea of what is going on, this chapter still helps you master some neat techniques to make your documents look better.

Applying Styles for Consistent Formatting

If you want to do any serious work whatsoever in Word, you need to know about styles. A *style* is a collection of formats that have been bundled under one name. Instead of visiting many different dialog boxes to reformat a paragraph, you can choose a style from the Style menu — and the paragraph is reformatted instantaneously. If you modify a style, Word instantly modifies all paragraphs in your document that were assigned the given style.

What's more, many Word features rely on styles. For example, before you can see the Document Map, organize a document with an outline, or generate a table of contents, you must have assigned heading styles to the headings in your document. Turning a Word document into a Web page is easy if you thoughtfully assigned styles to the different parts of the document.

By using styles, you make sure that the different parts of a document are consistent with one another and that your document has a professional look.

To understand how styles work, you have to know about templates. A *template* is a special kind of file that is used as the starting point for creating Word documents. All Word documents are created from templates, and each template comes with many predefined styles. When you choose File➪New, click General Templates in the New Document task pane, and choose a template in the Templates dialog box to create a document, you are really choosing a set of predefined styles for your new document. Each template comes with its own unique set of styles.

Applying a style to text and paragraphs

To see which styles are available in the document you are working on, either open the Style drop-down list on the Formatting toolbar or click the Styles and Formatting button to open the Styles and Formatting task pane. Want to know which style has been assigned to text or a paragraph? Click the text or paragraph and glance at the Style drop-down list or the Styles and Formatting task pane.

In the Style drop-down list and the task pane, each style name is formatted to give you an idea of what it does when you apply it in your document. Word offers four types of styles:

- **Paragraph styles:** Determine the formatting of entire paragraphs. A paragraph style can include these settings: font, paragraph, tab, border, language, and bullets and numbering. Paragraph styles are marked with the paragraph symbol (¶). The majority of styles are paragraph styles.
- **Character styles:** Apply to text, not to paragraphs. You select text before you apply a character style. You create a character style for text that is hard to lay out and foreign-language text. A character style can include these settings: font and language. When you apply a character style to text, the character-style settings override the paragraph-style settings. If the paragraph style calls for a 14-point Arial text but the character style calls for 12-point Times Roman font, the character style wins. Character styles are marked with an underlined *a.*
- **Table styles:** Apply to tables (see Chapter 10 for advice about creating and formatting tables). Table styles are marked with a grid icon.
- **List styles:** Apply to lists (see Chapter 5). List styles are marked with a list icon.

The beauty of styles is this: After you modify a style, all paragraphs or text to which the style has been assigned are instantly changed. You don't have to go back and format text and paragraphs throughout your document.

To apply a style, follow these steps:

1. **Click the paragraph you want to apply the style to, or, to apply a style to several paragraphs, select all or part of them. If you're applying a character style, select the letters whose formatting you want to change.**

2. Do one of the following to apply the style:

- Click the down arrow next to the Style drop-down list and select a style.

- Click the Styles and Formatting button to open the Styles and Formatting task pane, and then select a style, as shown in Figure 6-1.

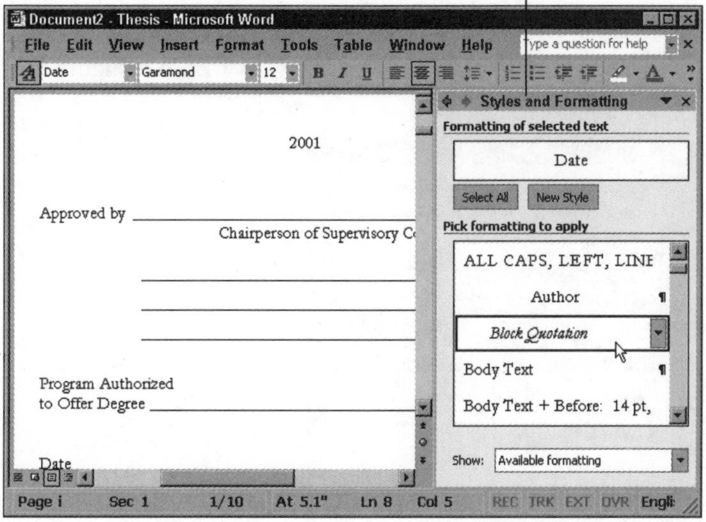

Figure 6-1: One way to apply a style — the Styles and Formatting task pane.

Creating a new style

You can create new styles in two ways: in the New Style dialog box and directly from the screen. First, the directly-from-the-screen method, which you can use to create paragraph styles for a document you are working on:

1. **Click a paragraph whose formatting you want to turn into a style and apply to other paragraphs in your document.**

   Remember, a heading is also a paragraph as far as Word is concerned, so if you're creating a style for a heading, click the heading.

2. **Click in the Style drop-down list and type a name for the style. Choose a meaningful name that you will remember.**

3. **Press the Enter key.**

A style you create directly from the screen becomes a part of the document you're working on — it isn't made part of the template from which you created your document. If you want to make a style available in other documents, make it part of a template, and use the New Style dialog box method.

To create a style by using the New Style dialog box, follow these steps:

1. **Click the Styles and Formatting button.**

   The Styles and Formatting task pane opens.

2. **Click the New Style button in the task pane.**

   The New Style dialog box appears, as shown in Figure 6-2.

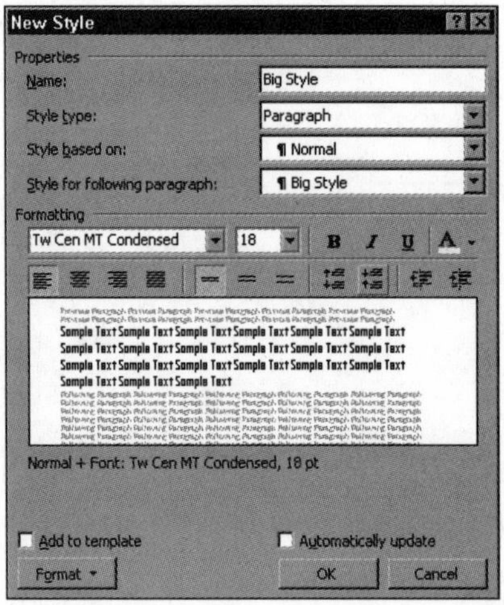

Figure 6-2: The New Style dialog box.

3. **Fill in the New Style dialog box.**

   As you do so, keep your eyes on the Preview box. It shows you what your new style will look like when you apply it to a document. You can modify the following options in the New Style dialog box:

   - **Name:** Enter a descriptive name for the style. The name you enter will appear in the Style drop-down list and the Styles and Formatting task pane.
   - **Style Type:** In the drop-down list in the dialog box, choose style type.

- **Style Based On:** If your new style is similar to a style that is already part of the template with which you created your document, choose the style to get a head start on creating the new one. Be warned, however, that if you or someone else changes the Based On style, your new style will inherit those changes and be altered as well. Remember: A template is the foundation file on which a document is built. Each Word document is founded on a particular template.
- **Style for Following Paragraph:** Choose a style from the drop-down list if the style you're creating is always followed by an existing style. For example, a new style called "Chapter Title" might always be followed by a style called "Chapter Intro Paragraph." If that were the case, you would choose "Chapter Intro Paragraph" from this drop-down list.
- **Formatting:** Choose options from the menus or click buttons to fashion or refine your style. (You can also click the Format button to do this.)
- **Add to Template:** Adds the style to the document's template so that other documents based on the template you are using can also make use of the new style.
- **Automatically Update:** When you make a formatting change to a paragraph, the style assigned to the paragraph normally doesn't change. The style does change, however, if you check this box. By checking this box, you tell Word to alter the style itself each time you alter a paragraph to which you've assigned the style. With this box checked, all paragraphs in the document that were assigned the style are altered each time you change a single paragraph that was assigned the style.
- **Format:** This is the important one. Click the button and make a formatting choice. Word takes you to dialog boxes so that you can create or refine the style.

4. **Click OK to close the New Style dialog box.**

Modifying a style

What if you decide at the end of an 80-page document that all 35 introductory paragraphs to which you've assigned the "Intro Para" style look funny? If you selected the Automatically Update check box in the New Style dialog box when you created the style, all you have to do is alter a paragraph to which you assigned the Intro Para style to alter all 35 introductory paragraphs. But if you decided against updating styles automatically, you can still change the introductory paragraphs throughout your document.

Follow these steps to modify a style that isn't updated automatically:

1. **Click any paragraph, table, or list to which you've assigned the style. If you want to modify a character style, select the characters to which you assigned the style.**

2. **Click the Styles and Formatting button.**

   The Styles and Formatting task pane appears. The style you want to modify should be selected in the task pane. If it isn't, select it.

3. **Select the name of the style that needs modifying, click the down arrow to open its drop-down list, and choose Modify.**

   You see the Modify Style dialog box, as shown in Figure 6-3. Does the box look familiar? That's because it is identical to the New Style dialog box you used to create the style in the first place.

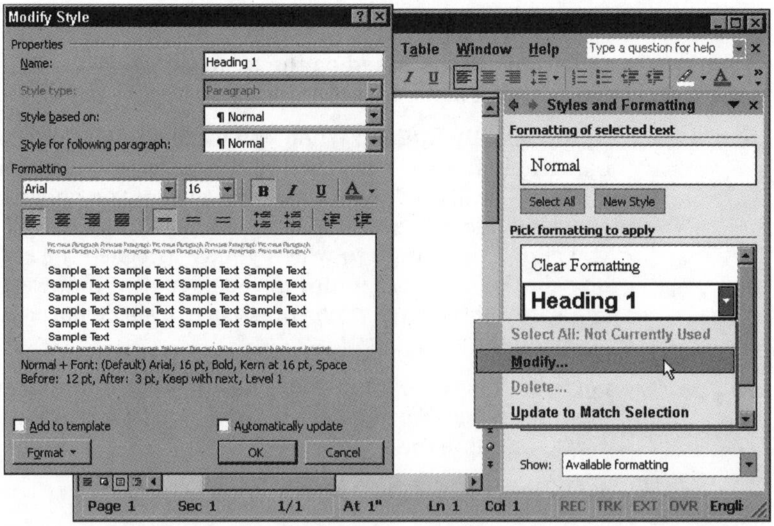

Figure 6-3: The Modify Style dialog box.

4. **Change the settings in the Modify Styles dialog box and click OK.**

While the Modify Style dialog box is open, you can click the Automatically Update check box if you want future modifications you make to the style to be made automatically. This way, when you change a paragraph or text to which the style has been applied, all other paragraphs and text in your document are changed accordingly. Select the Add to Template option if you want the style change to be made not only in the document you are working on, but in all documents that are founded on the same template.

Dropping In a Drop Cap

A *drop cap* is a large capital letter that "drops" into the text. Drop caps appear at the start of chapters in some books, and you can find other uses for them as well. In Figure 6-4, a drop cap marks the "A" side of a list of songs on a homemade reggae tape.

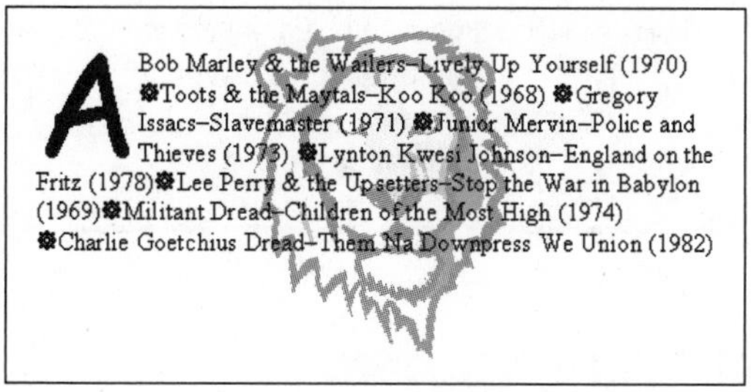

Figure 6-4: A drop cap can be used for special effects.

To create a drop cap, follow these steps:

1. **Click anywhere in the paragraph whose first letter you want to "drop."**
2. **Choose Format➪Drop Cap.**
3. **In the Drop Cap dialog box, choose which kind of drop cap you want by clicking a box.**

   The None setting is for removing a drop cap.
4. **Choose a font from the Font drop-down list.**

   Choose one that's different from the text in the paragraph. You can come back to this dialog box and get a different font later, if you want.
5. **In the Lines to Drop box, enter the number of text lines that the letter should "drop on."**
6. **Keep the 0" setting in the Distance from Text box unless you're dropping an I, 1, or other skinny letter or number.**
7. **Click OK.**

You see your drop cap in Print Layout View. The drop cap appears in a text frame. To change the size of the drop cap, choose Format➪Drop Cap again and play with the settings in the Drop Cap dialog box.

Juggling your columns

Sometimes it is easier to create columns by creating a table or by using text boxes, especially when the columns refer to one another. In a two-column résumé, for example, the left column often lists job titles (Facsimile Engineer) whose descriptions are found directly across the page in the right column (I photocopied stuff all day long). Creating a two-column résumé with Word's Format⇨Columns command would be futile because making the columns line up is impossible. Each time you add something to the left column, everything "snakes" — it gets bumped down in the left column and the right column as well.

Dividing a Document into Sections

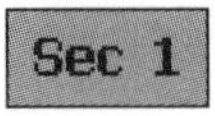

Every document has at least one *section.* That's why "Sec 1" appears on the left side of the status bar at the bottom of the screen. When you want to change page numbering schemes, headers and footers, margin sizes, and page layouts, you have to create a section break to start a new section. Word creates one for you when you create newspaper-style columns or change the size of margins. To create a new section, follow these steps:

1. **Click where you want to insert a section break.**
2. **Choose Insert⇨Break.**

   The Break dialog box appears, as shown in Figure 6-5.

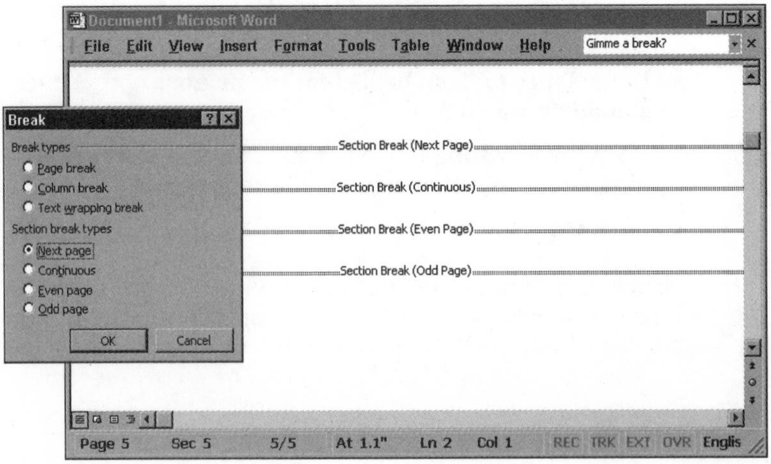

Figure 6-5: Creating section breaks with the Break dialog box.

3. **Under Section Break Types, tell Word which kind of section break you want.**

   All four Section break options create a new section, but they do so in different ways:

   - **Next Page:** Inserts a page break as well as a section break so that the new section can start at the top of a new page (the next one). Select this option to start a new chapter, for example.
   - **Continuous:** Inserts a section break in the middle of a page. Select this option, for example, if you want to introduce newspaper-style columns in the middle of a page.
   - **Even Page:** Starts the new section on the next even page. This option is good for two-sided documents where the headers on the left and right pages are different.
   - **Odd Page:** Starts the new section on the next odd page. You might choose this option if you have a book in which chapters start on odd pages. (By convention, that's where they start.)

4. **Click OK.**

In Normal view, you can tell where a section ends because `Section Break` and a double dotted line appear on-screen. The only way to tell where a section ends in Print Layout view is to glance at the "Sec" listing on the status bar or click the Show/Hide (¶) button. To delete a section break, make sure that you are in Normal view, click the dotted line, and press the Delete key.

Putting Newspaper-Style Columns in a Document

Columns look great in newsletters and similar documents. And you can pack a lot of words in columns. With columns, you can present more than one document on a single page so that readers have a choice of what they read.

TIP

Before you put text in newspaper-style columns, write it. Take care of the spelling, grammar, and everything else first because making text changes to words after they've been arranged in columns is hard.

FAST TRACK

You can create columns in two ways: by clicking the Columns button on the toolbar or by choosing Format⇨Columns. Choosing Format⇨Columns gives you considerably more leeway because the Columns button lets you create only columns of equal width. To use the Columns button, follow these steps:

1. **Select the text to be put in columns or simply place the cursor in the document to "columnize" all the text.**

2. **Click the Columns button on the toolbar.**

   A menu drops down so that you can choose how many columns you want.

3. **Click and drag to choose how many columns you want.**

Word creates a new section if you selected text before you columnized it, and you see your columns in Print Layout view. Very likely, they don't look so good. It's hard to get it right the first time. You can drag the column border bars on the ruler to widen or narrow the columns, as shown in Figure 6-6.

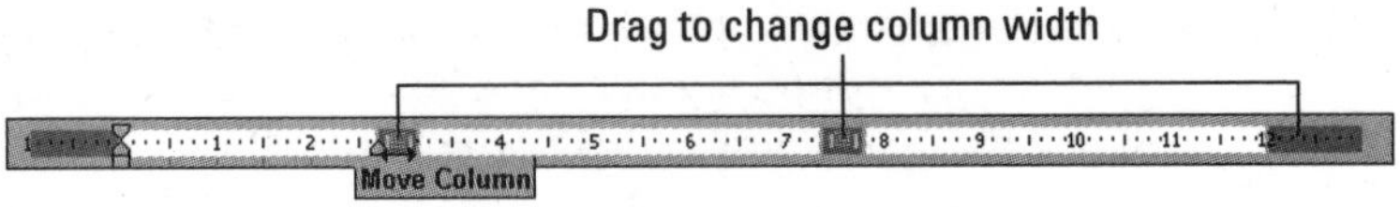

Figure 6-6: Drag the column border bars to increase or decrease column width.

Choosing Format⇨Columns and playing with options in the Columns dialog box is easier, of course. If you want to start all over, or if you want to start from the beginning with the Columns dialog box, here's how:

1. **Select the text to be put in columns, or put the cursor in the section to be put in columns, or place the cursor at a position in the document where columns are to start appearing.**

2. **Choose Format⇨Columns.**

   The Columns dialog box appears, as shown in Figure 6-7.

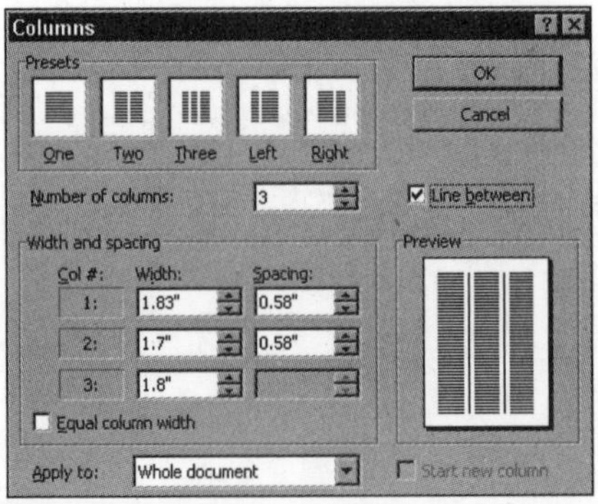

Figure 6-7: Laying out columns in the Columns dialog box.

3. **Choose options in the Columns dialog box.**

   As you do so, keep your eye on the Preview box in the lower-right corner. You can modify the following options:

   - **Presets:** Click a box to choose a preset number of columns. Notice that, in some of the boxes, the columns aren't of equal width. Choose One if you want to remove columns from a document.
   - **Number of Columns:** If you want more than three columns, enter a number here.
   - **Line Between:** Click this box to put lines between columns.
   - **Col #:** If your document has more than three columns, a scroll bar appears to the left of the Col # boxes. Scroll to the column you want to work with.
   - **Width:** If you click the Equal Column Width option to remove the check mark, you can make columns of unequal width. Change the width of each column by using the Width boxes.
   - **Spacing:** Determines how much blank space appears to the right of the column.
   - **Equal Column Width:** Click this box if you want columns to be the same width.
   - **Apply To:** Choose which part of the document you want to "columnize" — selected text, the section the cursor is in, this point forward in your document, or the whole document.
   - **Start New Column:** This box is for putting empty space in a column, perhaps to insert a text box or picture. Place the cursor where you want the empty space to begin, open the Columns dialog box, click this check box, and choose This Point Forward from the Apply To drop-down list. Text below the cursor moves to the next column.

4. **Click OK.**

TIP

Faster ways to "break" a column in the middle and move text to the next column are to press Ctrl+Shift+Enter or choose Insert⇨Break and click the Column Break radio button.

As you format your multicolumn newsletter or incendiary pamphlet, click the Print Preview button early and often. The best way to see what a multicolumn document really looks like is to see it on the Print Preview screen.

Chapter 7: Envelopes, Labels, and Form Letters

In This Chapter

- **Addressing envelopes**
- **Making labels**
- **Printing form letters, labels, and envelopes for mass mailings**

If you've ever wanted to know how Publisher's Clearinghouse and Ed McMahon could churn out millions of personalized letters and blanket the entire country, this chapter helps you understand how easy it is. And you can do it, too! Word lends itself to making mundane tasks easier, so you really have no excuse for not letting it help you with your correspondence. Word can do everything except come up with the money-making schemes!

Printing an Address on an Envelope

You don't have to address envelopes by hand, although it's often easier to do that. To print an address and a return address on an envelope, follow these steps:

1. **Open the document that holds the letter you want to send, and select the name and address of the person you want to send the letter to.**
2. **Choose Tools⇨Letters and Mailings⇨Envelopes and Labels.**

   The Envelopes and Labels dialog box appears, as shown in Figure 7-1.
3. **If necessary, click the Envelopes tab.**
4. **Type a name and address in the Delivery Address box (the address is already there if you selected it in Step 1).**

   Your name and address should appear in the Return Address box. (If it isn't there, type it for now, but be sure to read the Tip at the end of this section to find out how to put it there automatically.)
5. **Click the Omit check box if you don't want your return address to appear on the envelope.**

   Click this box if you're using preprinted envelopes.
6. **Click the Print button to print the envelope.**

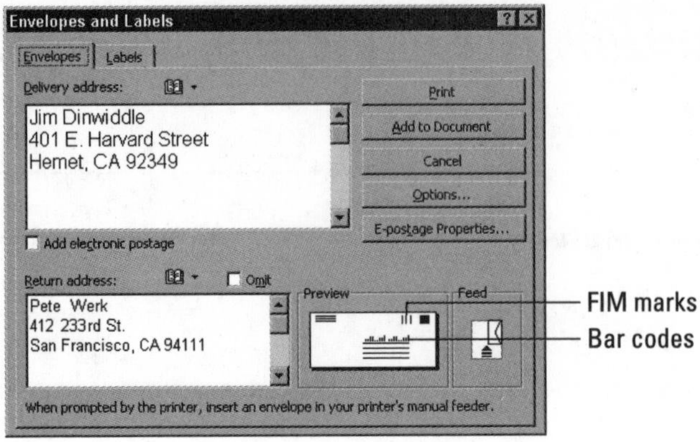

Figure 7-1: The Envelopes and Labels dialog box.

Two commands on the Envelopes tab tell Word how your printer handles envelopes and what size your envelopes are. If you haven't yet told Word how your printer handles envelopes, you can do that in the Envelopes and Labels dialog box.

On the Envelopes tab of the Envelopes and Labels dialog box, click the envelope icon below the word "Feed" to open the Envelope Options dialog box and choose the right technique for feeding envelopes to your printer (see Figure 7-2). Consult the manual that came with your printer, click one of the Feed Method boxes, click the Face Up or Face Down radio button, and open the Feed From drop-down list to tell Word which printer tray the envelope is in or how you intend to stick the envelope in your printer. Click OK when you're done.

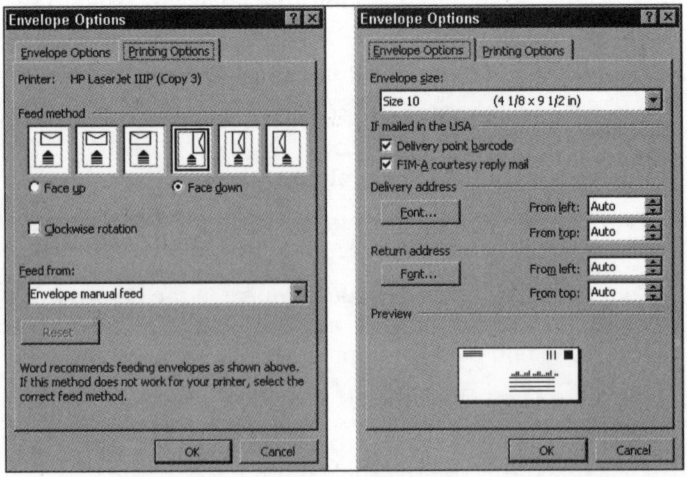

Figure 7-2: Telling Word how to print addresses on envelopes with the Envelope Options dialog box.

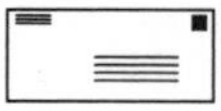

After you've fed the envelope to your printer, click the envelope icon below the word Preview — that's right, click the icon — to tell Word what size your envelopes are and choose other settings. You can modify the following settings:

- **Envelope Size:** Select a size from the drop-down list.
- **Delivery Point Barcode:** Click this box to put bar codes on the envelope and help the United States Postal Service deliver the letter faster.
- **FIM-A Courtesy Reply Mail:** Click here to put Facing Identification Marks on the envelope. These marks, which tell letter-processing machines at the post office whether the envelope is face up, also aid the speedy delivery of mail.
- **Delivery Address:** Change the font of the delivery address and the address's position. Change the From Left and From Top measurements to slide the address up or down on the envelope. The sample envelope under Preview shows what the measurements mean in real terms.
- **Return Address:** Ditto for the return address.

The Add to Document button on the Envelopes tab of the Envelopes and Labels dialog box (refer to Figure 7-1) creates a new section at the top of the document with the return and delivery address in it. In the new section, both addresses are formatted and made ready to go straight to the printer. Not everyone can take advantage of this feature. Click the Add to Document button only if you have a printer that can accept envelopes as easily as it can accept sheets of paper. (I want one for my birthday.)

TIP

To make your name and return address appear automatically in the Envelopes and Labels dialog box, choose Tools⇨Options, click the User Information tab, and type your name and address in the Mailing Address box.

Printing a Single Address Label (Or a Page of the Same Label)

Word enables you to print a single label or a sheet of labels that are all the same. Before you start printing, however, take note what size and what brand your labels are. You are asked about label brands and sizes when you print labels. (See the section "Churning Out Letters, Labels, and Envelopes for Mass Mailings," later in this chapter, to print many labels as part of a mass mailing.)

To print a single label or a sheet full of identical labels, follow these steps:

1. **Choose Tools⇨Letters and Mailings⇨Envelopes and Labels.**

   The Envelopes and Labels dialog box appears.

2. **Click the Labels tab, as shown in Figure 7-3.**

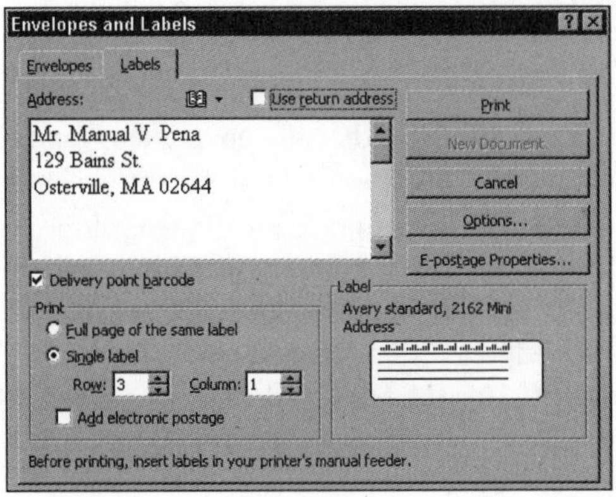

Figure 7-3: The Labels tab of the Envelopes and Labels dialog box.

3. **Type the label — the name and address — in the Address box.**

   If you're printing your return address on labels, click the Use Return Address check box. Your return address appears automatically if you entered it in the Options dialog box by choosing Tools⇨Options and entering it on the User Information tab. If your return address doesn't appear, however, enter it now.

4. **Either click the Options button or click the label icon in the Label box.**

   The Label Options dialog box appears, as shown in Figure 7-4.

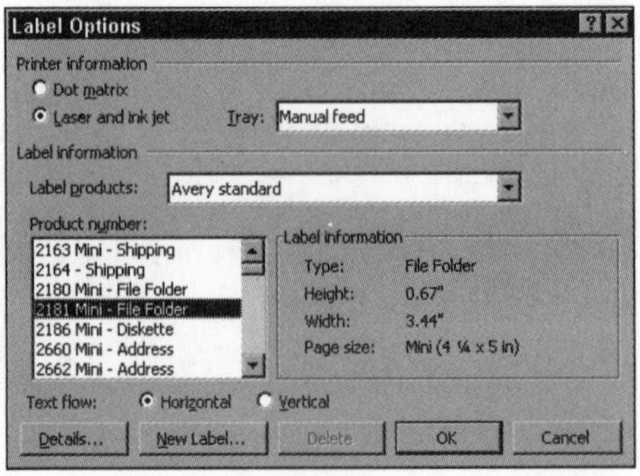

Figure 7-4: Telling Word what kind of label you will print on.

5. **In the Printer Information area, click either Dot Matrix or Laser and Ink Jet to say which kind of printer you have. Then choose the option that describes how you will feed labels to your printer in the Tray drop-down list.**

6. **In the Label Products drop-down list, choose the brand or type of labels that you have.**

   If your brand is not on the list, you can choose Other/Custom (found at the bottom of the list), click the Details button, and describe your labels in the extremely confusing Address Information dialog box. A better way, however, is to measure your labels and see whether you can find a label of the same size by experimenting with Product Number and Label Information combinations. Many label manufacturers put an Avery-compatible model number on their packaging. Look for an Avery-compatible number on your box of labels.

7. **In the Product Number box, select the product number listed on the box your labels came in.**

   Look in the Label Information box on the right to make sure that the Height, Width, and Page Size measurements match those of the labels you have.

8. **Click OK to return to the Envelopes and Labels dialog box.**

9. **Choose a Print option:**

   - **Full Page of the Same Label:** Select this option if you want to print a pageful of the same label. Likely, you'd choose this option to print a pageful of your own return addresses. Click the New Document button after you make this choice. Word creates a new document with a pageful of labels. Save and print this document.
   - **Single Label:** Select this option to print one label. Then enter the row and column where the label is and click the Print button.

Churning Out Letters, Labels, and Envelopes for Mass Mailings

Thanks to the miracle of computing, you can churn out form letters, labels, and envelopes for a mass mailing in the privacy of your home or office, just like the big companies do. Producing form letters, labels, and envelopes is easy, as long as you take the time to prepare the source file. The *source file* is the file that the names and addresses come from. A Word table, a Microsoft Access database table or query, or an Outlook Contacts list or Address Book can serve as the source file.

To generate form letters, labels, or envelopes, you merge the source file with a form letter, label, or envelope document. Word calls this process *merging.* In the merge, names and addresses from the source file are plugged into the appropriate places in the form letter, label, or envelope document. When the merge is complete, you can either save the form letters, labels, or envelopes in a new file or start printing right away.

The following sections explain how to prepare the source file and how to merge addresses from the source file with a document to create form letters, labels, or envelopes. You then find out how to print the form letters, labels, or envelopes.

Preparing the source file

If you intend to get addresses for your form letters, labels, or envelopes from an existing Outlook Contact List or Address Book on your computer, you're ready to go. But if you haven't entered the addresses yet or you're keeping them in a Word table, Access database table, or Access query, make sure that the data is in good working order. To ensure that your data is ready, do the following in the Word table, Access table, or query you intend to use as the data source:

- ✦ **Word table:** Save the table in its own file and enter a descriptive heading at the top of each column, as shown in Figure 7-5. In the merge, when you tell Word where to plug in addresses and other data, you will do so by choosing a heading name from the top of a column. In this figure, Last Name, First Name, Street, and so on are the column heading names. (See Chapter 10 if you need help constructing a Word table.)

Figure 7-5: Preparing the data source for a mass mailing.

Records Fields

Last Name	First Name	Street	City	State	Zip	Birthday	Sign
Haines	Clyde	1289 Durham Lane	Durban	MA	64901	January 1	Aquarius
Yee	Gladys	1293 Park Ave.	Waddle	OR	98620	May 3	Libra
Harmony	Esther	2601 Estner Rd.	Pecos	TX	34910	April 10	Taurus
Sings	Melinda	2789 23rd St.	Roburgh	NE	68912	June 14	Gemini
Stickenmud	Rupert	119 Scutter Lane	Nyad	CA	94114	August 2	Leo
Hines	Martha	1263 Tick Park	Osterville	MA	03874	March 16	Sagittarius

INTEGRATION

- ✦ **Access database table or query:** Make sure you know the field names in the database table or query where you keep the addresses. In the merge, you will be asked for field names. By the way, if you're comfortable in Access, query a database table for the records you will need. As you find out shortly, Word offers a technique for choosing only the records you want for your form letters, labels, or envelopes. But by querying first, you can start off with the records you need and spare yourself from having to choose records in Word.

A Word table or Access table or query can include more than address information. Don't worry about deleting information that isn't required for form letters, labels, and envelopes. As you soon find out, you get to decide which information from the table or query to include.

Merging the source file with the document

After making sure that the data source is in good working order, the next step in generating form letters, labels, or envelopes for a mass mailing is to merge the data source file with the document. Follow these general steps to do so:

1. **Open a new document if you want to print labels or envelopes en masse. If you want to print form letters, either open a new document or open a letter you have already written and delete the addressee's name, the address, and other parts of the letter that will differ from recipient to recipient.**
2. **Choose Tools⇨Letters and Mailings⇨Mail Merge Wizard.**

   The Mail Merge task pane appears, as shown in Figure 7-6. After you complete each step in the Mail Merge Wizard, click the Next hyperlink at the bottom of the task pane. Or, if you know your way around mail merging, you can give merge commands by way of the Mail Merge toolbar (right-click a toolbar and chose Mail Merge to display it).

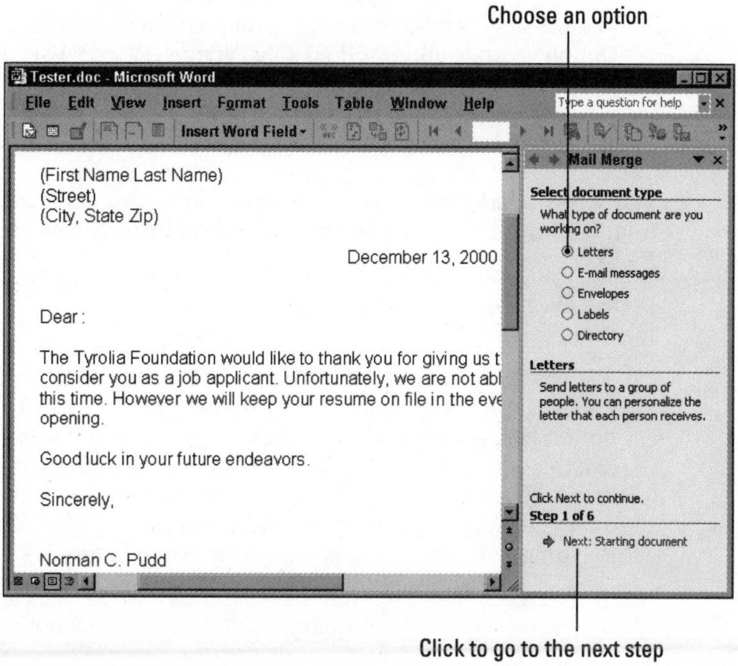

Figure 7-6: Telling Word what you will merge with the source file.

3. **Under Select Document Type in the task pane, click the Letters, Envelopes, or Labels option; then click the Next: Starting Document hyperlink.**

   The next step in the wizard appears in the task pane.

4. **Under Select Starting Document in the task pane, choose the type of document you're working with.**

   What you do now depends on what you are mail-merging:

   - **Form letters:** With the Use Current Document option already selected, you're ready to go. The text of your form letter already appears on-screen if you followed the directions for opening it or writing it in Step 1. (To use a form letter you have used before, select the Start from Existing Document option, click the Open button, find and select the letter in the Open dialog box, and click the Open button. Your form letter appears on-screen.)
   - **Labels:** With the Change Document Layout option already selected, click the Label Options hyperlink under Change Document Layout. The Label Options dialog box appears, where you tell Word what size labels you will print on. (See "Printing a Single Address Label [Or a Page of the Same Label]," earlier in this chapter, if you need advice for filling out this dialog box.) A sheet of sample labels appears on-screen.
   - **Envelopes:** With the Change Document Layout option already selected, click the Envelope Options hyperlink under Change Document Layout. The Envelope Options dialog box appears, where, on the Envelope Options and Printing Options tabs, you tell Word what size envelope you will print on. A sample envelope appears on-screen.

5. **Click the Next: Select Recipients link at the bottom of the Mail Merge task pane.**

6. **Tell Word what your source file or the source of your address and data information is (see the preceding section, "Preparing the source file").**

   Do the following in the Mail Merge task pane to tell Word how to obtain names and addresses from the data source file:

   - **Addresses from a Word table, Access database table, or Access query:** Under Select Recipients, make sure the Use an Existing List option is selected, and then click the Browse hyperlink under Use an Existing List. You see the Select Data Source dialog box. Locate the Word file with the table or the Access database with the table or query, select it, and click the Open button. The Mail Merge Recipients dialog box appears, as shown in Figure 7-7.

     If you select an Access database, you see the Select Table dialog box. Select the table or query you want and click the OK button.

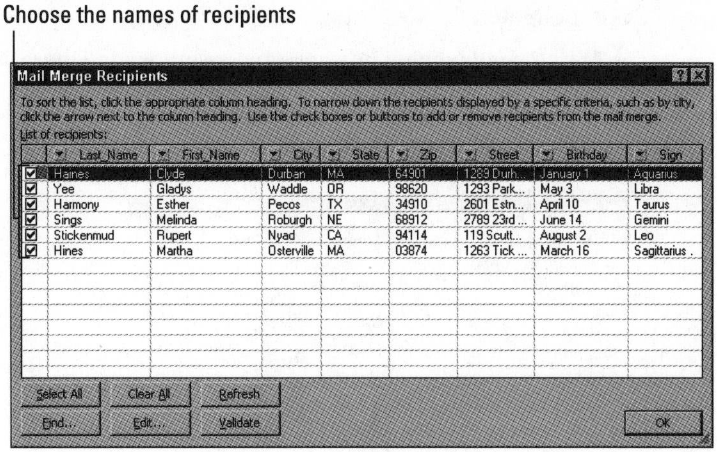

Figure 7-7: Choosing who in the source file will receive the mass mailing.

- **Addresses from Microsoft Outlook:** Under Select Recipients, choose the Select from Outlook Contacts option. Then under Select from Outlook Contacts, click the Choose Contacts Folder hyperlink. The Choose Profile dialog box appears. Click OK in this dialog box. You see the Select Contacts List folder dialog box. Double-click the Contacts folder there. Now you're getting somewhere. You see the Mail Merge Recipients dialog box, with its list of contacts.

7. **In the Mail Merge Recipients dialog box, select the names of people to whom you will send mail, and click OK.**

   To select recipients' names, click to select or deselect the check boxes on the left side of the dialog box. Or, click the Clear All button to remove all the checks and then click recipients names one at a time.

8. **Click the Next hyperlink in the bottom of the task pane to go to Step 4 of the mail-merge process.**

   You must now enter the *address block* on your form letters, labels, or envelopes. The address block is the address, including the recipient's name, company, title, street address, city, and zip code. If you are creating form letters, click in the sample letter where the address block will go. If you are printing on envelopes, click in the middle of the envelope where the delivery address will go.

9. **Either click Insert Address Block button on the Mail Merge toolbar, or click the Address Block hyperlink in the Mail Merge task pane.**

   The Insert Address Block dialog box appears.

10. **Choose a format for entering the recipient's name in the address block.**

11. **Click the Match Fields button.**

    The Match Fields dialog box appears, as shown in Figure 7-8.

Match these names with names from the source file

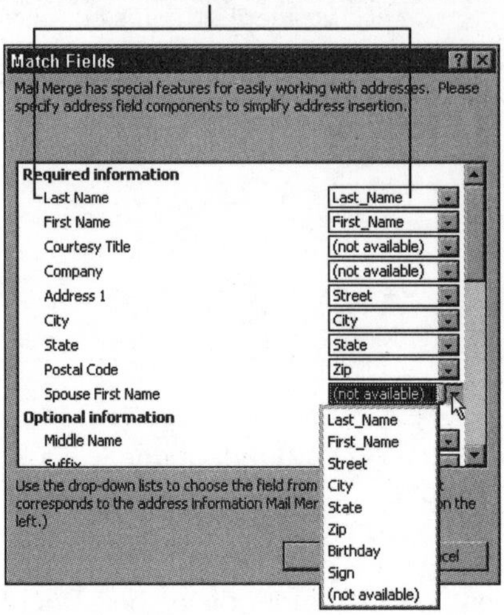

Figure 7-8: Describing the address block.

12. **Using the drop-down lists on the right side of the dialog box, match the fields in your source file with the fields on the left side of the dialog box.**

    In this figure, for example, the Street field is the equivalent of the Address 1 field on the left side of the dialog box.

13. **Click OK in the Match Fields dialog box and the Insert Block Address dialog box.**

    Fields appear in the sample document where the address block goes. Later, when you merge your document with the data source, real data will appear where the field is now. Think of a field as a kind of placeholder for data.

14. **Click the View Merged Data button on the Mail Merge toolbar to see real data instead of fields.**

    Now your screen shows clearly whether you entered the address block correctly. If you didn't enter it correctly, click the Match Fields button on the Mail Merge toolbar to open the Match Fields dialog box and make new choices.

15. **Put the finishing touches on your form letters, labels, or envelopes:**

    - **Form letters:** Click where the salutation will go and then click the Insert Greeting Line button on the Mail Merge toolbar or the

Greeting Line hyperlink in the task pane. You see the Greeting Line dialog box. Make choices in this dialog box to determine how the letters' salutations will read.

The body of your form letter may include other variable information such as names and birthdays. To enter that stuff, click where variable information goes and then click the Insert Merge Fields button or the More Items hyperlink. The Insert Merge Field dialog box appears and lists fields from the source file. Select a field, click the Insert button, and then click the Close button.

If you're editing your form letter and you need to see precisely where the variable information you entered is located, click the Highlight Merge Fields button. The variable information is highlighted in your document. Don't worry — the fields won't print. They're just to show you where variable information is.

- **Labels:** Click the Update All Labels button on the bottom of the task pane to enter all recipients' labels in the sample document. (You may have to click the down arrow on the bottom of the task pane several times to see the button.)

  To include postal bar codes on labels, click the Postal Bar Code hyperlink in the task pane, make sure a Zip Code field is selected in the Insert Postal Bar Code dialog box, and click OK. Postal bar codes help the mail get delivered faster.

- **Envelopes:** If you don't like the fonts or font sizes on the envelope, select an address and change fonts and font sizes with the drop-down lists on the Formatting toolbar.

  To enter a return address, click in the upper-right corner and enter it by hand.

  To include postal bar codes on envelopes, click below the delivery address, click the Postal Bar Code hyperlink in the task pane, and fill in the Insert Postal Bar Code dialog box.

16. **Click the Next Record and Previous Record buttons on the Mail Merge toolbar to skip from recipient to recipient and make sure that you have entered information correctly.**

    The items you see on-screen are the same form letters, envelopes, or labels you will see when you have finished printing. (Click the View Merged Data button if you see field names instead of peoples' names and addresses.) If an item is incorrect, open the source file and correct it there. When you save the source file, the correction is made in the sample document.

At last — you're ready to print the form letters, labels, or envelopes.

Printing form letters, labels, and envelopes

After preparing the data file and merging it with the document, you're ready to print your form letters, labels, or envelopes. You can save the material in a new document or send it straight to the printer:

- **Saving in a new document:** Click the Merge to New Document button on the Mail Merge toolbar (or press Alt+Shift+N) to create a new document for your form letters, labels, or envelopes. You see the Merge to New Document dialog box. Click OK. After Word creates the document, save and print it. You can go into the document later and make changes before printing.

- **Printing right away:** Click the Merge to Printer button (or press Alt+Shift+M) to print the form letters, labels, or envelopes without saving them in a document. Click OK in the Merge to Printer dialog box. Then, in the Print dialog box, tell Word how many copies to print and click the OK button.

Chapter 8: Making Your Work Go Faster

In This Chapter

- **Changing menus and keyboard shortcuts**
- **Rearranging toolbars to your liking**
- **Correcting typos as you type**
- **Repeating actions**
- **Getting around quickly in documents**
- **Inserting text and graphics automatically**

Faster, faster, faster! Work faster!

Does this sound familiar? If you can't seem to work smarter, you can always try to work faster. Word has ways to help you save time here and there. You can correct typos as you type, repeat actions, navigate quickly, insert text automatically, and perform many other time-saving tasks. Who needs to work smarter when they can take advantage of what Word has to offer?

Customizing Word

Never let software be the boss! You are the master of your word-processing fate! With a few simple changes, you can make Microsoft Word work for you instead of the other way around.

You can choose which buttons appear on a toolbar and fashion toolbars for your favorite commands. You can also put menu commands in different places, create your own menus, and invent your own keyboard shortcuts.

Choosing which buttons appear on toolbars

You may never do some of the tasks that the buttons on some of the toolbars were put there to help you do. If you're not using a button, you can take it off the toolbar and replace it with a button that you do use. Adding buttons to and removing buttons from toolbars are easy, and if you make a mistake, getting the original toolbars back is easy, too.

The fastest way to change the buttons on a toolbar is to click the Toolbar Options button on the right side of a toolbar, but you can also go to the Customize dialog box to do a more thorough job. First, the Toolbar Options method:

1. **Put the toolbar whose buttons you want to change on-screen. To do so, choose View⇨Toolbars and click the toolbar's name. (Or, you can right-click in the toolbar area and choose the name of the toolbar from the list that appears.)**

2. **Click the Toolbar Options button, the rightmost button on the toolbar.**
3. **Choose Add or Remove Buttons from the drop-down list, as shown in Figure 8-1.**
4. **Choose the name of the toolbar you want to customize on the submenu. (Picture is being chosen in Figure 8-1.)**

   Another menu appears with the names of buttons now on the toolbar. If you're dealing with the Standard or Formatting toolbar, a handful of extra buttons appears at the bottom of the menu.

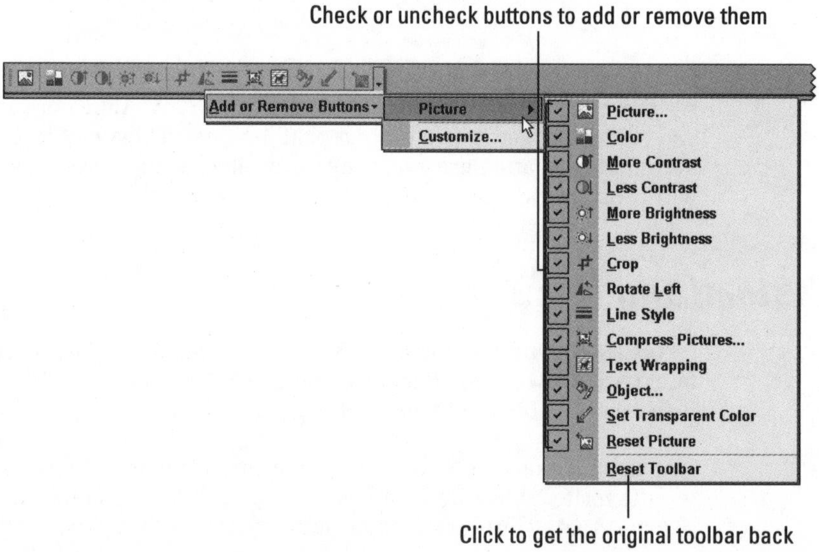

Figure 8-1: Add or remove toolbar buttons at your leisure.

5. **Click the check boxes next to button names to add or remove buttons from the toolbar.**

   A check mark next to a button means that it appears on the toolbar.

To get the officially certified Microsoft toolbar that came with the program, click the Toolbar Options button, choose Add or Remove Buttons, choose a toolbar name, and choose the Reset Toolbar option at the bottom of the buttons list.

So much for the Toolbar Options button method of customizing toolbars. To do a more thorough job of customizing toolbars, to rearrange the buttons on a toolbar, or to bring buttons from distant toolbars to rest on the toolbar of your choice, follow these steps:

1. **Put the toolbar that you want to customize on-screen.**
2. **Choose Tools⇨Customize, or right-click a toolbar and choose Customize from the shortcut menu.**

   The Customize dialog box appears.
3. **Click the Commands tab (see Figure 8-2).**

   The Categories list in this dialog box lists all the menus and several of the toolbars. At the bottom of the list are the styles, macros, AutoText entries, and fonts that are available in the template you're using. A *macro* is a set of command instructions recorded under a name. When a user executes the macro, the program carries out all the instructions.

   You can find every command in Word in this dialog box by clicking an item in the Categories box and then scrolling in the Commands box. If you aren't sure what a button does, click it in the Commands box and then click the Description button.

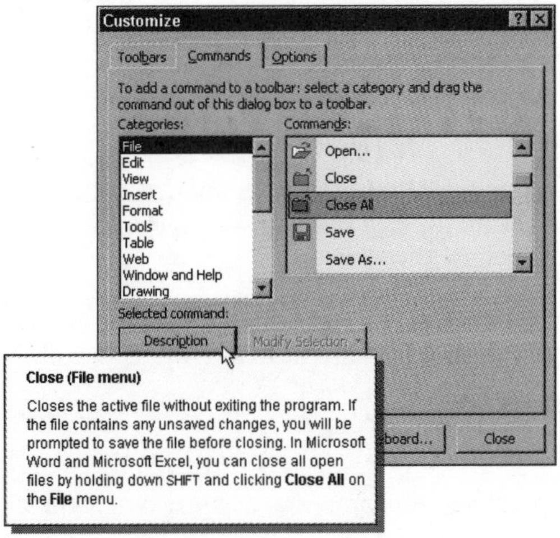

Figure 8-2: The Customize dialog box.

4. **Remove or add a button from the toolbar you displayed in Step 1. To do so, you move the pointer outside the Customize dialog box and click a toolbar:**

   - **Removing:** To remove a button from a toolbar, simply drag it off the toolbar. As you drag, a gray rectangle appears above the pointer, and an *X* appears below it. Release the mouse button, and the toolbar button disappears.

   - **Adding:** To add a button, find it in the Customize dialog box by clicking categories and scrolling in the Commands box. When you have found the button, gently drag it out of the Customize dialog box and place it on the toolbar where you want it to appear. A gray rectangle appears above the cursor. A plus sign appears below it when you move the button onto the toolbar.

5. **While the Customize dialog box is open, you can drag buttons to new locations on toolbars.**
6. **If you want your new toolbar arrangement to appear only in certain templates, click the Save In drop-down list and choose the template.**
7. **Click the Close button.**

You can also move buttons between toolbars by dragging them from toolbar to toolbar while the Customize dialog box is open. To copy buttons from one toolbar to another, hold down the Ctrl key as you drag the buttons.

TIP

If you make a boo-boo and wish that you hadn't fooled with the buttons on the toolbar, choose Tools⇨Customize or right-click a toolbar and choose Customize to get to the Customize dialog box. From there, select the Toolbars tab, click the toolbar whose buttons you fooled with, and click the Reset button. Click OK in the Reset Toolbar dialog box.

Creating your own toolbar

You can also create a new toolbar with your favorite buttons on it. If you want, you can even create toolbar buttons for styles, fonts, AutoText entries, and macros. Follow these steps:

1. **Choose Tools⇨Customize, or right-click a toolbar and choose Customize from the shortcut menu to see the Customize dialog box.**
2. **Click the Toolbars tab.**
3. **Click the New button.**

   The New Toolbar dialog box appears, as shown in Figure 8-3.

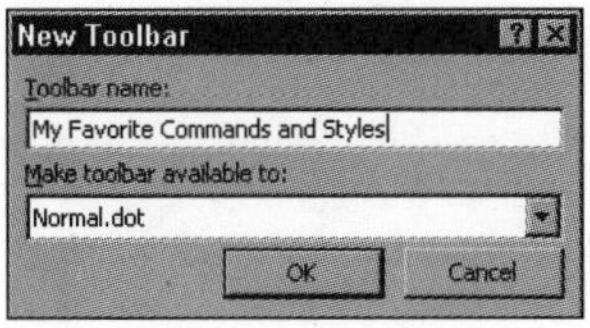

Figure 8-3: The New Toolbar dialog box.

4. **Type a name for your toolbar in the Toolbar Name box.**

   The name you type here will appear on the View⇨Toolbars submenu.

5. **If necessary, choose a template in the Make Toolbar Available To drop-down list.**
6. **Click OK. A tiny toolbar with the name you entered appears on the screen.**
7. **Double-click the title bar of your new toolbar to move it to the top of the screen.**
8. **Click the Commands tab in the Customize dialog box.**
9. **In the Categories box, find and click the category in which the command, style, font, macro, or AutoText entry you want to put on a toolbar is found.**
10. **To add a button, drag an item from the Commands box right onto your new toolbar.**

    Drag as many buttons onto the toolbar as you need. For now, don't worry about their position on the toolbar.

11. **After you've added all the buttons, drag them where you want them to stand on the toolbar.**
12. **If you've added styles or fonts to your toolbar, you may want to shorten their names to make them fit better. To do so, right-click the button whose name you want to shorten and enter a new name in the Name text box.**
13. **When your toolbar is just-so, click the Close button.**

TIP

You can always delete a toolbar you made yourself. Choose Tools⇨Customize, or right-click a toolbar and choose Customize to get to the Customize dialog box. Then click the Toolbars tab, click the toolbar you want to extinguish (self-made toolbars are at the bottom of the list), and click the Delete button. Click OK when Word asks if you really want to go through with it.

Changing the menu commands

You can decide for yourself which menu commands appear on which menus. You can also add macros, fonts, AutoText entries, and styles to menus. Doing so is easy, and if you make a mistake and want to go back to the original menus, that's easy, too.

The quickest (but scariest) way to remove a command from a menu is to press Ctrl+Alt+hyphen. When the cursor changes into an ominous black bar, simply select the menu command that you want to remove. Press Esc twice, by the way, if you decide after you press Ctrl+Alt+hyphen that you don't want to remove menu commands this way.

A more precise way to remove menu commands or alter the menus is to use the Commands tab of the Customize dialog box. To do so, follow these steps:

1. **Choose Tools⇨Customize.**

   The Customize dialog box appears

2. **Click the Commands tab (see Figure 8-4).**

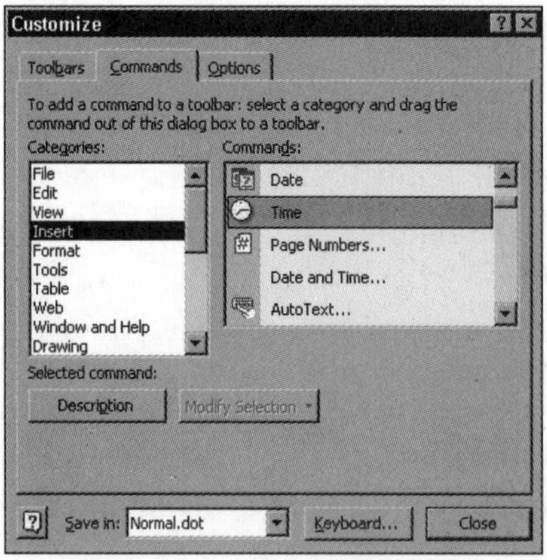

Figure 8-4: The Commands tab of the Customize dialog box.

3. **If you want the menu changes you make to be made to a template other than Normal.dot or the template you are working in, choose the template in the Save In drop-down list.**

4. **In the Categories list, select the menu you want to change.**

   If you're adding a macro, font, AutoText entry, or style to a menu, scroll to the bottom of the Categories list and select it. The commands that are on the menu you chose appear in the Commands list on the right.

5. **Choose the command you're changing in the Comman<u>d</u>s list.**

   You can click the Description button to read a description of the command if you aren't quite sure what it does.

6. **What you do next depends on whether you want to remove a command from a menu, add a command to a menu, or change its position on a menu. Changing menu commands requires moving the pointer out of the Customize dialog box and clicking menus on the menu bar.**

   - **Removing:** To remove a menu command, move the pointer over the menu that holds the command you want to remove and click. That's right — click the menu name as you would if you were pulling it down to choose one of its commands. When the menu appears, click the menu command you want to remove, and drag it off the menu. You see a gray rectangle above the pointer and an *X* below it. Release the mouse button after you have dragged the menu command away from the menu.
   - **Adding:** To add a menu command to a menu, drag it from the Commands list in the Customize dialog box to the menu itself. As you do this, you see a gray rectangle above the pointer and a plus sign below it. Move the pointer over the menu to which you want to add the command. The menu appears. Gently drag the pointer down the menu to the spot where you want the command to be listed. A black line appears on the menu to show where your command will go. When the command is in the right spot, release the mouse button.
   - **Changing position:** To change the position of a command on a menu, move the pointer out of the Customize dialog box and gently click the menu whose command you want to move. Then drag the pointer up or down the list of commands. A black line shows where the command will move when you release the mouse button. When the black line is in the right spot, let up on the mouse button.

7. **Click the Close button.**

If you wish that you hadn't messed with the menus and you want to repent, choose <u>T</u>ools–><u>C</u>ustomize, click the Commands tab, move the pointer out of the dialog box and right-click the name of the menu whose commands you fooled with, and choose Reset on the shortcut menu.

Changing the keyboard shortcuts

If you don't like Word's keyboard shortcuts, you can change them and invent keyboard shortcuts of your own. You can also assign keyboard shortcuts to symbols, macros, fonts, AutoText entries, and styles. Follow these steps:

1. **Choose <u>T</u>ools⇨<u>C</u>ustomize.**

2. **Click the Keyboard button.**

   The Customize Keyboard dialog box appears, as shown in Figure 8-5.

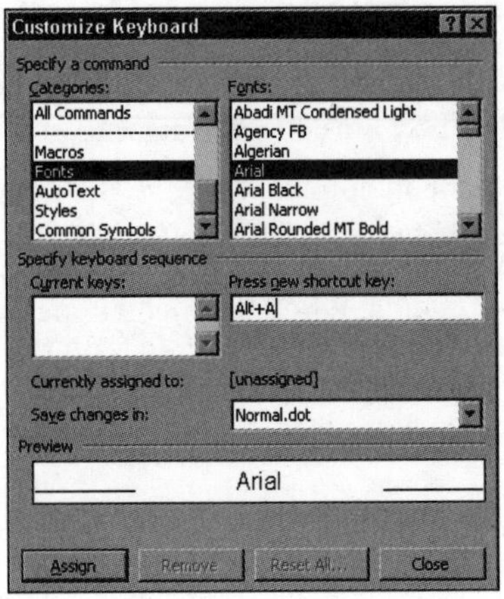

Figure 8-5: The Customize Keyboard dialog box.

3. **To make the changes to a template other than Normal.dot or the template you are working in, choose a template in the Save Changes In drop-down list.**

4. **In the Categories list, choose the menu with the command to which you want to assign the keyboard shortcut.**

   At the bottom of the list are the Macro, Font, AutoText, Style, and Common Symbols categories.

5. **Choose the command name, macro, font, AutoText entry, style, or symbol name in the Commands list.**

6. **Click in the Press New Shortcut Key box and type the keyboard shortcut. Press the actual keys. For example, if the shortcut is Ctrl+~, press the Ctrl key and the ~ key — don't type out C-t-r-l-+~.**

   If you try to assign a shortcut that is already assigned, the words `Currently assigned to` and a command name appear below the Press New Shortcut Key box. You can override the preassigned keyboard assignment by entering a keyboard assignment of your own.

7. **Click the Assign button.**

8. **After you're done, click the Close button.**

9. **Click Close in the Customize dialog box.**

To delete a keyboard shortcut, display it in the Current Keys box, click it, and click the Remove button.

You can always get the old keyboard shortcuts back by clicking the Reset All button in the Customize Keyboard dialog box. Click Yes when Word asks whether you really want the old keyboard shortcuts back.

Correcting Typos on the Fly

Unless you or someone else has messed with the AutoCorrect settings, the invisible hand of Word corrects certain typos as you enter them. Try misspelling *weird* by typing *wierd* to see what I mean. Try entering two hyphens (--) and you get an em dash (—). You can have Word correct the typos that you make often, and with a little cunning, you can even use the AutoCorrect feature to enter long company names and hard-to-spell names on the fly.

If Word makes an autocorrection that you don't care for, move the pointer over the spot where the correction was made. The AutoCorrect Options button appears, as shown in Figure 8-6. By clicking it, you can get a drop-down list with options for reversing the correction, telling Word never to make the correction again, and opening the AutoCorrect dialog box.

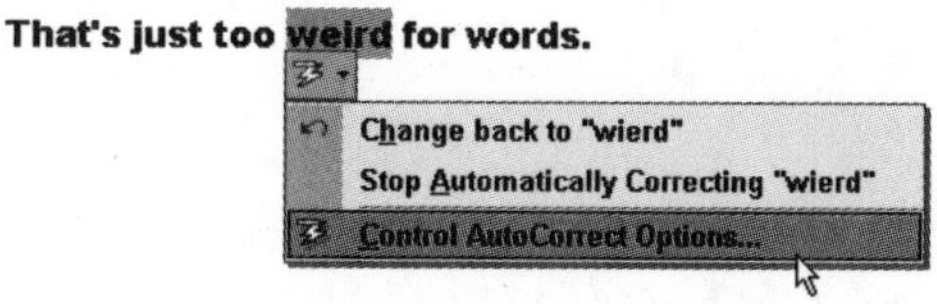

Figure 8-6: The AutoCorrect Options drop-down list.

The AutoCorrect dialog box offers a comprehensive list of words that are autocorrected, as well as options for telling Word what to autocorrect (you can open the dialog box at any time by choosing Tools➪AutoCorrect Options). When you have a spare moment, open the AutoCorrect dialog box and do the following:

- ✦ Remove the check marks from the AutoCorrect features that you don't want. For example, if you enter a lot of computer code in your manuscripts, you don't necessarily want the first letter of sentences to be capitalized automatically, so you should click the Capitalize First Letter of Sentences check box to deselect it.
- ✦ If you want, remove the check mark from the Replace Text as You Type box to keep Word's invisible hand from correcting idiosyncrasies in capitalization and spelling as you enter them.

- Scroll through the list and take a look at the words that are "autocorrected." If you don't want a word on the list to be corrected, select it and click Delete.
- If a word that you often misspell isn't on the list, you can add it to the list and have Word correct it automatically. Enter the misspelling in the Replace box, enter the right spelling in the With box, and click the Add button.
- If you don't like one of the replacement words, select the word on the list, enter a new replacement word in the With box, and click the Replace button.

If Word AutoCorrects a word that you don't want changed, just press Ctrl+Z or click the Undo button.

TIP

The Spelling and Grammar dialog box has an AutoCorrect option. Choose it when you're spell-checking a document to add the word you're correcting to the list of words that are "autocorrected." The AutoCorrect choice sometimes appears on the shortcut menu when you right-click a misspelled word, as shown in Figure 8-7. Choose AutoCorrect on the shortcut menu and choose a correct spelling to add the misspelling to the family of words in the AutoCorrect dialog box that get corrected automatically.

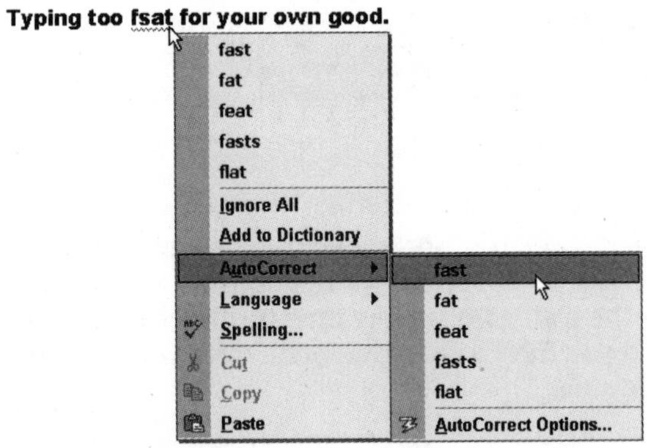

Figure 8-7: You can right-click to add a word to the AutoCorrect list.

Repeating an Action — and Quicker This Time

The Edit menu has a command called Repeat that you can choose to repeat your last action, and it can be a mighty time-saver. The command changes names, depending on what you did last.

For example, if you just changed a heading style and you want to change another heading in the same way, move the cursor to the heading and choose Edit⇨Repeat Style (or press F4 or Ctrl+Y). Rather than go to the trouble of clicking the Style menu and choosing a heading style from the drop-down list, all you have to do is choose a simple command or press a key or two.

If you had to type "I will not talk in class" a hundred times, all you would have to do is write it once and choose Edit⇨Repeat (or press F4 or Ctrl+Y) 99 times.

Going Here, Going There in Documents

Word offers three very speedy techniques for jumping around in documents: the Select Browse Object button, the Edit⇨Go To command, and the document map.

"Browsing" around a document

A really fast way to move around quickly is to click the Select Browse Object button in the lower-right corner of the screen. When you click this button, Word presents 12 "Browse by" icons.

Select the icon that represents the element you want to go to, and Word takes you there immediately. For example, click the Browse by Heading icon to get to the next heading in your document (provided that you assigned heading styles to headings). After you have selected a Browse by icon, the navigator buttons — the double-arrows directly above and below the Select Browse Object button — turn blue. Click a blue navigator button to get to the next example or the previous example of the element you chose. For example, if you selected the Browse by Heading icon, all you have to do is click blue navigator buttons to get from heading to heading backwards or forwards in a document.

Going there fast with the Go To command

Another fast way to go from place to place in a document is to use the Edit⇨Go To command. Choose this command or press Ctrl+G to see the Go To tab of the Find and Replace dialog box (see Figure 8-8).

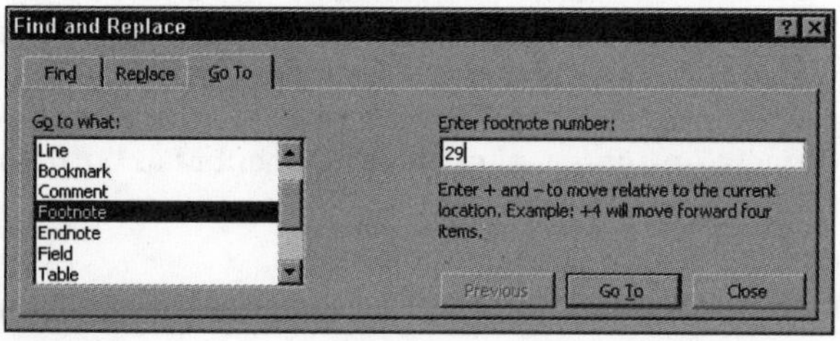

Figure 8-8: Go To tab of the Find and Replace dialog box.

The Go to What menu in this dialog box lists everything that can conceivably be numbered in a Word document, and other things, too. Everything that you can get to with the Select Browse Object button, as well as lines, equations, and objects, can be reached by way of the Go To tab. Click a menu item and enter a number or choose an item from the drop-down list to go elsewhere.

Click the Previous button to go back to the footnote, endnote, comment, line, or whatever you just came from. You can press + or – and enter numbers to go backward or forward by one or several numbered items at once.

Hopping from place to place in the document map

Yet another way to hop from place to place is by turning on the document map. To do so, click the Document Map button or choose View➪Document Map. Everything in the document that hasn't been assigned the Normal style — headings, captions, and so on — appears along the left side of the screen (see Figure 8-9).

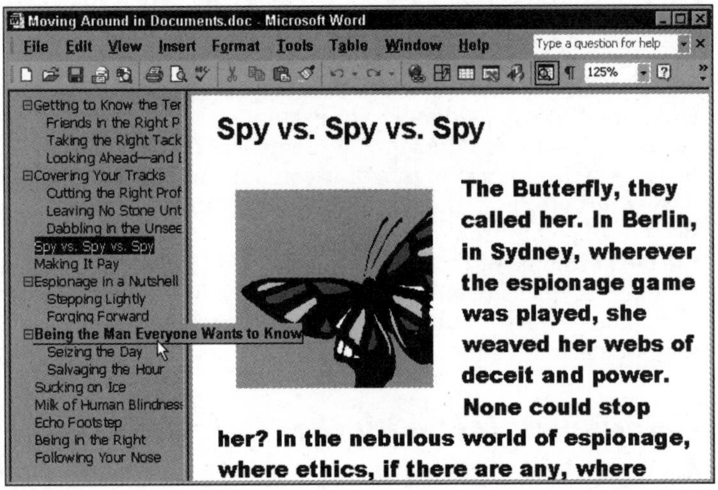

Figure 8-9: View your document's structure at a glance.

Select an item in the document map and Word takes you there in the twinkling of an eye. Right-click the document map and choose a heading level option on the shortcut menu to tell Word which headings to display in the map. You an also click the plus sign (+) or minus sign (-) next to a heading to hide or display its subheadings. To put away the document map and see only the document on-screen, click the Document Map button again.

Bookmarks for hopping around

Instead of pressing PgUp or PgDn or clicking the scroll bar to thrash around in a long document, you can use bookmarks. All you do is put a bookmark in an important spot in your document that you'll return to many times.

To place a bookmark in a document, follow these steps:

1. **Click where you want the bookmark to go.**
2. **Choose Insert⇨Bookmark (or press Ctrl+Shift+F5).**

   The Bookmark dialog box appears, as shown in Figure 8-10.
3. **Type a descriptive name in the Bookmark Name box.**

   You cannot include spaces in bookmark names.
4. **Click the Add button.**

Figure 8-10: The Bookmark dialog box.

When you want to return to that bookmark, follow these steps:

1. **Choose Insert⇨Bookmark (or press Ctrl+Shift+F5).**
2. **Double-click the bookmark in the Bookmark dialog box and click the Close (X) button to close the dialog box.**

You can arrange bookmarks in the list in alphabetical order or by location in the document by clicking the Name or Location options at the bottom of the Bookmark dialog box. Click the Hidden bookmarks check box to see cross-references in the Bookmark Name box, although hidden bookmarks appear as code and don't tell you much about what they are or where they are in the document.

To delete a bookmark, select it in the Bookmark dialog box and click the Delete button.

Entering Graphics and Text Quickly

Put the text and graphics that you often use on the Insert➪AutoText list (Word has already placed a few common entries there). That way, you can enter the long-winded text or a complicated graphic simply by clicking a few menu commands or typing a couple of letters. Addresses, letterheads, and company logos are ideal candidates for the AutoText list because they take so long to enter.

Creating your own AutoText entries

Follow these steps to create an AutoText entry:

1. **Type the text or import the graphic.**
2. **Select the text or graphic.**
3. **Choose Insert➪AutoText➪New or press Alt+F3.**

   The Create AutoText dialog box appears, as shown in Figure 8-11.

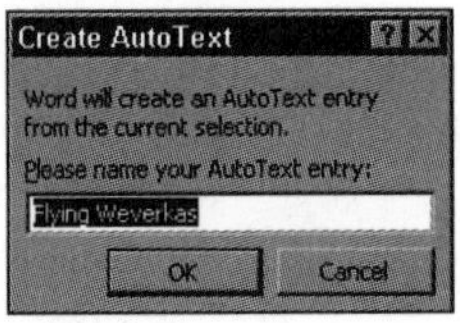

Figure 8-11: The Create AutoText dialog box.

4. **Type a name for the text or graphic in the text box and click OK.**

Inserting an AutoText entry

Word offers five ways to insert an AutoText entry. Place the cursor where you want the entry to go and choose one of these methods to enter it:

FAST TRACK

- Start typing the entry's name. Midway through, a bubble appears with the entire entry (see Figure 8-12). Press Enter to insert the whole thing.

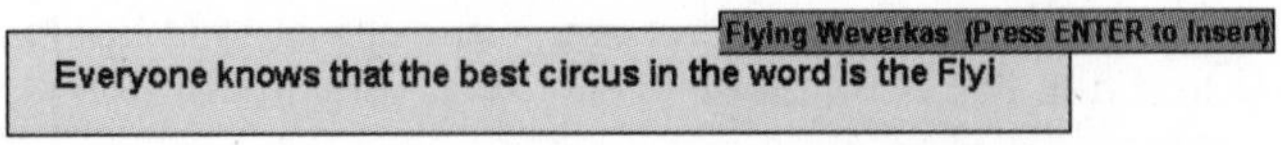

Figure 8-12: The fastest way to insert an AutoText entry.

- Type the entry's name and press F3.
- Display the AutoText toolbar, click the All Entries button, select a submenu name, and choose an AutoText entry.
- Choose Insert⇨AutoText, select a submenu name, and choose an AutoText Entry.
- Choose Insert⇨AutoText⇨AutoText, select an entry in the AutoCorrect dialog box, and click the Insert button. Go this route when you aren't sure which AutoText entry to make. The Preview box in the AutoCorrect dialog box clearly shows all the AutoText entries.

To delete an AutoText entry, choose Insert⇨AutoText⇨AutoText to open the AutoCorrect dialog box, click the entry that you want to delete, and click the Delete button.

TIP: Some people think that the AutoText bubbles are annoying. They pop up in the oddest places. Try typing the name of a month, for example, to see what I mean. To keep the bubbles from appearing, choose Insert⇨AutoText⇨AutoText and click to remove the check mark from the Show AutoComplete Suggestions check box.

Chapter 9: Getting Really Organized

In This Chapter

- Creating an outline
- Linking documents together

If you're working on a document that's more than one page long, you may notice that keeping track of your document's structure begins to become a bit more difficult. And if you're composing your masterpiece novel or your Ph.D. dissertation on *The Guardians in the 'Roman de la Rose' of Guillaume do Lorris and Jean de Meun,* you soon discover that you can use some serious help with organization!

Word not only outlines your work for you, but it can also make it possible for you to work on long documents — even on a group of documents — without losing your place or giving up in frustration.

Outlines for Organizing Your Work

Outline view is a great way to see at a glance how your document is organized and whether you need to organize it differently. To take advantage of this feature, you must have assigned heading levels to the headings in your document (see Chapter 6). In Outline view, you can see all the headings in your document. If a section is in the wrong place, you can move it simply by dragging an icon or by pressing one of the buttons on the Outline toolbar.

To see a document in Outline view, choose View➪Outline or click the Outline View button in the lower-left corner of the screen. Rather than text, you see the headings in your document, as well as the first line underneath each heading. And in Outline view, the Outlining toolbar appears along the top of the window, as shown in Figure 9-1. (The seven buttons on the right side of the Outlining toolbar are for handling master documents, a subject not covered in this book. To hide or display those buttons, click the Master Document View button on the toolbar.)

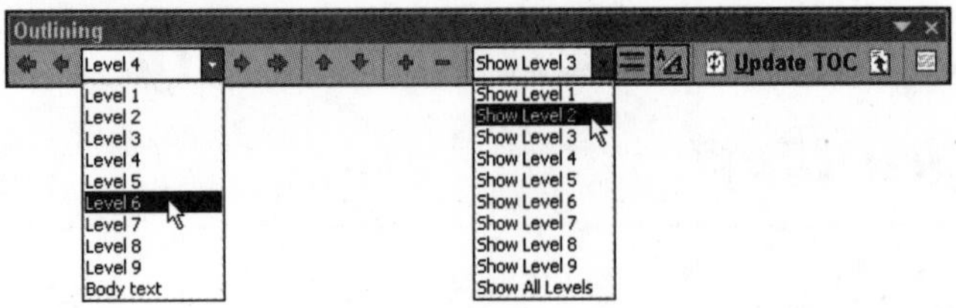

Figure 9-1: The Outlining toolbar.

Before you start rearranging your document in Outline view, get a good look at it by taking advantage of buttons and menus on the Outlining toolbar:

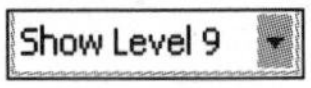

- **View some or all headings:** Choose an option from the Show Level drop-down list. To see only first-level headings, for example, choose Show Level 1. To see first-, second-, and third-level headings, choose Show Level 3. Choose Show All Levels to see all the headings.

- **View heading formats:** Click the Show Formatting button. After clicking this button, you can see how headings were formatted and get a better idea of their ranking in your document.

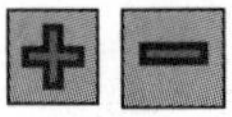

- **View or hide the headings in one section:** To see the headings and text in only one section of a document, select that section by clicking the plus sign beside it and then click the Expand button. To hide the headings and text in a section, click the minus sign beside its name and then click the Collapse button.

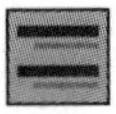

- **View or hide paragraph text:** Click the Show First Line Only button (or press Alt+Shift+L). After clicking this button, you see only the first line in each paragraph. First lines are followed by ellipses (. . .) so that you know that more text follows.

Notice the plus and minus icons next to the headings and the text. A plus icon means that the heading has subtext under it. For example, headings almost always have plus icons because text comes after them. A minus icon means that nothing is found below the heading in question. For example, body text usually has a minus icon because body text is lowest on the Outline totem pole.

You can do the following tasks with the lists and buttons on the Outlining toolbar:

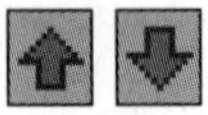

- **Move a section:** To move a section up or down in the document, click the Move Up or Move Down button. You can also drag the plus sign or minus sign to a new location. If you want to move the subordinate text and headings along with the section, click the Collapse button to tuck all the subtext into the heading before you move it.

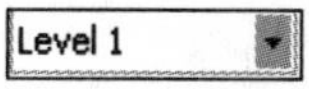

✦ **Choose a new level for a heading:** Click the heading and choose a new heading level from the Outline Level drop-down list.

✦ **Promote a heading by one level:** Click the heading and then click the Promote button. For example, you can promote a Level 4 heading to Level 3.

✦ **Promote a heading to the first level:** Click the heading and then click the Promote to Heading 1 button, the leftmost button on the Outlining toolbar.

✦ **Demote a heading by one level:** Click the heading and then click the Demote button to bust down a Level 1 heading to Level 2, for example.

✦ **Turn a heading into normal text:** Click the heading and then click the Demote to Body Text button to turn a heading into plain-Jane text.

Linking Documents to Make Your Work Easier

You can save a lot of time and effort by connecting two documents so that changes made to part of the first are made automatically to the second. This process is called *linking*. If a table in a memo you're working on happens to be useful in an annual report, you can link the documents, and updates to the table in the *source document* (in this case the memo) will also show up in the *linked document* (in this case the annual report).

Word offers two kinds of links, automatic and manual:

✦ With an *automatic link,* changes made to the source document are made in the linked document as well each time you reopen the linked document.

✦ With a *manual link,* you have to tell Word to update the link. It isn't updated automatically.

Creating a link

Before you create a link between documents, ask yourself whether either document is likely to be moved out of the folder where it is now. Links are broken when documents are moved. Although you can reestablish a link, doing so is a chore. The better strategy is to plan ahead and link only documents that are not going to be moved to different folders.

To create an automatic link between documents, follow these steps:

1. **Open the source document with the text you want to link to another document.**

2. **Select the text and copy it to the Clipboard by clicking the Copy button, pressing Ctrl+C, or choosing Edit⇨Copy.**
3. **Switch to the document where the linked text is to be pasted and put the cursor where you want the text to go.**
4. **Choose Edit⇨Paste Special.**

   The Paste Special dialog box appears, as shown in Figure 9-2.

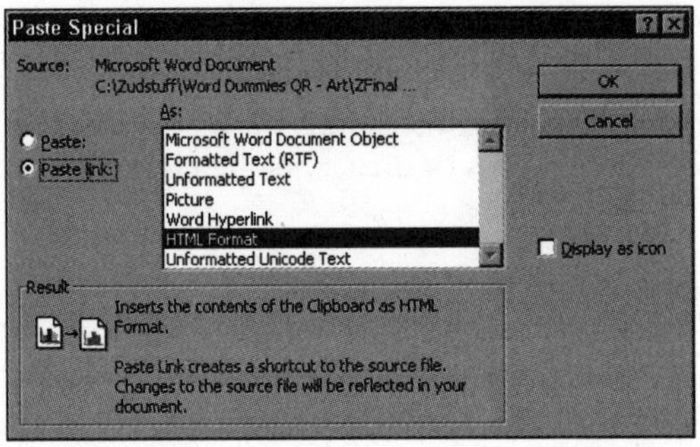

Figure 9-2: Get ready to link with the Paste Special dialog box.

5. **Click the Paste Link radio button.**
6. **Under As, choose a different option than the one Word chose for you, if necessary.**

   HTML is now the official format of Microsoft Word, so don't worry if HTML Format is the choice in the As box when you're trying to link normal text.

7. **Click OK.**
8. **Save the document.**

Updating, breaking, and changing links

With an automatic link, changes made to the original document are made to the linked document whenever the linked document is reopened. You can update automatic and manual links by clicking the link and pressing F9 or right-clicking the link and choosing Update Link.

To break or change a link — and do other things besides — go to the document that received the linked data and follow these steps:

1. **Choose Edit⇨Links.**

   The Links dialog box appears, as shown in Figure 9-3.

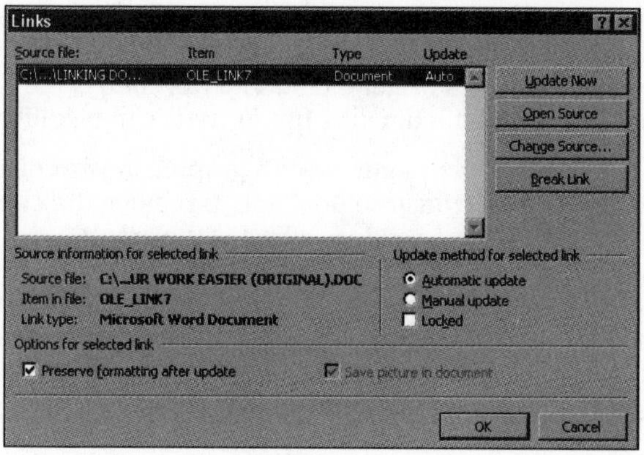

Figure 9-3: Telling Word to update a link.

2. **Click the link that you want to update.**

   Be sure to look at the Source File listing at the bottom of the dialog box to make sure that you're updating the right link.

3. **Choose from the following options and click OK:**

   - **Update Now:** Updates all the links so that they show what is currently in the source documents.
   - **Open Source:** Clicking this button opens the original document so that you can make changes to text or find out more about the original document.
   - **Change Source:** If you move the original document to another folder, Word doesn't know where to look for the document that contains the original text. Click this button (or double-click the source file's name under Source File) to open the Change Source dialog box. Then find the original document and click Open. The link is re-established.
   - **Break Link:** Severs the tie between the original document and the document with the link in it. After you click this button, the link is broken, and you can't get it back.
   - **Automatic Update:** Turns the link into an automatic link.
   - **Manual Update:** Turns the link into a manual link.
   - **Locked:** Makes it so that updates to the original text do not affect the linked text. Choose this option instead of Break Link if you want to break the link temporarily and still be able to reestablish the link later on.

- **Preserve Formatting After Update:** Enables you to make format changes to linked text — changing fonts, for example — independent of the formats in the original text. The raw data is the same in the source and linked documents, but formats can be different.
- **Save Picture in Document:** Saves a graphic in your document instead of a link to the graphic. Click to remove the check mark from this check box to a store a link to the graphic.

Suppose that you're in the linked document and you realize that you need to change the source text. To change it, click the linked text and choose Edit➪Linked Document Object➪Open Link, or right-click and choose Linked Document Object➪Open Link on the shortcut menu.

TIP

To make sure that all links are updated before you print documents, choose Tools➪Options, click the Print tab, and click the Update Links check box.

Chapter 10: Constructing the Perfect Table

In This Chapter

- Creating and modifying a table
- Changing the order of items in a table
- Formatting a table
- Joining and breaking up cells
- Putting math formulas in your tables

The time will come when you need to put text into little boxes that are organized into columns and row. Yes, we're talking about tables here. As everyone who has ever worked on one knows, tables are a chore. Getting all the columns to fit, making columns and rows the right width and height, and editing text in a table is not easy. So problematic are tables that Word has devoted an entire menu to constructing them: the Table menu. Fortunately for you, the commands on this menu make formatting and working with tables easy.

This chapter explains how to create tables, enter text into tables, change the number and size of columns and rows, sort tables, and format tables.

Constructing the Perfect Table

Like so much else in Computerland, tables have their own jargon. A *cell* is the box that is formed where a row and column intersect. Each cell holds one data item. The *header row* is the name of the labels along the top row that explain what is in the columns below. *Borders* are the lines in the table. The *gridlines* are the gray lines that show where the columns and rows are. Gridlines are not printed — they appear to help you format your table. (Choose Table⇨Show Gridlines or Table⇨_Hide Gridlines to display or hide them.) Word prints only the borders when you print a table. A sample table is shown in Figure 10-1.

Row Header row Borders Split cells

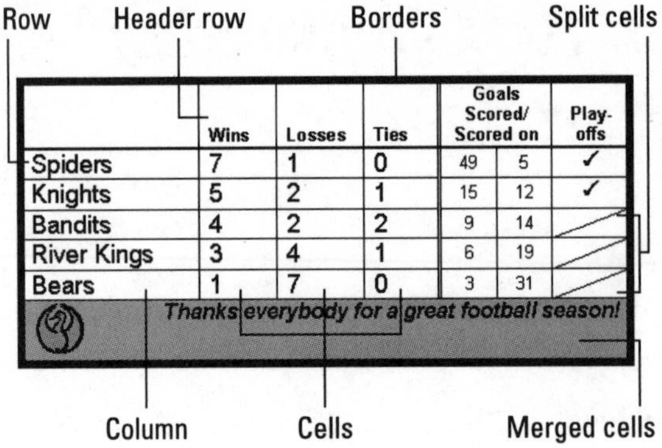

Figure 10-1:
This table
demon-
strates that
the Spiders
were big
winners.

	Wins	Losses	Ties	Goals Scored/ Scored on		Play-offs
Spiders	7	1	0	49	5	✓
Knights	5	2	1	15	12	✓
Bandits	4	2	2	9	14	
River Kings	3	4	1	6	19	
Bears	1	7	0	3	31	
	Thanks everybody for a great football season!					

Column Cells Merged cells

Creating a table

Word offers no less than four ways to create the cells and rows for a table: the Insert Table button, the Draw Table button, the Table⇨Insert⇨Table command, and the Table⇨Convert⇨Text to Table command.

The fastest way to create a table is to click the Insert Table button on the Standard toolbar:

1. **Place the cursor where you want the table to go.**

2. **Click the Insert Table button, drag out the menu to the number of rows and columns you want, and let go of the mouse button (see Figure 10-2).**

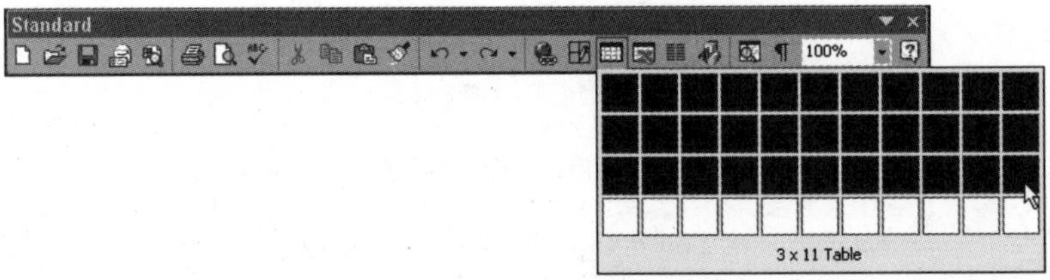

Figure 10-2:
Creating a
table by
using the
Insert Table
button.

Standard

3 x 11 Table

That's easy enough. Another easy way is to make like your computer is a scratch pad and draw a table. As the "Merging and Splitting Cells and Tables" section later in this chapter explains, merging and splitting cells with the Table menu commands is far more difficult than simply drawing merged and split cells. To create a table with rows and columns of different widths and heights, follow these steps:

1. **To draw a table, choose Table⇨Draw Table or click the Draw Table button on the Tables and Borders toolbar.**

   Choose a thick line from the Line Weight menu on the toolbar to see the lines better as you draw them. The pointer changes into a pencil. By the way, you can click the Tables and Borders button on the Standard toolbar to display the Tables and Border toolbar.

2. **Start drawing.**

   As you drag the pencil on-screen, you get columns and rows.

3. **If you make a mistake, click the Eraser button on the Tables and Border toolbar.**

   The pointer changes into an eraser. Drag it over the parts of the table you regret drawing.

4. **When you are finished drawing the table, press Esc or click the Draw Table button to put the pencil away.**

You can also create a table by using the Table⇨Insert⇨Table command. The only advantage of this command is that it gives you the opportunity to decide how wide to make the table. To create a table this way, follow these steps:

1. **Place the cursor where you want the table to be.**
2. **Choose Table⇨Insert⇨Table.**

   The Insert Table dialog box appears.

3. **In the Number of Columns box, enter the number of columns you want.**
4. **In the Number of Rows box, enter the number of rows you want.**
5. **Under AutoFit Behavior, you can enter a measurement in the Fixed Column Width text box to make all columns the same width.**

   The Auto setting creates columns of equal width and stretches the table so that it fits across the page between the left and right margin.

6. **Click the AutoFormat button to open a dialog box from which you can choose one of Word's table formats.**

   See "Formatting a table with Word's AutoFormats," later in this chapter, to find out about these formats.

7. **Click OK.**

The fourth way to create a table is to convert text that you've already entered. This is the way to go if you've created a list and you don't want to go to the trouble of re-entering the text all over again for the new table. To convert text into a table, follow these steps:

1. **Either press Tab or enter a comma in the list where you want columns to be divided.**

   For example, if you're turning an address list into a table, put each name and address on one line and press Tab after the first name, the last name, the street address, the city, the state, and the zip code. For this feature to work, each name and address — each line — must have the same number of tab spaces in it.

2. **Start a new paragraph — press Enter, that is — where you want each row to end.**
3. **Select the text you want to turn into a table.**
4. **Choose Table⇨Convert⇨Text to Table.**
5. **Under Separate Text At in the Convert Text to Table dialog box, choose Tabs or Commas to tell Word how the columns are separated.**
6. **Choose an AutoFit Behavior option, if you want.**
7. **Click OK.**

In Figure 10-3, five tab stops were entered on each line in an address list. Below the list is the table that was created from the address list.

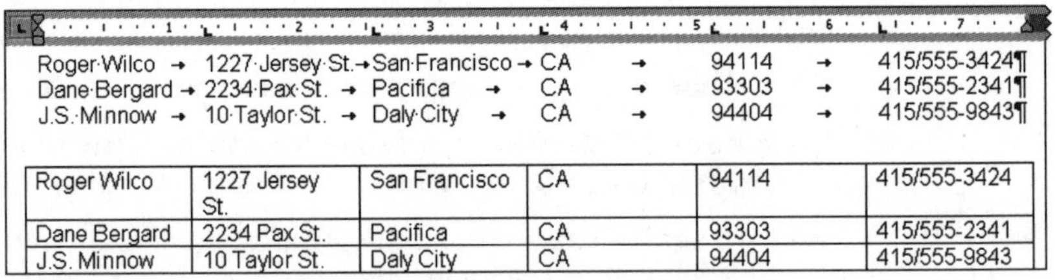

Figure 10-3: Turning a list into a table.

Entering text and numbers in a table

After you've created the table, you can start entering text. All you have to do is click in a cell and start typing. If you need to add a row at the bottom of the table to enter more text, place the cursor in the last column of the last row and press the Tab key.

Modifying the Table Layout

Very likely, you created too many or too few rows or columns for your table. Some columns are probably too wide, and others may be too narrow. If that is the case, you have to change the layout of the table by deleting, inserting, and changing the size of columns and rows. In other words, you have to modify the table layout.

Selecting different parts of a table

Before you can fool with cells, rows, or columns, you have to select them:

- **Cells:** To select a cell, click in it. You can select several cells at once by dragging the cursor over them.
- **Rows:** Place the cursor in the left margin and click to select one row, or click and drag to select several rows. You can also select rows by placing the cursor in the row you want to select and then choosing the Table⇨Select⇨Row command. To select several rows, select cells in the rows and then choose Table⇨Select⇨Row.

- **Columns:** To select a column, move the cursor to the top of the column. When the cursor changes into a fat down-pointing arrow, click once. You can click and drag to select several columns. The other way to select a column is to click anywhere in the column and choose Table⇨Select⇨Column. To select several columns with this command, select cells in the columns before giving the Select command.
- **A table:** To select a table, click in the table and choose Table⇨Select⇨Table; hold down the Alt key and double-click; or press Alt+5 (the 5 on the numeric keypad, not the one on the keyboard).

Inserting and deleting columns and rows

Here's the lowdown on inserting and deleting columns and rows:

- **Inserting columns:** To insert a blank column, select the column to the right of where you want the new column to go, right-click, and choose Insert Columns. You can also choose Table⇨Insert⇨Columns to the Left (or Columns to the Right). Word inserts the number of columns you select, so to insert more than one, select more than one before choosing the Insert Columns command.
- **Deleting columns:** To delete columns, select them. Then choose Table⇨Delete⇨Columns, or right-click and choose Delete Columns. (Pressing the Delete key deletes the data in the column.)

- **Inserting rows:** To insert a blank row, select the row below which you want the new one to appear. If you want to insert more than one row, select more than one. Then right-click and choose Insert Rows, or choose Table⇨Insert⇨Rows Above (or Rows Below). You can also insert a row at the end of a table by moving the cursor into the last cell in the last row and pressing the Tab key.
- **Deleting rows:** To delete rows, select them and choose Table⇨Delete⇨Rows, or right-click and choose Delete Rows. (Pressing the Delete key deletes the data in the row.)

A fast way to insert columns or rows is to insert one and then press F4 (or press Ctrl+Y or choose Edit⇨Repeat) as many times as necessary to insert all the columns or rows you need.

Moving columns and rows

Because there is no elegant way to move a column or row, you should move only one at a time. If you try to move several at once, you open a can of worms that is best left unopened. To move a column or row, follow these steps:

1. **Select the column or row you want to move.**
2. **Right-click in the selection and choose Cut on the shortcut menu.**

   The column or row is moved to the Clipboard.
3. **Move the column or row:**
   - **Column:** Click in the topmost cell in the column to the right of where you want to move the column. In other words, to make what is now column 4 column 2, cut column 4 and click in the topmost cell of column 2. Then right-click and choose Paste Columns on the shortcut menu.
   - **Row:** Move the cursor into the first column of the row below which you want to move your row. In other words, if you're placing the row between what are now rows 6 and 7, put the cursor in row 7. Then right-click and choose Paste Rows on the shortcut menu.

Resizing columns and rows

The fastest way to adjust the width of columns and the height of rows is to "eyeball it." To make a column wider or narrower, move the cursor onto a gridline or border. When the cursor changes into a double-headed arrow, start dragging. Tug and pull, tug and pull until the column is the right width or the row is the right height. You can also slide the column bars on the ruler or the rows bars on the vertical ruler (if you're in Print Layout view) to change the width of columns and height of rows.

Because resizing columns and rows can be problematic, Word offers these commands on the Table⇨AutoFit submenu for adjusting the width and height of rows and columns:

- **AutoFit to Contents:** Makes each column wide enough to accommodate its widest entry.
- **AutoFit to Window:** Stretches the table so that it fits across the page between the left and right margin.
- **Fixed Column Width:** Fixes the column widths at their current settings.

- **Distribute Rows Evenly:** Makes all rows the same height as the tallest row. You can also click the Distribute Rows Evenly button on the Tables and Borders toolbar. Select rows before giving this command to make the command affect only the rows you selected.

- **Distribute Columns Evenly:** Makes all columns the same width. You can also click the Distribute Columns Evenly button. Select columns before giving this command if you want to change the size of a few columns, not all the columns in the table.

Aligning text in columns and rows

The easiest way to align text in the columns or cells is to rely on the Align Left, Center, Align Right, and Justify buttons on the Standard toolbar. Select a cell, a column, or columns and click one of those buttons to align the text in a column the same way.

Sorting (Or Reordering) a Table

The fastest way to rearrange the rows in a table is to use the Table⇨Sort command or click one of the Sort buttons on the Tables and Borders toolbar. *Sorting* means to rearrange all the rows in a table on the basis of data in one column. For example, the first table shown in Figure 10-4 is arranged, or sorted, on the fifth column, "Total Votes." This column has been sorted in *descending* order from most to fewest votes. The second table has been sorted on the first column. It is sorted by the candidates' names in *ascending* order alphabetically. Both tables present the same information, but the information has been sorted in different ways.

	1st Ward	2nd Ward	3rd Ward	Total Votes
Demoste	2,567	7,399	10,420	20,386
Reputan	3,113	9,907	4,872	17,892
Libertas	67	211	89	367
Greensway	12	2	113	127

	1st Ward	2nd Ward	3rd Ward	Total Votes
Demoste	2,567	7,399	10,420	20,386
Greensway	12	2	113	127
Libertas	67	211	89	367
Reputan	3,113	9,907	4,872	17,892

Figure 10-4: Two tables sorted differently.

The difference between ascending and descending sorts is as follows:

- ✦ Ascending arranges text from A to Z, numbers from smallest to largest, and dates from the oldest in time to the most recent.
- ✦ Descending arranges text from Z to A, numbers from largest to smallest, and dates from most recent to the oldest in time.

WARNING!

When you rearrange a table by sorting it, Word rearranges the formatting as well as the data. Do your sorting before you format the table.

For simple sorts, select the column that is to be the basis of the sort and click the Sort Descending button on the Tables and Borders toolbar for a descending sort or the Sort Ascending button for an ascending sort. You can also select a column and choose Table⇨Sort, click the Ascending or Descending radio button in the Sort dialog box, and click OK.

Sprucing Up Your Table

After you enter the text, put the rows and columns in place, and make them the right size, the fun begins. Now you can dress up your table and make it look snazzy.

Almost everything you can do to a document you can do to a table by selecting parts of it and choosing menu commands or clicking buttons. You can change text fonts, align data in the cells in different ways, and even import a graphic into a cell. You can also play with the borders that divide the rows and columns and "shade" columns, rows, and cells by filling them with gray shades or a black background. Read on to find out how to do these tricks and also how to center a table or align it with the right page margin.

Formatting a table with Word's AutoFormats

The fastest way to get a good-looking table is to let Word do the work for you:

1. **Click a table.**
2. **Choose Table➪Table AutoFormat.**

   The Table AutoFormat dialog box appears, as shown in Figure 10-5.

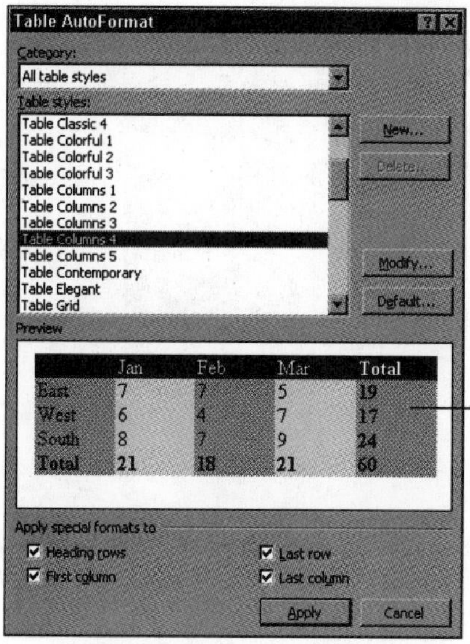

Figure 10-5: Word can format your tables automatically.

3. **Rummage through the Table Styles until you find a table to your liking.**

   The Preview box shows what the different tables look like. (On the Category drop-down list, you can choose an option to put a cap on the number of styles offered in the Table Styles menu.)

4. **Under Apply Special Formats To, click to select and deselect the check boxes to modify the table format.**

   As you do so, watch the Preview box to see what your choices do.

5. **When you have the right table format, click the Apply button.**

Getting your own borders, shading, and color

Instead of relying on Word's Table➪Table AutoFormat command, you can draw borders yourself and shade or give color to different parts of a table as well. Doing so by means of the Tables and Borders toolbar is easier than you might think.

Click the Tables and Borders button on the Standard toolbar to display the Tables and Borders toolbar, as shown in Figure 10-6. Then follow these steps to decorate a table with borders, shading, and color:

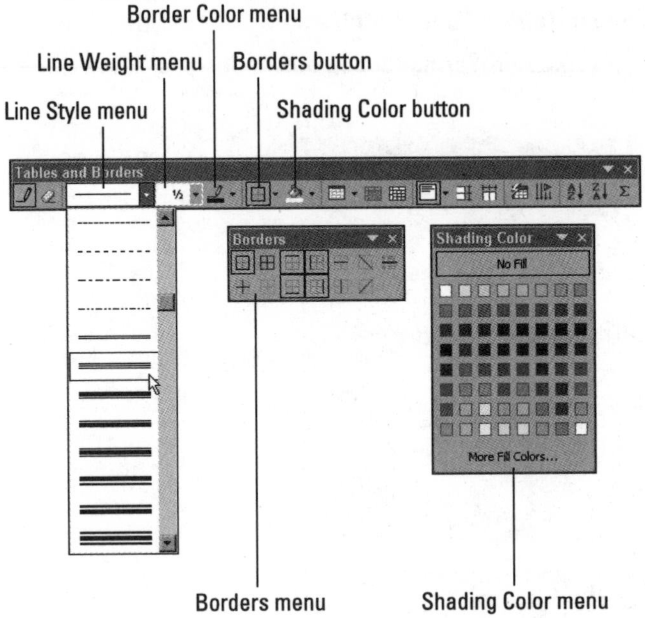

Figure 10-6: The Tables and Borders toolbar.

1. **Select the part of the table that you want to decorate.**

   For example, to put a border along the top or bottom of a row, select the row; to shade two columns, select them.

2. **Use the tools on the Tables and Borders toolbar to decorate your table:**

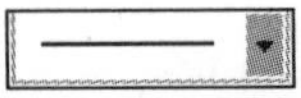

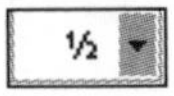

   - **Choosing lines for borders:** Click the down arrow beside the Line Style button and choose a line, dashed line, double line, or wiggly line for the border. (Choose No Border if you don't want a border or you are removing one that is already there.) Then click the down arrow beside the Line Weight button to choose a line width for the border.

   - **Choosing line colors:** Click the down arrow beside the Border Color button and choose one of the colors on the drop-down list. Use the Automatic choice to remove colors and gray shades.

- **Drawing the border lines:** Click the down arrow beside the Borders button and choose one of the border styles on the Borders menu. (Choose No Border to remove borders.) For example, click the Top Border button to put a border along the top of the part of the table you selected in Step 1; click the Inside Border button to put the border on the interior lines of the part of the table you selected. You will find the Borders button on the Formatting toolbar as well as the Tables and Borders toolbar.

- **Shading or giving a color background to table cells:** Click the down arrow beside the Shading Color button and choose a color or gray-shade on the Shading Color menu.

After you make a choice from a menu on the Tables and Borders toolbar, the choice you made appears on the button that is used to open the menu. Choose Blue on the Shading Color menu, for example, and the Shading Color button turns blue. If the choice you want to make from a menu happens to be the last choice you made, you can click the button instead of opening a drop-down list or menu. To make a blue background show in a table, for example, you can simply click the Shading Color button as long as the Shading Color button is blue.

Merging and Splitting Cells and Tables

The cells in the second row in the table shown in Figure 10-7 have been merged to create one large cell. Where the first and third row have six cells, the second has only one.

Figure 10-7: Merging small cells to create a larger cell.

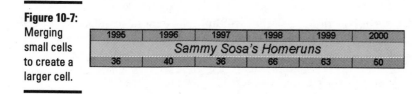

1995	1996	1997	1998	1999	2000
Sammy Sosa's Homeruns					
36	40	36	66	63	50

To merge cells in a table, follow these steps:

1. **Select the cells you want to merge.**

2. **Choose Table⇨Merge Cells or click the Merge Cells button on the Tables and Borders toolbar.**

In the same vein, you can split a cell into two or more cells. To do so, follow these steps:

1. **Click in the cell you want to split.**

2. **Choose Table⇨Split Cells or click the Split Cells button on the Tables and Borders toolbar.**
3. **In the Split Cells dialog box, declare how many cells you want to split the cell into and click OK.**

Follow these steps to split a table:

1. **Place the cursor in what you want to be the first row of the new table.**
2. **Choose Table⇨Split Table.**

Using Math Formulas in Tables

No, you don't have to add the figures in columns and rows yourself; Word gladly does that for you. Word can perform other mathematical calculations as well.

To total the figures in a column or row, place the cursor in the cell that is to hold the total and click the AutoSum button on the Tables and Borders toolbar.

The AutoSum button, however, is only good for adding figures. To perform other mathematical calculations and tell Word how to format sums and products, follow these steps:

1. **Put the cursor in the cell that will hold the sum or product of the cells above, below, to the right, or to the left.**
2. **Choose Table⇨Formula.**

   The Formula dialog box appears, as shown in Figure 10-8.

Units Sold	Price Unit ($)	Total Sale
13	178.12	$2,315.56
15	179.33	$2,689.95
93	178.00	$16,554.00
31	671.13	
24	411.12	
9	69.13	
11	79.40	
$ 196.00	$1,766.23	

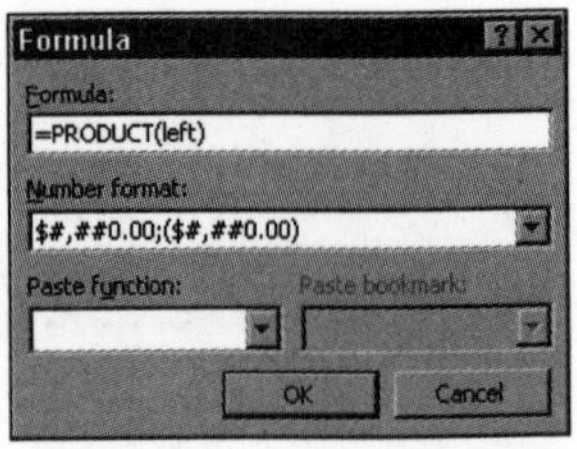

Figure 10-8: Entering a math formula.

3. **In its wisdom, Word makes a very educated guess about what you want the formula to do and places a formula in the Formula box. If this isn't the formula you want, delete everything except the equal sign in the Formula box, open the Paste Function drop-down list, and choose another function for the formula.**

   For example, choose PRODUCT to multiply figures. You may have to type **left, right, above,** or **below** in the parentheses beside the formula to tell Word where the figures that you want it to compute are.

4. **In the Number Format drop-down list, choose a format for your number.**

5. **Click OK.**

TIP

Word does not calculate blank cells in formulas. Enter a **0** in blank cells if you want them to be included in calculations. You can copy functions from one cell to another to save yourself the trouble of opening the Formula dialog box.

REAL WORLD

Repeating header rows on subsequent pages

Your new table sure looks great — until you turn to the next page and can no longer see the column headings and can't tell which figures are your earnings and which figures are your debts. Making sure that the header row appears on a new page if the table breaks across pages is absolutely essential. Without a header row, readers can't tell what the information in a table is or means. To make the header row (or rows) repeat on the top of each new page, place the cursor in the header row (or select the header rows if you have more than one) and choose Table➪Heading Rows Repeat. By the way, heading rows appear only in Print Layout view, so don't worry if you're in Normal view and you can't see them.

Chapter 11: Drawing and Inserting Things into Your Document

In This Chapter

- Drawing lines and shapes
- Inserting pictures and graphics

You thought that you were just going to type plain old text and make some nice looking memos and reports in Word, didn't you? Think again! Word is more than just the most expensive typewriter that you have ever purchased. Why not put that money to good use and take advantage of the desktop publishing capabilities in Word? With a little effort, you can go from memos and reports to neat newsletters and fancy brochures. (Or you can at least have the nicest looking memos and reports around!)

This chapter shows you how you can insert pictures, borders, charts, and anything else you can think of into documents that are sure to impress your friends and neighbors — unless you slip up and reveal to them just how easy it is.

Drawing Lines and Shapes

The Drawing toolbar offers many opportunities for decorating documents and Web pages with lines, lines with arrows on the end, shapes such as ovals and rectangles, and what Word calls *autoshapes* — stars, banners, and various other artistic tidbits. You can even create shadow backgrounds and 3-D effects for shapes. Figure 11-1 shows some of the things you can do with the buttons and menus on the Drawing toolbar.

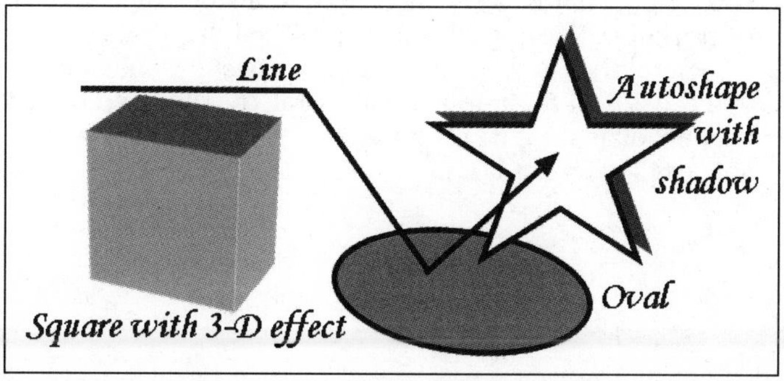

Figure 11-1: Word lets you express yourself in many ways.

To draw lines and shapes, follow these steps:

1. **Display the Drawing toolbar. To do so, click the Drawing button on the Standard toolbar, or right-click a toolbar and choose Drawing on the shortcut menu.**

   The Drawing toolbar, unlike other toolbars, appears along the bottom of the window.

2. **Click the appropriate button on the Drawing toolbar.**

   The drawing canvas appears on-screen.

3. **Drag the pointer across the screen to draw the line or shape.**

   See Chapter 12 to find out how to shrink or enlarge lines and shapes, move them, fill them with color, and change the width of lines on their borders.

Here are instructions for drawing all the different lines and shapes that you can create in Word:

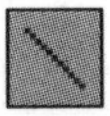

- **Drawing lines:** Click the Line button and drag the pointer across the screen to draw the line.

- **Drawing arrows on lines:** Start by clicking the Line or Arrow button and drawing a line. To choose an arrow style of your own, select the line by clicking it, click the Arrow Style button, and choose a style from the shortcut menu. Choose More Arrows from the shortcut menu to go to the Format AutoShape dialog box and select different arrows or different-size arrows for either side of the line.

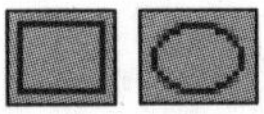

- **Drawing rectangles and ovals:** Click the Rectangle or Oval button and drag the cursor across the screen to draw the rectangle or oval. Hold down the Shift key as you drag to draw a square or circle.

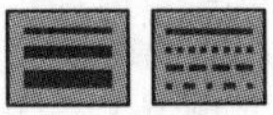

- **Choosing a line style or dash style:** After you draw a line or shape, click to select it. Then click the Line Style button and choose a thickness or style for the line or shape. Click the Dash Style button and make a choice to draw a dashed line.

- **Drawing an autoshape:** Click the AutoShapes button, move the pointer over a submenu, and click a shape. Then drag the cursor across the screen to draw it. A diamond appears beside some autoshapes so that you can adjust their appearance. Drag the diamond to make the auto-shape look just right. The AutoShapes submenus offer many different shapes (see Figure 11-2).

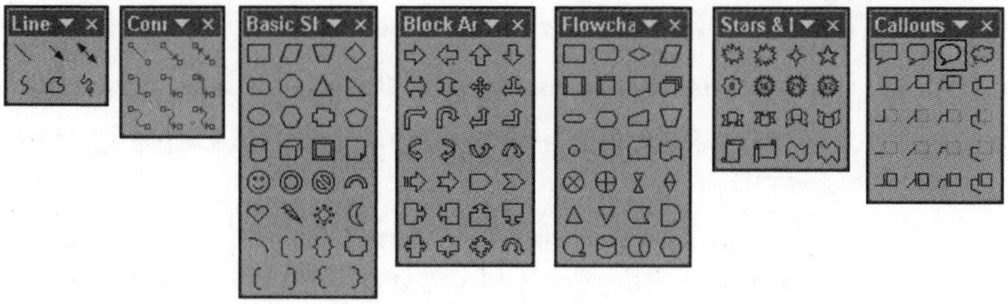

Figure 11-2: The different AutoShape submenus.

- **Putting shadows and three-dimensional effects on shapes:** Click a shape to select it, click the Shadow or 3-D button, and choose a shadow style or 3-D effect from the shortcut menu. Choose No Shadow or No 3-D to remove shadows and third dimensions.

Inserting Clip Art and Graphics in Documents

If you keep clip art, graphics, and photographs on your computer, you have a golden opportunity to embellish your documents with art created by genuine artists. And you don't have to tell anyone where this art came from, either, as long as you're a good liar.

This section explains how to insert a clip art image, change its resolution, and crop it. See Chapter 12 to find out how to move and change the size and shape of a clip art image, put borders and color shades on it, or wrap text around it.

TIP

The first time you try to insert a clip art image, Word asks if you want to catalog all the clip art, sound, and video files on your computer. By all means, do it! That way, you can access clip art and graphic files more easily. From time to time, as you acquire more clip art, ask Word to catalog your clip art collection. To do so, open the Microsoft Clip Organizer by clicking the Clip Organizer hyperlink at the bottom of the Insert Clip Art task pane (choose Insert⇨Picture⇨Clip Art to open the task pane). Then choose File⇨Add Clips to Gallery⇨Automatically.

Inserting a clip art image from your computer

Whether you know it or not, you installed several hundred clip art images on your computer when you installed Word. To insert a clip art image, follow these steps:

1. **Click in your document where you want the clip art image to go.**
2. **Click the Insert Clip Art button on the Drawing toolbar or choose Insert⇨Picture⇨Clip Art.**

   The Insert Clip Art task pane appears on-screen.

3. Tell Word how and where to search for the clip art image you want.

To search for clip art images in the Insert Clip Art task pane:

- **Search Text:** Enter a word that describes what kind of clip art you want.
- **Search In:** Open the drop-down list and tell Word where to search. As long as the Everywhere box is checked, Word searches for every piece of clip art it can lay hands on. Searches don't take very long, so you may as well keep the check mark in the Everywhere box.
- **Results Should Be:** Open the drop-down list and tell Word what to search for. If the All Media Types box is checked, Word searches for photographs, movies, and sounds, as well as clip art. Click the plus sign (+) beside the All Media Types folder and then click to deselect Photographs, Movies, and Sounds to search for clip art only.

4. Click the Search button.

If Word can find clip art images, they appear in thumbnail form in the Insert Clip Art task pane, as shown in Figure 11-3. If necessary, scroll down the list to examine all the images, or else click the small icon under the word Results to see the images in a box.

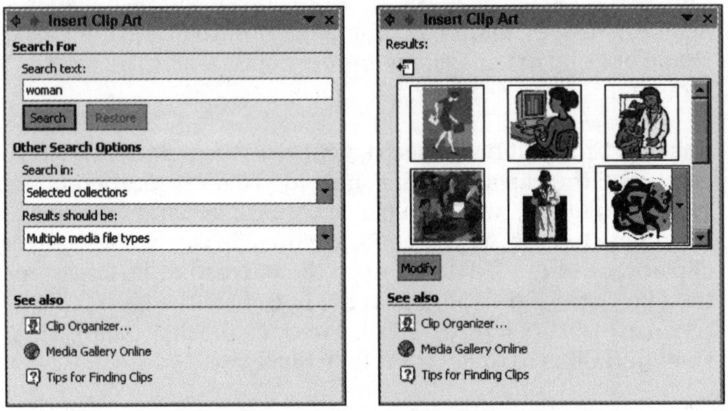

Figure 11-3: Searching for a clip art image for your document.

5. Click an image to insert it in your document.

If your search turns up nothing or turns up images you aren't happy with, click the Modify button to start all over.

If you find a clip art image whose appearance and style you like, select it, click its down arrow to open its drop-down list, and choose Find Similar Style. Images of the same style will appear in the Insert Clip Art task pane.

Inserting a photograph or graphic from your computer

You can insert a graphic or photograph that you keep on your computer by clicking the Insert Picture button on the Drawing or Picture toolbar or by choosing Insert➪Picture➪From File and, in the Insert Picture dialog box, finding and double-clicking the name of the graphic file whose image you want to insert.

Experimenting with brightness, contrast, and appearance

After you insert an image, you can alter it a bit by experimenting with its brightness and contrast or by turning it into a grayscale or black-and-white image. Here's how:

1. **Click the image to select it.**

   You know that an image is selected when its selection handles appear. *Selection handles* are the small, round circles or squares that appear on the corners and sides of an image. By dragging the handles, you can change the image's size.

2. **Display the Picture toolbar and experiment with the different buttons:**

   - **Color:** Click the Color button and choose Grayscale to see the image in shades of gray, Black & White to see the *film noir* version, or Washout to see a bleached-out image.

   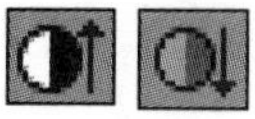

   - **More Contrast and Less Contrast:** These buttons either heighten or mute line and color distinctions. Use them in combination with the More Brightness and Less Brightness buttons to make the image clearer and easier to behold.

   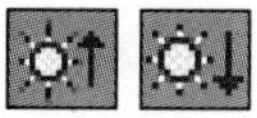

   - **More Brightness and Less Brightness:** These buttons either lighten or darken the image. They are especially useful when you're experimenting with black-and-white images.

To get the original picture back if you experiment too enthusiastically, either click the Reset Picture button on the Picture toolbar or click the Color button and choose Automatic on the drop-down list.

You can also experiment with clip art images by clicking the Format Picture button on the Picture toolbar or by choosing Format➪Picture. On the Picture tab of the Format Picture dialog box, choose an option from the Color menu or use the Brightness and Contrast sliders to alter your image. You can't see how good an artist you are, however, until you click OK and view your image on-screen.

Cropping off part of a graphic

You can *crop* — that is, cut off parts of — a graphic, but not very elegantly. To do that, select a graphic and click the Crop button on the Picture toolbar. The pointer changes into an odd shape with two intersecting triangles on it. Move the pointer to a selection handle and start dragging. The dotted line tells you what part of a graphic you are cutting off. Sorry, you can crop off only the sides of a graphic. You can't cut a circle out of the middle, for example, proving once again that the computer will never replace that ancient and noble device, the scissors.

Chapter 12: Desktop and Web Publishing

In This Chapter

- **Handling inserted objects**
- **Creating text boxes**
- **Using WordArt**
- **Using borders and colors on objects**
- **Turning a Word document into a Web page**
- **Putting hyperlinks in Web and Word documents**

Once upon a time, word processors were nothing more than glorified typewriters. They were good for typing and basic formatting, but not much else. Over the years, however, Microsoft Word and other word processors have become desktop publishing applications in their own right. Now you can even create a Web page with Word.

Chapter 12 explains advanced formatting techniques in Word. If you're in charge of the company newsletter, or you need to post a page on the company intranet or create a Web page to describe your exploits on the Internet, this chapter is for you.

Handling Objects in Documents

After you place a clip art image, graphic, text box, line, shape, autoshape, drawing canvas, or WordArt image in a document, it ceases being what it was before and becomes an *object.* That's good news, however, because the techniques for manipulating objects are the same. To move, reshape, draw borders around, fill in, lock in place, or overlap an object, use the techniques described on the following pages.

Selecting objects

Before you can do anything to an object, you have to select it. To do so, click the object. You can tell when an object has been selected because *selection handles* appear on the sides and corners (in lines, only two selection handles appear, one on either side of the line). To select more than one object at the same time, hold down the Shift key and click the objects.

When objects overlap, sometimes selecting one of them is difficult. To select an object that is stuck among other objects, click the Select Objects button on the Drawing toolbar and then click the object.

Moving and resizing graphics, text boxes, and other objects

Moving an object on a page is easy enough. All you have to do is select the graphic, text box, shape, or whatever, wait till you see the four-headed arrow, click, hold down the mouse button, and drag the pointer where you want the object to be on the page or the drawing canvas. Dotted lines show where you are moving the object. When the object is in the right position, release the mouse button. If you are moving a text box, place the pointer on the perimeter of the box to see the four-headed arrow.

If you can't move an object, it's because Word thinks that it is an inline image and shouldn't be moved. On the Picture toolbar or Drawing Canvas toolbar, click the Text Wrapping button and then click any button on the pop-up menu except In Line With Text. See "Wrapping Text Around a Graphic, Drawing Canvas, or Other Objects" later in this chapter if you need to know how text wrapping works.

How you change an object's size depends on whether you want to keep its proportions:

- **Changing size but not proportions:** To change the size of an object but keep its proportions, click the object and move the cursor to one of the selection handles on the *corners*. The cursor changes into a double-headed arrow. Click and start dragging. Dotted lines show how you are changing the size of the frame. When it's the right size, release the mouse button.
- **Changing size and proportions:** To change both the size of an object *and* its proportions, move the cursor to a selection handle on the side, top, or bottom. When the cursor changes into a double-headed arrow, click and start dragging. Dotted lines show how the object is being changed. When it is the size and shape you want, release the mouse button.

Figure 12-1 shows the same graphic at three different sizes. The original graphic is on the left. For the middle graphic, I pulled a corner selection handle to enlarge it but keep its proportions. For the one on the right, I pulled a selection handle on the side to enlarge it and change its proportions.

If you want to get very specific about how big an object is, go to the Size tab of the Format dialog box. To do that, right-click the object, choose Format, and click the Size tab. Then enter measurements in the Height and Width boxes. Go this route if you want to make text boxes or objects the exact same size, for example.

Figure 12-1: Tug at images to change their size.

Locking objects in place

Suppose that you want an object such as a text box, WordArt image, clip art image, or drawing canvas creation to stay in the same place. Normally, what is in the middle of page 1 is pushed to the bottom of the page or to page 2 when you insert paragraphs at the start of a document. What if you want the paragraph or graphic to stay put, come hell or high water? In that case, you can *lock* it to the page. After you lock it, text flows around your image or text box, but the image or text box stays put. To lock an object in place, follow these steps:

1. **Move the object to the position on the page where you want it to remain at all times.**
2. **Double-click the object or right-click it and choose Format.**

   The Format dialog box appears.
3. **Click the Layout tab in the Format dialog box.**
4. **On the Layout tab, choose any Wrapping Style option except In Line with Text.**

   (See "Wrapping Text Around a Graphic, Drawing Canvas, or Other Object" later in this chapter to find out about text wrapping.)
5. **Click the Advanced button.**
6. **In the Advanced Layout dialog box, click the Picture Position tab.**
7. **Click the Absolute Position radio button under Vertical.**
8. **Click the Lock Anchor check box.**
9. **Click the Move Object with Text check box to remove the check mark.**

   As soon as you do so, the Absolute Position Below setting under Vertical changes to Page.
10. **Under Horizontal, choose Page from the Absolute Position To the Left Of drop-down list.**

    Now the object is locked, horizontally and vertically, to the page, and Word knows to keep it at its current position on the page and *not* move it in the document when text is inserted before it. For now, don't worry about the To the Right Of and Below settings. In Step 12, you will drag the object on the page exactly where you want it to be.

11. **Click OK in the Advanced Layout dialog box and OK again in the Format dialog box. Back in your document, your object may have slid to a different position.**

12. **Drag the object where you want it to be on the page.**

To tell whether an object has been locked in place, click the Show/Hide ¶ button and look for the picture of an anchor and a tiny padlock in the left margin of the document.

Handling objects that overlap

Chances are, objects like the ones in Figure 12-2 overlap when more than one appears on the same page. And when objects are placed beside text, do you want the text to appear in front of the objects, or do you want the objects to cover up the text?

Figure 12-2: Overlapping objects.

Word offers special Order commands for determining how objects overlap with one another and with text. But before you know anything about the Order commands, you need to know about *layers*, also known as *drawing layers*. From top to bottom, text and objects can appear on these layers:

- **Foreground layer:** Objects on this layer cover up objects on the text layer and background layer. Only objects, not text, can appear on the foreground layer. When you insert a new object in a document, it appears on the foreground layer.
- **Text layer:** The text you type appears on this layer. No objects can appear on this layer. Text on this layer is covered by objects on the foreground layer but covers objects on the background layer.
- **Background layer:** Only objects can appear on this layer. Objects on the background layer are covered by objects on the foreground layer and by text.

To tell Word whether an object should overlap text or overlap other objects, follow these steps:

1. **Click the object to select it.**
2. **Click the Draw button on the Drawing toolbar, choose Order, and choose a Send or Bring command on the Order menu; or right-click, choose Order, and choose a submenu command.**

The commands on the Order submenu do the following:

- **Bring to Front:** When objects are on the same layer, either the foreground or background, moves the object in front of all others on the layer.

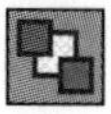

- **Send to Back:** When objects are on the same layer, moves the object behind all others on the layer.

- **Bring Forward:** When three or more objects are on the same layer, either foreground or background, moves the object higher in the stack of objects.

- **Send Backward:** When three or more objects are on the same layer, moves the object lower in the stack so that more objects overlap the object you selected.

- **Bring in Front of Text:** Moves the object from the background layer to the foreground layer, where it appears in front of text.

- **Send Behind Text:** Moves the object from the foreground layer to the background layer, where it appears behind text.

Book II Chapter 12

Desktop and Web Publishing

Working with Text Boxes

Put text in a text box when you want it to stand out on the page. Text boxes can be shaded, filled with color, and given borders. You can also lay text boxes over graphics to make for interesting effects (see Figure 12-3). I removed the borders and the fill color from this text box, but rest assured, the text in this figure lies squarely in a text box.

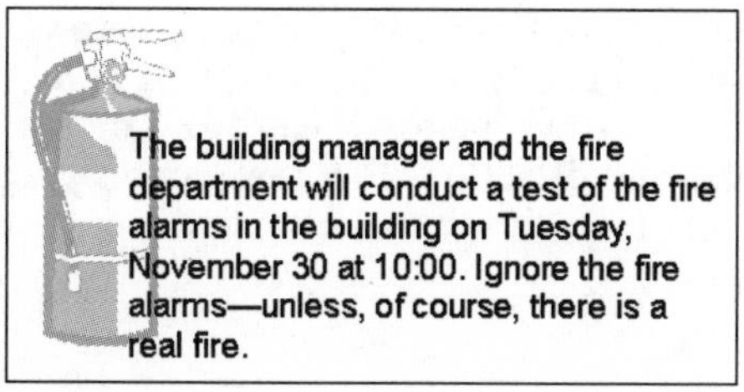

The building manager and the fire department will conduct a test of the fire alarms in the building on Tuesday, November 30 at 10:00. Ignore the fire alarms—unless, of course, there is a real fire.

Figure 12-3: You can use text boxes for neat effects.

Inserting a text box

To put a text box in a document, follow these steps:

1. **Choose Insert➪Text Box or click the Text Box button on the Drawing toolbar.**

   The pointer turns into a cross and the drawing canvas appears on-screen.

2. **Click and drag to draw the text box. Lines show you how big it will be when you release the mouse button.**
3. **Release the mouse button.**

After you insert the text box, you can type text in it and call on all the formatting techniques in Word to boldface it, align it, or do what you will with it.

Changing the direction of the text

On the Text Box toolbar is a little toy called the Change Text Direction button. Click a text box and click this button to make the text in the text box change orientation. Figure 12-4 shows what happens when you click the Change Text Direction button.

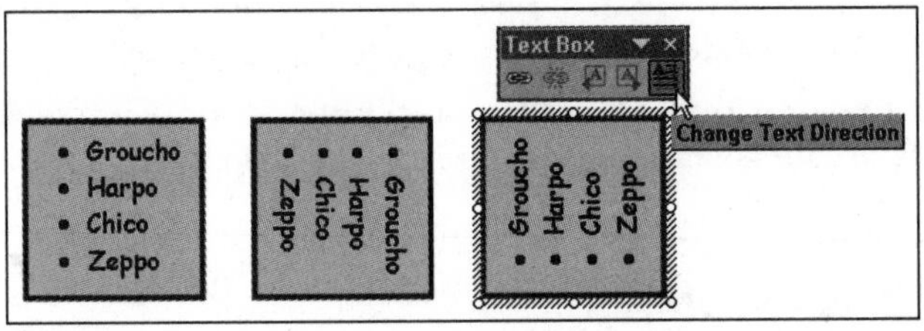

Figure 12-4: Your text can go any way you want it to.

Wrapping Text Around a Graphic, Drawing Canvas, or Other Object

Word gives you lots of interesting opportunities to wrap text around text boxes, graphics, drawing canvases, and other objects in a document. By playing with the different ways to wrap text, you can create very sophisticated layouts. When you wrap text, you pick a wrapping style and the side of the object around which to wrap the text. Figure 12-5 demonstrates several of the wrapping styles and directions that text can be wrapped.

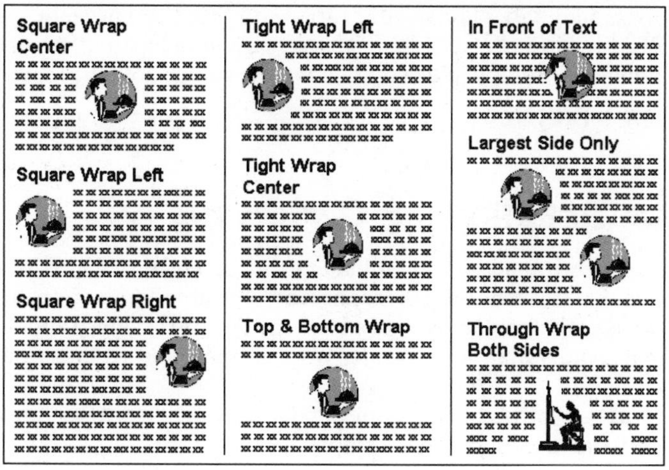

Figure 12-5: Text wrapped different ways for different needs.

The fastest way to wrap text is to click the object around which text is to be wrapped, click the Text Wrapping button, and choose an option from the drop-down list. You find the Text Wrapping button on the Picture and Drawing Canvas toolbars.

TIP

Wrapped text looks best when it is justified and hyphenated. That way, text can get closer to the object that is being wrapped.

To wrap text around an object, follow these steps:

1. **Select the object by clicking it.**
2. **Right-click and choose Format, or else choose Format on the menu bar and then choose the last option on the Format menu. (The option is named after the kind of object you are dealing with.)**
3. **Click the Layout tab in the Format dialog box.**
4. **Click a box under Wrapping Style to tell Word how you want the text to behave when it reaches the graphic or text box.**

   The In Line with Text option keeps text from wrapping around objects.
5. **Under Horizontal Alignment, tell Word where you want the object to be in relation to the text.**

   For example, choose the Left radio button to make the object stand to the left side of text as it flows down the page.

   If you want text to wrap to the largest side or to both sides without the object being centered, click the Other radio button and then click the Advanced button. In the Advanced Layout dialog box, click the Text

Wrapping tab, choose either the Both Sides or Largest Only radio button, and click OK. The Text Wrapping tab also offers choices for telling Word how close text can come to the object as it wraps around it.

6. **Click OK.**

WordArt for Embellishing Documents

You can bend, spindle, and mutilate text with a feature called WordArt. I believe that this feature was inspired by old superhero comics, in which words and images that may have come from the WordArt Gallery appeared whenever Batman, Spider-Man, and Wonder Woman brawled with the criminal element.

To create a WordArt image, put the cursor roughly where you want the image to go and follow these steps:

1. **Choose Insert⇨Picture⇨WordArt or click the Insert WordArt button on the Drawing toolbar.**

   You see the WordArt Gallery, as shown in Figure 12-6.

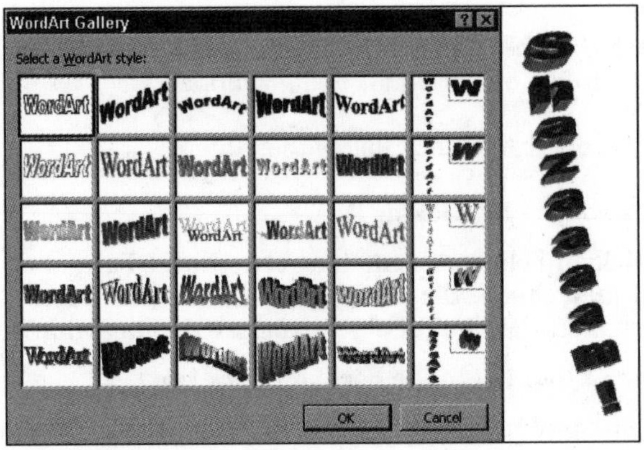

Figure 12-6: The WordArt Gallery dialog box awaits your choices.

2. **Click the image that strikes your fancy and then click OK.**
3. **In the Edit WordArt Text dialog box, type a word or words of your own.**
4. **Choose a new font from the Font menu or change the size of letters with the Size menu; then click OK.**

   You see the WordArt image and the WordArt toolbar.

5. **Click the WordArt image to select it**

6. **Click the Text Wrapping button on the WordArt toolbar and choose any option except In Line With Text.**

Now you see the image with its selection handles showing. To really bend the word or words out of shape, click and drag the diamond on the image. To change the wording, click Edit Text on the WordArt toolbar to reopen the Edit WordArt Text dialog box. To choose a new WordArt image, click the WordArt Gallery button. To change the shape of a WordArt image, click the WordArt Shape button on the WordArt toolbar and choose a shape from the pop-up menu.

Borders and Color Shades for Graphics, Text Boxes, and Other Objects

By putting borders around graphics, text boxes, shapes, and other objects, and by putting interesting gray shades and colors behind them as well, you can amuse yourself on a rainy afternoon. And you can sometimes create fanciful artwork. The text boxes and graphics shown in Figure 12-7 were created by a 7-year-old with help from his father. This section explains how to put borders and gray shades on objects.

Figure 12-7: Framed and unframed objects.

Putting borders on objects

The fastest way to put a border around an object is to select it, click the Line Style button on the Picture or Drawing toolbar, and choose a line from the pop-up menu. To change the color of borders, click the down arrow beside the Line Color button on the Drawing toolbar and then choose a color from the pop-up menu.

To get fancy with borders, select the object and follow these steps:

1. **Right-click the object and choose Format on the shortcut menu (or choose Format on the menu bar and then choose the bottom-most command on the Format menu).**

   Which command that is — Picture, Object, Text Box, AutoShape, or Drawing Canvas — depends on what kind of object you are working on.

2. **Click the Colors and Lines tab in the Format dialog box.**

   You can also get here by clicking the Line Style button on the Drawing or Picture toolbar and choosing More Lines.

3. **Under Line, click the Color drop-down list and choose a color; or click the No Line option to remove borders from an object.**

   Black is the first choice in the drop-down list.

4. **Click the Dashed down arrow and choose a dashed or dotted line, if you want.**

5. **Click the Style down arrow and tell Word what kind of line you want.**

   You find exotic choices at the bottom of the menu.

6. **Click arrows in the Weight box or enter a number yourself to tell Word how wide or narrow to make the borderlines.**

7. **Click OK.**

Filling an object with a color or gray shade

The fast way to "fill" a graphic or text box is to select it, click the down arrow beside the Fill Color button on the Drawing toolbar, and choose a color or gray shade. By clicking Fill Effects at the bottom of the menu, you can get to interesting gray shades and textures.

Or, if you are the kind who likes dialog boxes, select the thing you are filling and either right-click and choose Format, or else choose Format on the menu bar and then choose the bottom-most command on the Format menu — Picture, Object, Text Box, AutoShape, or Drawing Canvas. Then click the Colors and Lines tab in the Format dialog box, open the Color drop-down list (the one in the Fill area, not the Color area), and make a choice. Experiment with the Transparenacy settings if you want a soupy, fainter-looking color.

Converting Word Documents to Web Pages

A Web browser such as Internet Explorer or Netscape Navigator cannot "see" images and text or display them on a computer screen unless the images and text have been tagged with *hypertext markup language* (HTML) codes. Fortunately for you and for the teeming multitudes who want to see your work on the Internet, Word has made the dreary task of entering HTML codes very easy: Word can do it for you. It can code a document and do a good job of it, as long as you thoughtfully assign styles to the different parts of the document. When Word converts a document to HTML, it converts styles to HTML codes. (See Chapter 6 to find out about styles.)

Not all Word styles can be converted to HTML codes. Text effects, drop caps, text boxes and autoshapes, margins, page borders, footnotes and end-notes, and columns are not on speaking terms with HTML. And to convert Word documents to Web pages, Microsoft Internet Explorer must have been installed on your computer. To see what can and what can't be turned into a Web page, choose File➪Web Page Preview. Internet Explorer opens and you see your document dressed up as a Web page.

Turning a document into a Web page

To turn a Word document into a Web page, follow these steps:

1. **Open the document to be converted to an HTML document.**
2. **Choose File➪Save as Web Page.**

   The Save As dialog box appears.
3. **In the Save As dialog box, find the folder that will hold your HTML file and enter a name in the File Name box.**
4. **Click the Change Title button and, in the Set Page Title dialog box, enter a descriptive name for your Web page and click OK.**

   The name you enter appears in the title bar of the Web browser when your Web page is shown online.
5. **Click the Save button.**

   Word gives the file the *.htm* extension. When next you see the file, it appears in Web Layout View.

Choosing backgrounds and themes for Web pages

To decorate your Web page, you can give it a background color or what Microsoft calls a "theme" — a coordinated design with different colors assigned to headings, text, bulleted lists, and hyperlinks. You are hereby encouraged to experiment with backgrounds and themes until you hit paydirt and fashion a lively design.

REAL WORLD

Seeing your Web page in a browser

When you start making Web pages, you may soon realize that you have a very important task to do before you even think about putting your page on the Web for all to see. If you don't preview your page before it gets on the Web, you may find yourself in an embarrassing position! Save yourself the pain. Choose File➪Web Page Preview to see what your Web page looks like to someone viewing it with a Web browser. The Microsoft Web browser, Internet Explorer, opens, and you see your Web page in all its glory. A Web page as seen in Web Layout view in Word and the same page in Internet Explorer look remarkably alike.

To select a background color, choose Format➪Background and select a color from the Color menu, or else click the Fill Effects option and choose a background from the Fill Effects dialog box. The Texture tab offers some neat backgrounds that are highly suitable for Web pages. To remove a background, choose Format➪Background and select the No Fill option.

To choose a theme, follow these steps:

1. **Choose Format➪Theme.**

   The Theme dialog box appears.

2. **In the Choose a Theme list, click a few names until you see a theme you like.**

   The Sample of Theme box shows what the themes look like.

3. **Check and uncheck the Vivid Colors, Active Graphics, and Background Image check boxes in the lower-left corner of the dialog box and watch what happens in the Sample of Theme box.**

   By checking or unchecking these check boxes, you can customize the theme.

4. **Click OK.**

To remove a theme or change themes, choose Format➪Theme and select a new theme or choose the (No Theme) option.

Hyperlinking to Other Places

Most people know hyperlinks from Web sites. When you click a hyperlink, you go to another place — another Web site, another page on the same Web site, or another place on the same Web page. A *hyperlink* is an electronic shortcut from one place to another. You can tell where hyperlinks are because, in the case of text, they are blue and underlined. When you move the pointer over a hyperlink, a screen tip appears and explains where the hyperlink goes, as shown in Figure 12-8.

The Town Crier of Idyllwild, California
CTRL + click to follow link
Sometimes I pay a visit to my hometown newspaper on the Internet.

Figure 12-8: A typical hyperlink.

Word users can include hyperlinks in their documents. Readers who want to visit a link hold down the Ctrl key and click with the mouse (Ctrl+click). You can create these kinds of hyperlinks in a Word document:

- **A link to a Web page on the Internet:** When a reader Ctrl+clicks the link, his or her browser opens and the page appears.
- **A link to another document:** The document opens on-screen when a reader Ctrl+clicks the link.
- **A link to another place in the same document:** The document scrolls to a new location when a reader Ctrl+clicks the link.
- **A link to an e-mail address:** When a reader Ctrl+clicks the link, his or her e-mailing program starts. Your address and the subject of the e-mail message are already entered. All the reader has to do is enter the text of the message and send it on.

Whether you want to put a hyperlink in a Word document or a Web page, start by following these steps:

1. **Select the text or graphic that will comprise the link. In other words, drag the pointer over the word or words that will form the hyperlink. If a graphic will comprise the hyperlink, click to select it.**

2. **Click the Insert Hyperlink button, choose Insert⇨Hyperlink, press Ctrl+K, or right-click and choose Hyperlink.**

   The Insert Hyperlink dialog box appears, as shown in Figure 12-9.

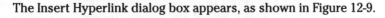

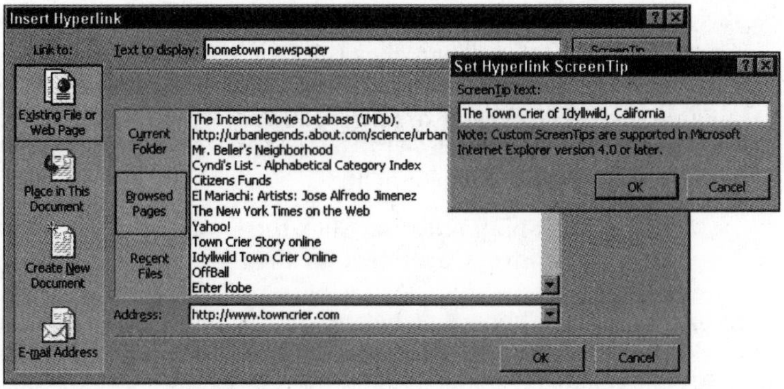

Figure 12-9: The Insert Hyperlink dialog box.

3. **Click the ScreenTip button and, in the Set Hyperlink ScreenTip dialog box, enter a brief two-or-three word description of the hyperlink and click OK.**

   When readers of your document move their mouse pointers over the link, they will see the description you enter along with the words `CTRL+click to follow link`. (For Figure 12-9, I entered "The Town Crier of Idyllwild, California.")

4. **Create the link (see the upcoming bulleted list).**
5. **Click OK.**

Here's a list of the different kinds of hyperlinks and how to create them:

- **A link to a Web page on the Internet:** Under Link To, click the Existing File or Web Page button. Then do one of the following to enter the address of the Web page:
  - Type it in the Address text box.
  - Open the Address drop-down list and choose it.
  -  Click the Browse the Web button. Your Web browser opens. Go to the Web page that you want to link to. When you return to the Insert Hyperlink dialog box, the address of the page appears in the Address text box.
  - Click the Browsed Pages button, look for the address on the page, and select it.
-  **A link to another document:** Click the Existing File or Web Page button. Then click the Browse for File button. In the Link to File dialog box, locate and select the document; then click OK. You can also click the Current Folder button and look for the file in the list or click the Recent Files button and look for the file in the Recent Files list.
- **A link to another place in the same document:** Click the Place in This Document button. Then click the plus signs next to the Headings and the Bookmarks label to see the headings and bookmarks on the page, find the one you want to link to, and click it. To link to a place in the same document, you must have assigned styles to headings or placed bookmarks in your document.
- **A link to an e-mail address:** Click the E-mail Address button. Then enter your e-mail address, a subject for the message, and click the OK button.

After you create a hyperlink, be sure to test it. If the hyperlink doesn't work, right-click it and choose Hyperlink⇨Edit Hyperlink. You see the Edit Hyperlink dialog box, which offers the same options as the Insert Hyperlink dialog box. Your hyperlink may not work because you entered a Web page address incorrectly or you linked to a document that no longer exists or was moved. Either edit your hyperlink or re-enter it.

To remove a hyperlink, right-click it and choose Remove Hyperlink.

Index

A

B

C

D

E

continued

T

U

V

W

Z

Book III

Excel 2002

The 5th Wave   By Rich Tennant

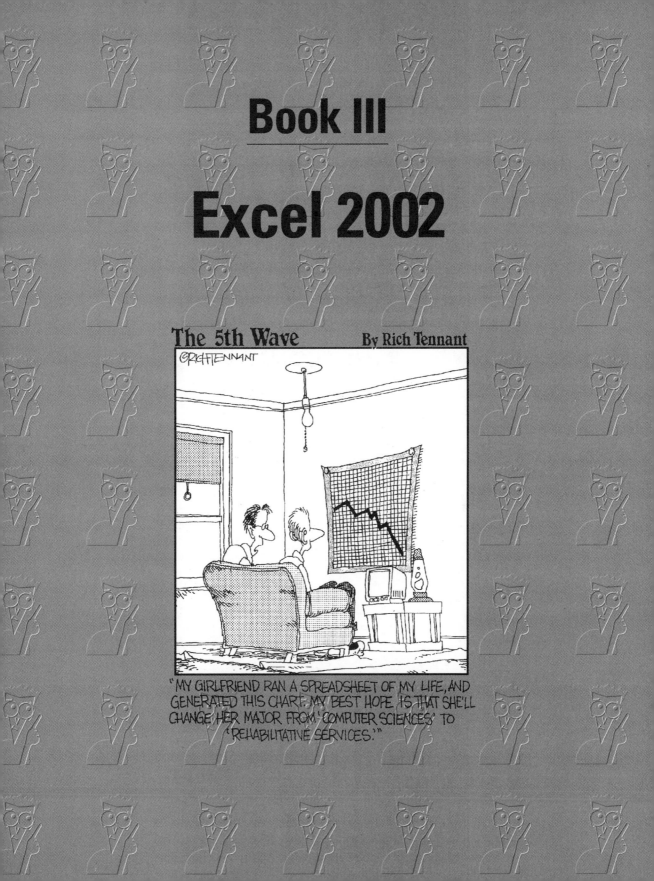

"MY GIRLFRIEND RAN A SPREADSHEET OF MY LIFE, AND GENERATED THIS CHART. MY BEST HOPE IS THAT SHE'LL CHANGE HER MAJOR FROM 'COMPUTER SCIENCES' TO 'REHABILITATIVE SERVICES.'"

Contents at a Glance

Chapter 1: Getting to Know Excel

In This Chapter

- Getting acquainted with the Excel screen
- Mastering cells and ranges
- Navigating in Excel

Microsoft Excel may not be the only spreadsheet program around, but it may be the only one you'll ever need. You can use Excel on many different levels. But most users find out what the program can really do after it gets going. Excel is a user-friendly program — especially for those who are comfortable getting right in and clicking things. But some parts of Excel can seem intimidating (especially when you just want to do something simple but don't know where to start).

This chapter serves as an initiation into the basics of Excel so that you can jump into the rest without fear.

Acquainting Yourself with the Excel Screen

Figure 1-1 shows a typical Excel screen, with some of the important parts pointed out. This terminology rears its ugly head throughout this book, so pay attention.

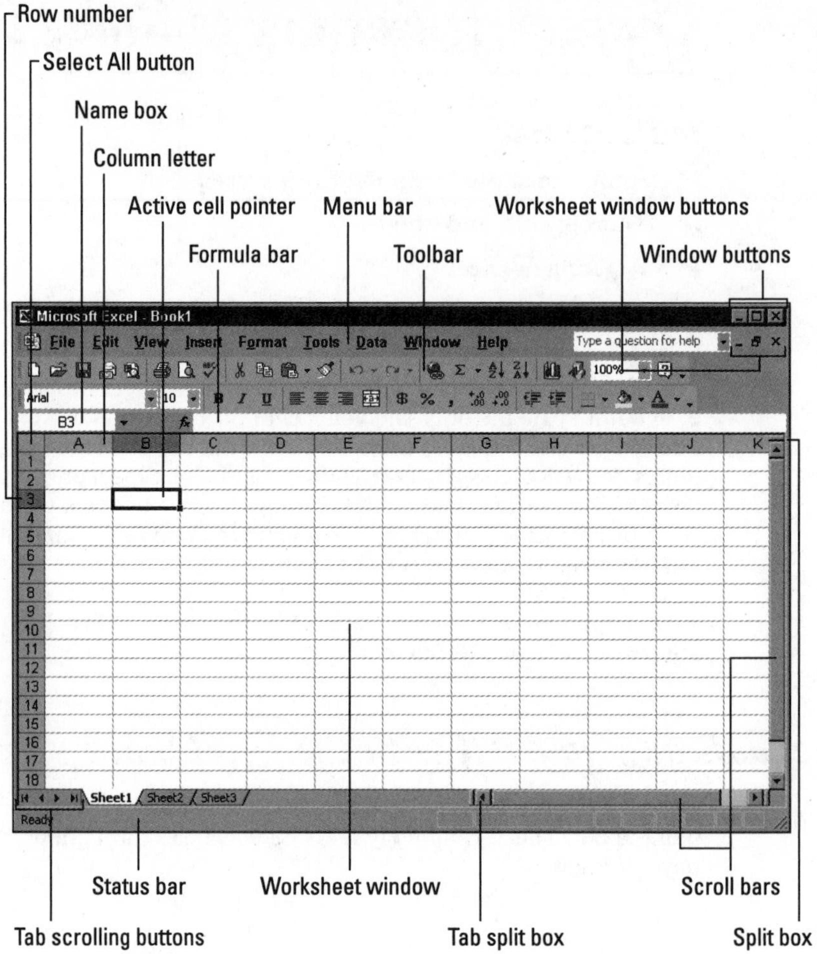

Figure 1-1: The important parts of the Excel screen.

Excel behind the Scenes

A *spreadsheet program* is essentially a highly interactive environment that lets you work with numbers and text in a large grid of cells. Excel also creates graphs and maps from numbers stored in a worksheet and works with database information stored in a record and field format.

Workbooks, worksheets, and chart sheets

Excel files are known as *workbooks*. A single workbook can store as many sheets as will fit into memory, and these sheets are stacked like the pages in a notebook. Sheets can be either *worksheets* (a normal spreadsheet-type sheet) or *chart sheets* (a special sheet that holds a single chart).

Most of the time, you work with worksheets — each of which has exactly 65,536 rows and 256 columns. A quick calculation with Excel tells me that this works out to 16,777,216 cells — which should be enough for most people. Rows are numbered from 1 to 65,536, and columns are labeled with letters. Column 1 is A, column 26 is Z, column 27 is AA, column 52 is AZ, column 53 is BA, and so on up to column 256 (which is IV).

Cells — and what you can put in them

The intersection of a row and column is called a *cell.* Cells have *addresses,* which are based on the row and column that they are in. The upper left cell in a worksheet is called A1, and the cell way down at the bottom is called IV65536. Cell K9 (also known as the dog cell) is the intersection of the eleventh column and the ninth row.

A cell in Excel can hold a number, some text, a formula, or nothing at all. You already know what numbers and text are, but you may be a bit fuzzy on the concept of a formula. A *formula* is a special way to tell Excel to perform a calculation using information stored in other cells. For example, you can insert a formula that tells Excel to add up the values in the first 10 cells in column A and to display the result in the cell that contains the formula.

Formulas can use normal arithmetic operators such as + (plus), – (minus), * (multiply), and / (divide). They can also use special built-in *functions* that let you do powerful things without much effort on your part. For example, Excel has functions that add up a range of values, calculate square roots, compute loan payments, and even tell you the time of day.

When you create a chart from numbers stored in a worksheet, you can put the chart directly on the worksheet or in a special chart sheet in the workbook. When you're working with a chart, some of Excel's menus change so that they are appropriate for chart-type operations.

If your worksheet contains geographic data, you can create maps from the data. Maps reside on a worksheet (there's no such thing as a map sheet).

The active cell and ranges

In Excel, one of the cells in a worksheet is always the *active cell.* The active cell is the one that's selected and it displays with a thicker border. Its contents appear in the *formula bar.* You can also select a group (or range) of cells by clicking and dragging the mouse over them. When you issue a command that does something to a cell or a range of cells, that something will be done to the active cell or to the selected range of cells.

REAL WORLD

Selecting noncontiguous cells as a range (huh?)

The selected *range* is usually a group of contiguous cells, but it doesn't have to be. Sometimes you may want to select a bunch of different cells here and there as a range. If you hold down the Ctrl key while you click a cell (or click and drag through some cells), you can select more than one group of cells.

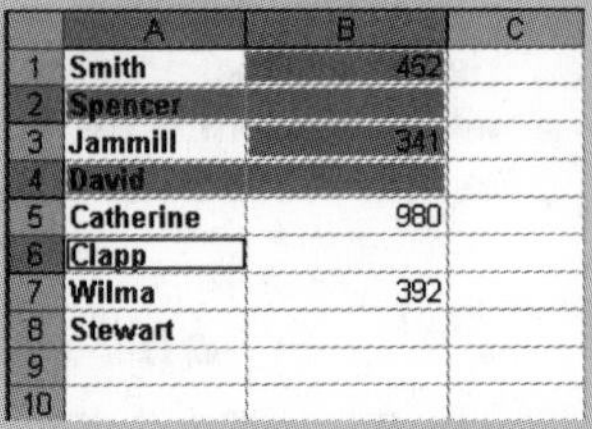

A
B
C
1 Smith 462
2 Spencer
3 Jammill 341
4 David
5 Catherine 980
6 Clapp
7 Wilma 392
8 Stewart
9
10

Navigational techniques

With more than 16 million cells in a worksheet, you need ways to move to specific cells. Fortunately, Excel provides you with many techniques to move around a worksheet. As always, you can use either your mouse or the keyboard on your navigational journeys. Table 1-1 lists the keystrokes that allow you to move through a worksheet.

Table 1-1 Moving around in Excel

Key	*Action*
Up arrow	Moves the active cell up one row
Down arrow	Moves the active cell down one row
Left arrow	Moves the active cell one column to the left
Right arrow	Moves the active cell one column to the right
PgUp	Moves the active cell up one screen
PgDn	Moves the active cell down one screen
Alt+PgDn	Moves the active cell right one screen
Alt+PgUp	Moves the active cell left one screen
Ctrl+Backspace	Scrolls to display the active cell
Up arrow*	Scrolls the screen up one row (active cell does not change)
Home	Moves the active cell to the first column
Ctrl+Home	Moves the active cell to the first column, first row
Ctrl+End	Moves the active cell to the last used cell

Key	Action
Down arrow*	Scrolls the screen down one row (active cell does not change)
Left arrow*	Scrolls the screen left one column (active cell does not change)
Right arrow*	Scrolls the screen right one column (active cell does not change)

* With Scroll Lock on

TIP

Press the End key and then an arrow key to travel in a particular direction to the nearest cell in the worksheet with data in it.

The actions for some of the keys in the preceding table may be different, depending on the transition options you've set. Choose Tools➪Options and then click the Transition tab in the Options dialog box. If the Transition Navigation Keys option is checked, the navigation keys correspond to those used in older versions of Lotus 1-2-3. Generally, it's better to use the standard Excel navigation keys than those for 1-2-3.

If you need basic help with dialog boxes, menus, icons, and the like, be sure to check out Chapter 1 of Book I.

Chapter 2: Working with Workbook Files

In This Chapter

- **Creating a workbook file**
- **Saving and closing a workbook file**
- **Using a workbook template**
- **Getting rid of a workbook file**
- **Viewing two different parts of a worksheet at one time**

An Excel file is called a *workbook.* A workbook is made up of one or more worksheets. And that's about the extent of it, right? Well, this brief introduction is only the beginning. To get something done in Excel, you have to know how to deal with workbooks: creating, saving, closing, and so on.

If you can start Excel, you're ready to begin working with workbooks (see Chapter 3 for the details on worksheets). This chapter shows you how to handle your workbooks so that your real work (the stuff you put into a workbook) remains safe and sound — and usable.

Creating an Empty Workbook File

When you start Excel, it automatically creates a new (empty) workbook called Book1. If you're starting a new project from scratch, you can use this blank workbook. You can create another blank workbook in any of three ways:

- ✦ Click the New button on the Standard toolbar.
- ✦ Press Ctrl+N.
- ✦ Choose File⇨New, if necessary, to open the New Work Workbook task pane, click the General Templates link, and double-click the Workbook icon in the General tab of the New dialog box.

Any of these methods creates a blank default workbook.

Opening a Workbook File

If you have a workbook file already created that you want to open, Excel makes this task easy for you.

1. **Choose File⇨Open (or press Ctrl+O) to bring up the Open dialog box (see Figure 2-1).**

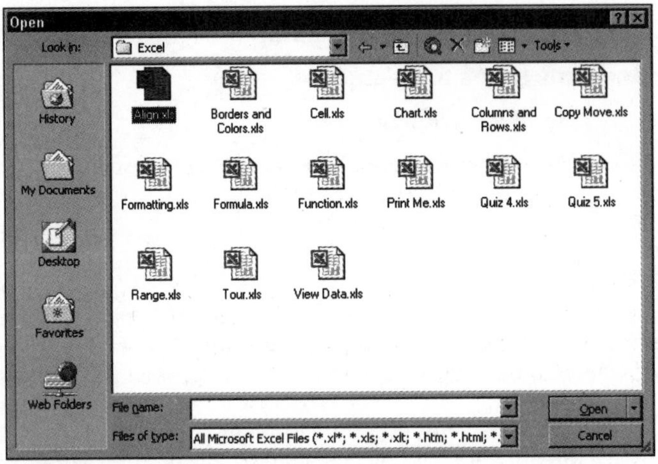

Figure 2-1: The Open dialog box in Excel.

You can also click the Open button on the Standard toolbar.

2. **Specify the folder that contains the file.**

If you have trouble finding the file, open the Views button drop-down list and choose an option to view files in different ways — as icons or as a list, for example. You find the Views button beside the Tools button. While you're at it, you can click and drag the corner of the dialog box to enlarge it, if enlarging it will help you find the file you are looking for.

3. **Select the workbook file and click Open or double-click the filename.**

You can select more than one file in the Open dialog box. The trick is to hold down the Ctrl key while you click the filenames. After you select all the files you want, click Open.

Excel comes with a new "Web browser-style" Open dialog box. On the left side of the dialog box is a vertical toolbar for quick access to commonly used folders. The blue arrow in the toolbar functions like a browser's back button. In the dialog box's toolbar, clicking the arrow takes you back to folders viewed previously.

Opening an Excel workbook for dialog box-challenged users

If you don't like rummaging through dialog boxes every time you want to open something, you can take advantage of other ways to open a workbook file:

- Double-click the workbook icon in any folder window. If Excel is not running, it starts automatically. Or you can drag a workbook icon into the Excel window to load the workbook.
- If you already have Excel running, open the File menu. Excel provides a list of files you've worked with recently at the bottom of the menu. If the file you want appears in this list, you can choose it directly from the menu.
- In the New Workbook task pane, look under Open a Workbook. There you will find the names of the last four workbooks you opened. Click a name to open its workbook.

Saving a Workbook File

When you save a workbook for the first time, Excel displays its Save As dialog box. When you save the same workbook anytime after that, Excel overwrites the previous copy of the file.

To save the active workbook to disk, follow these steps:

1. **Choose File⇨Save.**

   If the file has not yet been saved, Excel prompts you for a name using its Save As dialog box (see Figure 2-2).

   You may prefer to use any of the following methods to save:

   - Click the Save button on the Standard toolbar
   - Press the Ctrl+S shortcut key combination
   - Press the Shift+F12 shortcut key combination

2. **Select the folder that will hold the file.**
3. **Enter a name in the File Name box.**

   A filename can consist of as many as 255 characters, including spaces. You can't, however, use these characters in a file name: / ? : * " < > |.

4. **Click Save.**

Save As				? ☒
Save in:	☐ Excel	▼ ← · ⛶ ⊘ ✕ ☞ ☷ · Tools ·		

Name	Size	Type	Modified
Align.xls	14KB	Microsoft Excel Wo...	1/16/99 1:08 PM
Borders and Colors.xls	15KB	Microsoft Excel Wo...	12/26/98 4:37 PM
Cell.xls	14KB	Microsoft Excel Wo...	12/30/00 11:55 AM
Chart.xls	14KB	Microsoft Excel Wo...	7/24/98 10:31 AM
Columns and Rows.xls	16KB	Microsoft Excel Wo...	12/26/98 4:37 PM
Copy Move.xls	13KB	Microsoft Excel Wo...	12/26/98 4:36 PM
Formatting.xls	15KB	Microsoft Excel Wo...	12/26/98 4:37 PM
Formula.xls	16KB	Microsoft Excel Wo...	12/30/00 11:56 AM
Function.xls	15KB	Microsoft Excel Wo...	12/26/98 5:02 PM
Print Me.xls	16KB	Microsoft Excel Wo...	12/26/98 4:35 PM
Quiz 4.xls	15KB	Microsoft Excel Wo...	12/26/98 4:36 PM
Quiz 5.xls	15KB	Microsoft Excel Wo...	12/26/98 4:37 PM
Range.xls	17KB	Microsoft Excel Wo...	12/26/98 5:17 PM
Tour.xls	16KB	Microsoft Excel Wo...	12/26/98 4:36 PM
View Data.xls	16KB	Microsoft Excel Wo...	12/30/00 11:56 AM

Sidebar icons: History, My Documents, Desktop, Favorites, Web Folders

File name: Save Me **Save**
Save as type: Microsoft Excel Workbook (*.xls) Cancel

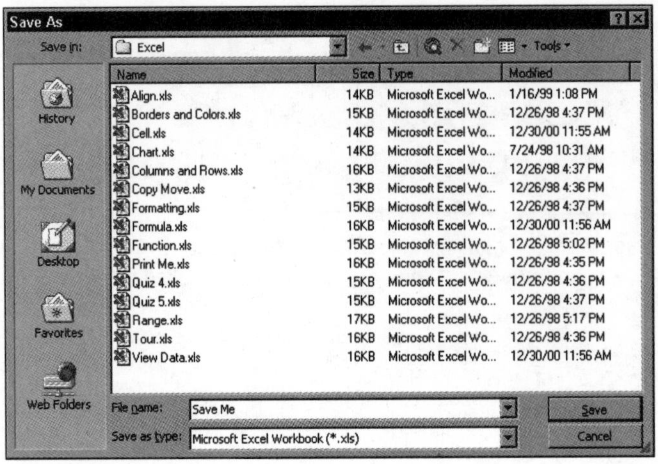

Figure 2-2:
The Save As
dialog box
lets you
name and
place your
file.

You should save your work at a time interval that corresponds to the maximum amount of time that you're willing to lose. For example, if you don't mind losing an hour's work, save your file every hour. Most people save at more frequent intervals.

Sometimes, you may want to keep multiple versions of your work by saving each successive version under a different name. No problem!

1. **Choose File⇨Save As to display the Save As dialog box.**

2. **Select the folder in which to store the workbook.**

3. **Enter a new filename in the File Name box.**

4. **Click Save.**

A new copy is created with a different name, but the original version of the file remains intact.

Closing a Workbook

After you're finished using a workbook, use any of these methods to close it and free up the memory it uses. (If you haven't saved it since the last time you made any changes, you are prompted to do so!)

✦ Choose File⇨Close.

 ✦ Click the Close Window button in the workbook's title bar. (Be careful not to click the Close button directly above it — clicking that button closes Excel as well as the workbook.)

✦ Double-click the Control button in the workbook's title bar.

✦ Press Ctrl+F4.

✦ Press Ctrl+W.

To close all open workbooks, press the Shift key and choose File⇨Close All. (This command only appears when you hold down the Shift key while you click the File menu.) Excel closes each workbook, unless you haven't saved your work. In that case, you are prompted to save it before closing.

Using a Workbook Template

A *workbook template* is a normal workbook that is used as the basis for other workbooks. A workbook template can use any of Excel's features such as charts, formulas, and macros. Normally, you set up a template so that you can enter some values and get immediate results. Excel includes several templates, and you can create your own. To set up a template, follow these steps:

1. **Choose File⇨Save As.**
2. **Select Template from the drop-down list box labeled Save As Type.**
3. **Save the template in your Templates folder (or a subfolder within the Templates folder).**

If you don't want to create your own templates but like the idea of ready-made workbooks, why not let good ole Excel help you? The Spreadsheet Solutions templates distributed with Excel are nicely formatted and relatively easy to customize.

To create a workbook from a template, follow these steps:

1. **Choose File⇨New.**
2. **Under New from Template in the New Workbook task pane, click the General Templates link.**

   The Templates dialog box appears.
3. **Click the Spreadsheet Solutions tab.**

   The tab offers several different templates.
4. **Select the template you want and click OK.**

Deleting a Workbook File

When you no longer need a workbook file, you may want to delete it from your hard drive to free up space and reduce the number of files displayed in the Open dialog box. You can delete files using standard Windows techniques, or you can delete files directly from Excel. To delete a file, follow these steps:

1. **Choose either File⇨Open or File⇨Save As to bring up a dialog box with a list of filenames.**
2. **Find and select the workbook file you want to delete.**
3. **Click the Delete button, press the Delete key, or right-click and choose Delete on the shortcut menu.**

   Depending on how your system is set up, you may have to confirm this action.

If your system is set up to use the Recycle Bin, you may be able to recover a file that you delete accidentally. Before you empty the Recycle Bin, open it up and restore items that need restoring. To do so, select an item and choose File⇨Restore.

Creating Multiple Windows (Views) for a Workbook

Sometimes, you may like to view two different parts of a worksheet at once. Or you may want to see more than one sheet in the same workbook. You can accomplish either of these actions by displaying your workbook in one or more additional windows.

To create a new view of the active workbook, choose Window⇨New Window. Excel displays a new window for the active workbook. To help you keep track of the windows, Excel appends a colon and a number to each window. When you want to close a window, click its Close Window button.

Chapter 3: Working with the Worksheets in Your Workbook

In This Chapter

- Adding and arranging worksheets
- Managing your worksheets
- Navigating in a worksheet
- Moving a worksheet
- Deleting a worksheet

If you look at an Excel workbook, you may notice that it's composed of one or more worksheets, each with its own little tab at the bottom of the workbook window. These tabs make worksheets look like upside-down folders (you know, those manila folders that fit neatly into a drawer, and whose tabs make them easy to find even if the folders are all stacked into tight rows). The similarity stops there, however, because worksheets are much more useful than a bunch of upside-down manila folders. Worksheets are the holders of the cells (explained in Chapter 1) into which you place your valuable, hard-earned data. Just try putting some valuable things into upside-down manila folders in your file cabinet!

In this chapter, you find out about fundamental worksheet management.

Working with Worksheets

A workbook can consist of any number of *worksheets.* To activate a different sheet, just click its tab (see Figure 3-1). If the tab for the sheet that you want to activate is not visible, use the tab scrolling buttons to scroll the sheet tabs.

You also can use these shortcut keys to activate a different sheet:

- **Ctrl+PgUp:** Activates the previous sheet, if there is one.
- **Ctrl+PgDn:** Activates the next sheet, if there is one.

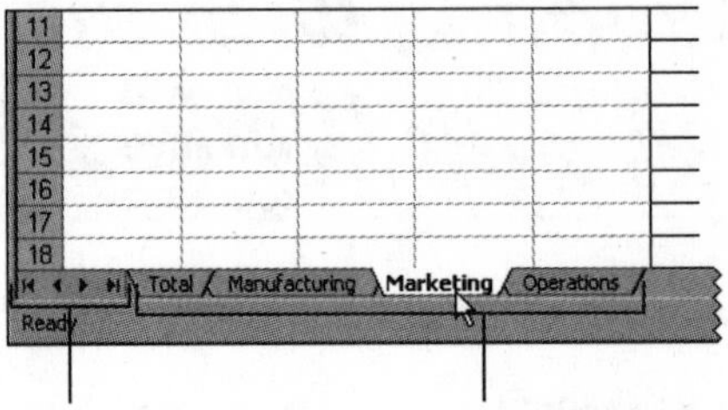

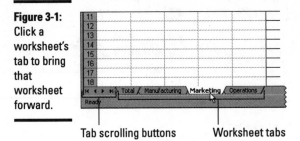

Figure 3-1: Click a worksheet's tab to bring that worksheet forward.

Adding a new worksheet

What? Three worksheets aren't enough for you! Fortunately, you can add a new worksheet to a workbook in several ways:

- ✦ Choose Insert⇨Worksheet.
- ✦ Right-click a worksheet tab, choose Insert from the shortcut menu, and select Worksheet in the Insert dialog box.
- ✦ Press Shift+F11.

Excel inserts a new worksheet before the active worksheet; the new worksheet then becomes the active worksheet.

Changing a sheet's name

Worksheets, by default, are named Sheet1, Sheet2, and so on. Providing more meaningful names helps you identify a particular sheet. To change a sheet's name, use any of these methods:

- ✦ Choose Format⇨Sheet⇨Rename.
- ✦ Right-click a worksheet tab and choose Rename from the shortcut menu.

Either method selects the text in the tab. Just type the new sheet name directly on the tab.

Sheet names can be up to 31 characters. Spaces are allowed, but the following characters aren't: [ ] (square brackets); : (colon); / (slash);\ (backslash); ? (question mark); and * (asterisk). Your computer may catch fire if you try to name your worksheet something like ?*?\ : /*]?[.

TIP

Keep in mind that the name you give is displayed on the worksheet tab; a longer name results in a wider tab. Therefore, if you use lengthy worksheet names, you can see fewer worksheet tabs without scrolling.

Manipulating Your Worksheets

That's right. You need to be manipulative with your worksheets. Show them who's boss. Read on to find out how to copy a worksheet, change your view of a worksheet, switch to Full Screen view, and zoom in and out to get a better look at your work.

Copying a worksheet

You can make an exact copy of a worksheet in either of two ways:

- ✦ Choose Edit⇨Move or Copy Sheet. Select the location for the copy and make sure that the check box labeled Create a Copy is checked. Click OK to make the copy.
- ✦ Click the worksheet tab, press Ctrl, and drag it to its desired location. When you drag, the mouse pointer changes to a small sheet with a plus sign on it.

If necessary, Excel changes the name of the copied sheet to make it unique within the workbook. For example, if you copy a sheet named Sheet1 to a workbook that already has a sheet named Sheet1, Excel changes the name to Sheet1 (2). To change the name of a sheet, see "Changing a sheet's name," earlier in this chapter.

Creating and using named views

Excel lets you name various *views* of your worksheet and switch quickly among these named views. A view includes settings for window size and position, frozen panes or titles, outlining, zoom factor, the active cell, print area, and many of the settings in the Options dialog box. A view can also include hidden print settings and hidden rows and columns.

To create a named view, follow these steps:

1. **Set up the worksheet the way you want it to appear.**
2. **Choose View⇨Custom Views.**

   The Custom Views dialog box appears, as shown in Figure 3-2.
3. **In the Custom Views dialog box, click the Add button and then enter a descriptive name for the view.**

To display a view that you've named, choose View⇨Custom Views, select the view from the list, and click the Show button.

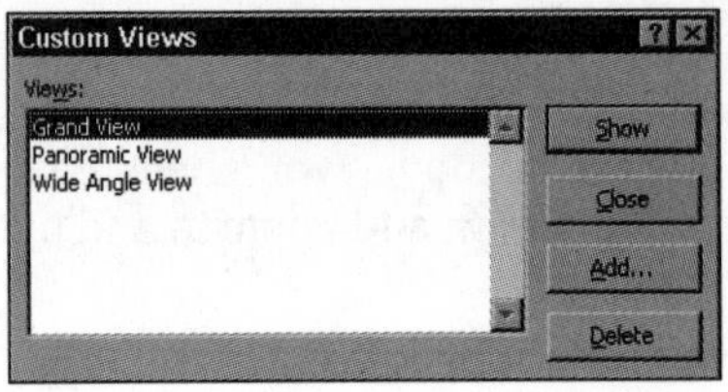

Figure 3-2: Go quickly to a named view from the Custom Views dialog box.

Using full screen view

If you want to see as much information as possible, Excel offers a full screen view. Choose View⇨Full Screen, and Excel maximizes its window and removes all elements except the menu bar. Click the Close Full Screen button to see Excel in all its glory again.

Zooming worksheets

Normally, everything you see in Excel is at 100 percent size. You can change the *zoom percentage* from 10 percent (very tiny) to 400 percent (huge). Using a small zoom percentage can help you get a bird's-eye view of your worksheet to see how it's laid out. Zooming in is useful if your eyesight isn't quite what it used to be and you have trouble deciphering those 8-point sales figures.

Here are techniques for zooming in and out of worksheets:

- Click the Zoom down arrow on the Standard toolbar and select the desired zoom factor from the list. Your screen transforms immediately. (You can also choose View⇨Zoom to bring up the Zoom dialog box and make a choice there.)
- Type a number directly into the Zoom box on the Standard toolbar and press the Enter key.
- If you have a Microsoft IntelliMouse, or equivalent device, zoom out on a worksheet by pressing Ctrl while you move the mouse wheel. Make sure the Zoom on Roll with IntelliMouse option is selected in the Options dialog box (choose Tools⇨Options and click the General tab).

TIP

If you choose the Selection option in the Zoom drop-down list, Excel zooms the worksheet to display only the selected cells. This option is useful if you want to view only a particular range.

Freezing row or column titles

Many worksheets (such as budgets) are set up with row and column headings. When you scroll through such a worksheet, getting lost when the row and column headings scroll out of view is easy. Excel provides a handy solution: freezing rows and/or columns. To freeze a row or column, follow these steps:

1. **Move the cell pointer to the cell below the row that you want to freeze and to the right of the column that you want to freeze.**

   For example, to freeze row 1 and column A, move the cell pointer to cell B2.

2. **Choose Window⇨Freeze Panes.**

Excel inserts dark lines to indicate the frozen rows and columns. These frozen rows and columns remain visible as you scroll throughout the worksheet. To remove the frozen rows or columns, choose Window⇨Unfreeze Panes.

Splitting panes

Splitting a window into two or four panes lets you view multiple parts of the same worksheet — as long as you think your mind can handle it.

- ✦ Choosing Window⇨Split splits the active worksheet into two or four separate panes.
- ✦ The split occurs at the location of the cell pointer.
- ✦ You can use the mouse to drag the pane and resize it.
- ✦ To remove the split panes, choose Window⇨Remove Split.

A faster way to split and unsplit panes is to drag either the vertical or horizontal split bar, shown in the Figure 3-3. To remove split panes using the mouse, drag the pane separator all the way to the edge of the window or just double-click it.

Moving and resizing windows

To move a window, first make sure that it's not maximized. If it is maximized, click its Restore Window button (shown in the margin). Move the window by clicking and dragging its title bar with your mouse. Note that the window can extend off-screen in any direction, if you like.

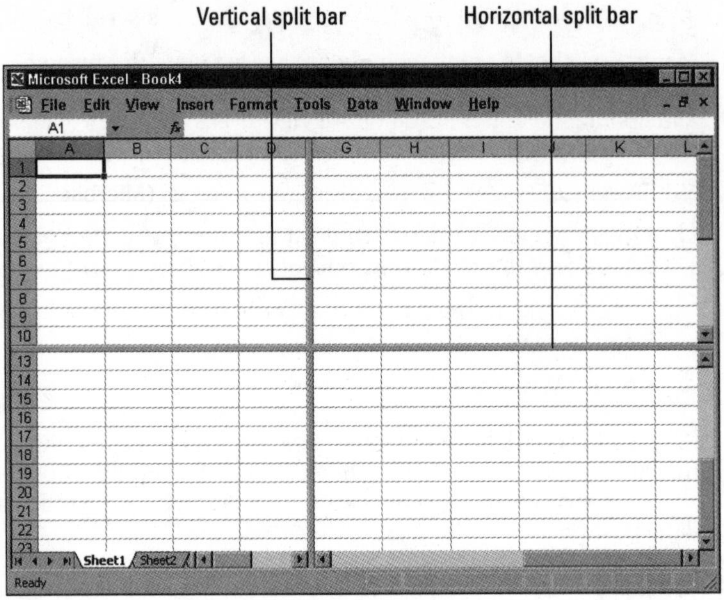

Figure 3-3: Now you can look at four different parts of your worksheet at one time.

To resize a window, click and drag any of its borders until it's the size you want it to be. When you position the mouse pointer on a window's border, the mouse pointer changes shape (into a double arrow) to let you know that you can then click and drag. To resize a window horizontally and vertically at the same time, click and drag any of its corners.

Moving Around in a Worksheet

Navigating through a worksheet with a mouse works just as you would expect. Just click a cell and it becomes the active cell. If the cell that you want to activate is not visible in the workbook window, you can use the scroll bars to scroll the window in any direction.

- To scroll one cell, click one of the arrows on the scroll bar.
- To scroll by a complete screen, click either side of the scroll bar's elevator button (the large center button).
- To scroll faster, drag the elevator button. And away you go!
- To scroll a long distance vertically, hold down the Shift key while dragging the elevator button.

Notice that only the active workbook window has scroll bars. When you activate a different window, the scroll bars appear.

Using the scroll bars doesn't change the active cell. It simply scrolls the worksheet. To change the active cell, you must click a new cell after scrolling.

Your mouse may be equipped with a small wheel (Microsoft's IntelliMouse is an example). If you have such a mouse, you can spin the wheel to scroll vertically. If this doesn't work, choose Tools⇨Options, click the General tab, and click the Zoom on Roll with IntelliMouse option to remove the check mark.

To scroll very quickly through a worksheet, hold down the IntelliMouse scroll wheel as you drag the mouse.

See Chapter 1 for some info on moving around by using the keyboard.

Moving a Sheet

Sometimes, you want to rearrange the order of worksheets in a workbook — or move a sheet to a different workbook.

First, select the sheet that you want to move by clicking the sheet tab. You can also move multiple sheets at once by selecting them: Press Ctrl while you click the sheet tabs that you want to move.

You can move a selected worksheet(s) in one of two ways:

- Choose Edit⇨Move or Copy Sheet. The Move or Copy dialog box pops up asking you to select the workbook and the new location (see Figure 3-4).
- Click the sheet tab and drag it to its desired location (either in the same workbook or in a different workbook). When you drag, the mouse pointer changes to a small sheet, and a small arrow guides you. To move a worksheet to a different workbook, both workbooks must be open.

Dragging is usually the easiest method, but if the workbook has many sheets, you may prefer to use the Move or Copy dialog box.

If you move a worksheet to a workbook that already has a sheet with the same name, Excel changes the name to make it unique. For example, if you move a sheet named Sheet1 to a workbook that already has a sheet named Sheet1, Excel changes the name to Sheet1 (2). To change the name of a sheet, see "Changing a sheet's name," earlier in this chapter.

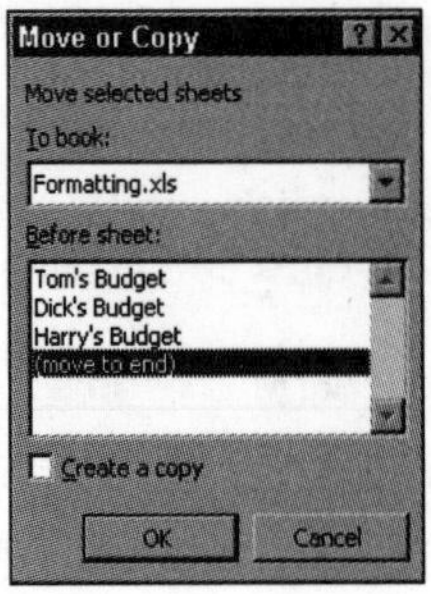

Figure 3-4: The Move or Copy dialog box lets you, well, move or copy.

Deleting a Worksheet

You can delete a worksheet in one of two ways:

- ✦ Activate the sheet and choose Edit➪Delete Sheet.
- ✦ Right-click the sheet tab and choose Delete from the shortcut menu.

In either case, Excel asks you to confirm that you want to delete the sheet. Every workbook must have at least one sheet so, if you try to delete the only sheet, Excel complains.

TIP: To select multiple sheets to delete, press Ctrl while clicking the sheet tabs that you want to delete. To select a group of contiguous sheets, click the first sheet tab, press Shift, and then click the last sheet tab.

WARNING! When you delete a worksheet, it's gone for good. This is one of the few operations in Excel that can't be undone. You may want to save a workbook before deleting worksheets. Then if you inadvertently delete a worksheet, you can revert to the saved version.

Chapter 4: Entering Worksheet Data

In This Chapter

- **Placing your data into worksheets**
- **Entering formulas into worksheets**
- **Putting fractions into worksheets**

With all those pretty horizontal and vertical lines, worksheets sure look impressive. And with those official-looking row and column indicators, worksheets seem to be saying, "Hey, I'm important. You'd better take me seriously."

A worksheet, however, is only as good as the data you put into it. Whether that data be Grandma's Secret Recipes or June 2001 Mid-West Sales Figures, a worksheet needs data to find fulfillment. This chapter reveals how to enter all sorts of data — from simple text to complex formulas — into your worksheets.

Entering Data into a Worksheet

Each worksheet in a workbook is made up of cells, and a cell can hold any of four types of data:

- A value (including a date or a time)
- Text
- A logical value (TRUE or FALSE)
- A formula, which returns a value, text, or a logical value

Entering text into cells

To enter text (rather than a value or a formula) into a cell, follow these steps:

1. **Move the cell pointer to the appropriate cell and click to make that cell the active cell.**

   The active cell is the one where data is entered when you start typing.

2. **Type the text.**
3. **Press Enter or any of the direction keys.**

In Excel, a cell can hold as many as 32,767 characters. (But who would want to put that much text into a cell?)

If you enter text that's longer than its column's current width, one of two things happens (see Figure 4-1):

- ✦ If the cells to the immediate right are blank, Excel displays the text in its entirety, spilling the entry into adjacent cells.
- ✦ If an adjacent cell is *not* blank, Excel displays as much of the text as possible. The full text is contained in the cell; it's just not displayed.

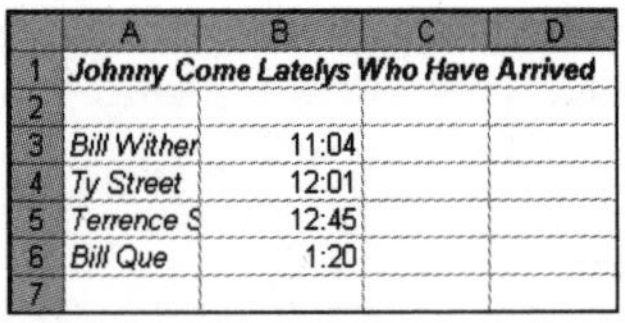

A
B
C
D
Johnny Come Latelys Who Have Arrived
Bill Wither
11:04
Ty Street
12:01
Terrence S
12:45
Bill Que
1:20

Figure 4-1: How Excel handles long cell entries.

In either case, you can always see the text that you're typing because it appears in the formula bar as well as in the cell.

If you need to display a long text entry that's adjacent to a cell with an entry, you can edit your text to make it shorter, increase the width of the column, or wrap the text within the cell so that it occupies more than one line.

If you have lengthy text in a cell, you can force Excel to display it in multiple lines within the cell. Use Alt+Enter to start a new line in a cell. When you add this line break, Excel automatically changes the cell's format to Wrap Text.

Entering values into cells

Enter a numeric value into a cell is just like entering text.

1. **Move the cell pointer to the appropriate cell.**
2. **Enter the value.**
3. **Press Enter or any of the direction keys.**

The value displays in the cell, and it also appears in the Excel formula bar. You can also include a decimal point, dollar sign, plus sign, minus sign, and comma. If you precede a value with a minus sign or enclose it in parentheses, Excel considers the value to be a negative number.

Sometimes the value isn't displayed exactly as you enter it. Excel may convert very large numbers to scientific notation. The formula bar always displays the value that you originally entered. If you make the column wider, the number displays as you entered it.

Entering the current date or time into a cell

If you need to date-stamp or time-stamp your worksheet, Excel provides two shortcut keys that do this for you (which is a lot easier than having to dig out your calendar or look at your watch — provided that your computer has the correct date and time entered).

- **Current date:** Press Ctrl+; (semicolon)
- **Current time:** Press Ctrl+Shift+; (semicolon)

Entering dates and times

To Excel, a date or a time is simply a value — but it's formatted to appear as a date or a time.

Excel's system for working with dates uses a serial number system. The earliest date that Excel understands is January 1, 1900 (which has a serial number of 1). January 2, 1900, has a serial number of 2, and so on. Dates previous to January 1, 1900 are recorded with negative numbers. December 31, 1899, for example, is given the serial number –1. This system makes it easy to deal with dates in formulas.

Normally, you don't have to be concerned with the Excel serial number date system. You can simply enter a date in a familiar format, and Excel takes care of the details.

If you plan to use dates in formulas, make sure that the date you enter is actually recognized as a date (that is, a value); otherwise, your formulas will produce incorrect results. Excel is quite smart when it comes to recognizing dates that you enter into a cell, and it recognizes most common date formats. But it's not perfect. For example, Excel interprets the following entries as text, not dates:

- June 1 2001
- Jun-1 2001
- Jun-1/2001

The Year 2000 issue deserves a mention here. Entering 1/1/29 is interpreted by Excel as January 01, 2029. Entering 1/30 is interpreted by Excel as January 30, 2001 (or whatever is the current year). To be safe, enter the year as a four-digit value, and then format it as desired.

Excel works with times by using fractional days. When working with times, you simply extend Excel's date serial number system to include decimals. For example, the date serial number for June 1, 2001, is 37043. Noon (halfway through the day) is represented internally as 37043.5.

The best way to deal with times is to enter the time into a cell in a recognized format. Table 4-1 features some examples of time formats that Excel recognizes.

Table 4-1 Excel Time Formats

Entered into a Cell	*Excel's Interpretation*
11:30:00 am	11:30 a.m.
11:30:00 AM	11:30 a.m.
11:30 pm	11:30 p.m.
11:30	11:30 a.m.

You also can combine dates and times, as shown in Table 4-2.

Table 4-2 Combining Dates and Times

Entered into a Cell	*Excel's Interpretation*
6/1/98 11:30	11:30 a.m. on June 1, 1998
7/31/01 3:30	3:30 p.m. on July 31, 2001

Entering the same data into a range of cells

FAST TRACK

If you need to enter the same data (value, text, or formula) into multiple cells, your first inclination may be to enter it once and then copy it to the remaining cells. Here's a better way:

1. **Select all the cells that you want to contain the data.**
2. **Enter the value, text, or formula into one cell.**
3. **Press Ctrl+Enter.**

   The single entry is inserted into each cell in the selection.

Entering Formulas

A *formula* is a special type of cell entry that returns a result: When you enter a formula into a cell, the cell displays the result of the formula. The formula itself appears in the formula bar (which is just below the toolbars at the top of the Excel window) when the cell is activated.

A formula begins with an equal sign (=) and can consist of any of the following elements:

- ✦ Operators such as + (for addition) and * (for multiplication)
- ✦ Cell references, including addresses such as B4 or C12, as well as named cells and ranges
- ✦ Values and text
- ✦ Worksheet functions (such as SUM)

You can enter a formula into a cell by manually typing it in or by pointing to cell references. See Chapter 8 for the lowdown on formulas.

Entering formulas manually

Entering a formula manually isn't as hard as it sounds. To do so, follow these steps:

1. **Move the cell pointer to the cell that you want to hold the formula.**
2. **Type an equal sign (=) to signal the fact that the cell contains a formula.**
3. **Type the formula and press Enter.**

As you type, the characters appear in the cell as well as in the formula bar. You can use all the normal editing keys (Delete, Backspace, direction keys, and so on) when entering a formula.

Entering formulas by pointing

The pointing method of entering a formula still involves some manual typing. The advantage is that you don't have to type the cell or range references. Rather, you point to them in the worksheet, which is usually more accurate and less tedious.

The best way to explain this procedure is with an example. To enter the formula **=A1/A2** into cell A3 by the pointing method, just follow these steps:

1. **Move the cell pointer to cell A3.**

   This is where you want the formula (and the result) to go.
2. **Type an equal sign (=) to begin the formula.**
3. **Press the up arrow twice or click in cell A1.**

   Notice that Excel displays a faint moving border around the cell and that the cell reference appears in cell A3 and in the formula bar.

4. **Type a division sign (/).**

   The faint border disappears and is replaced by a solid blue border. Meanwhile, the word `Enter` reappears in the status bar at the bottom of the screen.

5. **Press the up arrow once or click in cell A2.**

   A2 is added to the formula.

6. **Press Enter to finish entering the formula.**

Entering Fractions

To enter a fraction into a cell, leave a space between the whole number part and the fractional part. For example, to enter $6\frac{7}{8}$, follow these steps:

1. **Type** 6.
2. **Type a space.**
3. **Type** 7/8.
4. **Press Enter.**

If your fraction has no whole number (for example $\frac{1}{8}$), you must enter a zero and a space first, like this: **0 1/8**.

Inserting cells, rows, and columns

The time may come when you need to squeeze more stuff into a section of a worksheet already occupied by other cell entries. Inserting a new cell range is a snap.

1. **Select the cells (both occupied and unoccupied) where you want the new cells to appear.**
2. **Right-click the selection and choose Insert from the shortcut menu or choose Insert⇨Cells to bring up the Insert dialog box.**

   You have a choice of radio buttons to select: Shift Cells Right or Shift Cells Down.

3. **Select the proper choice and then click OK.**

You may notice that you can also choose the options of inserting an entire row or column from the Insert dialog box. Inserting a row or a column is even easier if you simply choose Insert⇨Rows or Insert⇨Columns. Rows are inserted below and columns are inserted to the right of where you have a cell selected. Insert as many rows or columns that you want at a time simply by selecting more than one row or column.

Chapter 5: Editing the Data You Enter

In This Chapter

- **Fixing your data**
- **Filling in data automatically**
- **Making comments on your data**
- **Searching and replacing your data**
- **Checking your spelling**

Imagine that you're perfect and that you have all the time in the world. You enter your data and you're done. You never need to go back and fix any mistakes. You never have to locate any stray data. You never have to check your spelling (because you were the fifth-grade spelling bee champion of Laura G. Hose Elementary School).

If you don't recognize yourself in the preceding paragraph, don't worry. Excel makes entering changes and correcting mistakes simple. Excel gives you lots of help entering data the easy way and even performing some automated tasks. And Excel makes it a breeze to find and repair data as well as to correct those spelling mistakes that seem to creep into even the most carefully prepared document. You don't need to do everything right the first time when you have Excel on your side. You just need to know a few Excel tips here and there, and this chapter strives to show you how to be productive without having to be perfect.

Basic Cell Editing

If you never have to go back and fix what you enter into a cell, you may as well skip this section. But if you're curious about what those other error-prone people must do to repair their mistakes, you may enjoy reading some of this advice.

Editing a cell's contents

After you enter information into a cell, you can change it — or edit it. When you want to edit the contents of a cell, you can use one of these ways to get into cell edit mode:

- Double-click the cell to edit the cell contents directly in the cell.
- Press F2. This enables you to edit the cell contents directly in the cell.
- Activate the cell that you want to edit; then click in the formula bar to edit the cell contents in the formula bar.

If nothing happens when you double-click a cell, or if pressing F2 puts the cursor in the formula bar instead of directly in the cell, the in-cell editing feature is turned off. To turn on in-cell editing, follow these steps:

1. **Choose Tools⇨Options.**
2. **Click the Edit tab.**
3. **Click to select the Edit Directly in Cell check box.**

When you're editing a cell that contains a formula, and you've clicked to place the cursor in the Formula bar, the Function list (located at the extreme left in the formula bar) displays a list of worksheet functions. You can select a function from the list, and Excel provides assistance entering the arguments, as shown in Figure 5-1.

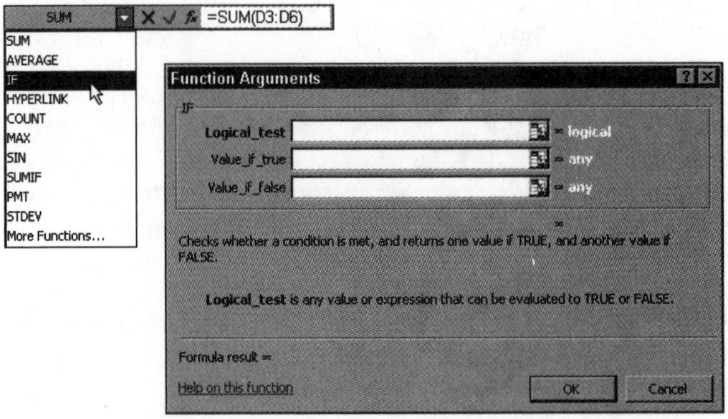

Figure 5-1: Choose a function from the Function list to learn how a function works.

When you're editing the contents of a cell in the Formula bar, the cursor changes to a vertical bar; you can move the vertical bar by using the direction keys. You can add new characters at the cursor location. After you're in edit mode, you can use any of the following keys or key combinations to perform your edits:

- **Left/right arrow:** Moves the cursor left or right one character, respectively, without deleting any characters.
- **Ctrl+left/right arrow:** Moves the cursor one group of characters to the left or right, respectively.

✦ **Shift+left/right arrow:** Selects characters to the left or right of the cursor, respectively.

✦ **Shift+Home:** Selects from the cursor to the first character in the cell.

✦ **Shift+End:** Selects from the cursor to the last character in the cell.

✦ **Backspace:** Erases the character to the immediate left of the cursor.

✦ **Delete:** Erases the character to the right of the cursor or erases all selected characters.

✦ **Insert:** Places Excel in OVR (Overwrite) mode. Rather than add characters to the cell, you *overwrite,* or replace, existing characters with new ones, depending on the position of the cursor.

✦ **Home:** Moves the cursor to the beginning of the cell entry.

✦ **End:** Moves the cursor to the end of the cell entry.

✦ **Enter:** Accepts the edited data.

If you change your mind after editing a cell, you can choose Edit➪Undo (or press Ctrl+Z) to restore the cell's previous contents.

TIP

You also can use the mouse to select characters while you're editing a cell. Just click and drag the mouse pointer over the characters that you want to select.

Replacing the contents of a cell

To replace the contents of a cell with something else, follow these steps:

1. **Select the cell.**
2. **Type your new entry (it replaces the previous contents).**

Any formatting that you applied to the cell remains.

Erasing data in cells and ranges

To erase the contents of a cell but leave the cell's formatting and cell comments intact, perform the following two steps:

1. **Select the cell or range you want to erase.**
2. **Press Delete.**

For more control over what gets deleted, you can choose Edit➪Clear, which leads to a submenu with four additional choices (see Figure 5-2):

- **All:** Clears everything from the cell
- **Formats:** Clears only the formatting and leaves the value, text, or formula
- **Contents:** Clears only the cell's contents and leaves the formatting
- **Comments:** Clears the comment (if one exists) attached to the cell

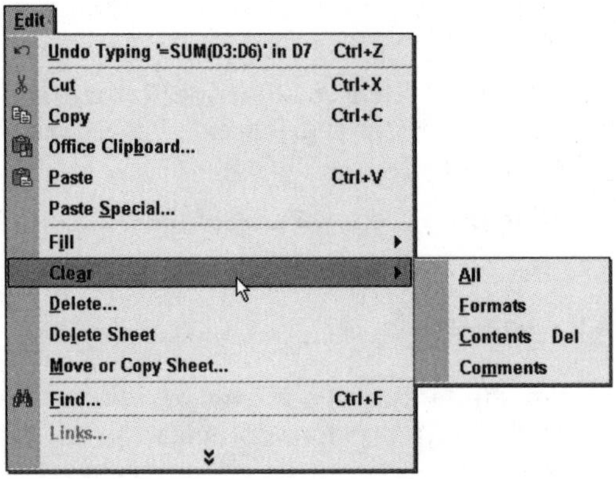

Figure 5-2: You can clear lots of things with this menu.

Undoing Changes and Mistakes

One very useful feature in Excel is its multilevel undo. This means that you can reverse your recent actions, one step at a time. For example, if you discover that you accidentally deleted a range of data several minutes ago, you can use the undo feature to backtrack through your actions until the deleted range reappears.

REMEMBER

You can undo your actions only in a sequential manner. In other words, if you want to undo an action you must also undo all of the actions that you performed after the action that you want to undo. You can undo the past 16 operations that you performed.

To undo an operation, use any of the following techniques:

- Choose Edit⇨Undo. The command tells you what you will be undoing.
- Press Ctrl+Z until you arrive at the action that you want to undo.
- Click the Undo button on the Standard toolbar until you arrive at the action that you want to undo.
- Click the arrow on the Undo button on the Standard toolbar. This displays a description of your recent actions (see Figure 5-3). Select the actions to undo.

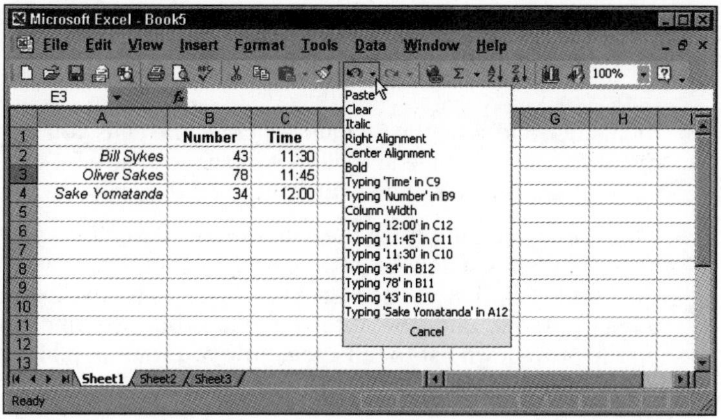

Figure 5-3: Look at all the things you can undo!

Using AutoComplete

AutoComplete enables you to type the first few letters of a text entry into a cell, and Excel automatically completes the entry based on other entries that you've already made in the column. AutoComplete works with no effort on your part:

1. **Begin entering text or a value.**

   If Excel recognizes your entry, it automatically completes it.

2. **Press Enter to accept Excel's entry if Excel guesses correctly. If you want to enter something else, just continue typing and ignore Excel's guess.**

TIP: You can also access this feature by right-clicking the cell and selecting Pick From List. With this method, Excel displays a drop-down list with all the entries in the current column. Just click the one that you want, and it's entered automatically.

If you don't like this feature, you can turn it off in the Edit tab of the Options dialog box. Choose Tools➪Options, click the Edit tab, and click to remove the check mark from the Enable AutoComplete for Cell Values check box.

Using AutoFill

AutoFill is a handy feature that has several uses. AutoFill uses the *fill handle* — the small square that appears at the bottom-right corner of the selected cell or range. After you enter the first in a series of data, AutoFill can fill in the rest. Try one of these techniques for autofilling the rest of the series:

- ✦ Right-click and drag the fill handle across the cells you need to fill. Excel displays a shortcut menu of fill options (see Figure 5-4). Choose an option that describes how you want to fill the cells.

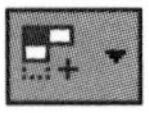

- ✦ Drag the fill handle across the cells you need to fill. As you do so, boxes appear to tell you how Excel proposes to complete the data series. Then the AutoFill Options button appears. If you don't like how Excel auto-filled the series, click the AutoFill Options button and choose an option on the drop-down list to tell Excel how you want to fill in the series (see Figure 5-5).

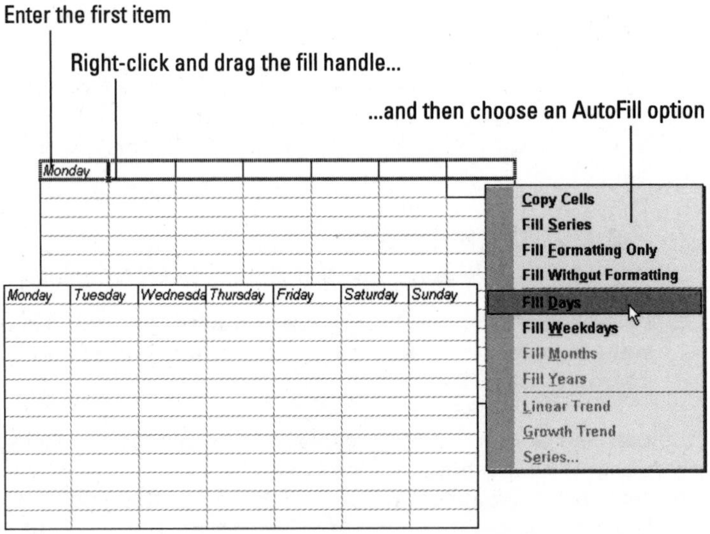

Figure 5-4: Right-click to fill in a data series.

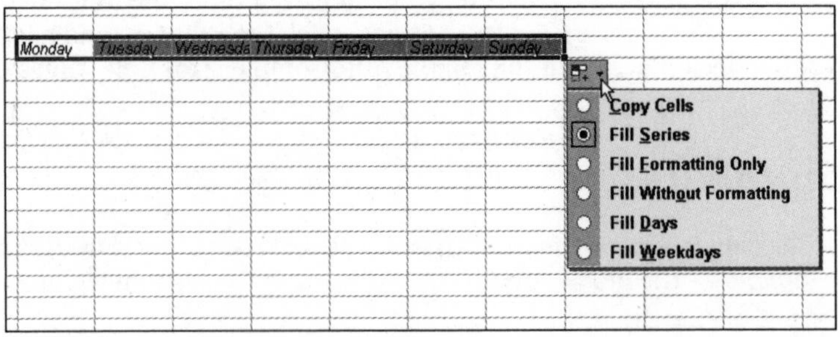

Figure 5-5: Using the AutoFill Options button to fill in a series.

Making a custom list

Are you tired of always retyping the starting lineup of your softball team or the home office's Pacific Rim sales staff? Why not teach Excel to recognize these lists? You can make a custom list for anything. Choose Tools⇨Options and click the Custom Lists tab. Then in the List Entries box, enter your list, placing commas and spaces between the entries. Click Add to store the list. Your custom list also works with AutoFill.

If the selected cell or range does not have a fill handle, it means that this feature is turned off. To turn AutoFill on, follow these steps:

1. **Choose Tools⇨Options.**
2. **Click the Edit tab.**
3. **Click the Allow Cell Drag and Drop check box.**

You cannot use AutoFill when you've made a multiple selection.

Entering a series of incremental values or dates

To use AutoFill to enter a series of incremental values, follow these steps:

1. **Enter at least two values or dates in the series into adjacent cells. These values need not be consecutive.**
2. **Select the cells you used in Step 1.**
3. **Click and drag the fill handle to complete the series in the cells that you select.**

   While you drag the fill handle, Excel displays a small box that tells you what it's planning to enter into each cell.

If you drag the fill handle when only one cell is selected, Excel examines the data and determines whether to increment the value or simply copy it. For more control, drag the fill handle while pressing the right mouse button. When you release the button, you get a list of options.

AutoFill also works in the negative direction. For example, if you use AutoFill by starting with two cells that contain –20 and –19, Excel fills in –18, –17, and so on.

If the values in the cells that you enter do not have equal increments, Excel completes the series by calculating a simple linear regression. This feature is handy for performing simple forecasts. ***Note:*** Excel calculates a simple linear regression or progression, depending on the direction (negative or positive) of the series.

Entering a series of text

Excel is familiar with some text series (days of the week, month names), and it can complete these series for you automatically. You no longer have to remember such things, thus freeing your mind for more important matters! Here's how to use AutoFill to complete a known series of text:

1. **Enter any of the series into a cell (for example, Monday or February).**
2. **Click and drag the fill handle to complete the series in the cells that you select.**

You can click the AutoFill Options button to keep or abandon the formatting of the first list entry.

Using Automatic Decimal Points

If you're entering lots of numbers with a fixed number of decimal places, you can save some time by letting Excel enter the decimal point (like the feature available on some adding machines). To do so, follow these steps:

1. **Choose Tools⇨Options.**
2. **Click the Edit tab.**
3. **Click to select the Fixed Decimal check box and make sure that it's set for the number of decimal places that you want to use.**

Excel now supplies the decimal points for you automatically. For example, if you have it set for two decimal places and you enter **12345** into a cell, Excel interprets it as 123.45 (it adds the decimal point). To restore things to normal, just uncheck the Fixed Decimal check box in the Options dialog box.

Using Cell Comments

The Excel cell comment feature enables you to attach a comment to a cell — useful when you need to document a particular value or to help you remember what a formula does. When you move the mouse pointer over a cell that has a comment, the comment pops up in a small box.

Adding a cell comment

To add a comment to a cell, follow these steps:

1. **Select the cell.**
2. **Choose Insert⇨Comment, press Shift+F2, or right-click and choose Insert Comment.**

   Excel displays a text box that points to the cell.
3. **Enter the text for the comment into the text box.**
4. **Click any cell when you're finished.**

The cell displays a small red triangle to indicate that the cell contains a comment, as shown in Figure 5-6.

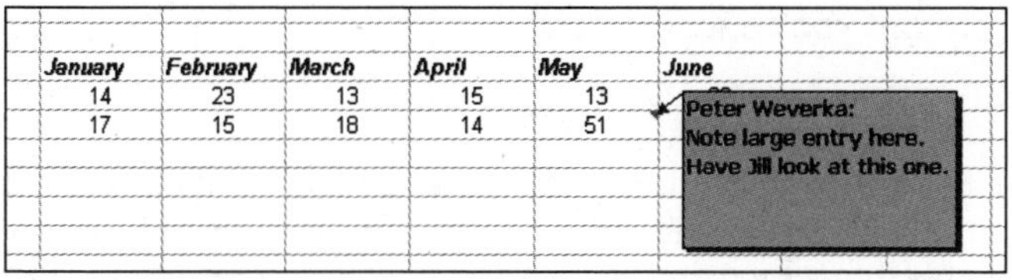

January February March April May June
14 23 13 15 13
17 15 18 14 51
Peter Weverka:
Note large entry here.
Have Jill look at this one.

Figure 5-6: Comments can tell you oh so much.

Editing and deleting cell comments

To edit a cell comment, select the cell that contains the comment and then choose Insert⇨Edit Comment. Or you can right-click the cell and choose Edit Comment from the shortcut menu.

To delete a comment, right-click the cell that contains the comment and choose Delete Comment.

Searching for Data

If your worksheet contains lots of data, you may find it difficult to locate a particular piece of information. A quick way to find that information is to let Excel do it for you. Make Excel earn its keep. To locate a particular value or sequence of text, follow these steps:

1. **Select the area of the worksheet that you want to search. If you want to search the entire worksheet, just select a single cell (any cell will do).**
2. **Choose Edit⇨Find or press Ctrl+F.**

   The Find and Replace dialog box appears, as shown in Figure 5-7.

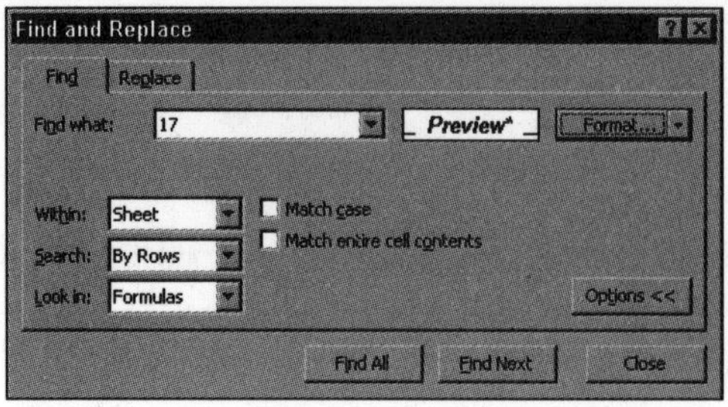

Figure 5-7: Find things with the help of the Find and Replace dialog box.

3. **In the Find What box, enter the characters to search for.**
4. **Click the Find Next button.**

   Excel selects the cell that contains what you're looking for.
5. **If there is more than one occurrence, repeat Step 5 until you find the cell that you're looking for.**
6. **Click the Close button to end.**

The Find and Replace dialog box offers a handful of options for pinpointing items that you are looking for. Clicking the Options button enables you to search for items by using more specific criteria. After you click the button, more search options appear in the dialog box:

- **Search by format:** Click the Format button and describe the format you are looking for in the Find Format dialog box. The dialog box offers ways to search for number formats, alignments, fonts, and even borders and patterns. Another way to describe the format you want is to click the down arrow beside the Format button, click the Choose Format From Cell option, and click a format in your worksheet. (Be sure to click the down arrow beside the Format button and choose Clear Find Format if you want to go back to search for unformatted data.)
- **Search the worksheet or workbook:** Click the Within drop-down arrow and choose Sheet or Workbook from the list.
- **Search by row or column:** For long searches, you can tell Excel to search by row or column by making a choice in the Search drop-down list.
- **Search in formulas, values, or comments:** Specify what to search for in the Look In drop-down list.
- **Search by case:** Click to select the Match Case check box if a case-sensitive search will make the search go faster.
- **Search for all cell contents or partial contents:** Click to select the Match Entire Cell Contents check box if you entered the entire contents of the cell you are looking for in the Find What box.

For approximate searches, use *wildcard characters.* An asterisk represents any group of characters in the specified position, and a question mark represents any single character in the specified position. For example, **w*h** represents all text that begins with *w* and ends with *h*. Similarly, **b?n** matches three-letter words such as *bin, bun,* and *ban*.

Searching and Replacing Data

Sometimes you may need to replace all occurrences of a value or text with something else. Excel makes this task easy to do:

1. **Select the area of the worksheet that you want to search. If you want to search the entire worksheet, just select a single cell (any cell will do).**
2. **Choose Edit⇨Replace or press Ctrl+H.**

   Excel displays the Find and Replace dialog box.
3. **In the Find What box, enter the characters to search for.**
4. **In the Replace With box, enter the characters to replace them.**
5. **Click the Replace All button to have Excel search and replace automatically.**

   If you want to verify each replacement, click the Find Next button. Excel pauses when it finds a match. To replace the found text, click Replace. To skip it and find the next match, click the Find Next button again.
6. **Click the Close button when you're finished.**

Spell Checking

Excel has a spell checker that works just like the feature found in word-processing programs. You can access the spell checker by using any of these methods:

- Choose Tools⇨Spelling.

- Click the Spelling button on the Standard toolbar.
- Press F7.

The extent of the spell checking depends on what was selected when you accessed the dialog box (see Table 5-1).

Table 5-1	How the Spell Checker Works
What Is Selected	*What Gets Checked*
A single cell	The entire worksheet, including cell contents, notes, text in graphic objects and charts, and page headers and footers
A range of cells	Only the selected range
A group of characters	Only those characters in the formula bar

If Excel encounters a word that isn't in the current dictionary or is misspelled, it offers a list of suggestions you can click to replace it with.

Chapter 6: Making Your Work Look Good

In This Chapter

- **Formatting cells and ranges automatically**
- **Formatting cells and ranges the old-fashioned way**
- **Copying formats for cells and ranges**
- **Working with numbers**

After you enter your data (described in Chapter 4) and make your various adjustments (as explained in Chapter 5), you can scoot your chair back and admire your work. But whether you're simply going to view your work on-screen or print a copy of it (see Appendix B for printing help), you may eventually realize that your precious data sure looks boring sitting there in those little cells. Everything appears the same! Why not let yourself get a little creative and make your data more appealing by doing some formatting? Align some text, apply some color, make some backgrounds, change column widths and row heights . . . in brief, let your data express itself. A touch of formatting makes your hard work look really good.

Using AutoFormats

The Excel AutoFormatting feature applies attractive formatting to a table automatically. You hardly have to move a muscle. To use AutoFormats, follow these steps:

1. **Select the range of cells that you want to format.**
2. **Choose Format⇨AutoFormat.**

   The AutoFormat dialog box appears, as shown in Figure 6-1.
3. **Select one of the 17 AutoFormats from the list and click OK.**

   Excel formats the table using the selected AutoFormat.

You can't define your own AutoFormats, but you *can* control the type of formatting that is applied. When you click the Options button in the AutoFormat dialog box, the dialog box expands to show six more options.

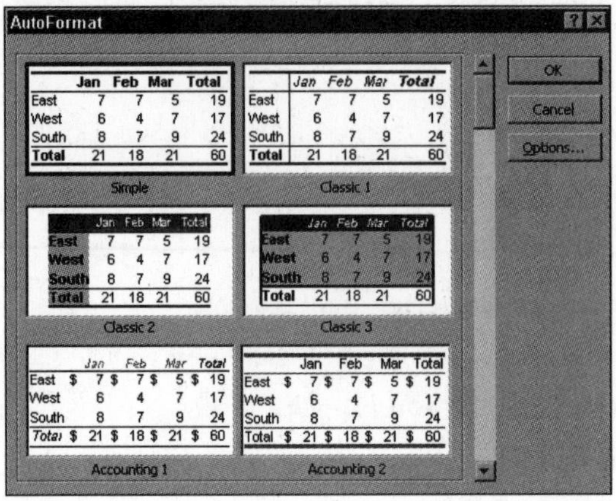

Figure 6-1: Let Excel help you with AutoFormat.

Initially, the six check boxes are all checked, which means that Excel applies formatting from all six categories. If you want it to skip one or more categories, just uncheck the appropriate boxes by clicking in them before you click OK.

Formatting Cells and Ranges to Your Liking

If AutoFormatting is not for you, realize that you have lots of control over the appearance of information that you enter into a cell. Excel provides three ways to format cells:

FAST TRACK

- **Toolbar buttons:** Common formatting commands are available on toolbar buttons on the Formatting toolbar.
- **Shortcut keys:** Some common formats can be applied by pressing shortcut key combinations. For example, Ctrl+B makes the text bold.
- **The Format Cells dialog box:** This tabbed dialog box provides all the cell formatting commands. Click one of the six tabs to access a particular panel in the dialog box.

You can bring up the Format Cells dialog box by choosing Format⇨Cells or by right-clicking the selected cell or range of cells and choosing Format Cells from the shortcut menu.

TIP

You can format cells before or after you enter information. For example, if you're entering a series of numbers, you can *preformat* the cells so the numbers will appear with commas and the desired number of decimal places.

Aligning cell contents

By default, cell contents appear at the bottom, numbers are right-aligned, text is left-aligned, and logical values are centered in cells.

You can apply the most common horizontal alignment options by selecting the cell or range of cells and using the tools on the Formatting toolbar: Align Left, Center, and Align Right. You can use the following procedure to align cell contents:

1. **Select the cell or range of cells to align.**
2. **Choose Format➪Cells (or press Ctrl+1).**
3. **Click the Alignment tab in the Format Cells dialog box (see Figure 6-2).**
4. **Choose the desired horizontal or vertical alignment option from the drop-down lists.**
5. **Click OK.**

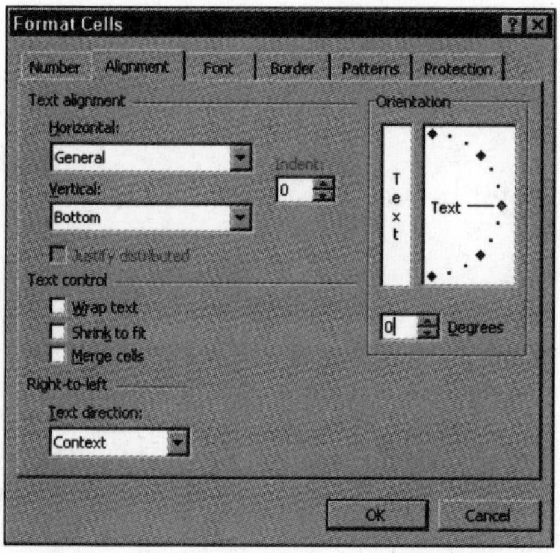

Figure 6-2: Align cells with the Format Cells dialog box.

Applying background colors and patterns

A cell with some background color or a pattern can really stand out. Changing the background color or pattern used in cells is a breeze. To do so, follow these steps:

1. **Select the cell or range that you want to format.**
2. **Choose Format➪Cells (or press Ctrl+1).**

3. **Click the Patterns tab in the Format Cells dialog box.**
4. **Choose a color from the Color box.**
5. **To add a pattern, open the Pattern drop-down box and choose one.**

   If you like, you can choose a second color for the pattern as well.
6. **Click OK to apply the color and/or pattern.**

A faster way to change the background color (but not a pattern) is to select the cells and then select a color from the Fill Color tool on the Formatting toolbar.

Applying colors to text

Perhaps you want certain cells to have important text or numbers in a different color. (Red, for example, just begs to be taken notice of.) The following steps are the fastest way to change the color of text:

1. **Select the cell or range.**

2. **Select a color from the Font Color tool on the Formatting toolbar.**

   If you click the down arrow button on the Font Color tool, it expands to show more colors.

You can also change text color in the Font panel of the Format Cells dialog box, if you aren't in a hurry.

Changing column width

You may want to change the width of a column if it's not wide enough to display values fully (you get a series of pound signs like this ####### if your cell entry is too long — and who wants to look at that?). Or you may simply want to space out the cells horizontally. Before changing the width, you can select a number of columns so that the selected columns will all have the same width.

Use any of these methods to change the width of selected columns.

- Choose Format➪Column➪Width and enter a value in the Column Width dialog box.
- Drag the right border of the column heading with the mouse until the column is the desired width.

- Choose Format➪Column➪AutoFit Selection. This adjusts the width of the selected column(s) so that the widest entry in the column fits.

- Right-click a column label and choose Column Width. Then, in the Column Width dialog box, enter a measurement and click OK.
- Double-click the right border of a column heading to automatically set the column width to the widest entry in the column.

To change the default width of all columns, choose Format⇨Column⇨Standard Width. This displays a dialog box into which you enter the new default column width. All columns that haven't been previously adjusted take on the new column width.

Changing row height

Row height is measured in *points* (a standard unit of measurement in the printing trade; 72 points equal one inch). Changing the row height is useful for spacing out rows; it's better to change the row height than to insert empty rows between rows of data. To change the row height of several rows, you can select them before using the following techniques to set row height:

- Drag the lower row border with the mouse until the row is the desired height.
- Choose Format⇨Row⇨Height and enter a value (in points) in the Row Height dialog box.
- Double-click the bottom border of a row to automatically set the row height to the tallest entry in the row. You can also choose Format⇨Row⇨AutoFit for this.

Changing text direction

Normally, the contents of a cell are displayed horizontally. How traditional! In some cases, you may want to display the text vertically or at an angle for a special effect — or to make it hard for your boss to figure out just where you messed up on last year's sales records.

1. **Select the cell or range to modify.**
2. **Choose Format⇨Cells (or press Ctrl+1).**
3. **Click the Alignment tab in the Format Cells dialog box.**
4. **In the Orientation section, adjust the angle by dragging the gauge or specifying an angle (in degrees).**
5. **Click OK to apply the formatting to the selection.**

	1999	1st Qtr	2nd Qtr	3rd Qtr	4th Qtr	2000	1st Qtr	2nd Qtr	3rd Qtr	4th Qtr
Rod		9	78	43	14		4	78	43	16
Todd		12	34	131	78		12	16	89	98
Maud		14	34	441	53		10	44	23	53

Changing fonts and text sizes

The easiest way to change the font or text size for selected cells is to use the Font and Font Size tools on the Formatting toolbar. Just select the cells, click the appropriate tool, and select the font or size from the drop-down list.

You can also use the following technique, which lets you control several other properties of the font from a single dialog box:

1. **Select the cell or range to modify.**
2. **Choose Format⇨Cells (or press Ctrl+1).**
3. **Click the Font tab in the Format Cells dialog box (see Figure 6-3).**
4. **Make the desired changes and click OK.**

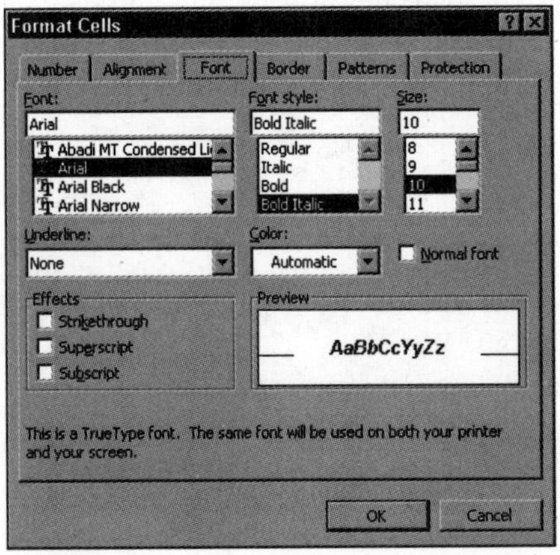

Figure 6-3: The Format Cells dialog box will help get your work looking nice.

Bold, italic, underline, and strikethrough

The easiest way to bold, italicize, underline, or strikethrough text is to select the cell or range and then click the appropriate tool on the Formatting toolbar (for Bold, Italic, or Underline).

Or you can use the shortcut keys shown in Table 6-1 to modify the selected cells.

Table 6-1	**Modifying Text in Cells**	
Format	***Shortcut Key***	***Toolbar Equivalent***
Bold	Ctrl+B	
Italic	Ctrl+I	
Underline	Ctrl+U	
~~Strikethrough~~	Ctrl+5	

These toolbar buttons and shortcut keys act as a toggle. For example, you can turn bold on and off by repeatedly pressing Ctrl+B (or clicking the Bold button).

Indenting the contents of a cell

Excel enables you to indent text in a cell. Using this feature is much easier than padding the cell with spaces to indent. Figure 6-4 shows six cells that are indented. To indent the contents of a cell, follow these steps:

1. **Select the cell or range of cells to indent.**
2. **Choose Format⇨Cells (or press Ctrl+1).**
3. **Click the Alignment tab in the Format Cells dialog box.**
4. **Specify the number of spaces to indent in the Indent text box.**
5. **Click OK.**

Indented text is always left-aligned.

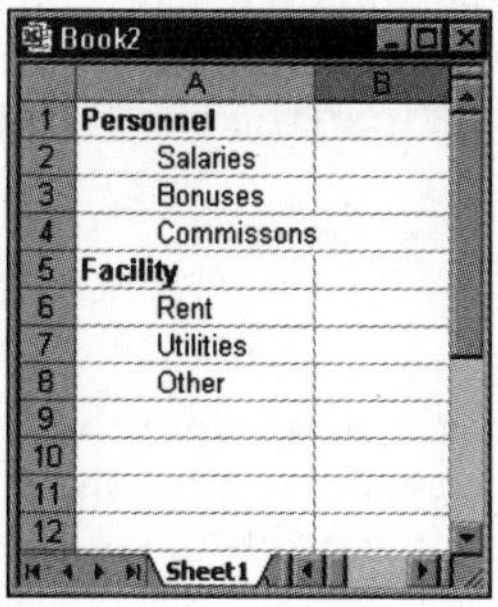

Figure 6-4: Indenting can make your text look more organized.

Merging cells

Excel offers a helpful feature that enables you to merge cells into a single, larger cell. This feature lets you have cells of unequal sizes. For example, if you have a table that spans six columns, you can merge six cells at the top to form a single larger cell for the table's title. In Figure 6-5, cells C4:E4 are merged horizontally, and cells A6:A9 are merged vertically. To merge a range of cells, follow these steps:

1. **Select the cells to be merged.**
2. **Choose Format⇨Cells (or press Ctrl+1).**
3. **Click the Alignment tab.**
4. **Click to select the Merge Cells check box.**
5. **Click OK.**

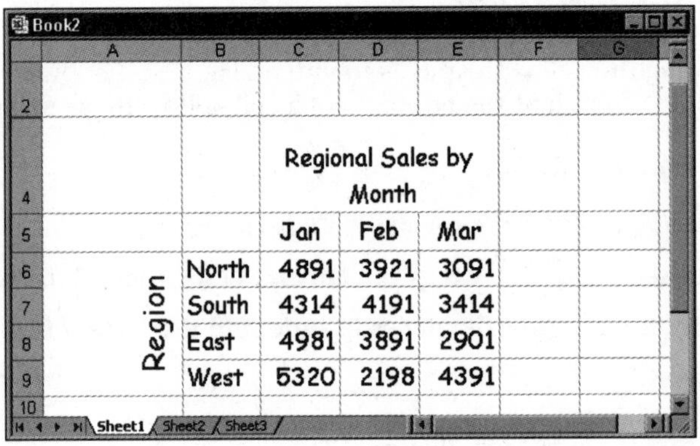

Book2
A
B
C
D
E
F
G
Regional Sales by Month
Jan Feb Mar
North 4891 3921 3091
South 4314 4191 3414
East 4981 3891 2901
West 5320 2198 4391
Region
Sheet1
Sheet2
Sheet3

Figure 6-5: Caution! Merging cells.

You can also merge cells by using the Merge and Center button on the Formatting toolbar. But the only way to "unmerge" cells is to use the Format Cells dialog box and remove the check mark from the Merge Cells check box.

Copying Formats

FAST TRACK

Instead of redoing all your formats every time you want other cells or ranges to have similar formats, you can copy formats the quick way — by clicking the Format Painter button on the Standard toolbar.

1. **Select the cell or range that has the formatting attributes that you want to copy.**

2. **Click the Format Painter button.**

   Notice that the mouse pointer appears as a miniature paintbrush.

3. **Select (paint) the cells to which you want to apply the formats.**
4. **Release the mouse button.**

   Excel copies the formats.

Double-clicking the Format Painter button causes the mouse pointer to remain a paintbrush after you release the mouse button. This lets you paint other areas of the worksheet with the same formats. To exit paint mode, click the Format Painter button again (or press Esc).

Formatting Numbers

Excel is smart enough to perform some number formatting for you automatically. For example, if you type **9.6%** into a cell, Excel knows that you want to use a percentage format and applies it for you automatically. Similarly, if you use commas to separate thousands (such as **123,456**), or a dollar sign to indicate currency (such as **$123.45**), Excel applies appropriate formatting for you.

Use the Formatting toolbar to quickly apply common number formats. When you click one of these buttons, the active cell takes on the specified number format. Table 6-2 lists these toolbar buttons.

Table 6-2 Number Formats

Button	*Button Name*	*Formatting Applied*
$	Currency Style	Adds a dollar sign to the left, separates thousands with a comma, and displays the value with two digits to the right of the decimal point
%	Percent Style	Displays the value as a percentage with no decimal places
,	Comma Style	Separates thousands with a comma and displays the value with two digits to the right of the decimal place
+.0 .00	Increase Decimal	Increases the number of digits to the right of the decimal point by one
.00 +.0	Decrease Decimal	Decreases the number of digits to the right of the decimal point by one

These five toolbar buttons actually apply predefined *styles* to the selected cells. This is not the same as simply changing the number format.

If none of the predefined number formats fits the bill, you need to use the Format Cells dialog box. To do so, follow these steps:

1. **Select the cell or range that contains the values to format.**
2. **Choose Format⇨Cells (or press Ctrl+1).**
3. **Click the Number tab.**
4. **Select one of the 12 categories of number formats.**

   When you select a category from the list box, the right side of the panel changes to display appropriate options.
5. **Select an option from the right side of the dialog box.**

   Options vary, depending on your category choice. The top of the panel displays a sample of how the active cell will appear with the selected number format.
6. **After you make your choices, click OK to apply the number format to all the selected cells.**

Chapter 7: Selecting, Copying, and Moving Your Data

In This Chapter

- Selecting cells and ranges
- Copying cells and ranges
- Moving cells and ranges

Unless you type 500 words per minute without mistake, one of the biggest time-savers you need to know is how to copy some data from one place to another, whether it be between places in the same worksheet, between worksheets in the same workbook, or even between worksheets of different workbooks. And if you can copy, you can also move data between places. No more retyping! What a breakthrough in spreadsheet management!

The key to copying and moving data, however, is knowing how to select data. This chapter gives you the lowdown on all these actions. You won't regret opening to this page.

Selecting Cells and Ranges

In Excel, you normally select a cell or range before performing an operation that works with the cell or range. This section describes how to make various types of cell and range selections.

Selecting a cell

To select a cell (and make it the active cell), use any of the following techniques:

- Move the cell pointer to the cell using the arrow keys.
- Click the cell with the mouse.
- Choose Edit⇨Go To (or press F5 or Ctrl+G), enter the cell address in the Reference box, and click OK.

The selected cell has a dark border around it, and its address appears in the Name box.

Selecting entire rows and columns

You can select entire rows or columns in several ways:

- ✦ Click the row or column heading to select a single row or column.
- ✦ To select multiple adjacent rows or columns, simply click a row or column heading and drag to highlight additional rows or columns.
- ✦ To select multiple (nonadjacent) rows or columns, press Ctrl while you click the row or column headings that you want.
- ✦ Press Ctrl+spacebar to select the column of the active cell or the columns of the selected cells.
- ✦ Press Shift+spacebar to select the row of the active cell or the rows of the selected cells.
- ✦ Click the Select All button (or Ctrl+Shift+spacebar) to select all rows. Selecting all rows is the same as selecting all columns, which is the same as selecting all cells.

Selecting a range

You can select a range in several ways:

- ✦ Click the mouse in a cell and drag to highlight the range. If you drag to the end of the screen, the worksheet scrolls.
- ✦ Move to the first cell of the range. Press F8 and then move the cell pointer with the direction keys to highlight the range. Press F8 again to return the direction keys to normal movement.
- ✦ Press the Shift key while you use the arrow keys to select a range.
- ✦ Choose Edit➪Go To (or press F5), enter a range's address in the Reference box, and click OK.

When you select a range in Excel, Excel shows the range in the See-Through View. Instead of appearing in reversed video like older versions of Excel, the cells appear as if behind a transparent colored shade. This transparent selection makes it easier to see the true colors and formatting underneath the selection.

Selecting noncontiguous ranges

Most of the time, the ranges that you select will be *contiguous* — a single rectangle of cells. Excel also lets you work with noncontiguous ranges, which consist of two or more ranges (or single cells), not necessarily next to each other (also known as a *multiple selection*), as shown in Figure 7-1.

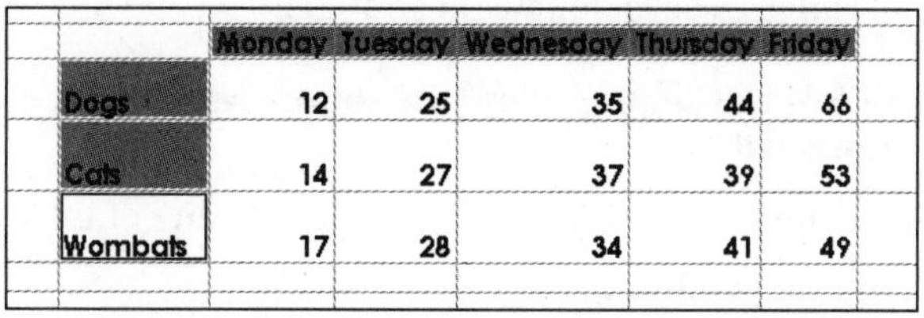

	Monday	Tuesday	Wednesday	Thursday	Friday
Dogs	12	25	35	44	66
Cats	14	27	37	39	53
Wombats	17	28	34	41	49

Figure 7-1: You can select noncontiguous ranges if necessary.

If you want to apply the same formatting to cells in different areas of your worksheet, one approach is to make a multiple selection. After you select the appropriate cells or ranges, Excel applies the formatting that you choose to all the selected cells. You can select a noncontiguous range in several ways:

- ✦ Hold down Ctrl while you click the mouse and drag to highlight the individual cells or ranges.
- ✦ From the keyboard, select a range by pressing F8 and then use the arrow keys. After selecting the first range, press Shift+F8, move the cell pointer, and press F8 to start selecting another range.
- ✦ Choose Edit⇨Go To (or press F5 or Ctrl+G) and enter a range's address in the Reference box. Separate the different ranges with a comma. Click OK, and Excel selects the cells in the ranges that you specified.

Copying Cells and Ranges

Copying cells is a very common spreadsheet operation, and several types of copying are allowed. You can do any of the following:

- ✦ Copy one cell to another cell.
- ✦ Copy a cell to a range of cells. The source cell is copied to every cell in the destination range.
- ✦ Copy a range to another range.

Excel uses the new Office Clipboard, which can store up to 24 data items at one time. That means you can keep 24 items on hand and copy them into a worksheet at will.

Copying a cell normally copies the cell contents, its cell comment (if any), and the formatting applied to the original cell. When you copy a cell that contains a formula, the cell references in the copied formulas are changed automatically to be relative to their new location. See Chapter 8 for help with formulas.

To copy a cell range of cells, follow these steps:

1. **Select the cell or range to copy (the source range) and copy it to the Office Clipboard.**

   To copy the item to the Clipboard, you can do any of the following:

   - Click the Copy button
   - Choose Edit⇨Copy
   - Press Ctrl+C
   - Right-click and choose Copy

2. **Move the cell pointer to the range that will hold the copy (the destination range).**
3. **Paste the cells.**

   To paste items from the Clipboard:

   - **Choose a standard Paste command:** With this technique, you paste in the last item you copied or moved to the Clipboard: Click the Paste button, choose Edit⇨Paste, press Ctrl+V, or right-click and choose Paste.
   - **Paste an item from the Office Clipboard:** Choose Edit⇨Office Clipboard. The Clipboard task pane opens (see Figure 7-2). Find the item you want to paste and either click it or open its drop-down list and choose Paste.

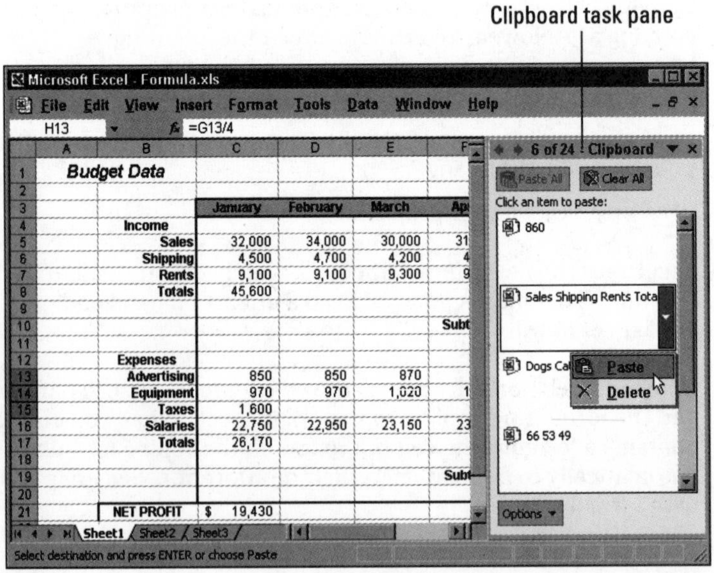

Figure 7-2: Pasting an item from the Office Clipboard.

Copying a cell to another cell or a range

To copy the contents of one cell to a range of cells, follow these steps:

1. **Move the cell pointer to the cell to copy.**

2. **Click the Copy button on the Standard toolbar (you can also press Ctrl+C or choose Edit⇨Copy).**
3. **Select the cell that you want to hold the copy.**
4. **Press Enter.**

If the range that you're copying to is adjacent to the cell that you're copying from, you can drag the cell's AutoFill handle to copy it to the adjacent range. (The AutoFill handle is that little black square in the lower right of a cell.)

Copying a range to another range

If you can copy and paste a cell's contents, why not an entire range? To copy the contents of one range to another range of the same size, follow these steps:

1. **Select the range to copy.**

2. **Click the Copy button on the Standard toolbar (you can also press Ctrl+C or choose Edit⇨Copy).**
3. **Select the upper-left cell of the range that you want to hold the copy.**
4. **Press Enter.**

Copying data to another worksheet or workbook

Someday you may want to copy something to another worksheet or even to another workbook. The routine may seem somewhat familiar to you if you've already copied data within the same worksheet.

1. **Select the cell or range to copy.**

2. **Click the Copy button on the Standard toolbar (you can also press Ctrl+C or choose Edit⇨Copy).**
3. **Click the tab of the worksheet that you're copying to.**

   If the worksheet is in a different workbook, activate that workbook (you can select the workbook from the Window menu) and then click the tab of the worksheet that you want to hold the copied data.

4. **Select the upper-left cell of the range that you want to hold the copy.**
5. **Press Enter.**

Paste options for handling data you copied or moved

After you paste data in a new location, the Paste Options button appears. Click the button and you see a drop-down list with options for formatting the cells you have copied to the new location (which options appear on the list depends on what you copied or moved). By choosing an option on the drop-down list, you spare yourself the trouble of having to format the copied or moved data.

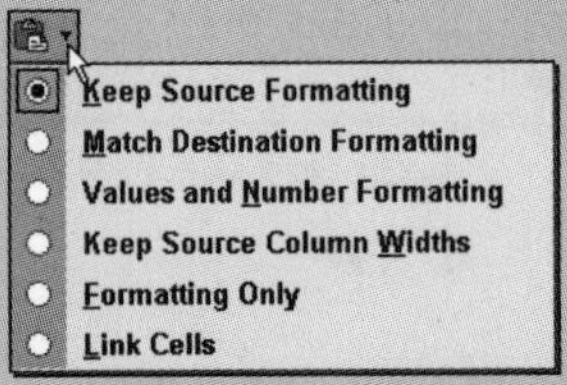

Moving Cells and Ranges

Moving the data in a cell or a range is common. For example, you may need to relocate a range of data to make room for something else. Or you just may have plunked down some data in the wrong place. It happens. Moving works on the same principle as copying (explained earlier in this chapter).

Moving data to a new location in the same worksheet

To move a cell or range, follow these steps:

1. **Select the cell or range to move.**

2. **Choose Edit⇨Cut. (You can also press Ctrl+X, click the Cut button on the Standard toolbar, or right-click and choose Cut from the shortcut menu.)**
3. **Move the cell pointer to the range that you want to hold the copy (you need only select the upper-left cell).**
4. **Press Enter.**

If the range that you're moving contains formulas that refer to other cells, the references continue to refer to the original cells. You almost always want references to continue to refer to the original cells.

Copying or moving by dragging

If the location that you're copying or moving to isn't too far away (and you want to conserve precious seconds or maybe just impress onlookers), you can drag data from place to place.

1. **Select the cell or range to copy.**
2. **Hold down the Ctrl key if you want to copy data. Don't hold down anything if you want to move data.**
3. **Move the mouse pointer to any of the selection's borders.**

   The mouse pointer turns into an arrow accompanied by a small plus sign (+) if you are copying. If you are moving, the mouse pointer turns into an arrow without anything.
4. **Drag the mouse to the location where you want to copy or move the cell or range.**

   Make sure that you place the cell correctly in the upper-left corner of the cell block you selected.
5. **Release the mouse button.**

   Your data is either copied or moved as if by magic.

Remember that the key (literally!) to copying or moving by dragging is the Ctrl key.

When you move data, make sure that there are enough blank cells to hold it. Excel overwrites existing data without warning.

If you change your mind after Step 2, press Esc to cancel the operation. If you change your mind after you've already moved the data, choose Edit⇨Undo Paste or press Ctrl+Z.

Moving data to a different worksheet or workbook

If you want to move the contents of a cell or range to a different worksheet or to a different workbook, follow these steps:

1. **Select the cell or range to move.**
2. **Choose Edit⇨Cut. (You can also press Ctrl+X, click the Cut button on the Standard toolbar, or right-click and choose Cut from the shortcut menu.)**
3. **Activate the worksheet that you're moving to. If you're moving the selection to a different workbook, activate that workbook and then activate the worksheet.**

4. **Move the cell pointer to the range that you want to hold the copy (you need only select the upper-left cell).**
5. **Press Enter.**

When you move data, make sure that there are enough blank cells to hold it. Excel overwrites existing data without warning.

If you change your mind after Step 2, press Esc to cancel the operation. If you change your mind after the data has already been moved, choose Edit⇨Undo Paste or press Ctrl+Z.

Chapter 8: Using Formulas and Functions

In This Chapter

- Creating your own formulas
- Discovering your formula errors
- Making absolute and relative cell references
- Entering functions

You haven't chosen to work in Excel just to type your diary into neat little cells or to conduct your business correspondence (and if you have, jump right back to the section of this book covering Word). You're certainly working in Excel in order to manipulate your data — adding, subtracting, multiplying, finding standard deviations (whatever those are), and the like. This chapter introduces you to the wonderful world of formulas — as well as to the Excel built-in functions that you can use to assist you in formula construction and to make your formulas perform some additional calculations.

Using Formulas

You use formulas to perform all sorts of calculations on the data that you enter. When you enter a formula into a cell, the cell displays the result of the formula. You see the formula itself in the formula bar when the cell is activated.

Table 8-1 provides a list of operators that you can use in formulas.

Table 8-1 Formula Operators

Operator	*Name*
+	Addition
–	Subtraction
*	Multiplication
/	Division
^	Exponentiation (raised to a power)

(continued)

Table 8-1 (continued)

Operator	*Name*
&	Concatenation (joins text)
=	Logical comparison (equal to)
>	Logical comparison (greater than)
<	Logical comparison (less than)

Operator precedence is the set of rules that Excel uses to perform its calculations in a formula. Table 8-2 lists the Excel operator precedence. This table shows that exponentiation has the highest precedence (that is, it's performed first), and logical comparisons have the lowest precedence. If two operators have the same precedence, Excel performs the calculations from left to right.

REMEMBER

You can override operator precedence by using parentheses in your formulas.

Table 8-2 Operator Precedence

Symbol	*Operator*	*Precedence*
^	Exponentiation	1
*	Multiplication	2
/	Division	2
+	Addition	3
–	Subtraction	3
&	Concatenation	4
=	Equal to	5
>	Greater than	5
<	Less than	5

Creating a formula is a snap — as long as you remember to begin every formula with an equal sign (=). For example, suppose that you have a column of numbers that you want to add (see Figure 8-1). Cell B4 seems like a good spot to place your total, right? So just follow these steps:

1. **Select the cell where you want to place your formula's results (in this case, cell B4).**
2. **Type your formula:** =B1+B2+B3.
3. **Press Enter.**

   Your formula disappears from the cell, and the result appears in the cell that you selected. Your formula (if you reselect that cell) appears in the formula bar.

Note: Don't worry about having to redo a formula if you make a change in the data. Excel automatically recalculates the results for you. Now that's service!

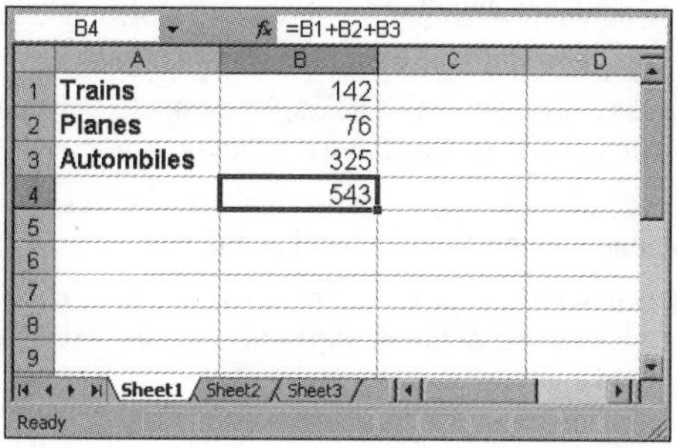

Figure 8-1: Let Excel do your calculations for you.

If you think that creating a formula is easy, the process gets even easier when you discover how to use functions, which are ready-made formulas. (You can read about functions later in this chapter.)

Identifying Formula Errors

Excel flags errors in formulas with a message that begins with a pound sign (#). The message part itself is in all capital letters so that you don't miss it. This occurrence signals that the formula is returning an error value. You have to correct the formula (or correct a cell that is referenced by the formula) to get rid of the error display.

If the entire cell is filled with pound signs, the column isn't wide enough to display the value. Check out Chapter 6 for info on how to widen a column.

Table 8-3 lists the types of error values that may appear in a cell that has a formula.

Table 8-3 Types of Error Values

Error Value	*Explanation*
#DIV/0!	The formula is trying to divide by zero (an operation that's not allowed on this planet). This also occurs when the formula attempts to divide by an empty cell.
#NAME?	The formula uses a name that Excel doesn't recognize. This can happen if you delete a name that's used in the formula or if you have unmatched quotes when using text.

(continued)

Table 8-3 *(continued)*

Error Value	*Explanation*
#N/A	The formula is referring (directly or indirectly) to a cell that uses the NA functions to signal the fact that data is not available.
#NULL!	The formula uses an intersection of two ranges that don't intersect.
#NUM!	There is a problem with a value; for example, you specified a negative number where a positive number is expected.
#REF!	The formula refers to a cell that isn't valid. This can happen if the cell has been deleted from the worksheet.
#VALUE!	The formula has a function with an invalid argument, or the formula uses an operand of the wrong type (such as text where a value is expected).

Using Absolute, Relative, and Mixed References

An *absolute reference* uses two dollar signs in its address: one for the column part and one for the row part. When you copy a formula that has an absolute reference, the reference is not adjusted in the copied cell.

Relative references, on the other hand, are adjusted when the formula is copied.

Excel also allows mixed references in which only one of the address's parts is absolute. Table 8-4 summarizes all of the possible types of cell references.

Table 8-4 Cell References

Example	*Type*
A1	Relative reference
A1	Absolute reference
$A1	Mixed reference (column part is absolute)
A$1	Mixed reference (row part is absolute)

To change the type of cell reference in a formula, follow these steps:

1. **Double-click the cell (or press F2) to get into edit mode.**
2. **In the formula bar, click any part of the cell reference.**
3. **Press F4 repeatedly to cycle through all possible cell reference types. Stop when the cell reference displays the proper type.**

Using Functions in Your Formulas

Excel provides more than 300 built-in functions that can make your formulas perform powerful feats and save you a great deal of time.

Functions do the following:

- Simplify your formulas
- Allow formulas to perform calculations that are otherwise impossible
- Allow "conditional" execution of formulas — giving them some rudimentary decision-making capability

Table 8-5 shows you a list of some of the most common functions. Why not all? Remember that Excel has more than 300 ready-made functions for all purposes, from math to engineering, from financial to statistical (and more). Take a look at the Help files in Excel for an explanation of all the functions. (Did you know that COSH returns the hyperbolic cosine of a number? Most humans don't need to do that, whatever it is — but someone somewhere is very happy that Excel can handle hyperbolic cosines!)

Table 8-5 Common Functions in Excel

Function	*Action*
SUM	The sum of the values
COUNT	The number of items
AVERAGE	The average of the values
MAX	The largest value
MIN	The smallest value
PRODUCT	The product of the values
STDDEV	An estimate of the standard deviation of a population, where the sample is all the data to be summarized
STDDEVP	The standard deviation of a population, where the population is all the data to be summarized
VAR	An estimate of the variance of a population, where the sample is all the data to be summarized
VARP	The variance of a population, where the population is all the data to be summarized

Entering functions manually

If you're familiar with the function that you want to use, you may choose to type the function and its arguments into your formula. Often this is the most efficient method. A function is composed of three elements:

✦ The equal sign (=) to indicate that what follows is a formula

✦ The function name, such as SUM or AVERAGE, which indicates what operation is to be performed

✦ The *argument*, which indicates the cell addresses of the data that the function will act on — you can indicate the range of a row or column by inserting a colon (:) between the starting and ending cell addresses, such as A1:A70

If you glance at the section, "Using Formulas," earlier in this chapter, you can see the simple formula:

=B1+B2+B3

You can more easily express this as a function by typing:

=SUM(B1:B3)

When you enter a function, Excel always converts it to uppercase. It's a good idea to use lowercase when entering functions: If Excel doesn't convert it to uppercase, it means that it doesn't recognize your entry as a function (you probably spelled it incorrectly).

Modifying a range reference used in a function

When you edit a cell that contains a formula, Excel color-codes the references in the formula and places an outline around each cell or range referenced in the formula. The color of the outline corresponds to the color displayed in the formula. Each outlined cell or range also contains a fill handle (a small square in the lower-left corner), as shown in Figure 8-2.

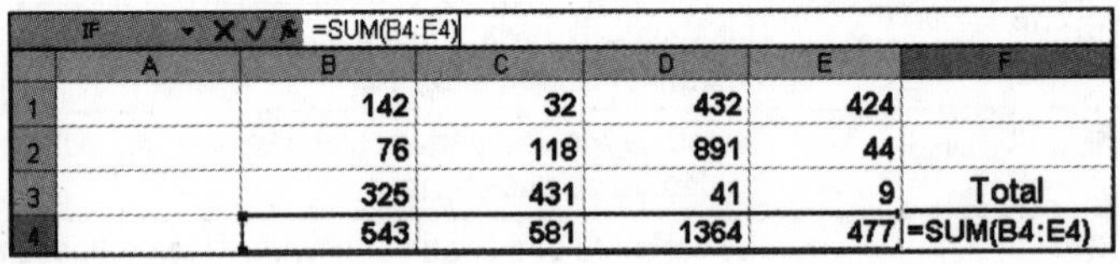

Figure 8-2:
Just imagine the pretty colors you can see when you edit a cell with a formula!

	A	B	C	D	E	F
			IF ▾ ✗ ✓ ƒ⨯ =SUM(B4:E4)			
1		142	32	432	424	
2		76	118	891	44	
3		325	431	41	9	Total
4		543	581	1364	477	=SUM(B4:E4)

REAL WORLD

Editing formulas and functions

If you make a typo when entering a formula or a function, you can edit your entry just like editing any other entry in Excel.

1. **Select the cell that contains your formula or function.**
2. **Click in the Formula bar and use the left or right arrow key to move your insertion point.**
3. **Use the Delete or Backspace keys to delete characters. You can also block text by dragging through it and then replacing the selected characters by simply typing in a new entry.**
4. **Press Enter when you're satisfied that you got it right this time.**

If you're in a big hurry to edit that cell, double-click the cell. The insertion point appears inside the cell, and you can undo your damage from there, saving a long trip up to the Formula bar.

If your formula contains a function that uses a range argument, you can easily modify the range reference by following these steps:

1. **Press F2 or double-click the cell to begin editing the formula.**
2. **Locate the range that the function uses (the range is outlined).**
3. **Drag the fill handle to extend or contract the range. Or, you can click a border of the outlined range and move the outline to a new range.**

   In either case, Excel changes the range reference in the formula.

4. **Press Enter.**

Using the Formula Palette

The Formula Palette makes it easy to enter a function and its arguments. Using this tool ensures that the function is spelled correctly and has the proper number of arguments in the correct order.

To enter a function using the Formula Palette, select the cell that will contain the function and then use either of these two methods:

fx

- Choose Insert⇨Function or click the Insert Function button. Then select a function in the Paste Function dialog box (see Figure 8-3).
- Enter an equals sign (=) in the Formula bar. When you do so, a drop-down list of functions appears where the Cell Name box used to be. Open the drop-down list and choose a function (see Figure 8-3).

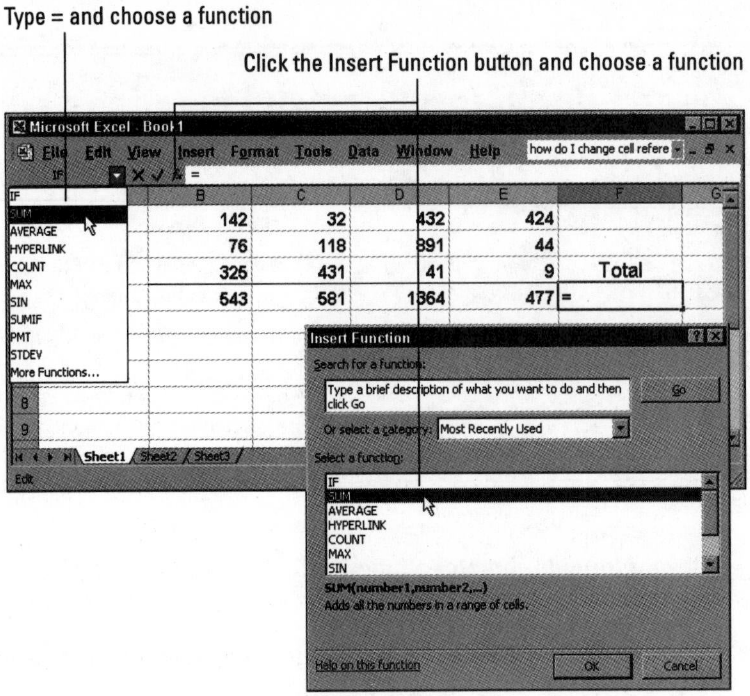

Figure 8-3: The two ways to choose a function.

After you choose a function, you see the Function Arguments dialog box (see Figure 8-4). The dialog box prompts you for each argument of the function you selected. You can enter the addresses of the arguments manually or, if the arguments are cell references, drag across them in the worksheet. The Function Arguments dialog box displays the result. When you've specified all of the required arguments, click OK.

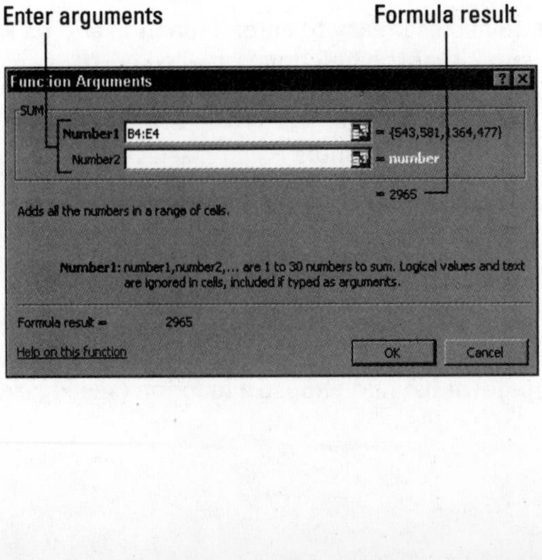

Figure 8-4: Entering arguments for a function.

Using templates to make your life easier

A *template* is a workbook that's all set up with formulas and ready for you to enter data. Lucky for you, Excel comes with templates for workbooks. To create a workbook from a template, follow these steps:

1. **Choose File⇨New to open the New Workbook task pane.**
2. **Under New from Template, click the General Templates link.**

   You see the Templates dialog box.
3. **Click the Spreadsheet Solutions tab.**
4. **Select the template that you want.**
5. **Click OK to open a copy of the template.**

If you can't find a ready-made template for what you want to do, you can simply create your own. You may be surprised how easy it is! To do so, follow these steps:

1. **Create a workbook to your liking to serve as a template for your future work.**
2. **With your workbook open, choose File⇨Save As.**
3. **In the Save As dialog box that appears, select Template from the Save As Type drop-down list.**
4. **Save the template in your Templates folder (or a subfolder within the Templates folder).**

You can insert a function into an existing formula. In the Formula bar, move the cursor to the location where you want to insert the function and then either click the Insert Function button or choose a function from the function list to open the Function Arguments dialog box.

Chapter 9: Managing and Analyzing Your Data

In This Chapter

- ✔ **Filtering and sorting lists of data**
- ✔ **Making a formula return a desired value**
- ✔ **Performing what-if analysis**

You can stare at your data for hours on end and still gain nothing for your time. Spreadsheet data is often not much good unless you can analyze it. If you're familiar with some of the actions that you can perform on a database, managing and analyzing your data in Excel is within your grasp. And even if you've never heard of a database, you can still filter and sort lists to your heart's content.

Besides filtering and sorting actions, you can also use this chapter to discover how to observe effects on formulas when you change input values.

If you enjoy this sort of stuff — and who doesn't? — get started on this chapter without delay.

Filtering and Sorting Lists

You can store information of just about any type in a *list.* If you're familiar with the concept of a *database table,* you'll recognize that a list has many similarities:

- ✦ Columns correspond to fields.
- ✦ Rows correspond to records.
- ✦ The first row of the table should have field names that describe the data in each column.

Applying database functions with lists

To create a formula that returns results based on filtered criteria, use the Excel database worksheet functions. For example, you can create a formula that calculates the sum of values in a list that meet certain criteria. Set up a criteria range in your worksheet and then enter a formula such as the following:

```
=DSUM(ListRange,FieldName,Criteria)
```

In this case, *ListRange* refers to the list, *FieldName* refers to the field name cell of the column being summed, and *Criteria* refers to the criteria range.

Table 9-1 describes the database functions.

Table 9-1 Excel Database Functions

Function	*Description*
DAVERAGE	Returns the average of selected database entries
DCOUNT	Counts the cells containing numbers from a specified database and criteria
DCOUNTA	Counts nonblank cells from a specified database and criteria
DGET	Extracts from a database a single record that matches the specified criteria
DMAX	Returns the maximum value from selected database entries
DMIN	Returns the minimum value from selected database entries
DPRODUCT	Multiplies the values in a particular field of records that match the criteria in a database
DSTDEV	Estimates the standard deviation based on a sample of selected database entries
DSTDEVP	Calculates the standard deviation based on the entire population of selected database entries
DSUM	Adds the numbers in the field column of records in the database that match the criteria
DVAR	Estimates variance based on a sample from selected database entries
DVARP	Calculates variance based on the entire population of selected database entries

Table 9-2 features some examples of text criteria:

Table 9-2 Text Criteria

Criteria	*Effect*
>K	Text that begins with L through Z
<>C	All text, except text that begins with C
January	Text that matches January
Sm*	Text that begins with sm

Criteria	*Effect*
s*s	Text that begins with s and ends with s (the * is a wildcard)
s?s	Three-letter text that begins with s and ends with s (the ? is a wildcard)

The text comparisons are not case-sensitive. For example, si* matches *Simon* as well as *sick*.

Computed criteria filters the list based on one or more calculations and does not use a field header from the list (it uses a new field header). Computed criteria essentially computes a new field for the list so that you must supply new field names in the first row of the criteria range.

Computed criteria is a logical formula (returns True or False) that refers to cells in the first row of data in the list; it does *not* refer to the header row.

Filtering a list with autofiltering

Autofiltering lets you view only certain rows in your list by hiding rows that do not qualify based on criteria you set. To autofilter a list, follow these steps:

1. **Move the cell pointer anywhere within the list.**
2. **Choose Data⇨Filter⇨AutoFilter.**

   Excel analyzes your list and then adds drop-down arrows to the field names in the header row, as shown in Figure 9-1.

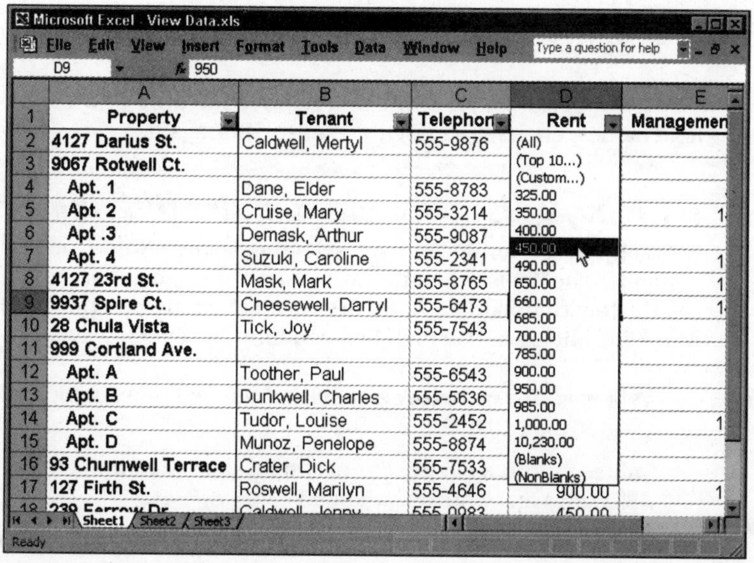

Figure 9-1: Autofiltering can hide unqualified rows for your convenience.

3. **Click the arrow on one of these drop-down lists.**

   The list expands to show the unique items in that column.

4. **Select an item.**

   Excel hides all rows except those that include the selected item. In other words, the list is filtered by the item that you selected.

After you filter the list, the status bar displays a message that tells you how many rows qualified. In addition, the drop-down arrow changes color to remind you that the list is filtered by a value in that column.

Each drop-down list includes five other items:

- **All:** Displays all items in the column. Use this to remove filtering for a column.
- **Top 10:** Filters to display the "top 10" items in the list. Actually, you can display any number of the top (or bottom) values.
- **Custom:** Lets you filter the list by multiple items (see the next section in this chapter).
- **Blanks:** Filters the list by showing only rows that contain blanks in this column.
- **NonBlanks:** Filters the list by showing only rows that contain nonblanks in this column.

TIP

The Blanks and NonBlanks options only appear if the list contains at least one blank field.

To display the entire list again, choose Data⇨Filter⇨Show All.

To get out of AutoFilter mode and remove the drop-down arrows from the field names, choose Data⇨Filter⇨AutoFilter again.

Filtering a list with custom autofiltering

Normally, autofiltering involves selecting a single value for one or more columns. The list is then filtered by that value. For more flexibility, choose the Custom option in an AutoFilter drop-down list to open the Custom AutoFilter dialog box, which lets you filter in several ways (see Figure 9-2):

- **Values above or below a specified value:** For example, sales amounts greater than 10,000.
- **Values within a range:** For example, sales amounts greater than 10,000 AND sales amounts less than 50,000.

✦ **Values outside of a range:** For example, sales amounts less than 10,000 or sales amounts greater than 50,000.

✦ **Two discrete values:** For example, state equal to New York OR state equal to New Jersey.

✦ **Approximate matches:** You can use the * and ? wildcards to filter in many other ways. For example, to display only those customers whose last name begins with a B, use **B***.

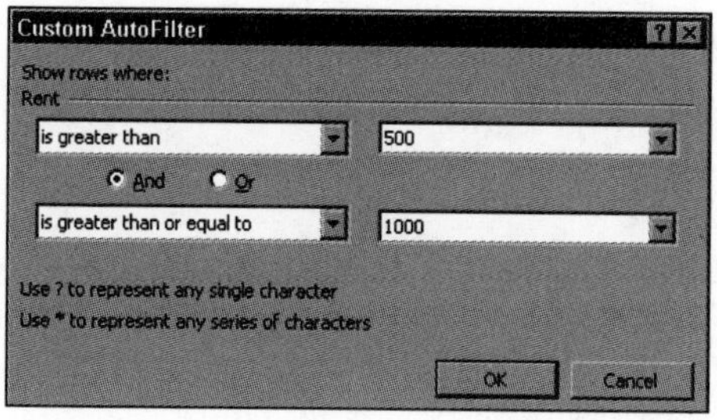

Figure 9-2: Use the Custom AutoFilter to customize your filtering.

Custom autofiltering is useful, but it has limitations. For example, if you want to filter the list to show only three values in a field (such as New York or New Jersey or Connecticut), you can't do it by using autofiltering. Such filtering tasks require the advanced filtering feature. Better read on.

Performing Advanced Filtering

Before you can use the advanced filtering feature, you must set up a *criteria range* — a range on a worksheet that holds the information Excel uses to filter the list. The criteria range must conform to the following specifications:

✦ The criteria range consists of at least two rows.

✦ The first row contains some or all of the field names from the list.

✦ The other rows consist of filtering criteria.

If you use more than one row below the field names in the criteria range, the criteria in each row are joined with an OR operator.

The entries that you make in a criteria range can be either of the following:

✦ Text or value criteria: The filtering involves comparisons to a value or text, using operators such as equal (=), greater than (>), not equal to (<>), and so on.

✦ Computed criteria: The filtering involves some sort of computation.

Advanced filtering is more flexible than autofiltering, but it takes some up-front work to use it. Advanced filtering provides you with the following capabilities:

- ✦ You can specify more complex filtering criteria.
- ✦ You can specify computed filtering criteria.
- ✦ You can extract a copy of the rows that meet the criteria to another location.

To perform advanced filtering on a list, follow these steps:

1. **Set up and select a criteria range.**
2. **Choose Data⇨Filter⇨Advanced Filter.**
3. **In the Advanced Filter dialog box (see Figure 9-3), specify the list range and the criteria range, and make sure to select the Filter the List, In-Place option.**
4. **Click OK.**

   The list is filtered by the criteria that you specified.

Figure 9-3: The Advanced Filter dialog box.

Sorting a list

Sorting a list involves rearranging the rows such that they are in ascending or descending order, based on the values in one or more columns. For example, you may want to sort a list of salespeople alphabetically by last name or by sales region. Or you may want to sort your relatives by how much money they owe you. The fastest way to sort a list is to use the Sort Ascending or Sort Descending buttons on the Standard toolbar:

1. **Move the cell pointer to the column upon which you want to base the sort.**

2. **Click the Sort Ascending button or the Sort Descending button.**

   You find these buttons on the Standard toolbar. Excel sorts the list by the current column.

You may need to sort a list by more than one column. For example, you may want to sort by state, by city within the state, and by zip code within the city. To sort a list on multiple columns, use the preceding procedure for each column that you want to sort. Always start with the "least important" column (for example, zip code) and end with the "most important" column (for example, state).

When you sort a filtered list, only the visible rows are sorted. When you remove the filtering from the list, the list will no longer be sorted.

If the sorted list contains formulas that refer to cells in other rows in the list, the formulas will not be correct after the sorting. If formulas in your list refer to cells outside the list, make sure that the formulas use an absolute cell reference.

To sort a list another way, follow these steps:

1. **Choose Data⇨Sort.**

   Excel displays the Sort dialog box (see Figure 9-4).

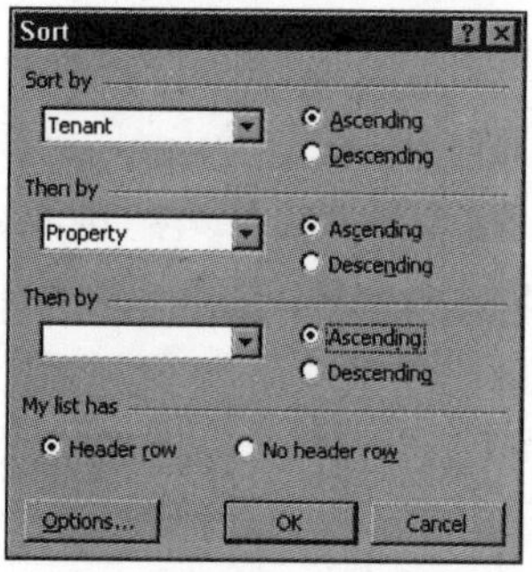

Figure 9-4: The user-friendly Sort dialog box.

2. **Select the first sort field from the Sort By drop-down list and specify Ascending or Descending order.**
3. **Repeat Step 2 for the second and third sort fields (if desired).**

4. **Click Options and select any of the following sort options:**
   - **First Key Sort Order:** Lets you specify a custom sort order for the sort.
   - **Case Sensitive:** Makes the sorting case-sensitive so that uppercase letters appear before lowercase letters in an ascending sort. Normally, sorting ignores the case of letters.
   - **Orientation:** Lets you sort by columns rather than by rows (the default).
5. **Click OK to return to the Sort dialog box.**
6. **Click OK.**

   The list's rows are rearranged.

If the Header row option is set, the first row (field names) is not affected by the sort.

Using a custom sort order

Sorting is done either numerically or alphabetically, depending on the data. In some cases, you may want to sort your data in other ways. If your data consists of month names, you probably want them to appear in month order rather than alphabetically. Excel, by default, has four custom lists, and you can define your own. To sort by a custom list, click the Options button in the Sort dialog box; then select the list from the First Key Sort Order drop-down list. Excel custom lists are as follows:

- **Abbreviated days:** Sun, Mon, Tue, Wed, Thu, Fri, Sat
- **Days:** Sunday, Monday, Tuesday, Wednesday, Thursday, Friday, Saturday
- **Abbreviated months:** Jan, Feb, Mar, Apr, May, Jun, Jul, Aug, Sep, Oct, Nov, Dec
- **Months:** January, February, March, April, May, June, July, August, September, October, November, December

To create a custom list, follow these steps:

1. **Choose Tools⇨Options.**
2. **In the Options dialog box, click the Custom Lists tab.**
3. **Enter your list in the List Entries box.**

   Enter a comma and a space between entries.
4. **Click Add and then click OK to close the Options dialog box.**

Goal-Seeking: Making a Formula Return a Desired Value

Excel's goal-seeking feature is designed to help you find an input value when you know the result you want but don't know which input value will produce the result. Suppose you want to invest $2,000 in such a way that it grows to $10,000 in ten years. By using the goal-seeking feature, you could determine by what percentage the investment would have to grow to meet the $10,000 goal. Here's a procedure that will give you hands-on experience with the goal-seeking feature:

1. **Start with any workbook in which you have entered formulas.**
2. **Choose Tools⇨Goal Seek.**
3. **Complete the Goal Seek dialog box (see Figure 9-5) by specifying the formula cell to change, the value to change it to, and the cell to change.**

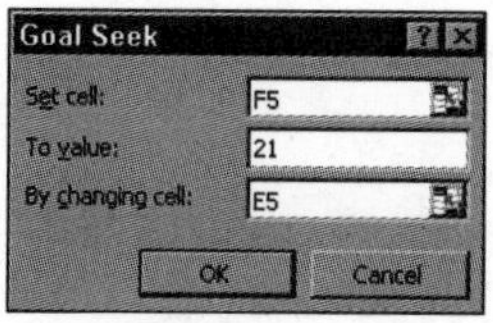

Figure 9-5: Goal-seeking with the Goal Seek dialog box.

4. **Click OK.**

   Excel displays the solution.

5. **Click OK to replace the original value with the found value; or click Cancel to restore your worksheet to the form that it was in before you chose Tools⇨Goal Seek.**

REMEMBER

Excel can't always find a value that produces the result that you're looking for (sometimes a solution just doesn't exist). In such a case, the Goal Seek status box informs you of that fact.

Performing What-If Analysis (Scenarios)

What-if analysis refers to the process of changing one or more input cells and observing the effects on formulas. An *input cell* is a cell that is used by a formula. For example, if a formula calculates a monthly payment amount for a loan, the formula would refer to an input cell that contains the loan amount.

Creating a data table (one-input)

A *one-input data table* displays the results of one or more result formulas for multiple values of a single input cell. For example, if you have a formula that calculates a loan payment at different interest rates, you can create a data table that shows the different monthly payment amounts. The interest rate cell is the input cell (see Figure 9-6).

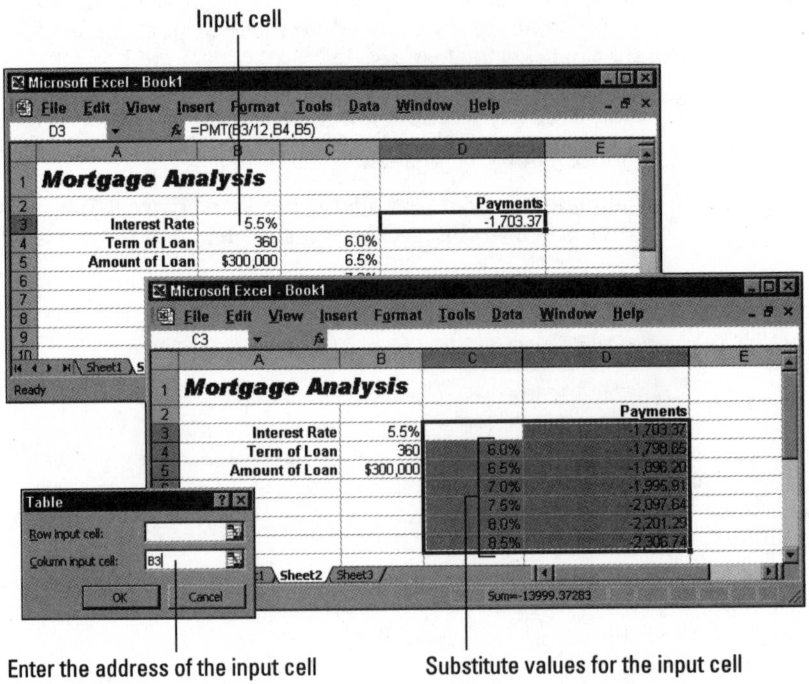

Figure 9-6: A one-input data table.

To create the table, follow these steps:

1. **Enter the list of values that you want to substitute for the value that is presently in the input cell, the one that is referred to in the formula.**

   Where you enter the substitute values depends on whether you are entering them in a column or row. If you enter the values in a column, enter them one cell below and one cell to the left of the cell where the formula is located (refer to Figure 9-6). If you enter the substitute values in a row, enter them one cell above and one cell to the right of the cell where the formula is.

2. **Select the table range.**

   That is, select the block of cells that includes the formula, the substitute values, and the cells directly to the right (in the case of a column) or directly below (in the case of a row) the substitute values.

3. **Choose Data➪Table.**

   The Table dialog box appears.

4. **Enter the address of the cell where the input value is located.**

   If the variables for the input cell are located in a column, enter the address in the Column Input Cell text box. If the variables are in a row, enter the address in the Row Input Cell text box.

5. **Click OK.**

   Excel performs the calculations and fills in the table.

REMEMBER

Excel uses an array formula that uses the TABLE function. Therefore, the table will be updated if you change the cell references in the first row or plug in different values in the first column.

Creating a data table (two-input)

A *two-input data table* displays the results of a single formula, but allows you to enter two input cells rather than one. For example, if you have a formula that calculates a loan payment, you can create a data table that shows not only how interest rates affect mortgage payments, but how mortgage payments are affected if you shorten or lengthen the life of the loan. Figure 9-7, for example, shows how monthly mortgage payments differ with different percentage rates and different time periods, in this case 15 years (180 months) and 30 years (360 months).

To create a two-input data table, follow these steps:

1. **Enter one set of substitute values below the formula in the same column as the formula.**
2. **Enter the second set of substitute values in the row to the right of the formula.**
3. **Select the cells that include the formula as well as the substitute values, both those in the column and those in the row (refer to Figure 9-7).**
4. **Choose Data➪Table.**

5. **In the Table dialog box, enter the input cell where row data is to be substituted and the input cell where column data is to be substituted.**
6. **Click OK.**

   Excel performs the calculations and fills in the table.

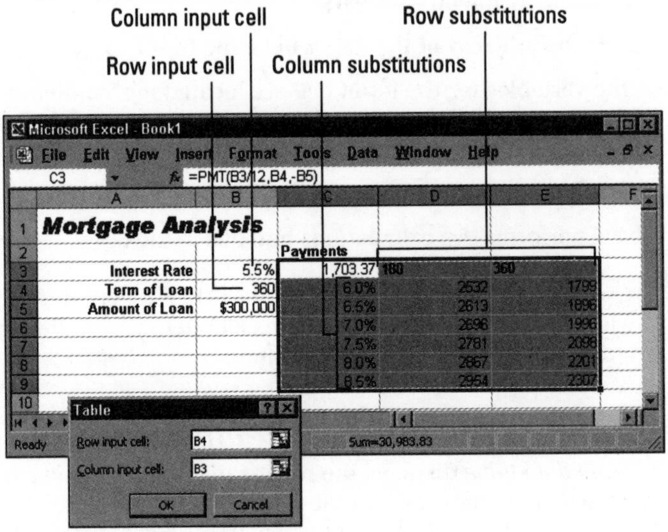

Figure 9-7: A two-input data table.

Chapter 10: Charting the Excel Way

In This Chapter

- **Creating charts by using the Chart Wizard**
- **Doing basic chart maintenance**
- **Changing charts and chart types**
- **Managing chart elements**
- **Viewing more of a 3-D chart**

If you intend to show your data to someone, wouldn't putting that data into a visual form be a great idea? Excel helps you convert data into chart form so that your data is more than an abstract jumble of text and numbers. You can create many different types of charts, including the standard favorites such as bar, pie, line, and scatter charts.

You can also choose from variants such as column and area charts or explore chart types such as bubble, cylinder, cone, and pyramid. To start working on a chart, use the Excel Chart Wizard to get you off and running.

Using the Chart Wizard

The Chart Wizard consists of a series of four dialog boxes that prompt you for various settings for the chart. By the time that you reach the last dialog box, the chart is usually exactly what you need. To begin using the Chart Wizard, follow these steps:

1. **Before you access the Chart Wizard, select the data that you want to include in the chart. Include in your selection items such as labels and series identifiers.**

   The data that you're plotting doesn't need to be contiguous. You can press the Ctrl key while making a multiple selection.

2. **After selecting the data, open the Chart Wizard by clicking the Chart Wizard button on the Standard toolbar or by choosing Insert➪Chart.**

Excel displays the first Chart Wizard dialog box, as shown in Figure 10-1.

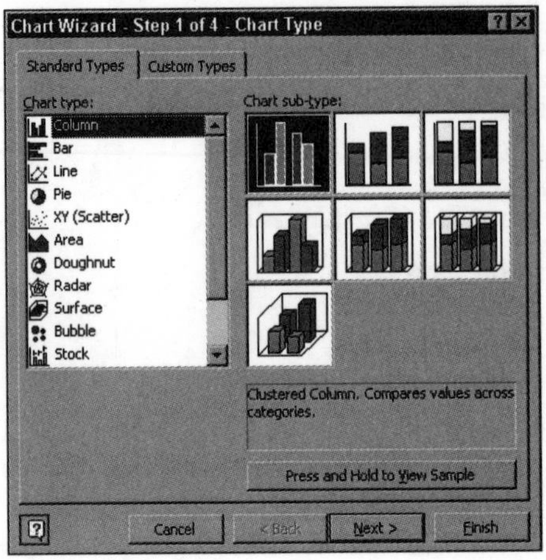

Figure 10-1: The first Chart Wizard dialog box.

To create your chart, you complete four steps in the Chart Wizard. You can always go back to the preceding step by clicking the Back button. Or you can click Finish to close the Chart Wizard. If you close it before completing all four steps, Excel creates the chart by using the information that you provide up to that point.

Chart Wizard Step 1 of 4

The first step of the Chart Wizard involves selecting the chart type.

1. **Select the chart type.**

   To use a standard chart type, make your selection in the Standard Types tab. Then choose one of the chart subtypes.

   To get a preview of how your data may look with the selected chart type, use the button below the list of chart subtypes. Click the button, but don't release it.

   To use a custom chart type, make your selection in the Custom Types tab.

2. **Click the Next button to move on to the next step.**

Chart Wizard Step 2 of 4

In the second step of the Chart Wizard, you verify (or change) the ranges that you want to use in the chart (see Figure 10-2).

1. **Make sure that the range appearing in the Data Range text box is the range that you want to use for the chart.**

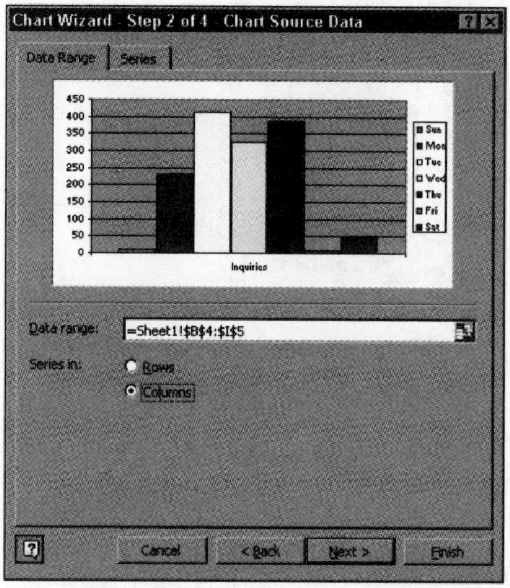

Figure 10-2: The second step of the Chart Wizard.

2. **If the data series are in rows, click the Rows option; if the data series are in columns, click the Columns option.**

The dialog box displays a preview of your chart.

3. **If you want to adjust the ranges that you're using for an individual series, click the Series tab and make the changes.**

On the Series tab, select a series and click the Remove button to remove it. To add a new series for plotting data on the chart, click the Add button, enter a name for the series in the Name box (the name you enter will appear in the chart's legend), and enter a cell range that describes the data you want to plot in the Values text box.

4. **Click the Next button to move on to the next step.**

REMEMBER

The Row or Column selection in Step 2 is an important choice that drastically affects the look of your chart. Most of the time, Excel guesses the data orientation correctly — but not always.

Chart Wizard Step 3 of 4

The third Chart Wizard dialog box (see Figure 10-3) consists of six tabs. Use these tabs to adjust various options for the chart. As you make your selections, the preview chart reflects your choices. The following list describes the function of each tab:

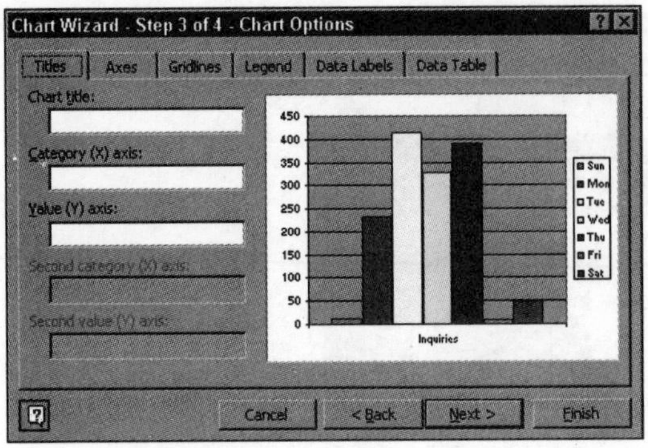

Figure 10-3: The third Chart Wizard dialog box.

- **Titles:** Enter titles for various parts of the chart. Enter the title, which appears above the chart. The Category and Value Axis entries appear on the side of the chart and describe the units that the chart measures.
- **Axes:** Select the type of values to display on the axes. The axes describe how the chart is laid out. In a chart that portrays the elevation of different mountains, mountain names can appear on either axis, as can elevations. By making choices here, you tell the Chart Wizard on which axis to place categories and values.
- **Gridlines:** Specify gridlines, if any. Gridlines are the lines on the chart that show measurements. In a bar chart, for example, gridlines show how high the bars reach. The Gridlines tab offers options for displaying horizontal as well as vertical gridlines, and major as well as minor gridlines.
- **Legend:** Specify whether to display a legend and its location on the chart. The legend is the box on the chart that describes what the parts of the chart — the bars, pie wedges, and so on — are.
- **Data Labels:** Specify whether to display data labels (and which type) for the data series. The labels appear on the chart to give viewers a clearer picture of what the bars, pie slices, or other chart parts represent.
- **Data Table:** Specify whether to display the table of values that the chart uses.

Click Next to move to the final step.

Chart Wizard Step 4 of 4

In Step 4 of the Chart Wizard, you specify where you want the chart to appear. You can display it as a new chart sheet in the workbook or as an object in an existing worksheet. To choose which worksheet, in your workbook, select a sheet from the As Object In drop-down list.

Click Finish, and Excel creates the chart per your specifications.

Charting Basics

After your chart is done, you still can't relax. Now is the time to do all those things that you didn't do right earlier! Before you can do anything with a chart, however, you must activate it, as follows:

- ✦ To activate a chart on a chart sheet, click the chart sheet's tab.
- ✦ To activate an embedded chart, click the chart.

Adding a new data series to a chart

You can add a new data series to a chart in several ways, as the following list describes:

FAST TRACK

- ✦ Select the range that you want to add and drag it into the chart. After you release the mouse button, Excel updates the chart with the data you dragged into it. This technique works only if the chart is embedded on the worksheet.
- ✦ Activate the chart and choose Chart⇨Add Data. Excel displays a dialog box that prompts you for the range of data to add to the chart.
- ✦ Activate the chart and then click the Chart Wizard button. You get the first Chart Wizard dialog box. Click the Next button to go to the second dialog box. Edit the range reference in the Data Range text box to include the new data series (or point to the new range in the worksheet). Click Finish, and Excel updates the chart with the new data.

Changing a chart's data series

Often, you create a chart that uses a particular range of data, and then you extend the data range by adding new data points in the worksheet. If you add new data to a range, the data series doesn't include the new data. Or you may delete some of the data points in a plotted range. If you delete data from a range, the chart displays the deleted data as zero values.

To update the chart to reflect the new data range, follow these steps:

1. **Activate the chart.**

   To do so, either go to the worksheet where it is located, or, if you embedded it, click the chart.

2. **Choose Chart⇨Source Data.**
3. **In the Source Data dialog box that appears, click the Series tab.**

4. **Select the data series that you want to modify from the Series list.**
5. **Use the range selection text boxes to change the data series. You may also need to modify the range that the Category values use.**
6. **Click OK, and the chart updates to include the new data range.**

In Step 3, you can also click the Data Range tab of the Source Data dialog box and specify the data range for the entire chart.

After you activate a chart, Excel outlines the ranges that the chart uses in the worksheet. To extend or reduce the range, simply drag the handle on the outline in the worksheet.

TIP

A better way to handle data ranges that change is to use *named ranges*. Simply create names for the data ranges that you use in the chart. Activate the chart, select the data series, and edit the `SERIES` formula by clicking the Formula bar. Replace each range reference with the corresponding range name. If you change the definition for a name, the chart updates.

Working with chart legends

If you create your chart by using the Chart Wizard, you can choose to include a legend (see "Chart Wizard Step 3 of 4" earlier in this chapter). If you change your mind, you can easily delete the legend or add one if you need one.

If you didn't include legend text when you originally selected the cells to create the chart, Excel displays *Series 1, Series 2,* and so on in the legend. To add series names, follow these steps:

1. **Activate the chart.**

   To do so, either go to the worksheet where it is located, or, if you embedded it, click the chart.

2. **Choose Chart➪Source Data.**
3. **In the Source Data dialog box that appears, click the Series tab.**
4. **Select a series from the Series list box and then enter a name in the Name text box.**

   For the name, you can use text or a reference to a cell that contains the series name.

5. **Repeat Step 4 for each series that you want to name.**
6. **Click OK, and the new names appear in the legend.**

Changing a chart's scale

Adjusting the scale of a value axis can dramatically affect the appearance of the chart. Excel always determines the scale for your charts automatically. You can, however, override the choice Excel makes. To do so, follow these steps:

1. **Activate the chart.**

   To do so, either go to the worksheet where it is located, or, if you embedded it, click the chart.

2. **Select the value (Y) axis.**

   To do so, open the Chart Object drop-down menu on the Chart toolbar and choose Value Axis.

3. **Choose Format⇨Selected Axis (or double-click the axis or press Ctrl+1).**
4. **In the Format Axis dialog box that appears, click the Scale tab, as shown in Figure 10-4.**
5. **Make the changes and then click OK.**

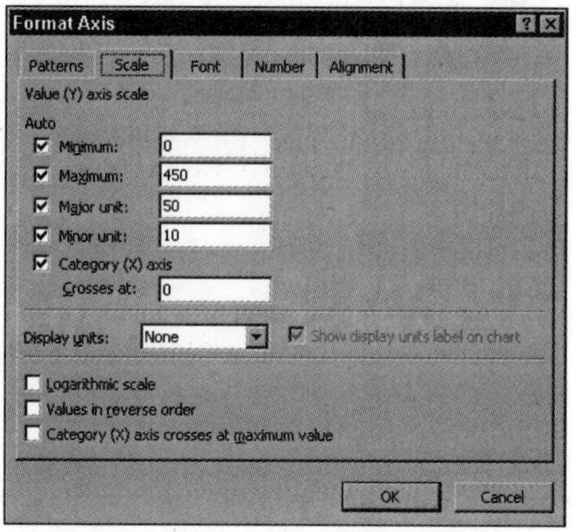

Figure 10-4: The Format Axis dialog box.

The dialog box varies slightly depending on which axis you select. The Scale tab of the Format Axis dialog box offers the following options:

- **Minimum:** Enables you to enter a minimum value for the axis. If you select this option, Excel determines this value automatically.
- **Maximum:** Enables you to enter a maximum value for the axis. If you select this option, Excel determines this value automatically.

- **Major Unit:** Enables you to enter the number of units between major tick marks. If checked, Excel determines this value automatically.
- **Minor Unit:** Enables you to enter the number of units between minor tick marks. If you select this option, Excel determines this value automatically.
- **Category (X) Axis Crosses At:** Enables you to position the axes at a different location. By default, Excel positions the axes at the edge of the plot area. The exact wording of this option varies, depending on which axis you select.
- **Display Units:** Enables you to set the display units for large numbers on the axis. Using this option can make numbers appearing on the axis shorter and more readable.
- **Show Display Units Label on Chart:** Enables you to add a label on the axis that describes the units that you selected in the Display Units drop-down list.
- **Logarithmic Scale:** Enables you to use a logarithmic scale for the axes. Useful for scientific applications in which the values that you intend to plot include an extremely large range; a log scale gives you an error message if the scale includes 0 or negative values.
- **Values in Reverse Order:** Makes the scale values extend in the opposite direction.
- **Category (X) Axis Crosses at Maximum Value:** Enables you to position the axes at the maximum value of the perpendicular axis. (Normally, the axis is positioned at the minimum value.) The exact wording varies, depending on which axis you select.

Changing a chart's gridlines

Gridlines can help you determine what the chart series represents numerically. Gridlines simply extend the tick marks on the axes.

To add or remove gridlines, follow these steps:

1. **Activate the chart.**

   To do so, either go to the worksheet where it is located, or, if you embedded it, click the chart.
2. **Choose Chart⇨Chart Options.**
3. **Click the Gridlines tab.**
4. **Click to select or deselect the check boxes that correspond to the desired gridlines.**

Each axis includes two sets of gridlines: *major* and *minor*. Major units are the ones displaying a label. Minor units are those in between. If you're working with a 3-D chart, the dialog box offers options for three sets of gridlines.

Changing a chart's location

If you embed your chart on a worksheet, you can click a border and drag it to a new location on the worksheet. To move the embedded chart to a different sheet or to a separate chart sheet, select the chart and choose Chart⇨Location. Specify the new location in the Chart Location dialog box and click OK. See "Chart Wizard Step 4 of 4" earlier in this chapter for a description of the options in the Chart Location dialog box.

Changing the Chart Type

Excel supports a wide variety of chart types (line charts, column charts, and so on). To change the chart type, follow these steps:

1. **Activate the chart.**

   To do so, either go to the worksheet where it is located, or, if you embedded it, click the chart.

2. **Choose Chart⇨Chart Type to display the Chart Type dialog box.**
3. **Click the desired chart type.**

   You can select from standard chart types (on the Standard tab) or custom chart types (listed on the Custom tab). You see a preview of how your chart looks.

4. **After you're satisfied with the chart's appearance, click OK.**

The chart types appearing on the Custom tab of the Chart Type dialog box are standard chart types that are modified in one or more ways. Excel comes with a variety of custom chart types, and you can create your own, too.

Another way to change the chart type is to use the Chart Type drop-down list on the Chart toolbar. Click the down arrow beside the button to open the list and choose a major chart type. (You can't select custom chart types if you use this button.)

If you customize some aspects of your chart, choosing a new chart type may override some of or all the changes that you make. If you add gridlines to the chart, for example, and then select a chart type that doesn't use gridlines, your gridlines disappear.

Dealing with Chart Elements

Working with an element in a chart is similar to everything else that you do in Excel: First you make a selection (in this case, select a chart part), and then you issue a command to do something with the selection.

After you activate a chart, you can select a chart element in one of the following three ways:

- ✦ Click the chart element.
- ✦ Press the up-arrow or down-arrow key to cycle through all the elements in the chart. If you select a data series, you can press the right-arrow or left-arrow key to select individual points in the series.
- ✦ Use the Chart Objects control in the Chart toolbar. This control opens a drop-down list that contains all the elements in the chart (see Figure 10-5).

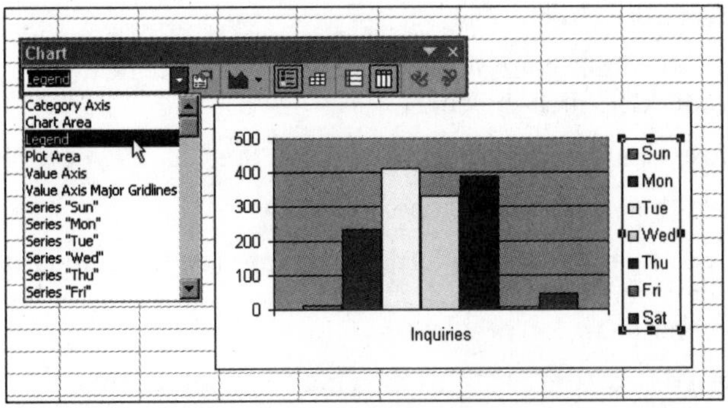

Figure 10-5: Use the Chart Objects drop-down list to select a chart element.

No matter which method you use, the name of the selected item appears in the Name text box (at the left of the Formula bar). Many of the chart element names include a number that further describes the element. The third point of the first data series, for example, carries the name Series 1 Point 3. You can't change the names of chart elements, and you can't select more than one element at a time.

TIP

After you move the mouse pointer over a chart element, a chart tip displays the name of the element. If the element is a data point, the chart tip displays the value. To control what appears in these chart tips, choose Tools➪Options and click the Chart tab in the Options dialog box. Make your selection in the Chart Tips section of the dialog box.

Modifying a chart element

You can modify most elements in a chart in several ways. You can, for example, change colors, line widths, fonts, and so on. You make modifications in the Format dialog box (which varies for each type of chart element).

To modify an element in a chart, follow these steps:

1. **Select the chart element.**
2. **Access the Format dialog box for that element by using any of the following techniques:**
   - Double-click the item.
   - Choose Format➪[*Item Name*] from the menu bar.
   - Press Ctrl+1.
   - Right-click the item and choose Format [*Item Name*] from the shortcut menu that appears.
3. **Click the tab of the Format dialog box that corresponds to what you want to do.**

   To change the font of the legend, for example, click the Font tab in the Format Legend dialog box.
4. **Make the changes.**
5. **Click OK.**

Moving a chart element

You can move some of the chart parts (any of the titles, data labels, and the legend). To move a chart element, follow these steps:

1. **Select the chart element that you want to move.**
2. **Click the border of the element and drag it to the desired location in the chart.**

Deleting a chart element or data series

You can delete any element in a chart. Heaven knows that you may change your mind often enough. To delete a chart element, follow these steps:

1. **Select the element or data series that you want to delete.**
2. **Press Delete.**

If you delete the last data series in a chart, the chart becomes empty.

Rotating 3-D charts

Sure, they're neat to look at, but as you work with 3-D charts, you may find that some data is completely or partially obscured. Drat! How can you convince the big executives at the Annual Sales Meeting that you aren't completely inept? Luckily for you, you can rotate the chart so that it shows the data better. To do so, follow these steps:

1. **Activate the 3-D chart.**
2. **Choose Chart⇨3-D View.**
3. **In the 3-D View dialog box that appears, make your rotations and perspective changes by clicking the appropriate controls.**

   To rotate the chart, for example, click one of the Rotate buttons; to tilt the chart, click a Tilt button.
4. **Click OK (or click Apply to see the changes without closing the dialog box).**

Index

Symbols & Numbers

A

B

C

G

I

L

M

N

O

P

R

S

T

U

V

W

Z

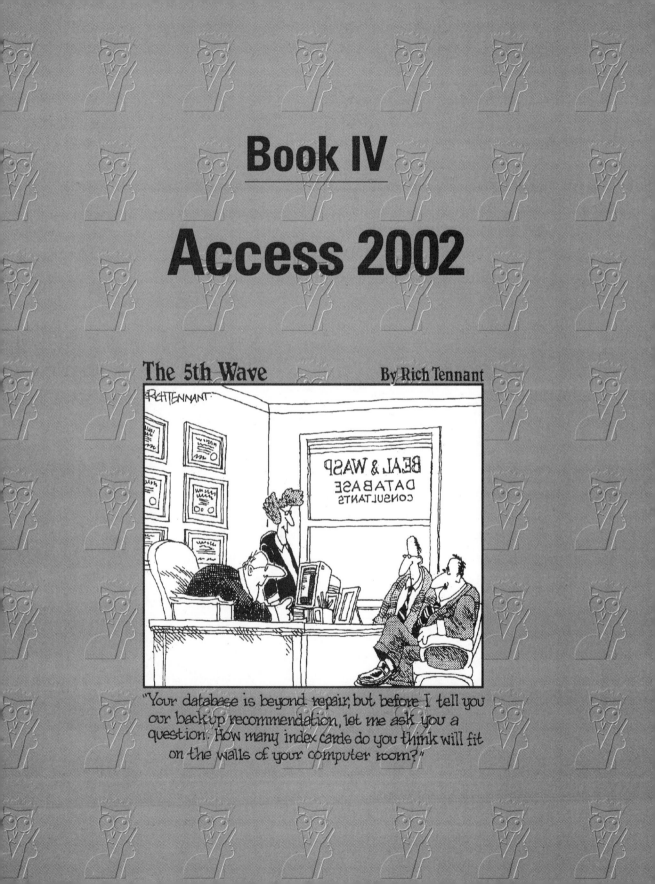

Book IV

Access 2002

The 5th Wave By Rich Tennant

"Your database is beyond repair, but before I tell you our backup recommendation, let me ask you a question: How many index cards do you think will fit on the walls of your computer room?"

Contents at a Glance

Chapter 1: Access Basics

In This Chapter

- Getting acquainted with databases
- Taking a look at the Access window
- Opening, saving, and closing a database
- Working with database wizards
- Quitting Access

You really need to know some things before getting started in Access — not because Access is an impossibly hard program to master, but the demands of database creation can sometimes be more involved than things you do everyday (unless you're a professional database designer, of course). Beginning with a brief explanation of databases in general, this chapter gives you a quick look at opening, saving, and closing an Access database. (By the way, be sure to check out Appendix A for refreshers on how to do basic Windows stuff in Access and in all other Office programs.) Finally, you get introduced to the ideas of Access Wizards (a concept for which you will surely be grateful!) as you also discover how to quit Access the recommended way.

About Databases

A *database* is an organized collection of related data. In a well-built database, you can organize your data so that you see only the data you need to see, in the order you need to see it. In technical terms, a database enables you to *filter* and *sort* data. You can also choose the format in which you want to view your data — a table, for example, or a form.

On the most basic level, databases are organized into records. A *record* is one batch of related information. If you think of your address book as a database, one record is the information about your best friend — her name, address, phone number, and any other information that you have about her in the address book.

Tables store records of data. A table consists of rows and columns. The rows are records, and the columns are fields. A *field* is one category of information that you collect for every record. In a database that stores your address book, the fields may be first name, last name, street address, birthday, and so on. The intersection of a field and a row is a cell (see Figure 1-1).

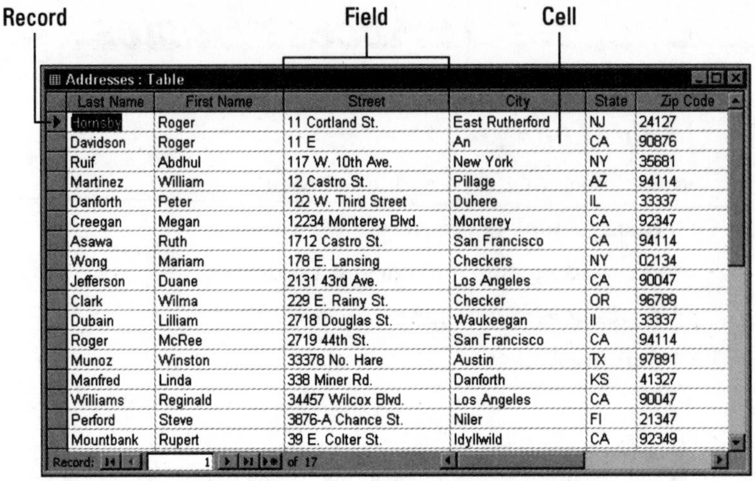

Last Name	First Name	Street	City	State	Zip Code
Hornsby	Roger	11 Cortland St.	East Rutherford	NJ	24127
Davidson	Roger	11 E	An	CA	90876
Ruif	Abdhul	117 W. 10th Ave.	New York	NY	35681
Martinez	William	12 Castro St.	Pillage	AZ	94114
Danforth	Peter	122 W. Third Street	Duhere	IL	33337
Creegan	Megan	12234 Monterey Blvd.	Monterey	CA	92347
Asawa	Ruth	1712 Castro St.	San Francisco	CA	94114
Wong	Mariam	178 E. Lansing	Checkers	NY	02134
Jefferson	Duane	2131 43rd Ave.	Los Angeles	CA	90047
Clark	Wilma	229 E. Rainy St.	Checker	OR	96789
Dubain	Lilliam	2718 Douglas St.	Waukeegan	Il	33337
Roger	McRee	2719 44th St.	San Francisco	CA	94114
Munoz	Winston	33378 No. Hare	Austin	TX	97891
Manfred	Linda	338 Miner Rd.	Danforth	KS	41327
Williams	Reginald	34457 Wilcox Blvd.	Los Angeles	CA	90047
Perford	Steve	3876-A Chance St.	Niler	FI	21347
Mountbank	Rupert	39 E. Colter St.	Idyllwild	CA	92349

Figure 1-1: A database table.

It's important to store each type of information in a separate field. Organizing your data into many different fields enables you to slice the data any way you want. For example, if you decide that having separate fields for first and last names is a waste of time, you lose out on the option of sorting the database by either first or last name.

Access Database Objects

An Access database can contain different types of Access *objects:* tables, forms, queries, and reports.

- Access stores data in *tables.*
- You use Access *forms* just like paper forms: to enter and display data.
- You create *queries* to gather the information you need about the data you've entered.
- Use *reports* to present the information you gather about your data.

Each of these types of objects is covered in this book.

Opening a Database File

When you start Access by clicking the Start button and choosing the Programs menu, the New File task pane appears listing the last four databases that you opened (see Figure 1-2). To open one of these databases, simply click its name. If the database you want to open isn't on the list, either click More Files or choose File⇨Open (or press Ctrl+O) to see the Open dialog box. In that dialog box, find your database file and open it.

Using Access as it was meant to be used

Access is a *relational database,* which means that one database file can consist of many tables of *related* data. For example, you may have a table called Orders that lists orders and includes the Product Number of each item ordered, and another table called Products that contains information about products, which identifies each product by using another Product Number field. When you tell Access that the two Product Number fields are related, you provide a link between the two tables that allows you to ask your database a question that requires data from both tables to answer. For example, you may want to know who ordered which products (information stored in the Orders table), and how much the product costs at wholesale (information stored in the Products table). The related Product Number fields allow you to pull the related data from two tables.

You can also open an Access file by double-clicking the file name in Windows Explorer or My Computer, or by clicking the Start button and choosing the file on the Documents menu. Opening an Access file also starts Access.

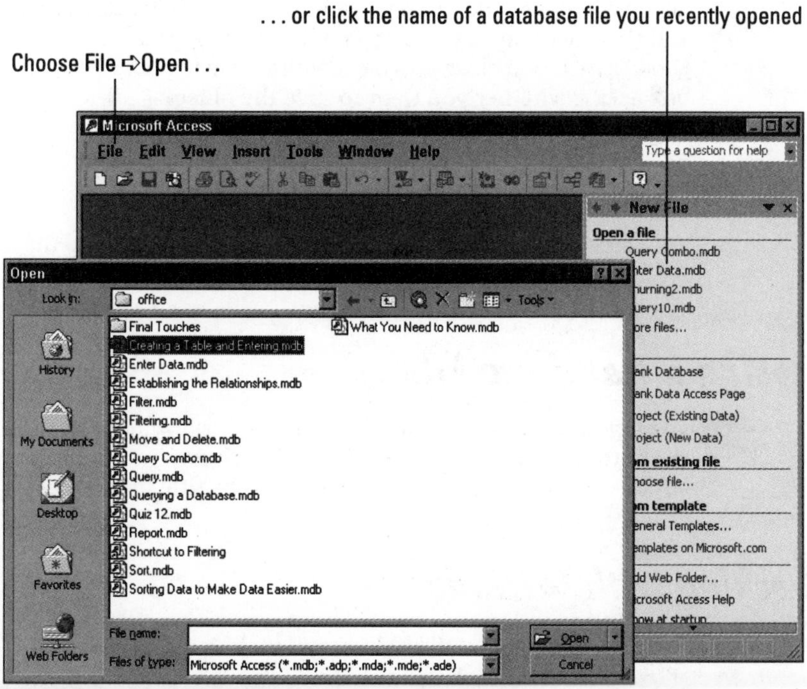
. . . or click the name of a database file you recently opened
Choose File ⇨ Open . . .

Figure 1-2: You can begin with a new or existing file.

To use the Open dialog box to open a database, follow these steps:

1. **Click the Open button (alternatively, choose File➪Open or press Ctrl+O) to bring up the Open dialog box (refer to Figure 1-2).**
2. **Select the file you want. (You may need to browse to it.)**

   Click the icons on the left of the Open dialog box to see different folders — History displays recently used files, Desktop displays desktop icons, Favorites displays the contents of the Favorites folder, and Web Folders displays defined Web folders.
3. **Click the Open button or simply double-click the filename.**

   Access opens the database.

Saving a Database File

Access is designed so that many people can use one database — and all at the same time, if they need to. So, unlike a spreadsheet or word processing program, Access doesn't require you to save the entire file — instead you save object definitions (such as a table or form definition) one at a time. Access takes care of saving data as soon as it's entered.

To save an object definition, make the object active (by clicking its window) and then click the Save button on the toolbar, press Ctrl+S, or choose File➪Save. If you close an object without saving it, Access displays a dialog box asking whether you want to save the object:

- ✦ Choose Yes to save the object.
- ✦ Choose No to close the object without saving changes to the definition.
- ✦ Choose Cancel to cancel the command and return to the unsaved object.

Closing a Database File

To close a database, simply close the database window by clicking its close (X) button. The database window is the window in which `Name of the database file: Database` appears in the title bar.

Working with Wizards

Access provides wizards to help you build and use databases. A *wizard* is a series of dialog boxes that ask you questions and then create something (such as a database, a query, or a report) based on your answers. The many wizards in Access do a variety of tasks, but they all work in a similar way: They present you with screens that ask you questions, such as which tables or fields you want to use and which format you prefer.

Specific wizards are covered in other parts of this book, but the following sections cover the basic techniques you must know in order to use any wizard.

Selecting fields

Many wizards have windows like the one in Figure 1-3, where you choose fields.

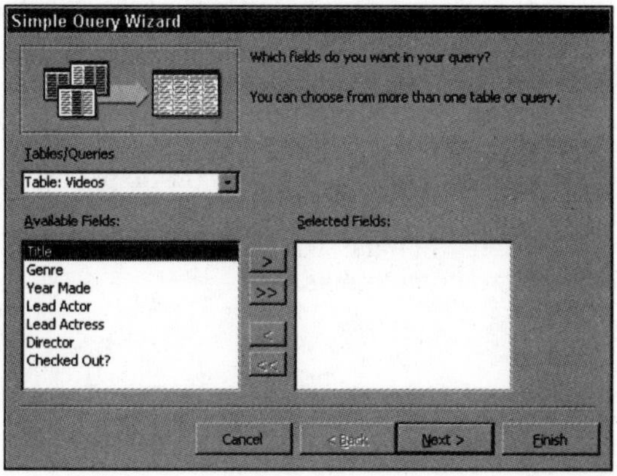

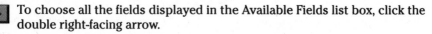

Figure 1-3: A typical Access wizard.

To tell Access that you want to use a field, you first have to tell it where to find the field by choosing a table or query from the Tables/Queries drop-down list. Access displays the fields from the table or query you choose in the Available Fields list box. Use one of the following methods to tell Access that you want it to use a field:

- ✦ Double-click the field.

- ✦ Select the field and click the single right-facing arrow button.

To choose all the fields displayed in the Available Fields list box, click the double right-facing arrow.

If you make a mistake and want to remove a field from the Selected Fields list box, double-click it, or select it and click the single left-facing arrow button.

To remove all fields from the Selected Fields list box, click the double left-facing arrow button.

To select fields from other tables or queries, choose another table or query from the Tables/Queries drop-down list and select the additional fields.

Viewing more windows

When you finish answering all the questions on one window of a wizard, you're ready to see the next window. The buttons at the bottom of the wizard enable you to proceed through the questions the wizard asks you:

- **Cancel:** Exits the wizard without letting the wizard complete its task.
- **Back:** Displays the previous window of the wizard.
- **Next:** Displays the next window of the wizard.
- **Finish:** Tells Access to complete whatever it is that this particular wizard does, using the information it already has, and using the default values on any windows that you skip by clicking the Finish button.

When you get to the last window of a wizard, you see the black and white checkered Finish flag. Access asks you if you want help, and it often asks you to name the object the wizard is creating and choose how you want to view the new object. When you finish with these options, click the Finish button to tell the wizard to complete its task.

Quitting Access

You quit Access the same way that you quit any other Windows program. Again, Windows offers a boatload of options. If you have parts of a database open, and you've made changes since the last time you saved the object, Access gives you the option of saving the object before you quit. Following are the most popular ways to close Access:

- Click the Close button in the top-right corner of the Access window (it looks like an X).
- Press Alt+F4.
- Choose File⇨Exit from the Access menu.

Chapter 2: Creating and Navigating a Database

In This Chapter

- **Creating a database by yourself or with wizards**
- **Getting to know the database window**
- **Using the database toolbars**

Unless you're lucky enough to have inherited a nice database to work on, you need to know how to create one. Fortunately, you can use a wizard if you don't want to build a database all yourself. After you have all your database objects in place, manipulating them is a breeze. (By the way, you read about database objects — tables, reports, queries, and forms — in later chapters.) This chapter doesn't guarantee to make you an expert database creator, but it can show you the ins and outs that you can later build on.

Creating a Database

Designing databases is a topic unto itself — this book certainly can't tell you everything you need to know. It can, however, give you some basic guidelines. It's important to give some consideration to the design of your database before you begin entering data into tables. Consider the data you have and how you want to use it — what kinds of queries, forms, and reports do you want to include in your database? What additional needs may crop up later? These questions help you figure out what data you need, and how to break up your data into fields and tables so that you can create the reports, forms, and queries that you will need.

Much of the work of designing a database to meet your needs is in deciding how to break your data into fields and which fields to store in each table; these can make or break your database. Use these guidelines for designing your database:

- Split data into its smallest logical parts. Usually this means the smallest unit that you may ever want to use. For example, give each name at least two fields; first name and last name. This allows you to work with either one or the other for sorting, form letters, and so on.

- Use multiple tables so that each table contains information on one topic. For example, one table may contain order information, while another contains the customer's billing information and shipping address. You can password-protect a table, so it makes sense to put sensitive information in a separate table.
- Make sure you know which fields in different tables are related. For example, the Customer Number field you use in the Orders table connects to the Customer Number field in the Customer table containing customer's shipping addresses and billing information.
- Avoid repeating data. If a table listing employee information has fields for both department name and department manager, you're repeating data. It may make more sense to list a department in the employee table and have a separate table for departments and department managers.

Developing a database

Follow these general steps to develop a database:

1. **Open a new database.**
2. **Create tables.**
3. **Tell Access how your tables are related.**
4. **(Optional) Create forms to make data entry clearer and to display a full record's worth of information at a time.**
5. **Enter your data.**
6. **Create queries to give you the information you need.**
7. **Create reports to transfer the information to paper in a clear format.**

Creating a database from scratch

If Access is closed, start Access by using the Start button menu (or your favorite method). Then follow these steps to tell Access that you want to create a database from scratch:

1. **Display the New File task pane if it isn't already displayed.**

   To display this task pane at any time, choose File➪New, press Ctrl+O, or click the New button.

2. **Click Blank Database in the task pane.**

   Access displays the File New Database dialog box, where you name the new database.

3. **Locate a folder for storing the database, name the database, and click the Create button.**

If you want to store the file in a folder other than the one displayed in the Save In box, change the folder.

Access takes a few seconds to create the new database; then it displays the Tables view of the Database window and the Database toolbar.

Access offers you a several new options in the New File task pane. You can create a new database, but you can also create a Data Access Page, a Project (using an existing database), and a Project using a new database. To create a new database starting from one you or someone else already created, click the Choose File link.

Creating a database with a wizard

Using wizards is a great way to get a jumpstart on creating a database. Even if they don't provide exactly what you want, wizards give you a framework to start from. Access comes with a number of database wizards:

Asset Tracking	Contact Management
Event Management	Expenses
Inventory Control	Ledger
Order Entry	Resource Scheduling
Time and Billing	Service Call Management

To create a database by using a wizard, follow these steps:

1. **Choose File⇨New (or press Ctrl+N) to open the New Task task pane, and then click General Templates in the task pane.**

   The Templates dialog box appears.

2. **Click the Databases tab.**

   A list of wizards appears. The name of the wizard gives you a general idea about what kind of data the wizard is set up to work with.

3. **Click a database name to get a graphical preview of the wizard.**
4. **To open a wizard, double-click the database icon (or name), or click the icon once to select it and then click the OK button.**

   Access displays the File New Database dialog box where you can name the database.

5. **Accept the name in the File Name box by pressing Enter, or edit the name and then press Enter.**

The wizard takes a few moments to set up and then displays the first window, which shows you some information about the database that you're setting up.

6. **Click Next to display the next window of the wizard.**

   You may see more than one screen of options. Follow the directions in each screen to determine which options to change. Access allows you to add additional fields, choose a form style, choose a report style, and give the database a name (which will appear in the Access title bar). The last screen gives you a setting to check if you want to view online help about the database.

   Click the Finish button immediately if you want to accept the wizard's defaults and create the database right away.

Finding Your Way around a Database

An Access database consists of data and database objects. Tables, reports, forms, and queries are the types of objects that you're most likely to work with. The Database window is the table of contents for all the objects in your database. From the Database window you can access each object in the database (see Figure 2-1).

Buttons for each type of object in the database.

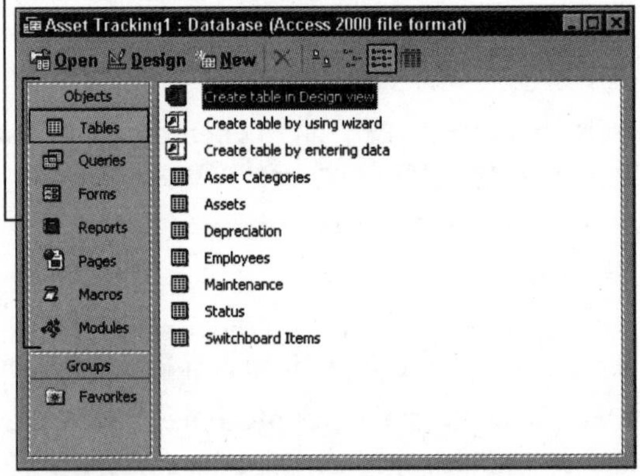

Figure 2-1: The Database window is like a table of contents.

Object types appear as buttons on the left side of the window. If you notice, the Database window resembles the Outlook window.

The view for each type of object contains at least two different types of icons — icons for creating a new object of this type, and icons for each defined object of this type in the database. For example, in addition to the seven tables defined in the database shown in Figure 2-1, you also see three icons for creating new tables. Notice that the icons for the tables and the icons that create new tables are different.

To see all the objects of a certain type, click the appropriate button. To see the names of all the forms in the database, for example, click the Forms button. To open a specific form after you've clicked the Forms button, click the form name to select it and then click the Open button on the toolbar.

Use any of these ways to view the database window:

- ✦ Click the Database Window button.
- ✦ Press F11.
- ✦ Open the Window menu and choose the name of your database.
- ✦ If you can see even part of the Database window, click it to make it the active window.

The Database Window Toolbar

In the Database window is the Database toolbar, which offers useful buttons for copying, printing, and creating objects, among other tasks (see Figure 2-2). If you've seen any Office application before, most of these buttons will seem familiar to you. Table 2-1 gives the rundown on those buttons.

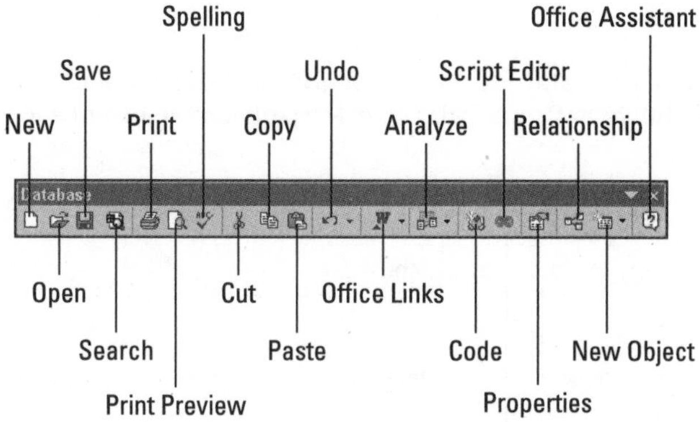

Figure 2-2: Useful database buttons abound.

Table 2-1 Toolbar Buttons

Button	*What It Does*
New	Opens the New File task pane so that you can create a new database
Open	Opens an existing database (and closes the currently open database)
Save	Saves data to the hard drive
Search	Opens the basic search task pane so that you can search for a missing file
Print	Prints the selected object
Print Preview	Displays the selected object as it will look when printed
Spelling	Checks the spelling of the selected object
Cut	Deletes the selected object and saves a copy in the Clipboard
Copy	Copies the selected object to the Clipboard
Paste	Pastes the contents of the Clipboard to the Database window
Undo	Undoes your last action
OfficeLinks	Opens another Office application
Analyze	Runs the Table Analyzer Wizard or another analyzer wizard
Code	Opens the Visual Basic Editor so that you can see the code with which an object was created
Script Editor	Opens the MS Script Editor so that you can view or add JScript to an Access page
Properties	Displays the properties of the selected object
Relationships	Displays the Relationships window
New Object: AutoForm	Creates a new object
Microsoft Access Help	Opens the Access Help program

In addition, the Database window has a secondary toolbar that contains the buttons shown in Figure 2-3. Table 2-2 explains the use of each button.

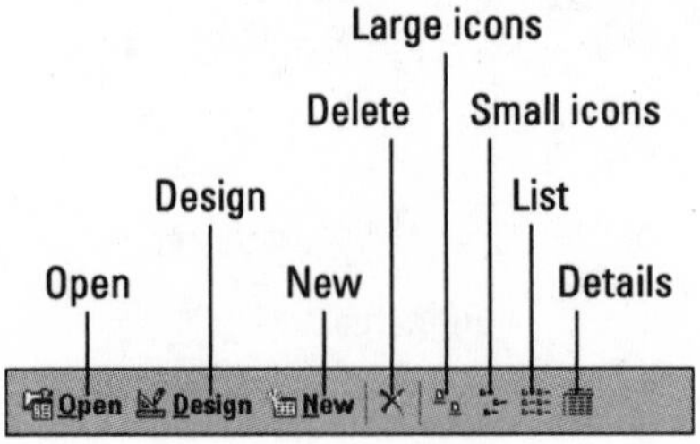

Figure 2-3: Buttons can do your every bidding.

Table 2-2 More Toolbar Buttons

Button	*What It Does*
Open or Preview	Displays the selected object
Design	Displays the design view of the selected object
New	Displays a dialog box of options for creating a new object of the type currently displayed
Delete	Deletes the selected object
Large Icons	Displays objects in the Database window as large icons
Small Icons	Displays objects in the Database window as small icons
List	Displays objects in the Database window in a list
Details	Displays objects in the Database window with details, including a description, last date modified, date created, and type of object

TIP

One advantage of using the Details view is that you can see when an object was last modified. You can also sort objects — just click the gray column header to sort by that column. And if you want to see which table was modified most recently, click the Modified column header.

REAL WORLD

Sample databases to play with

Access comes with a number of samples that can help you understand how Access databases work. The Northwind database is the most frequently used sample database. The database is an example of how to track products, suppliers, and sales for a company called Northwind Traders. Playing around with the Northwind database is one way to become familiar with different Access features.

The Northwind database is stored in `C:\Program Files\MicrosoftOffice\Office\Samples\Nwind.mdb` when it's installed. If it has not been installed, you can find it on your Access or Office CD.

Chapter 3: Tables: A Home for Your Data

In This Chapter

- ✓ **Discovering database tables**
- ✓ **Creating tables**
- ✓ **Navigating a datasheet**
- ✓ **Adding and editing data**
- ✓ **Changing data types**
- ✓ **Linking tables**
- ✓ **Identifying table records with a primary key**

Because tables hold your data, tables are the fundamental element of any database. If you can create and move around in your tables, the world of databases seems to open up to you. But hold on! You also need to do more than just create tables; you need the capability to link tables so that you can actually do something with your database. And for linking purposes, you must take into account your primary keys. Hey, this topic appears to be getting complicated very fast. Fortunately for you, I devote Chapter 3 to getting you off to a comfortable start in table basics.

About Tables

Tables are the basic building block of your database — they store the data. One *table* stores a collection of related data in records and fields. Fields define each piece of information about an item, and you store these related fields in records. Most databases have a number of tables. Each table stores a set of related data, and normally each table in the database relates to other tables through the repetition of a common field. You can work with tables in two different views: Datasheet view and Design view.

Working in Datasheet view

A table in Datasheet view looks similar to a spreadsheet — it stores a collection of similar data in records and fields (see Figure 3-1). To display the list of tables in the database that you're working on, click the Tables button on the left side of the Database window. Then, to display a table in Datasheet view, take any of the following actions:

- ✦ Double-click the name of the table in the Database window.
- ✦ Select the table in the Database window and click the Open button on the toolbar.
-  ✦ Click the Datasheet View button if the table's in Design view.

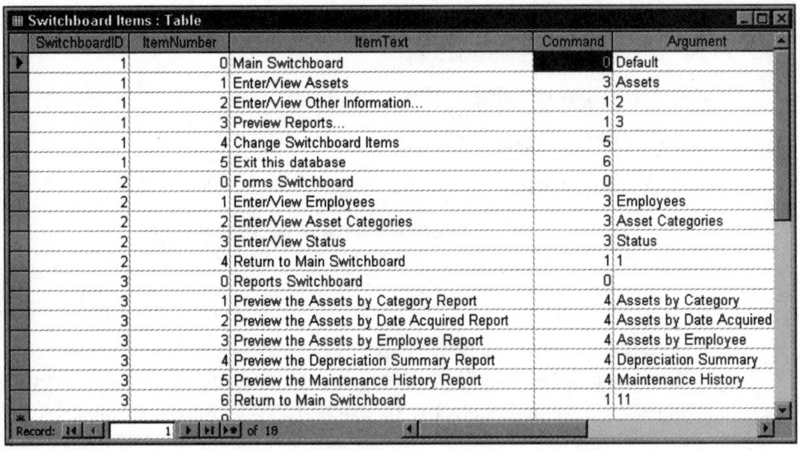

Switchboard Items : Table

SwitchboardID	ItemNumber	ItemText	Command	Argument
1	0	Main Switchboard	0	Default
1	1	Enter/View Assets	3	Assets
1	2	Enter/View Other Information...	1	2
1	3	Preview Reports...	1	3
1	4	Change Switchboard Items	5	
1	5	Exit this database	6	
2	0	Forms Switchboard	0	
2	1	Enter/View Employees	3	Employees
2	2	Enter/View Asset Categories	3	Asset Categories
2	3	Enter/View Status	3	Status
2	4	Return to Main Switchboard	1	1
3	0	Reports Switchboard	0	
3	1	Preview the Assets by Category Report	4	Assets by Category
3	2	Preview the Assets by Date Acquired Report	4	Assets by Date Acquired
3	3	Preview the Assets by Employee Report	4	Assets by Employee
3	4	Preview the Depreciation Summary Report	4	Depreciation Summary
3	5	Preview the Maintenance History Report	4	Maintenance History
3	6	Return to Main Switchboard	1	11
	0			

Record: 1 of 18

Figure 3-1: A table in Datasheet view.

Working in Design view

Design view gives you ways to specify field properties and refine the table definition (see Figure 3-2). You use Design view to define the type of data that you store in a field, define the format of a field, identify the primary key, and enter data validation rules. To display a table in Design view, take any of the following actions:

- ✦ Press and hold the Ctrl key as you double-click the name of the table in the Database window.
- ✦ Select the table in the Database window and click the Design button on the toolbar.
- ✦ Right-click the table name in the Database window and choose Design View from the shortcut menu that appears.
-  ✦ Click the Design View button if the table's in Datasheet view.

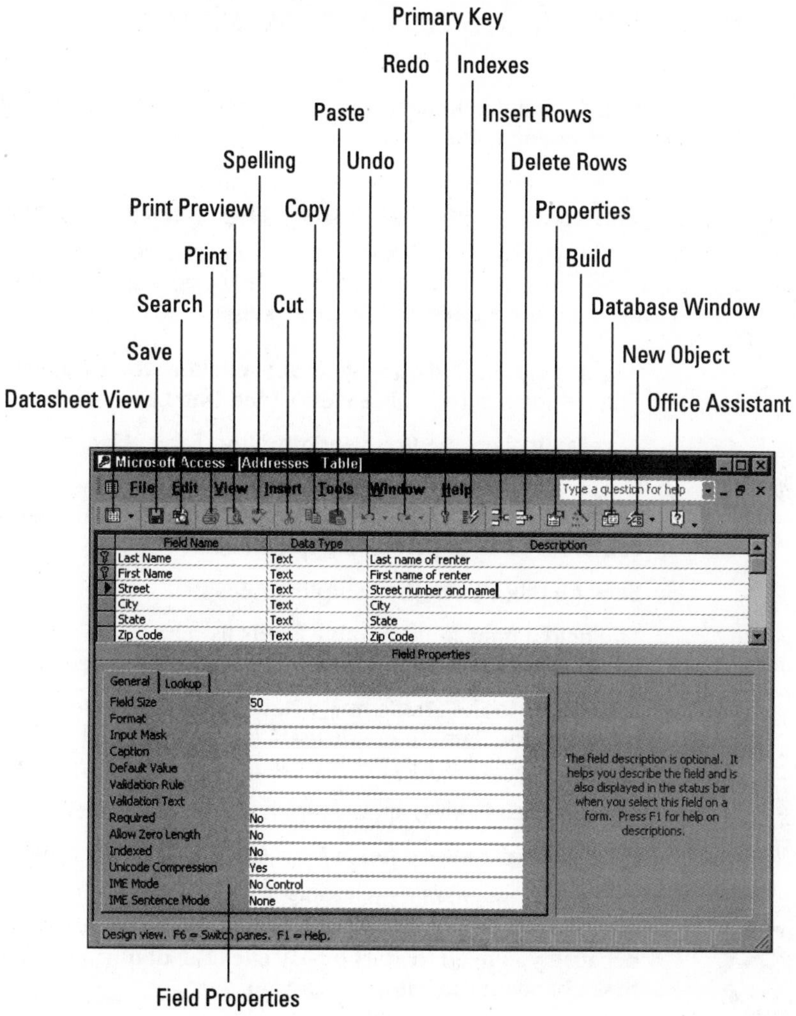

Figure 3-2: A table in Design view.

In Design view, each field gets a row, with the field name appearing in the first column, the type of data that you're storing in the field appearing in the second column, and a description of the field appearing in the third column. The bottom half of the Design view window is known as the Field Properties pane, and it displays additional options for the selected field (the one with a triangle in the row selector, immediately to the left of the field name).

Adding a New Table to Your Database

You can create a table by several different methods: by using a wizard, by entering data and field names in a datasheet, or by using Design view. This section gets you going.

Creating a table by using the Table Wizard

The Table Wizard simplifies the process of creating a table by enabling you to choose from some common tables and often-used fields. To use the Table Wizard to create a table, follow these steps:

1. **Begin the Table Wizard by double-clicking the Create Table by Using Wizard icon in the Table view of the Database window.**

   Access displays the first window of the Table Wizard.

2. **If your database is for personal rather than business use, click the Personal radio button to display tables and sample fields that you commonly use in personal applications.**

3. **Select a table from the Sample Tables list.**

   The field names in the Sample Fields list change to reflect the table that you select. (Don't forget to use the scroll bars to see all the options.)

4. **Add fields to the Fields in My New Table list by double-clicking field names in the Sample Fields list. You can select all the fields in the Sample Fields list by clicking the double-right-arrow button.**

   The selected field(s) appears in the Fields in My New Table list.

5. **If necessary, remove fields from the Fields in My New Table list.**

   To remove one field name, select it and click the left-arrow button to the left of the Fields in My New Table list. To remove all fields (maybe because you need to start over!), click the double left-facing arrow that's beneath the left-arrow button.

6. **(Optional) You can rename a field by selecting it in the Fields in My New Table list and clicking the Rename Field button.**

   Access displays the Rename Field dialog box. Type the new name or edit the name appearing in the dialog box and press Enter.

   Any time after you select the table and fields, you can click Finish to accept the Table Wizard defaults and create the table.

7. **Click Next to display the next Table Wizard window.**

8. **Change the name of the table (if you think it needs a better name) and use the radio buttons to tell Access whether you want it to set a primary key.**

See "Identifying Records with a Primary Key Field," later in this chapter, for an explanation of primary keys.

9. **Click Next to display the next window. (This window asks whether any fields in the new table relate to any existing tables in the database.)**
10. **If fields in the new table relate to fields in an existing table, select the table, click the Relationships button, and use the Relationships dialog box to tell Access how the tables relate; then click OK.**

    "Relating (Linking) Tables," later in this chapter, describes what table relationships are and how to link tables.
11. **Click Next to display the last window.**
12. **Click the radio button that describes what you want to do after Access creates the table.**
13. **Click Finish to create the table.**

Creating a table in Datasheet view

Using the Datasheet view is the most straightforward way to create a table. A datasheet looks like a spreadsheet — you can name your fields and begin entering data. Access figures out the type of data that each field holds.

TIP

Creating a table in Datasheet view doesn't prevent you from using the more advanced settings in Design view. To display Design view at any time, click the Design View button.

To create a table in Datasheet view, follow these steps:

1. **Display the Table view in the Database window and double-click the Create Table by Entering Data icon.**

   To see the list of tables in a database, click the Tables button in the Database window.

   After you click the Create Table by Entering Data icon, Access creates a table called Table1. Across the top of the table are field names: Field1, Field2, and so on.
2. **Enter one record of data (by filling in the first row). Move to the next field by pressing Tab or Enter.**

   Access displays a pencil icon in the left border of the row to indicate that you're entering or changing data.
3. **Save the table by clicking the Save button, pressing Ctrl+S, or choosing File⇨Save.**

   Access displays the Save As dialog box.

4. **Type a new name for the table (assigning the table a name that indicates what data you intend to store in it) and click OK.**

5. **After Access asks whether you want to define a primary key, choose Yes or No. If you're not sure, choose No — you can go back to the table later to define a primary key if you need to.**

   See "Identifying Records with a Primary Key Field," later in this chapter.

   After you save the table, Access gets rid of any additional columns in the datasheet. You can still add or remove fields later, however.

6. **Rename a field by double-clicking the field name, typing a new name, and pressing Enter.**

   Instead of Field1, Field2, and so on, assign fields names that reflect the data that they contain. Rename all the fields. Access automatically saves the new field names.

7. **Enter the rest of your data.**

   Access automatically saves the data as you move to the next cell.

   To move to the beginning of a row, press the Home key. To move to the next line after you complete a record, press Tab or Enter. (This method works only after you save the table the first time.) You can also move to the next row by pressing the ↓ key.

8. **Close the table by clicking its Close button.**

Creating a table in Design view

Design view is a good place to create your table if you want to use the more advanced settings, known as *field properties,* which are available only in this view. Otherwise, Datasheet view usually works best.

TIP

You can only define fields in Design view — you can't enter any data. You must use the Datasheet view or a form to do that.

To use Design view to create a table, follow these steps:

1. **Click the Table button in the Objects list of the Database window and double-click the Create Table in Design View icon.**

   Access displays a Design view for the new, blank table, which it names Table1. The cursor is in the first row, below the Field Name column heading (see Figure 3-3).

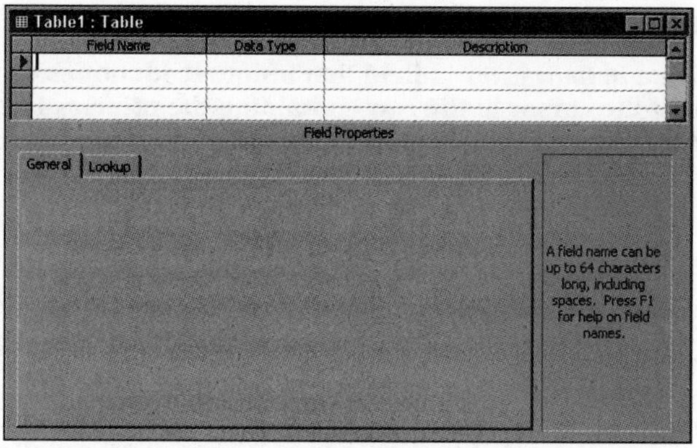

Figure 3-3: You can create a table in Design view.

2. **Type the name of the first field; then press Enter or Tab to move to the Data Type column.**

   Access displays the default Data Type, which is Text. As soon as you establish a data type for a field, Access displays field properties for that type of data in the Field Properties pane of the Design View window. The Field Properties pane is in the bottom of the window.

3. **To view all data types, click the down arrow to display the drop-down list of data type options and select the appropriate data type for the field (see Figure 3-4).**

   See "Changing Data Types," later in this chapter, if you need to change data types.

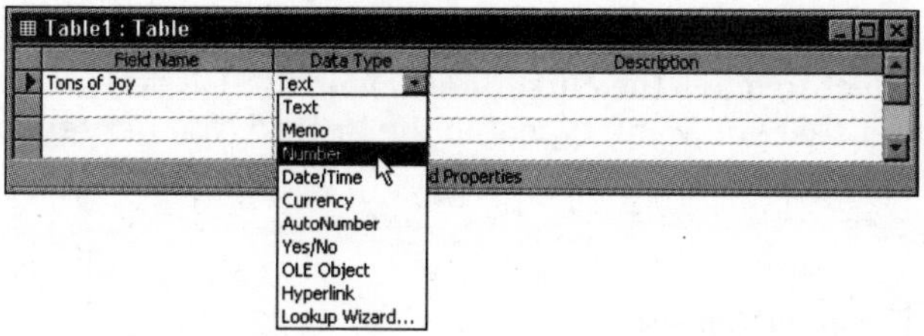

Figure 3-4: Selecting the appropriate data type.

4. **(Optional) Type a description in the third column (the one carrying the label Description).**

   TIP: The description that you type appears in the status bar whenever you select the field. Typing a description can give you and other users a hint about using the field.

5. **Define additional fields in the table by repeating Steps 2 through 4.**

6. **Define a *primary key* (a field that uniquely identifies each record) by putting the cursor in the row containing the primary key field and clicking the Primary Key button on the toolbar. Access displays a key to the left of the field name.**

   See "Identifying Records with a Primary Key Field," later in this chapter, for information about primary keys.

7. **Click the Save button or press Ctrl+S to display the Save As dialog box.**
8. **Type a new name for the table and then press Enter or click OK.**

To enter data after you design the table, click the Datasheet View button to display the table in Datasheet view.

Moving Around in a Datasheet

You can move around a datasheet in three ways: by using the mouse, by using keystrokes, and by using the VCR buttons at the bottom of the Datasheet window, as the following list describes:

- **Moving with the mouse:** Click the cell in the datasheet where you want the cursor to appear. You can also click the vertical and horizontal scroll bars to change the part of the datasheet that's on-screen.
- **Moving with keys:** In addition to using the arrow keys and Page Up and Page Down keys, you can use the keystrokes shown in Table 3-1 to move around a datasheet.
- **Moving with VCR buttons:** Use the VCR buttons at the bottom of the datasheet to move the cursor (see Figure 3-5). If you know the record number that you want, type it in the Record Number text box and press Enter.

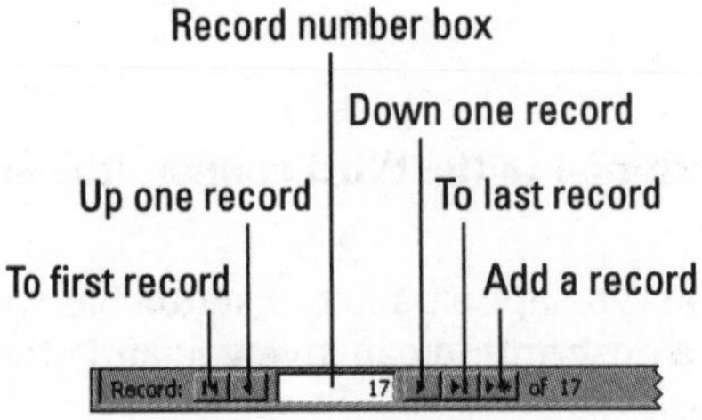

Figure 3-5: You can move around a datasheet by using its VCR buttons.

Table 3-1	Moving Around with Keys
Key to Press	*Where It Takes You*
Ctrl+PgUp	Left one screen
Ctrl+PgDn	Right one screen
Tab	Following field
Shift+Tab	Preceding field
Home	First field of the current record
End	Last field of the current record
Ctrl+Home	First record of the first field (the top-left corner of the datasheet)
Ctrl+End	Last record of the last field (the bottom-right corner of the datasheet)
F5	Specified record (type a record number and press Enter to go to a specific record)

Adding Data to Your Database

The easiest way to put data into a database or to work with the data already there is to use the Datasheet view, although you can also add data to the database through forms and queries. Here's how to add new records to an existing table:

1. **Open the table in Datasheet view.**

   The easiest way to open a table in Datasheet view is to double-click the table name in the Database window.

2. **Click the New Record button on the toolbar or at the bottom of the Datasheet.**

   Access moves the cursor to the last record, which is blank and waiting for input.

3. **Type the appropriate information in the first field.**
4. **Press Enter or Tab after you type data in a cell to move to the next field. You can also click a cell to move the cursor to that cell.**
5. **Enter data in all the fields in the record (as necessary) by repeating Steps 3 and 4.**

   To enter data for another record, simply press Enter after the cursor is in the last field — Access automatically creates a new record.

TIP

Access automatically saves the data in the database file as you move to the next record.

Editing Data in a Datasheet

Edit a value by moving the cursor to the value, pressing F2, or clicking the value to see a cursor. Delete characters by using the Delete and Backspace keys. Add new characters by typing them.

To replace the contents of a field, select the entire field by clicking at the beginning of the field, pressing and holding the mouse button, and dragging the mouse pointer to the end of the field. Then type the new entry — whatever you type replaces the selected characters.

Changing Data Types

Fields must have a *type,* which describes the kind of data that you can enter into the field. Common data types are *text, numeric,* and *date/time.* Table 3-2 describes each data type.

Table 3-2 Access Data Types

Data Type	*What It Holds*
Text	The Text type can contain numbers, letters, punctuation, spaces, and special characters (such as #, @, !, %). If you use hyphens or parentheses in phone numbers (and almost everyone does), Access defines the phone-number field as a text field. You can't use a number in a text field in calculations. (But who wants to add phone numbers?) A text field holds up to 255 characters.
Memo	The Memo type can contain numbers, letters, spaces, and special characters, just as the Text type can, but more of them fit in a Memo field than in a Text field — up to 65,535 characters. (You really need to work to fill up this type of field!)
Number	The Number type can contain only numbers. You may use + and – before the number and a decimal point as long as you follow it with at least one number. You can use Number fields in calculations.
Date/Time	The Date/Time type can hold, well, dates and times. You can do calculations in Date/Time fields.
Currency	The Currency type holds numbers with a currency sign in front of them ($, £, ¥, and so on). You can do calculations in Currency fields.

Data Type	*What It Holds*
AutoNumber	The AutoNumber type includes numbers unique to each record. Access assigns these numbers, starting at 1, and automatically increments subsequent records.
Yes/No	The Yes/No type holds any kind of yes-or-no data. You can set up a Yes/No field to contain other two-word sets, such as True/False, On/Off, and Male/Female, and so on.
OLE Object	The OLE Object type can hold a picture, a sound, or another object that someone creates by using OLE-compatible software other than Access.
Hyperlink	The Hyperlink type can hold links to World Wide Web addresses (URLs), objects within the database, files, and other kinds of hyperlink addresses.
Lookup Wizard	The Lookup Wizard type runs the Lookup Wizard, which enables you to select a table or type a list to display in a drop-down list that you use for data entry.

If you create your table in Datasheet view and enter data, Access selects a data type that it bases on the data you're entering. If you enter text, Access makes the data type of the field Text. If you enter numbers with a currency symbol in front, Access sets the data type to Currency. To change the data type that Access chooses, use the Data Type setting for the field in Design view. Follow these steps:

1. **If necessary, switch to Design view by clicking the Design View button.**
2. **Click the Data Type column of the field whose data type you want to change.**
3. **Display the drop-down list by clicking the down-arrow.**
4. **Choose the data type that you want by clicking it.**

TIP

You can also cycle through the data types without displaying the drop-down list by double-clicking the Data Type setting.

Relating (Linking) Tables

Most databases consist of a number of tables. Each table contains a number of fields that relate to one another. One table, for example, may contain customer information with fields for names, addresses, and phone numbers. Another table may contain customer orders with fields for the items that users ordered and the number of items that they ordered. Yet another table may contain detail information on the order with fields for the item number, description, and price. All the tables contain related data, but Access doesn't know that until you link the tables by defining related fields. You may use a customer number field, for example, to link the customer information table to the customer order table, which means that the customer number field must appear in both tables. And you may use an order number to link the customer order table to the order detail table.

After you link tables with related fields, you can create queries and reports that use fields from a number of tables. Telling Access about the relationships between tables is the key to making your relational database useful.

Pick your related fields carefully — make sure that both fields contain exactly the same type of data. Usually, a related field is the primary key in one table and simply information in the other table. A *primary key* is the field that uniquely identifies each record in the table. (See "Identifying Records with a Primary Key Field," later in this chapter, for more information about key fields.)

Related fields must contain the same data type, or the link doesn't work.

Types of relationships

You can relate fields that appear in more than one table in one of four ways. These four types of relationships are as follows:

- **One-to-one:** A record in one table has exactly one related record in another table. Each record in a table that lists employees by name, for example, has exactly one related record in a table that lists employees by employee number, and each employee number refers to only one employee.
- **One-to-many:** One record in the first table has many related records in the second table. One table that lists artists, for example, may have many related records in another table that lists CDs by artist.
- **Many-to-one:** This relationship is identical to one-to-many, except that you look at the relationship from the other side. Each record in a table that lists CDs by artist, for example, has only one related record in a table that lists artists, but many CDs may have the same artist.
- **Many-to-many:** This relationship is the most complicated type. A many-to-many relationship requires a linking table. The item field in a table listing items by the stores that sell them, for example, has a many-to-many relationship to the item field in a table listing stores and the items that they sell. An item may be sold by many stores, and many stores sell a particular item.

Creating and managing relationships

To define the relationships in your database, follow these steps:

1. **Choose Tools⇨Relationships or click the Relationships button on the toolbar.**

   If no relationships are defined in the database, Access displays the Show Table dialog box, where you choose which tables with fields you want to use in relationships. If you already defined relationships in the database, Access displays the Relationships window.

2. **Add tables to the Relationships window by selecting them in the Show Table dialog box and clicking the Add button.**

   TIP

   You can also add a table to the Relationships window by double-clicking the table name. You can select more than one table by selecting the first table and Ctrl+clicking the others. Then click the Add button.

3. **Click the Close button to close the Show Table dialog box. If you need to display it again, click the Show Tables button on the toolbar.**

4. **Pick two related fields. Use the scroll bars to display the fields that you want to link. Drag the field from one table and drop it on its related field in the second table.**

   If you drag the wrong field, just drop it on the gray background rather than dragging it to a field in a table. Then you're ready to start again.

   TIP

   After you release the mouse button, Access displays the Edit Relationships dialog box. It details the nature of the relationship (see Figure 3-6).

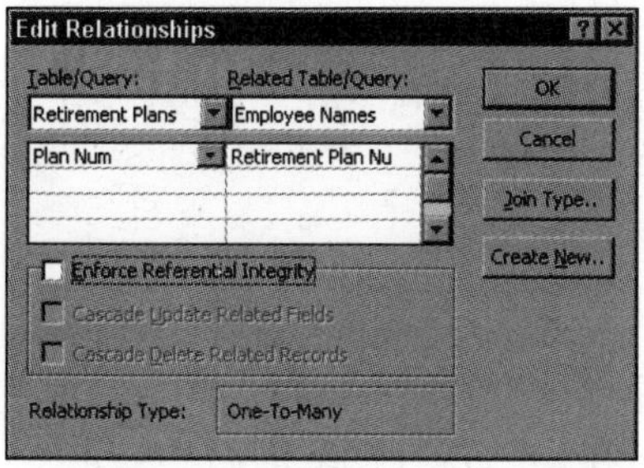

Figure 3-6: The Edit Relationships dialog box.

5. **Make sure that the table and field names are correct; then click Create New to tell Access to create the relationship.**

   If a field name is incorrect, you can change it by clicking the name of the field, clicking the arrow to display the drop-down list, and choosing another field name from the same table. If the relationship looks completely wrong, click Cancel and start over.

   TIP: To reopen the Relationships dialog box after you close it, double-click the line joining two fields in the Edit Relationships window.

6. **Repeat Steps 3 through 5 to create relationships between other fields.**

Access automatically saves the relationships that you create. You can view the relationships in the Relationships window (see Figure 3-7). You can print relationships by choosing File⇨Print Relationships whenever the Relationships window is active. To delete a relationship, click the line that connects two fields in the Relationships window and press Delete.

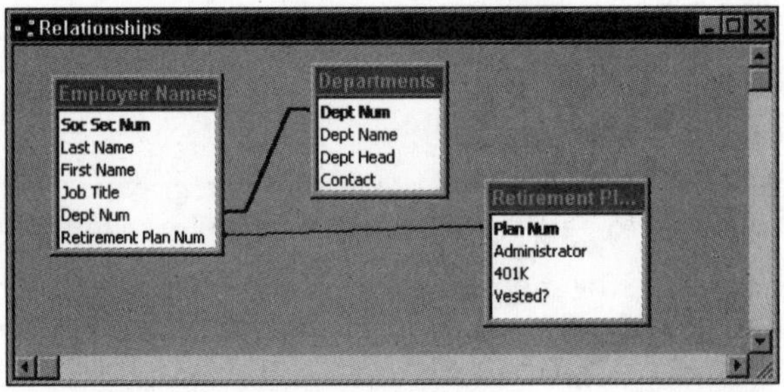

Figure 3-7: You can view your table relationships.

TIP: You can move tables around in the Relationships window so that the relationships are easy to understand; just drag the title bar of the table to move it. You can also size a table so that you can see more field names; just drag the border.

Identifying Records with a Primary Key Field

A *primary key* uniquely identifies every record in a table. Most of the time, the primary key is a single field, but it can also be a combination of fields, in which case it is known as a *multiple-field primary key.* Examples of a primary key field are Social Security Number, a unique customer number, or some other field that uniquely identifies the record.

REAL WORLD

Exporting and importing data

You can export an object from an Access database to a file that isn't an Access file — a dBase or Excel file, for example. You can also use this technique to create a static HTML file. To export an object, follow these steps:

1. **Open the database that contains the object.**
2. **Select the object in the Database window.**
3. **Choose File⇨Export or right-click the object and then choose Export from the shortcut menu that appears.**
4. **In the Export dialog box that appears, select the file type that you want to create by opening the Save as Type drop-down list and clicking the file type in the list.**
5. **Select the file to which you want to save the object by typing the name in the File Name box.**

   You can save to a file that already exists, or you can create a completely new file by typing a new name in the File Name text box. If you're creating a non-Access file, type a name for your brand-new file.
6. **Click the Export button.**

   If you're exporting an existing Access file, you see the Export dialog box, where you can rename the object (if you want to) and tell Access whether you want to export all the data or just the object definition (field names, format, and any expressions).

The easiest way to import data is to use the Import Data Wizard. This wizard enables you to see what you're working with and gives you more options than importing or linking with a simple menu command. Open the database that you want to add the imported or linked data to and follow these steps to import data:

1. **Click the New button in the Tables tab of the Database window and choose Import Table in the New Table dialog box that appears.**
2. **In the Import dialog box that appears, open the Files of Type drop-down list and select from the list the file type that you're importing from.**

   If you're importing data from an Excel file, for example, choose Microsoft Excel (*.xls). Access then displays the Excel files in the current folder.
3. **Navigate the folder structure (if necessary) to find the file that contains the data that you want to use and click the filename so that it appears in the File Name text box of the Import dialog box.**
4. **Click the Import button.**

   The wizard takes over and guides you through the process of choosing the data you that want to import. The windows you see depend on the type of file that contains the data you're importing.

You can identify an existing field as the primary key, or you can ask Access to create one. To have Access create a primary key for you, follow these steps:

1. **Click the Design View button, if necessary, to switch to Design view.**

2. **Click the cursor in the field that you want to make the primary key and click the Primary Key button.**

   Access displays the key symbol to the left of the field name.

If you neglect to create a primary key, Access creates one that it calls ID in the first field of the table. The field starts at 1 and increases by 1 for each record. (It's an AutoNumber field.) Access automatically inserts a new number each time that you add a new record to the table. See the section, "Changing Data Types," earlier in this chapter, for an explanation of AutoNumber fields.

To make an AutoNumber primary key field, create an AutoNumber field and designate it as the primary key.

To make a *multiple-field primary key,* select the fields in Design view. To select a field, click the row selector — the gray block to the left of the field name. Then Ctrl+click to select fields after you select the first field. After you select the fields, click the Primary Key button.

Chapter 4: Getting Your Tables Just Right

In This Chapter

- **Getting your columns and rows as you want them**
- **Inserting and moving columns**
- **Making your datasheets look good**
- **Deleting records**
- **Saving your table**

As smart as Access seems sometimes, it doesn't have a creative side. If Access had its way, everything in every table would look just the same. It doesn't know how wide you want your columns or how high you want your rows. In addition, it doesn't care that you can add colors and change fonts in your datasheets. Access never even reminds you that you can change how its gridlines look. Although these options are never crucial to the importance of your data, maintaining *some* control over the look and feel of your tables may just help you regain some human dignity. Besides, you're the one who must look at your tables on-screen, and you can make them easier to work with. In addition, you need to know how to delete unwanted records and — goodness forbid if you forget — save your tables.

Changing Column Width

Initially, Access gives all columns in a datasheet the same width. You can change the width one column at a time or a few columns at once.

To change the width of one column, follow these steps:

1. **Move the mouse pointer to the right border of the column and then up to the top of the column, where the field names appear.**

   The pointer turns into the change-column-width pointer.

2. **Click and drag the column border to a new position.**

FAST TRACK

You can change the width of several adjacent columns at the same time by using this method — simply select all the columns (by clicking the first column header and dragging to the header for the last column that you want to select). Change the width of one of the selected columns. All the selected columns become the same width as the one column whose width you change.

Changing Row Height

You can change row heights in the same way that you change column widths. Changing row height has a catch, however — if you change the height of one row, the heights of all the other rows in the datasheet change, too. You can wrap text on a datasheet by making the row tall enough to fit multiple lines.

You can change the height of rows in a datasheet by using one of the following methods:

- Click and drag between rows in the row selector boxes. (To make a row exactly two lines tall, use the row borders as a guide as you drag the change-row-height pointer.)
- Use the Row Height dialog box (refer to Figure 4-1). Display it by right-clicking a row selector and choosing Row Height from the shortcut menu.

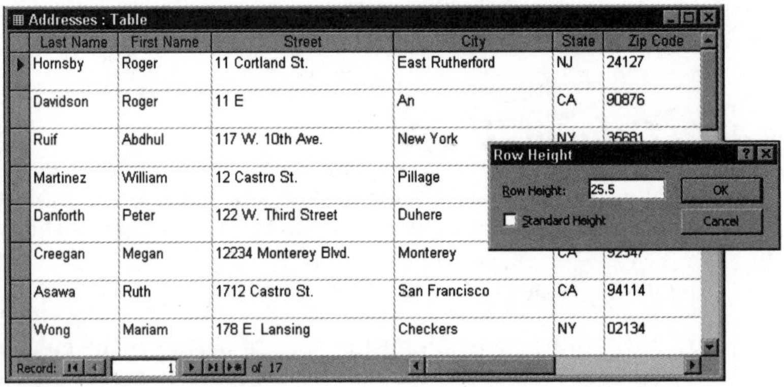

Addresses : Table
Last Name | First Name | Street | City | State | Zip Code
Hornsby | Roger | 11 Cortland St. | East Rutherford | NJ | 24127
Davidson | Roger | 11 E | An | CA | 90876
Ruif | Abdhul | 117 W. 10th Ave. | New York
Martinez | William | 12 Castro St. | Pillage
Danforth | Peter | 122 W. Third Street | Duhere
Creegan | Megan | 12234 Monterey Blvd. | Monterey
Asawa | Ruth | 1712 Castro St. | San Francisco | CA | 94114
Wong | Mariam | 178 E. Lansing | Checkers | NY | 02134
Record: 1 of 17
Row Height
Row Height: 25.5
OK
Standard Height
Cancel

Figure 4-1: Click and drag or right-click and choose Row Height to change the height of rows.

Inserting a Column/Adding a Field

Inserting a column into a datasheet gives you the space to add a new field to the table. You can add a field to your table by using either Datasheet or Design view. To add a column in Datasheet view, follow these steps:

1. **Click the field name of the column to the right of where you want the new column.**

   Access selects the column and displays the shortcut menu.

2. **Either right-click and choose Insert Column from the shortcut menu or choose Insert⇨Column.**

To add a field in Design view, follow these steps:

1. **Click the row selector of the field that is immediately to follow the field you're inserting.**

   Access selects the row and displays the shortcut menu.

2. **Either right-click and choose Insert Rows from the shortcut menu or choose Insert⇨Rows.**

   Access adds a row. Now you can define your field.

Moving a Column in a Datasheet

You can move a column heading (so that the entire column goes with it) in Datasheet view by dragging it. To do so, follow these steps:

1. **Click the field header of the column that you want to move to select the column.**

2. **Click the field name a second time and drag the column to its new position.**

   The mouse pointer turns into the "move pointer," and a dark line appears where the column is going.

3. **After the dark line is in the position you want the column in, release the mouse button.**

Formatting Datasheets

Although you don't have the flexibility in formatting datasheets that you do with reports and forms, you do have some options. You can change the font, row height, column width, and some other options. To change a datasheet's format, use the Format menu. (A datasheet must be the active window for you to see this menu.)

Changing the font

You can change the font and font size in your datasheet by using the Font dialog box. You can't change the font of just one cell, column, or row, however, because font choices apply throughout a datasheet. To display the Font dialog box, choose Format⇨Font (see Figure 4-2).

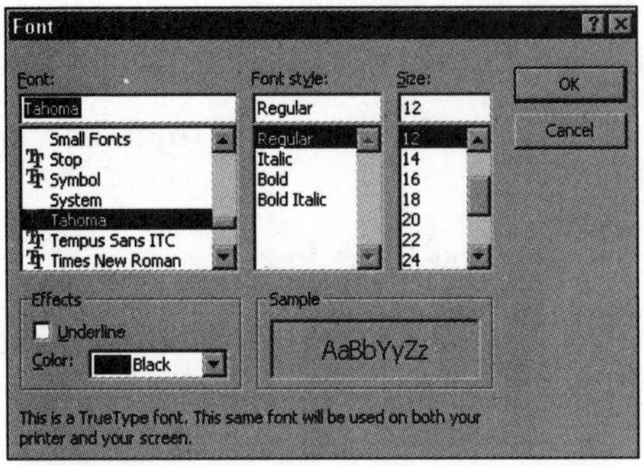

Figure 4-2: The Font dialog box gives you lots of leeway in changing fonts.

Displaying and removing gridlines

Gridlines are the gray horizontal and vertical lines that separate cells in a datasheet. You can change the color of the gridlines appearing in a datasheet or choose not to display gridlines at all. You can also give cells some special effects instead of simply separating them with gridlines.

To change gridlines, choose Format⇨Datasheet. Access displays the Datasheet Formatting dialog box. As you change the settings, the Sample box shows the effect of the changes on the datasheet. Table 4-1 shows what the options on the Datasheet Formatting dialog box do to your datasheet.

Table 4-1 Datasheet Formatting Options

Option	*What It Does*
Cell Effect	Displays the cells normally (Flat) or with a three-dimensional effect.
Gridlines Shown	Displays or hides horizontal and vertical gridlines.
Background Color	Enables you to choose a background color for cells.
Gridline Color	Enables you to choose a gridline color.
Border and Line Styles	Enables you to change the look of the border, horizontal gridline, vertical gridline, and column header underline. Select the line that you want to format in the first box and choose the line style in the second box.

Deleting Records

To delete a record in a datasheet, follow these steps:

1. **Right-click anywhere in the record or row that you want to delete.**
2. **Choose Delete Record from the shortcut menu.**

Alternatively, you can put the cursor anywhere in the row that you want to delete and then click the Delete Record button.

Deleting a record is permanent. After you delete data, you can't get it back — so make sure that you really want to delete it!

Saving a Table

Access automatically saves data that you enter in a table after you move to the next record. You do, however, need to save the table design — the field definitions and formats. To save a table design, follow these steps:

1. **Make sure that the table is active.**

   If the table is active, the color of its title bar matches the color of the Access title bar. You can click a window to make it active.

2. **Click the Save button, press Ctrl+S, or choose File➪Save.**

You can also save a table by closing it. If you've made changes in a table since the last time you used it, and you attempt to close the table, Access asks whether you want to save it. Remember that Access saves the data automatically each time that you move to another field. What you need to save at this point is the table design and the datasheet's formatting.

Chapter 5: Working with Fields

In This Chapter

- **Copying, naming, and opening fields**
- **Changing field names and size**
- **Freezing and hiding columns**
- **Formatting all types of fields**
- **Creating a lookup field**

Fields are categories of data in your database. Each field holds one kind of data. You may have a Birthdays field, for example, that stores all the birthdays of the people in your database. Then you're always prepared to send them birthday greetings as a cheap advertising gimmick. Or you can have a Delinquent Accounts field to include all your favorite customers. You can send them a sort of greeting, too. The different categories of data are simply unlimited.

To understand better the concept of a field, you may need to visualize one. If you think in terms of a table, fields are the columns of data, each column displaying a "heading" to indicate what type of data it holds. No matter which way you think, however, fields are the cornerstone of your database.

Field Management

If you control your fields, you're the master of your database. Basic field management isn't very complicated, however, and Access almost makes it an enjoyable task.

Copying a field

You can copy a field. This capability is particularly useful if you're creating several similar fields — instead of defining the data type and properties for each field, you can simply copy a field definition and edit the field as necessary. Or you may want to copy a field that you're using to link tables. This procedure ensures that the field maintains the same properties in both tables, a requirement for related fields.

To copy a field, follow these steps:

1. **Display the table in Design view.**

   If necessary, open the View button drop-down list and choose Design View.

2. **Select the field that you want to copy by clicking the row selector.**

3. **Copy the field by clicking the Copy button, choosing Edit⇨Copy, or press Ctrl+C.**

4. **Move to a blank row or create a blank row by right-clicking within a row and choosing Insert Rows from the shortcut menu. If you're copying the field to a different table, display that table in Design view and move to a blank row.**

5. **Click the Paste button, choose Edit⇨Paste, or press Ctrl+V.**

   Notice that Access copies the field properties as well as the information in the selected row.

6. **Type a new name to rename the copied field.**

   Access displays the field name selected, so typing a new name replaces the selected name.

7. **Press Enter to complete the new field.**

8. **Edit the Description, if necessary.**

9. **Save the table.**

You can copy the field again by moving to another blank row and clicking the Paste button.

Naming and renaming fields

The rules for naming Access fields are simple, as the following list describes:

- Start with a letter or a number. (Actually, this one isn't a hard and fast rule, but it's good practice.)
- Don't use more than 64 characters. And if you intend to export the table, field names should be no longer than one word. Some database programs have trouble handling blank spaces.

Changing the name of a field before you finish designing a table is a hassle-free task. To rename a field, start in Datasheet view and follow these steps:

1. **Double-click the field name.**

   Access selects the entire name.

2. **Type a new name for the field.**
3. **Press Enter to enter the new name or press Esc to cancel the renaming procedure.**

Setting field size

In the Field Properties pane is the Field Size text box. You can use this text box to restrict the number of characters that can be entered in a Text or Memo field. For Number data, the Field Size defines the type of number and tells Access how much space is necessary to store each value. In Design view, open the Field Size drop-down list and choose an option to tell Access how you want to treat numbers (see Figure 5-1). Table 5-1 gives the Field Size options for numeric data.

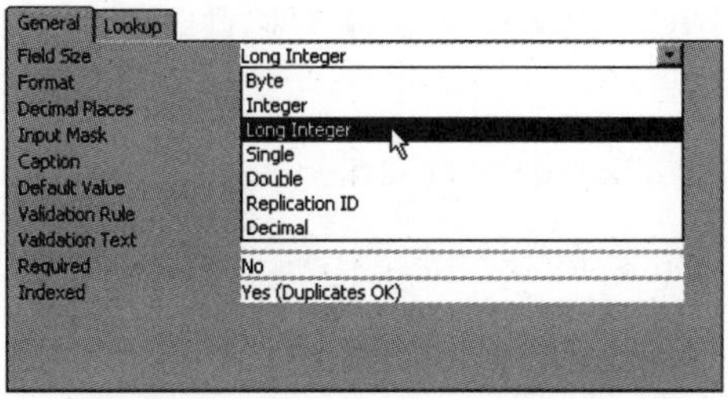

Figure 5-1: Choosing a field size for numeric data.

Table 5-1 Numeric Data Field Size

Numeric Field Size Settings	*What They Do*
Byte	Accepts values from 0 to 255 with no decimal places.
Integer	Accepts values from -32,768 to 32,767 with no decimal places.
Long Integer	Accepts values from about negative 2 billion to about positive 2 billion with no decimal places.
Double	Accepts really huge numbers, both positive and negative, with up to 15 decimal places.
Single	Accepts not-quite-as-huge numbers, both positive and negative, with up to seven decimal places.

If you shorten the field size after entering data, you risk losing data whenever Access truncates entries longer than the new field size. The default field size for Text data, for example, is 50 characters. If you change the field-size setting to 25, Access truncates all entries longer than 25 characters to 25 characters. Access warns you in the form of a message dialog box, however, if you're going to lose data as a result of shortening the field length.

Freezing a column in a datasheet

If you're working with a wide datasheet, you may want to freeze one column so that you can move all the way to the right edge of the table and still see that particular field. If you freeze a column, it moves to the left side of the window (no matter where it appears before that) and stays there, even if you scroll or pan all the way to the right. To freeze a column, follow these steps:

1. **Right-click the field name to select the column and display the shortcut menu.**
2. **Choose Freeze Columns from the shortcut menu to freeze the selected column.**

   To unfreeze a column, choose Format⇨Unfreeze All Columns.

Deleting a column/removing a field

You can delete a field from a table, but do so very carefully — a 24-hour waiting period may be in order. If you delete a field (a column) in a datasheet, you also irretrievably delete all the data in the field.

To delete a field from a table, follow these steps:

1. **Right-click the field name for the column.**

   Access selects the column and displays the shortcut menu.

2. **Choose Delete Column from the shortcut menu.**

   Access displays a warning box, telling you that you're permanently deleting the field and the data in it.

3. **Click Yes to delete the field (or No if you change your mind).**

To delete a field in Design view, follow the same procedure, except right-click the row selector for the field that you want to delete and choose Delete Rows from the shortcut menu.

Formatting Fields

If you're working with a table in Design view, you can format various fields by using the Format setting in the Field Properties pane. These options change how the data appears in the table and may affect how the data appears in queries, forms, and reports. Read on to discover how to format fields.

Formatting Text and Memo fields

If you're dealing with a Text field, the Format options of the Field Properties pane enable you to specify how the text in a field appears, as well as how many characters you may enter in the field. To format Text and Memo fields, type a character or characters from Table 5-2 into the Format line of the Field Properties pane.

Table 5-2 Formatting Options for Text and Memo Fields

Formatting for Text	*What You Type*
Display text in all uppercase	>
Display text in all lowercase	<
Display text left-aligned	!
Specify a color	[color] (Black, blue, green, cyan, magenta, yellow, and white are the color options.)
Specify a certain number of characters	@ (Type @ for each character that you want to include — including spaces.)
Specify that no character is required	&
Display text	/text

You can tell Access to add characters such as +, —, $, a comma, parentheses, or a space to the data that you enter. You may, for example, want to enter the following in the Format setting for a phone number:

```
(@@@)@@@-@@@@
```

If you then enter ten digits into this field, the numbers appear with parentheses and the hyphen, even though you don't type those extra characters.

TIP

You can even format fields to include additional text. Just enclose the text that you want to add in quotation marks or precede it with a slash (/).

Formatting Number and Currency fields

Access comes with common formats for Number and Currency fields built right in — all you need to do is choose the format that you want from the Format drop-down list in the Field Properties pane (see Figure 5-2). Table 5-3 describes the different formats from which you can choose:

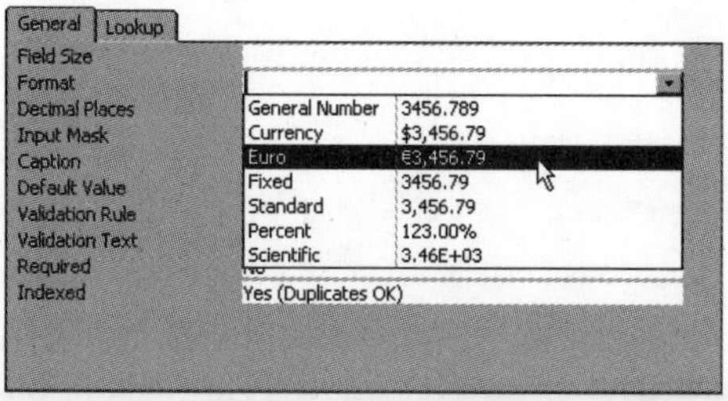

Figure 5-2: Access comes with formats for Number and Currency fields already built in.

Table 5-3	Formatting Options for Number and Currency Fields
Number Format	*How It Works*
General Number	Displays numbers without commas and with as many decimal places as the user enters.
Currency	Displays numbers with the local currency symbol (determining it from the Regional Settings in the Windows Control Panel), commas as thousands separators, and two decimal places.
Euro	Displays numbers as does the Currency format, but places the Euro symbol before the number.
Fixed	Displays numbers, specifying the number of decimal places in the Decimal Places setting (immediately below the Format setting); the default is 2.
Standard	Displays numbers with commas as thousands separators and specifies the number of decimal places in the Decimal Places property.
Percent	Displays numbers as percentages — that is, multiplying them by 100 and following them with a percent sign.
Scientific	Displays numbers in scientific notation.

REMEMBER

If the formatting for the numbers in the field doesn't seem to correspond to the Number Format property, you may need to change the Field Size property. If you set the Field Size property to Integer or Long Integer, for example, what value you use in the Decimal Places property doesn't matter; Access insists on displaying the value as an integer — with no decimal places. Try using Single or Double in the Format property instead.

Formatting Date/Time fields

Access includes built-in Date/Time formats from which you can choose. To see these formats, open the drop-down list in the Format section of the Field Properties pane (see Figure 5-3).

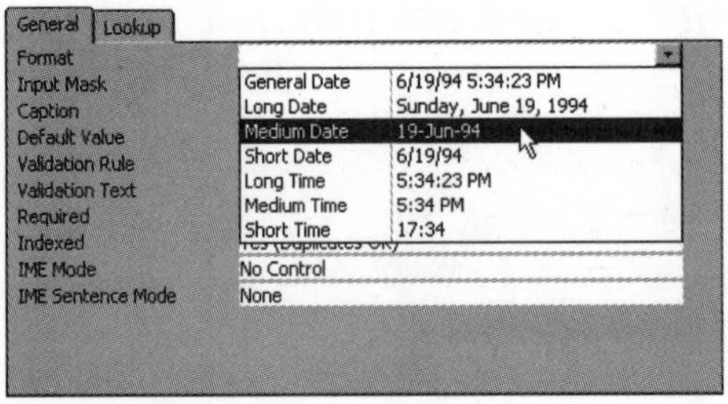

Figure 5-3: The drop-down list for choosing Date/Time field formats.

Next to each format name is an example of how the date and/or time appears. If you don't specify a format for a Date/Time field, Access uses the General Date format.

Creating a Lookup Field

You can create a *lookup field,* which is a drop-down list in a table to guide others (or yourself) as they enter data. A lookup field provides the user with a list of choices, rather than requiring users to type a value in the datasheet. Lookup fields enable you to keep your database small and the data that you enter in it accurate and consistent.

The items on the drop-down list can come from a list that you type or from a field in another table. You may want to input the customer number, for example, if you know the customer name. By using its Lookup Wizard, you can tell Access to display a drop-down list in the Customer Number field that shows the first and last name as well as the customer number, as shown in Figure 5-4. After you select a customer, Access puts the customer number in the table. (It's not as confusing as it sounds!)

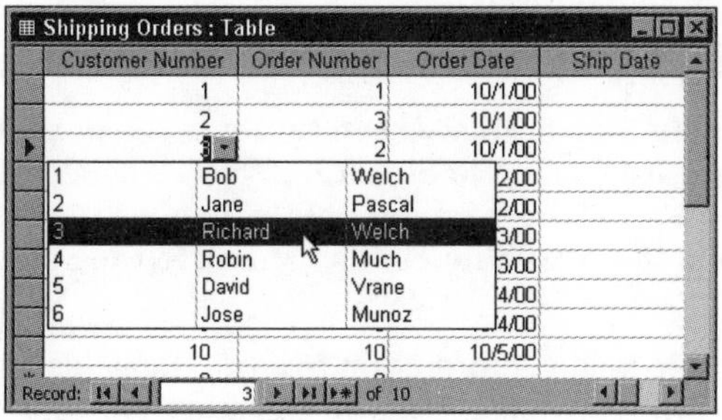

Figure 5-4: Access can display a drop-down list for a field.

To use the Lookup Wizard, follow these steps:

1. **Display the table in Design view.**
2. **Click the Data type column of the field that you want to hold the Lookup drop-down list and then open the Data Type drop-down list and select Lookup Wizard.**
3. **In the Lookup Wizard dialog box, select an option button to tell the wizard whether the values you want to appear on the field's drop-down list are coming from a field in another table or from a list that you type.**

   TIP: If the field simply consists of several choices, choose the second option. But if you want to store more information about those choices (maybe because you're entering the name of a customer who bought something, but you also want to store the customer's address and phone number in another table), store the values in a table.

4. **Click Next to display the next window of the Lookup Wizard.**

   What you see in the second window depends on the option you choose in the first window, as follows:

   - If you ask the lookup field to display values from another table, Access asks you for the name of the table.
   - If you tell Access that you want to type in the values, you get a table in which you can type the lookup list.

5. **If you're typing values to choose among, click the table in the wizard window (which currently displays only one cell) and type the first entry in the list. Press Tab — not Enter — to create new cells for additional entries.**

   If you want your lookup list to include values that a table or query stores, select the object containing the field with the values that you want to choose among. You can choose an existing query by clicking the Queries or Both radio button.

6. **Click Next to display the next window.**

7. **If you type a list in Step 5, this screen that you see now is the last screen of the wizard — skip to Step 13. If you're using a table for the lookup, you must tell Access which field(s) you want to use by moving field names from the Available Fields list box to the Selected Fields list box.**

   If you pick multiple fields, information from all the fields that you select appears on the drop-down list. But you can store only one field's information, so the next window asks you which field's value you want to store in the new field. You may, for example, display the Customer Number, First Name, and Last Name in the drop-down list, but you can store only one of those values — in the example in the figure, that value is the Customer Number.

8. **Click Next to display the next window.**

   This window shows you a table with the values in the lookup list and enables you to change the width of the columns. The window also contains a check box that, after you select it, hides the key field (if you select the key field). Depending on your application, you may want to display the key field by deselecting the Hide Key Column check box.

9. **Change the width of the column, if necessary.**

   TIP: You can change the width of the column to automatically fit the widest entry by double-clicking the right edge of the field name that appears at the top of the column.

10. **Click Next to display the final window of this wizard.**

11. **In the Available Fields list, choose the field that contains the value from the lookup list that you want to store in your database.**

    If you choose more than one field in Step 7, you see more than one field after you open the drop-down list to insert a value in your database table (refer to Figure 5-4). Choose the field from which you want to enter data.

12. **Edit the name that Access gives the lookup column, if you want, and then click Finish to create the lookup column.**

13. **Now check out your lookup list by viewing your table in Datasheet view. After you click the field for which you create the lookup list, you see an arrow that indicates that a drop-down list is available. Click the arrow to see options in the list.**

The default setting enables users to either choose from the drop-down list or type a value. To force users to choose from the drop-down list (or enter a value that's on the drop-down list) click the Lookup tab in the Field Properties pane and change the Limit To List setting from No to Yes.

You can add values to an existing lookup list. If you typed values for the lookup list yourself, switch to Design view, click the field with the lookup list, and click the Lookup tab in the Field Properties pane. You can add options to the Row Source by typing them in — just be sure to separate the options with a semicolon. If the lookup list gets its values from a table, you can add records to the table to see additional choices in the lookup list.

REMEMBER

The lookup field doesn't automatically update if you add additional items. Refresh the data in the lookup field by pressing F9.

Chapter 6: Manipulating Your Data

In This Chapter

- **Limiting data entry**
- **Finding data that you enter**
- **Filtering your data**
- **Sorting your data**
- **Blocking data that you don't want**

You don't always want people — or yourself — to enter data willy-nilly into your database. If you know what kind of data you want, Access can help you set limits on data entry and block unwanted data (to keep the riff-raff out, so to speak). Then, after you enter all this nice data into your database, Access can make finding and filtering your data according to your deep-rooted database needs a breeze. And while you're at it, feel free to go ahead and sort that data. This chapter gives you a head start on all these worthy activities.

Finding Data in a Table

To find a record that contains a particular word or value, use the Find and Replace dialog box. To display the Find and Replace dialog box, open a datasheet and perform one of the following tasks:

- ✦ Press Ctrl+F.
- ✦ Choose Edit⇨Find.

- ✦ Click the Find button on the Table Datasheet toolbar.

To use the Find and Replace dialog box, follow these steps:

1. **In Datasheet view, put the cursor in the field that contains the value you're searching for.**
2. **Use one of the preceding methods to display the Find and Replace dialog box.**
3. **In the Find What text box, type the text or value that you're looking for.**

4. **Use the Look In option to determine where to look — in the field your cursor's in or in the whole table.**

5. **Click Find Next to find the first instance of the value or text in the table.**

   Access displays the section of the table containing the values you enter in the Find What text box.

6. **If you don't find what you're looking for, click Find Next until you do.**

TIP

The Find and Replace dialog box also offers the following options, which can come in handy during a search:

- **Match:** Choose Any Part of Field, Whole Field, or Start of Field to tell Access whether the value or text that you type in the entire field, at the beginning of the field, or anywhere in the field (which means that the text may start somewhere in the middle of the field).
- **Search:** This option determines the direction in which Access searches. Choose Up, Down, or All. Choose All to find the text or value anywhere in the table — although Access starts the search at the cursor.
- **Match Case:** If you activate this check box, Access finds only text that matches the case of the text that you type in the Find What text box.
- **Search Fields As Formatted:** This option matches the contents of the Find What text box to the formatted data (the way that the data appears in the table, using the format and input mask properties, rather than the way that you enter it).
- **Replace With:** Use this option on the Replace tab of the Find and Replace dialog box to replace instances of the Find What text with the Replace With text. Replace one instance at a time by clicking the Replace button. Replace all instances by clicking the Replace All button.

Filtering Your Data

Filtering enables you to look at a subset of your table — records that match a particular criterion. (In English, filtering means that you can create a test for your data to pass and then look only at the rows in your table that pass your test.) In Access, a criterion for filtering is something such as "I want to find all the records with 2 in the Number of Items field." To use more advanced criteria, such as "2 or more" or "between 3 and 20," you need to use the Advanced Filter/Sort command or a query. If filtering doesn't give you the options you need, you probably need to use a query (see Chapters 7 and 8).

You can filter in three ways: Filter by Selection, Filter by Form, and Advanced Filter/Sort. Filtering creates a temporary table containing only those records that fit the criteria you choose. If you want a permanent table that updates as you add more records, you need to create a query.

You can tell whether a table uses a filter by looking at the bottom of the table — the status bar tells you how many records are in the table and displays `Filtered` in parentheses.

You can't save a filter — if you want to use a filtered table later, you need to create a query that contains the same criterion as your filter.

Filtering by selection

Filter by selection when you want to search using only one criterion and you know that the criterion is found in one field in your database table. To find all the Maine addresses in your address table, for example, you need to find an address that contains `ME` in the State field.

To filter by selection, follow these steps:

1. **In Datasheet view, put the cursor in the record and field that matches the criterion.**

   To find all the videos that were filmed in 1939, for example, you may put the cursor in the Year Made field to the year 1939.

2. **Click the Filter by Selection button, choose Records➪Filter➪Filter by Selection, or right-click and choose Filter By Selection.**

   Access creates a temporary table consisting of the records that meet the criterion. Access finds records that contain identical entries in the selected field (see Figure 6-1).

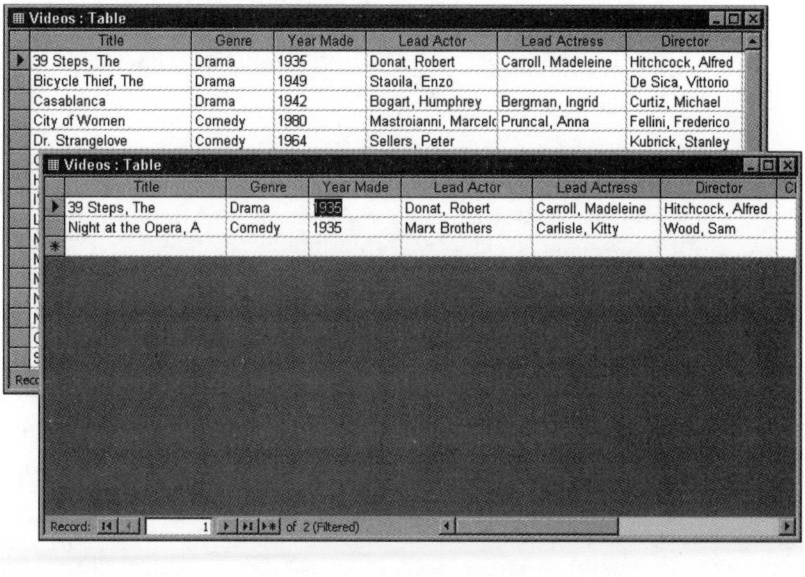

Figure 6-1: This table is filtered by the Year Made field.

If you don't narrow the list down enough, you can refilter the filtered table by using the same technique. You can choose a different field or even select just one word or part of a field before clicking the Filter by Selection button.

To see the entire table again, click the Remove Filter button. (It looks exactly like the Apply Filter button.)

You can select particular records that you want to filter out and then choose Records⇨Filter⇨Filter Excluding Selection (or right-click and choose Filter Excluding Selection) to exclude the selected records from the table. Use this technique in combination with the Filter by Selection command to see only the records that you want to see. To see the entire table, click the Apply Filter button again.

Filtering by form

If you have more than one criterion to match, you can filter by form. Say, for example, that you're looking for orders of more than $50 that customers sent before December 1. The Filter by Form window enables you to pick the values that you want for the filtered records. Unlike the Filter by Selection command, however, Filter by Form enables you to choose more than one value and to choose values to match for more than one field.

When you filter by form, you can use multiple criteria. If you specify more than one criterion on a Filter by Form tab, Access treats the criteria as AND criteria, meaning that a record must pass *all* the criteria to appear on the filtered datasheet.

If you use criteria on different tabs (by using the Or tab at the bottom of the window to display a clean grid), Access treats the criteria as OR criteria. A record must, therefore, meet the criteria on one tab or the other to appear on the filtered datasheet.

Using AND and OR criteria enables you to filter the records by using more than one rule or set of rules. You can find addresses from South China, Maine, for example, as well as you can addresses in Vermont by using the Or tab at the bottom of the Filter by Form window.

To filter a datasheet by form, follow these steps:

1. **In Datasheet view, click the Filter by Form button or choose Records⇨Filter⇨Filter by Form.**

   Access displays the Filter by Form window, which looks like an empty datasheet with some different buttons in the toolbar and some different menu choices.

2. **Move the cursor to a field in which you want to search for data.**

   A down arrow appears in the field the cursor's in.

3. **Click the arrow to see the list of all the values for that field.**

4. **Click the value that you want the filtered records to match (see Figure 6-2).**

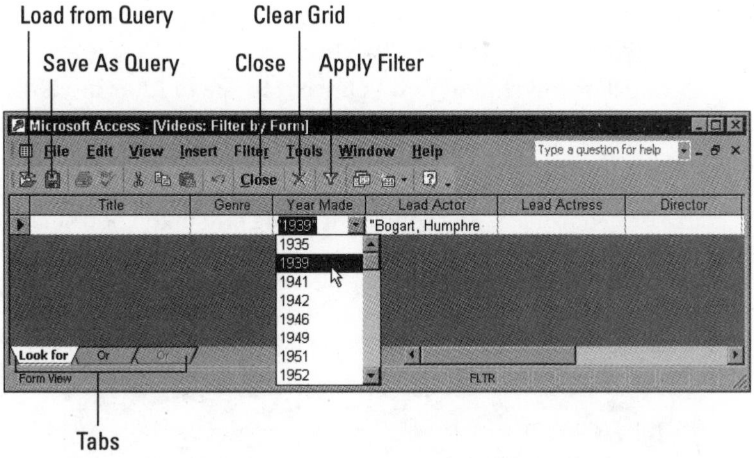

Figure 6-2: Filtering by form enables you to specify more than one criterion.

5. **If you have criteria for another field that you want to apply at the same time as the criteria you set in Step 4 (AND criteria), repeat Steps 3 and 4 for the additional field.**

   If you want to find movies made in 1939 starring Humphrey Bogart, for example, set the Year Made field to 1939 and the Lead Actor field to Bogart, Humphrey (see Figure 6-2).

6. **If you have another set of rules to filter records by, click the Or tab at the bottom of the Filter by Form window.**

   Access displays a blank Filter by Form window. If you set criteria on more than one tab, a record must meet all the criteria only on any one tab to appear on the filtered datasheet.

7. **Choose the criteria on the second tab in the same way that you chose those on the first — click the field and choose the value that you want to match.**

   Another Or tab appears, enabling you to continue adding as many sets of OR criteria as you need.

8. **To see the filtered table, click the Apply Filter button.**

Filtering by Advanced Filter/Sort

The easiest kind of query to create is one that filters records in only one table. You perform this simple query by using the Advanced Filter/Sort command. To do so, follow these steps:

1. **In Datasheet view, open the table that you want to filter.**
2. **Choose Records⇨Filter⇨Advanced Filter/Sort.**

   Access displays the Filter window, which contains two parts, just as it does in the Query Design view.
3. **Click the first field that you want to use to filter the table and drag it from the table window to the Field row. Put it in the first column of the grid in the bottom half of the window.**

   Or, instead of dragging a field, you can choose a field from the Field drop-down list. You will find it in the grid in the bottom half of the window (see Figure 6-3).

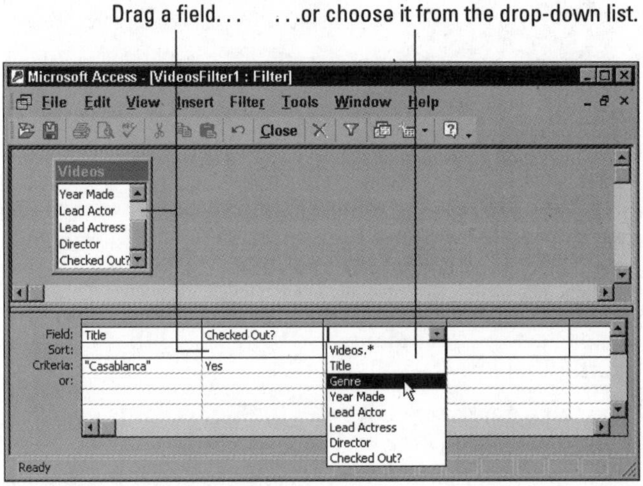

Figure 6-3: Constructing an advanced filter operation.

4. **Click the Criteria row in the first column and type the criteria to limit the records you see.**

   If you want to see only items that cost more that $10, for example, put the Cost per Item field in the Field row of the first column and enter **>10** in the Criteria row. To search for text, enclose the text in quotation marks (" ").

5. **Repeat Steps 3 and 4 to add other fields and criteria to the grid.**
6. **(Optional) Choose a field by which to sort the resulting table.**

   Set a sort order by opening the drop-down list for the Sort row in the column containing the field that you want to sort by — then choose Ascending or Descending. This option tells Access to sort the table that results from the advanced filter in ascending or descending order, using the field that you list in the same column as the sort key.
7. **After you finish creating all the criteria you need, click the Apply Filter button to see the resulting table.**

   Access displays only the records that meet the criteria.

You can do several things with the resulting table, as the following list describes:

- **Save it as a query:** If you want to save your advanced filter, you must save it in Design view. After you apply the filter, return to Design view by choosing Record⇨Filter⇨Advanced Filter/Sort and click the Save As Query button to save the advanced filter. You can access the filter after you save it through the Queries tab of the Database window.
- **Filter it:** Use the filter buttons or choose Records⇨Filter to filter the table even more.
- **Print it:** Click the Print button.
- **Sort it:** The best way to sort a table is to use the Sort row in the design grid. But you can click the Sort Ascending or Sort Descending buttons to sort the query-result table by the field that the cursor's in.
- **Fix it:** Choose Records⇨Filter⇨Advanced Filter/Sort to start over and change the filtering criteria or other information in the grid.
- **Add data to it:** Add data to the table you are filtering by clicking the New Record button and entering the data.
- **Edit data:** Edit data the same way that you do in a datasheet.
- **Delete records:** You can delete entire records if you want — click the record you want to delete and then click the Delete Record button.
- **Toggle between the filtered table and the full table:** Click the Apply Filter button. If you're looking at the full table, clicking the Apply Filter button displays the filtered table (according to the last filter that you apply). If you're looking at the filtered table, clicking the Apply Filter button displays the full table.

Sorting a Table

You may have entered your data randomly, but it doesn't need to stay that way. Use the Sort commands (or buttons) to sort your data.

Before you sort, you must know what you want to sort by. Do you want the Addresses table in order by last name, for example, or by zip code? If you know which field you want to sort by, sorting is a piece of cake.

You can sort in ascending order or descending order. *Ascending order* means that you start with the smallest number or the letter nearest the beginning of the alphabet and work up from there. When you sort in ascending order, fields starting with *A* appear at the top of the table (actually, blank fields, symbols, and numbers come first), and fields starting with *Z* appear at the bottom. *Descending order* is the opposite.

To sort a table in Datasheet view, follow these steps:

1. **Select the field that you want to sort by (sometimes known as the *sort key*) by clicking the field name.**

   If you don't select the column (and you don't need to), Access uses the field the cursor's in as the sort key.

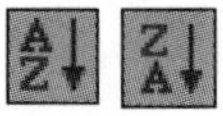

2. **Click the Sort Ascending or Sort Descending button, depending on which order you want to sort in.**

   Records are rearranged in the table according to the sorting command you entered.

Blocking Unwanted Data by Using an Input Mask

An *input mask* limits the information that can go in a field by specifying what characters someone can enter. An input mask is useful if you know the form the data needs to take — for example, if an order number has two letters followed by four digits. Phone numbers and zip codes are other examples of fields where input masks prove useful.

You commonly use input masks in tables, but you can also add them to queries and forms where people may enter data. In all cases, you must add an input mask from the Design view.

You can use an input mask to specify the first character in a field as a letter, for example, and every character after the first as a number. You can also use an input mask to add characters to a field — for example, use an input mask to display ten digits as a phone number, with parentheses around the first three digits and a dash after the sixth digit. If the data in a field varies or you can't easily describe it, it's probably not a good candidate for an input mask.

The input mask for the field is in effect whenever anyone's entering data into the field in a datasheet or a form.

You can create input masks for text, number, and currency data; other data types don't use the Input Mask field property.

To create an input mask, go to Design view and enter a series of characters in the Input Mask area of the Field Properties pane to tell Access what kind of data to expect. (Input Mask is the third area, right below Format.) No one can enter Data that doesn't match the input mask. To block data from a field, first figure out exactly what data you want a field to accept; then use the characters shown in Table 6-1 to code the data in the Input Mask field property.

Table 6-1 Input Mask Possibilities

Input Mask Character	*What It Accepts/Requires*
0	Requires a number; doesn't accept + and –.
9	Accepts a number; doesn't accept + and –.
#	Accepts a space and converts a blank to a space; accepts + and –.
L	Requires a letter.
?	Accepts a letter.
A	Requires a letter or number.
a	Accepts a letter or number.
C	Accepts any character or a space.
<	Converts the following characters to lowercase.
>	Converts the following characters to uppercase.
!	Fills field from right to left; characters on the left side are optional.
\	Displays the character following in the field (\Z appears as Z).
.,	Displays the decimal placeholder or thousands separator.
;:-/	Displays the date separator. (The symbol that you use depends on the setting in the Regional Settings area of the Windows Control Panel.)

Chapter 7: Queries: Getting Answers from Your Data

In This Chapter

- **Making queries by using a query wizard**
- **Using Query Design view**
- **Making a select query**
- **Saving a query**

Queries can help you narrow down and find the information that you need. So why not just use filtering and sorting (as explained in Chapter 6), you may ask? Well, you're not far off. Queries are nothing more than a heavy-duty way to filter and sort your data. You can use queries to select records from a database, for example, and to create summary calculations. Maybe you want to know the people to whom you owe more than $100 but less than $500 (if you just so happen to keep a database on such stuff). Access helps you with a query wizard if you don't want to go it alone. And if you want to get your feet wet, feel free to plunge ahead and create your own queries. This chapter starts you off on creating queries so that you, too, can join the fun.

About Queries

Queries enable you to select specific data from one or more tables. As do tables, queries have two views: Design view and Datasheet view. In the Design view, you tell Access which fields you want to see, which tables they come from, and the criteria that must be true for a record to appear on the resulting datasheet.

Criteria are tests that a record must pass — for example, you may want to see only records with a value in the Amount field greater than 100. The criterion, therefore, is that the value in the Amount field must be greater than 100.

In Datasheet view, you see the fields and records Access finds that meet your criteria.

A query doesn't store data — it just pulls data out of tables for you to look at. A query is *dynamic* — as you add to or change your data, the result of the query also changes. When you save your query, you're not saving the table that the query produces — you're just saving the query design so that you can ask the same question again.

The following are examples of queries:

- **Advanced filter/sort:** The Advanced Filter/Sort feature in Access is the simplest kind of query; it enables you to find and sort information from one table in the database. This option is available from the Datasheet view of a table by choosing Records⇨Filter⇨Advanced Filter/Sort.
- **Select:** A select query finds the data you want from one or more tables and displays it in the order in which you want it to appear. A select query can include criteria that tell Access to filter records and display only some of them.
- **Total:** These queries are similar to select queries, but they enable you to calculate a sum or some other aggregate (such as an average).
- **Action:** Action queries change your data based on some set of criteria. Action queries can delete records, update data, append data from one or more tables to another table, and make a new table.
- **Crosstab:** Most tables in Access, including ones that queries generate, display records down the side and field names across the top. Crosstab queries produce tables with the values from one field down the side and values from another field across the top of the table. A crosstab query performs a calculation — it sums, averages, or counts data that you categorize in two ways.

Using a Query Wizard

If you click the New button in the Queries tab of the Database window, you see not one but four wizards to help you build your query. The wizard that you use depends on what you want your query to do. Table 7-1 lists the four query wizards and tells when you may find each useful.

Table 7-1 Query Wizards

Query Wizard	*When to Use It*
Simple Query Wizard	Use this wizard to build a select query. If you want to perform summary calculations with the query, the wizard can help you. If you have criteria, however, you still must enter them in Design view, so the Simple Query Wizard isn't a huge improvement over designing the query yourself.
Crosstab Query Wizard	Use this wizard to create a crosstab query.

Query Wizard	*When to Use It*
Find Duplicates Query Wizard	Use this wizard to find duplicate data in the database.
Find Unmatched Query Wizard	Use this wizard to find records with no corresponding records in related tables.

Wizards help you create queries, but the queries that they create are just like the ones that you create — you can see them in Design or Datasheet view and do anything with them that you may do with any other query of the same type.

TIP

Using a query wizard and studying the Design view of the queries that they create is a good way to find out how to use some of the more advanced features of queries. To start a query wizard, follow these steps:

1. **Display the Queries view of the Database window.**

   To do so, click the Queries button.

2. **Click the New button.**

   Access displays the New Query dialog box.

3. **Click to select the wizard that you want to use.**

   On the left side of the dialog box, Access displays a brief summary of what the wizard does (see Figure 7-1).

4. **Click OK.**

   Access starts the wizard that you choose. That's it!

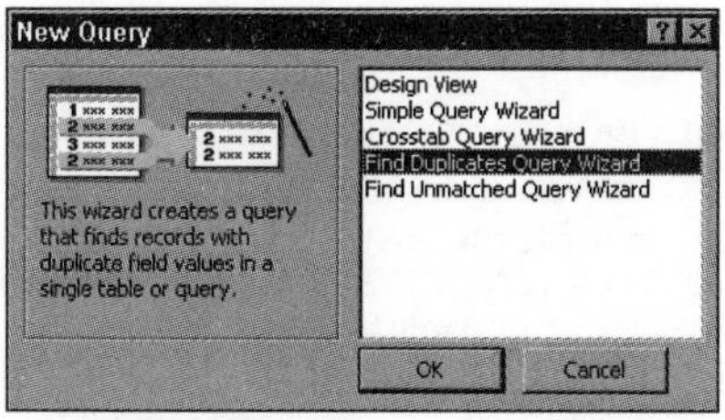

Figure 7-1: Using a wizard is simply a matter of choosing the right one.

The following sections help you start out using some of the more popular query wizards.

Find Duplicates Query Wizard

Use The Find Duplicate Query Wizard if you want to find duplicate entries in a field in a table or query. The Find Duplicates Query Wizard can, for example, help you find identical records as well as records with the same name and different addresses.

The Find Duplicates Query Wizard needs to know the following things:

- **The table or query that you want it to examine.** The wizard displays table names first — if you want to see query names, select the Queries or Both radio button. In other words, you can query a query.
- **The fields in the table or query that may contain duplicate information.** Select the names of fields that may contain duplicate entries and click the right arrow to move them into the Duplicate-Value Fields list box.
- **Any additional fields that you want to see in the datasheet that the query produces.** Seeing additional fields can prove useful if you're editing or deleting duplicated records.
- **The name of the query.** Enter a descriptive name.

After you click the Finish button and display the datasheet, you see a list of records. Access lists duplicates in groups. You can edit this datasheet to update the data in the database table or query. You can also delete records that you don't need by editing the datasheet or by using the tools in the Query Design window.

Find Unmatched Query Wizard

The Find Unmatched Query Wizard finds records in one table that contains no matching records in another, related table. You may, for example, store orders in one table and details about customers in another table. If, say, a Customer Number field links the tables, the Unmatched Query Wizard can tell you whether the Orders table lists any customers who don't appear in the Customers table.

The Find Unmatched Query Wizard needs to know the following things:

- **The table (or query) that you want to examine to see which of its records do not match records in the other table.** In the preceding example, this table is the Order table, where you store the details of each order. (You usually have a related record about each customer.) If you want to choose a query, select the Queries or Both radio button.
- **The name of the table that contains the related records.** In the example, this table is the Customer table, where you store the details about each customer. If you want to see queries in addition to tables, select the Queries or Both radio button.
- **The names of the related fields.** Access makes a guess, especially if a field in each table has the same name. (The fact that Access can't figure out the names of the related fields by itself seems a little odd, especially if you've defined relationships, but there it is.)

✦ **The fields that you want to see in the datasheet resulting from the query.**

✦ **The name for the query.** Enter a descriptive name.

Using the Simple Query Wizard

The Simple Query Wizard does a great deal of the work in creating a query for you. The most basic query that you can create by using the Simple Query Wizard pulls together related data from different fields. The Simple Query Wizard is a terrific way to create some summary calculations from your data — such as how much someone spent on an order or how many items people ordered.

The Simple Query Wizard gives you the option of creating a *summary* or *detail* query if the fields you choose for the query include both of the following:

✦ A field with values.

✦ A field with repetitions, which Access uses to group the values.

A *detail query* lists every record that meets your criteria. A *summary query* performs calculations on your data to summarize it. You can sum, average, count the number of values in a field, or find the minimum or maximum value in a field. A summary query creates new calculated fields that you can use in other queries or in reports.

If you have a field that lists the amount spent and a field that lists the dates on which the money is spent, for example, Access can create a summary query for you that sums the amount spent by date.

To use the Simple Query Wizard to create a query, follow these steps:

1. **Start by clicking the Queries tab of the Database window and then clicking the New button.**

   Access displays the New Query dialog box.

2. **Select Simple Query Wizard and click OK.**

   Access displays the first window of the query.

3. **From the Tables/Queries drop-down list, choose the first table or query from which you want to use fields.**

   After you choose a table or query, fields from the object you chose appear in the Available Fields list box.

4. **Move fields that you want to use in the query from the Available Fields list to the Selected Fields list by double-clicking a field name or by selecting the field name and then clicking the right-arrow button.**

5. **If you're using fields from more than one table or query, repeat Steps 3 and 4 to add fields from the additional tables or queries to the Selected Fields list.**

6. **Click Next after selecting all the fields that you need for the query.**

   Access displays the next window, which asks whether you want a Detail or Summary query. If summary calculations aren't possible with the fields you choose, Access skips this window. For simple queries, you may see the Finish window — skip to Step 11 if so.

7. **Choose the type of query that you want: Detail or Summary.**

   If you choose a Summary query, click the Summary Options button to display the window where you tell the wizard how to summarize each field (see Figure 7-2).

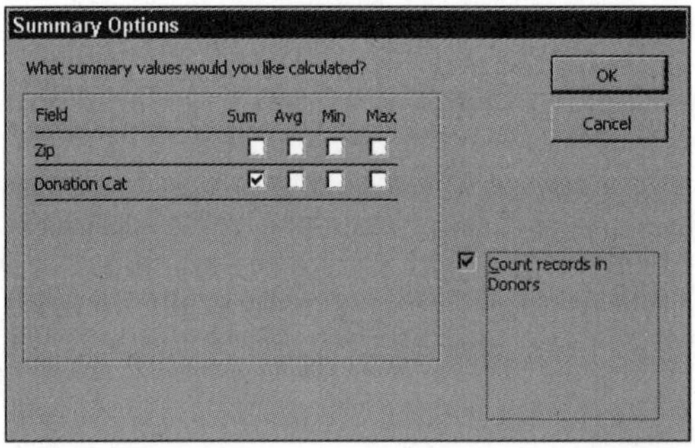

Figure 7-2: The Summary Options dialog box.

   Use the check boxes to indicate the new fields for Access to create with this query. If you want to add all the values in the Cost Per Item field, for example, click the Sum check box in the row for the Cost Per Item field.

   Don't overlook the Count check box(es) that may appear in this window — selecting a count check box tells the wizard to create a field that counts the records within each grouping.

8. **Click OK to leave the Summary Options window.**

9. **Click Next to view the next window.**

   If you're summarizing data, and if you can group the fields that you're summarizing by a Time/Date field, the wizard displays a window where you choose the time interval by which to group the records.

   If you choose to sum a field that details check amounts, for example, and you enter check amounts in a record that also contains a field telling the date that customers wrote each check, you can choose to display total check amounts by Day, Month, Quarter, or Year. Select the time interval by which to group your data.

10. **Click Next to see the final window.**

11. **Type a name for the query in the text box at the top of the window.**

12. **Choose whether you want to Open the query to view information, which shows you the query in Datasheet view, or to Modify the query design, which shows you the query in Design view.**

    If you want to see the Help screen about working with a query, click the Display Help on Working With the Query check box.

13. **Click Finish to view the query.**

TIP

You can't tell the Simple Query Wizard about criteria. If you want to include criteria in your query, open the query that the wizard created in Design view and add the criteria.

Using the Crosstab Query Wizard

A *crosstab query* is a specialized kind of query for displaying summarized data. Instead of creating a table with rows showing record data and columns showing fields, you can use a crosstab query table to use data from one field for the row labels and data from another field for column labels. The result is a more compact, spreadsheet-like presentation of your data.

REMEMBER

The Crosstab Query Wizard works only with one table or query. If the fields that you want to use in the crosstab query aren't in one table, you must create a query that combines those fields in one query before you use the Crosstab Query Wizard.

To start the Crosstab Query Wizard, follow these steps:

1. **Display the Queries in the Database window.**

   Access displays the names of any queries in your database.

2. **Click the New button.**

   Access displays the New Query dialog box.

3. **Select Crosstab Query Wizard and click OK.**

   Access starts the Crosstab Query Wizard.

The Crosstab Query Wizard asks you for the following information:

- The table or query that you want to use to create the crosstab table.
- The field that you want to use for row headings.
- The field that you want to use for column headings.

- The field that you want to summarize by using the row and column headings.
- How you want to summarize the field (count the entries, add them together, average them, and so on).
- Whether you want Access to sum each row (Access adds a Sum of *Field Name* column to the table to display the result).

About Query Design View

Whichever kind of query you're using, you must use Query Design view to tell Access about the data you're looking for and where to look for it (see Figure 7-3). Take one of the following actions to display a query in Design view:

- Click the Queries button in the Objects list on the Database window, select the query name from the list that appears, and click the Design button on the toolbar.
- Ctrl+double-click the query name in the Queries view of the Database window.

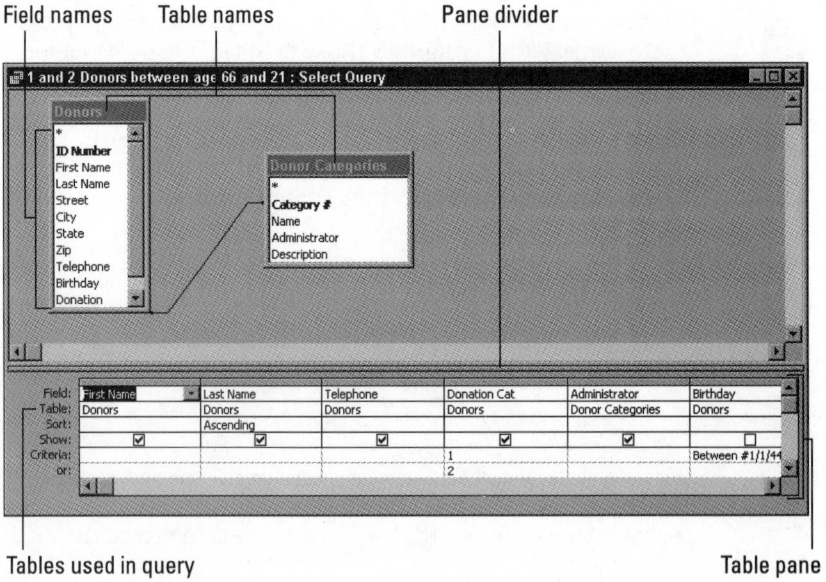

Figure 7-3: Query Design view.

Table 7-2 explains the functions of the buttons on the Query Design View toolbar that are unique to queries.

Table 7-2 Query Design View Toolbar Buttons

Toolbar Button	*Button Name*	*What It Does*
	View	Displays Datasheet view.
	Save	Saves the query so that you can view the design and the query datasheet again.
	Undo	Undoes your last undoable action. (Many actions you can't undo, so always keeping a backup is a good idea.)
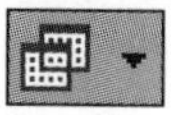	Select Query Type	Displays a drop-down list from which you can choose a query type: Select Query, Crosstab Query, Make-Table Query, Update Query, Append Query, or Delete Query.
	Run	Runs the query. (For a select or crosstab query, clicking the Run button displays the results in Datasheet view. For other types of queries, the Run button performs the action that the type of query requires — it changes, deletes, copies, or created data. Use this button carefully.)
	Show Table	Displays the Show Table dialog box so that you can add tables to the query.
	Totals	Displays the Total row in the query grid. (Use the total row to tell Access what kind of calculation you want.)
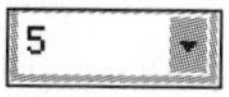	Top Values	Limits the result of the query appearing in the datasheet to the number of records or the percentage of records that appear in this option.
	Properties	Displays properties for the selected field or field list.
	Build	Displays the Expression Builder dialog box. (This button is "live" only if the cursor's in the Field or Criteria row.)
	Database Window	Displays the Database window.

The top half of the window displays the tables containing fields that you want to use in the query. Use the bottom half of the window to give Access specifics about the datasheet you want the query to produce — specifically, what fields to display, and how to decide whether to display a record.

Each row in the query grid has a specific purpose. Table 7-3 tells you how to use each of them.

Table 7-3 Query Grid Rows

Query Grid Row	*What It Does*
Field	Provides the name of a field that you want to include in a query.
Table	Provides the name of the table that the field comes from. (This row isn't always visible.)
Total	Performs calculations in your query. (This row isn't always visible — use the Totals button on the toolbar to display or hide it.)
Sort	Determines the sort order of the datasheet that the query produces.
Show	Shows a field. (If you want to use a field to determine which records to display on the datasheet but not actually display the field, remove the check mark from the Show column for the field.)
Criteria	Tells Access the criteria for the field in the same column.
Or	Use for additional criteria.

Adding a Select Query to the Database

The most frequently used type of query is the *select query.* A select query displays fields from one or more tables, based on criteria that you define. To create a select query from scratch, follow these steps:

1. **Display Queries in the Database window.**

   To do so, in case you need reminding, click the Queries button in the Database window.

2. **Double-click the Create Query in Design View icon.**

   Access displays Query Design view and the Show Table dialog box.

3. **Select the table(s) that contain fields that you want to display in the query datasheet or use to create criteria. To select the table(s), click them and then click the Add button in the Show Table dialog box.**

If you want to include a field that another query generates, you can add queries to a query by clicking the Queries or Both tab of the Show Table dialog box and double-clicking the query name.

4. **Click the Close button in the Show Table dialog box.**
5. **Select the fields that you want to use in the query table.**

   To select a field for the queries, either drag its name out of a table box and onto the design grid or double-click its name. You can also use the drop-down Field and Table lists in the query grid to select the fields that you want to use.
6. **In the Criteria row, enter the criteria that you want to use to create the query table.**

   Look carefully and you will see a row called Criteria on the query grid. That is where you describe the information you want to glean in the query.

   If you want to see only records with values in the Order Numbers field of more than 100, for example, type **>100** in the Criteria row of the column that contains the Order Numbers in a Field row. Or, if you want to see only those records with an Author field containing *Hemingway*, type **Hemingway** in the Criteria row for the Author column. By the way, don't let Access's placing of quotation marks around text criteria surprise you. Access does that on its own.
7. **Set the Sort and Show options to create your perfect query table.**

   To sort the results of a query on a particular field, click in the Sort row in the field in question and choose Ascending or Descending from the drop-down list.

   By default, results are shown for each field on the query grid. But if you want to exclude the results in a particular field, go to the Show row in a field and click to deselect the check box. (See the "Showing or hiding a field" sidebar for details.)

8. **Click the View button (or Run button) to view the results of the query in a datasheet.**
9. **Save the query by clicking the Save button in the query's Design or Datasheet view.**

If you're querying just one table, the easiest way to create the query is to select the table in the Database window and then click the New Object: Query button. (You may need to click the down arrow and choose Query from the drop-down list.) Then select Design View in the New Query dialog box. Access displays the Query Design view showing the table that you select.

Showing or hiding a field

You include some fields in your query simply so that you can base your filter or sort on them. But you may not always want to see those fields in your query results. You may, for example, want to find all customers who purchased items within the past six months — but you don't necessarily want to see the dates for all these purchases. To exclude a field from showing up in your query results, make sure that the check box in the Show row is blank. Click the check box again to make the field appear in query results.

Field:	ID Number	Last Name	Last Name	Donation
Table:	Donors	Donors	Donors	Donors
Sort:				
Show:	☐	☑	☑	☐
Criteria:				>250
or:				

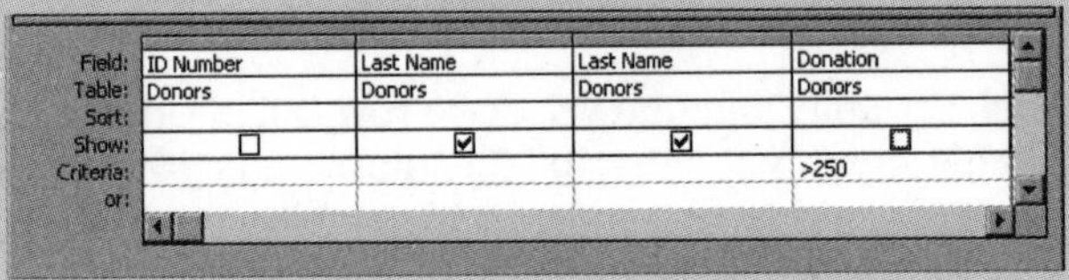

Saving a Query

You don't need to save a query. Often, you create queries on the fly to answer a question. You don't need to clutter your database with queries that you're unlikely to need again.

That said, you can certainly save a query design (but not the query data sheet) if you need to by using one of the following methods:

 ✦ In Design or Datasheet view, click the Save button or choose File⇨Save. If you haven't saved the query yet, Access asks you for a name for the query. Type the name and then click OK.

 ✦ Close the query. (Clicking the Close button is a popular method.) If you've never saved the query or if you've changed the query design since you last saved it, Access asks whether you want to save the query. If you've never saved the query, give it a name and then click OK; otherwise, click Yes to save the query.

Make sure that you give your new query a name that tells you what the query does. That way, you don't need to open one query after another to find the one you're looking for.

REAL WORLD

Printing an object

Views that you can print offer a Print button in the toolbar. You can't, however, print some views (notably Design view). In those views, the Print button is grayed out, indicating that you can't click it.

You can print an object such as a datasheet or a report in the following three ways:

✦ To print the object currently on-screen without changing any settings, click the Print button.

✦ If you want to change some settings in the Print dialog box before printing the object, choose File⇨Print or press Ctrl+P. Change settings as necessary in the Print dialog box that appears and click OK to print the object.

✦ To print an object without opening it, select it in the Database window and then click the Print button or right-click the object and choose Print from the shortcut menu. Access sends the object straight to the printer.

Note: For information on printing in general for Access or for any other Office application, see Appendix B.

If you want to create a query similar to one you already have in your database, select or open the query and choose File⇨Save As to save the query with a new name. Then you can keep the original query and make changes to the new copy.

Chapter 8: More Fun with Queries

In This Chapter

- Sorting queries
- Inserting fields into a query
- Correcting queries
- Attaching tables to queries
- Limiting the data that queries display

Queries are so much fun that this minibook devotes two entire chapters to them. Well, true, queries *are* important enough to require the extra space. In any case, you need to realize that you can do a lot more with queries than you may at first think. You can, for example, sort a table that a query produces. You can also correct a query if you make a mistake. And you can use criteria expressions to limit the data that your queries display. (Do you really need to see a list of all the people named Smith in Tennessee?) Read on for some help with these topics as well as a few more things that you may want to do with queries.

Sorting a Query

You can sort a table that a query produces in several ways. The first way is to use the Sort row in the query grid. Use the Sort row to tell Access which field to use to sort the datasheet. To sort by a field, display your query in Design view and follow these steps:

1. **Move the cursor to the Sort row in the column that contains the field by which you want to sort.**
2. **Click the down arrow to display the drop-down list for the Sort row.**

   Access displays the options for sorting: Ascending, Descending, and (Not Sorted), as shown in Figure 8-1.

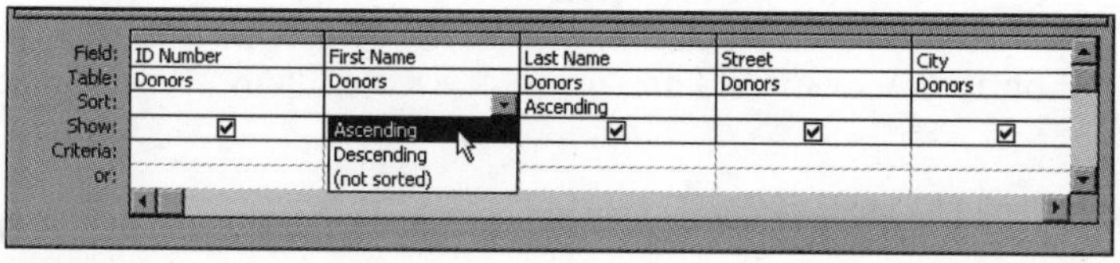

Figure 8-1: Sorting query results.

3. **Click Ascending or Descending.**

You can use the Sort row in the query grid to sort by more than one field. You may want to sort the records in the datasheet by last name, for example, but more than one person may have the same last name. You can specify another field (perhaps first name) as the second sort key. If you want, you can specify more than two fields by which to sort.

If you sort by using more than one field, Access always works from left to right, first sorting the records by the first field (the primary sort key) that displays Ascending or Descending in the Sort row and then sorting any records with the same primary sort key value by the second sort key.

You can also sort the datasheet that results from the query by using the same technique that you use to sort any datasheet: Click the field that you want to sort by and then click the Sort Ascending or Sort Descending button on the Query Datasheet toolbar.

Inserting Fields in a Query Grid

If you're working with queries in Design view, you can move a field from the table pane to the query grid in any of the following three easy ways:

- **Double-click the field name.** Access moves the field to the first open column in the grid.
- **Drag the field name.** You drag the field name from the table pane to the field row of an unused column in the query grid.
- **Use the drop-down list.** You click the down arrow in the Field row of the query grid and then select the field you want from the drop-down list. If you use this method with a multiple-table query, you find that choosing the table name from the drop-down Table list is easier if you do it before selecting the field name.

You can put all the field names from one table into the query grid in the following two ways:

- **Put one field name in each column of the grid.** If you have criteria for all the fields, you can put one field name in each column of the query grid in just two steps. Double-click the table name where it appears in the table pane of the Design view to select all the fields in the table. Then drag the selected names to the grid. After you release the mouse button, Access puts one name in each column.

✦ **Put all the field names in one column.** This method is useful if you want to find something that may be in any field or if you have one criterion for all the fields in the table. The asterisk (*) appears above the first field name in each Table window. Drag the asterisk to the grid to tell Access to include all field names in one column. The asterisk is also available as the first choice in the drop-down Field list — it appears as `TableName*`.

Editing a Query

You can do a few things in a query to edit it — you can move the columns around, delete a column, or delete all the entries in the design grid. To take any of those actions, however, you first must select the column in the grid by clicking the column selector — the gray block at the top of each column in the grid (see Figure 8-2). Table 8-1 breaks down some steps that you can take to make your query better.

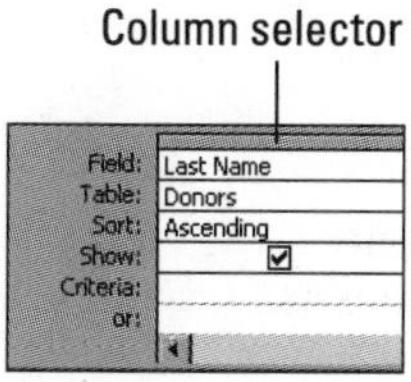

Figure 8-2: Use the column selector to select a column.

Table 8-1 Making a Better Query

When You Want to . . .	*Here's What to Do*
Move a column	Click the column selector to select the column, click a second time, and then drag the column to its new position.
Delete a column	Click the column selector to select the column; then press the Delete key.
Delete all columns	Choose Edit⇨Clear Grid.
Insert a column	Drag a field from the table pane to the column in the grid where you want to insert it. Access inserts an extra column for the new field.
Change the displayed name	Enter the display name and a colon before the actual name of the field in the Field row (**display name: field name**).

Adding Another Table to a Query

To use a table's fields in a query, you must "attach" the table to the query — that is, display the table name in the top half of the Query window.

That you use a Show Table dialog box to add a table to a query may seem a little odd — but that's how you do it. To display the Show Table dialog box, take one of the following actions:

- ✦ Right-click the table part of Query Design view and choose Show Table from the shortcut menu.
- ✦ Click the Show Table button.
- ✦ Choose Query➪Show Table.

After you display the Show Table dialog box, you add a table to the table pane of Query Design view by taking one of the following actions:

- ✦ Double-click the table name in the Show Table dialog box.
- ✦ Select the table and then click the Add button.

You can also add a query to the table pane if you want to use a field that a query creates or filters. Click the appropriate tab at the top of the Show Table dialog box to see all Tables, all Queries, or all tables and queries (Both).

To remove a table from a query, select the table and press the Delete key. Deleting a table from a query is absurdly easy and can have damaging consequences for your query — if you delete a table, you also delete all the fields from that table from the query grid. Take care when your fingers get close to the Delete key. You can't choose Edit➪Undo to bring the table back to life, although you can take a roundabout way of restoring the table: Close the file and choose not to save the changes you made to it. Next time you open the file, the table is still a part of the query.

Limiting Records by Using Criteria Expressions

Criteria enable you to limit the data that the query displays. Although you can use a query to see data from related tables together in one record, the power of queries is that you can filter your data to see only records that meet certain criteria. You use the Criteria and Or rows in the query grid to tell Access exactly which records you want to see.

Access knows how to *query by example* (QBE). In fact, the grid in Design view is sometimes known as the *QBE grid*. QBE makes creating criteria easy.

If you tell Access what you're looking for, Access goes out and finds it. If you want to find values equal to 10, for example, the Criteria is simply 10. Access then finds records that match that criteria.

The most common type of criteria are logical expressions. A *logical expression* gives a yes or no answer. Access shows you the record if the answer is yes but not if the answer is no. The operators that you commonly use in logical expressions include <, >, `AND`, `OR`, and `NOT`.

TIP

Although we use uppercase to distinguish operators and functions, case doesn't matter in the query design grid.

Querying by example

If you want to find all the addresses in Virginia, the criterion for the state field is simply the following:

```
Virginia
```

You may want to add another criterion in the next line (`OR`) to take care of different spellings, as follows:

```
VA
```

Access puts the text in quotes for you. The result of the query is all records that contain either *Virginia* or *VA* in the state field.

Using operators in criteria expressions

The simplest way to use the query grid is to simply tell Access what you're looking for by typing a value that you want to match in the Criteria row for the field. But often, your criteria are more complicated than "all records with Virginia in the state field." You use operators in your criteria expressions to tell Access about more complex criteria.

Table 8-2 lists the operators that you're likely to use in a criteria expression.

Table 8-2 Operators to Use in a Criteria Expression

Relational Operator	*What It Does*
=	Finds values equal to text, a number, or date/time.
<>	Finds values not equal to text, a number, or date/time.
<	Finds values less than a given value.
<=	Finds values less than or equal to a given value.

(continued)

Table 8-2 *(continued)*

Relational Operator	*What It Does*
>	Finds values greater than a given value.
>=	Finds values greater than or equal to a given value.
BETWEEN	Finds values between or equal to two values.
IN	Finds values or text included in a list.
LIKE	Finds matches to a pattern.

As you type your criteria, you don't need to tell Access that you're looking for **Costs<10**, for example. If you put `<10` in the Criteria row, Access applies the criteria to the field that appears in the Field row of the same column. Table 8-3 shows some examples of criteria that use operators.

Table 8-3 Examples of Criteria That Use Operators

Expressions with Operator	*What the Operator Tells Access to Do*
<10	Finds record with values less than 10.
>10	Finds records with values greater than 10.
<>10	Finds records with values not equal to 10.
>10 AND <20	Finds records with values between 10 and 20.
>=10 AND <=20	Finds records with values between 10 and 20, including 10 and 20.
BETWEEN 10 AND 20	The same as >=10 AND <=20.
IN ("Virginia", "VA")	Finds the values Virginia and VA.
LIKE "A*"	Finds text beginning with the letter A. You can use LIKE with wildcards such as * to tell Access in general terms what you're looking for.

Using AND, OR, and NOT

The most common way to combine expressions that tell Access what you're looking for is to use `AND`, `OR`, and `NOT` in your criteria. These three operators can be a little difficult to figure out unless you aced Logic 101 in college. Here's how they work:

- `AND`: Tells Access that a particular record must meet more than one criterion to appear in the datasheet.
- `OR`: Tells Access that a particular record must meet only one of several criteria to appear in the datasheet.
- `NOT`: Tells Access that a criterion must be false for the record to appear in the datasheet. For example, the expression `NOT "France"` in the Address field retrieves all records *except* those of people who live in France.

You can combine operators in one criterion expression, such as if you're looking for the following:

```
>10 OR <18 NOT 15
```

This expression produces records with the values 11, 12, 13, 14, 16, and 17 (assuming that all values in the field are integers).

Using multiple criteria

If you have criteria for only one field, you can use the OR operator in the following two different ways:

- Type your expressions into the Criteria row, separating them by OR.
- Type the first expression in the Criteria row and type subsequent expressions by using the Or rows in the query grid.

Whichever approach you take, the result is the same — Access displays records in the Datasheet that satisfy one or more of the criteria expressions.

If you use criteria in multiple fields, Access assumes that you want to find records that meet all the criteria — in other words, that you're in effect joining the criteria in each row with AND statements. If you type criteria on the same row for two fields, a record must meet both criteria to appear on the datasheet.

If you use the Or row, Access treats the expressions on each row as though you're joining that with AND, but it treats the expressions on different rows as though you're joining them with OR. Access first looks at one row of criteria and finds all the records that meet all the criteria on that row. Then it starts over with the next row of criteria, the Or row, and finds all the records that meet all the criteria on that row. A record must meet all the criteria on only one row to appear in the datasheet.

Using dates, times, text, and values in criteria

Access does its best to recognize the types of data that you use in criteria and encloses elements of the expression between the appropriate characters. You're less likely to create criteria that Access doesn't understand, however, if you use those characters yourself.

Table 8-4 lists types of elements that you may include in a criteria expression and the character to use to make sure that Access knows that the element is text, a date, a time, a number, or a field name.

Table 8-4 Types of Data to Use in Certain Expressions

Use This Type of Data	*In an Expression Such as This*
Text	"text"
Date	#1-Feb-97#
Time	#12:00am#
Number	10
Field name	[field name]

You can refer to dates or times by using any format that Access recognizes. July 31, 2001, 07/31/01, and 31-Jul-01, for example, are all formats that Access recognizes. You can use AM/PM or 24-hour time.

Chapter 9: Using Aggregate Calculations and Building Expressions

In This Chapter

- **Creating a calculation that works with a group of data**
- **Adding calculations to queries**

Using aggregate calculations and building expressions sure sounds a lot more complicated than topics such as opening your database or giving your database some color. You may be surprised, however, at how simple these complicated-sounding activities really are. If you want to create a calculation that works with a group of data, you need an aggregate calculation. You may want to count the number of orders that come in each day for potatoes on your potato farm, for example, or calculate an average amount for all orders. And as you're creating your database, you don't want to waste your time dragging out your calculator, doing the math yourself, and then typing in the result. Instead, you can tell Access to perform the calculation for you. The work gets done faster, and the result is always up to date — even if you later add, delete, or change records. Your potatoes never go bad in the barn again!

Calculating Summary Data for a Group of Data

An *aggregate equation* is one that uses a bunch of records to calculate some result. You may want to calculate the total cost of an order, for example, count the number of orders that come in each day, or calculate an average dollar amount for all orders.

If you create an aggregate calculation, you tell Access to *group* data by using a particular field. If you want to know the number of orders that come in each day, for example, you need to group the order data by date — that is, you use the field that contains the date to group your data. If you want to count the number of orders for each item, you need to group data by using the field that contains the item name or number.

FAST TRACK

The easiest way to create aggregate calculations is to use the Summary option in the Simple Query Wizard (see Chapter 7).

Using the Total row

The Total row in the query grid enables you to aggregate data. To perform a total calculation on your data, you must select one of the options from the row's drop-down list for each field in the query grid.

The first step in creating a total is displaying the Total row in the query grid by clicking the Totals button. You can tell whether Access is displaying the Total row because a square appears around the Total button whenever the row appears on-screen.

After the Total row is visible on-screen, you must open the Total drop-down list and select a setting in the Total row for each field in the query. Table 9-1 lists the choices for the Total row and how each works.

Table 9-1 Total Row Choices

Total Row	*How It Works*
Group By	Groups the values in this field so that like values are in the same group, enabling you to perform calculations on a group.
SUM	Calculates the sum (total) of values in the field.
AVG	Calculates the average of values in the field. (This choice doesn't include blanks in the calculation.)
MIN	Finds the minimum value in the field.
MAX	Finds the maximum value in the field.
COUNT	Counts the entries in the field (but doesn't count blanks).
STDEV	Calculates the standard deviation of values in the field.
VAR	Calculates the variance of values in the field.
FIRST	Finds the value in the first record in the field.
LAST	Finds the value in the last record in the field.
Expression	Tells Access that you plan to type your own expression for the calculation.
Where	Tells Access to use the field to limit the data that it includes in the total calculation.

Aggregating groups of records

To calculate aggregates, you must select one or more fields to group by. Say that you want to calculate the total cost of an order, so you group by the fields defined in the Order Summary table that contains one record for each order (see Figure 9-1).

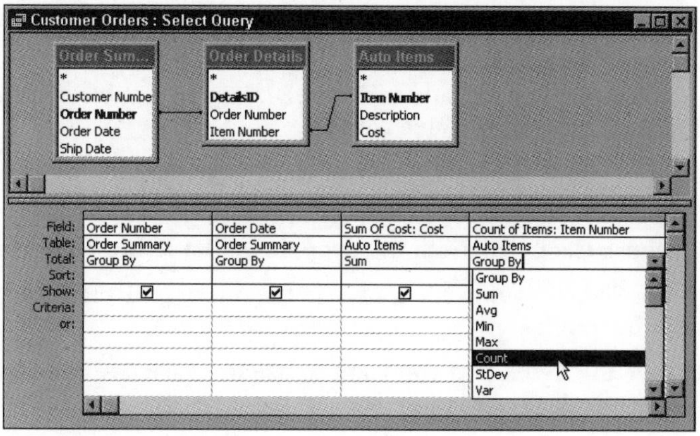

Figure 9-1: Grouping by the fields that the Order Summary table defines.

The Group By option in the Total row enables you to perform an aggregate calculation on a group of records. The result is a datasheet that displays one row for each value in the field (with no repetitions) and a calculated field for the value.

Each field with an aggregate function (`SUM`, `AVG`, `MIN`, `MAX`, `COUNT`, `STDEV`, `VAR`, `FIRST`, or `LAST`) in the Total row appears as a calculated field in the datasheet that results from the query (see Figure 9-2).

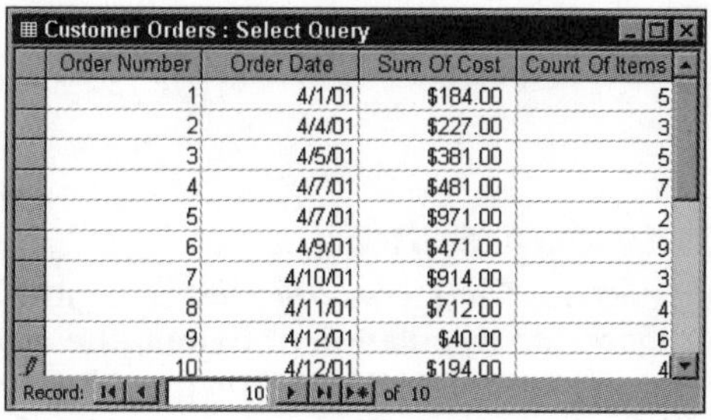

Order Number	Order Date	Sum Of Cost	Count Of Items
1	4/1/01	$184.00	5
2	4/4/01	$227.00	3
3	4/5/01	$381.00	5
4	4/7/01	$481.00	7
5	4/7/01	$971.00	2
6	4/9/01	$471.00	9
7	4/10/01	$914.00	3
8	4/11/01	$712.00	4
9	4/12/01	$40.00	6
10	4/12/01	$194.00	4

Figure 9-2: Fields resulting from a query appear in the datasheet as calculated fields.

Access creates new fields to hold the aggregate calculation. You can use these new fields in reports, forms, and other queries.

To create an aggregate calculation for grouped records, follow these steps:

1. **Create a new query in Design view.**

   Chapter 7 explains how to create a new query.

2. **From the Show Tables window, choose the tables that you need fields from and add them to the query. Close the Show Tables window.**

   Remember, you can add tables to a query by double-clicking their names in the Show Table window.

3. **Double-click the field that you want to group data by to display it in the query grid.**

4. **Choose Group By from the drop-down list in the Total row.**

   If the Total row doesn't appear in the query grid, click the Totals button on the toolbar.

5. **Move the fields that you want to use in aggregate calculations to the query grid.**

6. **Choose the type of calculation that you want for each field from the drop-down list in the Total row.**

Table 9-1 earlier in this chapter explains your choices.

TIP

To perform more than one type of calculation on a field, put the field in more than one column in the query grid and specify a different type of calculation in each Total row.

You can also group by more than one field. If you want aggregate information about people with the same last name who live at the same address, you can use the Group By setting in both the last name field and the address field.

REMEMBER

If you don't use the Group By option for any of the fields in the query grid, the result of any aggregation is the same — the "group" that you aggregate includes all records.

Limiting records to aggregate

You can use the Criteria and the Total rows together to limit the records that Access uses in the aggregate calculation or to limit the records that appear after Access performs the calculations. You must be careful, however, to make sure that Access does exactly what you want it to do. Following are some tips on using the Criteria and Total rows in one query:

- If you use Criteria in a Group By field, you limit the data that Access uses for the aggregate calculation. In other words, Access first finds the records that meet the criterion and then performs the aggregate calculation on just those records.
- If you use Criteria in a field with an aggregate function (`SUM`, `AVG`, `MIN`, `MAX`, `COUNT`, `STDEV`, `VAR`, `FIRST`, or `LAST`), Access uses the criteria to limit the result of the calculation. It first does the calculation and then selects the results that meet the criteria for the datasheet.

- Use the Where option in the Total row if you want to limit the records to use for the calculation by using a field that's not a Group By field. If you use the Where option, you can also use a criterion. The Where option limits the records that Access uses for the aggregate calculation to those that pass the criterion for the field — think of it as meaning "Limit the records to Where this criterion is true."

TIP

If you use the Where option, you use it only to limit records — Access knows this fact and deselects the Show check box. You can't, therefore, show a field that you use with the Where option in the Total row. If you want to display a field that you use with the Where option, use the same field in another column of the query grid with the Group By option in the Total row.

Creating your own expression for an aggregate calculation

Access doesn't limit you to the aggregate functions that it provides to perform a calculation in a query — you can write your own expression instead. To write your own expression for an aggregate calculation, select Expression in the drop-down list in the Total row and type the expression into the Field row of the grid. To create your own expression, follow these steps:

1. **Move your cursor to the Field row of a blank column in the query grid.**
2. **Type the name of the new field that you're creating and follow it with a colon.**
3. **Type the expression in the Field row after the colon.**

   Enter a blank space after the colon.
4. **Select Expression in the drop-down list in the Total row of the new field.**

Calculating Fields (Building Expressions)

You can add calculations to queries and reports by typing an expression, sometimes known as a *formula,* that tells Access exactly what to calculate. In a query, you put the expression in the Field row of one column of the query grid.

Most expressions include some basic elements, such as field names, values, and operators. You must enclose field names in brackets. Following is an example of an expression that calculates profit by using the Revenues and Expenses fields:

```
Profit: [Revenues] - [Expenses]
```

The name of the new field appears first, with a colon following it. You enclose the names of existing fields in square brackets.

You can also use values in an expression, as follows:

```
Retail Cost: [Wholesale Cost] * 1.50
```

Access doesn't limit you to performing calculations with values; you can also perform calculations with dates, times, and text data.

You must enclose some types of data between special characters so that Access knows what kind of data it is (see Table 9-2).

Table 9-2 Enclosing Data in Special Characters

Type of Data in an Expression	*How It Should Look*
Text	"Massachusetts"
Date/time	#15-jan-97#
Field name	[Cost]

To add a calculated field to a query, follow these basic steps:

1. **In the query grid, click the Field row of a blank column.**
2. **In the Field row, type the name of the new field and follow it with a colon.**
3. **Type the expression that you want Access to calculate after the field name you just entered.**

   In Figure 9-3, the new field is Item Cost, and the expression to calculate it follows the colon and a blank space.

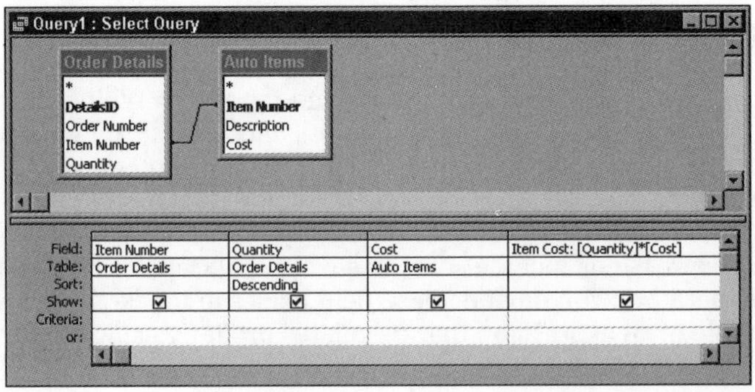

Figure 9-3: You can add a calculated field to a query.

4. To see the result, click the View button (see Figure 9-4).

After you create the new field, you can use it in other queries and in other calculations.

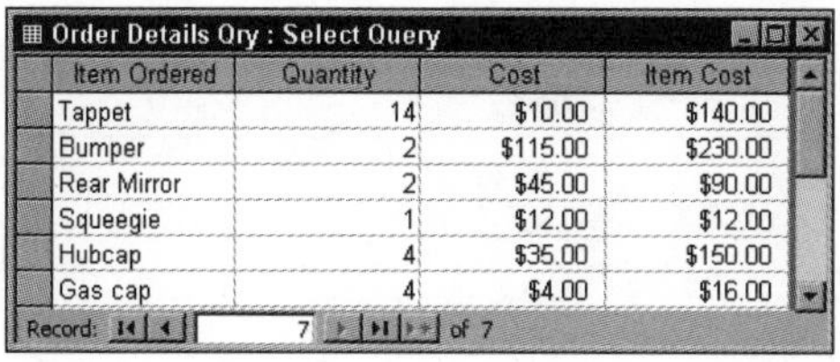
Order Details Qry : Select Query

Item Ordered	Quantity	Cost	Item Cost
Tappet	14	$10.00	$140.00
Bumper	2	$115.00	$230.00
Rear Mirror	2	$45.00	$90.00
Squeegie	1	$12.00	$12.00
Hubcap	4	$35.00	$150.00
Gas cap	4	$4.00	$16.00

Figure 9-4: The results of adding a calculated field to a query.

TIP

You can display a zoom window for your expression that enables you to see the whole expression. To display the contents of a cell in a zoom window, position your cursor in the cell and press Shift+F2. (This procedure works in a table, too.)

Using a parameter in an expression

TIP

You may want to change the value in a criteria or expression without needing to rewrite the expression in Query Design view each time. You may, for example, want to see the names of customers who ordered a particular product. You can do so by creating a *parameter query*. When you run a parameter query, Access displays the Enter Parameter Value dialog box and tells you the name of the field for which it needs a value.

Enter the value of the field name that Access asks for and click OK to see the datasheet.

You can use this feature to your advantage. If, for example, you're in retail and want the capability to calculate the markup for a variety of your products, you first make sure that you don't name any of your fields Markup and then create an expression that includes `[Markup]`. Then each time that you run the query, you get the Enter Parameter Value dialog box and can enter a different markup value.

Using operators in calculations

Access offers a slew of operators. The operators that you're most likely to already know are the *logical* and *relational* operators, which result in a true or false result. But Access also provides operators that you can use in calculations.

Mathematical operators work with numbers. Table 9-3 lists mathematical operators and what they do.

Table 9-3 Mathematical Operators

Mathematical Operator	*What It Does*
*	Multiplies
+	Adds
–	Subtracts
/	Divides
^	Raises to a power

Chapter 10: Reporting Results

In This Chapter

- Creating a report by using AutoReport
- Creating a report by using the Report Wizard
- Creating a report in Design View
- Editing objects in a report
- Sending a report to another Microsoft application
- Sorting records in a report

Compiling exactly the data you're looking for is all fine and good, but making that data look great so that you can print it, pass it around, impress your friends, and send it to your high school business teacher who said that you wouldn't amount to anything is the whole point, right? In Access, spiffy output comes in the form of reports.

Who wouldn't be impressed? Just imagine: You can create a report from one table or query or from several linked tables and queries. You can even create a report from a filtered table. Nothing can hold you back now.

About Reports

Reports can group information from different tables — for example, you can display the customer information just once and list all the items the customer's ordered. You can also use calculations in reports to create totals, subtotals, and other results. You can create invoices with reports as well as other output that summarizes your data. Thanks to the trusty Label Wizard, reports are also the best way to create mailing labels from the data in a database.

Adding a Report by Using AutoReport

AutoReports are an easy way to create a report out of one table or query. AutoReports don't have the flexibility that regular reports have — you can't create groups with an AutoReport, for example — but they're an excellent way to get your data into a report quickly. You can customize an AutoReport by using the formatting tricks that I describe throughout this chapter.

Access offers two kinds of AutoReports: columnar and tabular. A columnar AutoReport prints the field names in a column on the left and the data for the record in a column on the right (see Figure 10-1).

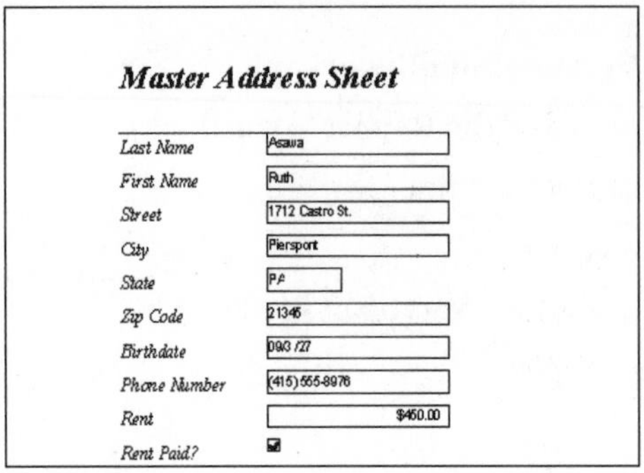

Figure 10-1: A columnar report.

A tabular AutoReport looks similar to a datasheet. Data appears in columns with field names as the column headers (see Figure 10-2).

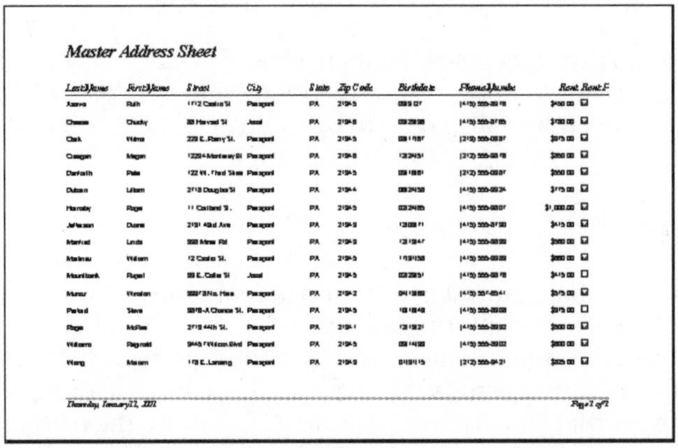

Figure 10-2: A tabular report.

To create a columnar AutoReport, follow these steps:

1. **In the Database window, select the table or query that contains the data that you want to display in a report.**

2. **Click the arrow next to the New Object button and choose AutoReport from the drop-down list.**

   Access creates the report.

Another way to create an AutoReport — and the only way to create a tabular AutoReport — is to click the New button on the Reports tab of the Database window. Access displays the New Report dialog box. From the Choose the Table or Query Where the Object's Data Comes From drop-down list at the bottom of the dialog box, select the table or query that you want it to use for the report. Then choose AutoReport: Columnar or AutoReport: Tabular and click OK. Access creates the report.

Creating a Report with the Report Wizard

Using the Report Wizard is the best way to create a report. You may be happy with the resulting report, or you may want to edit the report further, but if you use the Report Wizard, at least you have a report to work with.

One big advantage of using the Report Wizard is that you can choose fields for the report from more than one table or query — you don't need to gather all the data that you want in the report into one table or query.

The Report Wizard displays different windows depending on the data and options that you select, so don't be surprised if you don't see every window of the wizard. To create a report with the Report Wizard, follow these steps:

1. **Display the reports in the Database window and double-click the Create Report by Using Wizard icon.**

   To display Reports view, click the Reports button.

   Access displays the first Report Wizard window, where you select the fields that you want to use in your report.

2. **From the Tables/Queries list, select the first table or query from which you want to select fields.**

3. **Add the fields that you want to appear in the report to the Selected Fields list.**

   To do so, select a field name and click the arrow button, or click the double-arrows button to add all the fields in the table to the report.

4. **Repeat Steps 2 and 3 for fields in other tables or queries until all the fields that you want to display in the report appear in the Selected Fields list.**

5. **Click the Next button to see the next window of the wizard.**

   If the fields that you choose for your reports are grouped in some way (usually by a many-to-one relationship with another field that you choose for the report), you see the window shown in Figure 10-3. It enables you to choose which table you want to use to group your data.

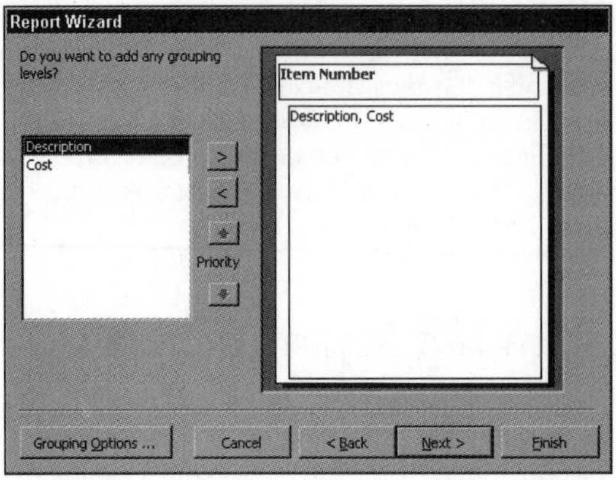

Figure 10-3: You can choose which table you want to use to group your data.

Double-click a table name to group the data in the report by using that table; then click Next to continue to the next window, which enables you to group by individual fields.

6. **Add grouping fields if you want by selecting the field and clicking the right-arrow button (>).**

   You can change the importance of a field in the grouping hierarchy by selecting the field on the right side of the window and then clicking the Priority up- and down-arrow buttons.

   Click the Grouping Options button to open the Grouping Intervals dialog box, where you can specify exactly how to group records by using the fields that you chose as grouping fields. The Grouping Intervals dialog box enables you to select grouping intervals for each field that you use to group the report. Click OK to leave the Grouping Intervals dialog box.

7. **After you finish grouping your data, click the Next button to see options for sorting and summarizing.**

   Access automatically sorts the report by the first grouping field.

   This window enables you to tell Access how you want to sort the detail section of the report. The detail section is the part of the report that displays the records within each group. You don't need to change anything in this window if you don't need to sort the detail section in any particular order.

   If you want to specify a sort order for the detail objects, display the drop-down list of field names next to the box labeled 1. Click the Sort button to change the sort order from ascending (A to Z, 1 to 10) to descending (Z to

A, 10 to 1). Click the button again to change the sort order back. You can sort by up to four fields — use the additional boxes to specify additional fields on which to sort. Access uses additional sort fields only if the initial sort field is identical for two or more records — then it uses the next sort field to determine in what order to display those records.

8. **Click Next in the Report Wizard window to view the next window.**

   Access displays the window that enables you to specify how to lay out your report.

9. **Choose the layout that you prefer and the orientation that works best with your report.**

   You can preview the layout options by clicking one of the Layout radio buttons. The example box on the left changes to show you what your chosen layout looks like.

10. **Click Next to see the next window, where you choose the style that you prefer.**

    Styles consist of background shadings, fonts, font sizes, and the other formatting used for your report.

11. **Select a style by choosing its name in the list of styles.**

    You can preview each style by clicking it.

12. **Click the Next button to view the last window of the wizard.**

13. **Type a new name for the report (if you don't like the name that the Report Wizard chooses).**

    If you want to view the report in Design view, click Modify the Report's Design; otherwise, the Preview the Report radio button is selected, and Access shows you the report in Print Preview. You can also tell Access that you want to see the Help window (which gives you hints on how to customize the report) by clicking the Display Help on Working with the Report? check box.

14. **Click the Finish button to view your report. Your computer may whir and grind for a minute before your report appears (see Figure 10-4).**

Although the Report Wizard does well setting up groups, it doesn't create a perfect report. Some controls may be the wrong size, and the explanatory text the wizard uses for calculated fields is a little pedantic. Display the report in Design view to fix anything that's wrong with it.

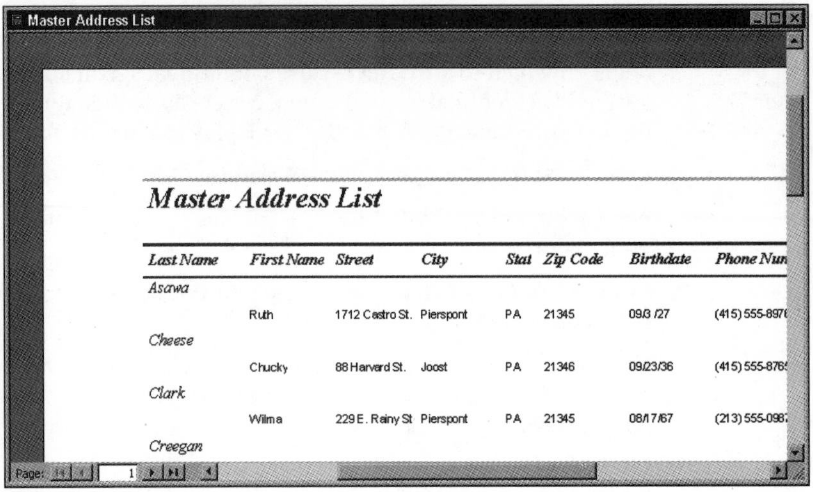

Master Address List
Master Address List
Last Name
First Name
Street
City
Stat
Zip Code
Birthdate
Phone Nun
Asawa
Ruth
1712 Castro St.
Pierspont
PA
21345
Cheese
Chucky
88 Harvard St.
Joost
PA
21346
09/23/36
Clark
Wilma
229 E. Rainy St
Pierspont
PA
21345
Creegan
Page:

Figure 10-4: Your report may just turn out nice if you use a wizard.

Creating a Report in Design View

You may have a personal thing against wizards, or you may just need to know how to create or edit a report in Design View. Whichever is the case, this section covers how to add *controls* that tell Access what to display on the report.

Controls tell Access what you want to see on your report: You add text, the contents of a field, and lines to reports by using controls. To create the report itself, follow these general steps:

1. **Display reports in the Database window by clicking the Reports button in the Objects list.**
2. **Click the New button.**

   Access displays the New Report dialog box.
3. **Select Design View (if it's not already selected).**
4. **Select the query or table on which you want to base the report from the Choose the Table or Query Where the Object's Data Comes From drop-down list at the bottom of the dialog box.**

   If you want to bind the report to more than one table, the easiest way is to create a query that includes all the fields that you want to display in the report. Chapter 7 describes querying.

TIP

Binding a report to a query can be very useful because you can create criteria for choosing the records that appear in your report so that Access doesn't include them all. You may want to make a report that includes only clients whose payments are overdue, for example, or you may want a report that includes only the addresses of people whom you're inviting to your wedding.

5. **Click OK.**

   Access displays the Report Design view (see Figure 10-5).

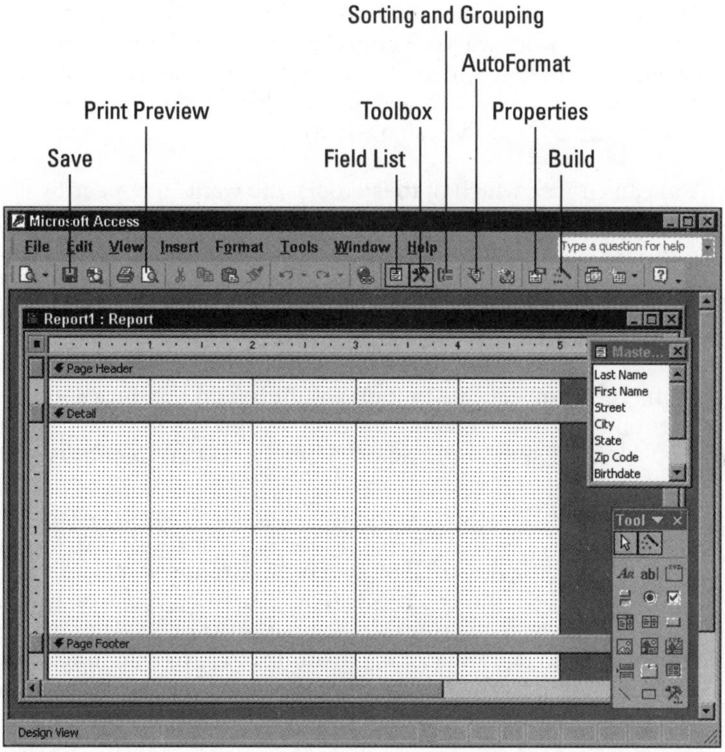

Figure 10-5: The Report Design view.

6. **Save the report design by clicking the Save button on the toolbar.**

   Give the report a name that helps you and others figure out which data it displays. Remember to save your report design often.

After you create the blank report, you're ready to start adding controls to it. (See the section "Adding a control," later in this chapter.)

Although you may think that you can easily create a report in Design view by double-clicking the Create Report in Design View icon, this method doesn't enable you to select the table or query to base the report on. If you create a report this way, you must select the table or query in the Record Source option of the report Properties dialog box that contains the data.

Using tools in Report Design view

Creating reports is complicated enough that Access gives you a group of new tools to work with in Report Design view: the buttons and boxes in the Formatting toolbar and in the Toolbox. Access also displays the grid in the background (to help you align objects in the report), as well as the rulers at the top and left of the Design window.

You can choose which of these tools you want to appear by using the View menu if you're in Design view. Items with a check mark appear in the Design window.

You can also display and close the Toolbox by clicking the Toolbox button on the toolbar.

Each type of object that you may want to add to your report displays a different button in the Toolbox — choose the type of object that you want and then click the spot in the report where you want to put the object.

You can move the Toolbox so that it appears along one edge of the Access window instead of floating free. To anchor the Toolbox to an edge, click its title bar and drag the Toolbox to one edge of the screen. A gray outline shows you where the Toolbox is to appear after you drop it. When the gray outline appears in one row or column against one side of the Access window, release the mouse. You can make the Toolbox free-floating again by clicking and dragging it by the top (if the Toolbox is vertical) or the left of the bar, or by double-clicking it. (In fact, you can perform this trick with any toolbar.)

You can also make the Toolbox a different size by clicking and dragging a border. The size that you choose affects the number of buttons that appear on each row.

Adding a control

A report consists of controls that tell Access what to display on the report. To display the contents of a field in a report, you must create a *bound* control. The control is bound to a field, which tells Access to display the contents of a field in that control.

The people who developed Access knew that you'd want to add fields to reports frequently. So they designed the program to enable you to add a field to a report by using a single drag-and-drop procedure instead of forcing you to use two steps — first creating the control and then telling Access to display the contents of a field in the control.

To add a control that displays the contents of a field to a report, display the report in Design view and follow these steps:

1. **Display the Field List window by, if necessary, clicking the Field List button on the toolbar.**

   Access displays a small window that contains the names of the fields available for use on the report. If you didn't bind a table or query to the report in the New Report dialog box, you don't see any fields here (see Figure 10-6).

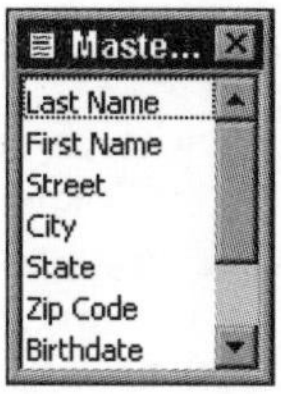

Figure 10-6: The Field List window.

2. **Drag the field that you want to use in your report from the Field List window to the report design and drop the field in the place where you want the contents of the field to appear.**

   Access puts a field control and a label control in the report. The label control contains the name of the field. It tells Access to display the contents of the field. You can edit or delete either control.

TIP: You can put several fields in the report by Ctrl+clicking to select multiple field names. You can also select consecutive fields by clicking the first field and then Shift+clicking the last field that you want to select. Then drag all the selected fields to the design grid where they appear one under the other. After they're in the design grid, you can edit and move the controls.

If you want to get rid of the label that Access adds automatically or move the label to a different place in the report, select the label and then press Ctrl+X. To display the label in a different position, click the report design where you want the label to appear and then press Ctrl+V. You can move the label by dragging the larger handle that appears on its upper-left corner after you select it.

Adding a line

Remember that what you see in Report Design view isn't exactly how the printed report appears. Not everything that you see in Design view prints — those little dots and the vertical and horizontal lines that you see in the background of the Design view, for example, as well as the boxes around the objects that you put in the report design, are all nonprinting elements of the design. To see what the printed report looks like, click the Print Preview button or the View button.

You can put a vertical, horizontal, or diagonal line into a report by adding it to the report design. If you want to create a box to surround an object, you actually want to work with the object's border.

Insert a line into a report by clicking the Line button in the Toolbox. Then move the mouse pointer into the report design, click where you want the line to begin, and drag to where you want the line to end. A line must begin and end in the same section of the report.

After you create a line, you can change its color and width by using the Line/Border Color and Line/Border Width buttons in the Formatting toolbar. You can delete the line by selecting it and pressing the Delete key. You can move the line by clicking it and dragging it to a new position or by using the Cut and Paste buttons on the toolbar.

Adding a label

If you want to create a text label that doesn't attach to a field control, you can do so by using the Label button in the Toolbox. You may, for example, want to create a label to display the name of the report. To add a label to a report, display the report in Design view and follow these steps:

1. **Click the Label button in the Toolbox.**
2. **Click and drag in the report design to create a box the right size and position for your label.**
3. **Type the text that you want to appear in the label.**
4. **Press Enter.**

TIP

If you want more than one line of text in your label box, press Ctrl+Enter to start a new line.

To edit the label, click the text box to select it, press F2, and then start editing. Press Enter after the edits are complete or Esc to cancel the edits you made.

Adding pictures and other objects

You can add a picture to a report in several ways; the method that you use depends on how you want to use the picture. You can bind or unbind a picture. (In fact, you can bind or unbind any object on the report.) An *unbound* object, such as a logo, is always the same. A *bound* object ties to one or more fields and changes for different records. You may store a picture of each person in your address database, for example, and display the appropriate pictures next to the addresses in your report by using a bound object. Or you may display your logo on each invoice by using an unbound object.

To insert a picture into a report, follow these steps:

1. **Display the report in Design view.**
2. **Click the Image button in the Toolbox.**
3. **Click the report where you want the picture to appear.**

   Access displays the Insert Picture dialog box, where you can find the file that contains the picture that you want to display on the report.
4. **In the Insert Picture dialog box, navigate your folders until you find the file that you need.**
5. **Select the file and then click OK.**

You can change the size and position of a picture the same way that you change the size or position of any object in the report.

You can delete a picture from the report by selecting it and pressing the Delete key.

Editing Objects in a Report

To edit any part of a report, you first must display the report in Design view, which you can accomplish by performing one of the following actions:

- Select the report on the Reports tab of the Database window and then click the Design button.
- Click the Design View button as you preview the report.

REMEMBER

To edit any object in a report, you first must select it. Clicking an object is the best way to select it.

By default, the label field object labels are named after field names, but you can change the wording of a label by clicking it, pressing F2, and then editing the words. Press Enter to put the changes on the report; press Esc to cancel your edits.

REAL WORLD

Sending a report to another application

Microsoft enables you to easily send a report (or a datasheet, for that matter) to another Microsoft application. All you need to do is click the OfficeLinks button, which appears on the Print Preview toolbar. The OfficeLinks default application is Word, but you can select Excel from the drop-down list.

After you click the OfficeLinks button, Access saves your report in the format that you choose (word-processing document or spreadsheet), opens the chosen application, and displays your report. Then you can edit, analyze, or print your report in that application.

You may prefer to use the drag and drop functionality to exchange data with Excel. You can drag Access tables and queries from the database window to Excel. You can also select portions of a datasheet and drag them to Excel.

Chapter 11: Changing the Look of Your Report

In This Chapter

- Deciding where your pages end
- Changing borders and colors
- Using dates and page numbers
- Changing your fonts
- Adjusting the report layout
- Using AutoFormat

Despite what you may read in Chapter 10, simply creating a nice report isn't always the fastest way to impress the lucky recipients of your data. You can do so much more than simply churn out nice reports. Why not try to add a little color to emphasize a point? How about giving some special text a unique font such as Baskerville Old Face? Would you consider adjusting the borders of your report? If you answer yes to any of the preceding questions, this chapter can show you how to make your reports the talk of the town.

Inserting Page Breaks in a Report

You can add a page break to a report in Design view. To do so, follow these steps:

1. **Click the Page Break button in the Toolbox.**

   To see the Toolbox, click the Toolbox button on the Report Design toolbar.

2. **Move the pointer to the part of the design where you want the page break to appear and click the mouse button.**

   Access inserts a page break, which looks like a series of dots that are slightly darker than the grid.

Take care where you insert a page break into a report design — you're working with the design, so the break repeats itself. A good place to use a page break is at the end of a section. If you have records that you group by month, for example, and you want each month on a separate page, put the page break at the bottom of the Date Footer section in Design view.

Playing with Borders

You can change the appearance of the border surrounding an object not only by changing its color, but also by changing the width and the style of the border. To change the width of the border (that is, the thickness of the line), follow these steps:

1. **Select the object.**

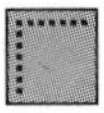

2. **Click the arrow next to the Line/Border Width button.**

   Access displays a drop-down list of border-width options. The first option is an invisible border.

3. **Click the border thickness that you want to use.**

   Access changes the border of the selected object to match the border that you select.

To change the style of the border, use the Special Effects button. Follow these steps:

1. **Select the object.**

2. **Click the arrow next to the Special Effects button.**

   Access displays a drop-down list of options.

3. **Click the option that you want to use.**

   Because the options in the drop-down list don't give you a very good idea of how the option actually appears in your report, the best way to see an effect is to try it.

Adding Color to a Report

The Formatting toolbar provides options for adding color to a report. You can change the color of text, backgrounds, and lines by using one of three buttons on the Formatting toolbar. Table 11-1 shows the buttons on the toolbar that control color and lists their names and how they work.

Table 11-1 Color Control Buttons

Button	*Name*	*What It Does*
	Fill/Back Color	Changes the color of the background of the selected object or the background of the selected section if no control is selected.
	Font/Fore Color	Changes the color of the text in the selected object.
	Line/Border Color	Changes the color of the border (the box around the object) of the selected object; also changes the color of a selected line.

You use each of these buttons the same way. To add color to a report, follow these steps:

1. **Select the object that you want to work with.**
2. **Click the arrow to the right of the button that changes colors.**

   Access displays a palette of colors.
3. **Click the color that you want to use.**

TIP

If you don't want the object visible on-screen or want it the same color as the general background, choose Transparent from the top of the color grid.

Adding Dates and Page Numbers

Access is a whiz at many things, including adding dates and page numbers. Access can number the pages of your report or put today's date in a report — all you need to do is ask.

The most sensible place to add the date and page number is in the page header or page footer of the report. The Report Wizard puts both the date and the page number (in the format *Page X of Y*) in the page footer for you.

Inserting the date and/or time

If you want to add the date and/or time yourself instead of relying on the Report Wizard, display the report in Design view and follow these steps:

1. **Click the section (or *band*) in which you want the date and/or time to appear.**
2. **Choose Insert⇨Date and Time to insert the date, the time, or both.**

The Date and Time dialog box appears. The Date and Time dialog box provides options for including the date, the time, or both, and enables you to choose the format.

3. **Select Include Date and/or Include Time and then select the format you want.**

   Check the Sample box to see how the date and/or time appears on your report.

4. **Click OK.**

   Access adds the date and/or time to the section of your report that you select in Step 1.

Inserting page numbers

To add page numbers yourself instead of relying on the Report Wizard, display the report in Design view and follow these steps:

1. **Choose Insert⇨Page Numbers.**

   The Page Numbers dialog box appears. It offers the following choices about how page numbers appear on your report:

   - **Format:** Select Page N to show only the current page number or select Page N of M to show both the current page number and the total number of pages.
   - **Position:** Decide whether the page numbers appear in the page header or the page footer.
   - **Alignment:** Click the down-arrow of this drop-down list box and choose Center (centers page numbers between the margins), Left (aligns page numbers with the left margin), Right (aligns page numbers with the right margin), Inside (prints page numbers alternately on the right and left sides of facing pages), or Outside (prints page numbers alternately on the left and right sides of facing pages).
   - **Show Number on First Page:** Deselect this option if you want to hide the page number on the first page of your report (a good way to keep your title page spiffy).

2. **Change the options in the dialog box to suit your purposes.**

3. **Click OK.**

   Access puts the page number in the position you select (Top of Page or Bottom of Page).

Aligning Report Objects

Access automatically aligns the contents of a bound control — that is, a control that displays the contents of a field: Text left-justifies and numbers and dates right-justify within the control. The three alignment buttons on the Formatting toolbar enable you to customize the alignment of the contents of a control.

To change the alignment of the contents of a control, follow these steps:

1. **Select the object.**
2. **Click the appropriate alignment button on the Formatting toolbar: Align Left, Center, or Align Right.**

Changing Date or Number Formats

To change the format of a date or number in a field control, you need to use the Format property for the control. To display the properties for the control and change the format, follow these steps:

1. **Select the control.**

2. **Display the control's properties by clicking the Properties button or pressing Alt+Enter.**
3. **Click the Format option (on the All and the Format tabs).**
4. **Choose the format that you want to use from the Format drop-down list.**
5. **Close the Properties box by clicking the Close button.**

Changing Font and Font Size

Changing the font and font size of text in a report is one of the easiest formatting tasks. All you need to do is select the control that contains the text that you want to format and choose the font and/or font size that you want from the Font and Font Size options on the Formatting toolbar.

You can make the text bold, italic, and/or underlined by clicking the Bold, Italic, and/or Underline button(s) while the object is selected.

Changing Page Layout

Use the Page Setup dialog box to change the way that Access prints your report on the page. Display the Page Setup dialog box by choosing File➪Page Setup working with the report in either Design view or Print Preview.

Choosing landscape versus portrait

To choose whether the report should appear in *landscape* (longer than it is tall) or *portrait* (taller than it is long) orientation, follow these steps:

1. **Display the Page Setup dialog box by choosing File➪Page Setup.**
2. **Click the Page tab at the top of the Page Setup dialog box.**
3. **Select the Portrait or Landscape radio button.**
4. **Click OK to close the dialog box.**

Adjusting margins

To change the margins for a report, follow these steps:

1. **Display the Page Setup dialog box by choosing File➪Page Setup.**
2. **Click the Margins tab at the top of the dialog box (see Figure 11-1).**
3. **Change the Top, Bottom, Left, and Right margins as necessary by entering measurements in the boxes.**
4. **Click OK to close the dialog box.**

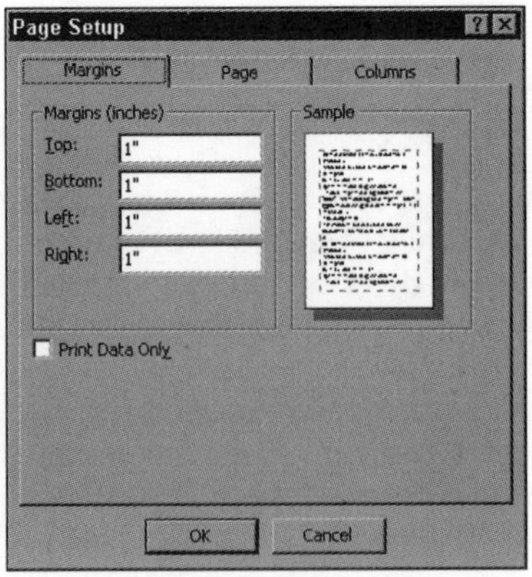

Figure 11-1: Adjusting the margins of a report.

Changing the Size of an Object

You can change the size of a control by clicking and dragging the border of the control while you're in Design view. Follow these steps:

1. **Select the object whose size you want to change.**

   Anchors (little black boxes) appear around the selected object.

2. **Move the mouse pointer to one of the anchors.**

   The pointer turns into a two-headed arrow, indicating that you can change the size of the box.

3. **Drag the edge of the box so that the object is the size that you want (see Figure 11-2).**

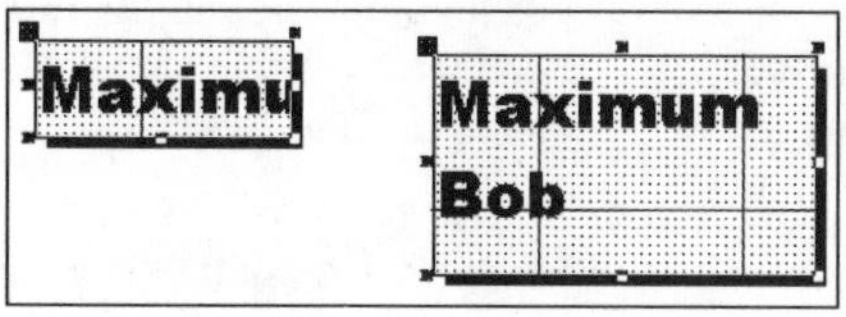

Figure 11-2: Before and after resizing an object.

The Format⇨Size menu offers the following additional options that enable you to change the size of an object:

- ✦ If you want an object just the right size to display its contents, choose Format⇨Size⇨To Fit.
- ✦ If you want several objects the same size, select all the objects and then choose Format⇨Size⇨To Tallest, To Shortest, To Widest, or To Narrowest. Access makes all the objects the same size. If you choose To Shortest, for example, Access changes all the objects to the same size as the shortest object that was selected when you chose the menu option.

Moving a Control

You can move a control by dragging it. To do so, follow these steps:

1. **Select the object that you want to move.**

   Anchors appear around the selected object.

2. **Move the mouse pointer to the edge of the box, but not over a handle.**

   The pointer changes into a hand to indicate that you can move the selected objects.

3. **Click and drag the objects to where you want them.**

REAL WORLD

Copying formatting from one control to another

After you go to the effort of prettifying one control, why reinvent the wheel to make another control match it? You can simply copy the formatting from one control to another by using the Format Painter. The Format Painter copies all formatting — colors, fonts, font sizes, border sizes, border styles, and anything else that you can think of. To copy formatting from one control to another, follow these steps:

1. **Select the object that has the formatting you want to copy.**
2. **Click the Format Painter button on the toolbar. If you want to format more than one object, double-click the Format Painter button.**

   When the mouse pointer is on an object that you can format, Access attaches a paintbrush to the pointer. If the mouse pointer is on a part of the report that you can't format with the Format Painter, the paintbrush displays a circle and line over it to indicate that you can't format there.
3. **Click the object to which you want to copy the formatting.**

   Access copies the formatting. If you used a single click to turn the Format Painter on, the mouse pointer loses its paintbrush. If you double-clicked to turn the Format Painter on, you can click additional objects to format them, too.
4. **To turn the Format Painter off, click the Format Painter button or press Esc.**

Formatting Reports by Using AutoFormat

By using AutoFormat, you can apply the same predefined formats that you saw in the Report Wizard to your report. You must tell Access which part of the report you want to format — you can choose the whole report, one section, or even just one control. Here's how to use AutoFormat to format your report:

1. **Display the report in Design view.**
2. **Select the part of the report that you want to format by using AutoFormat.**
3. **Click the AutoFormat button on the Report Design toolbar.**

   Access displays the AutoFormat dialog box.
4. **Choose the format that you want from the Report AutoFormats list.**
5. **Click OK to apply the format to the selected part of the report.**

Some additional options appear in the AutoFormat dialog box. If you click the Options button, Access displays check boxes that enable you to choose attributes of AutoFormat: Font, Color, and Border. The default is to apply all three, but you can choose not to apply the fonts, colors, or borders in the AutoFormat to your report by clicking to deselect the check box for the formatting option that you don't want Access to apply to your report.

The Customize button displays the Customize AutoFormat dialog box, where you can create and delete AutoFormats. You can create your own format, basing it on the current format of the selection, or change the AutoFormat so that it matches the format of the current selection.

Chapter 12: Forms for Displaying and Entering Data

In This Chapter

- **Getting to know forms**
- **Creating forms by using a wizard or by yourself**
- **Entering data into forms**
- **Putting controls in your forms**
- **AutoFormatting your form**
- **Using Design View to work on your form**

Tables are a great way to store data, but they aren't always great tools if you want to enter data — particularly related data that you want to store in separate tables. That's when you need a form.

Unlike tables, forms display only the fields that you want to see. You can create a form that shows all the data for one record on-screen at one time — something that's difficult to do if a number of fields are in a table. You can also add features such as check boxes and drop-down lists that make entering data easier. And making data entry into your database easy for people should be your life-long ambition.

About Forms

Forms are similar to reports, except that *forms* enable you to input and edit data, not just view and print it. You can easily create a form that enables you to work with linked tables — you can see and enter related data in the same place, and you can see all the fields in one record at the same time, instead of needing to scroll across a table. You can also create different forms for different people or groups of people who use a database.

Forms can range from relatively simple to complex. Really extravagant forms can include formatting, calculated fields, and controls (such as check boxes, buttons, and pictures) that make entering data easier. Forms are so similar to reports that many of the features you use to create a form are the same features you use to create a report.

Adding a Form to Your Database

Making a new form is similar to making any new Access object. The easiest way to create a new form is to follow these steps:

1. **Display the forms in the Database window.**

   To do so, click the Forms button.

2. **Click the New button.**

   Access displays the New Form dialog box, which gives you several choices for creating your form (see Figure 12-1).

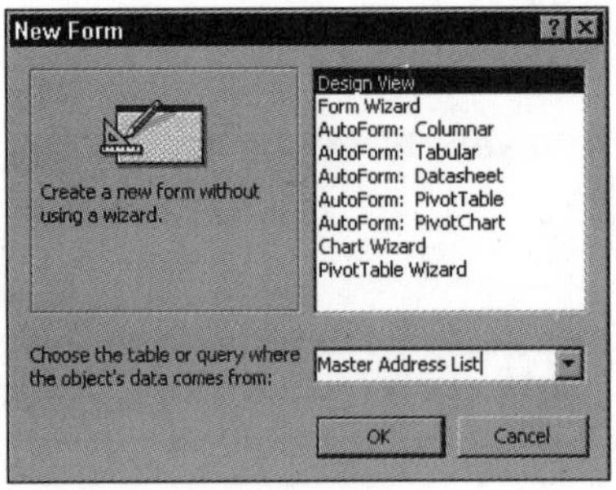

Figure 12-1: The New Form dialog box.

3. **Choose the method that you want to use to create the form.**
4. **Select the table or query on which you want to base the form.**
5. **Click OK.**

Table 12-1 describes the choices in the New Form dialog box and tells you when to use each of them.

Table 12-1 Choices in the New Form Dialog Box

Option	*When to Use It*
Design View	If you want to design your own form from scratch, with no help from Access. (Design view is great for putting your own stamp on a form, but getting started with a wizard really helps.)
Form Wizard	If you want help creating a form. The Form Wizard walks you through the creation of a form, enabling you to use fields from multiple tables and queries, to create groups, and to perform calculations for summary fields. The resulting form is bland, but editing an existing form is much easier than creating one from scratch.

Option	*When to Use It*
AutoForm: Columnar	If you want to create a quick and easy columnar form (in which the field names go in one column and the data in another) from the table or query that you specify.
AutoForm: Tabular	If you want to create a quick and easy tabular form from the table or query that you specify. A tabular form displays data in rows, like a datasheet, but with more room for each row.
AutoForm: Datasheet	If you want to create a datasheet form from the table or query that you specify. These forms look almost exactly like a datasheet. (Tabular AutoForms are similar but a little spiffier.)
AutoForm: PivotTable	If you want to create an Excel-style PivotTable form.
AutoForm: PivotChart	If you want to create an Excel-style PivotChart form.
Chart Wizard	If you want to create a form consisting of a chart.
PivotTable Wizard	If you want to create a form with an Excel PivotTable.

FAST TRACK

The quick way to create a form from a table or query is to select the name of the table or query that you want to use in the Database window, click the New Object button, and select Form or AutoForm from the list that appears. Choosing Insert⇨Form or Insert⇨AutoForm from the menu bar also creates a new form.

Adding a Form by Using the Form Wizard

The Form Wizard is a great way to create a simple or complex form — but especially a complex form. If you want to use fields from multiple tables in your form, the Form Wizard is the way to go. Here's how to create a form by using the Form Wizard:

1. **Display the Forms view of the Database window and double-click the Create Form by Using Wizard icon.**

   To switch to Forms view, click the Forms button in the Database window. Access displays the first window of the Form Wizard, where you can choose the fields that you want to use in the form.

2. **Use the Tables/Queries drop-down list to choose the first table or query from which you want to use fields.**
3. **Select the fields in the Available Fields list that you want to appear on the form and move them to the Selected Fields list by double-clicking or by selecting a field and clicking the right-arrow button.**
4. **Repeat Steps 2 and 3 to select fields from other tables or queries.**

5. **After all the fields that you want to display in the form appear in the Selected Fields list box, click Next.**

   The Form Wizard displays the next window. If you're selecting fields from only one table, this window asks you to choose a format for the form — skip right to Step 10. Otherwise, the window asks how you want to group your data.

6. **Choose the organization that you want for your form by double-clicking the table or query by which you want to group records.**

   Grouping items in a form is similar to grouping fields in a report. In the preceding figure, for example, many items relate to a single order, so grouping the data according to the data in the Order Summary table displays the summary information for the order only once and then shows all the items ordered (grouped by the catalog from which they were ordered) and the specific information about the order.

7. **Choose the Form with Subforms(s) or Linked Forms radio button at the bottom of the window.**

   If you want to see all the fields on the form at one time, click the Form with Subform(s) radio button. If you click Linked Forms, Access creates a separate form for the detail records. Users can then view this form by clicking a button in the first form. (If you're not sure which option to choose, go for Form with Subforms(s).)

8. **Click Next to see the next window.**

   Access displays a window that enables you to choose the layout for the form or subform, if you're creating one.

9. **Choose the layout.**

   You can click a layout option to see what it looks like. If you're not sure which layout to use, stick with Columnar — it's easy to use and easy to edit. If you're working with grouped fields, this window gives you only two options: Tabular and Datasheet.

10. **Click Next to see the next window, which enables you to choose a style for the form.**

11. **Choose one of the lovely styles that the Form Wizard offers.**

    Click a style name to see a sample of a form formatted with that style. (None of the styles is gorgeous, so pick one and get on with the real work.)

12. **Click Next to see the final window.**

13. **Give the form a name and decide whether you want to see the form itself (click the Open the Form to View or Enter Information option) or the form Design view (click the Modify the Form's Design option).**

    If you're creating subforms or linked forms, Access enables you to name those items, too (or you can accept the names that Access gives them).

14. **Click Finish to create the form (see Figure 12-2).**

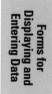

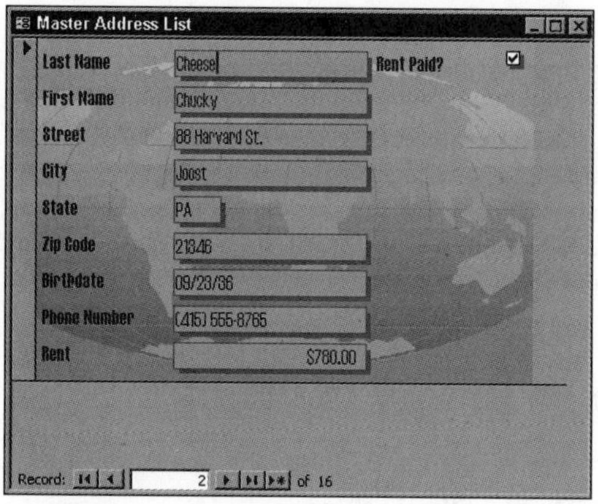

Figure 12-2:
Oh, what
forms you
can create.

> Master Address List
>
> Last Name Cheese Rent Paid? ☑
> First Name Chucky
> Street 88 Harvard St.
> City Joost
> State PA
> Zip Code 21346
> Birthdate 09/23/36
> Phone Number (415) 555-8765
> Rent $780.00
>
> Record: ◀◀ ◀ 2 ▶ ▶▶ ▶* of 16

Entering Data through a Form

After you create a form, you want to use it for its intended purpose: viewing and entering data. To use a form that you create, double-click the form name in the Database window — you're now in Form view. The data that a form displays comes directly from tables in the database, and the table reflects any changes that you make in that data. If you add data by using a form, Access adds the data to the table.

In general, you use the same skills to work with a form as you use to work with datasheets. You can use navigation buttons at the bottom of the form or subform to move to different records, and you press the Tab or Enter key to move from one field to another.

Editing and Formatting Forms

The steps for creating, editing, and formatting form controls are identical to those for performing the same tasks by using report controls. But some formatting tasks are even easier with forms than with reports because you can do them from the Form view without switching to the Design view.

You can do the following formatting in Form view:

✦ Change control properties (by right-clicking the control and choosing Properties from the shortcut menu to display the properties).

✦ Change fonts.

**Book IV
Chapter 12**

Forms for
Displaying and

- Change font sizes.
- Change text appearance by clicking the Bold, Italic, and Underline buttons.

The Formatting toolbar normally appears in Form view (unless you turn it off), and you can use any of its buttons to format the selected control. Notice that, in Form view, you have no visual clue that a control is selected — the selected control is the last one that you click. Design view is superior for making wholesale changes, because you can select only one control at a time in Form view, but the Formatting toolbar makes on-the-fly editing possible in Form view.

Viewing Your Form in Design View

If you want to work on the design of your form, you can display the form in Design view, as shown in Figure 12-3.

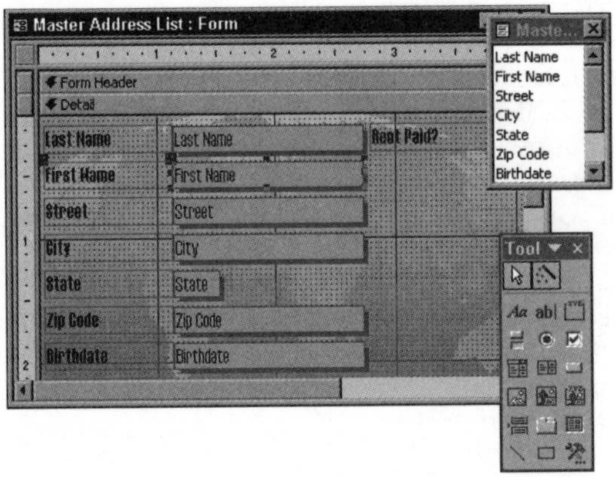

Figure 12-3: A form on display in Design view.

You can display the Design view of a form by doing either of the following:

- Select the form on the Forms tab of the Database window and click the Design button.
- Click the Design View button if you're working with the form in Form view.

You can also change control properties without displaying the form in Design view. To do so, right-click a part of the form that you want to alter and choose Properties on the shortcut menu.

AutoFormatting Your Form

You can use AutoFormat to give your form one of the format styles that Access provides. The styles that you see in the AutoFormat dialog box are the same ones that you see in the Form Wizard.

To format a form, you first must select what you want to format: the entire form, part of the form, or even just one control. Selecting part of a form in Design view is identical to selecting part of a report in Design view. To use AutoFormat to format your form, follow these steps:

1. **Display the form in Design view.**

   You can display a form by selecting it in the Database window and clicking the Design button.

2. **Select the part of the form that you want to format by using AutoFormat.**

   To select the whole thing, click the small box in it in the upper-left corner of the window.

3. **Click the AutoFormat button on the toolbar.**

   Access displays the AutoFormat dialog box.

4. **Select the format that you want to use by clicking its name on the Form AutoFormats list.**

   You can select a format to see an example of how your form looks with that format.

5. **Click OK to apply the format to the part of the form that you select in Step 2.**

Index

A

B

C

D

Continued

S

T

U

V

W

Y

Book V

Outlook 2002

"IT'S ANOTHER DEEP SPACE PROBE FROM EARTH, SEEKING CONTACT FROM EXTRATERRESTRIALS. I WISH THEY'D JUST INCLUDE AN E-MAIL ADDRESS."

Contents at a Glance

Chapter 1: All About Outlook

In This Chapter

- Getting acquainted with the look of Outlook
- Customizing the Outlook bar
- Adding specialized applications
- Archiving your old work

After the hordes of Microsoft programmers put the last touches on Outlook, they surely took a step back in awe of what they'd wrought. What most regular people saw as some fancy e-mail software was actually a "messaging and collaboration client." Microsoft realized that information was spread out in calendars, schedulers, planners, Rolodexes, folders, sticky notes — and in e-mail, of course. So why not create a single product that lets people share this information? Outlook is the result of this question.

Chapter 1 introduces you to the Outlook interface (how the thing actually appears on screen) and gets you going on some basic tasks.

Recognizing What You See in Outlook

After you start Outlook, you see a screen within a screen. The area along the top edge and left side of the screen offers a collection of menus and icons. These items enable you to control what you see and what you make happen on the other areas of the screen. The different parts of the Outlook screen have names, as shown in Figure 1-1.

Along the left side of the Outlook screen is the *Outlook bar.* It displays large, clearly marked icons for each of the Outlook modules: Outlook Today, Inbox, Calendar, Contacts, Tasks, Notes, and Deleted Items. (Click the down arrow at the bottom of the Outlook bar to scroll down and see all the module icons.) You can click any icon at any time to switch to a different module and then switch back — just like changing channels on your TV.

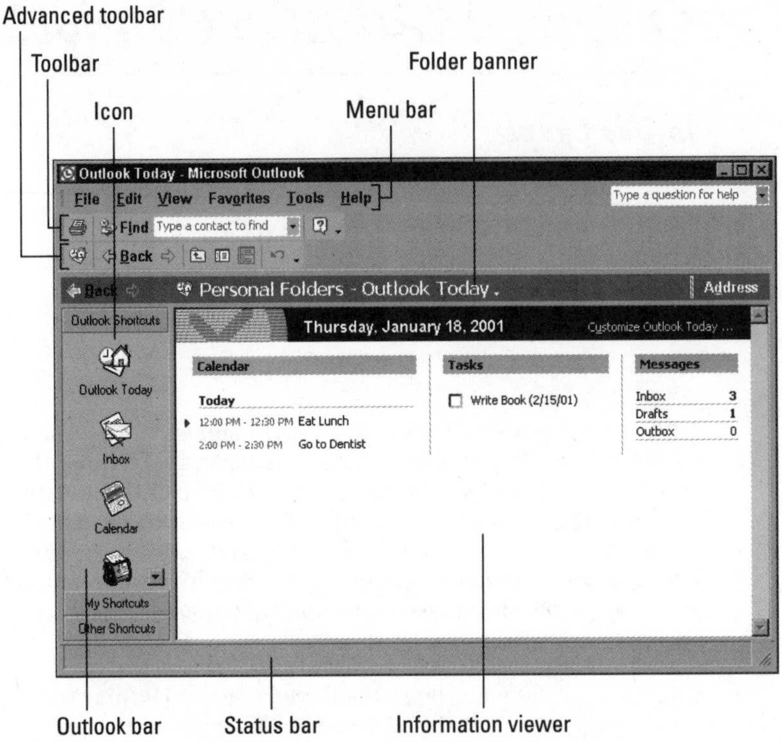

Figure 1-1: Your basic Outlook screen.

The Outlook bar also offers three gray separator bars: Outlook Shortcuts, My Shortcuts, and Other Shortcuts. You can click these separator bars to switch to a different section of the Outlook bar and see a different set of icons. You can add icons to any section of the Outlook bar. You can also add sections to the bar itself by right-clicking the Outlook bar and choosing Options from the shortcut menu.

Now that you know about the Outlook bar, here's a quick rundown of the other parts of the Outlook window:

- **The folder banner:** The folder banner is the name of the area that sits below the toolbars and above the main part of the Outlook screen (the *information viewer*). The name of the folder or module you're using appears in large letters at the left end of the folder banner, just to the right of the Back and Forward buttons.
- **The folder list:** The folder list gives you a quick peek behind the scenes at what's going on in Outlook. To open the folder list, click the name on the folder banner or choose View⇨Folder List. To close the folder list, click the name on the folder banner a second time or choose View⇨Folder List again.

Outlook organizes all the information that you enter in folders. Each Outlook module has its own folder. Although most people change modules by clicking an icon on the Outlook bar, speedsters do it by clicking the name on the folder banner and choosing a folder from the folder list. Every Outlook module that displays an icon on the Outlook bar has a folder on the folder list, but not every folder on the folder list has an icon on the Outlook bar. Because you can have more folders on the folder list than icons on the Outlook bar, you may need to use the folder list to go to a specific folder rather than click its icon on the Outlook bar.

✦ **The information viewer:** The biggest part of the Outlook screen is the information viewer. Whatever you ask Outlook to show you appears in the information viewer. Dates in your Calendar, messages in your Inbox, and names on your Contact list all appear in the information viewer.

✦ **Menus:** Like all Windows programs, Outlook has a menu bar across the top of the screen.

✦ **On-screen forms:** Every time that you either open an item or create a new item in Outlook, a form appears. This form either accepts the information that you want to enter or contains the information that you're viewing — or both. Each module has its own form, and each form has its own menus and toolbars.

✦ **Status bar:** The gray bar across the bottom of the Outlook screen is the *status bar,* which tells you how many items Outlook is displaying and a few other pieces of essential information.

✦ **Toolbars:** Toolbars offer a quicker way to control Outlook than clicking menus. The Outlook toolbar changes as you switch between different modules or views to offer you the most useful set of tools for the task you're doing at the moment. If you see a tool button and want to know what it does, hover your mouse pointer over the button but don't click it; a ToolTip box appears, revealing the name of the tool. Outlook offers two toolbars that you can choose from on the main screen: the Standard toolbar and the Advanced toolbar. The Advanced toolbar offers a larger selection of tools. You can pick the toolbar that you want to use by choosing View⇨Toolbars and clicking the name of the toolbar that you want to see or by right-clicking a toolbar and choosing a name from the shortcut menu.

Adding an Icon to the Outlook Bar

After you become familiar with Outlook, you may want to create more icons on the Outlook bar. Because each icon on the Outlook bar is a shortcut to a folder or resource on your computer, you can save some time by adding a few well-chosen icons. To add an icon, follow these steps:

1. **Right-click the Outlook bar and choose Outlook Bar Shortcut from the shortcut menu.**

   The Add to Outlook Bar dialog box appears, as shown in Figure 1-2.

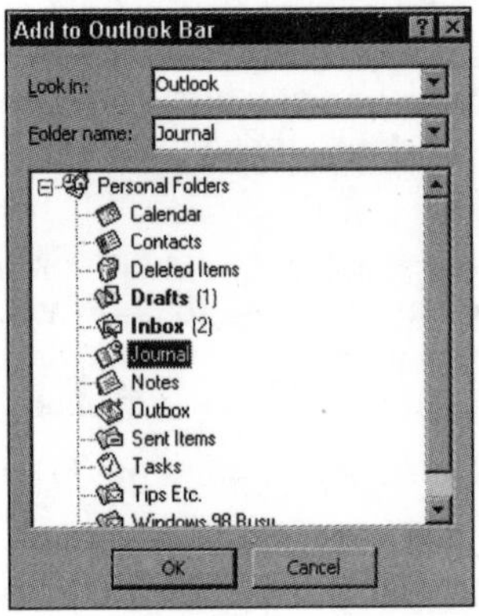

Figure 1-2: Use this dialog box to add an icon to the Outlook bar.

2. **In the Look In drop-down list, choose Outlook.**
3. **Select a folder from the Folder Name list or click a name in the list in the bottom half of the dialog box.**
4. **Click OK.**

To move an icon in the Outlook bar, drag it upward or downward. To remove an icon, right-click it and choose Remove from the Outlook Bar from the shortcut menu.

Archiving Your Work

You can save a great deal of information in Outlook. But after storing a lot of items, Outlook starts to slow down. To keep the program speedy, Outlook periodically sends older items to the archive file. Although the files are still available (You see how to access them later in this section), Outlook doesn't need to dredge them up every time that you start the program.

You can set up Outlook to send items to the archives automatically after the items reach a certain age. To do so, follow these steps:

1. **Choose Tools⇨Options to open the Options dialog box.**
2. **Click the Other tab.**
3. **Click the AutoArchive button to open the AutoArchive dialog box, as shown in Figure 1-3.**

REAL WORLD

Backing up your Outlook work

To avoid losing the work that you do in Outlook, better back it up. All the items that you create with Outlook and all the e-mail that you send and receive go into one enormous file, known as `outlook.pst`. If you're trying to find your Outlook files so that you can back them up, use the Windows Find utility and search for files by the name *.PST. The Outlook data file, however, can be very large, so don't plan to back it up on a floppy disk. You need a Zip drive or CD-RW for that.

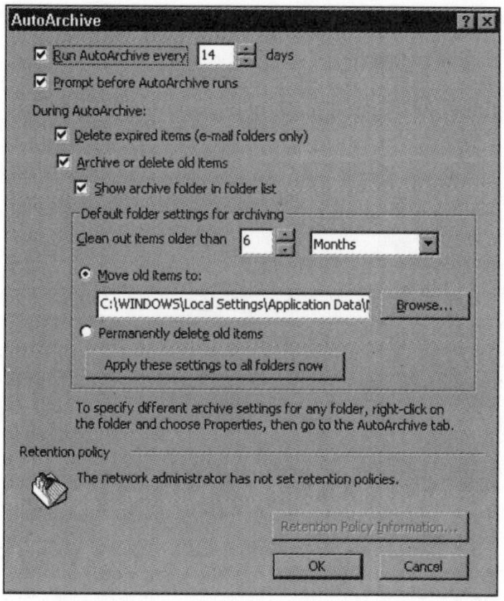

Figure 1-3: You can archive a lot of old stuff that you don't need by using this dialog box.

4. **Click the Run AutoArchive Every *XX* Days check box and fill in the number of days that you want between automatic archive sessions. If the check box is already selected and you want AutoArchiving on, leave the check box alone.**
5. **Click OK to close the AutoArchive dialog box.**
6. **Click OK again to close the Options dialog box.**

After AutoArchiving is set up, whenever Outlook is ready to send items to the archive, you see a dialog box that asks whether you want the items sent to the archive. The dialog box appears right after you start Outlook.

REMEMBER

If you choose not to use AutoArchiving, you can always archive items manually by choosing File⇨Archive.

To see an item that you archived, choose View⇨Folder List to open the Folder List. Then, in the Folder List, click the plus sign (+) beside the Archive Files icon. You see a list of Outlook Folders. Click the folder for the type of item you are looking for to display the item in the Information viewer.

Chapter 2: Getting Going with E-Mail

In This Chapter

- **Discovering your Inbox**
- **Creating and sending e-mail**
- **Checking your spelling**
- **Making a mailing list**

If you're like most people, you want to get (and keep) your e-mail up and running without any problems. E-mail may be your lifeline — an indispensable tool for your personal satisfaction or your business needs. Then again, you may simply want to exchange e-mail with your pals, send your opinions to the White House, and seek the wisdom of the Microsoft Product Support Staff. Setting up Outlook to send and receive mail is probably high on your priority list, just below eating and sleeping. This chapter helps you prepare for the e-mail barrage that may soon follow your foray into the online world.

The Outlook Inbox

The main Inbox screen enables you to look at a list of your e-mail and helps you manage the messages that you send and receive (see Figure 2-1). You can create folders for storing each message according to what the message is about, who sent it to you, or when you got it.

You can change the arrangement of what you see in the Inbox by changing the view. (A *view* is a method of organizing the information that you see in Outlook.) Each view has a name, such as Message, AutoPreview, or By Conversation Topic. To change from one view to another, simply choose View➪Current View and pick the view you want from the list of views that appears.

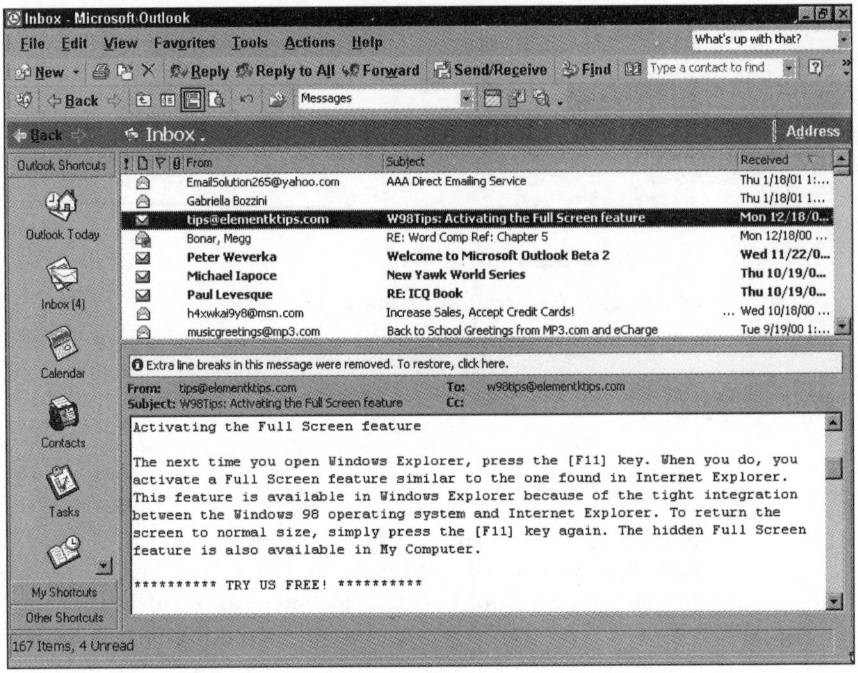

Figure 2-1: The Inbox is where you'll spend much of your time in Outlook.

Creating and Sending Messages

If you know an e-mail address, you can send a message. You don't even need to have anything to say, although having a thought or two worth sending is usually a good idea so that people find your e-mail worth reading. To create and send a message, follow these steps:

1. **Switch to the Inbox by clicking the Inbox icon on the Outlook bar to show your list of messages.**

2. **Click the New Mail Message button (or press Ctrl+N) to open the New Message form.**
3. **Click the To text box and enter the e-mail address of the person to whom you're sending the message.**

For people whose e-mail addresses you include on your Contact list (see Chapter 9), just enter the first few letters of the person's name. If Outlook knows the e-mail address of the person whose name you enter, Outlook fills in the rest of the name.

Another approach is to click the To button to open the Select Names dialog box. Then, on the left side of the dialog box, double-click the name of the person to whom you're sending the message; click OK to return to your New Message form.

4. **Click the Cc text box and enter the e-mail address(es) of the people to whom you want to send a copy of your message (if you want to send a copy, that is).**
5. **Enter the subject of the message in the Subject text box.**
6. **Enter the text of your message in the large text box.**
7. **Click the Send button (or press Alt+S) to close the New Message form and send your message on its way.**

Attaching files to your messages

Whenever you want to send someone a document, a picture, or a spreadsheet that you don't want to include in the message itself, you can add it to the message as an *attachment.* You don't even need to send an actual message; just save the file you're working on and send it as an attachment. To send an attachment, follow these steps:

1. **Switch to the Inbox by clicking the Inbox icon on the Outlook bar.**
2. **Choose File⇨New⇨Mail Message, press Ctrl+N, or click the New button on the Standard toolbar to open the New Message form.**

3. **Click the Insert File button on the New Message toolbar.**

   The Insert File dialog box appears, as shown in Figure 2-2.

Figure 2-2: Attach a file to an e-mail by using the Insert File dialog box.

4. **Locate and select the name of the file that you want to send.**

   The filename is highlighted to show that you selected it.

5. **Click the Insert button.**

   Back on the message form, an icon representing your file and the name of the file itself appear in the Attach box, a new box that you find below the Subject text box.

6. **Enter your message if you have one to send (although you don't need to send a message if you don't have anything to say).**

7. **Click the Send button to send your message and attachment.**

If you want to send a document by e-mail while you're creating the document in another Microsoft Office application, you can eliminate most of this procedure by clicking the E-mail button or choosing File⇨Send To⇨Mail Recipient from the application's menu bar. The command, however, isn't available in all Office applications.

Formatting message text

You can spice up your messages with text formatting — such as boldface, italics, or various typefaces — whether you use Outlook alone or with Microsoft Office. You can also tell Outlook to use Microsoft Word as your e-mail editor, which means that every time you open an e-mail message, Microsoft Word steps in and automatically adjusts the appearance of the message. Whenever you create a new message with Word as your e-mail editor, you can add fancy-looking elements to your message, such as tables and special text effects (for example, flashing text), and you can use all the other powerful features of Word.

In order to format messages in Word, you must instruct Outlook to send the messages in HTML format. What's more, the people who receive your messages must have e-mail software that is capable of interpreting HTML. To tell Outlook to send messages in HTML format, choose Tools⇨Options, click the Mail Format tab in the Options dialog box, and choose HTML from the Compose in This Message Format drop-down list.

To format text in a message, use the buttons on the Formatting toolbar on the Message form (see Figure 2-3). Book 2 explains how to format text in Word.

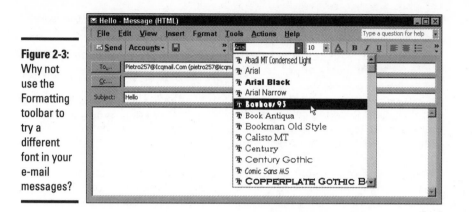

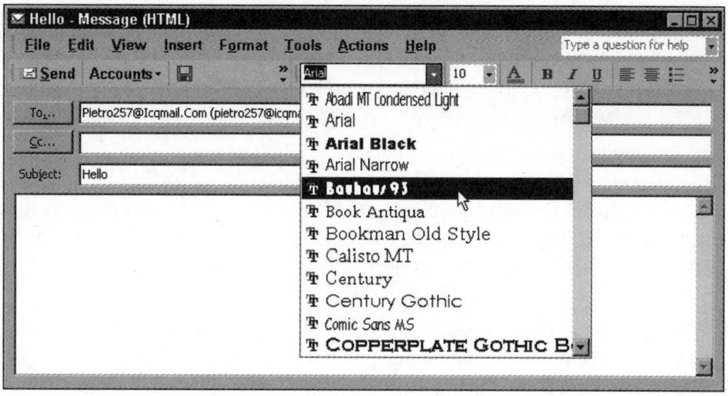

Figure 2-3: Why not use the Formatting toolbar to try a different font in your e-mail messages?

If you've ever used a word processor in Windows, the steps that you follow to format text in an Outlook message are familiar to you: Just click the toolbar button on the Formatting toolbar for the type of formatting that you want to add to your text, and then type your text. The following list provides details:

- **To format text you've already typed:** Press and hold the mouse button and drag the mouse pointer over the text to select it. Then click the button for the type of formatting that you want to add to your text, such as bold or italics.
- **To set the typeface of your text:** Click the down arrow to open the Font drop-down list and select the font that you want to use.
- **To set the size of your text:** Click the down arrow next to open the Font Size drop-down list and select a font size.
- **To set the color of your text:** Click the Font Color button and select a color from the color palette that appears. The Font Color button is next to the Bold button on the Formatting toolbar.
- **To make your text bold, italic, or underlined:** Click the Bold, Italic, or Underline button (or press Ctrl+B, Ctrl+I, or Ctrl+U, respectively) and then start typing your message text. Click the button again to return to regular type. (You can also select the type that you want to format and then click the button for that attribute.)
- **To align your text to the left, center, or right:** Click the Align Left, Center, or Align Right button on the Formatting toolbar.

- **To create a bulleted list:** Click the Bullets button. (This button is not the one to click if you want to shoot your computer.)
- **To indent your text:** Click the Increase Indent. To reduce the amount of space you indent your text, click the Decrease Indent button.

If you send e-mail to people who don't use Outlook, the formatting that you apply in Outlook often gets lost. Although you may enjoy seeing all your messages as you type them in bold fuchsia, many of your readers don't get the same pleasure as they read your messages.

Want to use Word as your e-mail editor (or quit using it for that matter)? In the Outlook window, choose Tools➪Options and then click the Mail Format tab in the Options dialog box that appears. Click to select or deselect the Use Microsoft Word to Edit E-mail Messages check box and then click OK.

Indicating a message's importance

Some messages are very important to both you and the person receiving the message. Other messages aren't so important, but you send them as a matter of routine to keep people informed. Outlook enables you to designate the importance of a message to help your recipients make good use of their time. After you open the Message form to create a message, two icons on the Message form toolbar enable you to select the importance of your message, as follows:

- **To assign High importance:** Click the Importance: High button on the Message form toolbar.
- **To assign Low importance:** Click the Importance: Low button on the Message form toolbar.

An icon corresponding to the importance of the message appears in the first column of the Message List.

Spell Checking

Heaven knows that you want to spell everything correctly when you send an e-mail message. Who knows how many people may see the message or whether someone on an archeological dig a million years from now may discover your old messages? Fortunately, you can spell-check all your messages before sending them out. To run the spelling checker, follow these steps:

1. **Choose Tools➪Spelling and Grammar (or press F7) to start the spelling checker.**

If everything is perfect, a dialog box opens, telling you that the spelling check is complete. If so, you can click OK and get on with your life.

2. **In the highly unlikely event that you misspelled something, the Spelling dialog box opens and shows you the error (which is probably the computer's fault) along with a list of suggested (that is, correct) spellings (see Figure 2-4).**

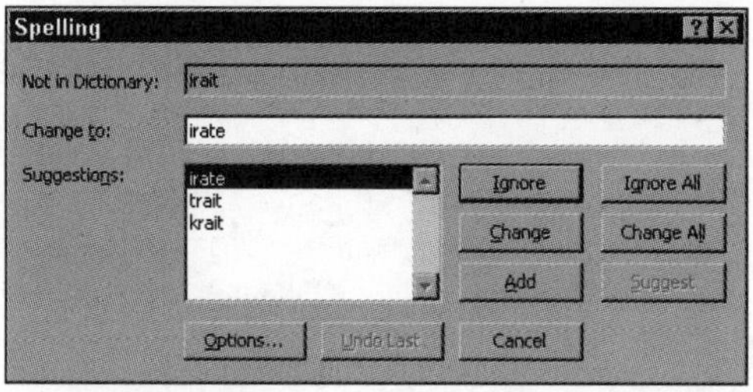

Figure 2-4: Spell-checking a message.

3. **If one of the suggested spellings is the one you really meant, click that spelling. If none of the suggested spellings is quite what you have in mind, type the spelling that you want in the Change To text box.**
4. **Click the Change button.**
5. **If Outlook finds any other errors, repeat Steps 3 and 4 until you eradicate all misspellings and Outlook tells you that the spelling check is complete, as in Step 1.**

Although the spelling checker thinks that certain technical terms (such as Linux or AutoFormat) and proper names (Englebert Humperdinck, for example) are misspellings, you can increase your spell-checker's vocabulary by clicking the Add button in the Spelling dialog box when the spell-checker zeroes in on such words. You can also click Ignore if the spell-checker stops on a weird word that you encounter infrequently.

INTEGRATION

If you choose to use Microsoft Word as your e-mail editor, a wavy red underline appears beneath misspelled words as soon as you type them. If you right-click a misspelled word, a shortcut menu appears with the correct spelling; click the correct spelling, and go right on entering text. (If you opted not to see the wavy red lines in Word, however, you won't see them when you compose e-mail messages in Outlook, either.)

Using stationery

If you get tired of the same, old e-mail day in and day out, try to personalize yours. *Stationery* is designed to make your messages convey a visual impression about you. You can make your message look uniquely important, businesslike, or just plain fun with the right choice of stationery. To add stationery to your e-mails, follow these steps:

1. **Choose Actions⇨New Mail Message Using⇨More Stationery.**

   The Select a Stationery dialog box appears with a list of each type of stationery that you can choose.

2. **Click the type of stationery you want to use and click OK.**

   The Message form appears and displays the stationery that you selected. Now you can enter your message and click Send to send it on its merry way.

Creating Personal Distribution Lists

If you repeatedly send e-mail to the same group of people, you can save lots of time by creating a *distribution list* that contains the addresses of all the people in the group. Then, to send your message, instead of entering the name of each person on your list, you need to enter only the name of the list.

To create a personal distribution list, follow these steps:

1. **Click the down arrow beside the New button and choose Distribution List on the drop-down list (or press Ctrl+Shift+L).**

   The Distribution List dialog box appears.

2. **In the Name text box, enter a name for your distribution list.**
3. **Click the Select Members button to open the Select Members dialog box (see Figure 2-5).**

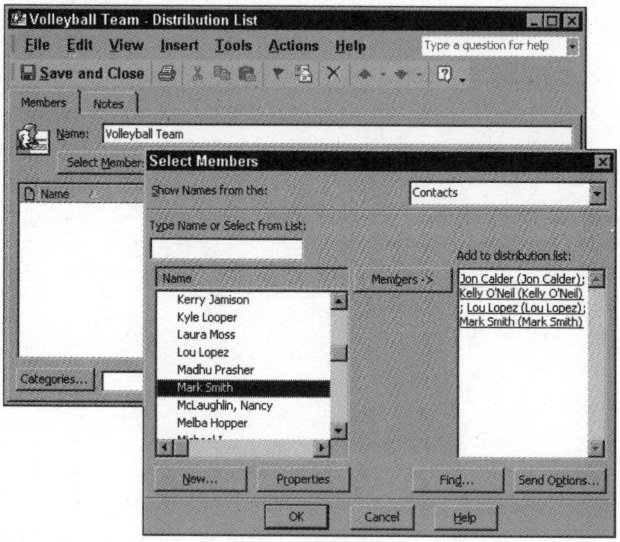

Figure 2-5: Set up distribution lists in this dialog box to make your life easier.

4. **Double-click the name of each person you want to include on your personal distribution list.**

   As you double-click each name, Outlook copies the names that you choose to the Add to Distribution List box.

5. **Click OK after you finish adding all the names that you want to include on your distribution list to close the Select Members dialog box.**

6. **Back in the Distribution List dialog box, click the Save and Close button.**

If you want to send a message to everyone in one of your groups or on your distribution lists, just type the list's name in the To box of your message form. You can also click the To button and choose the list's name in the Select Names dialog box. You can create as many distribution lists as you want.

Chapter 3: Reading and Replying to Your Mail

In This Chapter

- **Taking care of your incoming e-mail**
- **Replying to mail**
- **Forwarding mail**

If you send e-mail, you receive e-mail. It's as simple as that. Heck, you're probably going to receive e-mail even if you never send an e-mail message to anyone. That's the funny way the e-mail world works. And if you don't read your e-mail, you may miss out on something important — for example, a great joke that you heard long ago but forgot or notification that you can earn lots of money at home working on your computer. Do you want to take a chance?

Of course, if you receive e-mail, you may want to respond (at least to some of it). You may even want to forward some of your e-mail to others so that you aren't the only one to suffer. This chapter helps you with your incoming and outgoing e-mail chores.

Handling Incoming Messages

All your incoming mail piles up unless you do something about it. This section shows you how to read, delete, flag, and do all sorts of things with the e-mail you receive.

Reading your mail

Your Inbox contains your list of incoming e-mail. Even if you never exchanged e-mail with anybody or you don't even *know* anybody, you see at least one message in your Inbox the first time that you start Outlook — the "Welcome to Microsoft Outlook" message. Isn't that nice of Microsoft? To read your e-mail, follow these steps:

1. **Double-click the title of the message that you want to read.**

   The message is probably in your Inbox unless you stored it elsewhere. The message opens in a window so that you can read it (see Figure 3-1).

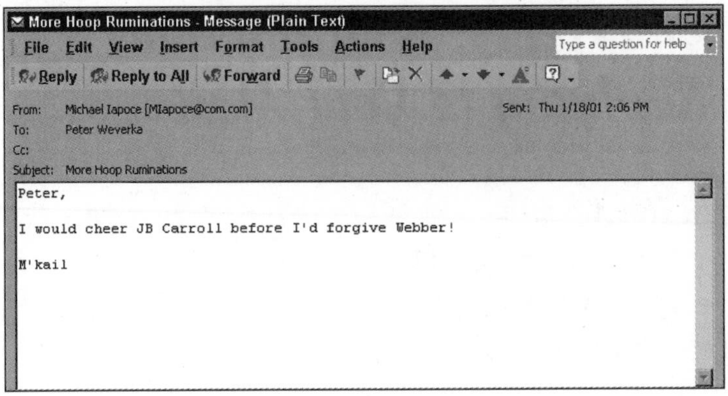

Figure 3-1: Reading an e-mail message.

2. **Press Esc or click the Close button to close the message screen.**

The little figures on the Message form toolbar do things that are specific to writing and reading e-mail messages, such as reply to it, print it, or mark it as high or low priority, and the up and down arrows enable you to read the next (or previous) message on your Inbox list.

Previewing messages

Because you can usually get the gist of an incoming e-mail message from the first few lines, Outlook enables you to see the first few lines of all unread messages in a special AutoPreview pane. To check out this AutoPreview feature, follow these steps:

1. **Switch to the Inbox by clicking the Inbox icon on the Outlook bar.**
2. **Choose View⇨AutoPreview.**

AutoPreview shows you the first few lines of the messages you haven't read yet. If you don't care to view messages this way, choose View⇨AutoPreview again.

REMEMBER

AutoPreview may be the only way that you ever want to view your Inbox. If you get a large number of messages, previewing them saves time. You can look at the contents of each message in the lower half of the information viewer while your list of messages appears in the upper half. To turn the preview pane on (or off) choose View⇨Preview Pane.

Deleting a message

If you get mail from the Internet, you can expect to receive junk mail. You may also get lots of e-mail at work. Bill Gates gets scads of e-mail. Maybe that's why deleting messages in Outlook is so easy. Just follow these steps:

1. **Switch to the Inbox by clicking the Inbox icon on the Outlook bar.**
2. **Select the title of the message that you want to delete.**
3. 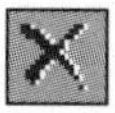 **Click the Delete button on the toolbar, press the Delete key, or choose Edit⇨Delete to make your message disappear.**

Flagging your e-mail messages as a reminder

Some people use their incoming e-mail messages as an informal task list. Flagging is designed to make it possible to use your Inbox as a task list. By adding reminders to each message that you get (or even to messages you send), you can prioritize them. A Reminder dialog box appears when the reminder falls due.

To flag an e-mail message with a reminder, follow these steps:

1. **Switch to the Inbox by clicking the Inbox icon on the Outlook bar.**
2. **Double-click the message that you want to flag, and the message reopens.**
3. **Choose Actions⇨Follow Up (or press Ctrl+Shift+G) to open the Flag for Follow Up dialog box, as shown in Figure 3-2.**

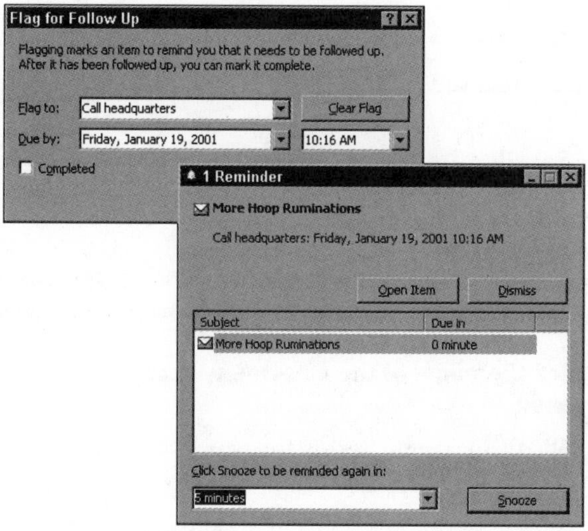

Figure 3-2: You can flag the e-mail that you receive by using this dialog box.

4. **Click the Flag To list box and enter your reminder, such as** Call headquarters. **You can also click the drop-down arrow on the Flag To box and choose a reminder from the list, such as Follow Up.**

5. **Click the Due By box and type the date on which you want the reminder flag to appear.**

   Remember that you can enter dates in plain English by typing something such as **Next Wednesday** or **In three weeks** and let Outlook figure out the actual date. You can also click the drop-down arrow and select a date from the calendar that appears.

6. **Enter a time in the Time text box, if you want.**
7. **Click OK.**

A little red flag appears next to your message in the Inbox. When the reminder falls due, you see the Reminder dialog box (refer to Figure 3-2). Another clever way that you can take advantage of flagging is to attach a flag to a message if you're sending it to someone else. If you flag a message that you're sending to someone else, a reminder pops up on that person's computer at the time that you designate.

Saving a message as a file

INTEGRATION

You may want to save the contents of a message you receive so that you can use the text in another program. You may want to use Microsoft Publisher, for example, to add the text to your monthly newsletter or to your Web page. To save a message as a file, follow these steps:

1. **Choose File⇨Save As (or press F12) to open the Save As dialog box.**
2. **Locate and select the folder where you want to store the message as a file.**
3. **Click the Save button.**

Reading attachments

If you receive a message with an attached file, you must open the attachment before you can read it. No problemo. To so, follow these steps:

1. **Double-click the name of the message with an attachment that you want to read.**

   The Message form opens. Beside the word `Attachments` are the names and icons of the files that someone sent to you (see Figure 3-3).

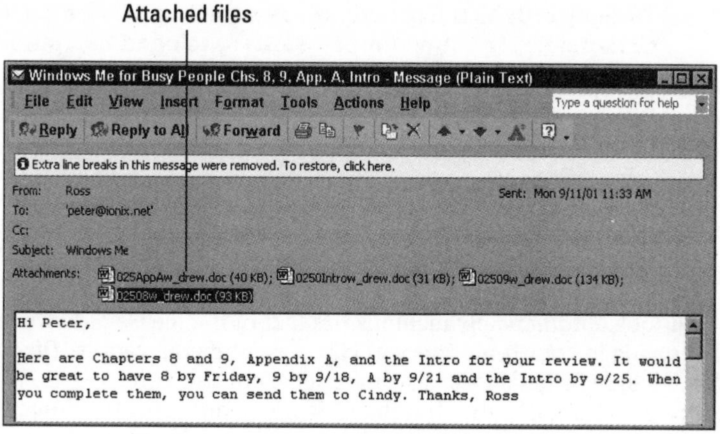

Figure 3-3: Handling a file that someone sent to you.

2. **Open a file or save it on your computer by taking one of the following actions:**

   - **To open the file now:** Double-click the file icon. You see the Opening File Attachment dialog box. Make sure that the Open It option is selected and then click OK.
   - **To save the file so that you can open it later:** Right-click the file icon and choose Save As. In the Save Attachment dialog box that appears, locate and select the folder on your computer where you want to store the file and click the Save button.

Replying to or Forwarding Messages

The e-mail wagon may not always stop in your Inbox. You often need to answer the e-mail messages that you receive or even forward them to others. The following sections tell you how.

Sending a reply

Replying to e-mail that you receive is a breeze. To reply to a message, follow these steps:

1. **Switch to the Inbox by clicking the Inbox icon on the Outlook bar.**
2. **Double-click the title of the message to which you want to reply.**

   Doing so shows the text of the message to which you're replying. You don't need to open a message to send a reply, however; you can click the name of a message once to select the message to reply to and then click the Reply button.

3. **To reply only to the people whose names appear on the From line, click the Reply button (or press Alt+R) to open the New Message form.**

To reply to the people whose names appear on the Cc line in addition to the people whose names appear on the From line, click the Reply to All button (or press Alt+L) to open the New Message form.

4. **Type your reply in the message box.**
5. **Click the Send button (or press Alt+S) to close the New Message form and send your message on its way.**

Outlook automatically includes the text of the message to which you're replying in your reply, but you can erase it if you want to. (If you don't care to include original messages in replies, choose Tools⇨Options, click the Preferences tab in the Options dialog box, and click the E-mail Options button. Then, in the E-mail Options dialog box, open the When Replying to a Message drop-down list and choose Do Not Include Original Message.)

Forwarding a message

If you get a message that you want to pass on to someone else, just forward it. (Yes, you can send mail without actually needing to create it!) To forward a message, follow these steps:

1. **Switch to the Inbox by clicking the Inbox icon on the Outlook bar.**
2. **Click the title of the message that you want to forward (thus highlighting the message).**

3. **Click the Forward button on the Outlook toolbar (or press Ctrl+F) to open the New Message form.**
4. **Click the To text box and enter the e-mail address of the person to whom you're forwarding the message.**
5. **(Optional) Click the Cc text box and enter the e-mail addresses of any additional people to whom you want to forward a copy of your message.**
6. **(Optional) In the text box, type any comments that you want to add to the message.**
7. **Click the Send button (or press Alt+S) to close the Message form and send your message on its way.**

You can also forward a message as you read it by clicking the Forward button on the Message form toolbar, which is visible after you open a message to read it.

REAL WORLD

Setting up online services

Before you can use Outlook to exchange e-mail through an online service — such as CompuServe, America Online, or the Microsoft Network — or through an Internet service provider — such as Netcom or AT&T WorldNet — you must set up Outlook to work with that particular service.

If you work in a large organization that uses Microsoft Exchange Server for its e-mail system, your system administrators set up the Outlook Corporate version for you. They probably don't want you setting up online services on the copy of Outlook on your desktop! You can still send e-mail to people on online services, such as CompuServe or AOL, by typing their addresses in the To text box of your message.

Although the method you use to set up any service is somewhat similar, the exact details differ, and those differences are important. Before setting up Outlook e-mail accounts, checking with the tech-support people from your online service so that you understand the details is a good idea. After you get the skinny from your online service, follow these steps to set up e-mail accounts:

1. **Choose Tools⇨E-mail Accounts.**
2. **Select the Add a New E-mail Account option and click Next to start the E-mail Account Wizard.**
3. **Follow the prompts in the wizard and enter the information that your online service or Internet service provider gives you.**

Chapter 4: Making Your E-Mail Life Easier

In This Chapter

- **Using folders to manage e-mail**
- **Automating your Inbox with the Rules Wizard**
- **Changing your Outlook view**

Because all incoming e-mail lands in your Inbox, you may soon end up with a list of messages whose sheer number makes staying on top of things seem almost impossible. But the battle is not yet lost! Before you become overwhelmed with e-mail and begin sinking into despair, find out how to manage your mail by using folders. Get on familiar terms with your Inbox and take advantage of what it can do for you. You can even automate some tasks so that you can sit back and relax as those e-mail messages come flooding in.

This chapter shows you how to take the initiative now so that your e-mail life is easier later.

Managing Your E-Mail by Using Folders

You can leave all incoming e-mail messages in your Inbox, but filing your messages in another folder makes more sense because you can quickly see which messages you've already dealt with and classified and which ones just arrived.

INTEGRATION

If you've used Windows for any amount of time, you may already be familiar with the concept of files and folders. (If you want to know about them or need a refresher, see Book I.) Outlook's capabilities for handling your files and folders really help you stay on top of your e-mail. For one thing, you need to be able to move files around — usually into folders — and then to move folders around — sometimes into other folders! Such an authority over your files and folders pays off as you get going in Outlook.

Creating a folder

Before you can file messages in a new folder, you must create the folder. To do so, follow these steps:

1. **Click the Inbox icon to switch to your Inbox (if you're not already there).**
2. **Choose File⇨New⇨Folder (or press Ctrl+Shift+E) to open the Create New Folder dialog box, as shown in Figure 4-1.**

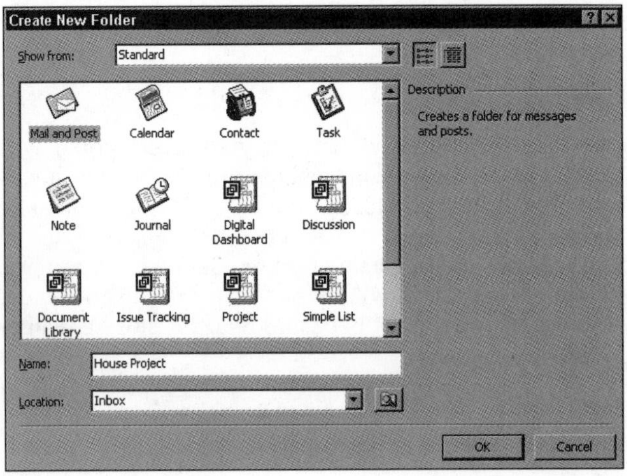

Figure 4-1: Create folders to store your mail in this dialog box.

3. **If necessary, select Inbox in the Location drop-down list.**
4. **In the Name text box, type a name for your new folder.**
5. **Click OK to close the Create New Folder dialog box.**
6. **Click Yes after Outlook asks whether you want to put a shortcut to the folder on My Shortcuts Outlook bar.**

   By putting it there, all you have to do to access it is click the My Shortcuts button in the Outlook bar.

Although you can create as many folders as you want, you can find things more easily if you minimize the number of folders you must search.

Moving messages to another folder

After you create extra folders for sorting and saving your incoming messages, you can move new messages to the different folders after they arrive. To move messages to a folder, follow these steps:

1. **Switch to the Inbox by clicking the Inbox icon on the Outlook bar.**
2. **Click the title of the message that you want to move to highlight the message title.**
3. **Click the My Shortcuts button in the Outlook bar to make the Outlook bar display the folders that you created.**
4. **Click and drag the message to the icon on the Outlook bar for the folder in which you want to store it. The name of the file disappears from the list in the Inbox.**

Another way to move an item to a folder is to choose Edit⇨Move to Folder or right-click and choose Move to Folder on the shortcut menu. The Move Items dialog box appears with a complete list of folders. Select the folder in which you want to file your message and press Enter.

After you make a habit of moving messages between folders, you can speed up the process by clicking the Move to Folder button. After you click the Move to Folder button, you see a list of the last ten folders to which you've moved items. Click the name of a folder on the list, and Outlook zaps your message directly to the folder of your choice.

Using the Sent Items folder

Outlook stores in the Sent Items folder a copy of every message that you send, unless you tell it to do otherwise. You can review and reread the messages you send by looking in the Sent Items folder. To get there, click the My Shortcuts divider on the Outlook bar and then click the Sent Items icon. The same collection of views is available in the Sent Items folder as is available in the Inbox or any other mail folder. (See the section "Using and Choosing E-Mail Views," later in this chapter.)

Using the Rules Wizard

The Rules Wizard reads your incoming and outgoing e-mail and takes an action of your choice. You can make Outlook display a pop-up announcement as important messages arrive or make a rude noise if you get messages from certain people, or it can just file certain types of messages in certain folders.

Wizards are little tools that Microsoft adds to all Office programs to guide you through multistep processes and help you make the choices that you need to make. The Rules Wizard asks you questions at each step in the process of creating a rule to help you create exactly the rule that you want.

You can create literally thousands of different kinds of rules by using the Rules Wizard. As you explore this feature, you discover many types of rules that you may find useful. You can, for example, block messages with certain words in the subject line, automatically flag certain kinds of messages, or automatically move certain kinds of messages to a folder.

To create a rule that moves a message from a specific person to a certain folder, follow these steps:

1. **If you're not in the Inbox, click the Inbox icon on the Outlook bar.**
2. **Choose Tools⇨Rules Wizard to open the Rules Wizard dialog box.**
3. **Click the New button to open the next Rules Wizard dialog box, which provides options for creating new rules (see Figure 4-2).**

   The Rules Wizard offers several rules that you may want to create, such as Move Messages from Someone, Assign Categories to Sent Messages, or Notify Me When Important Messages Arrive.

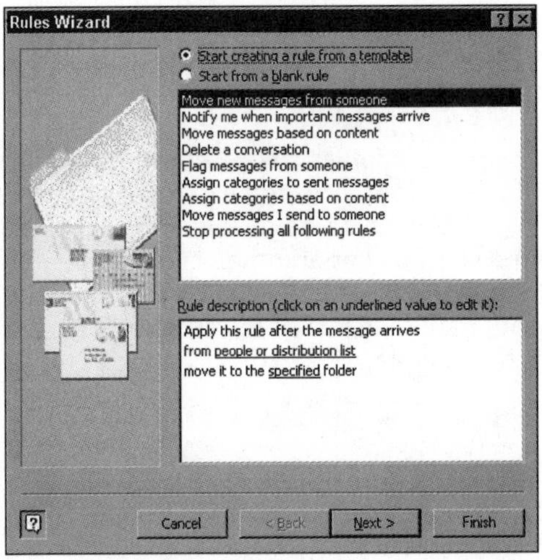

Figure 4-2: The Rules Wizard offers you many rules from which to choose.

4. **In the top box, click to select the type of rule that you want to create.**

   What happens after this depends on the kind of rule you want to set up. For our purposes, suppose you want to file messages from someone in a folder as they arrive.

5. **In the Rule Description box, click the first piece of underlined text: From People or Distribution List.**

   Your address book opens under the guise of the Rule Address dialog box to enable you to choose the name of a person to put into your rule (see Figure 4-3).

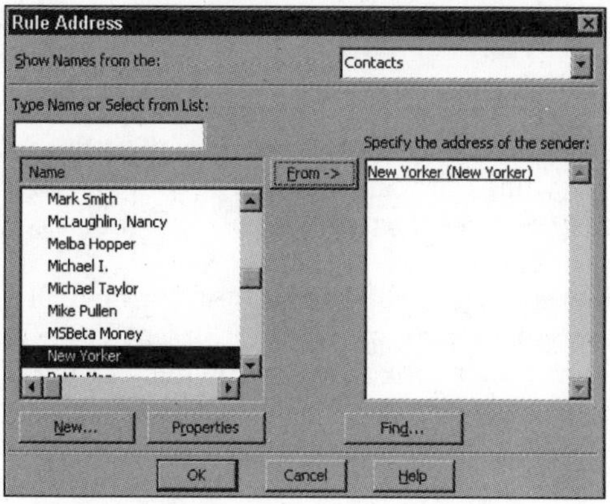

Figure 4-3: Click to select the person you want to include in a rule.

6. **Choose the name of the person whose messages you want to move to a new folder by selecting the person's name and then clicking the From button; then click OK.**

7. **Click the next piece of underlined text in the Rule Description box, Move It to the Specified Folder.**

   Another dialog box opens to enable you to choose the folder to which you want to move the message.

8. **Click the name of the folder to which you want to move messages (or create a new folder by clicking New); then click OK.**

   The name of the folder that you choose appears in the sentence in the Rule Description box. Now the name of the folder you choose replaces "Specified."

9. **Click Finish to complete your rule.**

   The first Rules Wizard dialog box appears with a list of all your rules. Each rule displays a check box next to it. You can turn rules on and off by clicking the check boxes; if a check mark appears next to a rule, the rule is turned on; otherwise, the rule is turned off.

10. **Click OK to close the Rules Wizard.**

REMEMBER

You don't need to limit yourself to making rules for incoming mail. You also can tell the Rules Wizard to act on the messages that you send out, such as attaching flags or assigning categories to messages that go to the people you designate or to messages that contain certain words in the subject line.

Using and Choosing E-Mail Views

One of the real benefits of Outlook is the variety of ways in which you can sort and arrange your collection of messages, as well as the several different ways that you can view what's in your messages. Your Outlook folders can serve as your filing system as well as your electronic mailbox.

You can use many different arrangements to view your e-mail messages. If you don't like the view, you can choose View➪Current View from the menu bar and pick a new view. Take a look at the following viewing options on the Current View submenu:

- **Messages:** A plain-vanilla list of your messages. The titles of unread messages appear in the message list in boldface, whereas messages you've read appear in a normal typeface.
- **Messages with AutoPreview:** Shows you the first few lines of all your unread messages.
- **By Follow-Up Flag:** Shows a list of your messages according to which kind of flag you've assigned to each message.
- **Last Seven Days:** A list of messages you've received within the past seven days.
- **Flagged for Next Seven Days:** Shows only flagged messages with due dates scheduled within the next week.
- **By Conversation Topic:** Organizes your messages by subject.
- **By Sender:** Groups your messages according to who sent the message.
- **Unread Messages:** Shows only unread messages. After you read a message, this view no longer appears.
- **Sent To:** Sorts messages according to receivers' names. In your Inbox, most messages come to you, so using this view in the Inbox makes little sense. In your Sent Items folder, however, you can use Sent To view to organize your outgoing messages according to the person to whom you sent each message.
- **Message Timeline:** Shows you a diagram with your messages organized by the time that you sent or received them. You can click the icon for any message and read that message.

Chapter 5: Using the Calendar

In This Chapter

- Getting to know the calendar
- Scheduling and changing appointments
- Scheduling an event
- Printing your calendar

Outlook is more than simply a convenient way for managing your e-mail. The Outlook calendar, for example, can help you with your busy life by organizing appointments, special events, holidays, meetings (ugh), and just about any other task that you must eventually face. You may never miss your dentist's appointment again, and your brother-in-law may actually get his birthday card *before* his birthday from now on. You can even use the Outlook calendar to help you *avoid* your commitments! Now that's a deal.

Reviewing the Calendar

You enter appointments in Outlook so that you can remember them later. Outlook enables you to view your appointment list in dozens of ways. (An Outlook *view,* by the way, is a method of presenting information in the arrangement that you need.) Outlook comes with six different views, and you can create your own views, too. This section describes the views that you get the first time that you use Outlook.

Basic calendar views

As you first use Outlook, you can choose among seven preprogrammed views. Although you can add views to your heart's content in any Outlook module, you can go a long way with the views Outlook starts with.

To change views, choose View➪Current View, and then choose one of these options on the submenu:

- **Day/Week/Month:** Looks like a calendar (see Figure 5-1). This view offers buttons on the toolbar that enable you to choose to view your appointments for one day, a week, a workweek, or an entire month. You'll probably use this view more than any other Outlook view.

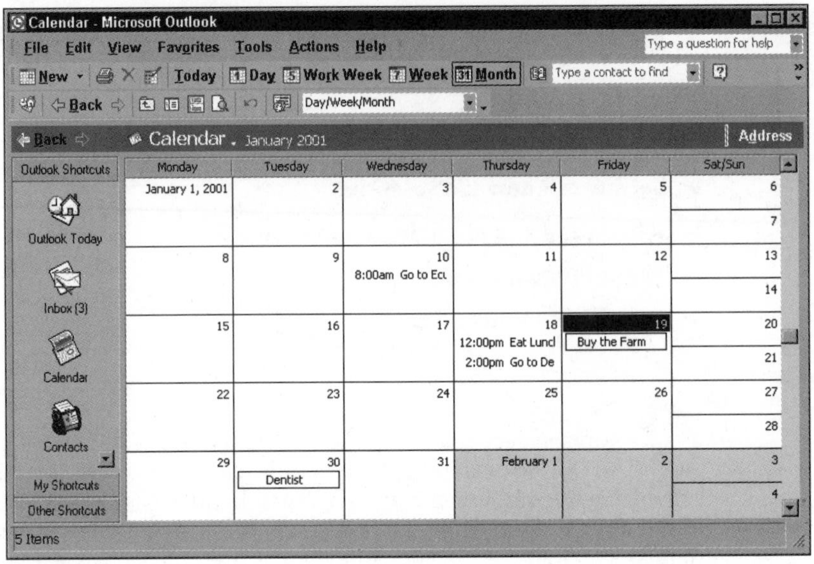

Figure 5-1: The Outlook Calendar view.

- **Day/Week/Month View with AutoPreview:** Works the same as Day/Week/Month view, except that it enables you to see a line or two of description as well as dates and times.
- **Active Appointments:** Shows you information about appointments and enables you to sort the list according to the location or subject you enter at the time that you create the appointment.
- **Events:** A list that shows you only items that you designate as All Day Events.
- **Annual Events:** Shows only the list of events that you make into recurring events that happen yearly. You can enter holidays and anniversaries as such annual events.
- **Recurring Appointments:** Lists all appointments and events that you set as recurring appointments.
- **By Category:** Groups your appointments according to the category that you assign to each appointment. Grouped views work the same way in all Outlook modules.

Another popular way to view your upcoming appointments is to click the Outlook Today icon on the Outlook bar. As its name suggests, Outlook Today pulls together everything you're doing today — appointments, tasks, and messages — and displays it all on a single page. You can print your Outlook Today page by clicking the Print button on the toolbar or by pressing Ctrl+P.

Changing the amount of time on display

Outlook enables you to choose from several calendar styles. Some styles show a bigger calendar with fewer dates, and some styles show a smaller calendar with more dates but include no notes about what you've scheduled on a certain date. The Date Navigator is a small calendar that enables you to see your schedule for the date of your choice simply by clicking the date with your mouse. To open the Date Navigator, follow these steps:

1. **Switch to the Calendar module by clicking the Calendar icon on the Outlook bar to make your calendar appear.**
2. **Choose View➪Current View➪Day/Week/Month.**
3. **Click the Day, Work Week, or Week button on the toolbar.**

The little calendar in the upper-right corner is the Date Navigator. The rest of the screen shows you your appointments for the current week (or the days you clicked in the Date Navigator). To see what's on your schedule for a different date, just click the date on the Date Navigator.

Going to one date

You can use the Outlook calendar to schedule appointments hundreds or even thousands of years from now. Because you can work with so many years, Outlook enables you to quickly go to a specific date. To do so, follow these steps:

1. **Click the Calendar icon on the Outlook bar (if you're not already in the Calendar module).**

   When you switch to the Calendar module from another module, Outlook always shows you the current date.
2. **Choose View➪Current View➪Day/Week/Month.**
3. **Choose View➪Go To➪Go to Date (or press Ctrl+G).**

   The Go To Date dialog box opens.
4. **In the Date drop-down list box, type the date you want to go to, such as** 4/1/01**, or a description for the date, such as** 1 year from now**, or even** 100 years from now.

   Outlook figures out what you mean.
5. **Click OK to make the calendar display the date you chose.**
6. **Click the Go to Today button on the toolbar to return to today's date.**

Scheduling an Appointment

Although Outlook gives you lots of choices for entering details about your appointments, the two most important aspects of scheduling are *what* and *when*. Everything else is optional. If you want to schedule two appointments at the same time, Outlook subtly warns you with a banner at the top of the form that says `Conflicts with another appointment`, although nothing stops you from scheduling yourself in two places at one time. To schedule an appointment, follow these steps:

1. **Click the Calendar icon on the Outlook bar if you're not already in the Calendar module.**
2. **Click the date on the calendar where you want to enter the appointment.**

   If the date where you want to enter the appointment isn't visible, either click the Back or Forward button on the calendar until you arrive at the date, or make use of the Go to Date command, as explained in the preceding section of this chapter.

3. **Click the New Appointment button on the toolbar, choose Actions⇨New Appointment, or press Ctrl+N.**

   The Appointment dialog box appears (see Figure 5-2).

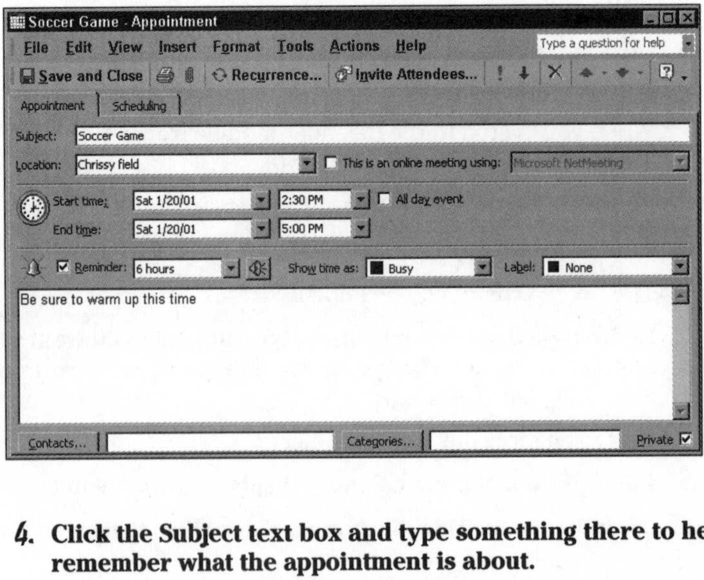

Figure 5-2: Scheduling an appointment.

4. **Click the Subject text box and type something there to help you remember what the appointment is about.**
5. **Click the Location text box and enter the location, if you want.**

6. **In the Start Time text boxes, enter the date and time the appointment begins.**
7. **In the End Time text boxes, enter the date and time the appointment ends.**

   If you ignore the End Time boxes, Outlook creates a 30-minute appointment.
8. **If you want Outlook to remind you of your appointment, click the Reminder check box and select an option from the drop-down list.**
9. **Click the Save and Close button on the toolbar.**

If you're on a network and don't want others to know about your appointment, click the Private check box in the lower-right corner of the dialog box.

Scheduling a Recurring Appointment

Some appointments keep coming back like a bad penny. Your Monday morning staff meeting or Wednesday night bowling league roll around every week unchanged (except for your bowling score), so why enter the appointment over and over? To schedule a *recurring appointment,* follow these steps:

1. **Click the Calendar icon on the Outlook bar if you're not already in the Calendar module and then click the first day of a recurring appointment.**

   If the weekly staff meeting is on Thursday, for example, click a Thursday.
2. **Click the New Appointment button on the left end of the toolbar to open the New Appointment form.**
3. **Fill in the dialog box. (The preceding section in this chapter explains how.)**
4. **Click the Recurrence button on the toolbar (or press Ctrl+G) to make the Appointment Recurrence dialog box appear, as shown in Figure 5-3.**

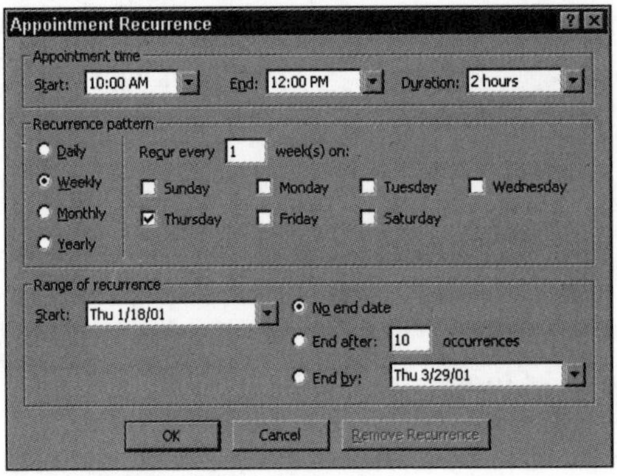

Figure 5-3: The Appointment Recurrence dialog box.

5. **In the Start drop-down list, choose the starting time.**
6. **In the End drop-down list, choose the ending time.**

   Don't worry about the Duration text box; Outlook calculates the duration for you. On the other hand, you can just enter the duration and have Outlook fill in the missing end time.
7. **In the Recurrence Pattern area, tell Outlook how often the appointment occurs and on which day it occurs.**

   The Recurrence pattern looks different depending on whether you chose Daily, Weekly, Monthly, or Yearly.
8. **In the Range of Recurrence area of the dialog box, enter the first occurrence in the Start text box.**
9. **Tell Outlook when the appointment is to end.**

   If you want the appointment to repeat indefinitely, you don't need to do anything; No End Date is selected by default if you don't choose something else.
10. **Click OK and then click Save and Close (or press Alt+S).**

A circle with arrows appears in the calendar next to recurring appointments.

Changing an Appointment

What? You say that your schedule never changes? You say that you never need to change your schedule? The world's pace is just too fast for anyone's schedule to last for even a short time without modification. Fortunately, Outlook makes changing appointments easy.

Changing an appointment by using drag-and-drop

Changing the starting time or the date of an appointment is just a matter of using the drag-and-drop technique. To select an appointment and slide it to the date or time that you want, follow these steps:

1. **Click the appointment in Calendar view.**
2. **Place the mouse pointer over the appointment.**

   In a moment, a gray bar appears.
3. **Click and drag the appointment to another day on the calendar.**

Changing the length of an appointment

When you're looking at One-Day view in your calendar, your appointments appear as boxes of different sizes, depending on the length of the appointment. If you want to shorten or lengthen an appointment, just use your mouse to drag the border of the box that represents the appointment to make the appointment longer or shorter. Follow these steps:

1. **Click the appointment in One-Day view.**

   Click the Day button on the Standard toolbar to switch to One-Day view.
2. **Move the mouse pointer over the line at the bottom of the appointment.**
3. **Click and drag the bottom line down to make the appointment time longer; click and drag the bottom line up to make the appointment shorter.**

Reopening an appointment to change it

Drag-and-drop isn't the ticket for changing appointment times if you can't view enough of the calendar to see both the original date and the rescheduled date. In that case, all you can do is reopen the appointment and change the particulars. To do so, follow these steps:

1. **In One-Day view, double-click the appointment to open the Appointment dialog box.**
2. **Change the Start and End times, or the date, as necessary, by typing new text in the appropriate boxes or by clicking the drop-down arrow and choosing a date or type from the list.**
3. **If necessary, make any other changes in the appointment by clicking the information that you want to change and typing new information over it.**
4. **Click the Save and Close button (or press Alt+S).**

Whenever you enter times in Outlook, you don't need to be particular about punctuation. If you type **5p**, for example, Outlook understands it as 5 p.m. and automatically converts the time to the correct format. Dates are even easier to enter; just type **next Wed**, and Outlook converts it to the correct date.

Deleting an Item from Your Calendar

Deleting items in Outlook is *intuitive,* which means that you can probably figure out how to do it without reading about it. In case you can't, however, follow these steps:

1. **Click the appointment that you want to delete.**
2. **Click the Delete button on the toolbar (or press Delete).**

If you want to delete several appointments at one time, press and hold the Ctrl key while clicking each appointment that you want to delete. Then press Delete. Selecting items in Outlook is no different than selecting items in Windows or any other Office application.

Chapter 6: Tasks for Everyone

In This Chapter

- Creating and deleting a task
- Modifying a task
- Creating recurring and regenerating tasks
- Attaching a file to a task
- Changing the appearance of your tasks list
- Keeping track of your tasks

Throw away all those notepads that you get for free from your car insurance company. Take down every sticky note that you stuck to your computer monitor or on your desk. You're no longer under the dominion of little pieces of paper that tell you what to do and when to do it. Outlook includes a tool that enables you to control your list of tasks and keep track of all your obligations and chores. And this chapter tells you how.

Creating a New Task

Outlook can handle all kinds of high-falutin' information and details about each task that you enter. You may find that, 90 percent of the time, you just need to type a quick note to jog your memory. For the other 10 percent, however, you may need to go whole hog and keep lots of information handy about tasks that you must perform — things such as travel directions and discussion notes.

Creating an abbreviated task quickly

Most of the time, you need only a word or two to jog your memory about a task — something such as **Call Mom**. Because you don't need much detailed information about how to do that, you can create a task the fast way. To do so, follow these steps:

1. **Click the Tasks icon on the Outlook bar to switch to the Tasks module (if you aren't already there).**

   If you don't see anything that reads `Click Here to Add a New Task`, switch to a different view of your task list by choosing View⇨Current View⇨Simple List.

2. **Click the text that reads** `Click Here to Add a New Task.`

   This step makes an insertion point (a flashing vertical bar) appear where the highlighted words were.

3. **Type the name of your task (see Figure 6-1).**

4. **Press the Enter key to make your new task drop down into the list of tasks.**

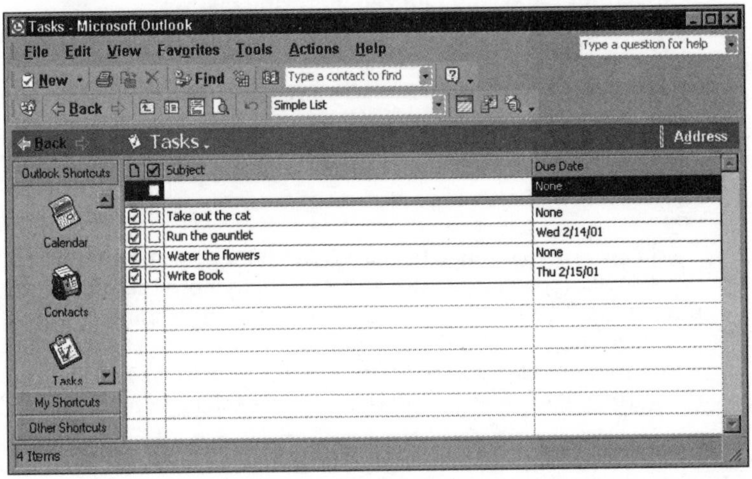

Figure 6-1: Fill in the tasks that you need to accomplish.

If you're using the calendar, you can use TaskPad, a miniature version of the task list — you find it in most views anyway. It's on the right side of the calendar window. You can enter tasks in the TaskPad by typing in the Click Here to Add a New Task text box.

Creating a detailed task slowly

Suppose that you need to enter more information about your task, such as driving directions, or you want Outlook to remind you just before the task is due. Outlook places no limits on the information that you can add to a task if you go the slow, complete way. To create a detailed task, follow these steps:

1. **Click the Tasks icon on the Outlook bar to switch to the Tasks module (if you're not already there).**

2. **Click the New Task button on the toolbar (or press Ctrl+N) to open the Task dialog box (see Figure 6-2).**

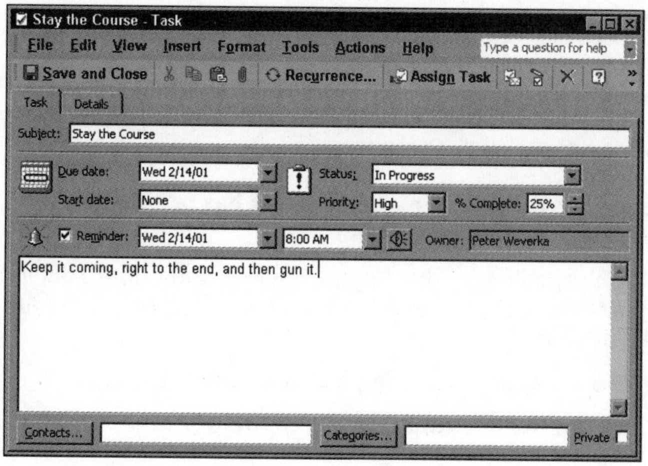

Figure 6-2: Look at all the information that you can attach to your task!

3. **Type the name of the task in the Subject text box.**
4. **To assign a due date to the task, enter it in the Due Date text box.**

   You don't need to be fussy about how you enter the date; Outlook understands **7/4/01**, **the first Saturday of July**, or **90 days from today** — however you want to type it.
5. **To assign a start date, enter it in the Start Date text box.**

   Not all tasks have start dates, so you can skip this step if you want.
6. **To keep track of the status of a task, open the Status drop-down list and select an option.**

   You must revise your task as the status of the task progresses. While you're at it, you can also enter a percentage in the % Complete text box.
7. **If the task you're entering is unusually important, urgent, or even relatively unimportant, open the Priority drop-down list and choose the priority of the task.**
8. **If you want Outlook to remind you before the task is due, click the Reminder check box and then enter the appropriate dates and times in the accompanying drop-down list box.**
9. **If you want, enter miscellaneous notes and information about this task in the text box near the bottom of this dialog box.**
10. **If you want to assign a category to your task, type the name of the category in the Categories text box.**

    Categories represent a way to organize tasks. You can group tasks by category and in so doing make reviewing them easier.
11. **Click the Save and Close button (or press Alt+S) to finish.**

Deleting a Task

Sometimes you change your mind about a task that you assign yourself and want to delete the task. Deleting tasks is *so* much simpler than doing them. To delete a task, follow these steps:

1. **Click the Tasks icon on the Outlook bar to switch to the Tasks module (if you're not already there).**

   If you're having trouble finding the task you want to delete, choose View➪Current View➪Simple List. This way, you see a comprehensive list of your tasks.

2. **Select the task by clicking it in the Task list.**

3. **Click the Delete button on the toolbar (or press Ctrl+D).**

Modifying an Existing Task

The weather changes. Social mores change. The height of hemlines changes. Your task list changes. Some aspect of an item on your to-do list is likely to change before you even finish entering the task in Outlook.

You can use the same method to change the information in a task that you use to enter the information in the first place. To modify an existing task, follow these steps:

1. **If you're not already in the Tasks module, go to it by clicking the Tasks icon on the Outlook bar.**
2. **Choose View➪Current View➪Simple List to list your tasks on-screen.**
3. **From the list of tasks, double-click the name of the task that you want to change.**

   The Task dialog box opens.

4. **In the Task dialog box, replace and change information, as necessary.**
5. **Click the Save and Close button (or press Alt+S) to finish.**

Creating a Recurring Task

You can set up tasks that occur over and over on a schedule as *recurring* tasks. You can designate a task as recurring as you enter the task for the first time. You can also create a recurring task by opening an existing task and following these steps:

1. **If you're not already in the Tasks module, go to it by clicking the Tasks icon on the Outlook bar; then choose View⇨Current View⇨Simple List to list your tasks on-screen.**
2. **From the list of tasks, double-click the name of the task that you want to designate as recurring.**

   The Task dialog box opens.
3. **Click the Recurrence button on the toolbar of the Task form (or press Ctrl+G) to open the Task Recurrence dialog box.**

   The Task Recurrence dialog box appears, as shown in Figure 6-3.

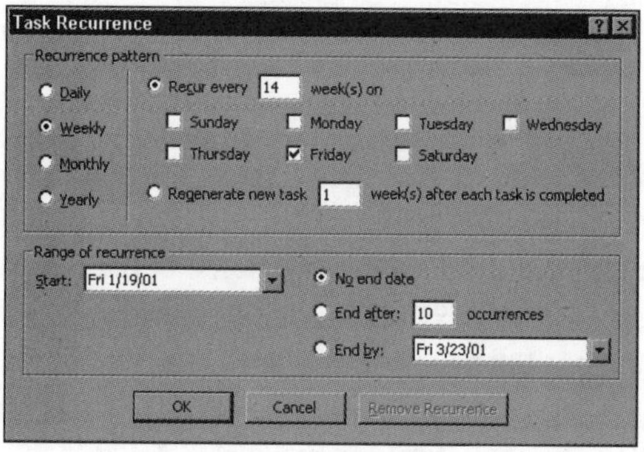

Figure 6-3: The Task Recurrence dialog box.

4. **Choose the Daily, Weekly, Monthly, or Yearly option to specify how often the task occurs.**

   The available options in the right pane of the Recurrence Pattern area change depending on whether you selected Daily, Weekly, Monthly, or Yearly in the left pane.
5. **Use the radio buttons, text boxes, and check boxes to specify how often the task occurs, such as every third day or the first Monday of each month.**
6. **In the Range of Recurrence area, enter the first occurrence in the Start drop-down list box.**
7. **Tell Outlook when the task is to stop by entering a number in the Occurrences text box or by choosing a date from the End By drop-down list.**
8. **Click OK to close the Task Recurrence dialog box.**
9. **Click Save and Close (or press Alt+S).**

Recurring tasks can prove confusing because the Task Recurrence dialog box changes appearance depending on whether you choose a Daily, Weekly, Monthly, or Yearly recurrence pattern.

Creating a Regenerating Task

Sometimes scheduling the next occurrence of a task doesn't make sense until you complete the preceding occurrence. If you get your hair cut every two weeks, for example, but you get busy and get one haircut a week late, you still want to wait two weeks for the following haircut. If you use Outlook to schedule your haircuts, you can set up your haircuts as a *regenerating* task. A regenerating task is "getting a haircut every two weeks," and a recurring task is "getting a haircut every Monday." To create a regenerating task, follow these steps:

1. **If you're not already in the Tasks module, go to it by clicking the Tasks icon on the Outlook bar; then choose View⇨Current View⇨Simple List to list your tasks on-screen.**
2. **From the list of tasks, double-click the name of the task that you want to designate as regenerating.**

   The Task dialog box opens.
3. **Click the Recurrence button on the toolbar of the Task dialog box (or press Ctrl+G) to open the Task Recurrence dialog box.**
4. **Click the Regenerate New Task radio button; then, in the text box, type the number of weeks or months between regenerating the task.**
5. **Click OK to close the Task Recurrence dialog box.**
6. **Click Save and Close (or press Alt+S).**

Attaching a File to a Task Item

INTEGRATION

You can include word-processing documents, spreadsheets, or any other type of file in a task by making the document an *attachment.* If you've had a bad day and type **Update Résumé** as your new task, for example, you can link your résumé to the task to find the résumé faster when you're ready to update it. To link a task to an attachment, follow these steps:

1. **If you're not already in the Tasks module, go to it by clicking the Tasks icon on the Outlook bar; then choose View⇨Current View⇨Simple List to list your tasks on-screen.**
2. **From the list of tasks, double-click the name of the task that you want to attach a file to.**

   The Task dialog box opens.

3. Click the Insert File button on the toolbar to open the Insert File dialog box.

4. In the Insert File dialog box, browse to the file that you want to attach to your task and then click the file name to select it.

5. Click the Insert button.

The dialog box closes, and you are returned to the Task dialog box, where the file has been inserted in the text box at the bottom of the form.

6. Click the Save and Close button (or press Alt+S).

Attaching files to tasks is similar to attaching files to any other Outlook item, such as an e-mail message. If you delete a task with an attached file, you delete only the task — not the file.

And how do you open the file that you attach to the task? Double-click the task to open the Task form and then double-click the file icon on the form.

Changing the Appearance of Your Task List

Task lists are just that: lists of tasks. You don't need fancy layouts in choosing a view; you just need a list that contains the information that you want. To switch between views, choose View⇨Current View and then pick the view that you want to use from the Current View menu. Here's a list of the views that come with Outlook:

- **Simple List:** Just the facts — the names that you give each task and the due date that you assign (if you assign one).
- **Detailed List:** A little more . . . uh, detail than in Simple List view. It's really the same information, plus the status of the tasks, the percentage completed of each task, and whatever categories you may assign to your tasks.
- **Active List:** Shows you only your unfinished tasks.
- **Next Seven Days:** Even more focused than Active List view. Next Seven Days view shows only uncompleted tasks scheduled for completion within the next seven days.
- **Overdue Tasks:** Shows (oops!) tasks that you let slip past the due date you assign. You ought to finish these up before the boss finds out.
- **By Category:** Breaks up your tasks according to the category you assign to each task.
- **Assignment:** Lists your tasks in order by the name of the person on whom you dump each task.

✦ **By Person Responsible:** Contains the same information as Assignment view, except that this view groups the list so that you can see the assignments of only one person at a time.

✦ **Completed Tasks:** Shows (you guessed it) only the tasks that you mark as complete.

✦ **Task Timeline:** Draws a picture of when you scheduled each task to begin and end. Seeing a picture of your tasks gives you a better idea of how to fit work into your schedule sensibly (see Figure 6-4).

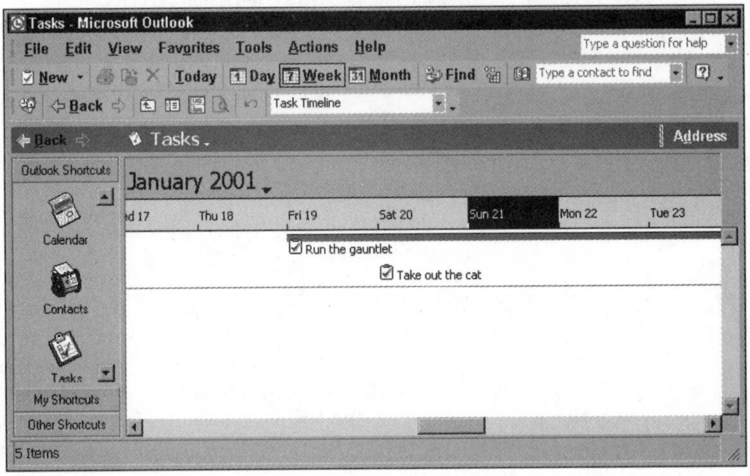

Figure 6-4: You can view your tasks by timeline.

Marking a Task as Complete

Noting your accomplishments for the day is satisfying. You can mark off each task that you complete by following these steps:

1. **If you're not in the Tasks module, switch to it by clicking the Tasks icon on the Outlook bar.**
2. **Choose View⇨Current View⇨Simple List to list your tasks on-screen.**
3. **Click the check box next to the name of the task that you want to mark as complete (see Figure 6-5).**

   All the tasks that you select appear with a check mark to show that they're complete. A line appears through the name of the task to drive the point home.

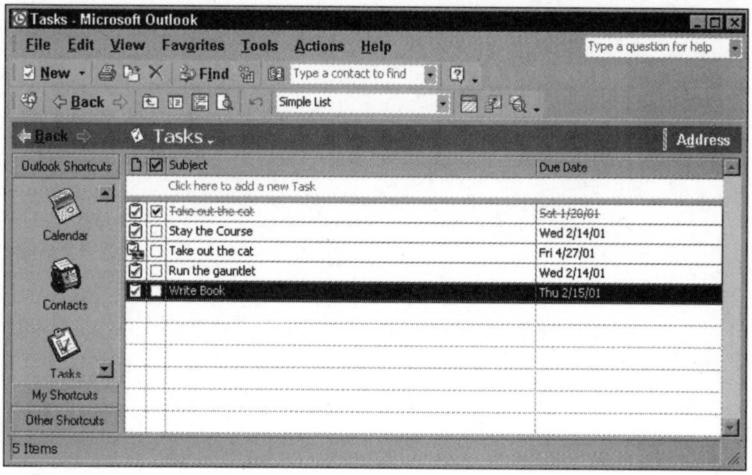

Figure 6-5: Click the check box to mark a task as complete.

Chapter 7: Working with Your Contacts

In This Chapter

- **Adding a contact**
- **Finding contact information**
- **Displaying and changing contact information**
- **Customizing your contact list**
- **Using a contact to call someone**

In Outlook, *contacts* are people about whom you keep some information (as if you were an FBI agent responsible for compiling a dossier on a select group of individuals). You can collect information that includes addresses, phone numbers, fax numbers, job titles, Web page addresses, and so on. You also find ample room to add free-form information for any contact on your list. Outlook enables you to communicate more easily with your contacts, whether they're friends, acquaintances, co-workers, or foreign spies.

Entering a New Contact

In the Contacts module, you can save and organize nearly any type of information about the people you deal with. You can then find everything again lickety-split. If you want, you can enter quick scraps of information without interrupting the flow of your work. You also can spend time entering minutely detailed information every time you create a new contact.

Adding names to your contact list is as simple as filling out a form. You only need to fill in the name of the contact you're entering. But while you're entering the name, you may as well enter other things that you need to know about the person, such as an address, phone number, e-mail address, Web page address, and whatever.

To add a name to your contact list, follow these steps:

1. **Click the Contacts icon on the Outlook bar (if you're not already in the Contacts module).**

2. **Click the New Contact button on the toolbar to access the New Contact dialog box.**
3. **Type the person's name in the Full Name text box.**

   After you open the New Contact dialog box, the insertion point already appears in the Full Name text box, so you don't need to click anywhere. Type the first name and then the last name.

   After you type a name in the Full Name text box, press Tab or click your mouse in any other text box. The name appears again in the File As text box — except that now the name appears last name first. The entry in the File As drop-down list box tells you how Outlook plans to file your contact — in this case, by the last name. You can also file a contact according to some other word. You can file the name George Washington under *F*, for example, for *f*ather of our country. More practical examples are filing the name of your plumber under the word *plumber*, your auto mechanic under *mechanic*, and so on.
4. **Click the Address button and type the person's address in the Check Address dialog box that appears (see Figure 7-1).**

   Outlook interprets addresses by using the same method that it uses to make sense of names. Breaking the address into street, city, state, zip code, and country enables you to use the Outlook contact list as a source of addresses as you're creating form letters in Microsoft Word.

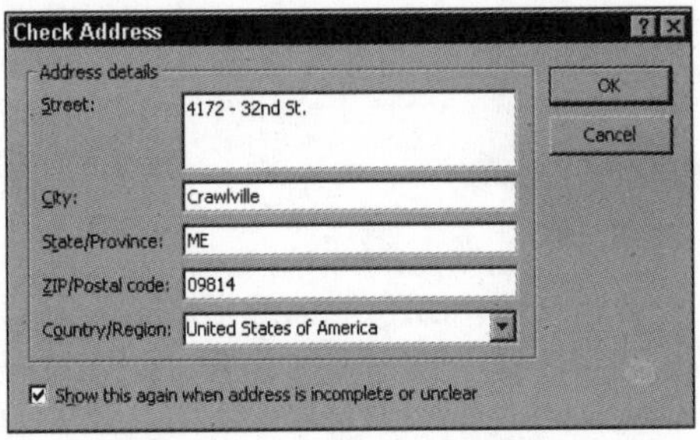

Figure 7-1: Entering the address information about a contact.

5. **When you finish typing all the parts of the address, click OK to return to the New Contact dialog box.**
6. **Click the This Is the Mailing Address check box if the address you just entered is the contact address to which you plan to send mail.**
7. **Click the other text boxes to type the contact's business phone number, home phone number, business fax, e-mail address, Web page, and so on.**
8. **Click the large text box at the bottom of the dialog box and type anything that you want.**

TIP

This text box is a good place to enter a little background information about the contact. In a contact list with many names, telling who's who can prove difficult without a brief description.

9. **Click the Categories button in the bottom-left corner of the screen to assign a category to the contact, if you want.**
10. **Click the check box next to each category that applies to your contact.**

    If none of the existing categories suits you, click Master Category List and, in the Master Category List dialog box that appears, enter the name of a new category, click the Add button, and click OK.
11. **Click the Private check box in the lower-right corner of the Contact dialog box if you're on a network and don't want others to know about your contacts.**
12. **After you finish entering the contact, click Save and Close (or press Alt+S) to close the New Contact dialog box.**

Outlook enables you to save and recall a huge list of items about your contacts. You always can go back and make changes to the list later.

Finding a Name, Address, or Phone Number

The purpose of creating a contact list is so that you can search it later on. The quick, simple way to find a contact is simply by looking up the name. But sometimes you can't remember the name. You may recall something else about the person on the list — such as the company she works for or the city where he lives. This section shows you several ways to dig up information about your contacts.

Finding a contact the quick, simple way

The quick, simple way of finding a contact assumes that you remember the last name or the word you used in the File As text box. To find a contact by last name, follow these steps:

1. **Click the Contacts icon on the Outlook bar (if you're not already in the Contacts module).**
2. **Choose View➪Current View➪Address Cards.**

   Address Cards view looks like a deck of address cards laid out across your screen.
3. **Press the first letter of the last name of the contact you want to locate.**

   The on-screen view moves to the alphabetical section of the Address Cards that contains people whose names begin with that letter.

4. **If you still don't see the person's name, press the right-arrow key to scroll through the list alphabetically or click one of the number or letter buttons displayed vertically down the right side of the window.**

If you enter something other than the contact's name in the File As text box, such as *plumber* or *dentist,* press the letter *p* for plumber or *d* for dentist.

Finding a contact by using the Advanced Find feature

You can use the Find button on the toolbar to find a contact, but the Advanced Find feature can perform a more detailed search. Suppose that you can't recall the name of the person you're looking for but you remember some fragment of the information you entered about about him or her. You remember that his name ends with Jr., for example, or that he lives in Omaha. The Advanced Find feature finds all items that contain the tiniest scrap of information you entered. To use this feature, follow these steps:

1. **Choose Tools➪Advanced Find (or press Ctrl+Shift+F) to open the Advanced Find dialog box, as shown in Figure 7-2.**

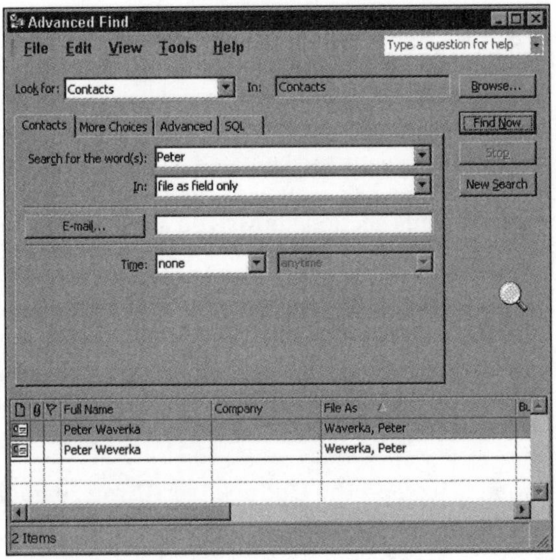

Figure 7-2: You can use the Advanced Find dialog box to conduct an advanced search for a contact.

2. **Open the Look For drop-down list and select Contacts.**
3. **In the Search for the Word(s) text box, enter the text that you want to find.**

   You can also use the other search options available on the Contacts tab and the other three tabs.

4. **Click the Find Now button.**

   A little magnifying glass turns in circles while Outlook finds contact items that contain the text you enter. After Outlook finds the items, their names appear on a list at the bottom of the Advanced Find dialog box.

5. **Double-click the name of a contact in the list at the bottom of the Advanced Find dialog box to see that person's contact record.**

Changing Information about a Contact

An advantage to saving names and addresses with a program such as Outlook is that you can easily update your records. Making changes to an item in your contact list is simple. To do so, follow these steps:

1. **Click the Contacts icon on the Outlook bar (if you're not already in the Contacts module).**
2. **From the displayed contacts (regardless of the view), double-click the name of the contact that you want to change.**

   The dialog box for that contact opens.

3. **Change the information that needs changing.**

   Enter information the same that you entered it when you recorded information about the contact the first time around.

4. **Click the Save and Close button (or press Alt+S).**

Customizing the Appearance of the Contact List

You can look at your contact list in a number of views, just as you can look at the information in all Outlook modules in a variety of ways. If you work a lot with contacts, you can save a great deal of time by using the options for sorting, grouping, and filtering the different items in an Outlook view.

About views

Although Outlook comes with dozens of views, and you can create hundreds more, Outlook features only a handful of basic view types. You can see what the choices are by choosing View⇨Current View⇨Define Views and then clicking the New button. (After you finish looking, press Esc twice to return to the screen where you started.)

You can cook up an endless variety of views, beginning with these five general types. The Create a New View dialog box enables you to choose from the following five basic types of view in any Outlook module:

- **Table:** Your plain arrangement of rows and columns. Phone List view in the Contacts module, Simple List view in the Tasks module, and Active Appointments view in the calendar are all examples of table-type views.
- **Timeline:** Draws a picture depicting each item in a view, either in order of their due dates or the date that you dealt with them. The Inbox, Tasks, and Journal modules all include Timeline views.
- **Card:** Looks like a collection of file cards. Address Cards view and Detailed Address Cards view in your Contacts module are the only examples of card views that come with Outlook.
- **Day/Week/Month:** Calendar-style views designed — you guessed it — for the Calendar module.
- **Icons:** Fill the screen with icons representing each item and a title that matches the title of the item. The Notes module uses Icons view.

Choosing a view

Outlook offers many different ways to view the Contacts folder. These views cover things for which most people use the contact list. You can add as many views as you need, however, so don't feel limited by the initial selection. Here are the views you have to begin with:

- **Address Cards:** Looks like a screen full of little file cards arranged in alphabetical order (see Figure 7-3).

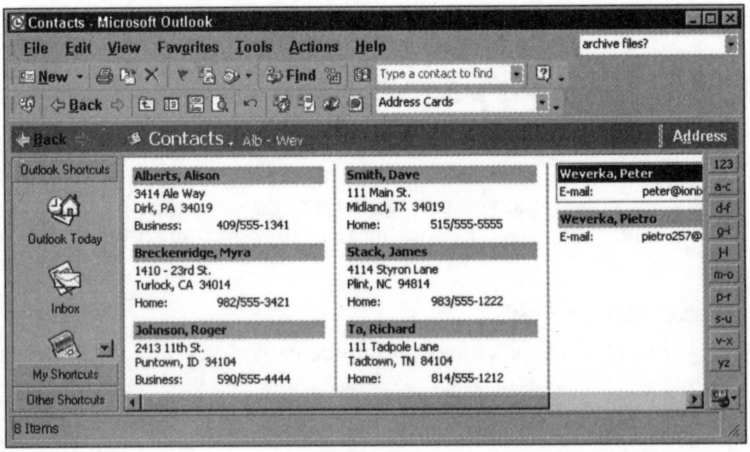

Figure 7-3: You may know more people than you think, as these electronic address cards display.

- **Detailed Address Cards:** A more detailed version of Address Cards view. This view shows everything on the first page of the Contact dialog box, including the person's title, company, and the first few lines of text from the text box at the bottom of the Contact dialog box.
- **Phone List:** Turns your collection of contacts into a plain-looking list of names, addresses, and phone numbers.
- **By Category:** This view clumps contacts together according to the category that you assign to each of them.
- **By Company:** Similar to the By Category view: They're both grouped views. (Grouped views in Outlook usually use a name that starts with the word *By*.)
- **By Location:** This view gathers contacts together — in this case, according to the country that you enter for each contact.
- **By Follow-Up Flag:** Shows a list of your messages according to which kind of flag that you assign to each message.

Switching between views in any Outlook module is as simple as changing channels on your TV. Choose View⇨Current View and then pick the view that you want from the Current View menu. If you don't like the new view, just switch back by using the same commands to choose the view you were looking at before.

Filtering views

Filtered views show only items with certain characteristics, such as a certain job title or a certain date. You can filter all views in all Outlook modules, and some modules include filtered views. Although the Contacts module doesn't come with any filtered views as you begin using Outlook, you can easily create filtered views of your contact list. Filtered views are useful if you frequently need to see a list of contacts who work at different companies but have the same job title, such as president or sales manager. You may also want to create a filtered view of contacts who live in your immediate vicinity if you need to call on customers in person. To filter items in a view, follow these steps:

1. **Click the Contacts icon on the Outlook bar (if you're not already in the Contacts module).**
2. **Choose View⇨Current View⇨Customize Current View to open the View Summary dialog box.**
3. **Click the Filter button to open the Filter dialog box (see Figure 7-4).**

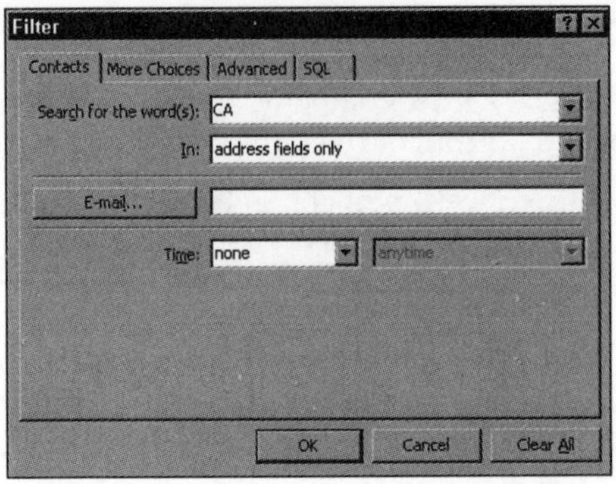

Figure 7-4: Filtering to find contacts in the Contacts folder.

4. **Enter the text that you want to filter in the Search for the Word(s) text box.**

   If you want to see only the names of people whose job title is president, for example, type the word **president** in the box.

5. **To search a specific area, open the In drop-down list and select a field from the list.**
6. **Click OK to close the Filter dialog box.**
7. **Click OK to filter your contact list.**

   Only the types of contacts you're looking for appear in the Outlook window.

To "unfilter" the view, follow the same steps that you follow to filter it, but click the Clear All button in the Filter dialog box (refer to Figure 7-4).

Putting new fields in a view

Most Outlook views display fewer than a dozen fields, although items in nearly every Outlook module can store several dozen fields. You can even create your own fields. You can add fields to any Outlook view and use the fields that you add to sort, group, or filter your collection of items. To add a field to a view, follow these steps:

1. **Choose View⇨Current View⇨Customize Current View to open the View Summary dialog box.**
2. **Click the Fields button.**

   The Show Fields dialog box opens (see Figure 7-5).

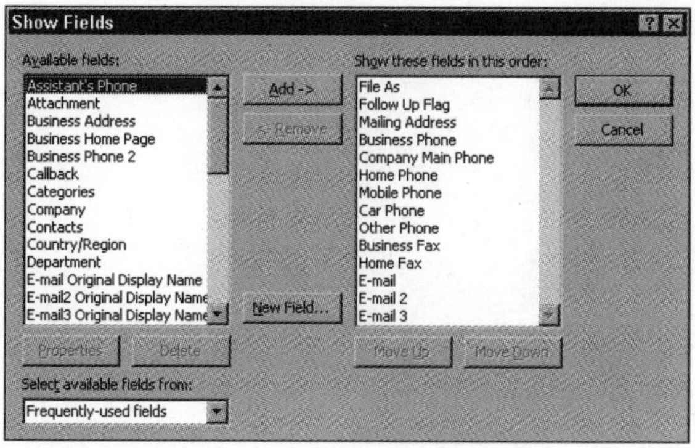

Figure 7-5: Feel free to add new fields to a view by using this dialog box.

3. **Click the name of the field that you want to add in the Available Fields list box and click the Add button.**

   Outlook copies the field that you choose to the bottom of the Show These Fields in This Order box list.

4. **Click Move Up to move the field that you chose higher on your list.**

   Every time that you click Move Up, your field moves up one position on the list. The highest items on the list appear closest to the top of any Address Cards view and farthest left in any Table view.

5. **Click OK to close the Show Fields dialog box.**

   Your new field appears in the position you selected.

Sorting a View

Each piece of information that you enter about a contact is known as a *field.* Each field shows up as a separate column in Phone List view. But each field shows up as a separate *line* in Address Cards view. If you use this method of sorting your contact list (or sorting the items in any Outlook module), the Sort dialog box refers to each item as a field (Name field or State field, for example).

Follow these steps to sort a view:

1. **Choose View⇨Current View⇨Customize Current View to open the View Summary dialog box.**
2. **Click the Sort button to open the Sort dialog box (see Figure 7-6).**

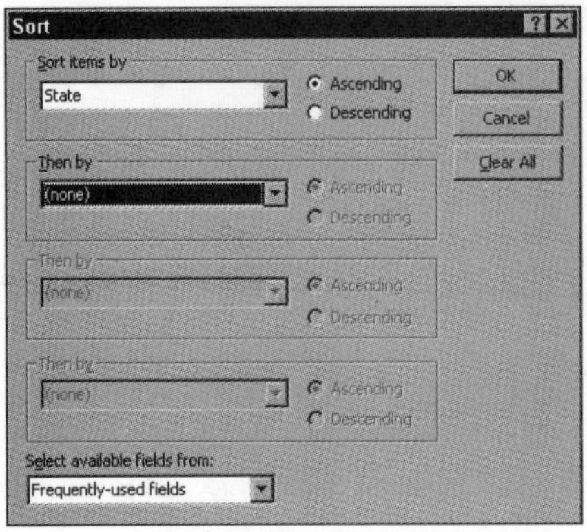

Figure 7-6: You can sort a view by many different fields in this dialog box.

3. **Open the Sort Items By drop-down list and select the item that describes how you want to sort your contacts.**

   In the other words, if you want to sort in state order, select State from the list.

4. **Click the Ascending option if you want to sort in alphabetical order or from smallest to largest; click the Descending option if you want to sort the opposite way.**

5. **Click OK twice (and choose Yes if a dialog box appears telling you that the field "state" that you want to sort by isn't shown in the view and asking whether you want to show it).**

Calling Someone from Outlook

After you enter the phone number for a contact, you don't need to settle for just looking up that person's number; you can make Outlook dial the number for you. You must have a modem installed to your computer and a phone attached to the modem and, of course, you must already have the person's phone number on your contact list. To call someone from Outlook, follow these steps:

1. **Click the Contacts icon on the Outlook bar to make the contact list appear.**

2. **Click the name of the contact that you want to call.**

3. **Choose Actions⇨Call Contact and choose which of the contact's phone numbers you want to dial from the submenu.**

   The New Call dialog box appears.

4. **If the number shown in the New Call dialog box is the number that you want to dial, click Start Call (or open the drop-down list and select the number that you want).**
5. **After the Call Status dialog box opens, pick up the phone.**
6. **After the person you're calling picks up the phone, click the Talk button in the Call Status dialog box to make the Call Status dialog box disappear.**
7. **After you finish the call, click the End Call button in the New Call dialog box.**

   The phone hangs up after you click the End Call button.
8. **Click the Close button to make the New Call dialog box disappear.**

Chapter 8: Tracking Activities with Journals

In This Chapter

- **Activating the Journal**
- **Viewing Journal entries**
- **Viewing a specific date**
- **Finding a Journal entry**
- **Recording automatically your Outlook activities**

The Journal is the one part of Outlook that's useful to you even if you never look at it. If you don't mess with the Journal at all other than to turn the feature on, you still have a record of every document that you create, every e-mail message that you send and receive, and a chronology of most of your important interactions with the people on your contact list.

Then again, if you actually use your Journal, you can keep track of meetings, phone calls, conversations, and a number of other routine events. Why would you want all this information? Because sometimes remembering what you name a document that you create or the folder in which you save a certain spreadsheet is hard. But you may remember when you did what you did — for example, last Thursday. The Journal comes in handy as a chronological record of all your activities.

Activating the Automatic Recording Feature

You're not lying if you say that you don't need to do anything to make the Journal work for you. But you are exaggerating a little. Although you do need to tell the Journal to record everything, you need to tell it only once. To activate the Journal's automatic recording feature, follow these steps:

1. **Choose Tools⇨Options to open the Options dialog box.**
2. **Click the Journal Options button to open the Journal Options dialog box (see Figure 8-1).**
3. **Click to place a check in the check box for the items and files that you want to record automatically and for the contacts about whom you want the Journal to record information.**

4. **Click OK.**

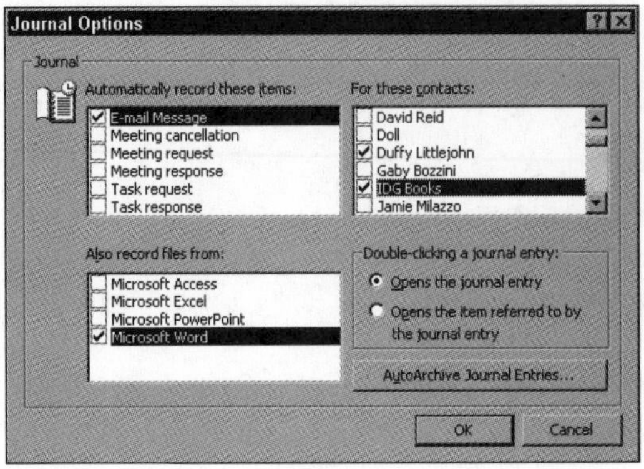

Figure 8-1: Make your Journal record things automatically.

WARNING!

Tracking too many procedures in the Journal can tax the memory resources of your computer.

Viewing the Journal

To view the Journal, choose View➪Folder List to open the Folder List. In the Folder List, click the plus sign (+) next to Outlook Today to see the folder names, and click Journal. The Journal appears in the Information window.

TIP

You can place the Journal icon on the Outlook bar and make opening the Journal easier. Chapter 1 explains how.

You can view your Journal entries in a variety of screen arrangements, known as *views*. After you first open the Journal, six views are already set up for you to use with the Journal. You can switch among them by choosing View➪Current View and picking the name of the view you want from the Current View submenu, or by opening the Current View drop-down list and choosing an option (see Figure 8-2). If one view doesn't suit you, switch to another view.

The following list describes each of the six built-in views:

- **By Type:** Groups your Journal entries on a timeline according to the type of entry, such as e-mail messages, Excel spreadsheets, or Word documents (see Figure 8-2). You can scroll forward and back in time to see different slices of your Journal.

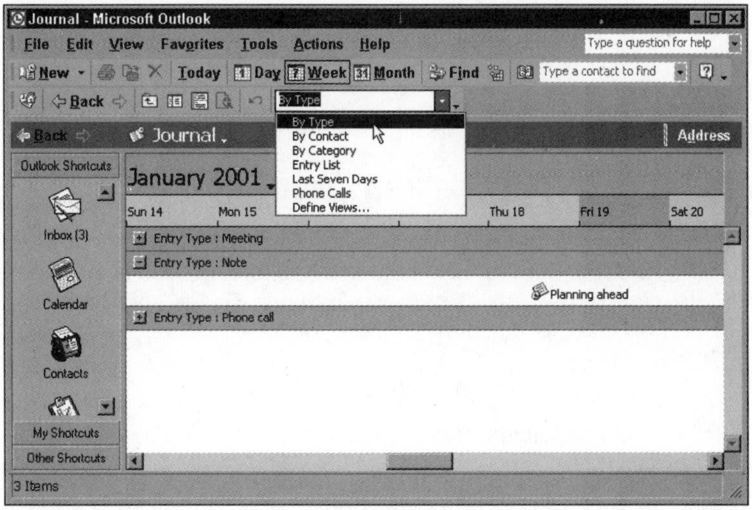

Figure 8-2: A Journal entry from a task.

- **By Contact:** Another grouped timeline view that organizes your Journal entries according to the contact that you associate with each entry. You can't print the By Contact view of the Journal.
- **By Category:** Looks much like the By Type view except that the entries are grouped according to the category you assign each entry. You can't print the By Category view of the Journal.
- **Entry List:** A simple list of all your Journal entries (see Figure 8-3). You can sort the Entry List according to any piece of information in the list, such as subject, contact, starting time, or duration. You also can select and copy a range of entries from the Entry List. You then can paste the range into an Excel spreadsheet to calculate the total time spent on work for a certain contact or on projects in a certain category.

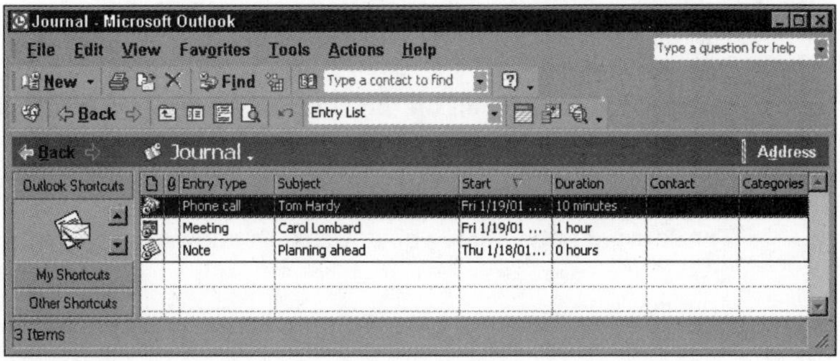

Figure 8-3: A simple list of Journal entries.

- **Last Seven Days:** Just like the Entry List except that it hides entries that occurred more than seven days ago.
- **Phone Calls:** Shows only the phone calls that you enter in your Journal.

Viewing a Specific Date in Your Journal

If you use the Journal to record your activities, you accumulate lots of information. Sometimes the amount of information is so great that sorting through all the entries becomes difficult. To see only the activities on a certain date, follow these steps:

1. **Open the Journal module.**

   The Journal appears.

2. **Choose any view that begins with the word *By* (By Type, By Contact, or By Category) by choosing View➪Current View and choosing the view that you want from the Current View menu.**

3. **Choose View➪Go To➪Go to Date (or press Ctrl+G).**

   The Go To Date dialog box opens.

4. **In the Date text box, enter the date you want to view, such as December 16, 2001, or type the amount of time since the date you have in mind, such as two weeks ago, and click OK.**

   The display shifts to the date that you ask for, and you see a collection of icons representing the Journal entries for the date that you specify. If no entries exist, no icons appear.

Creating Journal Entries with the New Journal Item Button

You can make a new Journal entry at any time. To do so, follow these steps:

1. **Click the Journal icon on the Outlook bar (if you're not in the Journal module).**

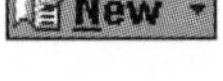

2. **Click the New Journal Entry button on the toolbar.**

   The Journal Entry dialog box opens, as shown in Figure 8-4.

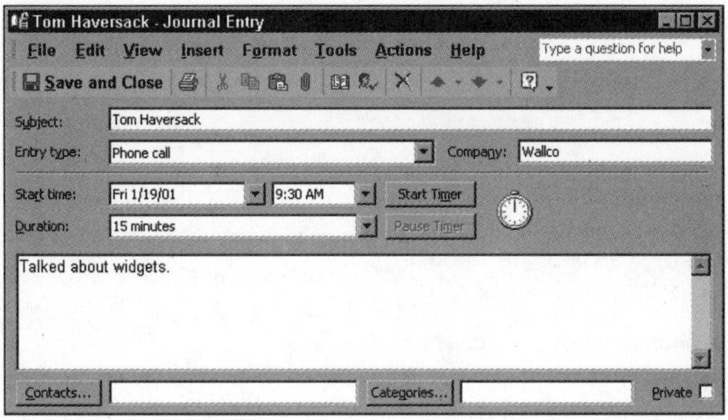

Figure 8-4: The Journal Entry dialog box, ready for input.

3. **In the Subject text box, type the topic of the Journal entry.**
4. **In the Entry Type drop-down list, pick an entry type.**
5. **If you want to add any other information to the Journal entry, enter it in the appropriate text boxes.**
6. **Click Save and Close (or press Alt+S).**

   Your new Journal entry now appears in your Journal.

Creating Journal Entries Manually by Using Drag-and-Drop

Although you may be skittish about keeping some computer record all your activities, having a record of important things (phone calls, e-mail messages) without needing to exert too much effort in compiling it can prove useful. You can use the manual (drag-and-drop) method to record individual events in your Journal. To do so, follow these steps:

1. **Drag to the Journal icon the item that you want to record (such as an e-mail message).**

   A new Journal Entry dialog box opens.

2. **Fill in any information that you want to record.**

   Enter how long a phone call lasted, for example, or where a meeting took place.

3. **Click Save and Close (or press Alt+S).**

Your e-mail message (or whatever you drag to the Journal icon) is now immortalized in your Journal. Congratulations!

Printing your Journal

Sometimes you just don't get the same picture from a screen that you do from a good ol' piece of paper. Fortunately, you can print the Journal. To print your Journal, follow these steps:

1. **Open the Journal by selecting its name in the Folder List.**
2. **Choose View⇨Current View, and from the submenu, choose the view that you want to print.**
3. **Click the names of the entries that you want to print (unless you want to print them all). To select more than one entry, use Ctrl+click.**
4. **Click the Print button on the toolbar (or press Ctrl+P).**

   The Print dialog box opens.
5. **Choose the Table or Memo option to decide which format you want.**
6. **Choose the All Rows or Only Selected Rows option.**
7. **Click OK to print your Journal entries.**

The Print dialog box displays a Preview button, which enables you to see what you're about to print before you commit everything to paper. Because a Journal can quickly develop thousands of entries, you may want to preview what you print before tying up your printer with a document that may run more than a hundred pages in length. (Check out Appendix B for the complete rundown on printing in Office.)

Finding a Journal Entry

The Journal is time-oriented (that is, it tracks items by time and date), but you may need to find a Journal entry without knowing when Outlook recorded the entry. To dig up the Journal entry that you want, simply use the Find button, as described in the following steps:

1. **Open the Journal module.**

   Your list of Journal entries appears. To open the Journal module, choose View⇨Folder List and select Journal in the Folder List.
2. **Click the Find button on the toolbar (or press Alt+I).**

   The Find bar opens.
3. **In the Look For text box, type a word or phrase that you want to find in your Journal.**

   If you conducted a similar search in the past, try opening the drop-down list and selecting a word or phrase.

4. **If the Journal entry you're looking for turns up, double-click the icon next to the entry to view the item's contents. If the entry you're looking for doesn't show up, try searching for different text.**
5. **Click the Find button again (or press Alt+I) to close the Find window.**

The icon that appears in the text box of your Journal entry is a shortcut to the document itself. You can open the document by double-clicking the shortcut.

Chapter 9: Managing Outlook Notes

In This Chapter

- Creating and reading notes
- Finding notes
- Choosing how to view notes
- Forwarding notes
- Deleting notes
- Manipulating notes

Jotting down an important note on a stray piece of paper is easy. You probably do it all the time. Finding those notes again when you really need them is a different matter! Now, where did you put that scrap of paper on which you jotted down the plans for your surefire moneymaking venture? Could someone have thrown away that napkin where you scribbled your important lunchtime thoughts? Unless you enjoy looking under piles of junk or digging through the trash for your important notes, get Outlook to help you organize your note-taking attempts.

Creating Notes

If you can click a mouse, you can create a note. To do so, follow these steps:

1. **If you're not already in the Notes module, click the Notes icon on the Outlook bar.**

2. **Click the New Note button on the toolbar (or press Ctrl+N).**

   A note appears, as shown in Figure 9-1.

3. **Type some text for your note.**
4. **Press Esc to close and save the note.**

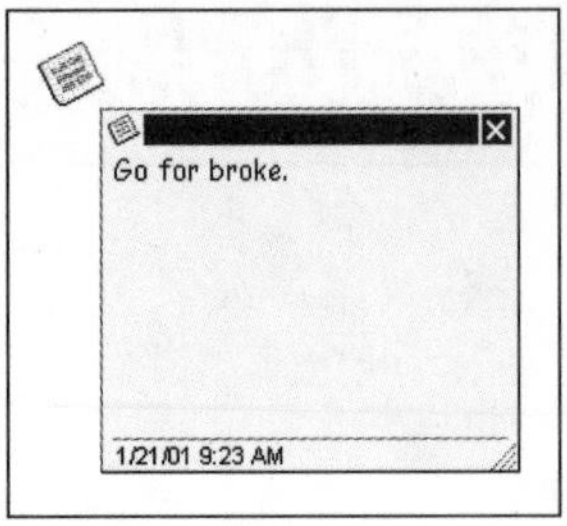
Go for broke.
1/21/01 9:23 AM

Figure 9-1: An Outlook note in all its glory.

Your new note takes its place in the collection of notes in the Notes module. Creating a note doesn't involve a great deal of fuss; just open, type, and close.

FAST TRACK

You don't even need to be in the Notes module to create a note. Just press Ctrl+Shift+N anywhere in Outlook and a blank note appears. After you finish writing your note, press Esc to close the note.

Reading (Or Changing) a Note

Opening a note so that you can read or edit it is as simple as possible. To open a note, follow these steps:

1. **If you're not already in the Notes module, click the Notes icon on the Outlook bar.**
2. **Double-click the note that you want to open.**

   The note appears.
3. **Read the note or make changes as you want.**

   To make changes, start typing words or deleting the words that are already there.
4. **Press Esc to close the note.**

Finding a Note

After seeing how easily you can create a note, you may begin adding notes all the time, quickly amassing a large collection. Finding one note in a large collection can be a needle-in-a-haystack proposition, which is why being able to find notes is so useful. To find notes, follow these steps:

1. **If you're not already in the Notes module, click the Notes icon on the Outlook bar.**

2. **Click the Find button on the toolbar (or press Ctrl+E).**

   The Find window opens (see Figure 9-2).

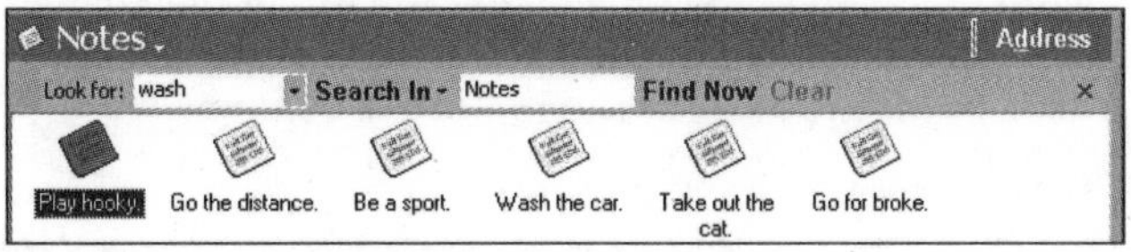

Figure 9-2: Finding a lost note.

3. **In the Look For box, enter the word or phrase you're looking for.**

   How much or how little text you use for your search doesn't matter. If you're looking for the words *George Washington,* for example, typing **geo** suffices. In this example, however, Outlook also finds *National Geographic* and a reminder to do your geometry homework (assuming that you write notes about all those sorts of things).

4. **Click the Find Now button.**

   An hourglass appears as Outlook searches for your specified text. After Outlook finishes, a list of items that satisfy your search appears.

5. **If the note you're looking for turns up, double-click it.**

   If the note you're looking for doesn't show up, try searching for different text.

6. **Click the Find button on the toolbar again (or press Ctrl+E) to close the Find window.**

REMEMBER

A nice thing about finding notes is that you don't need to enter a whole word. The Find feature can find any sequence of characters that you type. If you're searching for a note you saved about John Paul Kowznofsky, you can search for **John Paul** or just **Kowz.** Whether you use upper- or lowercase letters doesn't matter; Outlook just looks for the letters that you enter.

Viewing Notes

You can make Outlook display your multitude of notes in a variety of ways. Each type of screen style, known as a *view,* emphasizes something different about your collection of notes. You can switch among different views of your notes by choosing View⇨Current View and picking a different view from the Current View menu. You can choose among the following views:

- **Icons:** Splashes your collection of notes in little boxes all across the screen (refer to Figure 9-2). To open one, just double-click it.

✦ **Notes List:** As its name suggests, presents a two-column list of your notes (see Figure 9-3). One column lists the subject of each note, and the other column shows the date on which you created the note. You can sort the list according to the date you created each note by clicking the word `Created` in the gray box at the top of the column. You also can sort the list in alphabetical order by subject by clicking the word `Subject` in the gray box at the top of the column.

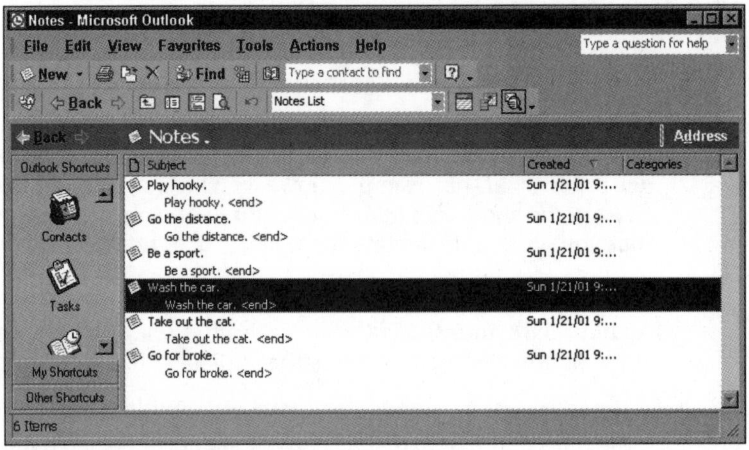

Figure 9-3: Notes can appear in a list.

✦ **Last Seven Days:** Shows only notes that you modified within the last seven days. After seven days have passed since you changed the text in a note or its color, size, or category, the note disappears from Last Seven Days view.

✦ **By Category:** Groups your notes according to the category that you assign to each one. (To assign a category to a note, click the small note icon in the upper-left corner of a note and choose Categories from the drop-down list. Then select a category in the Categories dialog box that appears.)

✦ **By Color:** Groups your notes according to the color that you assign to each one.

Forwarding a Note to Someone Else

You don't need to keep your treasure trove of notes to yourself. Forwarding a note by e-mail is simple. To forward a note by e-mail, follow these steps:

1. **Click the title of the note that you want to forward.**

   The title of the note is highlighted.

2. **Choose Actions⇨Forward (or press Ctrl+F).**

   The Message form opens, as shown in Figure 9-4.

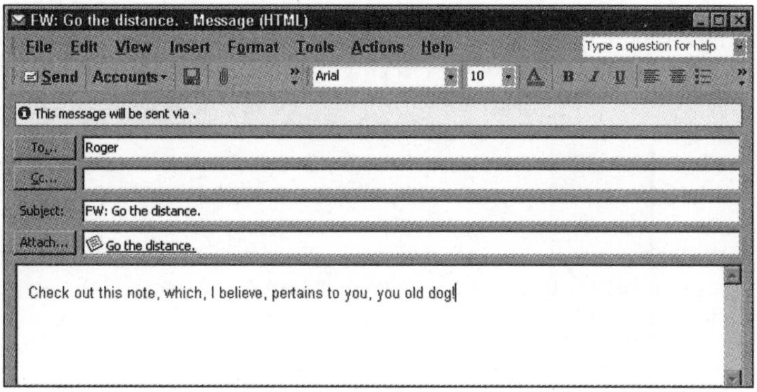

Figure 9-4: You can forward a note by using this form.

3. **Forward the note as you would an e-mail message.**

   For example, enter a word of explanatory text to describe what the note is about. Chapter 3 explains forwarding, if you need help with that.

4. **Click the Send button (or press Ctrl+Enter).**

   Your message is on its way to your recipient.

REMEMBER

By forwarding a note, you're really just sending an e-mail message with a note attached (which is quick and simple but not terribly magical). Keep in mind that for the recipient to read the Outlook note, he must be a happy user of Outlook.

Deleting a Note

Creating a huge collection of notes is so easy that someday you're probably going to need to delete some of them. (Years from now, you're unlikely to need that note to remind yourself to take out the trash or get your hair cut.) Deleting notes is even easier than creating them. To do so, follow these steps:

1. **If you're not already in the Notes module, click the Notes icon on the Outlook bar.**

2. **Click the title of the note that you want to delete.**

   The title (or the icon if you're viewing icons) is highlighted to show which note you're selecting.

3. **Click the Delete button on the toolbar (or press Delete).**

   The note disappears.

You don't need to limit yourself to deleting one note at a time. If you know how to select multiple items in Windows, you can apply this knowledge to any Office application. You can select a bunch of notes by pressing and holding the Ctrl key while clicking the different notes that you want to delete; then click the Delete button. You can also click one note and then hold down the Shift key and click another note farther down the row to select both notes that you click — as well as all the notes between them. After you click the Delete key, all the notes that you select go away.

To recover a note that you deleted, click the Deleted Items button in the Outlook bar. Your note, along with other items you deleted, appears in the information viewer.

Using Notes to Your Advantage

Outlook enables you to manipulate notes to make them even more useful. The following sections discuss some of the ways in which you can modify your use of notes.

Assigning a category to a note

You can assign a category to any note that you create in Outlook. Categories may prove more useful while you're using notes than as you're using other parts of Outlook — you can enter any type of information in a note, which can make it hard to find later. Assigning categories makes the stuff that you collect easier to use and understand. To assign a category to a note, follow these steps:

1. **Click the Notes icon in the Outlook bar to view your notes.**
2. **Click the Note icon in the upper-left corner of the note (see Figure 9-5).**

   The shortcut menu appears. If the note isn't open and you're viewing it in the Notes window, simply right-click the note.

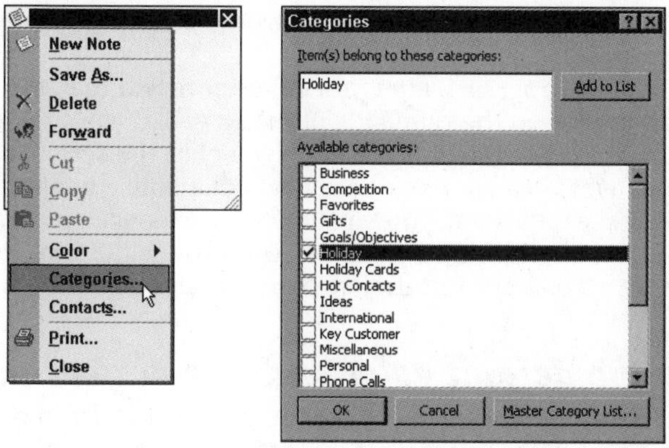

Figure 9-5: Assigning a category to a note by using the shortcut menu.

3. **Choose Categories from the shortcut menu that opens.**

   The Categories dialog box appears.

4. **In the Available Categories list, choose a category that describes your note.**

   If none of the categories suit you, type one in the text box and click the Add to List button.

5. **Click OK.**

   Your note looks the same, but now it has a category. You can arrange notes by category by choosing View➪Current View➪By Category.

Changing the size of a note

A note can appear as a teensy little squib, or it can cover your entire screen. The size of the text in the note is the same no matter how large you make the note. If the note is too small, however, much of your text is invisible, so you need to make the note larger. To change the size of a note, follow these steps:

1. **Click the Notes icon on the Outlook bar (if you're not already in the Notes module).**

2. **Double-click the title of the note whose size you want to change.**

   The note opens.

3. **Move your mouse pointer to the bottom-left corner of the note until the mouse pointer changes into a two-headed arrow pointing on a diagonal.**

4. Click and drag your mouse until the note is the size that you want.

In most Windows programs, after you enter more text than fits in a text box, a scroll bar appears at the right side of the screen. If you want to see text that scrolls off the bottom of the screen, you click the scroll bar to move the text up. Because notes don't use scroll bars, if a note contains more text than you can see on-screen, you must click your mouse on the text and press the arrow keys to scroll up and down through the text. Note boxes are cuter without scroll bars, but they're harder to use.

Setting the default color and size of your notes

Maybe yellow just isn't your color. Maybe you want a little more space as you create a new note. You can set up Outlook to start each note in the color and size that you want (within reason). To change the default settings for the color and size of your notes, follow these steps:

1. **Choose Tools⇨Options.**

   The Options dialog box opens.

2. **Click the Note Options button.**

   The Notes Options dialog box appears (see Figure 9-6).

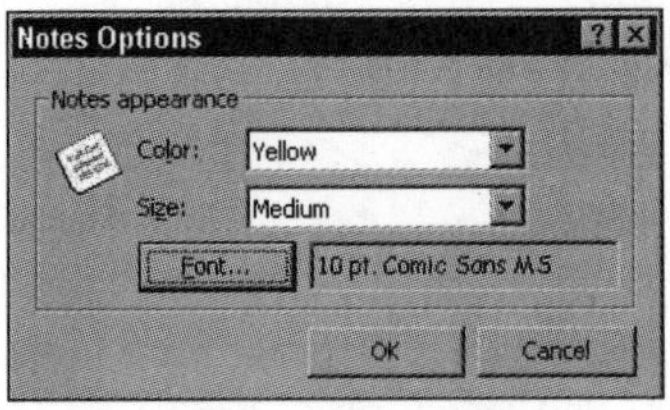

Figure 9-6: You can set many options for your notes in this dialog box.

3. **Open and select a color from the Color drop-down list.**
4. **Open and select a size for notes from the Size drop-down list.**
5. **Click the Font button to open the Font dialog box and choose a font and font size for the text in notes.**
6. **Click OK.**

Changing the default size and color of your notes doesn't affect the notes you've already created. If you want to change the color of a note after you create it, right-click the note, choose Color from the shortcut menu, and choose a color from the submenu.

REAL WORLD

Printing the contents of a single note

You're meant to read notes on-screen, but you may want to print one out. Remember that, although you can change the colors of your notes, the colors don't print on a black-and-white printer. To print a note, follow these steps:

1. **Click the title of the note that you want to print.**

   The title of your note is highlighted to show that it's selected.

2. **Click the Print button on the toolbar (or press Ctrl+P) to open the Print dialog box.**
3. **In the Print Style area, choose Memo Style in the Print Style box.**
4. **Click OK.**

If you print notes, they don't look like the cute little yellow squares that you see on-screen; each one looks like an office memorandum.

Index

A

B

C

D

M

N

O

P

R

S

Book VI

PowerPoint 2002

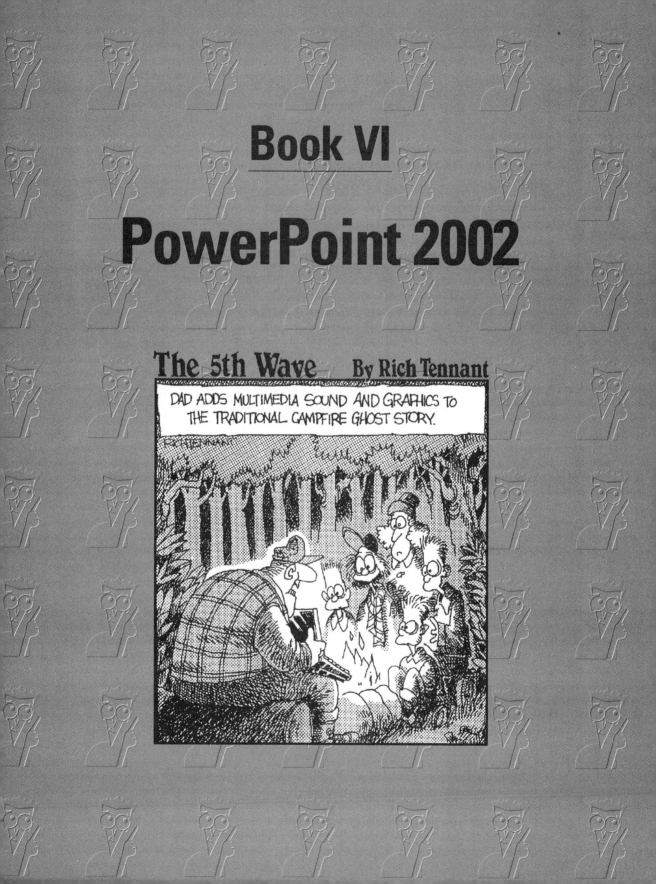

The 5th Wave
By Rich Tennant
DAD ADDS MULTIMEDIA SOUND AND GRAPHICS TO THE TRADITIONAL CAMPFIRE GHOST STORY.

Contents at a Glance

Chapter 1: Getting Started with a PowerPoint Presentation

In This Chapter

- Opening a presentation
- Making a new presentation
- Changing your view
- Saving and closing in PowerPoint

Remember the days when all you had to make presentations with were pictures, floppy poster boards, and maybe a handful of hard-to-read overhead transparencies?

Such simple presentations weren't fun to put together and even less enjoyable to sit through. Times have changed. By using PowerPoint, you can make almost any presentation worth watching. This chapter starts you out on the PowerPoint basics so that you're ready to take advantage of this great presentation program.

Opening a Presentation

PowerPoint provides you with a choice of several methods with which to create a new presentation. The easiest method — and perhaps best for beginners — is for a wizard to walk you through the process. If you don't want to use a wizard, however, you can use a template offering a standard group of slides that you personalize according to your needs. Finally, you can start from scratch and build your presentation from the ground up. Whichever method you choose, PowerPoint makes creating a presentation easier than ever before.

For the lowdown on how to use the mouse, as well as details on cursors and pointers for PowerPoint, check out Appendix A. I explain how to use dialog boxes and make menu choices in Chapter 5 of Book I. The basic routines are similar.

After firing up PowerPoint, you see the screen shown in Figure 1-1. Notice the New Presentation task pane on the right side of the screen. (If you don't see it, choose File⇨New, press Ctrl+N, or choose View⇨Task Pane.) You can begin developing a presentation by selecting from the following options in the task pane:

- **Presentations:** The Presentations option enables you to go back and work on any presentation that you previously named and saved.
- **Blank Presentation:** This option gives you blank slides with no color and no artwork, which is great for minimalists and artists. Go this route and you can create artistic elements from scratch.
- **From AutoContent Wizard:** The AutoContent Wizard yields a nearly complete set of PowerPoint slides. You just need to supply the wizard some basic lines of text, and the wizard does its thing. You can then tweak the final product.
- **General Templates:** This option provides you with cool predesigned layouts that offer you the flexibility to alter the layout elements.

While you're staring at the PowerPoint screen, you may as well get acquainted with its two most important parts, the Slide bar and the Slide pane:

- **Slide bar:** In Normal view, the Slide bar lists all the slides in the presentation in the order in which they appear. The slide bar appears along the right side of the screen.
- **Slide pane:** In Normal view, the Slide pane shows a single slide. You can see precisely what a slide looks like by glancing at the Slide pane.

Changing your view of a presentation is explained near the end of this chapter.

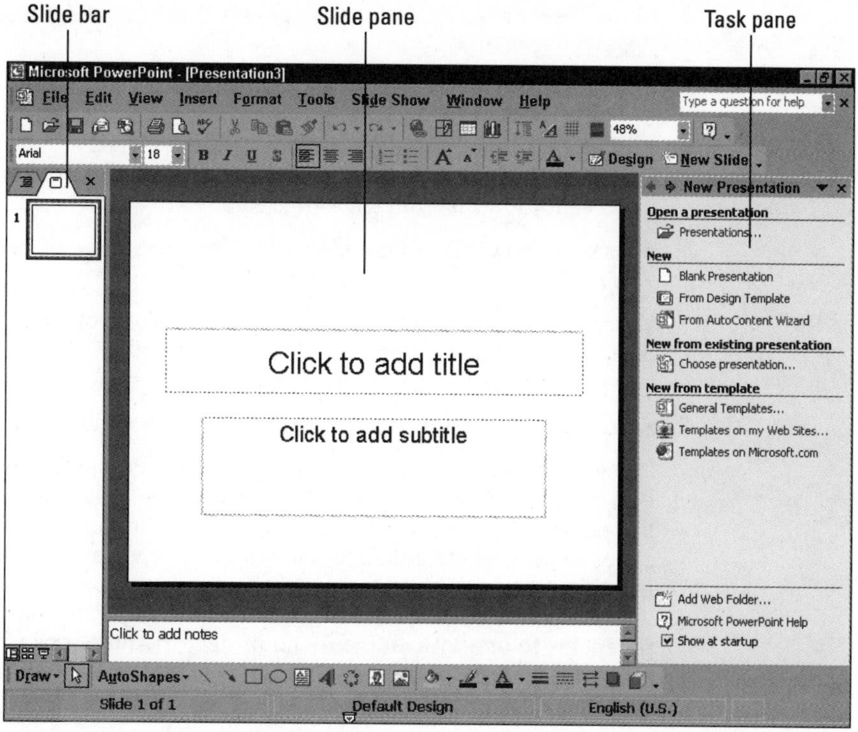

Figure 1-1: PowerPoint starts up ready to go.

Creating a presentation by using the AutoContent Wizard

The AutoContent Wizard is a simple program that builds a rudimentary set of PowerPoint slides based on a few tidbits of information that you input to the program. The wizard is a good way to get started with PowerPoint, but don't let its name fool you into thinking that it magically does all the work for you. Just accept the wizard for what it is — a quick and dirty way to generate a basic set of PowerPoint slides. To create a presentation by using this wizard, follow these steps:

1. **Start PowerPoint, if you haven't done so already.**

   To start PowerPoint, click the Start button on the taskbar and choose Programs⇨Microsoft PowerPoint.

2. **In the New Presentation task pane, click the From AutoContent Wizard hyperlink.**

   The AutoContent Wizard dialog box opens.

3. **Click Next.**

   The wizard now asks you a series of questions about the type and style of presentation that you want to create.

4. **Select a presentation type from the Select the Type of Presentation You're Going to Give list; then click Next.**

   Your choices consist of All, General, Corporate, Projects, Sales/Marketing, and Carnegie Coach. After you click the Next button, you see a list of presentation styles.

5. **Select a presentation style from the list; then click Next.**

   Presentation style choices include On-Screen Presentation, Web Presentation, Black-and-White Overheads, Color Overheads, or 35mm Slides. Select On-Screen Presentation if you plan on presenting your slides in front of an audience (face-to-face) or via a computer-networked meeting. Choose Web Presentation if you plan to post your slides to the Web for online access. Choose Overheads if you want to print transparencies to use with an overhead projector. And choose 35mm Slides if you want to show your presentation by using a traditional slide carousel.

6. **Type a descriptive title in the Presentation Title text box.**

   You can also enter a footer in the Footer text box or click the appropriate check boxes to list dates and place slide numbers on your slides.

7. **Click Next.**

   The wizard presents a final wrap-up screen.

8. **Click the Finish button.**

   Your completed presentation appears on-screen in Normal view. (You can read about views in the section "Changing Your View of a Presentation" later in this chapter.) Notice the generic text on the slide. Make sure that you enter your own text — unless you want a generic presentation, but who wants that?

Creating a presentation by using templates

Another way to create a slide presentation is to start with a template. By going this route, you get predesigned slides. The PowerPoint templates offer visually appealing colors and design elements. Some templates go one step further and provide generic text — text that you need to make your own, of course.

To create a PowerPoint presentation from a template, follow these steps:

1. **Click General Templates in the New Presentation task pane. (Choose File⇨New if you don't see the task pane.)**

   The Templates dialog box appears (see Figure 1-2).

2. **On the Design Templates or Presentations tab, click the name of any template to see a thumbnail sketch of how the design appears on your computer screen.**

3. **After picking a template that suits your fancy, click OK.**

   If you choose a template on the Presentations tab, PowerPoint provides generic text as well as a design.

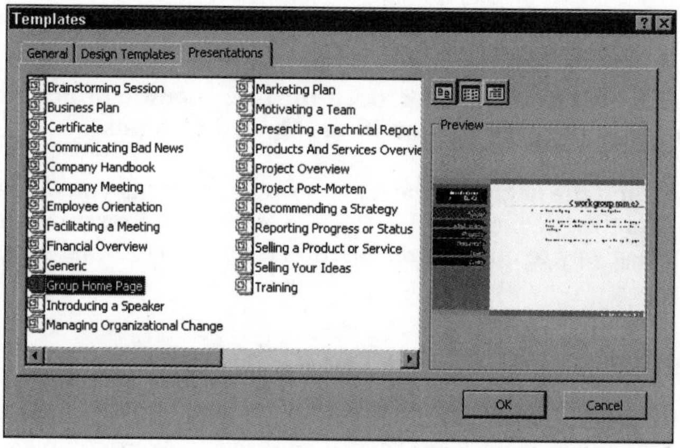

Figure 1-2: Look at all the templates that you can choose from!

To create a presentation from a template you've used recently, click the name of the template in the New Presentation task pane. You can find the name under the New From Template option.

Creating a blank presentation

You can click Blank Presentation in the New Presentation task pane to create a PowerPoint presentation from scratch.

Blank presentations can provide placeholders for adding text and graphic objects, but they're otherwise barren of images, colors, and artistic designs. Blank presentations are ideal for building complete layouts from scratch or for building simple, text-only presentations.

Opening an Existing Presentation

PowerPoint offers you the flexibility of saving presentations to — and opening presentations from — a variety of locations. If you're like most users, you may frequently save files to and open files from your own hard drive or a shared network drive. To open a saved PowerPoint presentation, follow these steps:

1. **Click the Open button on the Standard toolbar, choose File⇨Open, press Ctrl+O, or click the More Presentations option on the New Presentation task pane.**

   The Open dialog box appears.

2. **Select a presentation that you want to open.**

   A thumbnail picture appears of the first slide in the presentation that you select.

3. **Click the Open button to open the presentation or double-click the name of the presentation in the Open dialog box.**

You can find the names of the last four presentations you opened at the bottom of the File menu and at the top of the New Presentation task pane. The fastest way to open a presentation is to open it from those locations.

Changing Your View of a Presentation

Next to the horizontal scrollbar sits a collection of buttons from which you can choose your view. You can also choose a view from the View menu. The rest of this book helps you to understand how to use these views, but you may just want to know what's available. You can choose among any of the following views:

- **Normal view:** This view shows you one slide at a time (see Figure 1-3). On the left side of the screen is the *Slide bar.* Click the Outline tab on the Slide bar to see and edit text on the slides in Outline view. Click the Slides tab to see numbered, thumbnail images of slides. By clicking a thumbnail image, you can make a slide appear in the Slide pane on the right side of the window.
- **Slide Sorter view:** This view shows thumbnails of all your slides simultaneously. The slides are presented in orderly rows and columns. Slide Sorter view enables you to quickly change the order of your slides by dragging and dropping them into new positions.
- **Slide Show:** This view presents the completed stack of slides to a viewing audience. Switch to this view when you want to give a slide presentation.

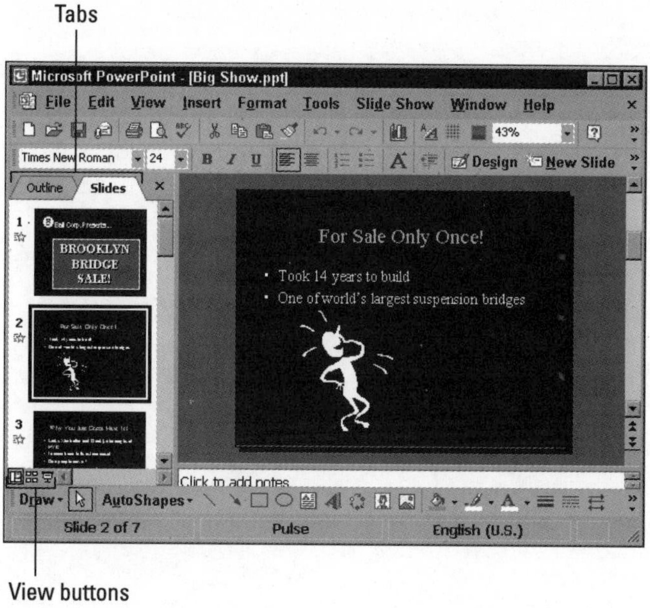

Figure 1-3: The Normal view of the PowerPoint screen.

Saving Your Work

As you compose an award-winning presentation or lecture, you're going to want to save your work. Save often. If you close your file or exit PowerPoint without saving your slides, consider them gone forever. Saving also buys you insurance against losing everything in the event that you experience a power surge or that your computer crashes. To save your goods, click the Save button on the Standard toolbar or choose File➪Save.

Exiting PowerPoint

When you're ready to close up shop, kick back for the evening, and bask in a little Microsoft glory, close the PowerPoint files that you're working on by choosing File➪Exit or by clicking the Close button.

PowerPoint doesn't enable you to quit the program without asking whether you want to save changes. Answer politely to complete the exiting process.

Chapter 2: Sliding into Your Presentation

In This Chapter

- Getting to know PowerPoint slides
- Managing your slides
- Using the Outline tab

Slides aren't just little square things that all too often jam in noisy carrousel projectors while you try to remain awake in a dark room. PowerPoint enables you to make slides that you can see on a computer screen. In this chapter, you find out some of the basics of working with slides.

Creating and Working with Slides

Showing PowerPoint slides is much more exciting than clicking through traditional slides. That's because a PowerPoint presentation can include text, graphics, movies, and audio clips, all of which you can present in animated steps to convey your information in a precise, engaging sequence. It can also include television-quality cuts and fades between slides.

So what does a PowerPoint slide look like? Basically, a slide looks like anything that you want it to look like. Sometimes, it looks like a simple piece of text, such as your company mission statement. Other times, it looks like a list of bulleted items — similar perhaps to the ingredients for guacamole — that fly in animated steps, one bullet item at a time, onto the slide. And other times, it looks like a graph of product sales forecasts or a labeled diagram of earthworm innards. If you can dream it up, you can probably stick it on a slide and show it to your audience. All the information in your presentation appears either directly on a slide or attaches to a slide as reference material. The following few sections tell you how to add new slides and move around a collection of slides in a presentation.

Adding a new slide

As you begin a new presentation — except for a presentation that you create by using an AutoContent Wizard — PowerPoint provides you with one fresh slide to work with. (New presentations that you create by using the

AutoContent Wizard sometimes provide you with ten or more slides to contend with.) But unless you're the most painfully concise human on the planet, you may want more than a single slide in your PowerPoint presentation.

To add a new slide to your presentation, click the New Slide button, choose Insert➪New Slide, or press Ctrl+N. The Slide Layout task pane appears (see Figure 2-1). The task pane offers 27 *AutoLayouts,* which are slide layouts that PowerPoint automatically sets up for you. The AutoLayouts offer various combinations of title slides, text bullets, clip art, and other features. If you want to fully customize the slide yourself, choose the blank AutoLayout slide.

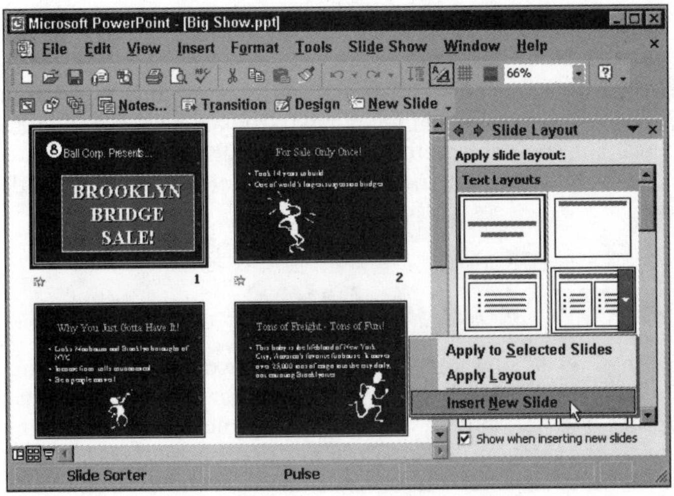

Figure 2-1: Creating a new slide in PowerPoint.

After you find the slide you want, either click it or open its drop-down list and select Insert New Slide. If you don't see a drop-down list, move the pointer over the slide you want and it will appear.

Typing text on a slide

Most new slides reserve blank space for you to type text (except for those times when you choose to create a completely blank slide). These "type-here" zones are known as *text boxes.* Notice that placeholders — `Click to add title`, `Click to add subtitle`, and `Click to add text` — occupy the text boxes until you replace the boxes with your own words (see Figure 2-2).

Move the cursor into a text box and click. The cursor changes into an I-beam. Start typing. Now PowerPoint acts as a word processor. The left and right arrow keys move you around, and the Delete key erases your typing.

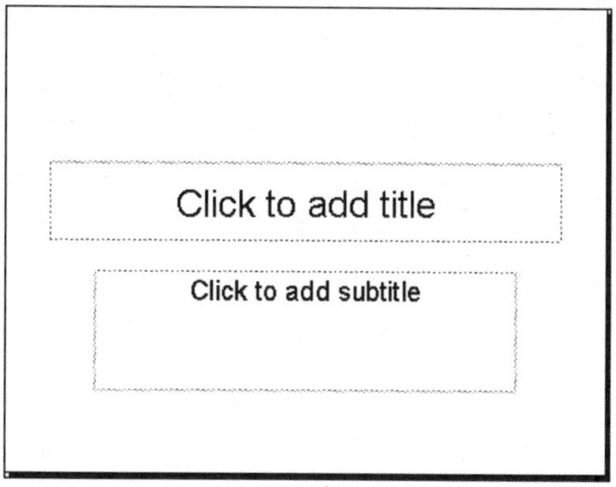

Figure 2-2: Place-holders are ready to accept your slide's text.

TIP: PowerPoint tries to fit any text that you type within the boundaries of the text placeholder. If the amount of text that you type can't fit in the boundaries comfortably, PowerPoint decreases the point size of the text to create a better fit.

Pasting clip art onto a new slide

You may want to add a relevant picture that "tells the story" to your slides. You may choose to add clip art, photos, drawings, or scanned images to your slides — the possibilities are endless! The simplest way to add a picture to a new slide is to grab one out of the Microsoft Clip Gallery that accompanies PowerPoint. Just follow these steps:

1. **In Normal view, insert a new slide into your presentation that includes a clip-art placeholder.**

   This placeholder doesn't limit you to adding pictures only in the form of clip art — *clip-art placeholder* is just an old and beloved name for the type of AutoLayout that includes a picture. You can actually add any image — a photograph, a scanned drawing, a piece of clip art — in using this AutoLayout.

2. **Double-click the placeholder to open the Select Picture dialog box.**
3. **Click to select a picture.**

   If you have trouble finding a picture, type a word that describes what you're looking for in the Search text box and click the Search button. You can also click the Import button to enter a clip art image that you're storing elsewhere on your computer.

4. **Click the OK button.**

   PowerPoint magically glues your chosen image to your slide.

Using a color scheme

Color schemes enable you to exercise your creative muscle to alter slide background colors, text colors, and accent colors. For each scheme, PowerPoint provides you with eight coordinated colors that complement one another in an aesthetically pleasing combination. The schemes ensure that the colors match and that the background of a slide doesn't obscure the text.

To apply a new color scheme to the slides in your presentation, follow these steps:

1. **Click the Design button or choose Format⇨Slide Design.**

   The Slide Design task pane opens.

2. **Click the Color Schemes hyperlink in the task pane.**

   Color Schemes is the second hyperlink. The task pane shows various color schemes (see Figure 2-3).

3. **Scroll to and double-click the scheme that you want.**

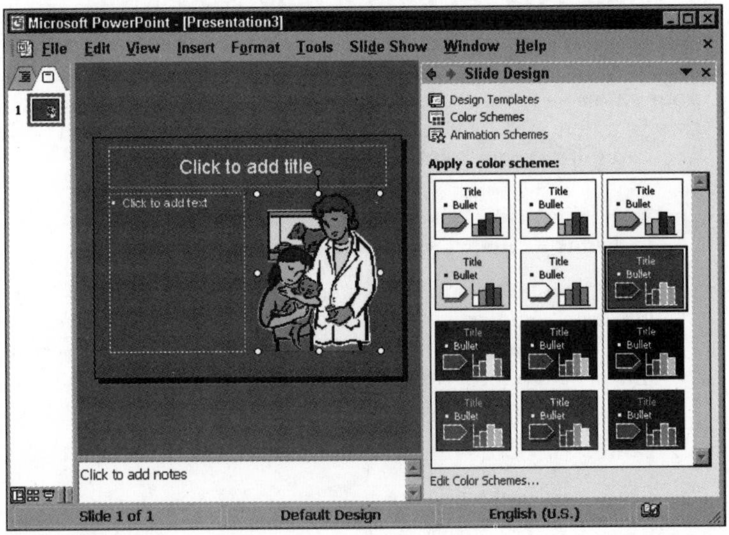

Figure 2-3: Applying a new color scheme to your slides.

If none of the schemes appeals to you, click Edit Color Schemes at the bottom of the Slide Design task pane. The Custom tab of the Edit Color Scheme dialog box appears. This tab enables you to create your own color scheme by changing different elements of the slides — the Background, Text and Lines, Shadows, Title Text, Fills, Accent, Accent and Hyperlink, and Accent and Followed Hyperlink. To change an individual color, go to the

Custom tab, click the color, click the Change Color button, and then choose a new color in the dialog box that appears and click OK. After making your changes, make sure that you click the Apply button in the Edit Color Scheme dialog box.

TIP

To save a scheme that you create on the Custom tab of the Color Scheme dialog box, click the Add As Standard Scheme button. PowerPoint adds your new scheme to the Slide Design task pane.

Duplicating a slide

Duplicating a slide is an easy way to reuse the formatting of one slide as a guide for other slides. You may find duplicating particularly useful for churning out slides with the same title and images and variations only on bullet items.

To duplicate a slide, select its thumbnail and choose Edit➪Duplicate or press Ctrl+D. PowerPoint duplicates the currently selected slide and places it immediately following its original slide. You then move to the duplicate slide in the presentation.

If you select more than one slide, PowerPoint duplicates every slide in the selection and places them immediately following the last selected slide.

Deleting a slide

You can eliminate a slide in any view — but not while you're running a slide show. (You're too late then!) To trash a slide that you no longer want, just follow these steps:

1. **Select the slide that you want to delete by clicking its thumbnail.**

   To select more than one slide, switch to Slide Sorter view (see the following section for information) and Ctrl+click the slides.

2. **Choose Edit➪Cut. You can also press the Backspace or Delete key to delete selected slides.**

Moving from slide to slide

You can move from slide to slide during the construction of your PowerPoint presentation in several ways, as follows:

- **In Normal view:** Click the slide to which you want to move. You can also take one of the following actions:
  - Click the Next Slide or Previous Slide arrow at the bottom of the vertical scroll bar.

- Drag the scroll-box up or down.
- Press PgUp or PgDn to move through your stack one slide at a time.

✦ **In Slide Sorter view:** Double-click the slide that you want to move to.

Changing the Order of Slides

So you want to move an entire slide to a different position in the outline? You're never too late to fine-tune a presentation. To change slide order, follow these steps:

1. **In Normal view or Slide Sorter view, click to select the slide that you want to move.**

   From the view buttons at the left edge of the PowerPoint window (under the Slide bar), you can click the button for the view you want to see.

2. **Drag the selected slide to a new position and let go.**

The entire presentation of slides reorders itself to reflect the repositioning of the moved slide. PowerPoint is just that accommodating!

Rearranging Text on the Outline Tab

When you click the Outline tab in Normal view, your entire presentation appears as an outline that comprises the titles and body text from each slide.

The purpose of the Outline tab is to concentrate on the text of the slides; you can edit text content, text formatting, and text organization. The benefit of working in the Outline tab is that it enables you to easily see how information progresses from slide to slide. And so that you don't forget, the Slide pane still shows the aesthetics of how each slide looks during the slide show.

TIP

You can make the Slide bar wider or narrow and, by doing so, be able to see slide text better on the Outline bar. To change the size of the Slide bar, drag its border to the left or right.

How slides and text are organized

The Outline tab lists slides vertically, from the first slide to the last. A number and a slide marker appears beside each slide.

The slide title appears to the right of each slide marker, and body text, indented up to five levels, appears below the slide title. The body text may appear as paragraphs or bullet items and you can easily move it by rearranging it within a slide or moving it to other slides. You accomplish some repositioning tasks by clicking and dragging the selected slide or text and others by using buttons on the Outlining toolbar.

Working with the Outlining toolbar

As you're working on the Outline tab in Normal view, you may want to open the Outlining toolbar. It offers specialized buttons for working with the outline of a presentation. Display the Outlining toolbar by choosing View⇨Toolbars⇨Outlining or right-clicking a toolbar and choosing Outlining from the shortcut menu.

Outlining buttons on the toolbar deal primarily with repositioning text so that the text's position relative to other text appropriately conveys its significance. The Outlining buttons, for one example, enable you to move text bullets higher or lower on a bulleted list. Outlining buttons also enable you to move a bulleted item of text so that it becomes a major bullet (a procedure known as *promoting text*) or a minor bullet (known as *demoting text*).

Buttons on the Outlining toolbar do the following:

- **Promote:** Elevates the position of the selected paragraph or bullet item by moving it up and left one heading level. Clicking this button makes a level-two heading, for example, become a level-one heading.

- **Demote:** Diminishes the position of the selected paragraph or bullet item by moving it down and right one heading level. Clicking this button makes a level-two heading, for example, become a level-three heading.

- **Move Up:** Repositions the selected paragraph or bullet item — and any collapsed subordinate text — up, positioning it above the preceding paragraph or bullet item. Clicking this button makes the second bullet item on a list, for example, become the first bullet item.

- **Move Down:** Repositions the selected paragraph — and any collapsed subordinate text — down, positioning it below the following paragraph. Clicking this button makes the second bullet item on a list, for example, become the third bullet item.

- **Collapse:** Hides body text to show only the title of the selected slide or slides. A slide with collapsed text displays a thin gray line underlining its title.

- **Expand:** Redisplays collapsed text of selected slides.

- **Collapse All:** Collapses the body text of all slides in the presentation.

- **Expand All:** Shows the body text of all slides in the presentation.

- **Summary Slide:** Builds a new slide from the titles of selected slides. The title of the new slide is Summary Slide, and the button inserts the summary slide in front of the first selected slide (serving more as an agenda slide than a summary slide).
- **Show Formatting:** Toggles on or off to show or hide text formatting (such as font and point size) in Outline view.

TIP

Many of the Outlining buttons that you use most frequently also appear on other toolbars, including the Formatting and the Standard toolbars.

Changing the position of a title or paragraph

You can change the position of a slide title or paragraph whenever you want — and you're undoubtedly sure to do so over and over. Follow these two tiny steps:

1. **On the Outline tab in Normal view, select the title or paragraph that you want to move.**
2. **Drag the selected text to a new position or click the Promote, Demote, Move Up, or Move Down button on the Outlining toolbar to reposition the selected text.**

Chapter 3: Laying the Groundwork with Templates

In This Chapter

- **Discovering templates**
- **Applying templates**

Just for the sake of the argument, suppose that you enjoy doing the same task over and over again. You want your name to appear in the top-right corner of every slide that you show during your presentation. You also want a picture of your cat on every other page. These requirements are no problem if you enjoy repeating the same actions: entering the text and adding the picture on every slide where you want these things to appear. But if you prefer to save time and avoid errors that occur as you try to do the same thing more than once, this chapter on templates is custom made for you.

Applying a New Template

PowerPoint comes with tons of premade *templates* — artistic blueprints for constructing your slide presentations. Templates are set up with predefined formatting settings (color schemes, graphic elements, and styled fonts) to minimize the time and effort that you spend building slides.

Applying a template to a new presentation

If you're just starting a new presentation and you want the slides to follow a template, follow these steps:

1. **Click General Templates in the New Presentation task pane.**

   To display the New Presentation tab, choose File⇨New. And to start PowerPoint if you haven't done so already, click the Start button and choose Programs⇨Microsoft PowerPoint.

2. **In the Templates dialog box that appears, click one of the following tabs and select a template:**

   - **General tab:** This tab contains a Blank Presentation template and the AutoContent Wizard template. A Blank Presentation means that you're working with a template of black text on a white background with no artistic design elements. You can either leave this template as is (a good option if you plan to print your presentation as black and white overhead transparencies) or embellish the template with your own colors and design elements.

- **Design Templates tab:** This tab contains 44 ready-to-go templates without content. The styles differ from those in the Presentation folder, and the designs are just gorgeous. Check out Ribbons and Romanesque.
- **Presentations tab:** This tab contains 24 content-inclusive templates, such as Communicating Bad News or Motivating a Team. Most of these templates use different colors and layouts. The content text provides suggested talking points for the template that you select. You can use the content or dump it by deleting the text on each slide and typing in your own information.

Click a template to check out a thumbnail sketch of it.

3. **Click OK to apply the template.**

   If you chose a template from the Design Templates tab, the Slide Layout task pane appears. If you chose a Presentation template, a multislide presentation of the type that you selected now appears in Normal view.

If PowerPoint presents you with the Slide Layout task pane, choose an AutoLayout for your first slide. To do so, double-click the slide that you want in the task pane.

AutoLayouts provide options for arranging information on your slide. One AutoLayout, for example, provides an area for typing title text at the top of the slide and another area for typing bulleted items of text below the title. Another AutoLayout provides an area for typing title text and an organization chart. You can choose among 27 AutoLayouts, including a blank AutoLayout that enables you to add whatever types of text or objects you want to the slide.

Applying a template to an existing presentation

You can easily change templates at any point while creating your presentation. But before you do so, you need to be aware of the following things:

- PowerPoint applies the template to all slides in the presentation. The program doesn't offer a mix-and-match approach, so you can't use one template for a few slides and another template for a few others.
- Applying a new template obliterates any modifications that you made to the Slide Master for the previously used template. Applying a new template copies the template's background colors, text formatting, decorations — everything — onto your Masters and all slides throughout the presentation.

✦ The application of the new template doesn't, however, affect changes that you made to the colors and formatting of non-Master items on individual slides. Any custom-tailoring of non-Master elements on individual slides (except background color) remains safe, as PowerPoint preserves such deviations regardless of changes in the Master. If you add a clip art to a particular slide, for example, the clip art is still there after you apply a new template.

To apply a template to an existing presentation, follow these steps:

1. **Click the Design button or choose Format⇨Slide Design.**

   The Slide Design task pane opens.

2. **If necessary, click Design Templates at the top of the Slide Design task pane to see the design templates.**

   Thumbnail images of templates appear in the task pane (see Figure 3-1).

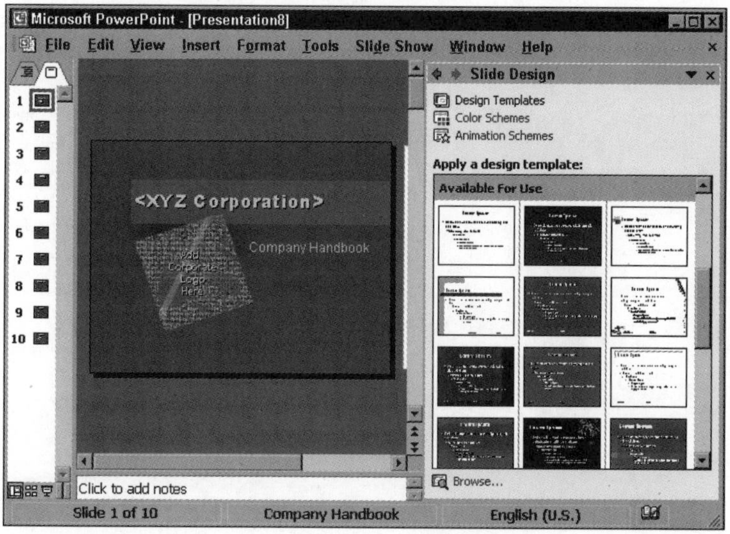

Figure 3-1: Choosing a template from the Slide Design task pane.

3. **Double-click a thumbnail to apply a template to your presentation.**

   Notice that the top of the task pane lists templates you recently used. What's more, you can click the last option, Addition Template Designs, to load more PowerPoint templates onto your computer.

   You now see the new template as PowerPoint applies it to your slides. If you want to tweak the template, see Chapter 4 for further details.

Chapter 4: Using and Abusing Masters

In This Chapter

- Editing the all-important Slide Master
- Editing Handout and Notes Masters
- Overriding the master style

In PowerPoint, a *master* controls the appearance of all the slides in your presentation. Three different types of master slide dictate your slide formats, the layout of the presentation's slides, the look of printed handouts, and the format of printed speaker notes. You can, however, override the formatting of objects for a particular slide. This chapter shows you how to live with masters but also how to defy their authority.

Editing the Slide Master

The *Slide Master* controls all aspects of how slides appear: background color; font, size, and color of the text; any decorations, borders, or logos; and the position of all elements on the slide. By formatting the Slide Master, you can ensure that all the slides in your presentation are consistent in look and style.

Every slide in a presentation uses the Slide Master format as a layout (unless you specify otherwise). Changing the Slide Master alters every slide in the presentation — adding a polka-dot border to the master, for example, adds a polka-dot border to each and every one of your slides.

The Slide Master contains text placeholders for these elements: a slide title, the main text of the slide, the date, the slide number, and the footer. You can format text as you please within these text placeholders, and your formats apply throughout. But specific text that you enter in a placeholder doesn't actually appear on your slides. Placeholder text appears only as an example of the formatting and placement of text on your slides.

To modify the Slide Master, follow these steps:

1. **Choose View➪Master➪Slide Master or press the Shift key and click the Normal View button to view the Slide Master (see Figure 4-1).**

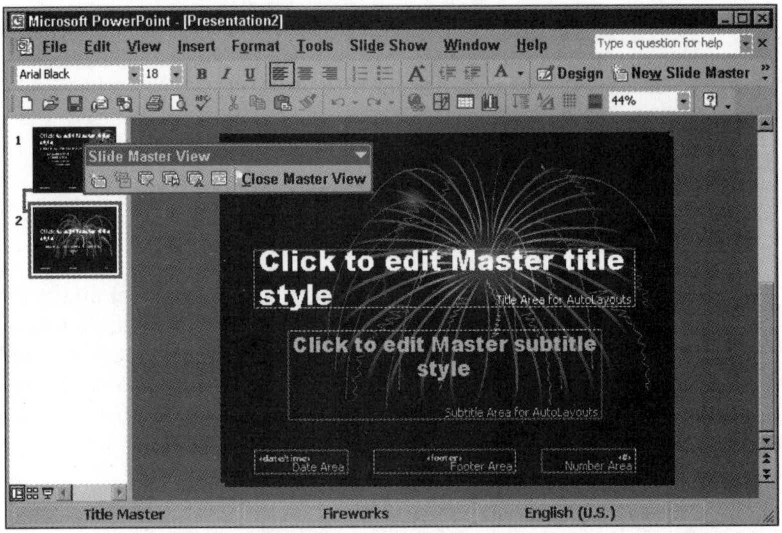

Figure 4-1: Change your Slide Master as you see fit.

2. **Edit the Slide Master as you like by clicking in the boxes and formatting the text and backgrounds.**

   PowerPoint applies text formatting changes to entire paragraphs in the master — just click anywhere within the paragraph, and your formatting changes apply to the whole shmear. This text formatting on the master applies to all paragraphs in the same position on slides throughout your presentation.

3. **Click the Close Master View button on the Slide Master View toolbar or click a View button to leave the Slide Master behind.**

Voilà! Your slides magically morph according to your changes on the Slide Master.

If the text boxes on your Slide Master are bumping into other master items (such as clip art), just click each text box and reposition it by dragging it to a new location. Another option is to resize a text box by selecting it and then adjusting one of the *handles* that mark the edges of the box. You know that you can select a handle when your regular cursor arrow converts to a small double-tipped arrow. After selecting a handle, the double-tipped arrow converts to a small cross (and stays that way) as you resize the box. Adjust the handle by clicking and dragging it to shrink or stretch the text box. To maintain the proportions of a text box, press and hold the Shift key during resizing. (By the way, resizing via the object handles applies not only to text boxes, but also to all other objects that you add to the master.)

Inserting headers and footers

A *footer* is a line of text that appears along the bottom of all the slides in a presentation. Typically, footers list company names or the names of presenters. A *header* does what a footer does, but it appears at the top of slides. You can enter headers only on notes and handouts.

As I discuss in the preceding section, you can enter footers on slides by using the Slide Master. PowerPoint also offers a special command for entering footers and headers — the Header and Footer command. You can also add headers and footers to slides, notes, and handout pages. To do so, follow these steps:

1. **From any view, choose View➪Header and Footer to open the Header and Footer dialog box (see Figure 4-2).**

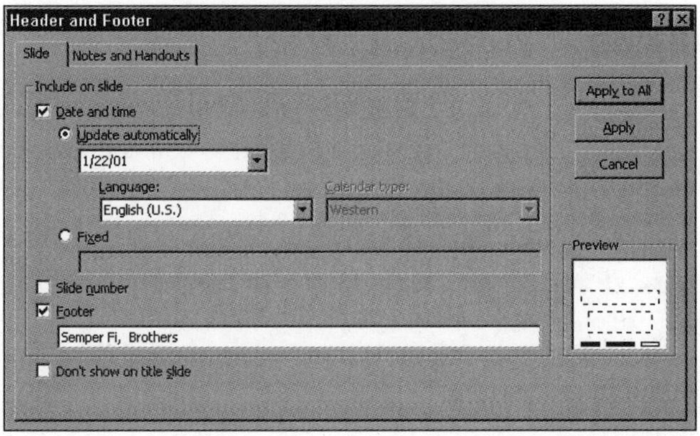

Figure 4-2: The Header and Footer dialog box.

2. **Click the Slide tab or the Notes and Handouts tab.**

   After working on one tab, you can click the remaining tab to work on it.

3. **Negotiate the following options:**

   - **Date and Time:** Displays the date and time. You can select Update Automatically or Fixed. If you choose the Fixed option, PowerPoint enters the date and time you type in the Fixed text box, regardless of what day you actually give the presentation.
   - **Slide Number (Slide tab only):** Displays the slide number.

   - **Page Number (Notes and Handouts only):** Displays the page number.
   - **Header (Notes and Handouts only):** Displays any recurring text that you want to place at the top of your notes and handouts.
   - **Footer:** Displays any other recurring text that you want to place on your slides or notes and handouts.

4. **Click the Apply to All button to make the changes take effect throughout your presentation.**

   On the Slide tab, you can click the Don't Show on Title Slide check box to keep headers, footers, and whatnot from appearing on the title slide — that is, slides that you introduce by using the Title Slide AutoLayout option. On the Slide tab, you can also click Apply (instead of Apply to All) to make the changes applicable to the current slide only. Chapter 2 describes how to enter slides with the AutoLayout option.

You can reposition headers and footers anywhere on the slides by switching to the Slide Master and dragging the placeholders to new locations. You can also edit the header and footer placeholders directly by displaying the master, clicking each placeholder, and typing in your information.

Picking master color schemes

PowerPoint offers flexible options for tinting your slides. You can fuss with minute details of coloring the masters, but setting PowerPoint up to serve as your personal designer is a whole lot easier. You can even choose a different color scheme for each master. To pick a color scheme, follow these steps:

1. **Choose View⇨Master⇨Slide Master or press the Shift key and click the Normal View button to view the Slide Master.**
2. **Click the Design button on the Formatting toolbar or choose Format⇨Slide Design.**

   The Slide Design task pane opens.
3. **Click Color Schemes hyperlink.**

   Color schemes appear in the task pane.
4. **Open the drop-down list of the scheme that you want and select Apply to All Masters.**

If none of the schemes tickle your fancy, click Edit Color Schemes, the hyperlink at the bottom of the task pane. Then construct a scheme of your own (see Chapter 2). After you finish, your scheme appears at the bottom of the task pane. Open its drop-down list and choose Apply to All Masters.

Shading background colors

You can change the shading of a slide's background color to obtain a richer feel than you achieve with ordinary brown or orange. To alter background shading, follow these steps:

1. **Choose Format⇨Background.**

   The Background dialog box appears.

2. **Click the down arrow in the box at the bottom of the Background Fill area and choose a background color from the drop-down list that appears (see Figure 4-3).**

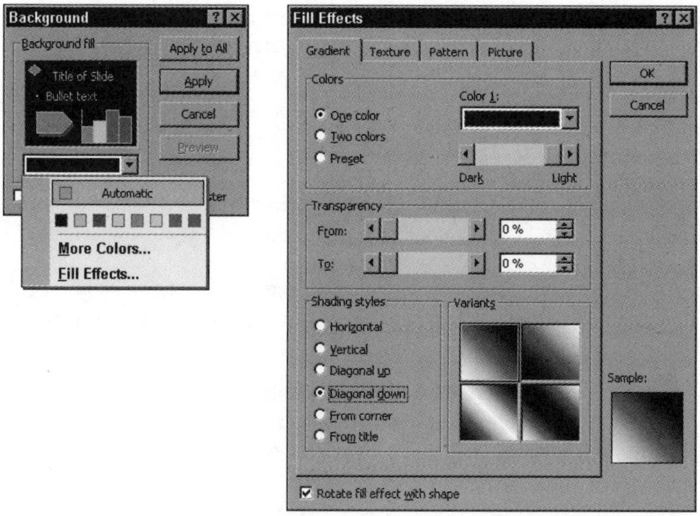

Figure 4-3: Choosing a background color for slides.

Which color you want depends on how much trouble you want to go through. The drop-down list gives you these options:

- **Simple color:** Select a color from the palette.
- **Richer color:** Select More Colors to open the Colors dialog box. Then click to choose just about any color imaginable.
- **Shading and textures:** Select Fill Effects to open the Fill Effects dialog box. From this box, you can choose a shading style, texture, pattern, or picture by clicking the appropriate tab. On the Texture tab, try out several of the textures as backgrounds — some of them are absolutely beautiful! Stay away from patterns on the Pattern tab, however, because they make text extremely hard to read. As for the Picture tab, which enables you to use pictures for backgrounds, use pictures only if they don't compete with the text that appears on top of the picture.

Deleting master components

Deleting an object on the Slide Master is a snap. To do so, follow these steps:

1. **View the Slide Master by choosing View⇨Master⇨Slide Master.**
2. **Select the object that you want to delete. To wipe out an entire text object, first click the text anywhere; then click the object frame.**
3. **Press the Backspace or Delete key, choose Edit⇨Cut, or click the Cut button on the Standard toolbar.**

You can't move or edit Slide Master elements from the slides themselves. You don't want to waste time trying to delete a theme picture on Slide #7 only to realize (after much frustration) that you can't grab the darn thing because it's not on the slide — it's on the Slide Master.

Editing the Handout Master

The Handout Master enables you to lay out the appearance of your presentation as a hard copy. You have the following options for your handouts:

- **The presentation outline:** Your handouts show only a collapsed outline of your presentation material. Instead of the text and headings, only the headings appear on the handout.
- **Small versions of the presentation slides:** This option shows the full text of your handouts in miniature. You can choose how many slide images appear on the printed page: 2, 3, 4, 6, or 9 slides per page.

You can also add placeholders on the Handout Master for the following items:

- **Headers and footers:** Headers go at the top of the handouts, and footers go at the bottom. You can click the placeholder for any header or footer to change the font, format, and content of the text within that placeholder.
- **Date or page number:** These fields automatically update.

To begin with, the Handout Master includes a place for the date, page numbers, a header, and a footer, but you can remove these elements by following these steps:

1. **From any view, Choose View⇨Master⇨Handout Master.**

   The Handout Master and the Handout Master View toolbar appear, as shown in Figure 4-4.

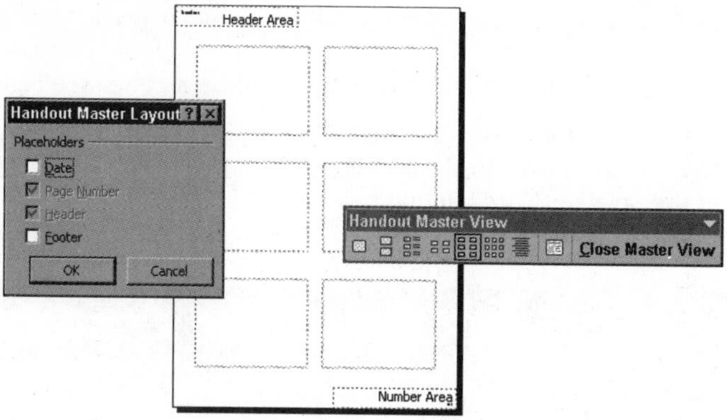

Figure 4-4: Handling the Handout Master.

2. **Choose which elements you want to appear on handouts.**

   PowerPoint offers the following ways to make your choices:

   - **Removing elements:** Click an element that you want to remove and then press the Delete key.

   - **Adding elements that you remove:** Click the Handout Master Layout button on the Handout Master View toolbar or choose Format➪Handout Master Layout. You see the Handout Master Layout dialog box (refer to Figure 4-4). Select elements that you want on your slides and click OK.

3. **On the Handout Master View toolbox, click a button to tell PowerPoint whether you want 2, 3, 4, 6, or 9 slides per page or the presentation outline appearing on the handouts.**

   The Handout Master generates dashed outlines showing where the slides or outline are to print.

   After you finish formatting the Handout Master, click any view button to return to your presentation. You may want to print and peruse your handouts by choosing File➪Print.

Editing the Notes Master

Notes pages are printed pages that you create to remind yourself what you want to say about each slide during your presentation. Notes pages are also known as *speaker notes,* and the speaker giving the PowerPoint presentation typically reads from speaker notes — they're not for distribution to the audience. After you write the notes, you can print them by choosing File➪Print and selecting Notes Pages from the Print What drop-down list in the Print dialog box. The notes appear under slide images in the printout.

You can add notes to a slide in the following two ways:

- **In Normal view:** Type the notes in the Notes pane (see Figure 4-5).
- **In Slide Sorter view:** Click the slide where you want to add notes, click the Speaker Notes button on the Slide Sorter toolbar, and type your text in the Speaker Notes dialog box.

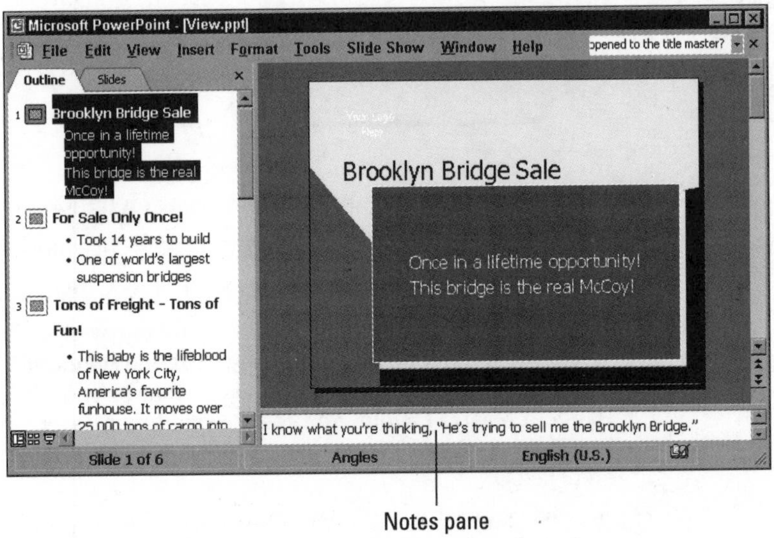

Figure 4-5: Writing a note to help with the presentation.

Overriding the Master Style on a Single Slide

You can disregard the master format for a particular slide. By doing so, you can modify individual slides as necessary without altering the rest of your presentation. The processes of adding and moving text and objects on an individual slide is the same as the process for altering the master slides.

Changing the text formatting

Suppose that you create nine slides that lead to a critical, culminating key point, and to ensure that every participant's brain captures and processes this super-important key point, you want to use bright-gold, italic, 60-point Impact font — but just on this one slide. Use the following steps to make changes to the master style of text on one particular slide:

1. **Select the slide in Normal view.**
2. **Click the text box and, when you see the selection handles that frame the box in which the text is found, select (highlight) the text that you want to edit.**
3. **Use the Formatting toolbar to make your changes.**

   Click, for example, the Bold button or the Center button.

Changing the background color

If you want to change the background color on a single slide, follow these steps:

1. **In any view, select the slide on which you want to use a different background.**
2. **Choose Format⇨Background.**

   The Background dialog box appears.
3. **Click the Background Fill drop-down arrow to reveal a list that you can use for changing the background color of slides.**
4. **Click to select a color from the palette.**
5. **Click the Apply button to make the changes on the current slide.**

Do *not* click the Apply to All button, or the changes affect every slide in your presentation. (Clicking the Apply to All button at this stage, however, is a convenient way of editing the Slide Master without opening up the master itself.)

Chapter 5: Adding Text to Your Presentation

In This Chapter

- **Getting to know text boxes**
- **Aligning and indenting text**
- **Finding and replacing text**
- **Spell-checking your text**

Unless you're planning a 100-percent visual presentation without text, you opened the right chapter. The written word is necessary to convey things that pretty pictures can't express. In this chapter, you discover how to add text to your presentation in creative and meaningful ways. And if you happen to err while adding your text, PowerPoint also offers ways to help you correct your mistakes.

Introducing Text Boxes

All slides, except the blank AutoLayout option, appear with at least one *text box* (a zone for adding text).

INTEGRATION

You can manipulate your text in PowerPoint in the same ways that you do in a word-processing program such as Office. (You can check out Book 2 for extra help.)

Adding text boxes

You can add as many text boxes to a slide as you like. You can format and move each text box independently from all the other text boxes. To add a text box, follow these steps:

1. **In Normal view, click the Text Box button on the Drawing toolbar or choose Insert⇨Text Box.**
2. **Point the I-beam cursor to the position on your slide where you want the upper-left corner of your new text box.**

3. **Click and hold the mouse button as you drag the cursor to position the lower-right corner of your new text box.**

   The cursor appears as a crosshair during the positioning, and you see solid edges appear as the borders of the box.

4. **Release the mouse button after you give the text box the proportions that you want.**

The new text box is now complete. Click inside the box to type text or click the edge of the box to format how text appears inside the box. What's the green dot above the text box for? Click and drag it to rotate or tilt a text box and the text inside it.

Selecting text boxes to modify

Before you can modify a text box (such as moving or resizing it), you must identify for PowerPoint which text box you want to work on. To select a text box, follow these steps:

1. **In Normal view, click the Select Objects button on the Drawing toolbar.**

2. **Point the arrow anywhere along the border of the text box that you want to edit; then click the left mouse button.**

   The text box suddenly sprouts *handles* — dots marking the corners and sides of the box (see Figure 5-1) — as well as the green rotation handle. The appearance of handles indicates that the text box is selected.

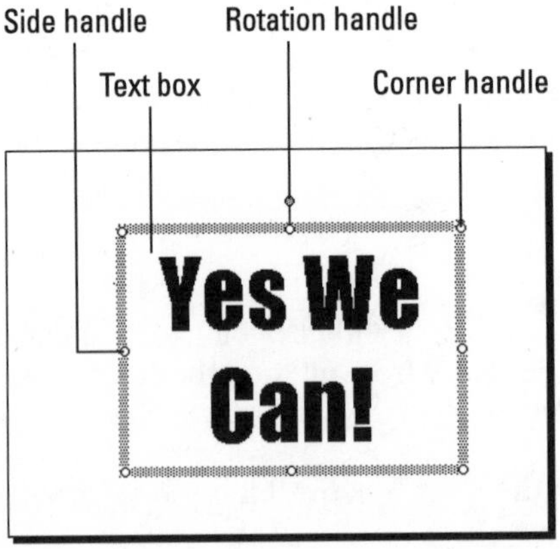

Figure 5-1: A selected text box, ready for modification.

Resizing, moving, and rotating text boxes

After you select a text box, you're free to resize and move the box as you want. Go wild! Follow these simple guidelines along the way:

✦ **To move a text box:** Click and hold the mouse button anywhere along the edge of the text box — except on a handle! Drag the box anywhere on the slide and release the mouse button.

✦ **To change the size of a text box while keeping the original proportions:** As you hold down the Shift key, click and hold the mouse button on any of the corner handles, drag the handle to enlarge or shrink the text box, and then release the mouse button. To keep the center of the box positioned in the same spot during resizing, press the Ctrl key while dragging a sizing handle.

✦ **To change the proportions of a text box:** Click and hold the mouse button on any of the side handles. Drag the top or bottom handle to increase or decrease the text box's height; drag the left or right handle to adjust the width.

✦ **To rotate a text box:** Move the pointer over the green circle, click, and start dragging.

Moving around and typing inside a text box

You type and edit text in a PowerPoint text box in virtually the same way that you use a word processor. But first you must tell PowerPoint that you want to manipulate the text. To do so, follow these steps:

1. **Click the Select Objects button on the Drawing toolbar.**

   If you don't see the Drawing toolbar, right-click any toolbar and choose Drawing on the shortcut menu.

2. **Click inside the text box that contains the text that you want to modify.**

   A thick border appears around the text box and the pointer changes to an I-beam inside the text box — all of which indicate that you can now start typing.

You need to know the following tips about typing and editing in a text box:

✦ As you reach the end of a line, keep typing — PowerPoint automatically moves to the next line. You press Enter only if you want to begin a new paragraph.

✦ If you attempt to type more text than can fit in your text box, PowerPoint automatically adjusts the point size of the text to fit the box.

✦ Use the ↑, ↓, ←, and → keys on your keyboard to move the cursor up or down one line or left or right one character.

✦ Move the mouse until you position the little I-beam where you want to make an edit and then click the left mouse button. The I-beam cursor instantly repositions itself to your chosen destination.

✦ To delete text, highlight the text that you want to delete and then press the Backspace key or the Delete key to delete the text.

Aligning Paragraphs of Text

Adjust the way that your text lines up by selecting an entire text box or selecting only specific lines of text within a text box. Then choose Format⇨Alignment and a command on the Alignment submenu to align your selected text. PowerPoint provides you with several ways to align text on your slides, as follows:

✦ **Center:** Clicking the Center button centers the text in the text box. (You can also press Ctrl+E to center text.)

✦ **Align Left:** Click the Align Left button to left-align bulleted text and short sentences and line up text neatly against the left edge of the text box. (You can also press Ctrl+L to left-align text.)

✦ **Align Right:** Click the Align Right button for something different. Clicking that button lines up text neatly down the right side of the text box. (You can also press Ctrl+R to right-align text.)

Finding and Replacing Text

The Find and Replace commands are helpful whenever you need to change one piece of text that appears several times throughout your slides — for example, the date on a series of slides from a long-ago presentation that you want to reuse. To find and replace text, follow these steps:

1. **Choose Edit⇨Find (or press Ctrl+F) to open the Find dialog box (see Figure 5-2).**
2. **In the Find What text box, type the text that you want to locate.**

   If you're looking for an exact match of capital and lowercase letters, click the Match Case check box. If you want to locate only whole words — not pieces of larger words (such as the *cat* in catalog) — click the Find Whole Words Only check box.
3. **Click the Find Next button to start the search.**

   If your chosen text resides anywhere among your slides, the Find command moves to the first slide containing that text. It also highlights the text that if finds so that you can then edit it or continue searching for the next occurrence.

   You're finished if all you want to do is find text. But if you want to replace text, you can do that as well from the Find dialog box.
4. **If you want to replace your found text with something else, click the Replace button.**

   A Replace dialog box appears (see Figure 5-2).

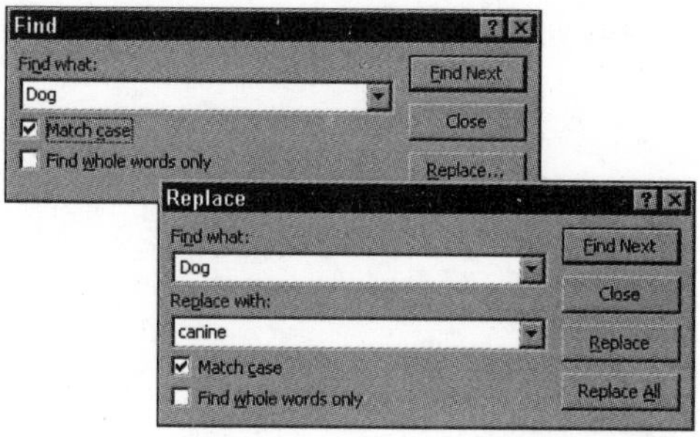

Figure 5-2: The Find dialog box and the Replace dialog box.

5. **In the Replace With text box, type your replacement text.**
6. **Click the Replace button to replace just the current instance of your found text or click Replace All to replace every instance of your found text.**

   If you click the Replace button, PowerPoint scrolls to the next instance of the text you're looking for so that you can replace or bypass it.

   Be careful about clicking the Replace All button. Doing so replaces text throughout your slide presentation and you don't get the chance to see what is being replaced. Clicking the Replace All button sometimes introduces errors in a presentation.
7. **After you're done finding (or replacing) text, click Close to close the Find dialog box.**

If you already know that you want to replace all instances of a given word — for example, substituting next year's date for this year's date — use the Replace command instead of the Find command. To do so, choose Edit⇨Replace to open the Replace dialog box from the start.

Spell Checking

Correct spelling is vital in communicating to your audience. If you're going to go through the effort of creating crisp, professional slides, you may as well ensure that you spell your text correctly. Besides, nothing's more embarrassing than misspelling a word and displaying your error to a roomful of watchful colleagues.

After typing all your text, you can open the spell-checker to look for spelling mistakes throughout the document by following these steps:

1. **Choose Tools⇨Spelling or click the Spelling button on the Standard toolbar.**

   If PowerPoint finds an error, the program shows the faulty slide and highlights the potentially misspelled word. PowerPoint also recommends possible corrections for your error (see Figure 5-3).

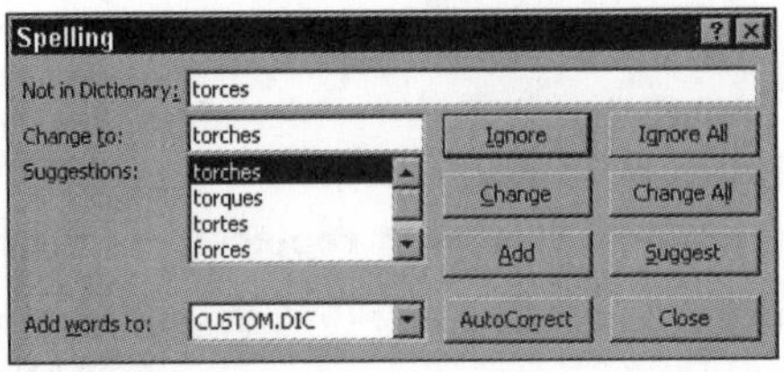

Figure 5-3: PowerPoint tries its best to help correct your misspellings.

2. **Accept one of PowerPoint's corrections and click the Change button, click Ignore to leave the word as it is, or type your own correction in the Change To text box.**

   If PowerPoint red-flags a word that you know is spelled correctly, click Ignore All to make PowerPoint ignore that word throughout the presentation.

   If you know that you misspelled a certain word throughout the presentation, click the Change All button and correct all instances of your error in one fell swoop.

   For any red-flagged misspelled word, you can type your own correction in the Change To text box and click the Change button. This option is useful if none of the changes that PowerPoint suggests are correct spellings for your word.

3. **Repeat Steps 1 and 2 until PowerPoint informs you that the spelling check is complete.**

INTEGRATION

PowerPoint, as does Word, can perform a spell check on the fly. You can actually see misspellings before your very eyes — a red wavy line appears under misspellings. Make sure that you check out the spell check on-the-fly function in Book 2.

Chapter 6: Making Your Text Look Presentable

In This Chapter

- **Formatting text with color, fonts, and more**
- **Making a numbered list**
- **Making a bulleted list**

So you add text to a presentation and still nobody bothers to read it? You may have forgotten that people, if they must read, like to read text that *looks* good. Fortunately, PowerPoint enables you to easily surpass the talents of 17th-century typesetters who did this stuff the hard way! You can jazz up your text in no time.

Formatting Text

FAST TRACK

The fastest way to format text for an entire presentation is to format text in the text boxes that you find on the Slide Master. Text on all slides in the presentation follows this formatting, eliminating the need for you to format text on a slide-by-slide basis. You can reformat individual text boxes on any slide as necessary, overriding the formatting that the masters prescribe for them.

Changing the overall look of text

To adjust how your text looks (the formatting), select the text and then choose one of the following methods:

- Open the Font dialog box (see Figure 6-1), which offers one-stop shopping for any and all formatting features, by choosing Format➪Font or by right-clicking the text and choosing Font from the shortcut menu.
- Click a button on the Formatting toolbar to change a single formatting feature. The Formatting toolbar offers buttons for boldfacing, italicizing, underlining, shading, and aligning text.

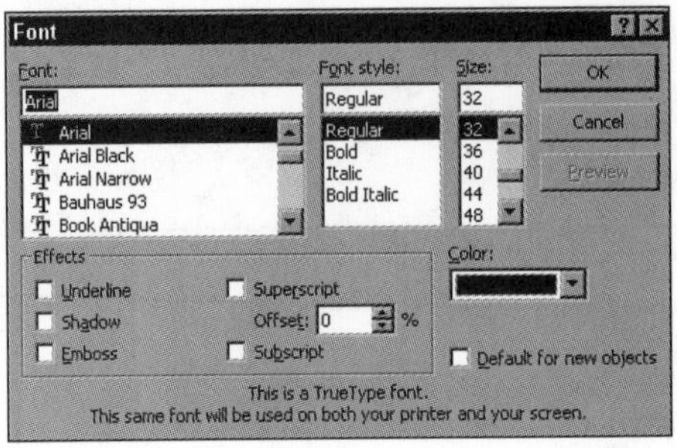

Figure 6-1: The Font dialog box can help your text look better.

✦ Use a keyboard shortcut to change a formatting feature (see Table 6-1).

Table 6-1	**Keyboard Shortcuts for Formatting**
Keyboard Shortcut	***Format or Function***
Ctrl+B	Makes text **Bold.**
Ctrl+I	Makes text *Italic.*
Ctrl+U	Makes text Underlined.
Ctrl+spacebar	Makes text normal (removes the formatting). Ctrl+spacebar clears font attributes, such as bold and underline, but it doesn't reset the font or point size of your text.
Ctrl+Shift+P	Highlights the current point size in the Font Size list box on the Standard toolbar. Typing a new number and pressing Enter changes the size of the currently selected text.
Ctrl+Shift+>	Increases point size.
Ctrl+Shift+<	Decreases point size.

To reset the point size of selected text, click the Font Size area on the Formatting toolbar and type a new point size in the text box. You can also click the Font Size drop-down arrow to reveal a list of point-size choices.

The fastest way to change the point size of text is to select the text and click the Increase Font Size or Decrease Font Size button on the Standard toolbar until your text is just right.

Changing capitalization for blocks of text

To quickly change the capitalization of text — a single character or a block of text — follow these steps:

1. **Highlight the text that you want to capitalize.**

2. **Choose Format⇨Change Case to open the Change Case dialog box (see Figure 6-2).**

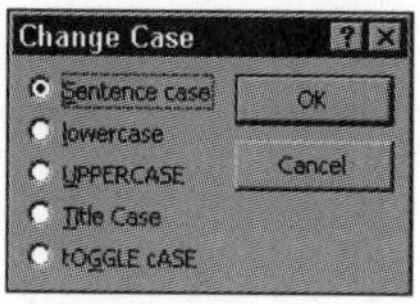

Figure 6-2: The Change Case dialog box.

3. **Select a capitalization option in the Change Case dialog box and click OK.**

   - **Sentence case:** Capitalizes the first letter of the first word in each sentence. Changes all other text to lowercase.
   - **lowercase:** Changes all text to lowercase.
   - **UPPERCASE:** Changes all text to uppercase.
   - **Title Case:** Capitalizes the first letter of each word except for articles, such as *a* and *the.*
   - **tOGGLE cASE:** Changes uppercase letters are to lowercase and vice versa. The toggle case option comes in handy if you discover that you've been typing away with the Caps Lock key on.

The fastest way to change the case of letters is to select them and keep pressing Shift+F3 until the letters appear in the case that you want.

Color

To change the color of highlighted text, click the drop-down arrow next to the Font Color button and select a color from the palette. You find the Font Color button on the Drawing and Formatting toolbars.

If the font colors that appear on the palette don't suffice, click More Font Colors for even more color choices. If these colors don't meet your needs either, click the Custom tab and create the perfect shade that you're searching for by clicking the appropriate portion of the spectrum of Colors and clicking OK.

Font

To change the font of highlighted text, click the drop-down arrow next to the Font text box on the Formatting toolbar and choose a font from the list that appears. You can also select a new font in the Font dialog box by choosing Format⇨Font. Remember to first select the text that you want to change or to select the text box the contains the text.

PowerPoint places the fonts that you use most frequently at the beginning of the font list so that you don't waste time scrolling through the list.

Shadows

Shadowing text adds a touch of class to your slides. It may also improve readability for some slides by making text characters stand out against their PowerPoint background. You can apply a shadow to selected text by clicking the Shadow button on the Formatting toolbar.

Size

To change the size of highlighted text, click the drop-down arrow next to the Font Size box on the Formatting toolbar; then click a preset point size (sizes range from 8 points to 96 points). You can also click the Font Size text box and type the point size that you want.

Numbering Lists

PowerPoint offers a quick and easy way to number items in a list, to change numbering styles from Arabic to Roman numbers, and to change numbers to a lettered outline. To number a list, follow these steps:

1. **Highlight the lines or paragraphs of text that you want to number.**

   You must separate text items with paragraph returns to give them separate numbers.

2. **Click the Numbering button on the Formatting toolbar.**

   The Numbering button toggles so that clicking it again removes numbering from the text.

To select the type of numbering that you want, choose Format⇨Bullets and Numbering to open the Bullets and Numbering dialog box (see Figure 6-3). In the Bullets and Numbering dialog box, click the Numbered tab and choose the size and color of your numbers, as well as the starting number, if necessary. (Clicking None removes numbering from the selected text.)

Numbered lists automatically renumber if you change the order of items in the list.

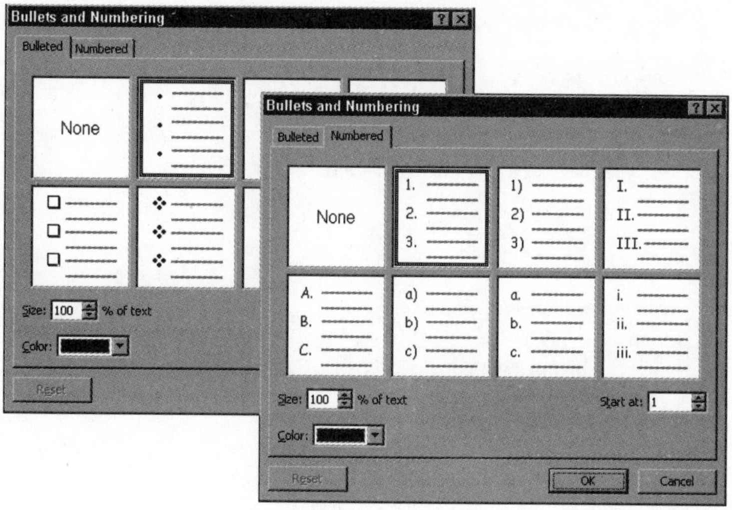

Figure 6-3: Bulleting lists (left) and numbering lists (right).

Bulleting Text

A bullet marks the start of a line to indicate a new text item. Bullets come in many styles, including spots, check marks, and arrows. To create a bulleted list, follow these steps:

1. **Select the lines or paragraphs of text that you want to bullet.**

   You must separate each bullet with a paragraph return. If you want a bulleted list of three text items, for example, make sure that you separate those three items with paragraph returns.

2. **Click the Bullets button on the Standard toolbar.**

   The Bullets button operates like an on/off switch (a toggle). Repeat the preceding steps to remove the bullets.

If you don't like the style of the bullets that appear on-screen, choose Format⇨Bullets and Numbering to open the Bullets and Numbering dialog box (refer to Figure 6-3). In the Bullets and Numbering dialog box, you can select a default bullet character and adjust its font, size, and color. (Clicking None "unbullets" the bulleted text.)

TIP

For fancy bullets, click the Picture button in the Bullets and Numbering dialog box and select a Web-style picture bullet in the Picture Bullet dialog box that appears.

Chapter 7: Getting Visual

In This Chapter

- Getting to know the Drawing toolbar
- Making all sorts of lines
- Adding WordArt
- Using clip art

You work long hours on your new presentation. The lights go out, and your slide presentation begins. Ten minutes into your presentation, however, you notice that the lights aren't the only things that are extinguished. Your audience is also out — lost who knows where and obviously not absorbing anything from your presentation. You may have the neatest looking text in town (see Chapter 6), but sometimes you must take further measures to keep your audience alert.

In this chapter, you find out about the basics of improving your presentation with some graphic elements. You don't necessarily need to replace your text; you simply need to complement it so that your message stands out even better.

About the Drawing Toolbar

Each button or menu on the Drawing toolbar offers a unique tool to assist you in creating something Picasso-esque.

You can use the Drawing toolbar in Normal view only. You access the Drawing toolbar by choosing View⇨Toolbars⇨Drawing or by right-clicking a toolbar and choosing Drawing from the shortcut menu. You can use the buttons in Table 7-1 to create your drawings.

Table 7-1 Drawing Toolbar Buttons

Button	*Name*
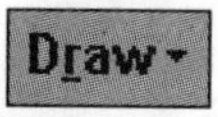	Draw menu button
	Select Objects button

(continued)

Table 7-1 *(continued)*

Button	***Name***
	AutoShapes menu button
	Line button
	Arrow button
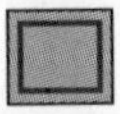	Rectangle button
	Oval button
	Text box button
	Insert WordArt button
	Insert Diagram or Organizational Chart
	Insert Clip Art button
	Insert Picture
	Fill Color button
	Line Color button
	Font Color button
	Line Style button
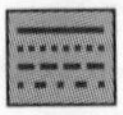	Dash Style button
	Arrow Style button
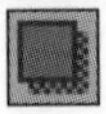	Shadow Style button
	3-D Style button

Drawing Lines

PowerPoint enables you to make your mark by using a variety of line styles. The following sections explain how to use each of the different styles.

Straight lines

To draw a straight line, follow these steps:

1. **Click the Line button on the Drawing toolbar or choose AutoShapes⇨Lines and then click the Line button on the submenu.**
2. **Click and hold the mouse at the point where you want the line to start.**
3. **Drag the mouse to create a line of the desired length and position and release the mouse after you reach the point where you want the line to end.**

Curved lines

To draw a curved line, follow these steps:

1. **On the Drawing toolbar, choose AutoShapes⇨Lines and then click the Curve button (the one that resembles an *S*) on the submenu.**
2. **Click the point in your slide where you want the curve to start; then start drawing.**
3. **Click each time that you want to create a turn or bend in your line. (You can add as many turns as you want.)**
4. **Double-click to end the line.**

Freehand lines

To draw a freehand (squiggly) line, follow these steps:

1. **On the Drawing toolbar, choose AutoShapes⇨Lines and then click the Scribble button on the submenu.**
2. **Click and drag the mouse to create your line.**
3. **Release the mouse button to end the line.**

Changing line style

After you draw a line, you can change its style — making it thin or thick, solid or dashed, and with or without arrows. To set line style, click the line that you want to change. Then click one of the following buttons on the Drawing toolbar:

✦ **Line Style button:** After you click the Line Style button on the drawing toolbar, a line-style menu appears. You can choose a new thickness or click the More Lines command, which provides you with millions of other choices in a dialog box.

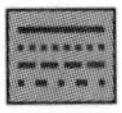

✦ **Dash Style button:** Choose a new dash style if you want to use something other than a solid line. Clicking the Dash Style button on the Drawing toolbar opens a menu that enables you to select whether your line appear as a series of dots, short dashes, long dashes, or dots alternating with dashes (sort of like Morse code).

✦ **Arrow Style button:** Choose arrows as end points for your line. Click the Arrow Style button on the Drawing toolbar to open a menu. Click the More Arrows command on the menu for additional arrow options.

Drawing by Using AutoShapes

The PowerPoint AutoShapes menu on the Drawing toolbar enables you to choose predrawn line styles and common shapes, such as hexagons, banners, moons, and flowchart arrows. To draw by using AutoShapes, follow these steps:

1. **Click the AutoShapes button on the Drawing toolbar.**

   A shopping mall of shape selections appears (see Figure 7-1).

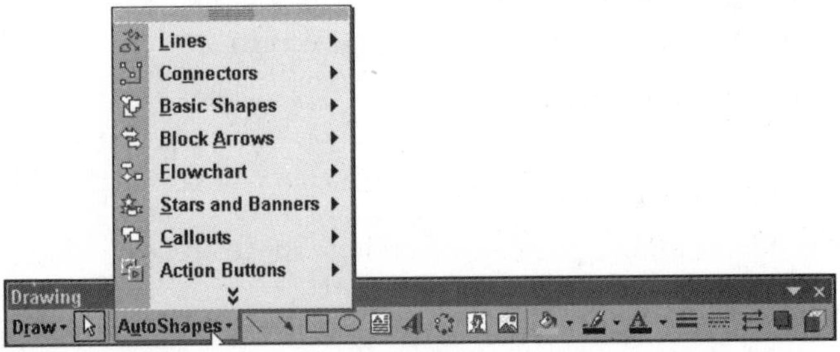

Figure 7-1: The AutoShapes menu.

2. **Select the AutoShapes menu that you want, as the following list describes:**

   - **Lines:** Every type of line from straight to swervy.
   - **Connectors:** Line segments with strangely shaped end points. You commonly use such lines for drawing road maps and electrical circuits.

- **Basic Shapes:** Hearts, moons, and parallelograms. Get yer Lucky Charms here, laddy!
- **Block Arrows:** Shapes that you can use to indicate directions such as north, south, and U-turn.
- **Flowchart:** Directional signs that track the flow of money from the wallets of your consumers into the profit pool of your company and out to the wallets of your shareholders.
- **Stars and Banners:** Symbols for patriots and American history teachers.
- **Callouts:** Bubble captions like the kind you see in cartoons. You can type text inside these shapes; the text may describe an image that the shape is pointing to or represents what the image is saying or thinking.
- **Action Buttons:** Navigation icons for slide-show and Web-based presentations. Some of these little guys resemble buttons on your VCR.
- **More AutoShapes:** This choice opens the Insert Clip Art task pane, where you can obtain additional AutoShapes.

3. **Click a shape on a submenu.**
4. **Create your chosen shape by clicking your slide and dragging the mouse until your AutoShape reaches the size you want it to be.**

   TIP

   To maintain the same height-to-width proportions as you resize an AutoShapes clip, press and hold the Shift key as you drag the mouse.
5. **Release the mouse button to finish creating your AutoShape.**

TIP

Yellow diamonds appear on some AutoShapes after you create them. By dragging a yellow diamond, you can subtly change an AutoShape. You can alter its interior and exterior lines and create something new and interesting.

Adding WordArt

WordArt is a nifty feature that enables you to place fancy, three-dimensional, shadowed text on your slides. You can even give the text a perspective quality, as if you're standing at the *H* looking toward the rest of the letters in the HOLLYWOOD sign.

WARNING!

Because WordArt images don't function as normal text, they don't appear on the Outline tab in Normal view. What's more, you can't spell-check them.

To add a WordArt clip to a slide, follow these steps:

1. **On the Drawing toolbar, click the WordArt button or choose Insert➪Picture➪WordArt.**

   The WordArt Gallery dialog box appears, as shown in Figure 7-2.

Figure 7-2: Creating a WordArt image.

2. **Click the thumbnail representing the WordArt style that you want to use and click OK.**

   The Edit WordArt Text dialog box appears (see Figure 7-2).

3. **In the Edit WordArt Text dialog box, type your text.**

4. **Select a font in the Font drop-down list and point size in the Size drop-down list and choose Bold or Italic formatting options if you want.**

5. **Click OK.**

   PowerPoint places the WordArt text on your slide.

TIP

To edit your WordArt, use the tools on the WordArt toolbar.

About Clips

PowerPoint refers to multimedia goodies — things that you put on your slides other than text — as multimedia clips or just *clips.* Clips can include simple drawings, graphic images (clip art and photos), sounds, or movies — all of which serve to enhance the content and quality of your presentation.

Using clips from the Clip Organizer

The Clip Organizer is a valuable resource, with thousands of free, high-quality pictures, sounds, and movies. It's neatly organized into categories such as Animals, Business, Maps, Photographs, and Transportation, and it provides a helpful little thumbnail sketch of each clip. You can also use the Clip Organizer to look for specific clips. To add a clip from the Clip Oraganizer, follow these steps:

1. **Go to the slide where you want to add a clip (and if you want your clip to appear on all your slides, go to the Slide Master by choosing View➪Master➪Slide Master).**

2. **Click the Insert Clip Art button on the Drawing toolbar or choose Insert➪Picture➪Clip Art.**

   The Insert Clip Art task pane appears.

3. **Tell PowerPoint how and where to grab the clip-art image by selecting or using the following options:**
   - **Search Text text box:** Type a word in this text box that describes what kind of clip art you want.
   - **Search In drop-down list:** Choose an option from the drop-down list to explain where you want to search for clips. Leave the check mark in the Everywhere check box and you search, well, everywhere. Click the My Collections check box to search collections you assembled yourself in the Microsoft Clip Organizer (how to assemble clips there is not covered in this book); search Office Collections to search for clips you loaded on your computer when you installed Office; search Web Collections to search the Design Gallery Live, a Web site on the Internet (you must be connected to the Internet to take advantage of this search option).
   - **Results Should Be drop-down list:** Choose an option from the drop-down list to describe what kind of clips you need. Select the All Media Types check box to obtain clip art, photographs, movies, and sound clips. By selecting a single check box — Clip Art, Photographs, Movies, or Sounds — you can search for a specific kind of clip.

4. **Click the Search button.**

   If PowerPoint can find clip-art images, they appear in thumbnail form in the Insert Clip Art task pane, as shown in Figure 7-3.

5. **Click an image to insert it in your presentation.**

PowerPoint places the clip in the middle of your slide. You may need to move it to a more favorable position. To do so, just click and drag it to your chosen destination. You may also need to resize the image.

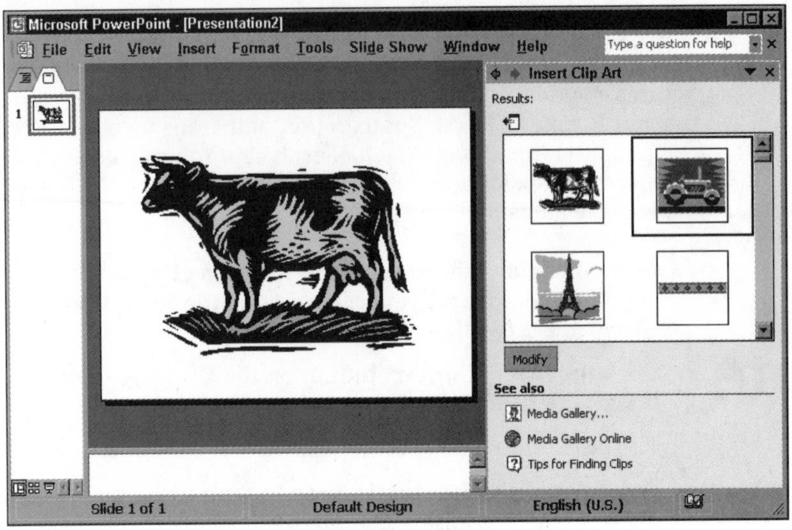

Figure 7-3: Putting a clip-art image in a presentation.

Lining up clips with guides

PowerPoint provides a set of horizontal and vertical *crosshairs* that aid you in lining up clips on your slides. These guides serve the same helpful purpose as grid lines on a sheet of graph paper. When you drag a clip close to a guide, the clip automatically aligns its edge to fit snuggly against the guide. When you drag a clip close to the intersection of two guides, the clip automatically aligns its center at the guides' point of intersection.

Starting in Normal view, choose View⇨Grid and Guides. The Grid and Guides dialog box appears (see Figure 7-4). From there, you can choose among the following options for handling the grid:

- ✦ **Snap Objects to Grid:** Aligns clips with the gridlines automatically.
- ✦ **Snap Objects to Other Objects:** Aligns clips horizontally and vertically with the edges of other objects.
- ✦ **Grid Settings:** Enables you to choose how tight or loose to make the grid.
- ✦ **Display Grid On Screen:** Displays gridlines on-screen.
- ✦ **Display Drawing Guides on Screen:** Places guides — dotted lines — that you can move on-screen as you align clips.

You can place a new drawing guide on-screen by clicking an existing guide, pressing Ctrl, and dragging the new guide away. You can delete a guide by dragging it toward the edge of the slide: After it reaches the edge, it vanishes.

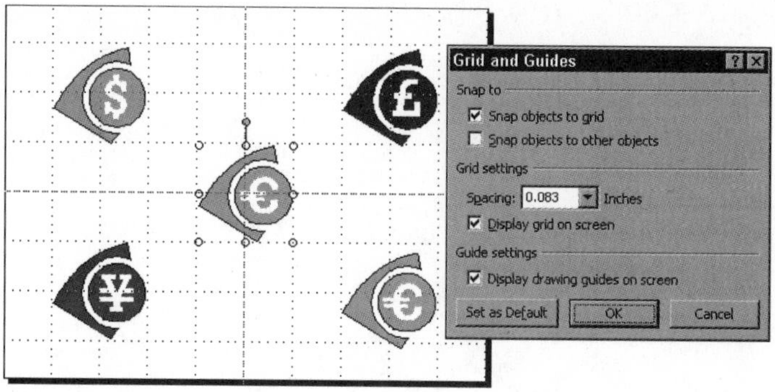

Figure 7-4: Gridlines make aligning clips on your slides easier.

Moving and resizing clips

PowerPoint adds clips to your slides the same way that the cafeteria worker adds food to your tray in the buffet line: It glops the clip down smack dab in the middle. You may want to move your clip to a more appetizing location, as well as stretch or shrink it to fit nicely on your slide.

After you insert a clip, it appears on-screen as a selected clip — with resizing handles surrounding it like a picture frame. If you click outside the clip, the handles vanish. Click the clip to make handles reappear. Handles must remain visible for you to move and resize your clip. Follow these instructions to handle clip art images:

- **Move the clip:** Click it and drag it to a new spot.
- **Enlarge the clip:** Click a corner handle and drag the handle outward from the clip.
- **Shrink the clip:** Click a corner handle and drag the handle in toward the clip.
- **Make the clip taller or shorter without changing the width:** Click a top or bottom center handle and drag the handle up or down.
- **Make the clip wider or narrower without changing the height:** Click a left or right center handle and drag the handle horizontally.

Chapter 8: Manipulating Your Multimedia

In This Chapter

- Getting to know multimedia possibilities
- Adding images to your presentation
- Adding sounds to your presentation

Multimedia is a magic word. Tell someone that your presentation incorporates multimedia elements and you perk up some interest. (Tell the same person that your presentation involves reading black text on a white background and notice the difference in reactions.) Text and pictures are fine, sure, but sounds and movies are the icing on the cake. Perhaps your lecture on New Zealand cinema can include a few film clips. Or maybe your outlining of the new Human Resources policies at the next staff meeting can feature sounds of employees cheering and clapping.

You don't want to overdo it, but just a little effort with multimedia can place you in the ranks of the great high-tech presenters.

Adding Movies and Motion Clips

PowerPoint enables you to add small movies to slides in your presentation. You can also include a special kind of animated movie known as a *motion clip* in a presentation.

You can choose to add a movie from other files that are available on your hard drive, on disk, or on other removable media. You can make a movie play automatically during a slide show or only after you click the movie on the slide where it resides.

Adding a motion clip from the Clip Organizer

To add a motion clip from the Clip Organizer to your slide, follow these steps:

1. **In Normal view, move to the slide where you want to add a motion clip.**

2. **Choose Insert⇨Movies and Sounds⇨Movie from Clip Organizer from the PowerPoint menu bar.**

   The Insert Clip Art task pane opens, but instead of clip-art images, the task pane offers movies and movie clips.

3. **Scroll through the gallery and find a clip that interests you.**

4. **Click the down arrow to open the clip's drop-down list and select Preview/Properties.**

   The Preview Properties dialog box appears (see Figure 8-1). In this dialog box, you can click the Play button to see what the movie clip looks like in your presentation. Click the Next or Previous button to preview the previous or next clip in the Insert Clip Art task pane. Click the Close button after you finish examining a clip.

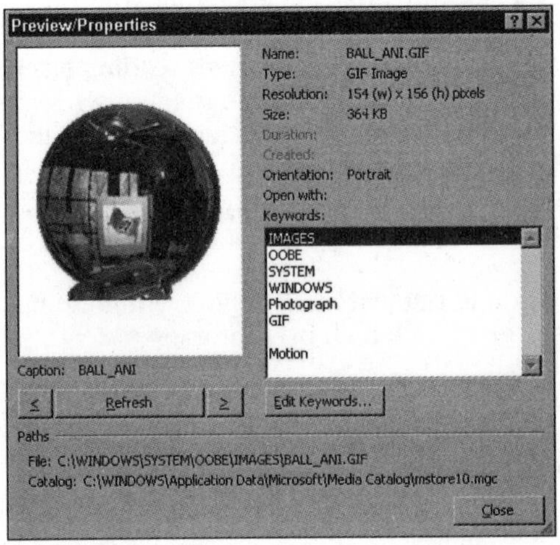

Figure 8-1: Previewing a movie clip.

5. **Click the clip that you want to place it on your slide.**

   PowerPoint inserts the motion clip right in the middle of your slide.

6. **(Optional) Resize the motion clip and reposition it by dragging it to a new location.**

   Because people can both hear *and* see a motion clip, you need to give it some room to physically reside on your slide. Be aware that you may need to rearrange slide elements — text boxes, clip art, and other objects — to accommodate a motion clip that you add to a slide.

Whenever it's not playing, the motion clip shows only the first frame as a placeholder on the slide where you locate it. In this sense, the motion clip appears similar to other graphic elements on a slide. Start the slide show and move to the motion clip-embellished slide to see how the motion clip appears while it's playing.

Adding a movie from a file

So you can't find what you want from the Clip Organizer? No need to despair. The following steps show you how to add a movie from a file to your slide:

1. **In Normal view, select the slide that needs a movie.**
2. **Choose Insert➪Movies and Sounds➪Movie from File from the PowerPoint menu bar.**

   The Insert Movie dialog box appears.
3. **Find and click the movie that you want to add and click OK.**

   PowerPoint inserts the movie right in the middle of your slide. PowerPoint then asks whether you want the movie to play automatically in the slide show.
4. **Click Yes to make the movie play automatically on the slide or click No to play the movie only after you click it.**
5. **(Optional) Resize the movie and reposition it by dragging it to a new location.**

   Be careful about enlarging movies. If you enlarge a movie too much, it can look blurred or jaggy when you or someone else plays it.

REMEMBER

Whenever it's not playing, the movie shows only the first frame as a placeholder on the slide where you locate it.

Playing a movie

You can play many movies in Normal view or Slide Show view by double-clicking them. Motion clips that you add to a slide from the Insert Clip Art task pane, however, you can't play in Normal view. If you're running the slide-show presentation, just single-click the movie to play it. If you choose to have the movie play automatically, it begins playing after you reach the slide where it resides.

REAL WORLD

Add sound and motion with caution

A movie clip takes up tons of memory and can really drag down the performance of your computer. File sizes are typically 1MB or more, even for a teensy-weensy movie snippet. Sound files also take up a fair amount of disk space. Each second of sound can occupy 10K or more — a small enough space to make use of sound but not so small a space that you can go completely nuts with it. Use sound and motion with care!

Adding Sound

Adding music, sound effects, and other audio snippets to a PowerPoint slide electrifies a presentation more than mere text and images can. PowerPoint comes with a small library of sound files that you can raid whenever you need a foghorn, phone ring, or rooster. You can find more sounds on the Internet (even beyond Design Gallery Live), where you can locate Web sites that offer sound clips for virtually every sound imaginable.

Adding a sound from the Clip Organizer

Inserting a sound into a PowerPoint presentation is as simple as choosing a sound and pasting it onto a slide. Whenever you run the slide show, you can set up the sounds to play either during slide transitions or at the click of a Sound icon. To add a sound from the Clip Organizer, follow these steps:

1. **Move to the slide that you want to jazz up with sound.**
2. **Choose Insert⇨Movies and Sounds⇨Sound from Clip Organizer from the PowerPoint menu bar.**

   The Insert Clip Art task pane opens, but now it presents sounds.
3. **Scroll through the task pane until you find the sound that you want.**
4. **Click the down arrow to open the sound's drop-down list and select Preview/Properties.**

   The Preview/Properties dialog box appears and you hear the sound. You can click the Play button to hear it again. For that matter, click Previous or Next button to hear more sounds in the Clip Art task plane. Click Close to shut down the dialog box.
5. **Click the sound that you want to include in your presentation.**

   A dialog box asks whether you want the sound to play automatically or only after you click its icon.

6. **Click Yes to play the sound automatically, or No to play it only once when you click a sound icon.**

   PowerPoint pastes the sound on the slide. Notice that a little sound icon appears on the slide to show you that your sound is present.

Adding a sound from another source

If you want to insert a sound that isn't listed in the Clip Organizer (such as one you download from the Internet, or one you digitize and store yourself), follow these steps:

1. **Move to the slide where you want to add a sound.**
2. **Choose Insert⇨Movies and Sounds⇨Sound from File.**

   The Insert Sound dialog box appears.
3. **Find and click the sound file that you want to add and then click OK.**

   PowerPoint asks whether you want the sound to play automatically or after you click it (see Figure 8-2).
4. **Click Yes to play the sound automatically, or No to play it only once when you click a sound icon.**

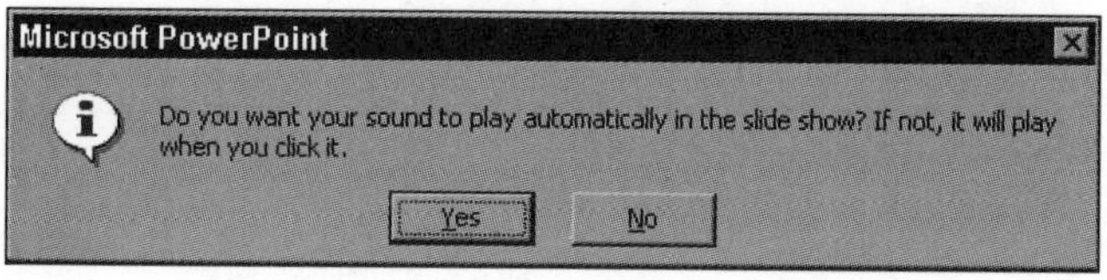

Figure 8-2: You make the call about how sounds play on your slide.

Playing a sound

To play a sound on a slide as you're working in Normal view, double-click the sound icon.

To play the sound during a slide show presentation, single-click the sound icon whenever it appears on a slide (unless you choose to make the sound play automatically on a slide).

You can also cause sounds to play in between slides, during a slide transition. (See Chapter 10 for information on how to do so.)

Chapter 9: Making a Graph(ical) Presentation

In This Chapter

- Using a datasheet to start a graph
- Making a graph
- Inserting a table

Multimedia is a wonderful tool for improving your PowerPoint presentations. But sometimes a presentation is better served by using a simple, cut-and-dried graph or table. In this chapter, you find out how to make convincing presentations even better.

Starting with the Datasheet

Microsoft Graph uses information that you supply in the datasheet to construct the graph that ultimately ends up (looking beautiful) on your slide. The datasheet functions as a simple spreadsheet, providing rows and columns where you insert your data (see Figure 9-1). Numbers designate rows, and letters designate columns. Each data point that you enter is cubbyholed in a unique cell of the datasheet. Simply click a cell and start typing to enter information into the cell.

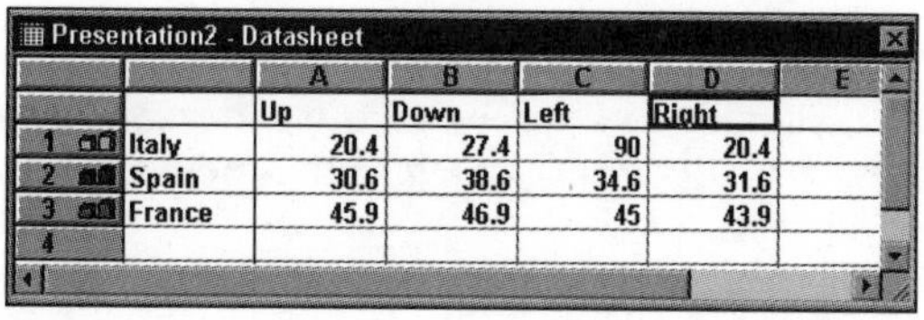
Presentation2 - Datasheet

		A	B	C	D	E
		Up	Down	Left	Right	
1	Italy	20.4	27.4	90	20.4	
2	Spain	30.6	38.6	34.6	31.6	
3	France	45.9	46.9	45	43.9	
4						

Figure 9-1: The datasheet is a simple spreadsheet.

After filling your datasheet with numbers, you can transform those numbers into a graph. Microsoft Graph offers you 14 graph types, from those you're likely to use frequently (line and scatter) to the weird (bubble, cone, and tube) and the really strange (doughnut and radar). It also offers you a handful of unusual, custom graph types in case none of the standard types suits your needs. Figure 9-2 shows a graph deriving from the data in the datasheet shown in Figure 9-1.

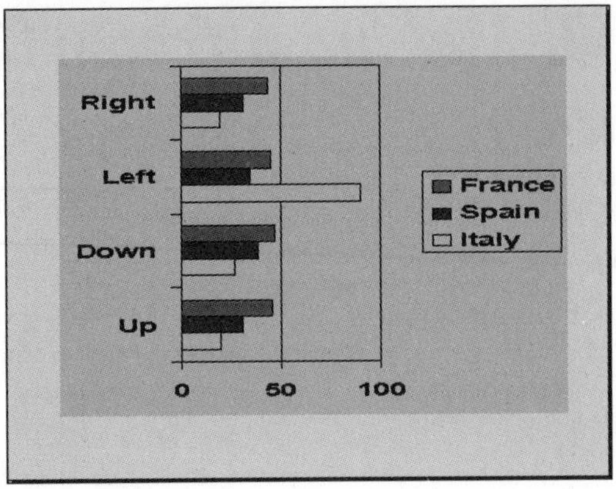

Figure 9-2: A graph that you can create by using Microsoft Graph.

Creating Graphs

Microsoft Graph is the program that you use to create graphs for PowerPoint slides, but don't worry about needing to open a second program. PowerPoint offers commands for starting Microsoft Graph and getting right to work.

Adding a slide with a graph placeholder

Before you can create a graph, you must enter a slide with a graph placeholder and fill in the datasheet. Chapter 2 explains how to insert a new slide and what placeholders are. Follow these steps:

1. **In Normal or Slide Sorter view, move to the location in your presentation where you want to insert a new slide with a graph.**
2. **Choose Insert⇨New Slide or press Ctrl+M.**

   The Slide Layout task pane appears.
3. **Click a slide design that includes a graph.**

   Scroll down the task pane to examine all the slides. Slides with a graph placeholder show a small picture of a graph. A new slide appears with a placeholder for a graph.
4. **Double-click the text that reads** `Double-click to add a chart.`

   Microsoft Graph opens and displays a sample graph along with a sample datasheet.
5. **Input your own data into the datasheet, which functions the same as a spreadsheet (refer to Figure 9-1).**

   Delete the generic data and enter your own data in its place.

6. **Accept your datasheet (that is, close the datasheet) by clicking the X in the upper-right corner of the datasheet.**
7. **Click outside the graph area to return to the slide.**

   Microsoft Graph redraws the graph with the data that you entered in the datasheet.

Suppose that you need to go back to the datasheet to enter new data or edit the data that's there? First, double-click the graph to start Microsoft Graph. Notice how the menu commands change — you're in a new program. Choose View⇨Datasheet or click the View Datasheet button to make the datasheet appear.

Adding a graph to an existing slide

To add a graph to a slide already in your presentation, follow these steps:

1. **In Normal view, move to the slide where you want to add a graph.**

2. **Click the Insert Chart button on the Standard toolbar or choose Insert⇨Chart.**

   A sample datasheet and graph appear on the slide.
3. **Replace the data in the sample datasheet with your actual information.**
4. **Accept your datasheet (that is, close the datasheet) by clicking the X in the upper-right corner of the datasheet.**
5. **Click outside the graph area to return to the slide.**

   Microsoft Graph redraws the graph with the data that you entered in the datasheet.

Choosing a type of graph

To choose a graph type after completing your datasheet, follow these steps:

1. **Double-click the graph on the slide to activate the Microsoft Graph program.**

   If you're already working in Microsoft Graph, just single-click the temporary graph that you see on-screen to select it.
2. **Choose Chart⇨Chart Type to open the Chart Type dialog box (see Figure 9-3).**
3. **Click either the Standard Types tab or the Custom Types tab.**

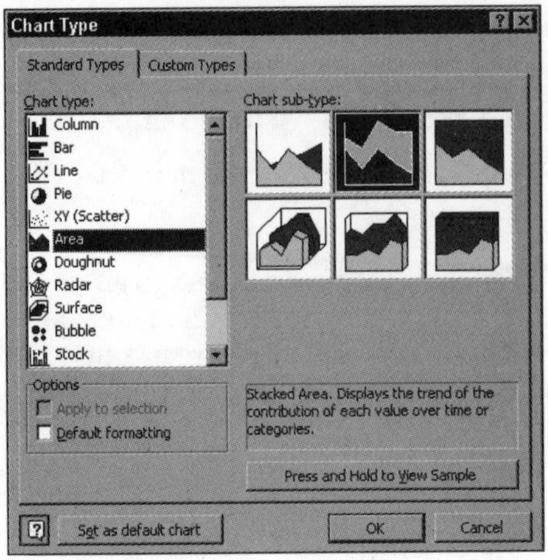

Figure 9-3: Choose among the many available chart types in this dialog box.

4. **Choose a graph option from the Chart Type list box.**

   On the Standard Types tab, you may also click an option in the Chart Subtype area, which offers variations on the Standard themes.

   On the Standard Types tab, you can also obtain a thumbnail preview of how your data appears in a selected graph type by clicking the Press and Hold to View Sample button.

5. **Click OK to accept your choice.**

You can also use a shortcut method to select a graph type while working in Microsoft Graph. Click the down arrow to open the drop-down list attached to the Chart Type button. A small palette appears from which you can choose the most commonly used graph types.

Labeling a graph

After you add a graph to your slide, you need to complete the graph by adding labels: a title, labels for the axes, and a deciphering legend. The datasheet enables you only to type names for column and row labels — you must add the other labels to the graph itself. To add labels to your graph, follow these steps:

1. **Double-click your graph to activate the Microsoft Graph program.**

   If you're already working in Microsoft Graph, just single-click your graph to select it.

2. **Choose Chart⇨Chart Options to open the Chart Options dialog box (see Figure 9-4).**

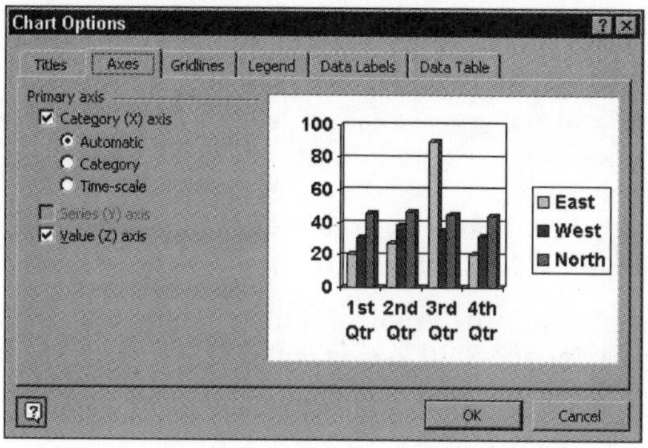

Figure 9-4: Choose your chart options in this dialog box.

This dialog box tabs offers many options for altering charts. (As you fiddle with the tabs, watch your chart take shape in the Preview area.) The following list describes what you can do on the different tabs:

- **Titles:** Add a title for the graph and titles for the axes by entering label names in the text boxes.
- **Axes:** Hide or show the labels that you gave the data on the datasheet by choosing options on the tab.
- **Gridlines:** Activate and deactivate the graph paper-style horizontal and vertical gridlines lines that appear with the graph by checking or unchecking check boxes.
- **Legends:** Click the Show Legend check box to include a legend on your graph. You can also click a radio button to position the legend in the Bottom, Corner, Top, Right, or Left of the Graph.
- **Data Labels:** Display the numerical data for each data point in your datasheet on the graph itself by checking or unchecking text boxes.
- **Data Table:** If you want to show actual data from the datasheet, choose the Show Data Table option as an accompaniment for your graph.

3. **Close the Chart Options dialog box and click your slide (outside the graph) to view your completed slide.**

TIP

While working on your graph, you can double-click any element — axes labels, data points, gridlines, and so on — to open a dialog box that offers you extensive customizing options for that element. These dialog boxes provide you with complete control over the color, size, and other formatting attributes of every element in your graph.

Moving and resizing a graph

Because Microsoft Graph may or may not position your newly created graph in the appropriate location, you may want to move or resize your graph, as follows:

- **To move a graph:** Click and drag the graph — not on the sizing handles — to move it to a new destination.
- **To resize a graph:** Click the graph and then pull on one of its handles. Pressing and holding the Shift key as you resize the graph maintains the proportions of the graph. Be aware that resizing may alter text readability.

Using Tables

Inserting massive quantities of text on your PowerPoint slides is rarely a good idea. Too many words means that you must use a small text point size to fit everything in, which may make reading your slides difficult for audience members. If you absolutely must present text-intensive information, consider organizing that information into a tidy table.

Inserting a new slide by using a table

The easiest way to insert a simple table on a PowerPoint slide is to create a new slide by using a table placeholder. To do so, follow these steps:

1. **In Normal view, move to the location in your presentation where you want to insert a new slide with a table.**
2. **Choose Insert➪New Slide or press Ctrl+M.**
3. **In the Slide Layout task pane, go to the Other Layouts section, click to select the Title and Table AutoLayout and click OK.**
4. **In the new slide, double-click the text that reads** `Double-click to add table.`

   The Insert Table dialog box appears (see Figure 9-5).
5. **Enter the number of columns in the Number of Columns text box and the desired number of rows in the Number of Rows text box in the Insert Table dialog box and then click OK.**

   Don't forget to include an extra row for the header row and column labels.
6. **Type and format text in each cell just as you do in a text box.**

   To do so, call upon the buttons on the Formatting toolbar.
7. **Click outside the table to return to your slide.**

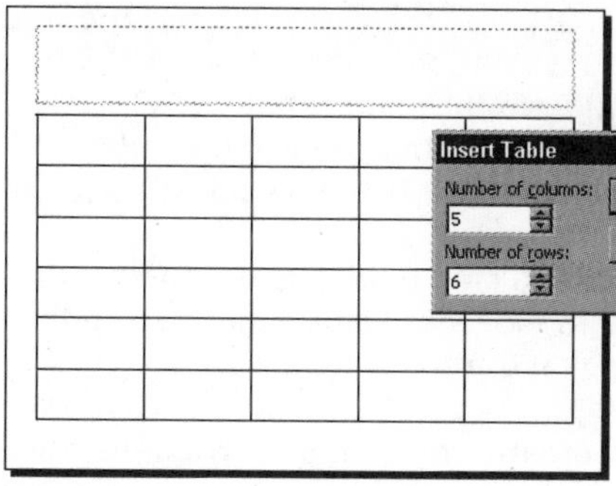

Figure 9-5: Creating a table by using the Insert Table dialog box.

Inserting a simple table on an existing slide

Just as the title of this section promises, you can add a simple table to any existing slide. Just follow these steps:

1. **In Normal view, move to the slide where you want to insert a simple table.**

2. **Click the Insert Table button on the Standard toolbar.**
3. **Press and hold the mouse button and drag the mouse to select the number of rows and columns that you want. Release the mouse button to accept your chosen dimensions.**
4. **Type and format text in each cell.**
5. **Click outside the table to return to your slide.**

Formatting a simple table

Several techniques can help you format your simple table. (If you're not already editing the table, click the table once to start editing.) The following list describes these techniques and what they can do for you:

- **To resize row height or column width:** Click and drag a line that defines the border of the row or column.
- **To insert a new row (or column):** Click where you want to insert the row or column. Then right-click and choose Insert Rows or Insert Columns. If you don't see the command you need on the shortcut menu, highlight a row or column before right-clicking.
- **To delete a row (or column):** Drag to highlight the row or column that you want to delete. Then right-click and choose Delete Rows or Delete Columns from the shortcut menu.

- **To format the borders, fill, text orientation, and other attributes:** Select the cells that you want to format. Right-click the mouse and choose Borders and Fill from the shortcut menu. The Format Table dialog box appears. The Format Table dialog box offers three tabs — Borders, Fill, and Text Box — that help you adjust table formatting.

Click outside the simple table to stop editing and return to the slide. Click and drag your simple table to move it to a new location on the slide. Resize your simple table by pulling on the sizing handles.

TIP

Perhaps the easiest way to create a table in PowerPoint is to start in Word or Excel. Create the table or chart there, select it, and copy it to the Clipboard (by pressing Ctrl+C). Then on a PowerPoint slide, choose Edit⇨Paste or Press Ctrl+V.

Chapter 10: Planning the Presentation

In This Chapter

- **Adding buttons to your presentation**
- **Adding slide transitions to your presentation**

A presentation doesn't run itself. You control how the slides appear and how much time passes between them. If you leave a slide on-screen for too short a period, you risk getting ahead of your viewers. If you leave a slide on-screen too long, you risk losing your viewers to other forms of entertainment (sleeping, talking to their neighbors, doodling, and so on). You also decide how the text appears on the slides. Do you want text to pop up suddenly, or do you want it to roll on dramatically? In this chapter, you find out ways to further plan your presentation.

Adding Action Buttons

PowerPoint offers you some way-cool *action buttons* that you can click during a slide show to perform certain specialized functions. You can use action buttons to perform a range of functions, such as running external programs or moving to certain slides.

The process of adding an action button to a slide involves first creating the button itself, and then defining its function. To add an action button to a slide, follow these steps:

1. **In Normal view, select to the slide where you want to add an action button.**
2. **Choose AutoShapes⇨Action Buttons from the Drawing toolbar to open the Action Buttons toolbar (see Figure 10-1).**
3. **In the Action Buttons toolbar, click a button shape.**

   You can choose buttons that represent actions, such as Home, Forward, Backward, Document, and Movie. You can also embellish the blank button with text to customize your choices (see Step 6).

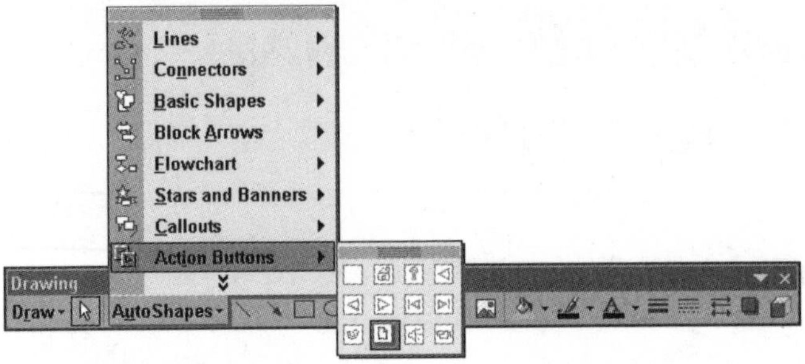

Figure 10-1: Action buttons on the Action Buttons submenu.

4. **Click your slide.**

   The Action Settings dialog box appears (see Figure 10-2).

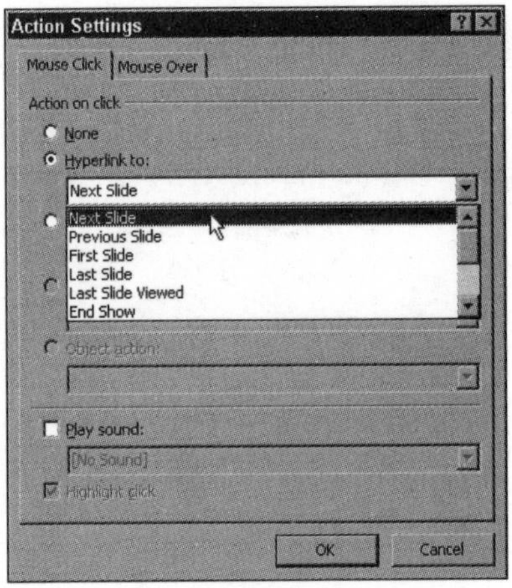

Figure 10-2: The Action Settings dialog box.

5. **In the Action Settings dialog box, click the Mouse Click or Mouse Over tab to start describing what you want the button to do.**

   Choosing Mouse Click requires that you click the button to execute its action, while choosing Mouse Over requires only that you move the mouse on top of the button (without clicking) to perform the button's action.

6. **Assign an action to your newly created button, if necessary.**

   Default actions are preset for many buttons. Returning to the home slide (the first slide in the presentation), for example, is the default action for the action button that looks like a house.

   TIP: To determine the default action of a button, consult the Hyperlink To area of the Action Settings dialog box.

You may want to redefine button actions according to your specific needs. Use the following options in the Action Settings dialog box to redefine button actions:

- **None:** No action occurs.
- **Hyperlink To:** Opens a drop-down list with options for describing what you want to happen when someone clicks the button. Choose Last Slide, for example, if you want to be able to click the button to go to the last slide in the presentation.
- **Run Program:** Enables you to choose a program that runs after you click the action button. ***Note:*** If you choose this option, you need to make certain that the program is available on whatever system you run your presentation.
- **Run Macro:** Produces a list of all available macros in the presentation.
- **Object Action:** Applies to a slide object to which you can assign the action of Open, Play, or Edit. You can assign the Play action to a movie clip, for example, or assign the Open or Edit action to an Excel chart. To use this option, switch to Slide or Normal view and click the object that you want to attach an action to. Right-click the object and choose Action Settings from the shortcut menu. On the Mouse Click or Mouse Over tab, click the Object Action radio button and choose Open, Play, or Edit from the drop-down list.
- **Play Sound:** Plays a sound in conjunction with any other action that occurs. Choose a sound from the drop-down list.
- **Highlight Click/When Mouse Over:** Applies to an object other than an action button to which you attach an action. Because action buttons highlight as you click or mouse over them, selecting this option makes other objects — such as movies or text boxes — look as if you're clicking or mousing over them, too. In other words, they are highlighted just like action buttons are.

After you make your selections, click OK to close the Action Settings dialog box.

7. **(Optional) Tweak the button's appearance by pulling the handles to adjust button size and yanking on the diamond handle to alter the 3-D effect of the button. Move the entire button by clicking it and dragging it to another place on your slide. Adjust the fill color as you do for any drawing object.**

   You can add text to any selected button by right-clicking the action button, choosing Add Text from the shortcut menu, and then typing at the cursor. After text exists, you simply need to click the text and start typing or editing. You can format button text by using the Formatting toolbar. Click the Bold button, for example, to boldface text; click the Underline button to underline it.

If you want to change a button's action setting at a later time, right-click the action button and select Action Settings from the shortcut menu.

Adding Slide Transitions

Slide transitions dictate how slides enter and exit as you present your on-screen slide show.

You can opt to use one type of transition consistently throughout your entire presentation, or you can choose unique transitions for individual slides. You can also adjust the speed at which a transition occurs — slow, medium, or fast — and even make a sound play as the transition takes place. PowerPoint provides you with more than 40 cool transitions to use in your presentations.

REMEMBER

Adding a transition to a slide dictates how that slide enters on-screen — not how it exits. PowerPoint doesn't enable you to set up an exit transition.

To add transitions to your presentation, follow these steps:

1. **In Slide Sorter view, click a slide that needs a transition.**

   To select multiple slides, press and hold Shift as you click. To select all slides, choose Edit⇨Select All or press Ctrl+A.

2. **Choose Slide Show⇨Slide Transition.**

   The Slide Transition task pane appears, as shown in Figure 10-3.

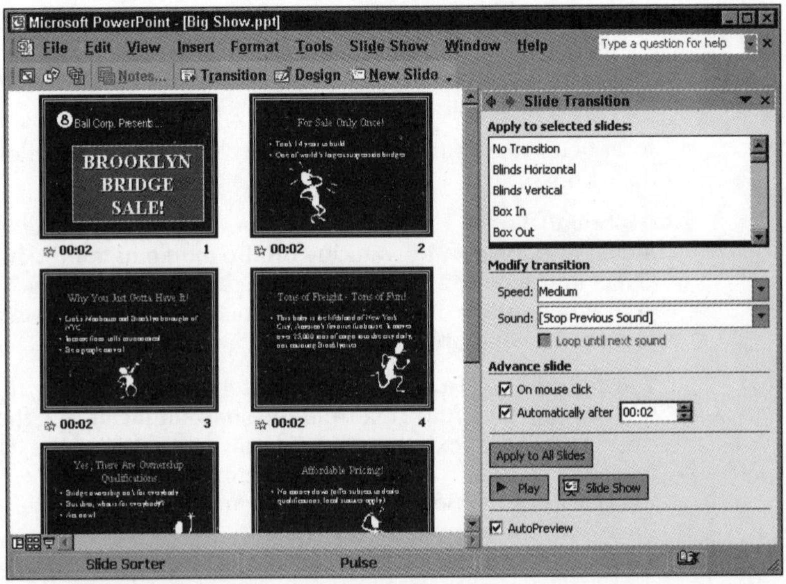

Figure 10-3: Choose your transitions in the Slide Transition task pane.

3. **Click to select a transition in the Apply to Selected Slides scroll list.**

   As soon as you choose it, PowerPoint demonstrates the transition on the slide or slides that you select in Step 1.

4. **In the Modify Transition area, select a speed for the transition in the Speed drop-down list.**

   Again, PowerPoint demonstrates your choice by showing it to you on the slides you select.

5. **If you want a sound to accompany your transition, select a sound from the Sound drop-down list (or select Other Sound to use non-PowerPoint sound files).**

   Chapter 8 explains how to choose non-PowerPoint sounds. The Loop Until Next Sound option causes the sound to play repeatedly until another sound in the presentation plays.

6. **In Advance Slide area, select the On Mouse Click check box if you want the transition to occur on the click of a mouse, or select the Automatically After check box and enter a number of seconds in the text box if you want a certain number of seconds to elapse during the transition.**

   Choosing Automatically After enables you to specify the number of seconds before the transition occurs. You can leave the number of seconds at 0 — the default — which causes each transition to play directly after the previous transition finishes.

7. **Click the Apply to All Slides button if you want your choices to apply to every slide in the presentation.**

Notice the transition icons (as well as the time designations, if you choose for the slides to appear after a certain amount of time) underneath the slides in Slide Sorter view. By clicking a transition icon, you can view a slide's transition.

TIP

PowerPoint enables you to apply any transition to any slide. But if you want to look like a real PowerPoint pro, pick one transition type and apply it consistently throughout your entire presentation. Don't use any transition with the adjective *random* in its name. Be creative, but don't overdo it, because then your audience pays more attention to your wacky transitions than to the information on your slides. You appear most professional if you choose something elegant, such as a straight cut (the No Transition choice), a Fade Through Black or a Dissolve, Cover, Uncover, Wipe, or Strip. Avoid the Blind and Checkerboard effects — they're certain to totally annoy your audience!

Chapter 11: Showing Off Your Work

In This Chapter

- Using a computer to show your slides
- Presenting automatically or manually

One of the best things about giving a PowerPoint presentation is that you no longer need to get your hands messy drawing on a flip chart or on one of those dry-erase boards. Most important, you can spend less time turning your back on your audience — which is always a dangerous thing, especially on a warm Friday afternoon. If you can turn on a computer, you can give your presentation. (And if you can't turn on a computer, how the heck did you manage to make a PowerPoint presentation?) In any case, this chapter gives you the lowdown on how to give your presentation by using a computer — not the only option with PowerPoint, but perhaps the most common.

Showing Your Slides via Computer

After creating your presentation, you're ready to take your message to the world. PowerPoint gives you lots of control over your presentation if you deliver it on your computer.

Preparing your show for presentation

After you create your slides, you must make some final decisions about how to present your show. To prepare your slides for presentation, follow these steps:

1. **Choose Slide Show⇨Set Up Show.**

   The Set Up Show dialog box appears (see Figure 11-1).

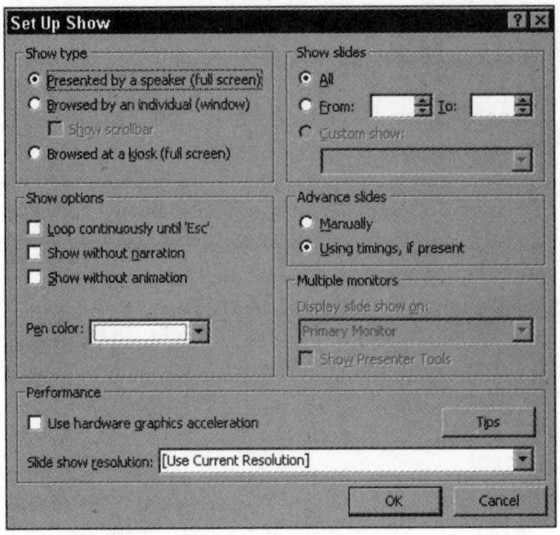

Figure 11-1: Set up your show by using the Set Up Show dialog box.

2. **Click one of the following three radio buttons in the Show Type section:**

   - **Presented by a Speaker:** The speaker controls the pace of the presentation by clicking through slides at his or her own pace.
   - **Browsed by an Individual:** Sets up a smaller screen presentation, which appears in its own window along with commands for navigating the show and for editing and printing slides. This option permits the user of the show to choose navigation commands and go from slide to slide at will.
   - **Browsed at a Kiosk:** Creates a full-screen self-running presentation of the kind that appears in an unattended display at a convention or a mall. The show restarts after five minutes of inactivity. You can include navigation commands (hyperlinks and action buttons) to give users who peruse the show control over how they view the presentation — but users can't modify the presentation itself.

3. **Click one or more of the following three check boxes in the Show area:**

   - **Loop Continuously Until 'Esc':** Starts the presentation at the first slide when the show finishes until the presenter or user presses the Esc key.
   - **Show Without Narration:** Enables you to turn off recorded narration that you record by using the Record Narration command on the Slide Show menu. Selecting this option enables you to present face-to-face a slide show that typically runs without a speaker at a kiosk or over an intranet.

- **Show Without Animation:** Shows each slide in its final form, as if all animations are done. Check this option to show an animation-free version of your presentation. Showing your slide show without animations speeds up the presentation. This option is important if you suddenly discover that you must reduce your half-hour presentation to ten minutes.

  If and only if you select the Browsed by an Individual radio button in Step 2, you can also select a Show Scrollbar check box. This option places a scrollbar on the slide show window to make all parts of the window accessible to the person who views the show.

4. **In the Slow Slides area, choose the All radio button to show all the slides in the presentation, or choose the From radio button and then specify a range in the From and To text boxes.**
5. **In the Advance Slides area, choose the Manually radio button if you want the presenter to proceed from slide to slide by clicking; choose the Using Timings, If Present option button to run the slide show automatically, using timings that are established when you run the slide show and PowerPoint times it.**
6. **Click OK.**

REMEMBER

Selecting the Loop Continuously Until 'Esc' option in Step 3 is always a good idea. If you select this option, you return to your first slide after you complete your presentation. Without looping back, your audience ends up staring at an ugly old slide construction view (whatever you start the show from — for example, from Slide Sorter view) after you click off your final slide. If you choose the Browsed by an Individual option and don't loop back, the viewer sees the words `End of slide show, click to exit` after the last slide.

Presenting slide shows manually

If you choose to run your show manually (see the preceding section for your other options), move to the first slide in your presentation and perform one of the following actions to start the show:

- Choose Slide Show⇨View Show.
- Click the Slide Show view button from the row of view buttons in the lower-left corner of the PowerPoint window.
- Press F5.

Besides speaking eloquently and making eye contact with your audience members, you spend the majority of your time delivering a manually run PowerPoint slide show in performing the following tasks:

- **Moving along:** The first slide of your show appears and stays on-screen until you click the left mouse button. You can also press PageUp and PageDown to move from slide to slide.

  If you created animation that builds your slide one bullet at a time, only the unanimated objects appear at the start of each slide. Click the mouse button to show the first animation and continue clicking to advance to each additional animation. After all animations on a slide are complete, click the mouse button to move to the next slide.

- **Writing notes on the slides:** PowerPoint offers a pen for scribbling on slides (see Figure 11-2). To use it, right-click and choose Pointer Options⇨Pen from the shortcut menu. Then drag the pointer to draw on-screen. (Don't worry; you're not rendering your doodles permanently on slides. They disappear as soon as you move ahead to the next slide in the presentation.) To advance to the next slide after you use the Pen, press the PageDown key. To get rid of the Pen, right-click the screen and choose Pointer Options⇨Pen again.

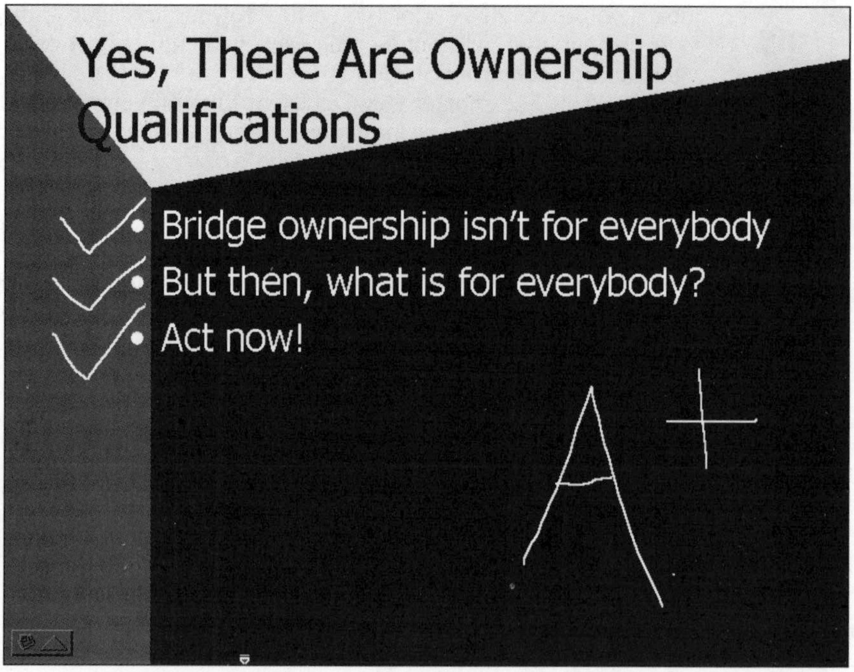

Figure 11-2: You can scribble on slides by using the Pen.

Automating the slide show by using slide timings

Use slide timings whenever you want to create a stand-alone show. This option enables you to designate how long each slide appears on-screen before the next slide appears. To automate the slide show with slide timings, follow these steps:

1. **Choose Slide Show⇨Rehearse Timings.**

   The show starts and a small Rehearsal dialog box with a timer appears in the corner of the screen. The Rehearsal dialog box times how long each slide appears on-screen, as well as the total time for the entire presentation. PowerPoint displays both times in the dialog box.

2. **Display Slide 1 for whatever duration you choose; click to advance to the next animation or next slide.**

   After you click to Slide 2, PowerPoint records how long you keep Slide 1 on display. PowerPoint resets the timer to zero to start recording how long Slide 2 appears on-screen.

   TIP: If you mess up timing a slide, click the Repeat button in the Rehearsal dialog box and try timing the slide again. Clicking the Pause button in the Rehearsal dialog box pauses the timing process. Resume timing by pressing Pause again.

3. **Continue clicking to advance your slides until you reach the end of the show.**

   PowerPoint times how long each slide appears. It also times how long the entire show runs from start to finish.

4. **After you time the last slide, PowerPoint informs you of the total time for the show and asks whether you want to record the presentation as timed. Click Yes to accept your timings or No to ditch them.**

Set the show to run with timings by clicking the Using Timings, If Present radio button in the Set Up Show dialog box (refer to Figure 11-1). Now you can play hooky while PowerPoint does all the work! Each slide appears on-screen for the amount of time that it appeared onscreen during the rehearsal.

Chapter 12: Publishing Your Presentation

In This Chapter

- **Making handouts for the audience**
- **Placing your presentation on the Web**

Poof! You give your presentation, the lights go on, and your audience scatters. Is that it? Is your presentation nothing more than a 15-minute splash that's soon forgotten? No! If your presentation demonstrates an enduring quality, why not use PowerPoint to help you publish it? Besides giving your audience something tangible to hang on to, you can also convert your presentation into a Web presence that can carry your message far and wide.

Printing Audience Handouts

Audiences appreciate copies of your slides — handouts make following your presentation easier for the audience, plus they represent a permanent record of what you say. Audience handouts present miniatures of your slides, and if you want, you can include on each handout a header, a footer, and even lines where audience members can jot down notes. To print handouts, follow these steps:

1. **Choose File⇨Print.**

   The Print dialog box appears.

2. **Select Handouts from the Print What drop-down list.**

   Doing so activates the Handouts area of the Print dialog box.

3. **In the Handouts area, select the number of Slides Per Page that you want from the drop-down list.**

   Your choices consist of 2, 3, 4, 6, or 9 slides per page.

4. **If available, click the radio button indicating whether you want slides to appear in Horizontal or Vertical order.**

   These radio buttons are available if you choose to print 4, 6, or 9 slides per page.

5. **Click OK to start printing.**

Make sure that you check out Appendix B for additional printing hints that PowerPoint shares with other Office applications.

Publishing on the Web

You can give your presentation some longevity and add to its accessibility by posting it on the Web. Thanks to PowerPoint, you don't need to know how to write HTML code to publish your show online. PowerPoint offers a quick and easy option for translating your slide shows into the HTML language necessary for publishing Web pages online.

Saving a presentation as a Web page

To post your PowerPoint presentation to the Web, you must save the file in HTML format — the language of the Web. Saving your presentation in HTML makes displaying and viewing your presentation in a Web browser such as Netscape or Internet Explorer possible.

Saving your slide show as a Web page also sets the Web page title and the location where you store the file. The following saving procedure doesn't automatically make your presentation available for viewing online. You must save it to a Web server for other people to access it. (See the section "Placing a presentation on a Web server," later in this chapter, for additional instructions.)

To save your presentation as a Web page, follow these steps:

1. **Choose File⇨Save as Web Page.**

   The Save As dialog box appears. Any other PowerPoint presentations that you save as Web pages appear in the list here. (You may need to browse to see the other presentations that you've saved.)

2. **Enter a descriptive name for your presentation in the File Name text box.**

3. **Click the Publish button.**

   The Publish as Web Page dialog box appears, as shown in Figure 12-1.

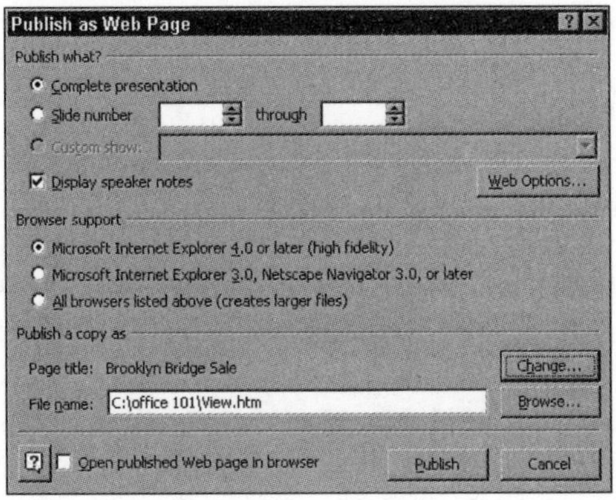

Figure 12-1: The Publish as Web Page dialog box.

4. **In the Publish as Web Page dialog box, you can make adjustments to the following attributes that affect how you save your presentation:**

   - **Publish What?:** Choices consist of Complete Presentation; a specific range of slides that you select by typing in start and end slides in the Slide Number text boxes; or a Custom Show that you select from the drop-down list. You can also click the Display Speaker Notes check box to include speaker notes on the Web page.

     Clicking the Web Options button opens a Web Options dialog box where you can make additional choices on six different tabs about how your presentation appears in the Web browser and how users navigate the presentation.

   - **Browser Support:** Choose which browsers the presentation can appear in. Choosing Microsoft Internet Explorer Version 4.0 or Later (High Fidelity) ensures that users can take advantage of advanced Web browser features such as animations, sounds, and movies.

   - **Publish A Copy As:** Accept the title on the first page of your presentation or press the Change button to summon the Set Page Title dialog box and type in a different name for viewers to see in the title bars of their browsers. Type a name for your presentation in the File Name text box as well or click Browse to change the location where you store your resulting Web files.

   - **Open Published Web Page in Browser:** Click this check box to view your presentation as a Web page on saving it.

5. **Click the Publish button to accept your choices and save your presentation.**

Saving your file as a Web page organizes all the components of your presentation (such as text, graphics, and sound) into a special Web folder. The default name of this folder is the name of the presentation file followed by the word *files.*

TIP: The very first time that you save a presentation as a Web page, PowerPoint converts all graphic images to one of three Web-supported formats: GIF, JPEG, or PNG. The more graphics that you include in your presentation, the more time this initial save takes.

Placing a presentation on a Web server

If you want to make your PowerPoint presentations available online, you need access to a Web server where you can save your presentations. Placing a presentation on a Web server can also make it available to colleagues on your company intranet.

To create a Web folder where you can save Web page files on a Web server, choose from the following options:

- **To create a new Web folder while you're working in PowerPoint:** Choose File➪Open and click Web Folders on the Places Bar in the Open dialog box that appears. Double-click the Add New Folder icon and type the information that the Add Web Folder Wizard requests (see Figure 12-2).
- **For a URL already on a Web server:** Choose File➪Save As to open the Save As dialog box. Type a Web address (such as `http://Camilleserver/public/`) in the File Name text box and click the Save button to create a Web folder at that location on the Web. You must have the appropriate access rights to create the folder on the Web server.

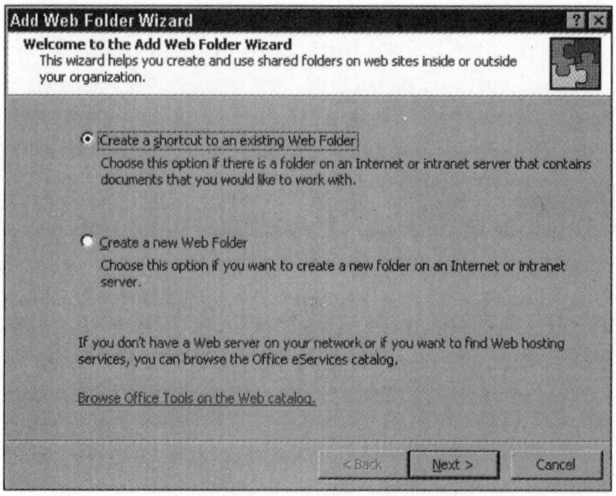

Figure 12-2: The Add Web Folder Wizard helps you place your Web page on the Web.

Index

A

B

C

D

E

F

O

P

Q

R

S

Book VII

FrontPage 2002

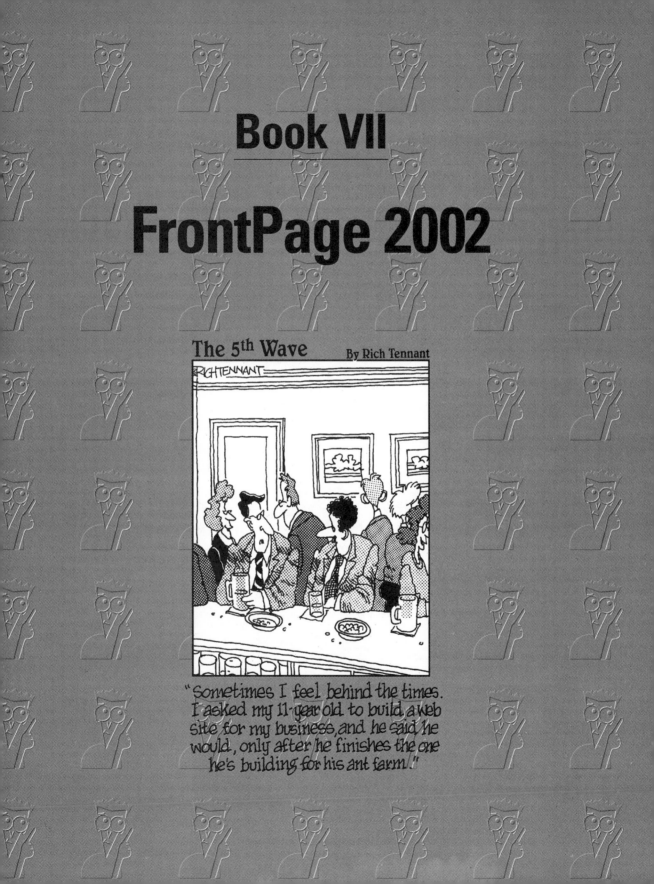

"Sometimes I feel behind the times. I asked my 11-year old to build a web site for my business, and he said he would, only after he finishes the one he's building for his ant farm."

Contents at a Glance

Chapter 1: Getting to Know FrontPage

In This Chapter

- ✔ **Discovering the power of FrontPage**
- ✔ **Assessing the Views bar**
- ✔ **Using the FrontPage Editor**

You don't need to be a whiz kid to churn out a quality Web page. By using FrontPage, you can join the ranks of Web-page designers. FrontPage is a powerful program that enables you to create almost any type of Web page. This chapter covers the FrontPage basics and introduces you to some of the program's essential tools.

What Is FrontPage, and What Can I Do with It?

FrontPage is an all-in-one Web publishing tool for big-time Web companies (such as Yahoo! or ESPN), small companies, and personal users. By using FrontPage, you can create individual Web pages and publish them to the Internet, generate tracking reports about those Web pages, and effectively administer the Web site after it's on the Net . . . all from within the same program.

Of course, you may never want to administer an entire Web site and use all that functionality, and that's okay. If you just want to build ordinary HTML pages and put them up on the Internet or the company intranet, that's fine, too. FrontPage is exceptionally flexible and scalable; it can grow with you as your Web site needs grow.

How FrontPage Is Organized

FrontPage contains a multitude of features, mini-applications, and menus, all wrapped up in one tidy little package. Still, maneuvering around FrontPage can baffle anyone. So to better orient you, Figure 1-1 shows you a typical FrontPage interface. You also see figure callouts for a number of features. Pay particular attention to the callouts, because you're going to find yourself using those features the most.

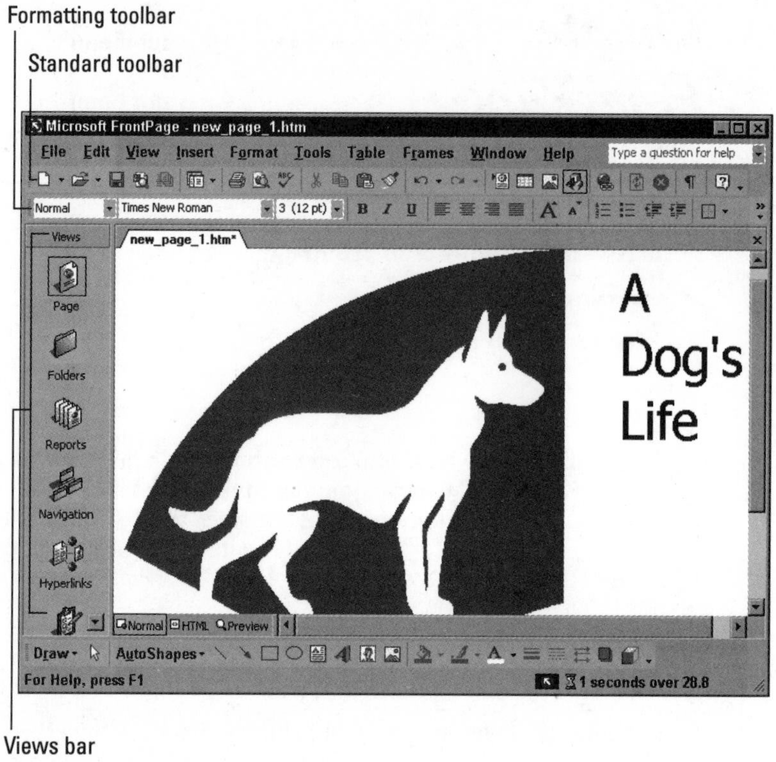

Figure 1-1: Welcome to the FrontPage Interface.

Exploring the Views Bar

You need to work pretty hard not to notice the Views bar after you fire up FrontPage for the first time. The Views bar's big menu, with its icons running down the left side of the screen, makes accessing the vast majority of features in FrontPage easy.

Each Views bar icon represents a different feature in FrontPage. To jump to a FrontPage feature, simply click the icon. The new feature appears in the right three-quarters of the screen, below the menus and toolbars.

If you don't like the Views bar, you can turn it off by right-clicking the bar and choosing Hide Views Bar from the shortcut menu. Presto! The Views bar disappears. After you turn off the Views bar, you can still toggle your view within FrontPage by choosing one of the six views from the View menu. To see the Views bar again, choose View➪Views Bar.

If you want to change the size of the icons in the Views bar, right-click the Views bar and select Small Icons from the shortcut menu.

FrontPage features six key *views* to represent major components that you may or may not use, depending on your Web project. The following list describes these views:

- **Page view:** The Page view is where you build all your Web pages (refer to Figure 1-1). Within Page view, you can review a Web page in three different ways: Click the Normal button to use FrontPage's drag-and-drop visual HTML Editor; click the HTML button to edit HTML directly; or click the Preview button to preview the pages in the Preview tab and see how they look in the Internet Explorer Web browser.

  You can preview your Web site in Internet Explorer at any time by choosing File➪Preview in Browser or clicking the Preview in Browser button on the Standard toolbar.

- **Folders view:** Folders view is pretty much what it says it is (see Figure 1-2). This view displays a typical Windows Explorer menu, making all your Web project's files and folders easily accessible within FrontPage. From this view, you can also drag and drop files, which makes adding and deleting content easy.

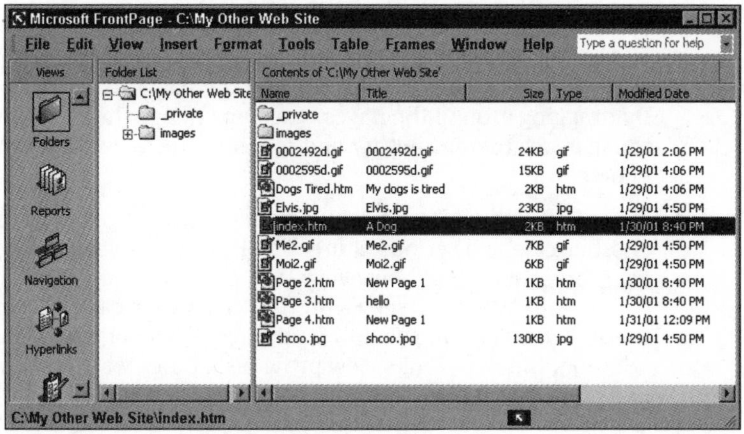

Figure 1-2: The FrontPage Folders view displays your folders.

A Folder List also appears in the Folders view. You can access the Folder List in other FrontPage views by clicking the Folder List button or by choosing View➪Folder List.

✦ **Reports view:** If you select the Reports view, as shown in Figure 1-3, you get an immediate Site Summary, which gives you a bird's-eye view of what's working within your Web site (or not working, if, for example, your site contains some broken hyperlinks). From the Reports view, you can also run a more detailed series of reports that give you immediate information on the status of various aspects of your Web site, such as load times or hyperlink status.

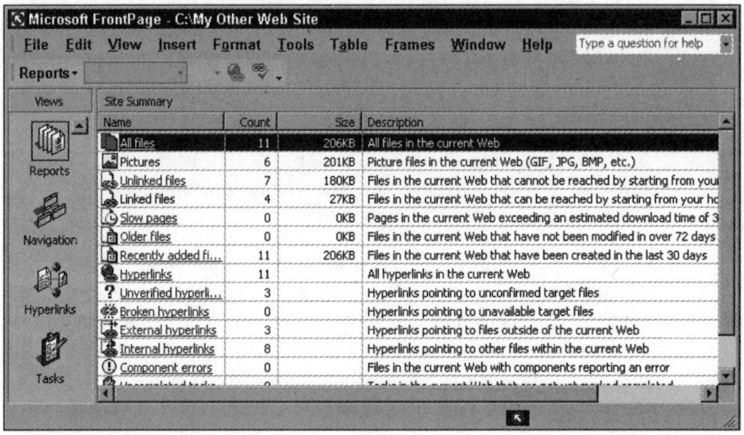

Figure 1-3: Reports view enables you to manage your site at a glance.

✦ **Navigation view:** The Navigation view provides a visual representation of all the pages on your Web site and the pages' hierarchical order. By dragging around the pages, you can change the relationships of those pages to one another and organize the pages of your site more effectively.

✦ **Hyperlinks view:** Figuring out how your Web pages connect to one another can be a serious chore. The Hyperlinks view gives you a graphical representation of how every Web page connects to every other page within your Web site (see Figure 1-4). This view can prove particularly useful if you want to see how your pages connect to one another. In addition, the Hyperlinks view provides a quick way to see which pages link to other sites outside your own.

✦ **Tasks view:** If you're going to use FrontPage in a multiuser environment, the Tasks View no doubt becomes a common sight. The Tasks view enables you to assign tasks to individuals on your team, check the status of tasks that are already underway, and manage the workflow and the publishing of new elements to the site. You can also use it to stay on top of tasks that you have to do yourself. Tasks view makes a very good to-do list.

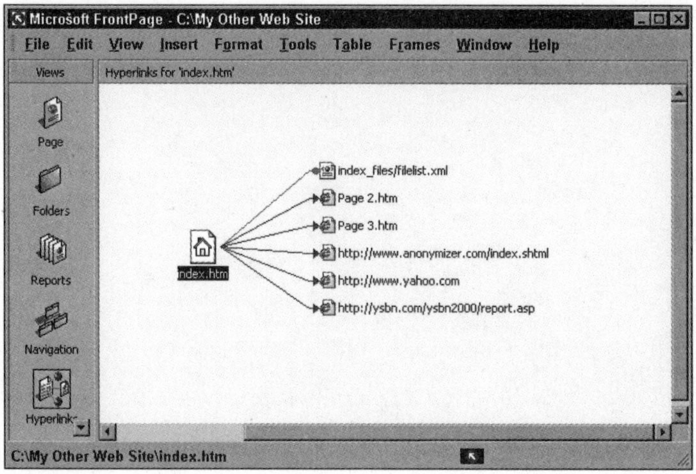

Figure 1-4: Check out your links by using the Hyperlinks view.

Introducing the FrontPage Editor

The FrontPage Editor is the program's built-in tool for creating and viewing Web pages. You can switch to Page view and then click a button at the bottom of the window — Normal, HTML, or Preview — to switch among the following modes:

- **Normal Mode:** Normal Mode is FrontPage's visual editor for Web development. In Normal Mode, you can place elements — meaning text, graphics, applets, or whatever — on-screen in any location, and FrontPage automatically generates HTML to account for the location of every object on-screen.
- **HTML Mode:** For the purist, HTML Mode enables you to edit raw HTML by hand, just as you did in the bad ol' days.
- **Preview Mode:** Preview Mode enables you to see what your pages look like in a Web browser window before you put them up on the Internet. The FrontPage default browser is Internet Explorer.

Chapter 2: Starting Your Webbing

In This Chapter

- Creating a new Web yourself or with a template
- Creating a Web page yourself or with a template
- Naming (and renaming) your Web page
- Saving your Web page
- Opening files in odd formats with FrontPage

Oh what a tangled Web you can weave — but FrontPage makes starting out and keeping track of what you're doing easy. Whether you plan to create a Web page on your own or use one of the Web templates that the program provides, this chapter shows you the basics. If you can figure out how to open, save, and close your Web pages, you're well on the road to Webmastery.

Creating a New Web

In FrontPage terminology, a *Web* is a Web site. As you create a Web site, FrontPage asks you to create a folder to store the files that make up the Web site.

REMEMBER

FrontPage, if you let it have its way, names the folder *My Web.* Although this name may seem nice and homey, it isn't particularly effective in helping you remember what your Web contains. And after you name your Web site, changing the name can prove a hassle if you decide that you don't like the current name. Naming your Web, therefore, is one of the more important decisions that you can make. Before you save your Web for the first time, think of a good name for it.

Whenever you start FrontPage, the program creates a default HTML page, `new_page_1.html` and then opens that page for you. Although FrontPage does some of this work for you, you want to create your own Web project. To do so, follow these steps:

1. **Choose File⇨New⇨Page or Web to open the New Page or Web task pane, as shown in Figure 2-1.**

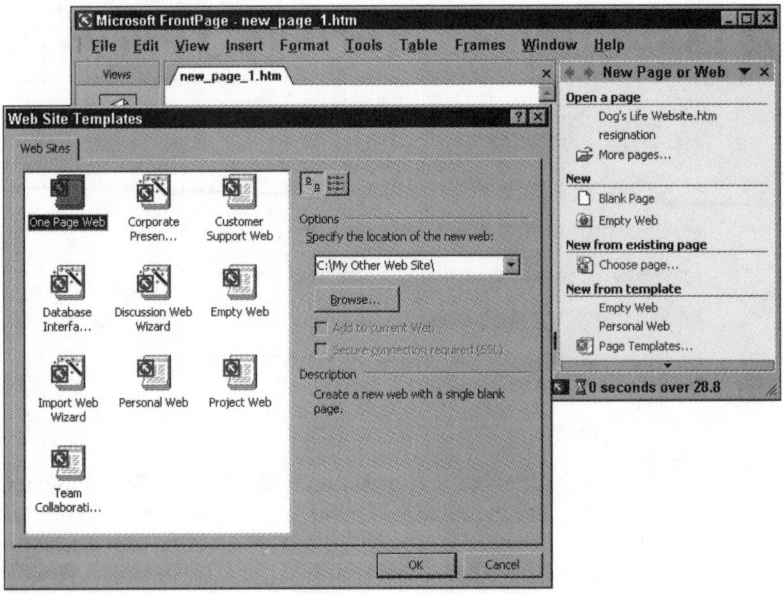

Figure 2-1: The New dialog box.

2. **Under New in the task pane, click Empty Web.**

   The Web Site Templates dialog box appears (see Figure 2-1).

3. **Enter a name for your Web site in the Specify the Location of the New Web text box.**

   In fact — and this part is confusing — what you enter determines both the location *and* the name of your new Web. After you finish naming it, FrontPage creates a new folder with the name that you choose, and then FrontPage generates the Web contents in that folder.

4. **Select a type of Web from one of the available templates.**

   The templates appear in icon form in the Web Site Templates dialog box. Each has a descriptive name (refer to Figure 2-1).

   The templates make possible different kinds of Web sites that you may want to build. The default selection — the one that FrontPage loads on startup — is One Page Web, a simple, one-page-long Web site. But FrontPage comes with several Web templates that enable you to design a Web site that you can tailor to your business or personal needs. Choose the Personal Web template, for example, to create a Web site that describes your family and its adventures. Table 2-1 describes these Web templates.

5. **Click OK or press Enter to create your new Web.**

Note: As you create a Web, you notice that FrontPage creates a few extra items, including an Images folder and a Private folder. The Images folder is the default location for housing images in your Web. The Private folder (it's actually called _Private) is where FrontPage puts the majority of the code it generates automatically to create your Web site.

Table 2-1 Web Templates in FrontPage

Template	*Description*
One Page Web	Includes just a single Web page.
Corporate Presence Wizard	Includes pages for products and services, feedback, and a search page, as well as pages for mission statements and contact information.
Customer Support Web	Includes the tools necessary for building a compelling customer support site, including pages for discussion groups, FAQs, bug-list reports, a searchable database, and bulletin-board postings.
Database Interface Wizard	Includes tools for interfacing with a database so that you can view, add, and update records in the database.
Discussion Web Wizard	Includes search forms, a discussion area, and user registration.
Empty Web	Includes only the empty default folders.
Import Web Wizard	Walks you through the process of importing an existing Web into a new Web.
Personal Web	Includes a home page, plus pages for a photo album, your personal interests, and your favorite sites on the World Wide Web.
Project Web	Includes such things as schedules, task status, discussion pages, and team-member information.
Team Collaboration Web Site	Includes a calendar, library for documents that you share with others, and a task list so that you can build a Web site with your colleagues.

Creating Web Pages

Creating new Web pages is perhaps the most common task that you perform in FrontPage, especially if you have a good-sized Web site. Not surprisingly, then, FrontPage offers you a plethora of options for generating new Web pages, whether you want to create merely an empty page or something as sophisticated as a page involving frames.

Creating an empty Web page

You can create a new, empty HTML page to add to your Web in several ways, but the following methods may prove the easiest:

- **From the New Page or Web task pane:** To create a Web page by using the task pane, choose File⇨New⇨Page or Web to see the task pane. Then click Blank Page.

- **From the toolbar:** Just below the File menu lies the New Page button. Click it (or press Ctrl+N) to create a new Web page.
- **From the Folder List:** Anytime the Folder List is active, you can generate a new, blank Web page by right-clicking a blank part of the Folder List and choosing New⇨Page from the shortcut menu.

After you create a new page, a tab appears along the top of the window in Page View. Click a tab to go from page to page.

Creating a Web page from a template

FrontPage gives you many more options for creating Web pages than just making an empty page. In fact, FrontPage includes 36 different Web page templates that make choosing a Web page for almost any of your needs easy. Table 2-2 lists some of these templates. To create a Web page from a template, choose File⇨New⇨Page or Web, click Page Templates in the New Page or Web task pane that appears, and double-click a template in the Page Templates dialog box that opens. The Preview box in the dialog box shows you what kind of Web page you get with each selection.

The fastest way to open the Page Templates dialog box is to open the New Page button drop-down list and choose Page.

Table 2-2 Web Page Templates

Web Page Template	*Features*
Bibliography	A page with entries in the correct form for a bibliography.
Confirmation Form	A customer-service reply page for users to submit a query.
Feedback Form	A form for submitting and receiving feedback.
Form Page Wizard	A customized page containing a form that Web surfers can submit.
Frequently Asked Questions	A blank table of contents and links to major sections. (You get to fill them in, however.)

Web Page Template	*Features*
Guestbook	A form that visitors can use to post comments to your Web site.
Narrow Body	A page with a slender column along the side.
One-column Body	A page with a column in the middle, a title at the top, and some default text down the middle of the page.
Photo Gallery	A page laid out for presenting photographs.
Search Page	A search form with instructions.
Table of Contents	A set of topics and built-in links for your Web pages.
Three-column Body	Three columns and a header at the top.
Two-column Body	Two text columns and a header at the top.
User Registration	A default set of text fields for registering new visitors to your Web site.

REAL WORLD

Saving an HTML file as a template

Say that you're working on a Web page and you suddenly realize, "Zoinks! All my other Web pages should have these same basic elements!" FrontPage enables you to save an HTML page as a template, which you can then load the same as other HTML templates. To save an HTML page as a template, follow these steps:

1. **Switch to Page View and select the page.**
2. **Choose File⇨Save As.**

   The Save As dialog box appears.
3. **Select FrontPage Template (*.tem) from the Save As Type drop-down list.**

   The dialog box opens to the C:\Windows\Application Data\Microsoft\FrontPage\Pages folder, the folder where FrontPage keeps its templates. (Depending on which version of Windows you're running, the templates may be in a different folder. You can look for the folder, however, starting in the C:\Windows path. Look in C:\Window*your name* to find the folder where FrontPage keep its templates.)
4. **Click the Save button.**

   The Save As Template dialog box appears.
5. **Enter a title, name, and description for your template and click OK.**

   The title, name, and description that you enter appears in the Page Templates dialog box along with the titles, names, and descriptions of other templates.

After you save your file, you can see and choose your new template on the General tab of the Page Templates dialog box, which is the one that you see after you click Page Templates in the New Page or Web task plane.

Creating framed Web pages

Ever see a Web page where you can scroll down the page, but the menu at the top never moves and the scrolling page seems to disappear underneath the menu? A feature known as *frames* controls these nifty tricks — and it's one of the great secrets of HTML. Frames aren't as popular as they once were, but you can still create frame pages with FrontPage by following these steps:

1. **In the Page View, choose File⇨New⇨Page or Web to open the New Page or Web task pane.**
2. **Click Page Templates.**

   The Page Templates dialog box appears.
3. **Click the Frames Pages tab.**
4. **Select the frame-style you want.**

   Be sure to glance at the Preview window — it shows precisely what your choice is.
5. **Click OK to generate the framed pages.**

After you select your framed page, you don't automatically see the page the way that it's eventually going to look. After you choose a frame page style, FrontPage creates a control page for the frame style, leaving the selection of the pages in the frame up to you. On-screen, you see borders breaking up the page according to the frame style that you select. Within each framed area on-screen, you find two buttons. You use these buttons to select the pages for each framed area in the style that you select. Figure 2-2 shows how these buttons look on-screen after you create a framed page.

Here's what the two buttons do:

- **Set Initial Page:** Click this button to select a page in your Web to include in the framed area.
- **New Page:** Click this button to create a new, empty HTML page for the framed area.

TIP

Click the Preview button along the bottom of the screen in Page View to see how a page with frames looks in real terms.

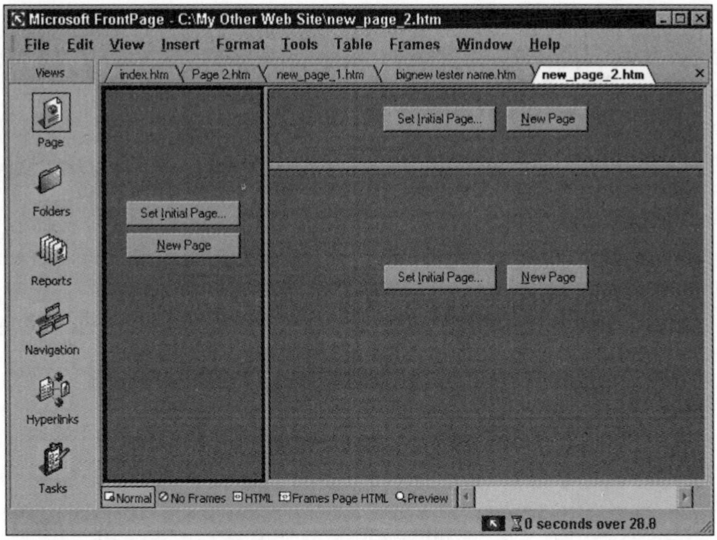

Figure 2-2: Select the pages for each framed area.

Changing a File Name

If you're familiar with the way Windows enables you to rename files, FrontPage is sure to seem awfully familiar, because it works almost identically. To change the name of a file, follow these steps:

1. **If you don't already have the Folder List open, choose View➪Folder List.**

   The Folder List area appears.

2. **Right-click the name of the file in the Folder List that you want to change.**

3. **Choose Rename from the shortcut menu that appears.**

   The file whose name you want to change is highlighted.

4. **Type the new name for the file.**

5. **Press Enter.**

If you change the name of a Web page, you break the links that connect the page to any other pages in your Web site. Fortunately, FrontPage knows exactly how all your Web pages link, so after you change the name of a file, FrontPage asks whether you want to automatically update your other pages as well.

Keep those file names short

Although you live in the wonderful world of Windows, where you can have long file names that even include spaces between words, keep your Web names short. Many servers out there on the Internet still use the 8.3 file-name/extension lengths (that is, those still using DOS and Unix syntax . . . ack!) for their file names, so the closer that you stay to the 8.3 convention, the fewer problems you experience in the long run.

Saving Your Web Pages

An old saying in software-development circles goes a little something like this: Save and save often. Well, saving and saving often is a great idea in FrontPage, too. The number of times that you save a file is directly proportional to how mad you get if you lose all the work you just finished. Keeping that in mind, use one of the following three easy ways to save a file in FrontPage:

- ✦ Choose File⇨Save.
- ✦ Click the Save button on the Standard toolbar.
- ✦ Press Ctrl+S.

If you haven't yet saved the file, the Save As dialog box appears.

From the Save As dialog box, you can give your file a name and choose where to save it. After you save the file the first time, you no longer see the Save As dialog box if you use any of the preceding three methods of saving.

Opening Files from Other Programs with FrontPage

Because FrontPage is part of Microsoft Office, the program can read and edit a large number of different file formats in addition to HTML. To open a file in FrontPage, follow these steps:

1. **Choose File⇨Open to access the Open File dialog box (see Figure 2-3).**

   You can also press Ctrl+O to access the Open File dialog box.

Figure 2-3: The Open File dialog box.

2. **Select the file type that you want to open from the Files of Type drop-down list.**
3. **Use the Look In drop-down list to find the file that you need.**
4. **Click the name of the file that you want from the list and then click the Open button.**

Chapter 3: Getting Organized Before It's Too Late

In This Chapter

- **Getting to know the FrontPage Editor**
- **Setting up your toolbars**
- **Dealing with your folders**
- **Importing Web elements**

Before you get too far along into churning out Web pages like a well-oiled machine, take a step back and set things up in FrontPage to your liking. Get your toolbars just right because you may end up clicking lots of buttons during your Web creating. Organize your file folders so that you can at least remember where you're putting your masterpieces. And don't forget to use some of the Web stuff that you may have already lying around. With a little advanced thought, your future efforts don't seem so hard.

A Quick Guide to the Three Modes of the FrontPage Editor

As with most things in FrontPage, you can make the Editor as simple or as complex as you want. The Editor is designed to appeal to HTML editing newbies as well as to HTML masters and purists. It achieves this delicate balance between the new kids on the block and the veterans by enabling users either to use drag-and-drop tools for composing pages or to edit the HTML directly.

The FrontPage Editor is split into three basic modes, which you can access by clicking one of the following three tabs in the bottom-left corner of the editing window:

- **Normal Mode:** This mode is the default for the Editor and undoubtedly the way Microsoft prefers that you create your Web pages.

  In the Normal Mode, as shown in the Figure 3-1, you can create Web page elements on-screen and position them anywhere you want. As you do so, FrontPage autogenerates the necessary HTML to make the page that you're creating.

Figure 3-1: FrontPage in Normal Mode.

The idea is that FrontPage takes HTML editing out of the HTML creation process and replaces it with menus, toolbars, wizards, and other elements that Office users are accustomed to seeing.

✦ **HTML Mode:** Prefer to do your own HTML editing? You can use HTML Mode, as shown in Figure 3-2, to edit your HTML directly and bypass all the automated features that the Normal Mode offers. This mode works the same as a more traditional HTML editor, but it also offers a number of handy features to make editing a little more user-friendly, such as HTML coloring and tag viewing.

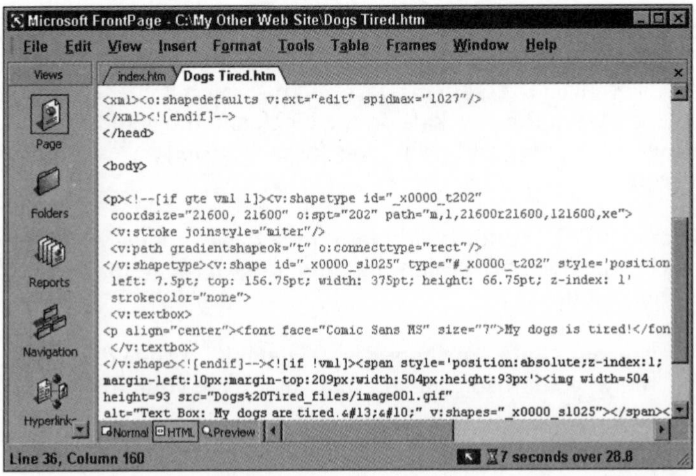

Figure 3-2: The lovely HTML Mode.

✦ **Preview Mode:** Preview Mode eliminates the need to open up a browser to see what your pages look like. This mode gives you an immediate idea of whether a page that you're creating is working correctly, because Preview Mode shows what your Web page looks like in the Internet Explorer browser.

WARNING!

Preview Mode is a good idea . . . almost. The downside is that it emulates Internet Explorer, which means that, if you use the Preview Mode as the only method of previewing your work, you're neglecting the large number of Web users who use some form of Netscape Navigator.

Using FrontPage Toolbars

INTEGRATION

FrontPage comes with the requisite Office toolbars, including the Standard and Formatting toolbars. In addition to these two toolbars, FrontPage supports seven other toolbars that you can display and customize. If you get to know these toolbars, your life may become much easier later. Table 3-1 highlights the functions of each toolbar.

Table 3-1 FrontPage Toolbars

Toolbar	*Features*
Standard	Includes such general Office functions as Open, Save, and Print.
Formatting	Provides font-style and formatting functions.
DHTML Effects	Assigns Dynamic HTML events to things such as mouse-clicks and rollovers.
Drawing	Offers tools and buttons for drawing and formatting shapes and lines.
Drawing Canvas	Presents tools for expanding, collapsing, and cropping the drawing canvas.
Navigation	Enables you to control the layout and size of the Navigation view. You can also use this toolbar to add external links.
Picture	Gives you point-and-click access to all the image-editing tools built into FrontPage.
Positioning	Enables you to set locations and move the position of objects on a page.
Reporting	Makes all the FrontPage reports accessible through a drop-down list.
Style	Launches the Cascading Style Sheet dialog box.
Tables	Generates quick and easy HTML tables.
Task Pane	Opens the task pane. Click the down arrow in the task pane and select which pane you want from the drop-down list.
WordArt	Offers buttons and tools for creating and editing WordArt images.

To display a toolbar, choose View⇨Toolbars⇨*Name_of_the_toolbar* or right-click a toolbar and choose a name from the shortcut menu that appears. After you choose the toolbar that you want, a check mark appears in the menu next to the name of the toolbar, and the toolbar that you choose either floats on-screen or sits next to the Standard and Formatting toolbars.

TIP

If a toolbar appears to be floating randomly on-screen, you can drag it up to the location of the other toolbars. After you get the toolbar up there, the toolbar area grows to accommodate the new toolbar. You can also double-click the title bar of a floating toolbar to mount it with the other nonfloating toolbars.

Creating Folders

FrontPage offers you two ways to create new folders for a Web project. The easiest way is to go to the Folders view and choose File⇨New⇨Folder. In this case, FrontPage generates the new folder in the directory that's currently selected in the Folders view.

Switching back over to the Folders view to create a new folder isn't always convenient. Fortunately, you can generate new folders in any view in which you can access the Folder List. Here's how you do it:

REAL WORLD

Collapsing and expanding folders

If you use Windows, seeing your folders arranged in a hierarchy that you can collapse and expand may already be familiar to you. Such an arrangement makes grasping the overall structure of your folders easy. FrontPage also offers the capability to view data through collapsing and expanding folders. To expand and collapse folders, follow these steps:

1. **Activate the Folders List by choosing View⇨Folder List.**
2. **Click any folder with a plus sign next to its name to expand the folder and view the contents of that folder.**

   After you click the plus sign, you notice that it changes to a minus sign.
3. **To collapse the folder, click the minus sign.**

You can also copy and move files by using the Folders List, just as you can in the Windows Explorer. Simply right-click the file, drag it into the desired folder, and choose either Copy Here or Move Here from the shortcut menu.

1. **If the Folder List isn't already open, choose View⇨Folder List to activate it.**
2. **Right-click the folder in which you want to place your new folder and then choose New⇨Folder from the shortcut menu that appears.**

   FrontPage creates the new folder and prompts you to enter a name for it.
3. **Enter a name for your new folder in the active text box next to your new folder.**

   The text box appears as a black box with a blinking white cursor at the end of the box.
4. **Press Enter to set the name of your new folder.**

Deleting Files and Folders

FrontPage offers a number of ways for you to delete files and folders. To delete any file or folder from your project, choose any of the following methods:

- **Deleting from the Folder List:** Click an item and press the Delete key. The Confirm Delete dialog box appears to make sure that you're really serious about wanting to delete the file or folder (see Figure 3-3).

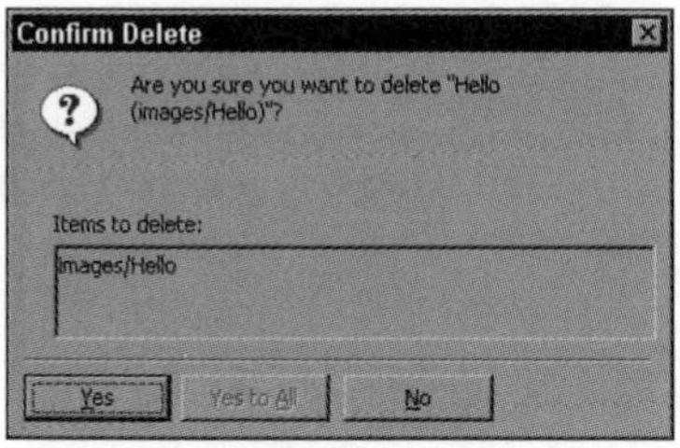

Figure 3-3: FrontPage always checks to make sure that you really want to delete an item.

- **Deleting from the Folders view:** This procedure works just the same as the Folder List option that I describe in the preceding paragraph.
- **Deleting from the Reports view:** You can also delete various HTML pages on which you generate reports. Just click the HTML page in a report and press Delete. Again, the Confirm Delete dialog box appears to confirm that you want to delete the HTML page. You can't, however, delete a page from the Site Summary report.

- **Deleting from the Navigation view:** Deleting from this view is slightly different. Select the page that you want to delete and then press Delete. The Delete Page dialog box appears. Select the Remove Page from the Navigation Structure option to keep the page in the Web but delete all links to the file or select the Delete This Page from the Web option to eliminate the page entirely.
- **Deleting from the Hyperlinks view:** Select the page that you want to delete and press the Delete key. The Confirm Delete dialog box appears to make sure that you want to delete your selection.

WARNING! After you delete a page from your Web, you can't undo the action. You're always better off eliminating the page from the active Web by stripping the page out of the Navigation view first and then removing the page. This method eliminates the file from use but keeps it in the Web. That way, you can check to see whether deleting it causes any unintended repercussions. The same rule applies for other kinds of files.

Importing Webs and Web Pages

If you're working with a number of different Web sites, you may want to import important Web pages, graphics, and even other Web sites into your current Web site. FrontPage enables you to import such accessories easily.

WARNING! You always need to specify the destination into which you want to import files first! To do so, first activate the Folder List by choosing View⇨Folder List. Then select the folder into which you want to import the data.

By the way, before you can use material that someone else created on your Web site, you must get the creator's permission. Presenting others' work without their permission is a violation of the copyright laws.

Importing files that you created elsewhere

To import a file into FrontPage, follow these steps:

1. **Choose File⇨Import.**

   The Import dialog box appears, as shown in Figure 3-4.

2. **Click the Add File button.**

   The Add File to Import List dialog box appears.

3. **Use the Look In drop-down list to tell FrontPage where you want to get the file(s), and then select the file(s) that you want to import from either your local drive or the network.**

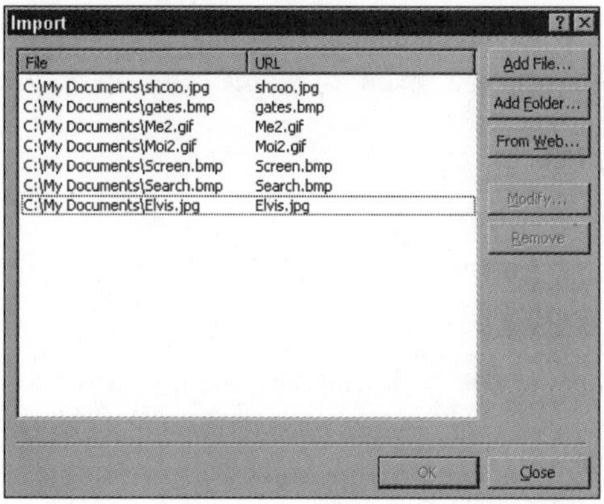

Figure 3-4: You can import a file by using this dialog box.

4. **Click the Open button to add the file(s) to your Import List.**

   You return to the Import dialog box.

5. **Click OK to import the files into your Web.**

Importing folders that you created elsewhere

After you have selected a folder in the Folder List, follow these steps to import a folder into the folder you selected:

1. **Choose File⇨Import.**

   The Import dialog box appears.

2. **Click the Add Folder button.**

   The File Open dialog box appears.

3. **Select the folder from which you want to add files by searching through the available local and network drives.**

4. **Click the Open button to add that folder and its contents to the Import List.**

   You return to the Import dialog box.

5. **Click OK in the Import dialog box to import the folder into your Web.**

TIP: You don't need to import files and then import folders separately. You can make a collection of files and folders by adding them to the Import List first. After you collect all the items that you want to import, click OK in the Import dialog box to import the whole collection.

Importing a Web that you created elsewhere

To import another Web into your existing FrontPage Web, follow these steps:

1. **Choose File⇨Import.**

   The Import dialog box appears.

2. **Click the From Web button.**

   The Import Web Wizard opens.

3. **Choose the location of the Web that you want to import.**

   The wizard provides two simple import options. If you select the From a Source Directory option, the Browse button appears on-screen. Click that button to search your local and network drives for available Webs. If you choose the From a World Wide Web Site option, the wizard provides a field for you to enter the URL from which you want to import the Web.

4. **Click Next.**

   The Choose Download Amount dialog box appears.

5. **Set the download options for the Web that you want to import.**

   You can limit the size of the Web you want to download by choosing from a series of check boxes. These check boxes enable you to specify the number of layers of the Web that you want to import, the size (in kilobytes) that you want to import, and the kinds of files that you want to import.

6. **Click Next.**

   The Finish dialog box appears.

7. **Click the Finish button to import the Web.**

Chapter 4: Laying the Groundwork for Your Web Pages

In This Chapter

- Giving your Web a theme
- Editing your theme
- Setting up page properties

If you thought you could just jump right in and make a Web page, you've probably figured out that it's not that easy. To do a thorough job, you need to consider the elements that may seem secondary to you but that make a big difference — especially as you try to apply them later and realize that you should have done these things first! Before getting too far along, you need to consider whether you need a theme for your page, additional background images and colors, and page margins. To save yourself grief later, establish your Web groundwork today.

Applying a Theme to a Web

Themes are compelling graphics and varying text styles that help provide a common look and feel for your Web. FrontPage comes with more than 60 different themes that you can apply to individual pages, as well as to an entire Web. To add a theme to a Web or Web page, follow these steps:

1. **Choose Format⇨Theme to open the Themes dialog box (see Figure 4-1).**
2. **In the list of theme names, select the theme that you want.**

   The four check boxes that occupy the bottom-left corner of the Themes dialog box give you the following additional options:

   - **Vivid Colors:** Uses more vibrant colors as you create your theme graphics and text.
   - **Active Graphics:** Creates more interesting and dynamic-looking graphics for such elements as a banner, the large heading that sometimes appears along the top of Web pages.
   - **Background Picture:** Adds a background image to the pages.
   - **Apply Using CSS:** Uses Cascading Style Sheets instead of HTML to create your text and graphics styles.

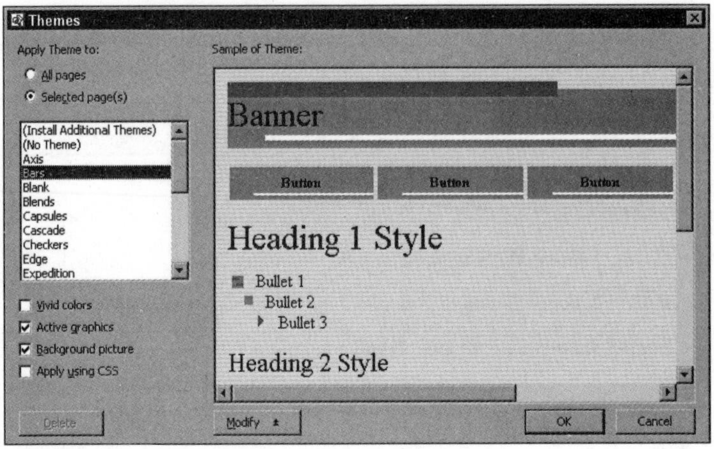

Figure 4-1: What theme do you want to use today? Choose one in this dialog box.

3. **To choose any of these options, click the check box next to the text that describes the option that you want.**
4. **Click OK to apply your chosen theme.**

Editing a Theme

What if you like the look of a theme, but the color just doesn't work for you? FrontPage enables you to modify any of the more than 60 themes in FrontPage, providing hours of fun for the entire family! To edit a theme, follow these steps:

1. **Choose Format⇨Theme to open the Themes dialog box.**
2. **In the list of theme names, select the theme that you want.**
3. **Click the Modify button.**

   The new level of options that appear enable you to change the colors, graphics, and/or text of your theme.
4. **Click the Colors, Graphics, or Text button to edit the color, graphic, or text properties of your theme.**

   After clicking one of these buttons, a Modify dialog box appears. From there, make choices to make your Web page spiffier.
5. **Click the Save button to save any changes to the theme or click the Save As button to save your theme under a new name.**

   If you click the Save As button, the Save Theme dialog box appears (see Figure 4-2). Choose a new name for your theme and then click OK to save the new theme.

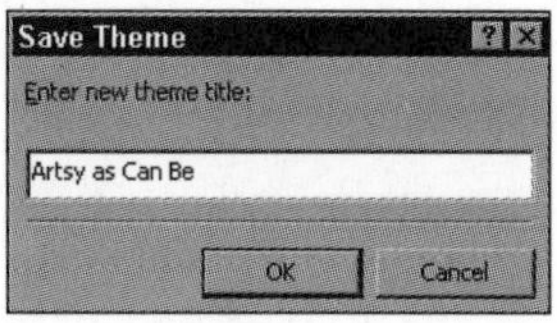

Figure 4-2: The Save Theme dialog box enables you to save a new theme.

Editing Page Properties

Every Web page offers a number of options that you can modify to fit the needs of the site that you're building. These options range from choosing Web page background images to specifying the color of hyperlinks. FrontPage organizes these options in one convenient place so that accessing them is a snap.

In the Page view with the Normal Mode selected, you can right-click a Web page and choose Page Properties from the shortcut menu. The Page Properties dialog box appears, as shown in Figure 4-3. You can also choose File➪Properties to access the same dialog box.

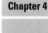

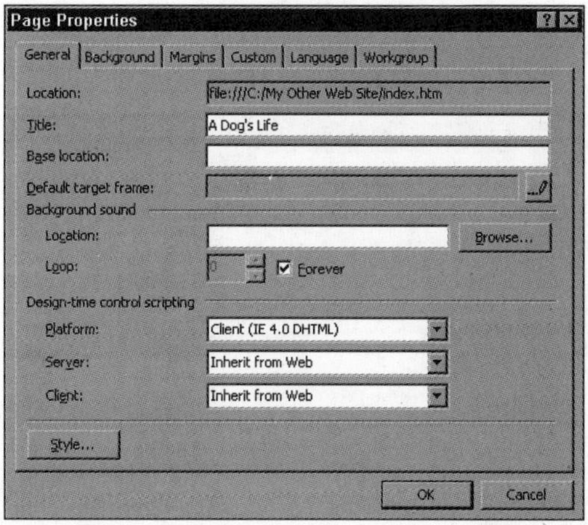

Figure 4-3: Choose your page options in this dialog box.

You can perform a number of detailed tasks in the Page Properties dialog box, most of which I describe in the following sections. Some of the simpler options that you can easily change include the following:

✦ **Changing a page title:** You can change a page title by typing a new name in the Title text box on the General tab.

- **Specifying a default page sound:** Also on the General tab, you can click the Browse button to place a sound in your Web. Unless you deselect the Forever check box and insert a value in the Loop text box, the sound loops continuously after the page loads. In other words, it keeps right on playing.

  Sounds are platform-dependent, so if you specify a PC sound file (for example, a WAV file), Macintosh and Unix Web users can't hear it.

- **Specifying the page language:** On the Language tab, you can choose the language for both the page text and the HTML coding.
- **Assigning categories to the page:** You use categories to track a page as someone's working on it in a multi-user environment. On the Workgroup tab, you can specify the categories that a page falls under, as well as the current review status of the page and who's assigned to work on it.

Setting a background image

Go to the Background tab of the Page Properties dialog box, as shown in Figure 4-4, to set a background image for a page. (You can access the dialog box by choosing File⇨Properties.) After you click the tab, follow these steps:

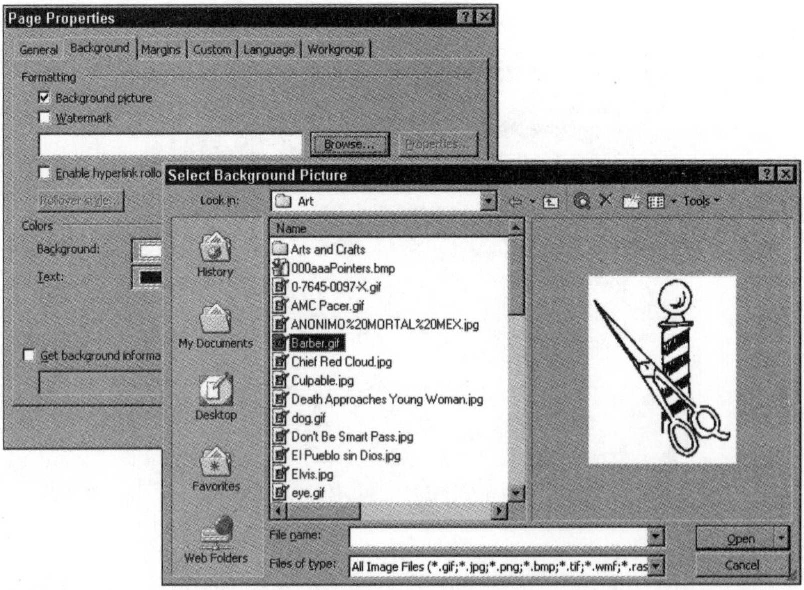

Figure 4-4: The Page Properties dialog box shows background options and enables you grab to background images for your Web page.

1. **In the Formatting area of the Page Properties dialog box, click the Background Picture check box.**

2. **Click the Browse button to locate and select the background image that you want to use.**

   After you click this button, the Select Background Picture dialog box appears (see Figure 4-4). As does every other dialog box in FrontPage that requires you to find a file, the Select Background Picture dialog box defaults to enabling you to choose files from your Web only. By rooting around and going to different folders on your computer or a network, however, you can look for background images until you find the right one.

3. **Click OK.**

   The image that you choose isn't visible until you click OK to close the Page Properties dialog box.

TIP

If you already set a background image for another page on your Web site, you can use the same background image for the page you're currently in by importing the page settings. To do so, start from the Background tab in the Page Properties dialog box, click the Get Background Information from Another Page check box, and then click the Browse button to find the page from which you want to import the background image.

WARNING!

If you choose to import a background image, you also import your background colors and hyperlink colors (see the following section).

If you're using a theme, you find that the Background tab in the Page Properties dialog box is missing. That's because you're using a theme, and themes require that all the pages using the theme also use the same background settings.

Setting background colors

From the Background tab in the Page Properties dialog box (right-click the page and choose Page Properties to see it), you can set the background colors and the various hyperlink colors for a Web page. For each option, a drop-down list enables you to choose from a series of default colors as well as to specify your own Web-safe color by clicking the More Colors button and choosing a color in the More Colors dialog box (see Figure 4-5).

Do the following under Colors on the Background tab of the Page Properties dialog box to set the colors of various parts of a Web page:

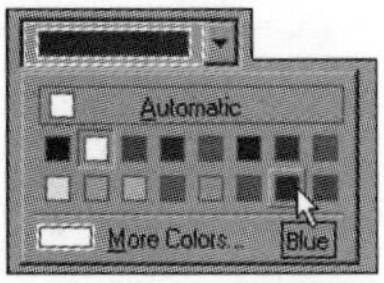

Figure 4-5: Specifying a Background color.

- **Background option:** If you didn't select a background image, the color shown here appears on the page. You can open the drop-down list and choose a new color.
- **Text option:** This menu sets the default color for text on your Web page, but you can open the drop-down list and choose a new color.
- **Hyperlink option:** The hyperlink color is the color that appears for either text that represents a link or the border around an image that's a link. This color appears only if no one's yet visited the link. Choose a new color form the drop-down list if you want.
- **Visited Hyperlink option:** Identical to the Hyperlink option, except that this color appears if the person who is visiting your Web page *has* previously clicked the link. You can choose a new color form the drop-down list.
- **Active Hyperlink option:** This color appears on a link if a visitor selects but does not visit the link. You can choose a new color from the drop-down list.

Setting page margins

Say that you want to indent an entire Web page, either from the top or from the left. What may otherwise prove a bear of an HTML problem, FrontPage makes an exceptionally trivial task. Here's how you do it:

1. **Choose File⇨Properties to access the Page Properties dialog box and then click the Margins tab.**
2. **Click to select the check box of the margin that you want to indent. FrontPage enables you to indent only the top and left-hand margins.**
3. **In the Pixels text boxes, type the desired margin sizes.**

   All images on computer screens are constructed of pixels, the tiny dots that, taken together, form images. On a 640 x 480 screen — the standard screen and the one for which Web site designers typically plan their work — indenting by ten pixels on the right margin moves the page about a sixth of the way across the screen.
4. **Click OK to see how your new margins look.**

Chapter 5: Getting the Basics on Your Page

In This Chapter

- Getting your text just right
- Making and modifying tables
- Creating and updating hyperlinks

During its infancy, pages on the World Wide Web offered only a few common elements. One constant was text on the page — nothing too fancy, but with a little bit of variety (maybe some color, a nice bullet list, and so on). Some designers chose to present their text in columns and rows, so tables, which are a great way to arrange text on a page, became the rage. Finally, the Web would never have become the Web without its capability of enabling you to use hyperlinks — you click here and go there.

These concepts are still the fundamentals of the Web today and the focus of this chapter.

Changing Text Attributes

INTEGRATION

FrontPage, by and large, looks and feels like Microsoft Word if you're changing text attributes. In the Page view with the Normal button selected, creating text is as simple as placing the cursor where you want it on-screen and then typing away. Editing your newly typed text is merely a matter of selecting the text and then choosing the appropriate text-editing feature.

TIP

You can change most of the basic attributes of a piece of text by highlighting it and then selecting the appropriate button from the Formatting toolbar, as shown in Figure 5-1.

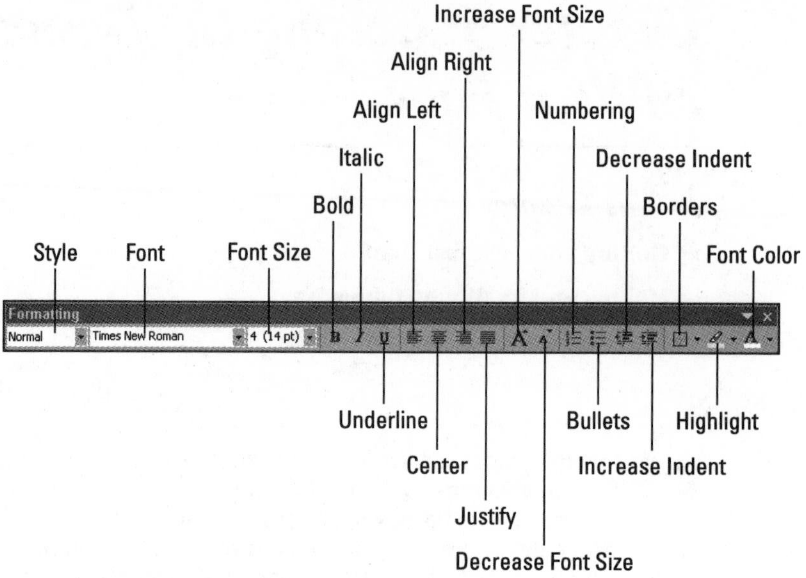

Figure 5-1: The Formatting toolbar.

Changing font properties

To change the text attributes for text that you create in the Page view with the Normal button selected, follow these steps:

1. **Highlight the text that you want to change.**
2. **Choose Format⇨Font.**

   The Font dialog box appears, as shown in Figure 5-2. (You can also open the Font dialog box by pressing Alt+Enter or by right-clicking the selected text and choosing Font from the shortcut menu.)
3. **Choose the new attributes for the selected text.**

   On the Font and Character Spacing tabs, you can change the font type, style, color, and size, as well as modify things such as character positioning and spacing. You can also choose from a number of effects, which enable you to modify such aspects as the text's visibility and its emphasis.

One of the biggest problems with Web-site development involves fonts. If you change fonts by using the Font dialog box, you're changing to fonts that reside on *your* machine. Those fonts may not be installed on someone else's machine. As a result, what the user sees may look entirely different from what you see as you're creating the page. The two safest fonts to use, therefore, are Arial and Times New Roman, because those fonts are installed on everyone's computer.

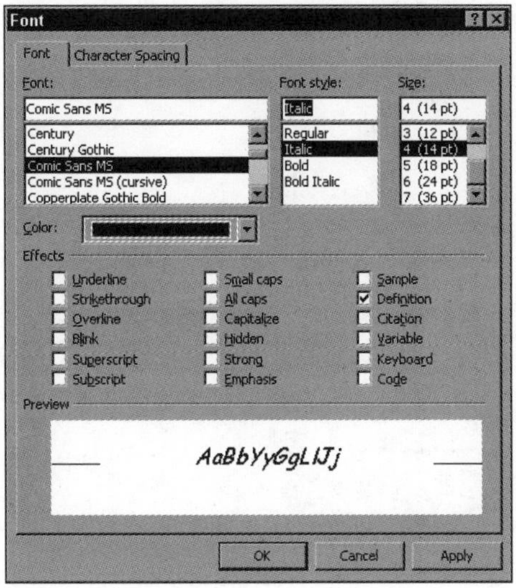

Figure 5-2: The Font dialog box gives you complete freedom to change your text attributes.

WARNING!

Many of the items in the Effects category don't work with the older 3.0 browsers or with WebTV.

4. **Click OK to activate your text changes.**

Changing paragraph settings

You change paragraph settings in the same manner that you change font attributes, so if these steps seem familiar, that's because they *are* the same! (Well, almost.) To change the paragraph setting for a chunk of text, follow these steps:

1. **Highlight the text that you want to change.**
2. **Choose Format⇨Paragraph or right-click and choose Paragraph.**

   The Paragraph dialog box appears, as shown in Figure 5-3.
3. **Enter the new paragraph settings in the Paragraph dialog box.**

   You can change the alignment, line spacing, and indentation of the paragraph.

   WARNING!

   As do font attributes, paragraph settings use Cascading Style Sheets and newer versions of HTML to set property values, making many of these settings nonfunctional for the 3.0 and earlier versions of Netscape Navigator and Internet Explorer, as well as WebTV.
4. **Click OK to change the paragraph settings.**

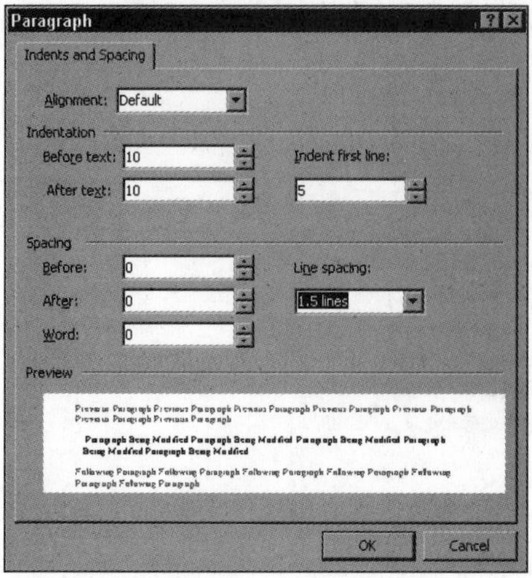

Figure 5-3: You can change your paragraph settings with a few deft clicks in this dialog box.

Creating bulleted and numbered lists

Bulleted and numbered lists are a simple, yet effective way to communicate an idea or concept with emphasis. And yes, FrontPage handles them just the same as the rest of the Microsoft Office programs. To turn a series of text items into a bulleted or numbered list, follow these steps:

1. **Highlight the text that you want to change.**
2. **Choose Format⇨Bullets and Numbering.**

   The Bullets and Numbering dialog box appears.
3. **Click the appropriate tab for the kind of list that you want.**

   FrontPage provides three basic kinds of lists: picture bulleted, plain bulleted, and numbered.
4. **Select the bullet or number style that you want by clicking it in the dialog box.**
5. **Click OK to change the text to a bulleted or numbered list.**

You can click the Numbering or Bullets button on the Formatting toolbar to create a numbered or bulleted list. By going this route, however, you get plain numbers or bullets unless you chose a theme for your Web pages.

Changing borders and shading properties

FrontPage provides a number of text border and shading options. The value in changing these settings is that you can create more emphasis on a particular piece of text by contrasting it with other text elements. Putting emphasis on particular pieces of text is especially useful for important elements that you want visitors to your site to see, such as navigation menus, sidebars, and forms. To change borders and shading, follow these steps:

1. **Highlight the text that you want to change.**
2. **Choose Format⇨Borders and Shading.**

   The Borders and Shading dialog box appears (see Figure 5-4).

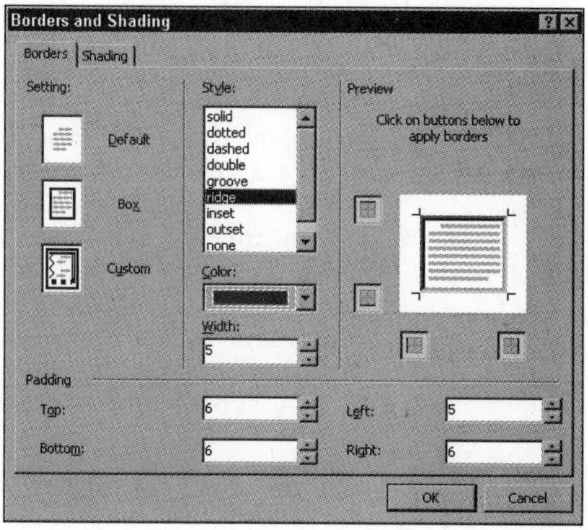

Figure 5-4: Go wild with the various Borders and Shading options.

3. **On the Borders tab, specify the border style that you want for the text box. You can choose from the following options:**
   - **Setting:** You can select one of three options: no border, a complete border around the text, or a custom border.
   - **Style:** This box lists all the border styles that you can choose, including solid lines, dashed lines, and groove lines (my favorite), just to name a few.
   - **Color:** You can select a color for your border from the many Web-safe colors that this option offers.
   - **Width:** In this text box, you can specify how wide (in pixels) you want the border.
   - **Padding:** You can set how much padding (in pixels) you want between all sides of the border and the text inside it by entering a value in this text box.
   - **Preview:** In this area, you can see what your borders look like, as well as add or remove individual sides of the border. To add or remove sides, click the one of the four buttons that surround the sample page.

4. **Choose your shading options.**

   On the Shading tab, you can set the foreground and background colors, as well as select an image as the background for the text box. To choose a background image, click the Browse button to find an image on your local drive, a network drive, or the World Wide Web. With each color selection, you get several default choices, but you can also specify any color from the Web palette.

5. **Click OK to set your border and shading options.**

Working with Tables

When it comes to laying out a Web page, tables are the backbone of nearly all Web-page development. The notion of a table with rows and columns was one of the first concepts introduced in the first version of HTML. Tables still offer the easiest way of presenting data within a Web browser. Instead of carefully laying out everything, you just plop each item in a table.

Not surprisingly, FrontPage offers a host of utilities that make generating and maintaining tables a reasonably easy task. The syntax and methodology for creating tables is, in fact, very similar to that of the other Office programs.

Creating a new table

To create a table in FrontPage, follow these steps:

1. **Choose Table➪Insert➪Table.**

   The Insert Table dialog box appears (see Figure 5-5).

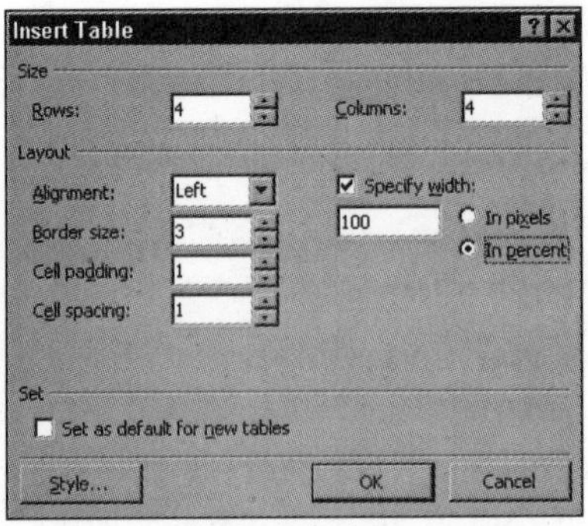

Figure 5-5: You can use this dialog box to insert tables into your page the easy way!

2. **Choose the number of Rows and Columns that you want for your table.**

   To do so, enter a number in the Rows text box and the Columns text box.

Remember: If you need more rows and columns after you create your table, you can just right-click a cell and choose Insert Row or Insert Column from the shortcut menu.

3. **Set your layout options from the Layout area of the Insert Table dialog box:**

   * **Alignment:** Determines how you want the table to be aligned on the page. You choices are Left, Right, and Center. Choosing Left, for example, places the table against the left margin.
   * **Border Size:** Establishes the thickness of the line border around both the cells and the outside of the table. Enter a number in this text box. If you don't want a border, set the value to 0.
   * **Cell Padding:** Sets the distance, in pixels, between the borders of a cell and the text within the cell. Enter a number in this text box.
   * **Cell Spacing:** Sets the distance, in pixels, between cells. Enter a number in this text box.
   * **Specify Width:** Sets the width of the table. You can specify the width as a percentage of the page or as a set pixel width by choosing the In Pixels or In Percent option button.

4. **Click OK to insert the new table.**

After you create a table, you can go back and change the properties you just set by placing your cursor anywhere in the table and choosing Table⇨Table Properties⇨Table to open the Table Properties dialog box (see Figure 5-6). For that matter, you can right-click the table and choose Table Properties on the shortcut menu.

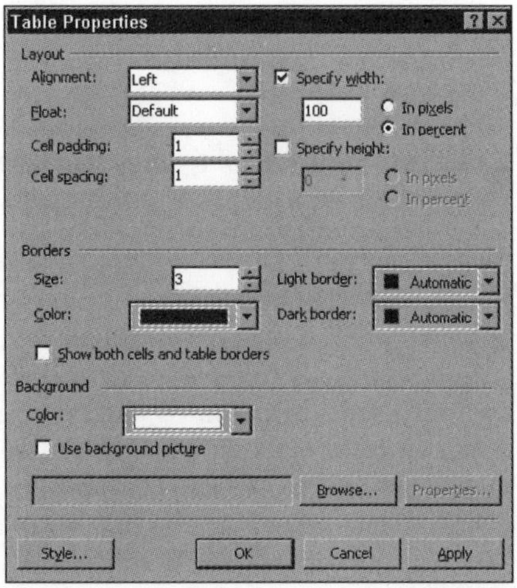

Figure 5-6: The Table Properties dialog box.

You can also choose Table⇨Table Properties⇨Cell to change the properties you just set for individual cells. Make your changes in the Cell Properties dialog box that appears.

Modifying tables

In addition to generating tables, FrontPage offers a host of tools for modifying tables after you create them. The following list describes the ways in which you can modify a table:

- **Adding cells:** You can add individual cells, rows, or columns. In all cases, first place the cursor where you want to create the new cells, rows, or columns.
  - To insert new cells, choose Table⇨Insert⇨Cell. FrontPage places a new cell directly to the right of the cell in which you placed the cursor.
  - To insert new rows or columns, choose Table⇨Insert⇨Rows or Columns. The Insert Rows or Columns dialog box appears (see Figure 5-7). Choose the number of rows or columns that you want to insert, as well as their location, and then click OK to insert them.

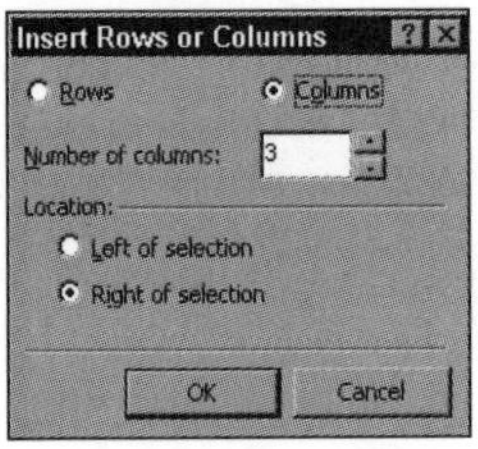

Figure 5-7: Use this dialog box to insert a row or column wherever you want.

- **Deleting cells:** Select a cell (or group of cells) and then choose Table⇨Delete Cells to eliminate the cell and its contents from the table.
- **Merging cells:** Select the cells that you want to merge and then choose Table⇨Merge Cells to collapse the two cells and combine their contents.
- **Splitting cells:** Select the cells that you want to split and then choose Table⇨Split Cells. From the Split Cells dialog box that appears, choose whether you want to split into rows or columns and how many rows or columns you want to split the cell(s) into and then click OK.

- **Distributing cells:** Select rows or columns of uneven size and then choose either Table⇨Distribute Rows Evenly or Table⇨Distribute Columns Evenly to make the rows or columns equal sizes.
- **AutoFit to Contents:** The AutoFit to Contents command tries to find the optimal size for the cells in the table based on their contents. This way, the table contains no wasted space. AutoFit to Contents is a good tool to use if you replace text or a graphic of a different size within a table cell. Select the cells and choose Table⇨AutoFit to Contents to set the optimal table.

Creating and Using Hyperlinks

Hyperlinks sounds like such an impressive word . . . very futuristic . . . the kind of thing you'd expect Captain Kirk or Captain Picard to burst out with on any given episode of *Star Trek.* Truthfully, however, hyperlinks are just a way of jumping from location to location within a series of Web pages.

Hyperlinks are the navigational building blocks of any Web site. Without hyperlinks, you'd never get off the home page of a Web site. So, not surprisingly, FrontPage offers a vast array of tools for generating and maintaining hyperlinks. To create a hyperlink in a Web page, follow these steps:

REAL WORLD

Checking spelling on a Web page

Don't wait to check the spelling on your pages until they're up on the Web! Check your spelling before others find your mistakes. You can run a spell-check on a page to make sure that it doesn't contain spelling errors. You can also tell FrontPage to fix those spelling errors and track them so that you can see them in the Tasks View. To track spelling errors in FrontPage, follow these steps:

1. **Choose Tools⇨Spelling.**

   The Spelling dialog box appears if FrontPage detects a spelling error. (As in other Office products, you can also press F7 to open the Spelling dialog box.)

2. **Click the correct spelling in the Suggestions list box or type it in the Change To box.**
3. **Click the Change button.**
4. **Keeping correcting errors until you see the** `Spelling Check Is Complete` **message.**

You also find Ignore buttons for ignoring what FrontPage thinks are spelling errors, and an Add button for entering words in the dictionary and preventing the spell-checker from stopping on them in the future.

1. **Highlight the text or image that you want to turn into a hyperlink. (You can also create a link to a page without highlighting anything at all. In this case, the link uses the title of the page that you're linking to for a text description.)**

2. **Choose Insert⇨Hyperlink, click the Insert Hyperlink button, or press Ctrl+K.**

   The Insert Hyperlink dialog box appears (see Figure 5-8).

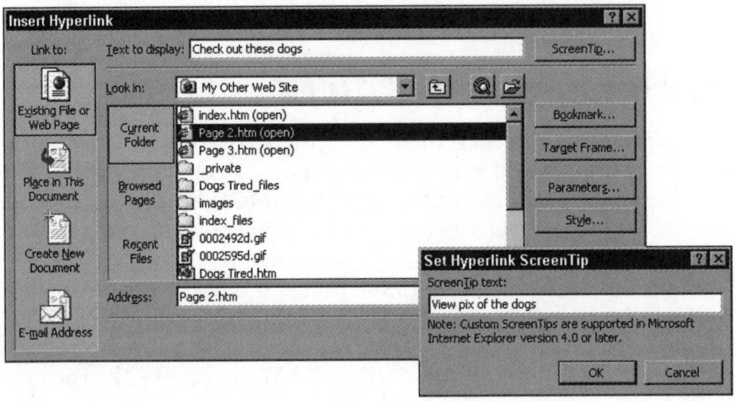

Figure 5-8: Hyper-linking's never been so easy.

3. **Click the ScreenTip button. In the Set Hyperlink ScreenTip dialog box that appears, type a brief two-or-three word description of the hyper-link and click OK.**

   When visitors to your Web site move their mouse pointers over the link, they see the description that you enter in a pop-up box.

4. **Create the link (see the next bulleted list).**
5. **Click OK.**

Here's how to create the different kinds of hyperlinks in the Insert Hyperlink dialog box:

✦ **A link to a Web page on the Internet:** Under Link To, click the Existing File or Web Page button. Then type the address of the Web page by doing one of the following:

  • Type it in the Address text box.

  • Open the Address drop-down list and select it.

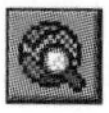

- Click the Browse the Web button. Your Web browser opens. Go to the Web page that you want to link to. After you return to the Insert Hyperlink dialog box, the address of the page appears in the Address text box.
- Click the Browsed Pages button, look for the address of the page, and select it.

✦ **A link to another page in your Web:** Click the Existing File or Web Page button. Then click the Current Folder button. The dialog box lists the files that make up your Web. Find the Web page that you want to link to and select it.

✦ **A link to another place in the same Web page you are on:** Click the Place in This Document button. Then click the plus sign next to the Bookmarks label, if necessary, to see the bookmarks on the page; find the one that you want to link to and click it. To link to a place in the same document, you must have bookmarks in your document. To place a bookmark, click where you want the bookmark to go, choose Insert➪Bookmark, enter a name for the bookmark in the Bookmark dialog box that appears, and click OK.

✦ **A link to an e-mail address:** Click the E-mail Address button. Then enter your e-mail address, suggest a subject for the messages that others send you, and click the OK button.

After you create a hyperlink, make sure that you test it by pressing the Ctrl button and clicking it. If the hyperlink doesn't work, right-click it, choose Hyperlink Properties from the shortcut menu, and fix the link in the Edit Hyperlink dialog box that appears. This dialog box works exactly like the Insert Hyperlink dialog box (refer to Figure 5-8). Click the Remove Link button to remove a hyperlink.

Working with the Hyperlinks view

One of the nice things about the Hyperlinks view is that you can choose any object in your Web site — including HTML pages and graphics — and see exactly what pages or other objects link into that object. You can also see where the object links. With the Folder list open, all you need to do is click an object, and the Hyperlinks view displays all the links to and from that page, as shown in Figure 5-9.

FrontPage comes with a Web browser built into its editor, but sometimes, you just can't beat the real thing. In FrontPage, you can preview a Web page in any of the browsers on your computer.

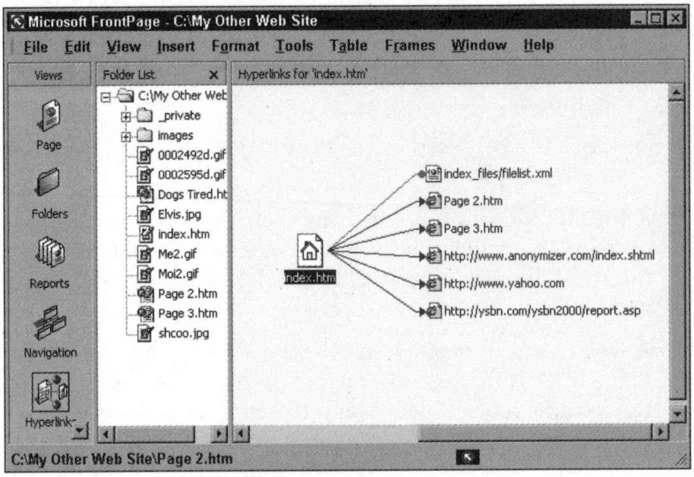

Figure 5-9: Hyperlinks view displays all your links.

Recalculating a project's hyperlinks

Through the process of building pages, moving folders around, and generally doing the work that maintaining a Web site requires, some things are liable to get broken. Hyperlinks are usually the first things to go. To combat this problem, FrontPage depends on Hyperlinks view, which enables you to see the links to and from every page and graphic on your site.

REAL WORLD

So what's your page looking like?

You probably don't like the idea of working on something that you can't see. Well, FrontPage doesn't keep you in the dark. To preview a Web page from any browser on your desktop, follow these steps:

1. **Switch to the Folders view by clicking the Folders icon in the Views bar or choose View⇨Folder List to open the Folder list from your current view.**
2. **Click the page that you want to preview in an external Web browser.**
3. **Choose File⇨Preview in Browser.**

   The Preview in Browser dialog box appears.
4. **Select the browser in which you want to preview the page.**
5. **Designate a window size by selecting one of the 6409 x 480, 800 x 600, or 1024 x 768 options in the Window Size area.**

   FrontPage supports four viewing ranges: the browser Default size, 640 x 480, 800 x 600, and 1024 x 768.
6. **Click the Preview button to view your Web page in the specified browser.**

Ah, but if it's broken and you can't see it amid the links, how do you know that it's broken? That's where the FrontPage Recalculate Hyperlinks feature comes in handy.

To recalculate hyperlinks, choose Tools➪Recalculate Hyperlinks. FrontPage warns you that recalculating may take a while and asks whether you really want to do it. Click Yes after you see the prompt, and you're off. Although a progress indicator doesn't appear, the bottom-left corner shows you that FrontPage is recalculating your hyperlinks.

Chapter 6: Making Your Pages Worth Looking At

In This Chapter

- **Adding ad banners, buttons, counters, and marquees**
- **Adding clip art and other graphics**

If people want to see black text on a white background, they can read a book. On the Web, people like to push things, watch things move, and see neat pictures. If you want to make your Web page a success, you need to make it visually pleasing. In this chapter, you find out how to add exciting graphics and navigation aids to your Web site.

Inserting Some Extra Effects

You may have admired some Web pages that feature moving messages, animated buttons, hit counters, and the like. These effects are easily within your reach, and this section shows you the way.

Adding a banner ad

So what is a banner ad? Well, mostly, it's how companies make their money on the Web — but that's a different story! Actually, a banner is a set of similarly sized images, usually appearing at the top or bottom of a Web page.

Banners are commonly used as a method of promoting advertising messages as well as key pieces of information that you want users to know. Adding a banner in FrontPage is simple. To do so, follow these steps:

1. **Choose Insert➪Web Component.**

   The Insert Web Component dialog box appears.

2. **Under Choose an Effect, double-click Banner Ad Manager.**

   The Banner Ad Manager Properties dialog box appears (see Figure 6-1). In this dialog box, you can specify all the different settings for your ad banner.

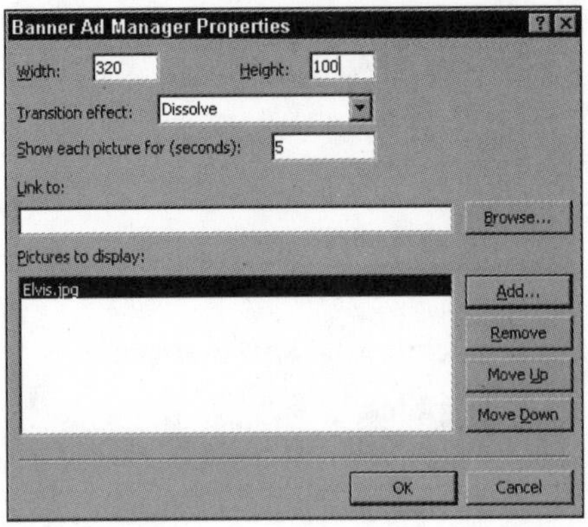

Figure 6-1: The Banner Ad Manager Properties dialog box.

3. **Choose the settings for your banner ad.**

   Table 6-1 explains the various settings.

4. **Click OK to insert the banner ad into your Web page.**
5. **Select the Preview view in the FrontPage Editor to preview your banner.**

Table 6-1 Banner Ad Settings

Setting	*What It Means*
Width/Height	The size of the banner. If your images are large, FrontPage crops them to fit. Enter the dimensions of your banner to be in the Width and Height text box.
Transition Effect	How the banner ads transition from one to the next. The more complicated the images are, the slower the page downloads. Choose an option from the drop-down list.
Show Each Picture For	The duration of time that users can view each image. Enter a number in the text box.
Link To	If you want the banner to link to another page, you can specify in this text box where you want it to link. Click the Browse button, and in Select Banner Ad Hyperlink, select the Web page (Chapter 6 explains how to establish a hyperlink).
Pictures to Display	By using the Add, Remove, Move Up, and Move Down buttons, you can specify from this area the number of images that you want to appear, as well as their viewing order.

WARNING!

Banner ads work by adding a Java applet to your Web. The advantage to using Java is that the ad transitions look nicer. But if you start using a lot of transitions, adding an applet makes your Web page run slower.

Adding a hit counter

A *hit counter* tracks the number of times people access a page and displays the number of "hits" on the Web page itself. It's a nice way of saying, "Hey, look how popular my Web page is!" (That is, unless nobody's visiting your Web site, in which case you probably don't want to include a hit counter.) To add a hit counter, follow these steps:

1. **Choose Insert⇨Web Component.**

   The Insert Web Component dialog box appears.

2. **In the Component Type area, click to select Hit Counter.**

   The right side of the dialog box offers different counters that you may choose for your Web page.

3. **Click to select the style and number of digits that you want in your hit counter.**

4. **Click the Finish button.**

   The Hit Counter Properties dialog box appears (see Figure 6-2).

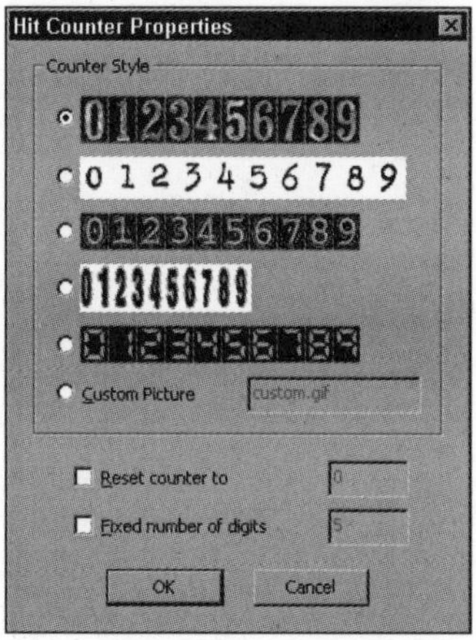

Figure 6-2: The Hit Counter Properties dialog box.

5. **Under Counter Style, select an option to specify the style and number of digits that you want; then click OK.**

TIP

If you're editing an existing hit counter and you want to reset the counter, click the Reset Counter To check box and, in the text box next to it, type the number to which you want to the counter to be reset.

Adding a hover button

If you don't have buttons that animate or highlight as you roll your mouse cursor over them, something's definitely wrong with your Web site — at least that's what conventional wisdom preaches. A number of methods exist for adding this kind of graphical quality to a Web page, including using JavaScript and Dynamic HTML. Not to be outdone, FrontPage offers you a way to use Java to create the same effect! To add a hover button, follow these steps:

1. **Choose Insert➪Web Component.**

   The Insert Web Component dialog box appears.

2. **In the Choose an Effect area, double-click Hover Button.**

   The Hover Button Properties dialog box appears (see Figure 6-3).

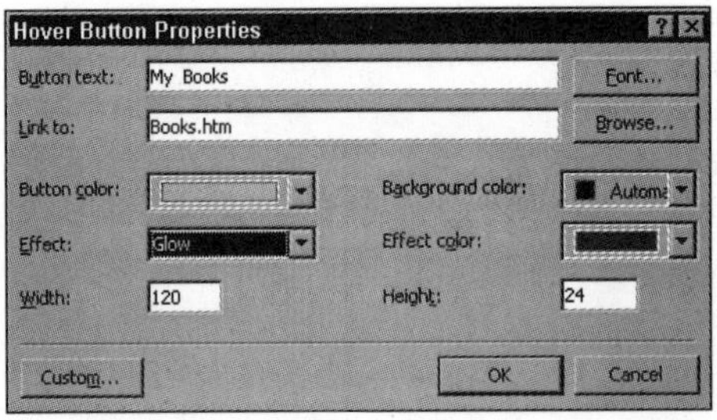

Figure 6-3: The Hover Button Properties dialog box.

3. **Specify the properties for your hover button.**

   You can set a number of different options for the button, including the size and color of the button and its highlight state, the *rollover effect* (what happens as the mouse cursor rolls over the button), and the page to which the button links after you click it.

4. **Click OK to insert the hover button into your Web page.**

Adding a marquee

Have you ever seen the stock listings whoosh by on a digital board or at the bottom of your television screen? Those are two examples of a marquee, which you can easily embed in your Web page. To add a marquee to a Web page in FrontPage, follow these steps:

1. **Choose Insert➪Web Component.**

   The Insert Web Component dialog box appears.

2. **In the Choose an Effect area, double-click Marquee.**

   The Marquee Properties dialog box appears (see Figure 6-4).

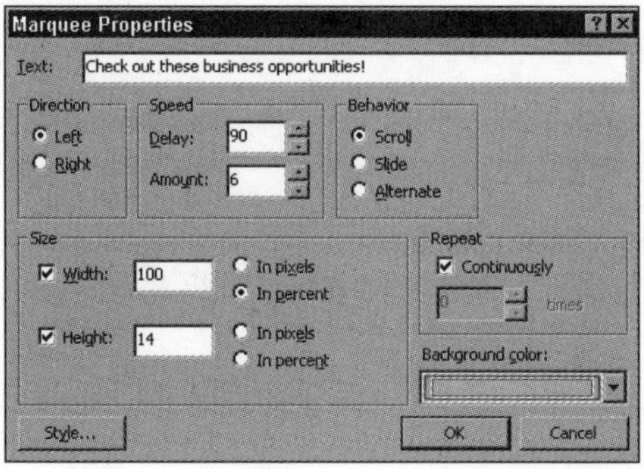

Figure 6-4: The Marquee Properties dialog box.

3. **Specify the properties for your marquee.**

   Table 6-2 explains your options. In addition to these options, you can change the text style associated with the banner. To do so, click the Style button and then either select from the available styles or select Format to create a new style.

4. **Click OK to insert the marquee into your Web page.**

Table 6-2 Marquee Settings

Setting	*What It Means*
Direction	Specify the direction in which you want the text to move across the screen by selecting the Left or Right option.
Speed	Choose the speed at which you want the text to move. In the Delay text box, enter the amount of time in milliseconds that the marquee pauses before it starts moving. In the Amount text box, enter the distance in pixels that the marquee is to move.
Behavior	Indicate how you want the text to move on-screen by choosing the Scroll, Slide, or Alternate option. If you choose the Alternate option, the marquee alternates between scrolling and sliding.
Size	Choose the size of the banner by entering its dimensions in the Width and Height text boxes. By choosing an option, you can specify whether the dimension measurement you are entering is in pixels or a percentage. Percentage is the better option, because by choosing it, you can take into account the visitors Web browser.
Repeat	Decide whether the banner repeats continuously or appears only once. Deselect the Continuously check box if you want it to appear once. To make it repeat, enter the number of times that you want it to repeat in the Times text box.
Background Color	Indicate the background color for the marquee by choosing a color on this drop-down list.

Adding Graphics to Web Pages

Now that FrontPage looks more like Word than anything else, the similarities between adding graphics to a Web page in FrontPage and adding graphics to a document in Word aren't surprising. In fact, adding graphics in FrontPage is very similar to adding graphics in Word. If, however, you can't adjust your preferences to using the Word-like interface in FrontPage, you can still use the FrontPage HTML capabilities.

TIP

Although FrontPage supports a host of file formats for graphics, older browsers don't support many of the file formats that FrontPage supports. As a result, you're better off making sure that the graphic that you want to import is in either GIF or JPG format before you import it into FrontPage. (Besides, those graphics load faster than the others.)

If you're looking for graphics for your Web page, you can either get one from your computer or use one from the Microsoft Clip Organizer.

Adding a graphic on your own

To add a graphic that you're storing on your computer, follow these steps:

1. **Click the location on the active Web page where you want to put your graphic. (If your page is blank, your only choice is to place your cursor in the top-left corner.)**
2. **Choose Insert➪Picture➪From File to open the Picture dialog box (see Figure 6-5).**

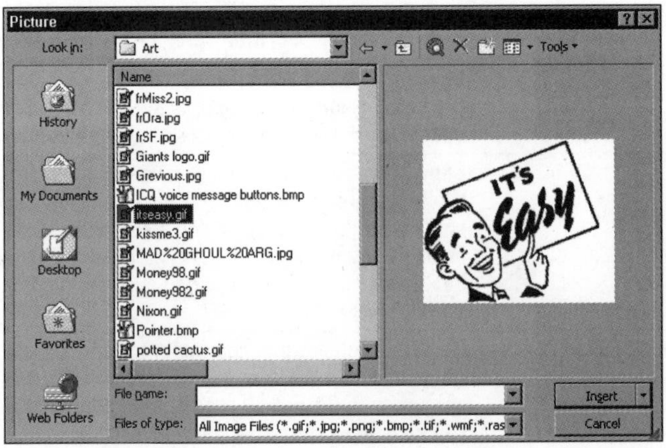

Figure 6-5: If you can find it, you can insert it by using the Picture dialog box.

3. **Select the graphic that you want to insert.**

   From the Picture dialog box, you can browse your Web, the rest of your computer, or the Internet to find the graphic that you want to insert. FrontPage also provides thumbnail previews for each graphic that you click, so you can see what you're adding before you add it.

4. **Click the Insert button to add the graphic to your Web page.**

   You can also add graphics to a Web page via the traditional Windows drag-and-drop interface. To do so, go to the folder on your desktop that houses the graphic that you want to insert. Click and drag the graphic onto the active Web page and voilà! There it is . . . good to go!

Adding clip art from the Clip Organizer to a Web page

FrontPage comes with an extensive Clip Art gallery that helps you create buttons and banners, as well as communicate all kinds of different themes and emotions. To add clip art to your Web page, follow these steps:

1. **Click the Web page where you want the clip art to appear.**
2. **Click the Insert Clip Art button on the Drawing toolbar or choose Insert⇨Picture⇨Clip Art.**

   The Insert Clip Art task pane appears on-screen, as shown in Figure 6-6.

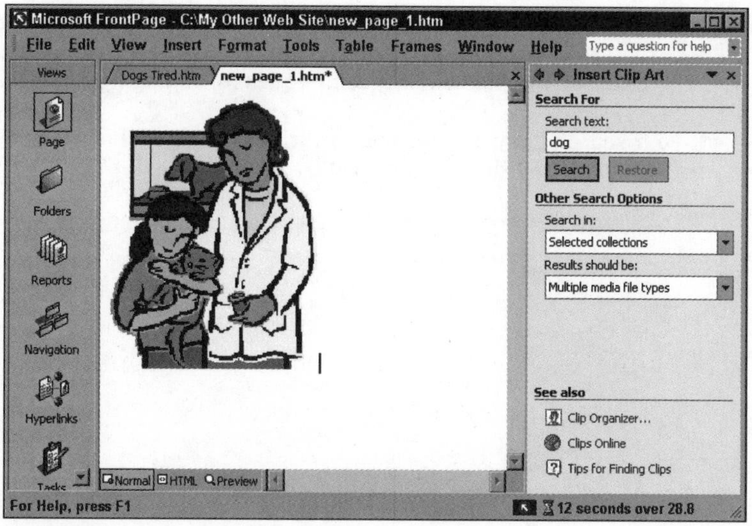

Figure 6-6: The Insert Clip Art task pane.

3. **Tell FrontPage how and where to search for clip-art images.**

   Choose among the following options in searching for clip-art images in the Insert Clip Art task pane:

   - **Search Text:** Type a word in this text box that describes what kind of clip art you want.
   - **Search In:** Open the drop-down list and choose options to tell FrontPage where to search. As long as the Everywhere check box is selected, FrontPage searches for every piece of clip art it can lay hands on, including clip art from the Microsoft Web site. You can, however, click check boxes beside the names of specific areas where you want to search.
   - **Results Should Be:** Open the drop-down list and make choices to tell FrontPage what kind of clip art you want. If the All Media Types check box is selected, FrontPage searches for photographs, movies, and sounds, as well as clip art. Click the plus sign (+) beside the All Media Types folder and then deselect Photographs, Movies, and Sounds to search for clip art only.

4. **Click the Search button.**

   If FrontPage can find clip-art images, they appear in thumbnail form in the Insert Clip Art task pane. If necessary, scroll down the list to examine all the images or click the small icon under the word *Results* to see the images in a box.

5. **Click an image to insert it in your document.**

   The image is probably too large and you need to make it smaller. To do so, drag a corner handle on the image toward the image's center. (Chapter 7 explains many techniques for changing the size of images.)

If your search turns up nothing or turns up images that you aren't happy with, click the Modify button to start all over.

Chapter 7: Image Editing for Everyone

In This Chapter

- **Using the Pictures toolbar**
- **Manipulating and editing your images**
- **Making an image map**

Simply grabbing or creating an image and then plopping it as-is into your Web page doesn't enable you to take full advantage of the FrontPage editing capabilities. You may find a great image to use, but think about what else you can do to it. You can scale it, flip it, move it, bevel it, brighten it, and more! You may even want to place some text over it or turn the image itself into a hyperlink. You can even turn different parts of the image into hyperlinks and make a clickable image map. This chapter walks you through the process of editing your images in FrontPage.

Activating the Pictures Toolbar

In FrontPage, you can't edit a graphics image without first activating the Pictures toolbar. Unlike a number of the other toolbars in FrontPage, the Pictures toolbar doesn't have any corresponding keyboard or menu options. To activate the Pictures toolbar, choose View⇨Toolbars⇨Pictures or right-click a toolbar and choose Pictures from the shortcut menu.

REAL WORLD

Working with Auto Thumbnails

An *Auto Thumbnail* is a handy tool that enables you to create a miniversion of a picture. This tool is particularly useful if you want to use an image as a button that then links to a larger version of the picture. To create an Auto Thumbnail, select an image and click the Auto Thumbnail button on the Pictures toolbar.

After you create a thumbnail and go to save the page, FrontPage prompts you to save the new thumbnail image. After you load the page in a browser, you see the thumbnail rather than the original image. Then, after you click the thumbnail, the larger version appears in the Web browser by itself.

Figure 7-1 shows the basic functionality of each button on the Pictures toolbar.

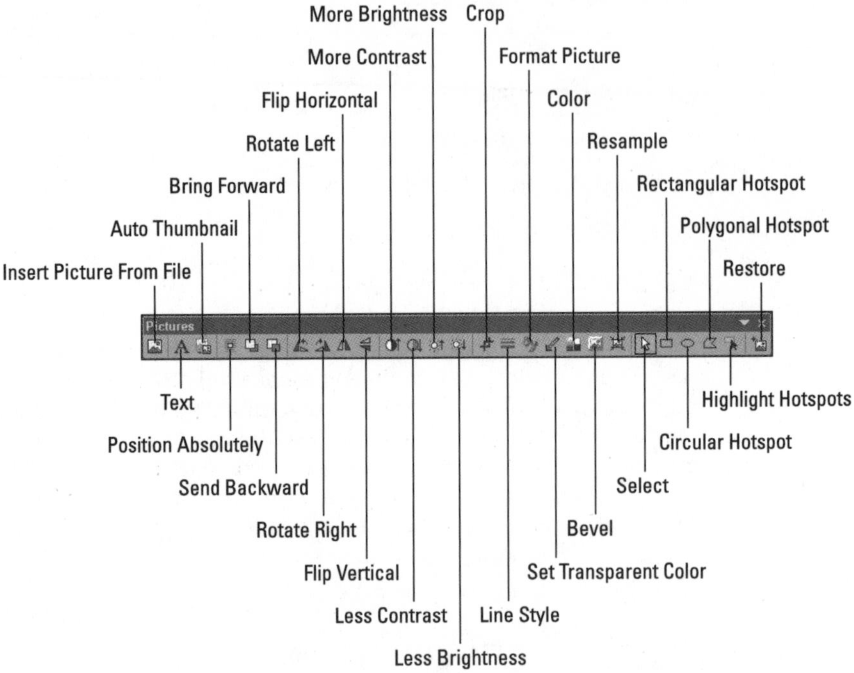

Figure 7-1: The Pictures toolbar.

Image Manipulation Made Easy

If FrontPage doesn't make image manipulation easy, it at least makes image manipulation easier than ever before. Although image editing in FrontPage isn't as powerful as in PhotoShop or some of the other popular graphics software, you can't beat the convenience — and the price — of getting this editing capability already built into your Web-creation application.

Scaling an image

Scaling is the process of making an entire image either larger or smaller. No cutting away of the image is involved here. In fact, you don't even find a button for this function! You can scale an image just by clicking it.

After you click an image, you see anchor points appear around the border of the image. To scale the image, click and drag one of these anchor points. The image resizes itself according to where you release the anchor point.

To scale an image and keep its proportions intact, choose one of the corner anchor points and then scale the image. Scaling in this manner keeps the *aspect ratio* (the height-to-width ratio of an image) consistent as the image gets bigger or smaller.

After you scale your image, you can resample it by clicking the Resample button on the Pictures toolbar. The Resample tool analyzes the image that you just scaled. If, for example, the image became bigger, the pixels that make up the image are stretched. The Resample tool then breaks up the stretched pixels into smaller pixels to create a crisper, cleaner image. Similarly, if you shrink the image, you end up with more pixels than are really necessary for a smaller image. In this case, using the Resample tool eliminates any unnecessary pixels without sacrificing image quality.

If you don't like how your new-scaled image looks, you can click the Restore button to reset the image to its original size.

You can use the Restore button on a number of other Pictures toolbar features as well, including the Color, Brightness, Contrast, Rotate, and Flip tools.

Changing brightness and contrast

Changing a graphic's *brightness* makes the graphic appear lighter or darker. Changing a graphic's *contrast* makes the graphic's individual pixels either stand out more or become more muted. Usually, setting a graphic's contrast goes hand in hand with changing the graphic's brightness. So, for example, the brighter a graphic becomes, the more contrast you need to avoid it becoming washed out. To change an image's brightness and contrast, follow these steps:

1. **In the Page view, click the image that you want to modify.**
2. **Click any of the following four Contrast or Brightness options on the Pictures toolbar:**
   - **More Contrast:** This option increases the color distinctions between pixels.
   - **Less Contrast:** This option makes the colors blend together.
   - **More Brightness:** This option washes the image out.
   - **Less Brightness:** This option darkens the image.

   Every time that you click a button, the brightness or contrast either increases or decreases incrementally. The more times that you click the brightness button, for example, the brighter the image gets.

You can undo your work by pressing Ctrl+Z or clicking the Undo button on the Standard toolbar. In fact, FrontPage supports multiple undos, so if you're fiddling with an image and you want to return it to its previous condition, open the Undo button drop-down list and choose how many actions you want to undo.

Setting an image's transparent color

GIF images support transparency, which means that you can choose to make a particular color on your image invisible. This feature is helpful if you have a square graphic and you want to display only the logo in the middle of the image. In FrontPage, setting the transparent color is a cinch! Here's what you do:

1. **In Page view, click the graphic that contains the color that you want to make transparent.**
2. **Click the Set Transparent Color button on the Pictures toolbar.**
3. **Click the color on the image that you want to make transparent.**

   After you do so, all instances of that color in the image become invisible, and you can see the Web page background through it.

Only GIF images can be made transparent, but all is not lost if you're using other image types in your Web page — a JPEG image, for example — because FrontPage tries to turn images into a GIF files after you click the Set Transparent Color button on the Pictures toolbar. In addition, you can set only one transparent color by using this tool. If you select the tool again and click another color, that color becomes the transparent color, and the preceding transparent color is no longer transparent.

Beveling an image

Beveling adds both a border and three-dimensional depth to a graphic. The most frequent reason to bevel an image is to create a button effect. To bevel an image in FrontPage, follow these steps:

1. **With the Normal button selected in Page view, click the image that you want to bevel.**
2. **Click the Bevel button on the Pictures toolbar.**

   The button adds a bevel to your graphic, as shown in Figure 7-2.

3. **If you want to make the bevel darker and add more emphasis to it, click the Bevel button again.**

Click the Undo button on the Standard toolbar if you regret clicking the Bevel button too many times.

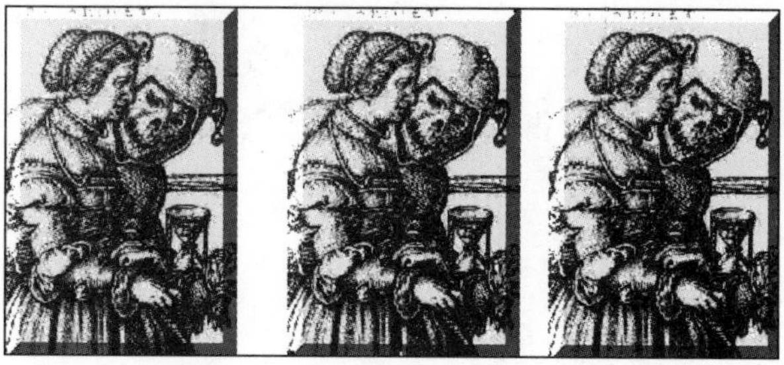

Figure 7-2: An image can have a beveled edge.

Cropping an image

Cropping reduces an image in size. Cropping images comes in handy if, for example, you have a picture of you and your mother-in-law and you want to eliminate your mother-in-law from the picture. To be honest, the FrontPage cropping features are limited in that you can crop only rectangular areas. To crop an image, follow these steps:

1. **In Page view, click the image that you want to crop.**

2. **Click the Crop button on the Pictures toolbar.**

   After you click the button, a rectangular box appears inside the image's border.

3. **Click and drag a selection handle to form a rectangle around the part of the graphic that you want to keep (see Figure 7-3).**

   There are eight selection handles, one at each corner and one in the middle of each side of the image. You can drag more than one selection handle and in so doing form the rectangle around only the part of the image that you want.

4. **Press Enter to crop the image to the size of the rectangle.**

Cropping cuts away everything that remains outside the cropping rectangle. If you specify an area, you're specifying the area of the image that you want to keep and not the area that you want to cut.

If you decide that you don't want to crop an image, press the Esc key or click outside the image to disengage the cropping tool.

Figure 7-3: You can crop any part of an image.

Flipping and rotating images

FrontPage makes flipping and rotating images easy. To do so, follow these steps:

1. **In Page view, click the graphic that you want to flip or rotate.**
2. **Click the Rotate Left, Rotate Right, Flip Horizontal, or Flip Vertical button on the Pictures toolbar, depending on the action that you want to initiate.**

   You get the following options with each button:

   - **Rotate Left:** This option rotates the image 90 degrees to the left.

   - **Rotate Right:** This option rotates the image 90 degrees to the right.

   - **Flip Horizontal:** This option mirrors the image left to right.

   - **Flip Vertical:** This option mirrors the image top to bottom.

Placing text over an image

FrontPage supports a clever little way of placing text in images to achieve a nice effect. To do so, follow these steps:

1. **In Page view, click the graphic over which you want to place text.**

2. **Click the Text button on the Pictures toolbar.**

   Clicking the Text button generates a text box in the middle of your graphic (see Figure 7-4). To resize the text box, drag the box's anchor points by using your pointer.

Figure 7-4: You can place text over an image.

3. **Type the text that you want in the text box.**

   You can change the font or font size of text by selecting the text and choosing options from the Font and Font Size drop-down lists on the Formatting toolbar.

4. **Press Esc.**

To generate another text box on that image, click the image and then click the Text button again. If you want to move a text box around on the image, click and hold the mouse button while the cursor's in the middle of the text box and then move the text box to its new location.

TIP

Because this graphic is essentially an image map with text, you can also turn these text boxes into hyperlinks. Just press Ctrl+K to open the Edit Hyperlink dialog box after you create a text box in a selected image. Then enter the link location and click OK to add the link to the text on the image.

WARNING!

If you're using other image types in your Web page — a JPEG image, for example — FrontPage tries to turn the image into a GIF file after you click the Text button on the Pictures toolbar. In most cases, this change compromises the graphical quality of the image you're adding text to, because converting from a JPEG to a GIF reduces the number of colors in the image.

Adding a hyperlink to an image

Using images as hyperlinks can add pizzazz and flair to a Web site. To add a hyperlink to an image, follow these steps:

1. **With the Normal button selected in Page view, click the image that you want to make a hyperlink.**

2. **Choose Insert⇨Hyperlink or press Ctrl+K.**

   The Insert Hyperlink dialog box that appears may look familiar; it's the same dialog box that FrontPage uses to create text hyperlinks (see Figure 7-5).

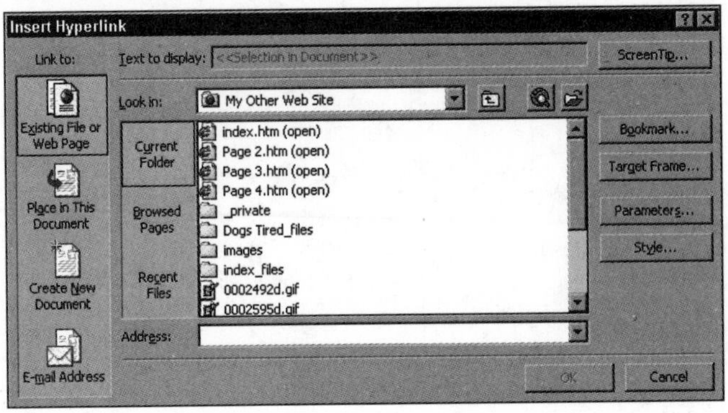

Figure 7-5: The Insert Hyperlink dialog box.

See Chapter 6 for more information about creating text hyperlinks.

3. **Click OK.**

   You can now use the image as a hyperlink on your Web page.

Creating Image Maps

Image maps are great navigation tools that you see in many Web sites. You load a Web page, and a big graphic appears smack dab in the middle of the page. On the graphic are a host of hot links to various locations. How did the Web designers create such a helpful tool, you ask? The answer lies in *image maps.*

You create image maps by specifying regions of a graphic and then setting links for those regions. In the past, you needed to create image maps in a separate program and then load the map into your Web page. Times change. The following steps show you how to create an image map in FrontPage:

1. **With the Normal button selected in Page view, click the graphic for which you want to create an image map.**
2. **Select one of the Image Map shapes tools from the Pictures toolbar.**

   FrontPage provides the following shape tools for creating image maps:

   - **Rectangular Hotspot:** This button creates squares and rectangles. To create a square or rectangular link, click the image and then drag the mouse while holding the mouse button. FrontPage creates a square image from the point where you first click the mouse.

   - **Circular Hotspot:** This button creates circles and ovals. You create a circular link precisely the same as you do a rectangular hotspot.

   - **Polygonal Hotspot:** This button enables you to create multisided polygon areas. Click the image first to create a path and then click it again to specify each point for the linked area. You finish creating the polygon by selecting the first path point. Doing so encloses the polygonal image.

3. **Create the shape that you want.**

   After you create the shape, the Insert Hyperlink dialog box appears.

4. **Create the hyperlink.**

   Chapter 6 explains in detail how to create a hyperlink.

5. **Click OK to set the hyperlink.**

TIP

You may want to move your link around on the graphic after you create it. To do so, click the Select button (the arrow) on the Pictures toolbar and then click and hold the mouse button on the link. As long as you continue to hold the mouse button, you can drag the link around on the graphic.

To change the size of the link, click and hold any of the link's *anchor points* — the square dots along the outline of the link area. Then drag the anchor to the desired location, and the link automatically scales according to where you move the anchor point. Releasing the mouse button changes the link's size.

Chapter 8: Publishing Your Web Pages

In This Chapter

- **Publishing via HTTP**
- **Publishing via FTP**

Eventually, you need to put your hard work on the World Wide Web for everyone to see. The process of publishing on the Web may seem difficult, but it's probably one of the easiest steps in creating a Web page — which explains why so much junk is already out there. This chapter shows you how to join the fray.

Publishing a Web by Using HTTP

HTTP sounds new and nifty, but if you've ever loaded a Web page, you already know what HTTP does. HTTP, which stands for HyperText Transfer Protocol, is simply a way of transferring data from a server to your Web browser (and vice versa). In fact, HTTP is the preferred way of transferring files in FrontPage.

To use this method of file transfer, your Internet service provider must support the FrontPage server extensions. Use the FTP method of uploading files if you Internet service provider doesn't support the server extensions.

To publish a Web by using HTTP, follow these steps:

1. **Choose File➪Publish Web.**

   The Publish Destination dialog box appears.

2. **Type the URL where you want to publish your Web content in the Enter Publish Destination text box.**

   Click the hyperlink in the dialog box if you're not sure whether your ISP provides the appropriate server extensions to support the FrontPage publishing features. Clicking the hyperlink sends you to the Microsoft Web site for the most current list of ISPs that support the extensions.

   If you're not sure of the location to which you want to publish your Web, click the Browse button in the Publish Destination dialog box to search for FrontPage servers from the New Publish Location dialog box.

3. **Click OK to submit the new Web content.**

   FrontPage tracks the progress of the upload and shows you which pages are transferring. After the upload is complete, an alert box appears, telling you so.

If you're publishing your Web to a Web server, it's likely to be password-protected. As you first see the Publish Web dialog box, you're more likely than not going to get another dialog box prompting you for your user name and password. This safeguard is to prevent people from coming along and posting content on any Web site they want.

Publishing a Web by Using FTP

People were publishing Web sites by using the Internet File Transfer Protocol long before Microsoft came along and tried to make the whole process transparent to the user. Now, by using FrontPage, you can finally connect to any server and publish your content on the Internet by using FTP. *FTP* is a software interface that enables you to send (and also receive) files to a remote computer over the Internet. Thanks to the protocol, you don't have to enter detailed commands about which files you want to send. All you have to do is designate a folder on your computer.

Publishing by using FTP consists of two parts. The first is to set up your FTP connection, and the second is to publish the content.

Setting up an FTP connection

To set up an FTP connection, follow these steps:

1. **Choose File⇨Open Web to access the Open Web dialog box.**

   Or, if you prefer, you can perform these same steps from the Open File dialog box, which you open by choosing File⇨Open.

2. **Open the Look In drop-down list and select Add/Modify FTP Locations.**

   Doing so opens the Add/Modify FTP Locations dialog box, as shown in Figure 8-1.

3. **In the Name of FTP Site text box, type the name of the FTP site.**

   For the Dummies FTP site, for example, you type `ftp.dummies.com`.

4. **In the Log On As area, choose how you want to log on to the FTP site.**

   If you want to log on anonymously, select the Anonymous option. If you're a registered user, select the User option and then type your name in the text box to the right of that button.

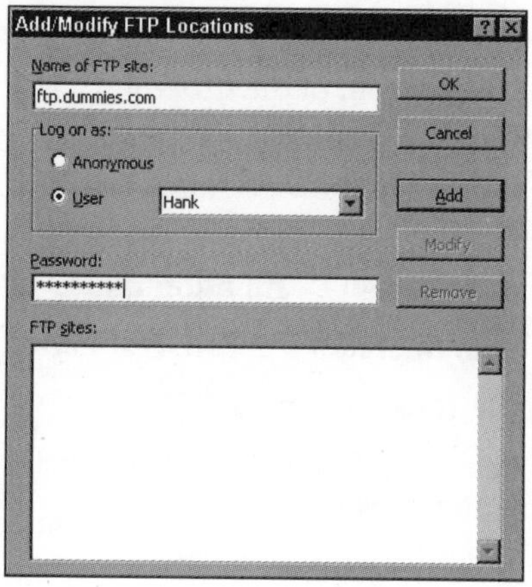

Figure 8-1: Establishing an FTP connection.

5. **Type your password in the Password text box.**

   TIP: If you log on anonymously, most FTP sites either request or require that you use your e-mail address as your logon password.

6. **Click the Add button to add your FTP location to the FTP Sites area in the dialog box.**

   You can also change the particulars of a location by clicking it in the FTP Sites area and then clicking the Modify button. Similarly, you can delete a location by selecting it and clicking the Remove button.

7. **Click OK in the Add/Modify FTP Locations dialog box to activate the connection and return to the Open Web dialog box.**
8. **Click Cancel to return to FrontPage.**

Publishing your Web

After you set up the FTP connection, you can publish your Web content by following these simple steps:

1. **Choose File⇨Publish Web.**

   The Publish Destination dialog box appears.

2. **Click the Browse button to access the New Publish Locations dialog box.**

   The following steps explain how to enter the publish destination by clicking the Browse button. But if you happen to know the location, you can type it in the Enter Publish Destination text box.

3. **Open the Look In drop-down list and select an FTP location.**

   You find FTP locations at the bottom of the drop-down list, below Add/Modify FTP Locations.

   The site that you select appears in the Web Name text box at the bottom of the dialog box.

4. **Click Open to return to the Publish Destination dialog box.**

   Your FTP location appears in the Enter Publish Destination text box.

5. **Click OK to FTP your content to the server.**

   If you see the Name and Password Required dialog box, type your user name and password there and click OK.

Index

G

H

I

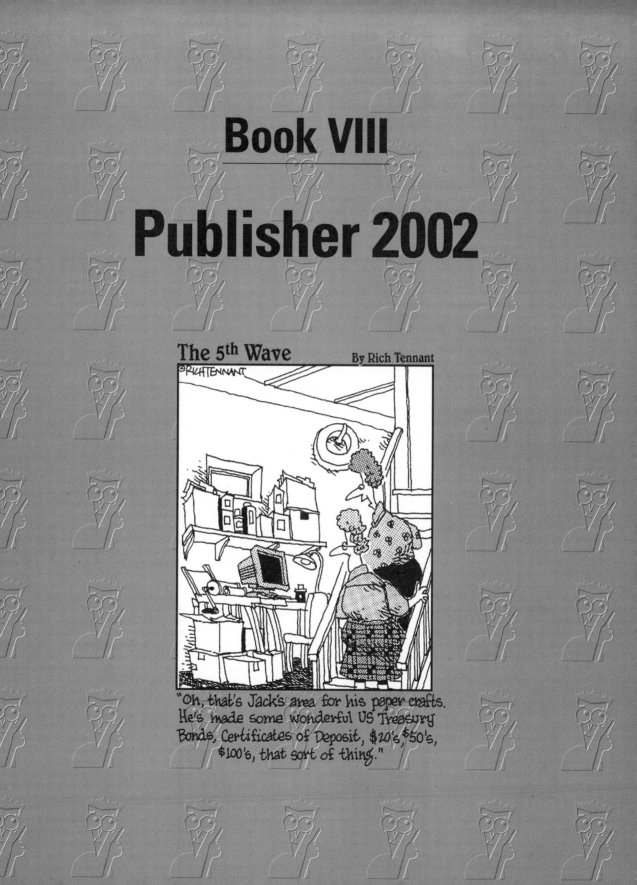

Book VIII

Publisher 2002

The 5th Wave

By Rich Tennant

"Oh, that's Jack's area for his paper crafts. He's made some wonderful US Treasury Bonds, Certificates of Deposit, \$20's, \$50's, \$100's, that sort of thing."

Contents at a Glance

Chapter 1: Getting Started with Publisher

In This Chapter

- **Creating a publication**
- **Saving your files**

This chapter covers the Publisher basics. Here you find out how to do the day-to-day stuff, such as creating publications, using the wizards, and so on. If you've been using Publisher for a while, feel free to skip this section. A word of warning, however: This material is on the test. Okay, so I'm not really giving you a test. But read the chapter anyway, and you may just discover something new!

Creating a Publication

A *publication* is any document that you create by using Publisher. Publications range from newsletters to flyers to business cards. Even Web sites are publications if you're using Publisher. And Publisher gives you several ways to create publications.

INTEGRATION

Starting Publisher and getting help with any part of the program is much like starting or getting help in other Office applications. Make sure that you check out Appendix A for details.

After you first start Publisher, you see the New Publication task pane, as shown in Figure 1-1. This task pane is the starting point for creating a publication. No matter what you're doing in Publisher, you can display the New Publication task pane and start a new publication by choosing File➪New from the Publisher menu bar.

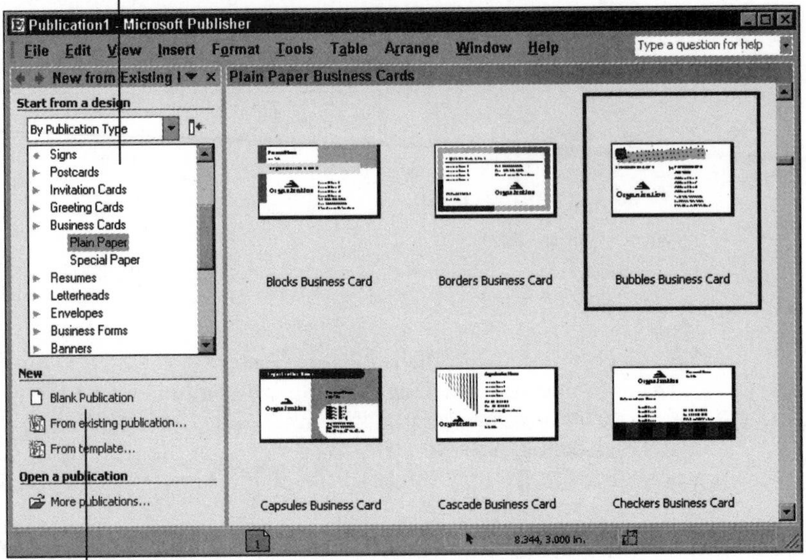

Figure 1-1: Reviewing your options in the New Publication task pane.

Starting with a wizard

The easiest way to create a publication is to start with a *wizard,* a prefabricated publication in which the program does most of the layout and decoration work is for you. All you need to do is replace the text — and the pictures, if you want — to make the publication your own. To create a publication by using a wizard, select By Publication Type in the Start From Design drop-down list of the New Publication task pane and then select the name of the publication type that you want to create. On the right side of the Publisher screen, you see designs for publications. By double-clicking one of these designs, you can activate a wizard and get a head start in creating a publication. Table 1-1 describes these wizards.

Table 1-1 Wizards for Creating Publications

Wizard	*Publications You Can Create*
Quick Publications	One-page publications, including notices, invitations, and posters.
Word Documents	Microsoft Word documents.
Newsletters	Multipage, multicolumn newsletters.
Web Sites	Web sites with sophisticated layouts.

Wizard	*Publications You Can Create*
Brochures	Professional-looking brochures, with all the folding problems solved for you.
Catalogs	Product catalogs — complete with pictures of your products — to send to clients.
Flyers	Informational flyers and flyers for special events, including sales and fund-raisers.
Signs	A variety of signs for businesses.
Postcards	Postcards for all occasions, including holidays and tent-fold postcards.
Invitation Cards	Invitations especially designed for different occasions, including baby showers and birthdays.
Greeting Cards	A passel of different greeting cards.
Business Cards	Business cards that you can print on plain paper or on special paper you purchase from Papers Direct.
Resumes	Resumes in different layouts.
Letterheads	Letterheads that you can print on plain paper or on special paper that you can purchase from Papers Direct.
Envelopes	Envelopes to match letterhead publications. Select plain paper or special paper from Papers Direct.
Business Forms	Professional-looking forms for businesses, including invoices, inventory lists, and statements.
Banners	Banners of all kinds and varieties.
Calendars	Choose between Full Page and Wallet Size calendars. These make great promo items to give to clients.
Advertisements	Lay out your own ads.
Award Certificates	Award certificates, well-decorated and dedicated to commemorating different occasions.
Gift Certificates	Gift certificates, colorfully decorated.
Labels	Mailing-address, shipping, return address, computer disk, cassette, compact disc, video, jar/product, and other labels.
With Compliments Cards	Cards for sending gifts and promo items to clients.
Menus	Take-out menus, fancy menus, and other kinds of menus.
Programs	Music, religious service, and theater programs.
Airplanes	Very neat paper airplanes for children and adults.
Origami	Origami made easy, with paper folds distinctly shown.

After you find the type of publication that you want, double-click it on the right side of the screen. Publisher opens the wizard, and you get the chance to choose the design, color scheme, page size, layout, or Personal Information set that your publication uses. Figure 1-2 shows the wizard for creating a business card. You see tools, including rulers, for laying out the card. In some cases, you see dialog boxes that ask you direct questions about how you want your publication to look.

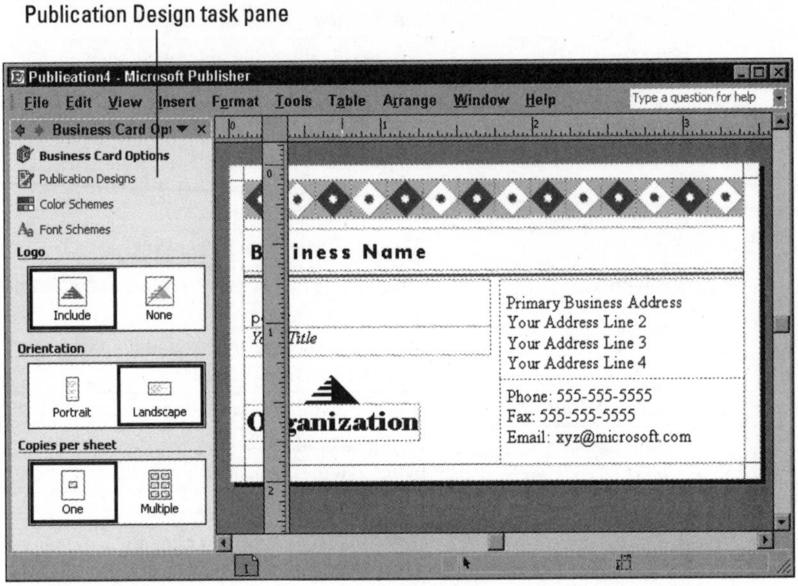

Figure 1-2: Creating a business card by using a wizard.

The design decision that you make as you create a publication by using a wizard isn't set in stone. By choosing options in the top of the Publication Design task pane (which I tell you how to open in a minute), you can alter the design that you choose. (You can't, however, change publication types. After you choose Business Card, for example, you can't go back and turn your business card into a banner.)

Choose View➪Task Pane to see the Publication Design task pane. Then, keeping your eyes on the sample design on-screen, choose from the following options in the task pane to alter your design:

- **Options:** Choose what to include in the publication. (The name of this option changes depending on what you're designing.)
- **Publication Designs:** Click this option and choose a new design from the thumbnails that appear on the task pane.
- **Color Schemes:** Click this option and choose a new color scheme from the drop-down list that appears. Don't be afraid to experiment. You certainly get enough choices!
- **Font Schemes:** Click this option to adjust the fonts used in your design.

TIP

If you need more real estate for working on your publication, you can tell the task plane to go away by clicking its Close button or choosing View➪Task Pane.

Starting from scratch

Maybe you're a do-it-yourself type. In that case, click Blank Publication in the New Publications task pane. (Choose File⇨New to access the task pane.) You see a plain-looking blank document, as shown in Figure 1-3. Start from scratch if you want to create a publication with a new design and you know your way around Publisher.

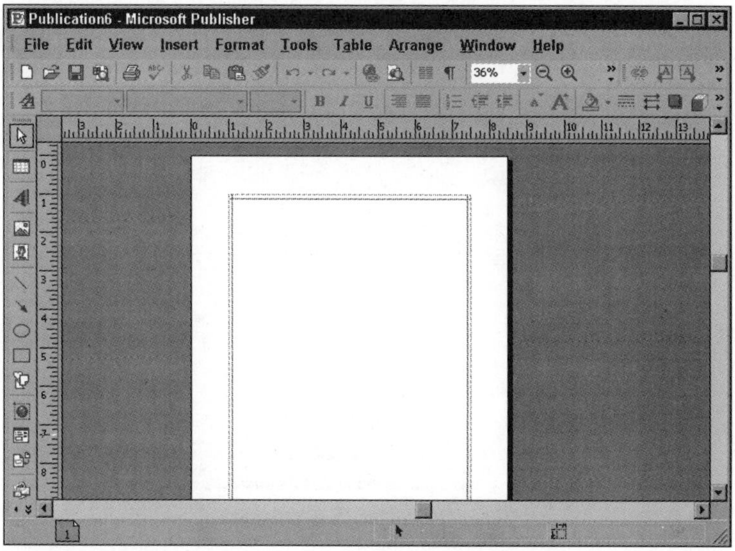

Figure 1-3: Creating a publication from scratch.

Saving Your Files

You can spend hours creating the greatest business publications ever to grace the computer screen, but until you save them, they don't really exist.

File-saving formats

You can save your Publisher publications in any of four different formats: Publisher Files, Publisher Template, Publisher 98 Files, and Publisher 2000 files. Publisher Files is the default. This format is how you normally save your publications. The Publisher Template type is useful if you create a publication that you want to save and base other publications on. Save your file as Publisher 98 or Publisher 2000 Files if you intend to give the publication file to someone who has Publisher 98 or Publisher 2000 installed.

The other file types save the text from your publication in various formats. Most of these file types — except plain text — retain character and paragraph formatting but lose layout and graphics.

File-saving mechanics

Saving is as easy as clicking the Save button on the Standard toolbar. If you prefer to use the menu bar, choose File⇨Save. Or you can press Ctrl+S. The first time that you save a publication, you're get the Save As dialog box, as shown in Figure 1-4. Type a name for your publication in the File Name text box and click the Save button. That's all you need to do! After you save a publication, you can save any changes that you make by choosing your favorite method of issuing the Save command. Publisher saves your publication without bothering you with the Save As dialog box.

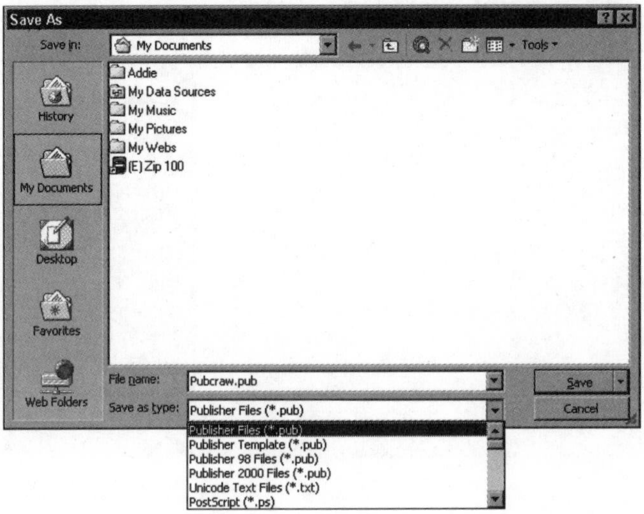

Figure 1-4: The Save As dialog box with the Save As Type drop-down list box open.

Chapter 2: Working with Pages

In This Chapter

- Moving around in your publication
- Changing your point of view
- Using rulers and guides to align objects
- Using backgrounds for a consistent look
- Modifying a page layout
- Altering publication types

Whether you use one of the wizards to create a publication or start with a blank publication, Publisher establishes defaults for the number of pages, the page size, margin guides, and so on. If these defaults suit your needs, great! If you need to change things a bit, this chapter is here to help. You also find out how to add and delete pages, change margins, and more.

Moving from Page to Page

Every publication must have at least one page. In a one-page publication, the current, or active, page is the page you're working on. In multipage publications, you determine the active page by checking the Page Navigation controls on the Status bar, as shown in Figure 2-1. In the figure, the 1 icon is selected, so page one is showing, and the publication has four pages altogether.

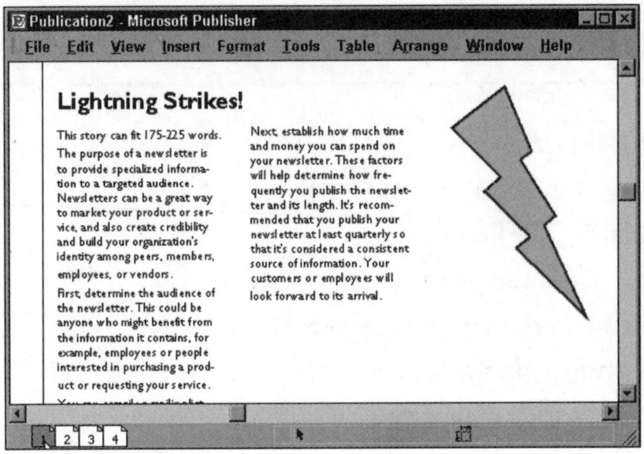

Figure 2-1: The Page Navigation controls, showing page 1 as the current page.

If you choose View➪Two-Page Spread, two pages in the Page Navigation controls are highlighted.

Publisher often provides several ways to accomplish a task. Moving among pages is no exception. To move to a different page, take one of the following actions:

- ✦ In the Page Navigation controls, click the page button that represents the page that you want to go to.
- ✦ Choose Edit➪Go To Page, press F5, or press Ctrl+G and then type the number of the page that you want to work on in the Go To Page dialog box, as shown in Figure 2-2. Press Enter or click OK to close the Go To Page dialog box and move to the page number that you enter.
- ✦ Press Shift+F5 to move to the next page or Ctrl+F5 to move to the previous page.

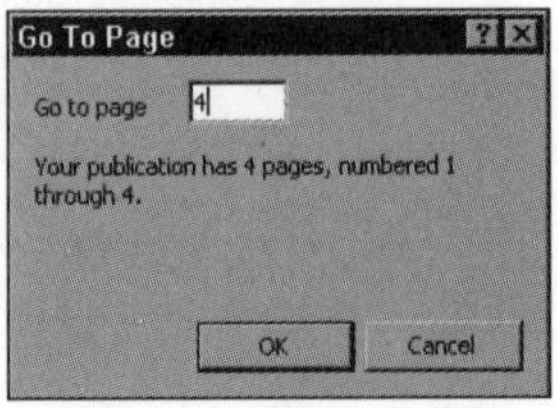

Figure 2-2: The Go To Page dialog box.

Changing What You See On-Screen

As you design a page layout, it's important to be able to change views. As you work with text or a graphic, for example, you want to be able to change the magnification so that you can see the details of what you're working on. To review the page as a whole, you need a magnification that lets you view the entire page.

Publisher makes changing your view of a page easy. You can change the size of the page as it's displayed on-screen, or you can change to a view that enables you to see two facing pages at once. The following sections tell you how to adjust your page view.

Two-page spreads

A two-page spread is simply a pair of facing pages. To see a two-page spread for your publication, choose View➪Two-Page Spread from the menu.

If you're working on a single-page publication, nothing seems to happen. And if you're working on page 1 of a multipage publication, nothing seems to happen there, either. What's going on? Publisher displays odd-numbered pages on the right side and even-numbered pages on the left side of the spread. Page 1 being an odd-numbered page appears on the right, and because it is the first page, it has no opposite to appear on the left side. Click page 2 in the Page Navigation controls. That's more like it. You see page 2, the even-numbered page, on the left, and page 3, the odd-numbered page, on the right. If the last page in your publication is an even number, you see only that page if you select it in Two-Page Spread view.

The Two-Page Spread command is a toggle. Choose View➪Two-Page Spread a second time to return to single page view.

Whole Page and Page Width views

In addition to Two-Page Spread view, Publisher offers two views that you may find useful: Whole Page and Page Width views. The following list describes these views:

- **Whole Page view:** Choose View➪Zoom➪Whole Page to see the layout of the entire page.
- **Page Width view:** Choose View➪Zoom➪Page Width to see the entire width of your document on-screen all at once. You may need to scroll vertically to see the entire document, but you won't have to scroll horizontally. This view comes in handy if you're working with text or objects that fill the page from left to right.

On the subject of zooming, Publisher offers two more helpful Zoom commands that are worth mentioning:

- ✦ Click the Zoom In or Zoom Out buttons on the Standard toolbar to make your publication look bigger or smaller on-screen and thereby get a better look at it.
- ✦ Open the Zoom menu on the Standard toolbar and choose a percent option. In this way, you can see precisely as much of your publication as you want to see. You can also click in the Zoom menu box, type a percentage, and press the Enter key to choose a percentage of your own.

Lining Things Up

Even the most proficient user sometimes encounters difficulty getting objects to align just right on the page. (As Chapter 3 explains, an object is simply a publication design element.) Luckily, Publisher offers several features to help you line things up on the page. The following sections describe these features and how to use them.

Margin and grid guides

Layout guides create a grid that you can use to organize objects into neat rows and columns to help give your publication a consistent look. Layout guides repeat on each page of your publication. These layout guides appear on-screen as pink and blue lines but don't show up as you print your publication. Use the Tools➪Snap To command on the Publisher menu bar to automatically align objects with these guides.

Publisher offers the following two types of layout guides:

- ✦ **Boundary guides:** Show the boundary of your printable area.
- ✦ **Grid guides:** Enable you to create a grid with any number of rows and columns.

Every publication uses boundary guides. These blue lines help you align text and graphics along the outside edges of your publication. Although you can place objects anywhere that you want, placing them outside the boundary guides may cause unpredictable results.

Grid guides help you align objects that you don't want to align with the boundary guides.

Don't be surprised if a publication that you create with one of the wizards already displays layout guides. The wizard is just trying to be helpful. If you don't like the placement of these guides, change them. To set up or change layout guides, choose A_r_range⇨_L_ayout Guides. The Layout Guides dialog box appears, as shown in Figure 2-3.

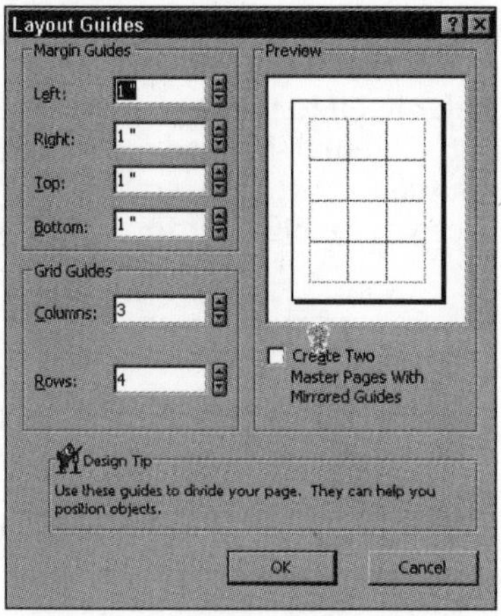

Figure 2-3: The Layout Guides dialog box, set for three columns and four rows.

Enter the number of columns and rows that you want for your grid. Grid guides evenly divide the space that the margin guides contain.

TIP

To remove or display boundaries and guides, choose _V_iew⇨_B_oundaries and Guides (or press Ctrl+Shift+O).

Ruler guides

Grid guides can come in very handy, but they don't give you much flexibility in their placement. Ruler guides enable you to align objects anywhere on the page. You can create as many ruler guides as you need and use them to align objects, as shown in Figure 2-4.

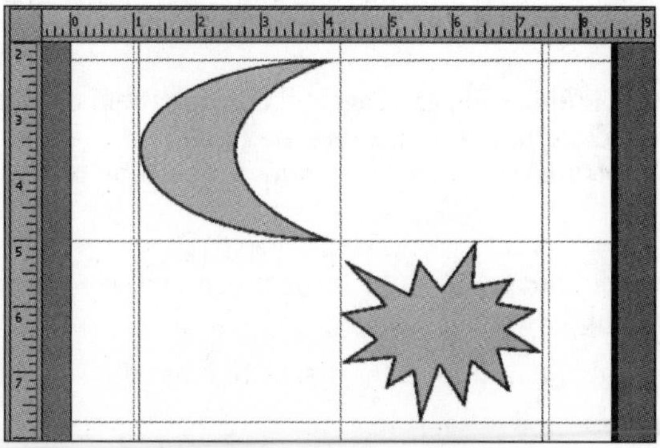

Figure 2-4: Using ruler guides to align two objects.

One drawback to ruler guides is that they don't automatically appear on every page, as the margin and grid guides do. You must create them separately for each page. Fortunately, that task isn't very difficult. Here's how ruler guides work:

- To create a vertical guide, press and hold the Shift key and then click and drag from the vertical ruler itself to the desired position on your layout. The pointer changes to a double-headed arrow and the word *adjust* appears below the pointer. As you drag, you see a green vertical line — the ruler guide. Release your mouse button after the guide is where you want it to be.
- To create a horizontal guide, press and hold the Shift key and click and drag from the horizontal ruler itself.
- To place a vertical guide in the exact center of your view, choose Arrange⇨Ruler Guides⇨Add Vertical Rule Guide.
- To place a horizontal guide in the exact center of your view, choose Arrange⇨_Ruler Guides⇨Add Horizontal Rule Guide.
- To move a ruler guide, just click and drag it while holding the Shift key.
- To remove a ruler guide, press and hold the Shift key and drag the ruler off the page.
- To remove all ruler guides, choose Arrange⇨Ruler Guides⇨Clear All Ruler Guides.

Snap to it!

After decorating the page with those pretty blue and green lines, you use the Snap to Guides to automatically align objects that you place close to a guide.

The Snap To Guide feature helps to ensure that the objects you drag close to a guide automatically attach to the guide. This feature makes lining up several objects easy because you don't needing to "eyeball" it. You can also make objects snap to the nearest ruler mark (increment) or to other objects.

The Snap To Guide commands are toggles. Choose them once to turn them on. Snap To Guide commands that are turned on display a check mark next to them on the Tools menu. Choose them a second time to turn them off. Here's how:

- Choose Arrange⇨Snap⇨To Guides (or press Ctrl+W) to align objects with your layout guides.
- Choose Arrange⇨Snap⇨To Ruler Marks to align objects with your ruler marks.

✦ Choose Arrange➪Snap➪To Objects to align objects with selected objects on-screen.

The Master Page for Handling Page Backgrounds

Sometimes as you design a multipage publication, you need objects to appear on every page. Such objects include page numbers, copyright information, and company logos. The good news is that you don't need to place the objects on each page individually. Instead, you can place the objects on the *master page*.

Think of the master page as a piece of preprinted letterhead. The company name and logo may appear at the top, and the company address may appear on the bottom. Every page that you print by using this letterhead presents these same items, although the text on each page is different. The master page works in a similar fashion. Objects on the master page appear in the background on every page, as shown in Figure 2-5.

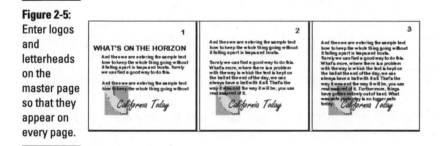

Figure 2-5: Enter logos and letterheads on the master page so that they appear on every page.

Working on the master page

To open the master page and place objects on the background of your publication, choose View➪Master Page or press Ctrl+M. Repeat these steps to close the master page and return to the foreground of your publication.

How can you tell that you're looking at the master page? Look at the Page Navigation controls in the bottom-left corner of your screen. If the Page Navigation controls — the page-number buttons — are there, you're in the foreground. But if you see a master page button with an *R* (for right) on it, you're looking at the master page.

Mirrored master pages for page spreads

In designing a publication with facing pages, creating two master pages is often convenient: one for the left-facing pages and another for the right-facing pages. To create a second master page, choose Arrange⇨Layout Guides to open the Layout Guides dialog box and click to select the Create Two Master Pages with Mirrored Guides check box.

If you create a second master page, the original master becomes the master page for right-facing pages, the new master page becomes the one for left-facing pages, and Publisher copies everything on the original master page (right) to the second master page (left).

To move between two master pages in Single Page view, click the L or R Page Navigation. As for Two-Page Spread view, don't worry about it. The left- and right-facing master pages are both visible.

Two master pages are great for creating facing-page publications. Unfortunately, having twice as many means doing twice as much setup work.

Adding background objects to pages

The procedure for adding objects to backgrounds by way of the master page is the same as adding objects to foreground pages (see Chapter 3). Try to keep your background objects close to the margins. Background objects that you place in the middle of the page tend to get covered up. To avoid needing to rearrange your foreground objects, set up your master pages first.

Putting headers and footers on master pages

If you've worked with word processors, you probably know that headers and footers contain text and graphics that repeat along the top and bottom of each page, respectively. Headers and footers may contain logos, page numbers, publication title, current chapter, author's name, company information, and so on. Anyone know a good place to put stuff that repeats on each page? That's right, the background! To add headers and footers on master pages, follow these steps:

1. **Choose View⇨Master Page or press Ctrl+M to open the master page.**
2. **Add an object(s) where you want your header or footer to appear.**

   Text boxes are probably the most common objects that you add to headers and footers, but you can add any object that you want to appear at the top bottom of each page.
3. **If appropriate, fill and format the object and then format its contents.**

   To do so, choose commands on the Formatting toolbar.
4. **Choose View⇨Master Page or press Ctrl+M again to return to the foreground of your publication.**

The two-master-page advantage

In addition to providing separate areas for different sets of layout guides, using facing master pages enables you to set up separate sets of background objects — one set that repeats on left-hand pages and another that repeats on right-hand pages. Separate left- and right-hand repeating objects are quite common in facing-page publications.

You want headers and footers to line up with the top or bottom margin. Set ruler guides for the bottom of the header and the top of the footer and turn on the Snap To Guides command to make lining them up easier. (See the section "Lining Things Up," earlier in this chapter, for information.)

Adding and Removing Pages

Publisher makes inserting and removing pages easy — maybe too easy.

You can insert more than one or two pages at a time. Publisher enables you to insert up to 999 pages at a shot. To insert multiple pages into your publication, follow these steps:

1. **Choose Insert⇨Page or press Ctrl+Shift+N.**

   The Insert Page dialog box appears, as shown in Figure 2-6.

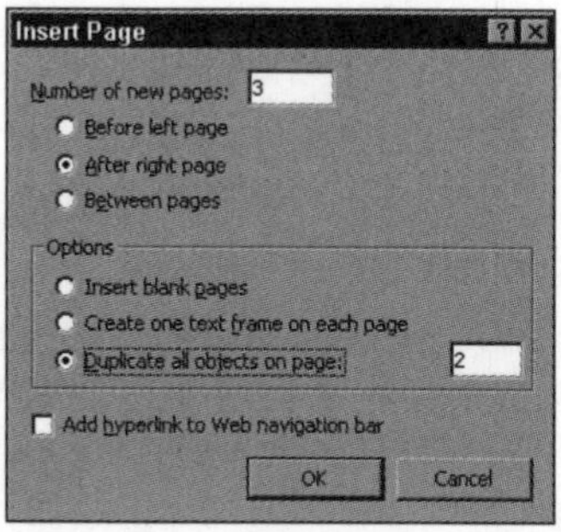

Figure 2-6: The Insert Page dialog box.

2. **In the Number of New Pages text box, type the number of pages that you want to insert.**

   Type any number up to 999.

Insert pages in even numbers so that your left-hand pages don't become right-hand pages and vice versa. This process becomes more important as your publication nears completion. Inserting pages in odd numbers can cause you quite a lot of work after your publication is set up.

3. **Click the Before Left Page, After Right Page, or Between Pages option to tell Publisher where to put the pages.**
4. **In the Options area, choose the kind of pages you want to insert, as follows:**
   - **Insert Blank Pages:** Inserts pages that are devoid of objects.
   - **Create One Text Frame on Each Page:** Places a blank text box on each new page that you create. Each text box matches your publication's margin guides. Keep in mind that this text box probably covers up any objects that you place in the background by way of the master page.
   - **Duplicate All Objects on Page:** Makes a copy of whatever objects already exist on the page number that you specify in the option box and places those objects on each of the new pages.
5. **Click OK.**

If you delete a page, you also delete all the objects on that page. Only objects off the page, on the scratch area, remain. The *scratch area* is the part of the Publisher screen that isn't occupied by pages. You can move objects into the scratch area and keep them there temporarily until you decide what to do with them.

After you delete a page, Publisher automatically renumbers the remaining pages so that you don't end up with pages out of sequence. To delete a page, follow these steps:

1. **Move to the page that you want to delete.**
2. **Choose Edit⇨Delete Page.**

   Notice that this command isn't available if you're currently viewing the background of your publication.

   After you choose Edit⇨Delete Page in Single Page view, Publisher displays a confirmation box asking whether you really want to delete the page. Click OK to delete the page. Click Cancel if you're having second thoughts. Use this command with caution. Press Ctrl+Z if you accidentally delete a page.

   After you choose Edit⇨Delete Page in Two-Page Spread view, Publisher opens the Delete Page dialog box, as shown in Figure 2-7.

Figure 2-7: The Delete Page dialog box for a two-page spread.

3. **Click the option that you want: Both Pages, Left Page Only, or Right Page Only.**
4. **Click OK.**

WARNING!

Delete pages in even numbers so that you don't mess up your left- and right-hand pages. If you delete just a left- or right-hand page in Two-Page Spread view, Publisher opens a dialog box asking whether you really want to delete just one page.

Changing Publication Types

"Don't change horses in the middle of the stream," the saying goes. The same is true for publication types. You can change publication types after you finish your layout work, but changing publication types late in the game can mean hours of work rearranging objects on pages.

To choose a new publication type, choose File⇨Page Setup. The Page Setup dialog box appears, as shown in Figure 2-8. Choose a new publication type from the drop-down list and select the requisite options. The available options change depending on the publication type you choose.

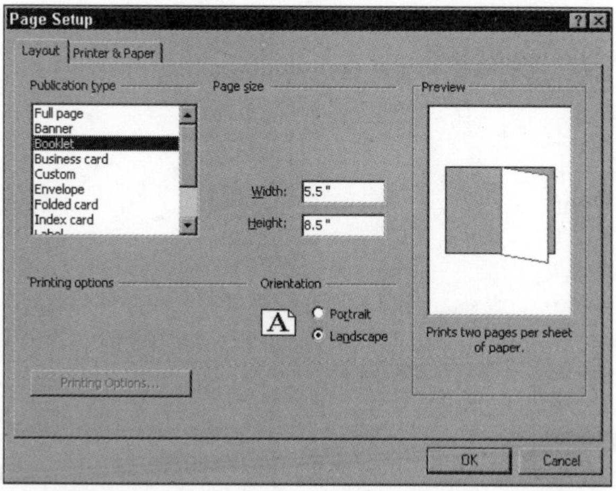

Figure 2-8: The Page Setup dialog box for a normal layout.

Chapter 3: Operating with Objects

In This Chapter

- **Building objects**
- **Manipulating objects**
- **Aligning objects**
- **Drawing objects**
- **Wrapping text around objects**

An *object* is simply a publication design element. For the purpose of laying out a publication, text boxes, graphics, a line, a circle, and other items that you find on pages are all objects. This chapter offers basic instructions for creating an object. You find out how to change the size of objects and position them on pages. You also discover how to align objects and wrap text around an object.

Creating an Object

No matter what kind of object you want to create, the basic steps for doing so are the same. You start from the Objects toolbar, as shown in Figure 3-1. To create an object, follow these steps:

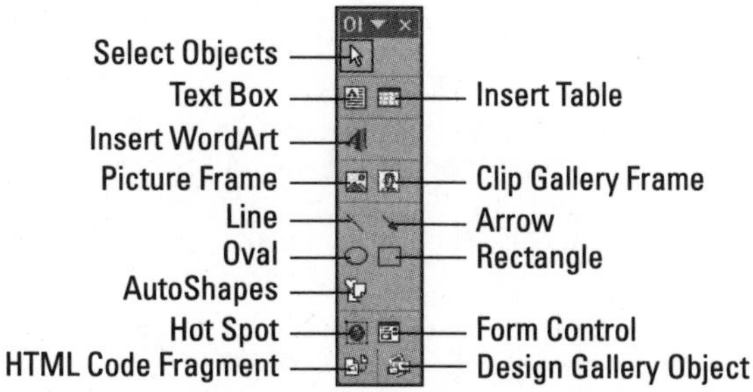

Figure 3-1: The Objects toolbar.

1. **Click the button for the kind of object that you want to create.**

   Your cursor changes to a crosshair.

2. **Move the pointer over a publication page or scratch area.**

The pointer changes into a crosshair. The scratch area, by the way, is the area to the side of the pages. You can create objects there, no matter what kind of publication you're working on.

3. **Click and drag to create the outline of your object.**

   As you drag, the program draws a sample to show you the size and shape of your new object.

   TIP: To draw an object from the center out, press and hold the Ctrl key as you draw. To draw a perfectly square or round object, press and hold the Shift key. To do both, press and hold both the Ctrl and Shift keys as you drag.

4. **Release the mouse button to finish creating the object.**

   Publisher creates your text or picture frame and selects it (makes it active) so that you can work with it further.

Figure 3-2 shows an *explosion*, an object that you can create by way of the AutoShapes button on the Objects toolbar. (Click the AutoShapes button, choose Starts and Banners, and choose Explosion 1 or Explosion 2 from the submenu.)

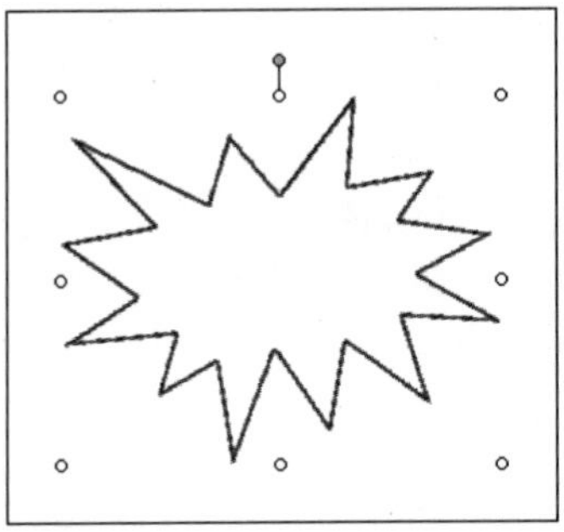

Figure 3-2: An auto-shape — one object that you can create by using the Objects toolbar.

Techniques vary for creating objects, but they all pretty much boil down to the following: On the Objects toolbar, click a button and then drag the mouse pointer across a publication page.

To delete an object — any kind of object — click to select it and then choose Edit⇨Delete Object or simply press the Delete key.

Moving and Resizing Objects

To move an object, start by clicking to select it. Then move the pointer over the object and watch the pointer turn into a truck with the word *Move* on it.

Finally, click and drag the object to a new location. As you drag, a dotted outline shows where your object is going to land if you release the mouse button.

To move several objects at once, Ctrl+click to select them all and then start dragging.

If you want to move an object or set of objects to a different page in your publication, drag the object or set off the publication page and onto the scratch area. Then go to the page where you want to move the object or set of objects and drag the stuff from the scratch area to a page.

To resize an object, click to select it and then move the pointer over one of the eight selection handles. The mouse pointer becomes a resize pointer, which consists of a double-arrow and the word *Resize.* Click the handle and start dragging it to resize the object, as the following list describes:

- ✦ To change the shape but keep the object's proportions, drag a corner handle.
- ✦ To squeeze or stretch the objects as you change its size, drag a side handle.

To change the size of several objects at once by the same degree, Ctrl+click to select all the objects and then resize one of them. All change size accordingly.

Suppose that you need to move an object just a tiny bit? To do so, click to select the object and choose Arrange⇨Nudge. You get a submenu with four choices: Up, Down, Left, and Right. Choose an option to nudge the object ever so slightly. The Nudge submenu appears as a floating toolbar. Move the pointer over the top of the submenu and, after you see the four-headed arrow, click and drag the submenu onto the screen. Now you can click a Nudge command as many times as necessary to get the object in the right place.

Aligning and Distributing Objects

A publication in which objects don't line up squarely with one another looks sloppy. Similarly, if you try to spread objects evenly across the page and you fail to do so, you get a sloppy-looking page. To keep pages from looking sloppy, Publisher offers the Align and Distribute commands.

Aligning objects on the page

You can align an object in two ways:

- **Align objects with respect to one another:** Objects can line up along their left or right edges, their top or bottom edges, or down the center either vertically or horizontally. In Figure 3-3, the objects — clip-art images in this case — align along the bottom.

Figure 3-3: Objects aligning with respect to one another along the bottom.

- **Align objects with respect to the page margins:** You can place objects against a margin, down the center of the page (between the left and right margin), or through the middle of the page (between the top and bottom margin).

Whether objects align with respect to one another or the page margin depends on whether you choose the Arrange⇨Align or Distribute⇨Relative to Margin Guides command. When the command is selected and a check mark appears beside its name on the menu, objects align with respect to the margin.

To align objects on the page, follow these steps:

1. **Decide whether to choose the Arrange⇨Align or Distribute⇨Relative to Margin Guides command.**

   Whether you choose this command or not determines whether objects align with one another or with respect to the margins of the page. Choose the command if you want the objects you will select in Step 2 to be aligned with respect to the margin. If you want the objects that you will select in Step 2 to align with one another, don't choose the command to remove the check mark beside the command's name.

2. **Click to select the objects that you want to align.**

   Press and hold the Ctrl key as you click the objects.

3. **Choose Arrange⇨Align or Distribute and then one of the Align commands from the submenu.**

Click the Undo button and try again if you choose the wrong Align command.

TIP

You can choose Arrange⇨Align or Distribute, move the pointer over the top of the submenu, click after you see the four-headed arrow, and drag the submenu to turn it into a toolbar. After that, you can click Align buttons to line up the objects correctly. You don't have to dig into the Arrange menu and its submenu.

Distributing objects on the page

As do the Align commands, the Distribute commands work with regard to the objects themselves or the page margins. Choose the Arrange⇨Align or Distribute⇨Relative to Margin Guides command to tell Publisher whether you want to distribute objects evenly from margin to margin or evenly between the first and last object in the set of objects you select.

To distribute objects on the page, follow these steps:

1. **Decide whether to choose the Arrange⇨Align or Distribute⇨Relative to Margin Guides command.**

   Choose the command if you want to distribute objects from margin to margin; don't choose the command if you want to distribute objects so that there is an equal distance between each of them. The command is chosen if a check mark appears beside its name.

2. **Click to select the objects that you want to distribute.**

   To select more than one object at a time, press and hold the Ctrl key and click the objects.

3. **Choose Arrange⇨Align or Distribute and then one of the Distribute commands on the submenu.**

REAL WORLD

Flipping and rotating objects

Who can resist the Flip and Rotate commands? After you place an object on a page or select an object, Publisher shows you the green rotation handle and practically begs you to give it a spin. And if you don't want to do the job by hand, you can choose Arrange⇨Rotate or Flip and then choose a Rotate or Flip command from the submenu. You can even rotate text boxes. Rotating and flipping objects is a great way to add a little pizzazz to your publications.

Drawing an Object

Publisher offers six tools on the Objects toolbar for drawing objects: Line, Arrow, Oval, Rectangle, AutoShapes, and Design Gallery Object. To draw an object, you click a button on the Objects toolbar and start dragging the pointer across the page. The following list describes what the tools do:

- **Line tool:** Used to create lines on your layout. Click and drag the pointer to draw a line.
- **Arrow tool:** Used to create lines with an arrow on the end. To change the size or shape of the arrowhead, right-click the line and choose Format AutoShape from the shortcut menu. Then choose a style for the arrowhead on the Colors and Lines tab of the Format AutoShape dialog box that appears.
- **Oval tool:** Used to create an oval. If you want to create a perfect circle, press the Shift key while you click and drag the pointer.
- **Rectangle tool:** Used to create a rectangle. Press the Shift key while you click and drag the pointer to create a square.
- **AutoShapes tool:** Used to create more complex shapes. After clicking the button, a drop-down list appears. Choose a submenu on the drop-down list and then, from the second submenu, choose an object (see Figure 3-4). Then start dragging.

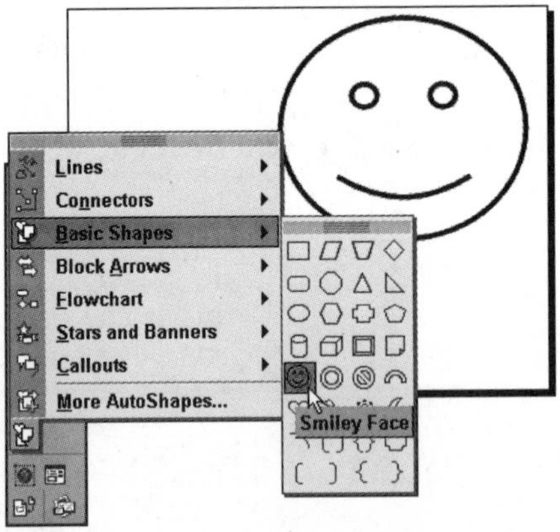

Figure 3-4: Drawing the Smiley Face, which is an autoshape in Publisher.

- **Design Gallery Object tool:** Enables you to select from a library of objects. Click the Design Gallery Object button to open up the Publisher Design Gallery, as shown in Figure 3-5, which enables you to select from a number of objects to insert into your publication.

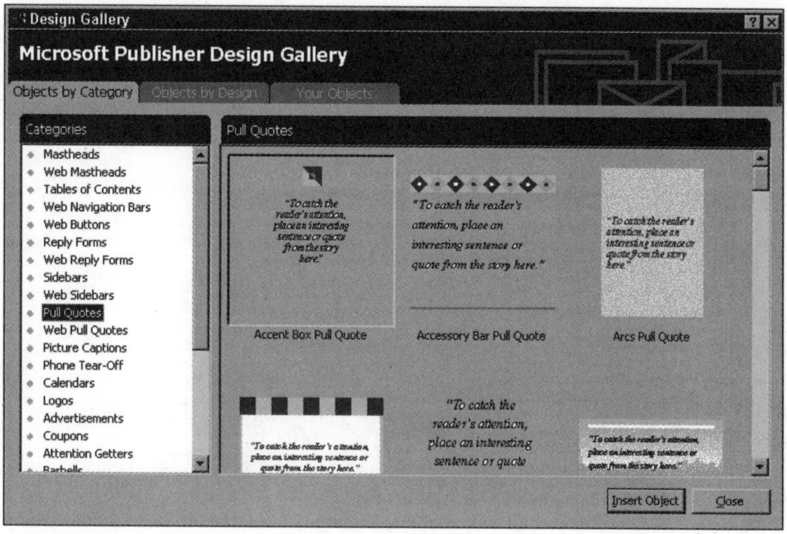

Figure 3-5: The Design Gallery.

Creating Regular Text Wraps

In Publisher, wrapping text is easy. Just place any type of object — even a second text box — on top of an object, and the text underneath automatically wraps around the object above it.

WARNING!

Sometimes Publisher wraps text too closely or too loosely around an object. Closely wrapped text can prove difficult to read, whereas loosely wrapped text can waste space and create big gaps on the page. Fortunately, changing the amount of space between the wrapping text and the object it wraps around is easy. All you need to do is change the margins of the wrapped-around object.

To increase the margins of an object, click to select it, choose Format from the menu bar, and then choose the last option on the Format menu. (The option changes depending on what kind of object you are dealing with.) The Format dialog box appears, as shown in Figure 3-6. Click the Layout tab and select a different Wrapping Style option.

By default, Publisher wraps text in a rectangular pattern around the perimeter of objects. If you're working with a picture or WordArt object, however, you can make your text wrap to the actual shape of the object by selecting the Through option in the Format dialog box.

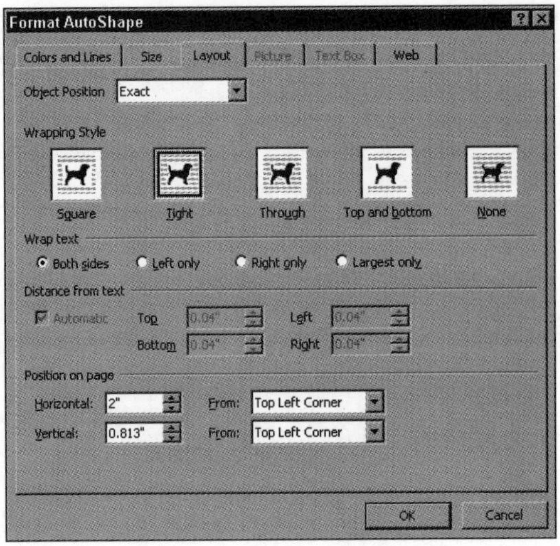

Figure 3-6: The Layout tab of the Format dialog box.

Chapter 4: Getting the Word Out

In This Chapter

- Working with text objects
- Developing tables

This chapter focuses on two types of objects: text objects and table objects. You use *text objects* to place and manage text in your publication. You use *table objects* to hold data in tabular form. The end result is getting text into Publisher.

Using Text Objects

Those of you familiar with word-processing software may find the fact that you can't type on the page in Publisher a bit disconcerting. (At least you can't do it directly.) Before you start typing in Publisher, you must create a text object. This task is easy enough to perform. Just click the Text Box tool in the Objects toolbar and then click and drag anywhere on the layout to draw a box. That's it! Start typing. After you create a text box, you can type text directly into it, paste text in from the Clipboard, or import text from your word processor or a text file.

Typing text

After you create a text box to hold your text, typing the text in Publisher is not much different from typing it in a word processor and is very similar to typing it in Microsoft Word. In fact, Publisher shares some features with Word, such as similar menus and toolbars, AutoCorrect Options, and Spell Check.

As you type, your text fills the text box from left to right, top to bottom in the same way that text fills a word-processed page. If the text box isn't large enough to accommodate all your text, you eventually reach the bottom of the box. After that happens, the *overflow icon* appears at the bottom of the box, as shown in Figure 4-1. Don't worry, the overflow text is not lost. You just can't see it.

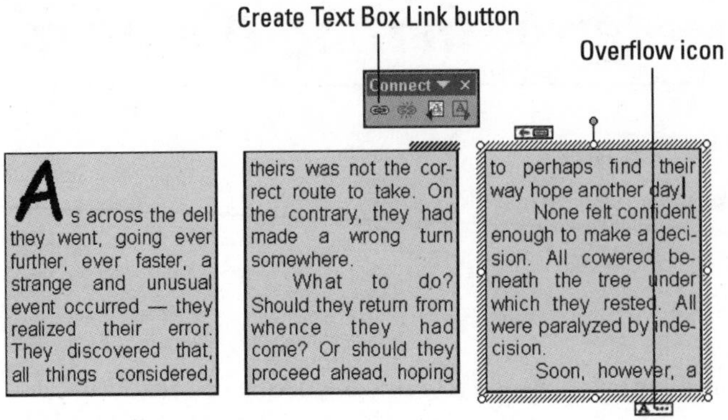

Figure 4-1: Linking text boxes so that text can flow from box to box.

To tell Publisher to make overflow text go to another text box in your publication, follow these steps:

1. **Click to select the text box containing the overflowing text.**

2. **Click the Create Text Box Link button on the Connect Frames toolbar (see Figure 4-1).**

   Figure 4-1 shows what the toolbar looks like. It should appear automatically, but if you don't see it, right-click any toolbar and choose Connect Frames on the shortcut menu.

3. **Move the pointer over the box that you want the text to flow into.**

   The pointer turns into an overflowing pitcher — or is that a beer stein?

4. **Click the target text box to make the text flow there.**

In Publisher-speak, text boxes that link this way are known as a *story*. Here are techniques for handling text boxes that link in a story:

- **Going from text box to text box so you can edit text:** Either click the Go To Next Frame or Go To Previous Frame icons, which you find at the bottom and top of text boxes, or click the Previous Text Box or Next Text Box buttons on the Connect Frames toolbar.
- **Selecting the text in all the text boxes:** Press Ctrl+A or choose Edit⇨Select All.
- **Breaking the link between boxes:** Select the text box that you want as the last one in the chain and click the Break Forward Link button on the Connect Frames toolbar.

Importing text

If you create text in another program, such as Word, and bring it into Publisher, you *import* the text. Importing text can prove a great time-saver. If you enter text in a program and decide that you need that same text in a publication, you don't need to retype it. An easy way to import text into Publisher is simply by copying and pasting. Or you can use the Insert⇨Text File menu command to import files that you save in other programs. You don't need to store those programs on your computer to import their files.

Creating and Formatting Tables

Table frames enable you to quickly create tables to hold your tabular data. The following sections explain how to create a table frame, enter the numbers and words, enter columns and rows, and format a table.

Creating a table box

If you know how to create a text box in Publisher, creating a table box isn't going to cause you any trouble. Click the Insert Table tool on the Objects toolbar and then click and drag anywhere on the layout to create the table. The Create Table dialog box appears, as shown in Figure 4-2. You must make three selections in this dialog box: Number of Rows, Number of Columns, and Table Format.

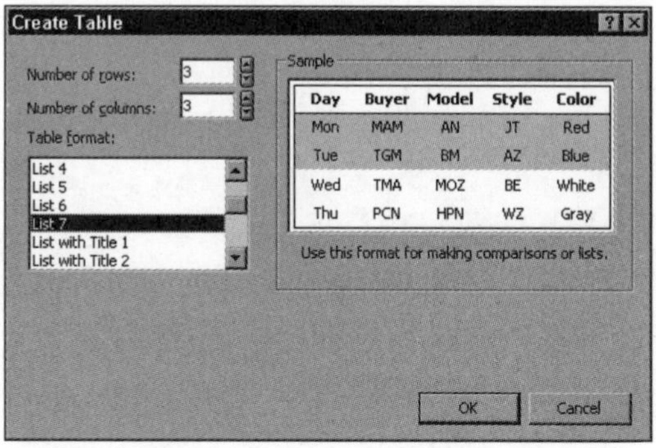

Figure 4-2: The Create Table dialog box.

Tables can contain up to 128 rows and columns. Publisher offers you 22 different table formats. As you select a format, the program shows you a sample of the format in the Sample portion of the dialog box. The None format is for stripping a table of its formats.

TIP

Suppose that you change your mind about the table format you choose? No problem. Select the table, choose Table➪Table AutoFormat, and choose a new format in the AutoFormat dialog box that appears.

Resizing tables, columns, and rows

A table box consists of a grid of many separate text compartments known as *cells.* As are just about everything else in Publisher, table boxes are subject to change. You can resize the entire table box; resize, insert, or delete columns and rows; merge many cells into a single cell; and split a cell into many cells. In short, you can restructure a table just about any way that you want.

To resize a table, click and drag any of its selection handles. Publisher automatically adjusts the height of each row to fit each row's contents. If you choose Table➪Grow to Fit Text, the table's row height expands to accommodate the text that you enter.

To resize a column or row, move your pointer over a column or row boundary line. After the pointer changes to a double-headed arrow, click and drag until the column or row is the size that you want.

Inserting and deleting columns and rows

You can insert and delete all the columns and rows that you want. If you run out of table cells while entering data, just press the Tab key after you get to the last cell. Publisher adds a new row at the bottom of the table frame and places the insertion point in the first cell of that row. You're now ready to type in that cell.

To add rows or columns to your table, follow these steps:

1. **Place the insertion point in the column or row adjacent to where you want to insert a new column or row.**
2. **Choose Table➪Insert➪Columns or Table➪Insert➪Rows.**

   Publisher inserts the column or row.

Deleting a column or row is just as easy. To do so, follow these steps:

1. **Click anywhere in the row or column that you want to delete.**
2. **Choose Table➪Delete➪Columns or Table➪Delete➪Rows.**

TIP

As you're inserting or deleting rows and columns, you can save time by selecting a number of columns or rows first. If you select four columns and give the command to insert columns, Publisher inserts four columns instead of one.

Want to delete an entire table? Choose Table⇨Delete⇨Table or click the table and then press the Delete key.

Working with table text

As you can text boxes, you can fill a table box either by typing the text directly into the frame or by importing existing text from somewhere else. With just a couple exceptions, typing and importing text into both types of boxes is pretty darn similar.

Each cell in a table works much like a miniature text box. As you reach the right edge of a cell, for example, Publisher automatically word-wraps your text to a new line within that cell. If the text that you type disappears beyond the right edge of the cell, you've probably locked the table to keep it from changing. Choose Table⇨Grow to Fit Text to unlock it. If you want to end a short line within a cell, press Enter. Filling in your table box row by row is usually easiest; after you finish one cell, just press Tab to move on to the next one.

Retrieving table frame text

Just as you can with text frames, you can paste a text file into a table. Cut or copy the text to the Windows Clipboard; then click the cell that you want as the upper-left cell of the range and choose Edit⇨Paste or press Ctrl+V.

Moving and copying table text

You can use the Clipboard or drag-and-drop text editing to copy and move text within and between table cells. If you want, you can even copy text between text and a table.

Because of how Publisher overwrites destination cells, rearranging entire columns and rows of text requires some extra steps. First, insert an extra column or row where you want to move the contents of an existing column or row. Then move the contents. Finally, delete the column or row that you empty.

Two commands on the Table menu, Fill Down and Fill Right, enable you to copy the entire contents of one cell into any number of adjacent cells either below or to the right.

To fill a series of cells in a row or column, follow these steps:

1. **Select the cell containing the text that you want to copy and the cells to which you want to copy the text.**

   To use the fill commands, you must select cells adjacent to the cell containing the text that you want to copy. To copy cells, hold down the Ctrl key and drag.

2. **Choose Table⇨Fill Down to copy the value in the topmost selected cell to the selected cells in the column below it or, choose Table⇨Fill Right to copy the value in the leftmost selected cell to selected cells in the row to the right.**

Formatting table text manually

All the character- and paragraph-formatting options that are available for use with text boxes are available with tables as well. You can change fonts and the size of text. You can use text effects, change the line spacing, and align text in different ways. You can even hyphenate text.

The key difference in applying paragraph formatting in tables and text is that Publisher treats each table cell as a miniature page. Thus if you align text, the text aligns within the cell and not across the entire table. And if you indent text, that text indents according to that cell's left and right edges.

To improve the look of cells, you can change cell margins, thus changing the amount of space between a cell's contents and its edges. To change cell margins, choose Format⇨Table and click the Cell Properties tab of the Format Table dialog box that appears (see Figure 4-3). Then change the Left, Right, Top, and Bottom margin measurements.

TIP

You can change the margins for multiple cells at the same time. Just select the cells before choosing Format⇨Table.

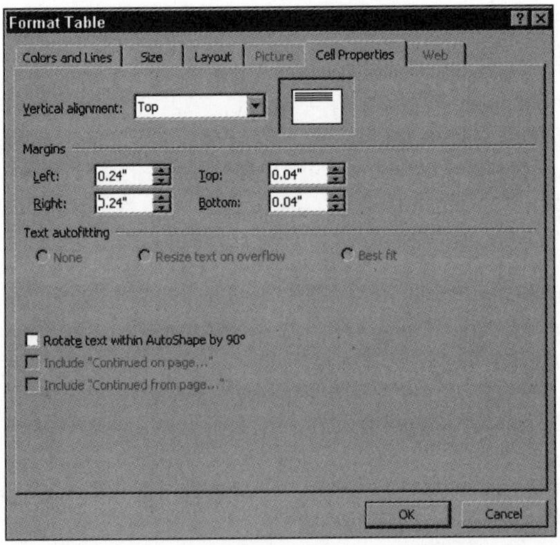

Figure 4-3: Changing cell margins in a table.

Chapter 5: You Ought to Be in Pictures

In This Chapter

- ✔ **Creating and working with graphics**
- ✔ **Resizing and cropping graphics**
- ✔ **Using BorderArt and the Design Gallery to enhance your publications**

Although Publisher really isn't the place to draw complex graphics, it's mighty flexible when it comes to importing graphics that you create elsewhere. Some desktop publishers rely heavily on collections of electronic clip art and libraries of photographs, whereas others are daring enough to create their own graphics by using specialized programs. Whether you're working from a clip-art collection or creating your own graphics, this chapter shows you how to get graphics into and out of your publications and how to work with graphics after they're in Publisher.

Ways to Insert or Import Graphics

Publisher provides the following five ways to insert or import graphics:

- Copy a graphic from another Windows program onto the Windows Clipboard and then paste it into a picture frame.
- Choose Insert➪Object and create an embedded object by selecting a program name in the Insert Object dialog box and creating the graphic with that program.
- Choose Insert➪Picture➪Clip Art (or click the Clip Gallery Frame button on the Objects toolbar) to obtain a graphic from the Clip Organizer.
- Choose Insert➪Picture➪From File (or click the Picture Frame button on the Picture or Objects toolbar) to import a graphic in a format that Publisher can recognize.
- Choose Insert➪Picture➪From Scanner or Camera to scan a hard copy of an image or capture an image from a digital camera.

TIP: No matter how you put a graphic into a picture frame, you can use any of the methods in the previous list to replace that picture.

Using the Microsoft Clip Organizer

The Microsoft Clip Organizer offers thousands of pieces of clip art. To place clip art in your publication, you simply click a miniature version of a graphic in the Organizer. To insert a graphic by using the Clip Organizer, follow these steps:

1. **Click the Clip Gallery Frame button on the Objects toolbar or choose Insert⇨Picture⇨Clip Art.**

   The Insert Clip Art task pane appears on the left side of the Publisher window, as shown in Figure 5-1.

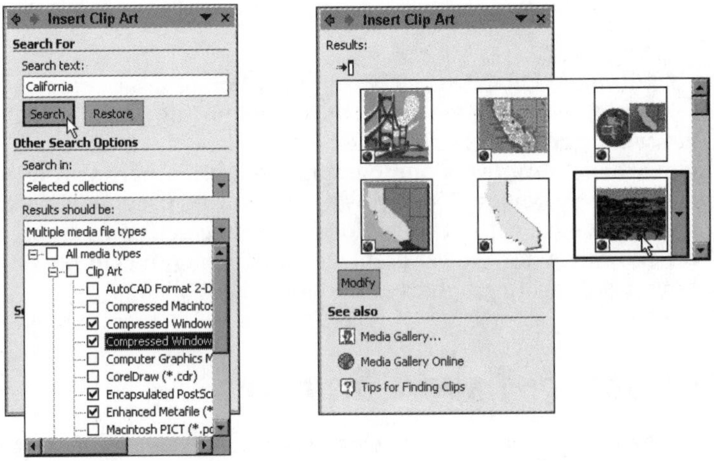

Figure 5-1: The Insert Clip Art task pane.

2. **Tell Publisher how and where to search for clip-art images.**

   You can do so by choosing any of the following options:

   - **Search Text:** Type a word in the text box that describes what kind of clip art you want.
   - **Search In:** Open the drop-down list and choose an option to tell Publisher where to search for images. As long as the Everywhere check box is selected, Publisher searches for every piece of clip art that it can find, including clip art from the Microsoft Web site. You can, however, click check boxes beside the names of specific areas — My Collections, Office Collections, and Web Collections — where you want to search. If you select Web Collections, make sure that your computer is connected to the Internet and that your browser is running because, with that option, you search a Microsoft Web site for images.

- **Results Should Be:** Open the drop-down list and tell Publisher what kind of clip art you are looking for. Check the Clip Art check box in this list and the Photographs check box as well if you're interested in putting one of them in your publication. To be specific about the kind of clip art that you want, click the plus sign (+) next to Clip Art or Photographs to open the list of file types and choose among them by clicking to check a particular box.

3. **Click the Search button.**

   If Publisher can find clip-art images, they appear in thumbnail form in the Insert Clip Art task pane. If necessary, scroll down the list to examine all the images or click the small icon under the word *Results* to see the images in a box.

4. **Click an image to insert it in your publication.**

If your search turns up nothing or turns up images you aren't happy with, click the Modify button to start your search over.

Inserting graphic files

Suppose that you assemble a great collection of graphics yourself, and you want to put one in a publication. To import a picture you're storing on disk into your publication, follow these steps:

1. **To import the graphic in place of a graphic object that's already on the page, select the graphic object that you want to replace.**

   Otherwise, make sure that no object is selected.

2. **Choose Insert⇨Picture⇨From File.**

   The Insert Picture dialog box appears, as shown in Figure 5-2. Publisher builds a preview of the picture for you in the dialog box.

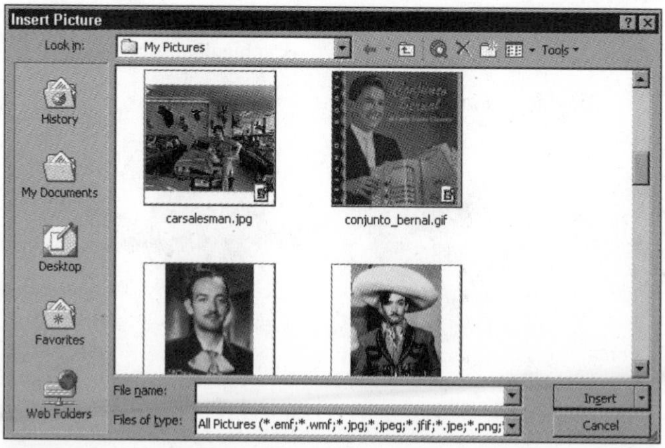

Figure 5-2: The Insert Picture dialog box.

3. **Find and select the file that you want to insert and then click the Insert button.**

   Publisher inserts the graphic into your publication. You can always resize the graphic, as I explain in the following section.

If you import a picture and later decide that you want a different picture, just double-click the existing picture. The Insert Picture dialog box reopens. Click a different file name and then click Insert.

If Publisher doesn't understand the format of the picture that you're trying to import, it whines out the following message: `Cannot convert this picture`. If you have access to the program that created that picture, try saving the picture in a different format. Or if you can open the picture in any other Windows program, try copying the picture to the Windows Clipboard and pasting it into your picture frame.

Resizing and Cropping Graphics

After you import a graphic, you can adjust it in Publisher by resizing it or chopping off parts of it (which is known as *cropping*).

To resize a graphic, start by clicking it to display the selection handles, and then drag one of its selection handles. As Figure 5-3 shows, a graphic maintains its proportions as you resize it by dragging a corner selection handle, but it's distorted if you drag a size handle. Sometimes, however, the distortions look kind of neat!

To maintain the proportions of a picture and its frame, drag a corner selection handle. In fact, when you're dealing with GIF and JPEG images, you almost need to maintain their proportions as you change size. If you don't, you end up with a distorted picture.

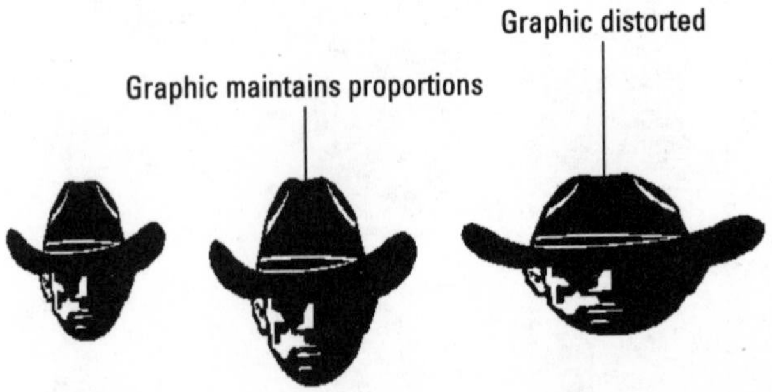

Figure 5-3: Choose a corner handle to resize a graphic and keep its proportions intact.

You can also use Publisher to crop a picture electronically. To do so, follow these steps:

1. **Click the picture to display its selection handles.**

2. **Click the Crop button on the Picture toolbar.**
3. **Point to one of the picture frame's selection handles.**

   Your mouse pointer changes to a *cropper pointer* — two scissors with the word *Crop.*

4. **Click and drag toward the center of the graphic until you see, in the dotted line that appears, the part of the graphic that you want to keep.**

   Figure 5-4 shows Publisher cropping a graphic. As you can see, what appears inside the dotted line is what's left after you finish your cropping.

5. **Release the mouse button.**

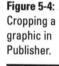

Figure 5-4: Cropping a graphic in Publisher.

Cropping a picture doesn't permanently remove any picture parts; it only hides them from view. To restore a picture part that you crop, repeat the preceding steps but drag the dotted lines outward. Regardless of whether you crop it, you can drag outward on any picture to *reverse crop* — that is, add space around the graphic.

Applying Borders and BorderArt

Publisher enables you to add a border to a graphic. You can make the border a thick line or something a little fancier. In Publisher, fancy borders are called BorderArt. To put a border around a graphic, follow these steps:

1. **Click to select a graphic.**
2. **Either right-click and choose Format from the shortcut menu that appears or choose Format⇨*last command* from the menu bar.**

   The last command on the Format menu changes names, depending on what kind of object you're dealing with. After you choose the command, the Format dialog box appears.

3. **If necessary, click the Colors and Lines tab, as shown in Figure 5-5.**

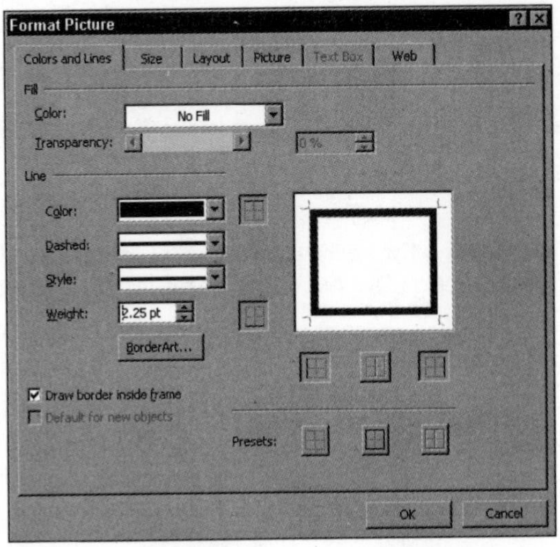

Figure 5-5: Putting a border around a graphic in the Colors and Lines tab of the Format dialog box.

4. **Choose among the following options the kind of line that you want for the border:**
   - **Color:** Choose a color for the border lines.
   - **Dashed:** Choose what kind of line you want.
   - **Style:** Chose a width for the line.
   - **Weight:** If the choices in the Style drop-down list don't do the job, enter a width of your own in this text box.
5. **Click OK.**

And those fancy borders? If you want one of those, click the BorderArt button in the Format dialog box. The BorderArt dialog box appears so you can choose a fancy border. Keep your eye on the Preview box so that you can see what kind of border you're choosing.

Chapter 6: Spinning a Web Site

In This Chapter

- Utilizing the Web Sites Wizard
- Working with hyperlinks
- Modifying the background with color and texture

If you don't know how to write HTML code but you want to create professional-looking Web pages, Publisher can help. In fact, if you can click a few buttons, you can create some great-looking Web pages in minutes! How? Read on.

Using the Web Sites Wizard

FAST TRACK

The easiest way to create a publication in Publisher is to use a wizard. Creating a Web site is no exception. Can you create a Web site from scratch by using Publisher? Sure. Do you want to? Probably not. So follow these steps to create a Web site in Publisher by using the Web Sites Wizard:

1. **Choose File➪New to open the New Publication task pane; then choose Web Sites from the Start From a Design list.**

   Publisher offers 60 styles of Web sites. You can peruse them all by scrolling down the screen.

2. **Click the Web site style that appeals to you.**

   After a few seconds, Publisher creates the first page of your Web site and shows you the Introduction panel of the Web Sites Wizard, as shown in Figure 6-1.

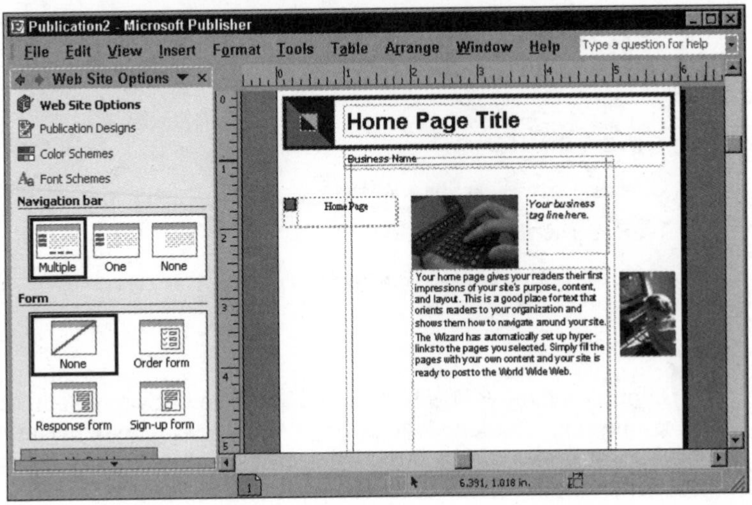

Figure 6-1: The Introduction panel of the Web Sites Wizard.

3. **In the Web Site Options task pane, click Web Site Options and then select the options that you want for your Web site.**

   The Web page on the right side of the screen shows what your choices mean in real terms. You can choose among various navigation bars and forms for your Web site.

4. **Click the Color Schemes option in the Web Site Options task pane and choose colors for your Web site.**

   Publisher enables you to choose from more than 60 color schemes. Microsoft paid big money for the design of these color schemes, so you can hardly go wrong in selecting one.

5. **Click the Font Schemes option in the Web Site Options task pane and choose fonts for your Web site.**

   Again, you can tell how the different font schemes appear by selecting one and studying the Web page on the right side of the screen. Try to choose a font scheme that sets the tone for your Web site.

WARNING! Be careful about choosing exotic fonts. When others view your Web site in their browsers, they see only the fonts that have been installed on their computers. If you choose Bondoni MT as a font, for example, and someone who views your Web site doesn't have that font on his or her computer, a substitute font is used in place of Bondoni MT. By choosing common fonts such as Arial and Times Roman, you can rest assured that others will see your Web site precisely as it appears on your screen.

Creating a Web site is pretty easy if you use the Web Sites Wizard. After you finish in the wizard, however, comes the hard part — putting content on your Web site to attract visitors. To do so, fill in the placeholder stuff — the graphics and words — with graphics and words of your own. Good luck.

Adding and Removing Hyperlinks

Hyperlinks enable a visitor to your Web site to click an object (text or a graphic) and jump to another document on your Web site or elsewhere on the Internet. Hyperlinks also enable visitors to send you e-mail messages.

Adding hyperlinks

You can choose from several methods to add a hyperlink to an object on your Web page. You can add hyperlinks to text, pictures, WordArt, and even the contents of table boxes. To add a hyperlink to a text box or table, you must first select the individual text that you want to turn into a hyperlink. Selecting just the text box or table doesn't work. To create a hyperlink, follow these steps:

1. **Select the text or object that you want to serve as the launching point for your hyperlink.**

2. **Choose Insert⇨Hyperlink, press Ctrl+K, or click the Insert Hyperlink button.**

   The Insert Hyperlink dialog box appears, as shown in Figure 6-2.

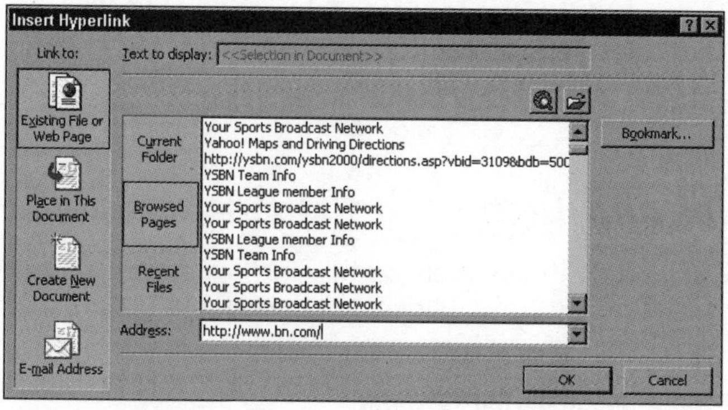

Figure 6-2: The Insert Hyperlink dialog box.

3. **Create the hyperlink.**

   Exactly how you create the hyperlink depends on where your link goes, as the following list describes:

- **A link to a Web page on the Internet:** Click the Existing File or Web Page button and then do one of the following to enter a Web page address in the Address text box: Type the address of the Web page in the Address text box; open the Address drop-down list and choose an address; click the Browse the Web button and go to a page in your browser (the address of the page you go to appears in the Address text box); or click the Browsed Pages button and select an address.
- **A link to another page in your Web site:** Click the Existing File or Web Page button, click the Current Folder button, and select the file where the Web page is located.
- **A link to an e-mail address:** Click the E-mail Address button, type an e-mail address in the E-mail Address text box and suggest a subject for the message in the Subject text box. After someone clicks the e-mail hyperlink on your Web page, his or her default e-mail program opens so a message can be sent.

4. **Click OK.**

Removing hyperlinks

Removing a hyperlink from an object is a snap. To do so, follow these steps:

1. **Select the object from which you want to remove a hyperlink.**

   If you're dealing with a text hyperlink, highlight the text.

2. **Choose Insert⇨Hyperlink, press Ctrl+K, or click the Hyperlink button.**

   The Edit Hyperlink dialog box appears.

3. **Click the Remove Link button in the Hyperlink dialog box and click OK.**

Adding Color and Texture to the Background

You can produce dramatic effects by applying texture and/or color to a Web page's background. To add or change the color or texture of the background, follow these steps:

1. **Choose Format⇨Background.**

   The Background task pane opens on the left side of the screen, as shown in Figure 6-3.

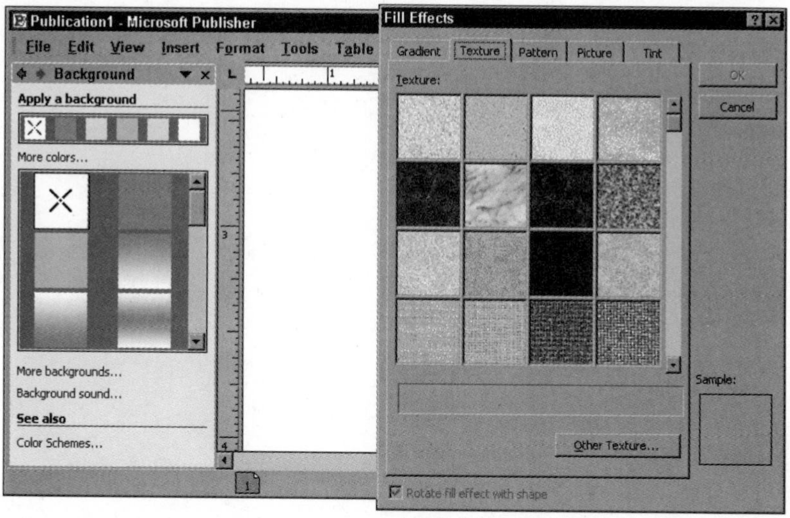

Figure 6-3: Choosing a background for Web pages that you create in Publisher.

2. **Look for a background that appeals to you and click to select it.**

   The background that you choose appears on your Web page. If you can't find an appealing background, go to Step 3.

3. **(Optional) Near the bottom of the task pane, click More Backgrounds.**

   The Fill Effects dialog box, also shown in Figure 6-3, appears. You find many interesting backgrounds here, especially on the Texture tab.

4. **After selecting a background for your Web page, click OK.**

Index

V

W

Z

Book IX

Bringing It All Together

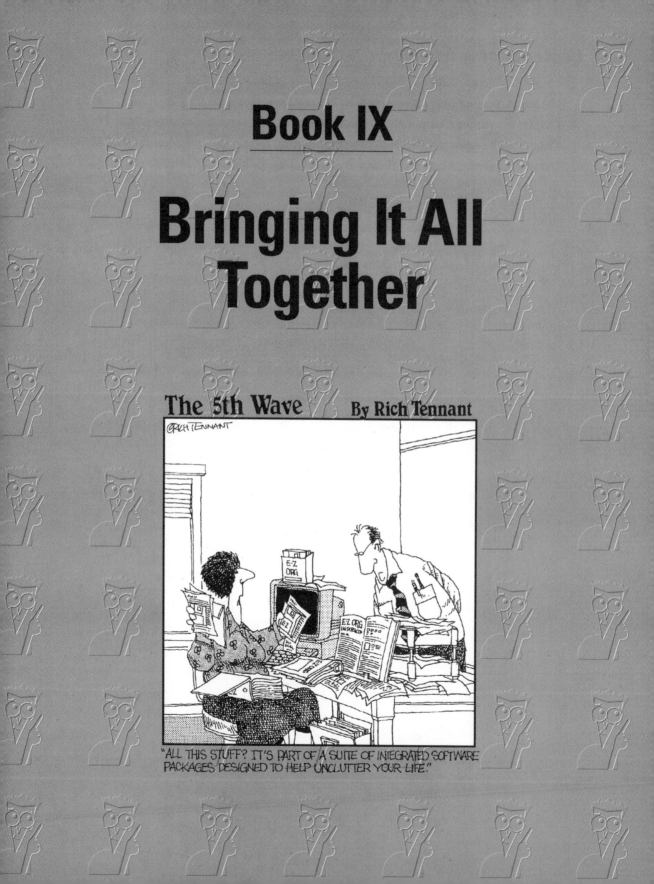

The 5th Wave
By Rich Tennant
©RICH TENNANT
E-Z ORG
E-Z ORG INSTRUCTIONS
"ALL THIS STUFF? IT'S PART OF A SUITE OF INTEGRATED SOFTWARE PACKAGES DESIGNED TO HELP UNCLUTTER YOUR LIFE."

Contents at a Glance

Chapter 1: Keeping Tabs on Your Files

In This Chapter

- **Searching for a file**
- **Keeping information about your files**

Files, like socks in a drawer, have a way of disappearing. The schedule that you took so much time to put together goes missing. The memo you want to print has flown the coop. How can you find the missing files that you need so badly?

One way is to use the Office Search command. This chapter explains how to conduct both basic and advanced searches. You also find out how to obtain information about a file — when you created it, how long you worked on it, and when you last modified it.

INTEGRATION

Book I covers how to find missing files by using the Windows Find (or Search) command. Searching in Windows entails looking for files by name. If you search with the Office Search command, you search by declaring what you think is inside the file that you so desperately seek.

Finding a Missing File

Suppose that you forget the name of a file that you want to open. Or you remember the name but forget the name of the folder that you put the file in. When that happens, you can search for the file by choosing File⇨Search. Office programs offer two means of searching: basic searches and advances searches. Start with a basic search, and if that turns up too many files, try an advanced search to pinpoint the file you're looking for.

TIP

If you know the name of the file you've lost, search for it in Windows, not Word: Click the Start button and choose Search⇨For Files or Folders. (In versions of Windows prior to Windows Me, choose Find⇨Files or Folders.)

Conducting a basic search and reading the results

Click the Search button or choose File⇨Search to conduct a basic search for a file. The Basic Search task pane appears on-screen, as shown in Figure 1-1. Use the following tools in the task pane to help with the search:

- **Search Text:** Type a word that you know is in the file in this text box. Type as many words as necessary to pinpoint the file that you're looking for. Office turns up only files that include all the words that you enter.

Enter a word or piece of data in the file you are looking for

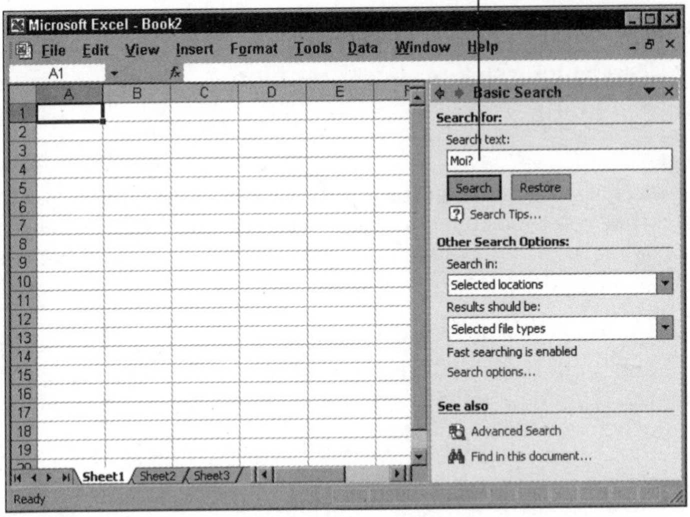

Figure 1-1: Search for missing files in the Basic Search task pane.

- **Search In:** Tell Office in which folders to look on your computer. After you open this drop-down list, you see a tree structure of the folders on your computer (refer to Figure 1-2). A search of *Everywhere* — all the folders on your computer, your A drive, and other drives — can take a long time. To narrow the search, start by deselecting the Everywhere check box. Then click the plus signs (+) to locate the folder or folders that you want to search, and click to select their check boxes. In Figure 1-2, the C:\Fiction folder is the target of the search. If you have no idea where the file resides on your computer, don't worry about it. Just click to select the Everywhere box. Your search takes longer, that's all.

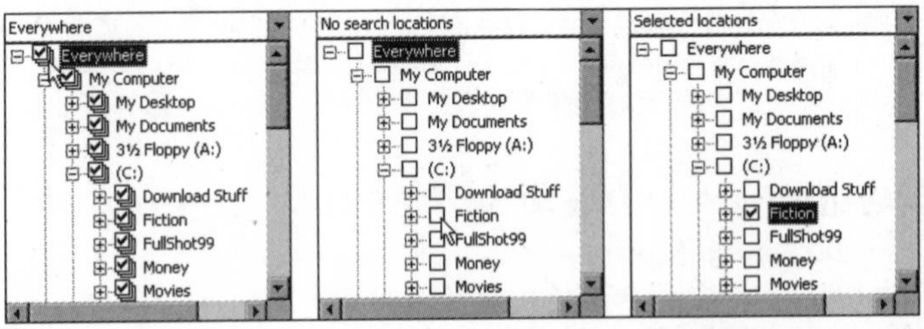

Figure 1-2: Telling Office where to search on your computer.

- **Results Should Be:** In this drop-down list, choose what kind of file you're looking for. To search for Word documents, for example, deselect the Anything check box. Then, if necessary, click plus signs (+) to display the other folders and deselect the Office Files, Outlook Items, and Web Pages check boxes. Finally, click to select the Word Files check box.

Click the Search button to conduct the search. The search results appear in the task pane. If you get no results or the wrong results, click the Modify button to start all over. (You find this button at the bottom of the task pane.) If your search turns up too many files, try conducting an advanced search.

Move the pointer over a file in the Search Results to see a pop-up box that tells you the file's location and the day you last edited it. Does that give you some idea if you've found the file you're looking for? If not, click the down arrow next to the file's name to open a drop-down list and complete these tasks:

- **Open the file:** Choose Edit from the drop-down list.
- **Open a new file with the contents of the file you searched for:** Choose New From This File from the drop-down list. A new file opens that includes all the content of the file you searched for. Now you can edit the file and save it under a different name.
- **Create a hyperlink to the file and store it on the Clipboard:** Choose Copy Link to Clipboard from the drop-down list. By choosing Edit⇨Paste, you can copy the hyperlink into a file. Then press and hold the Ctrl key and click the hyperlink that opens the file you searched for.
- **Learn more about the file:** Choose Properties from the drop-down list. The Properties dialog box appears so that you can get statistics about the file. (See the section, "Entering and Reviewing Information about a File," later in this chapter, for more information about the Properties dialog box.)

Conducting an advanced search

If your search turns up too many files, you may need to conduct an advanced search. To do so, click Advanced Search at the bottom of the Basic Search task pane. (Click the Modify button, if necessary, to return to the Search options and see Advanced Search.) After you click Advanced Search, the Advanced Search task pane appears, as shown in Figure 1-3. The Advanced Search task pane offers the same tools as the Basic Search task pane, as well as the means to describe search conditions. (A *search condition* is a specific description of a file.)

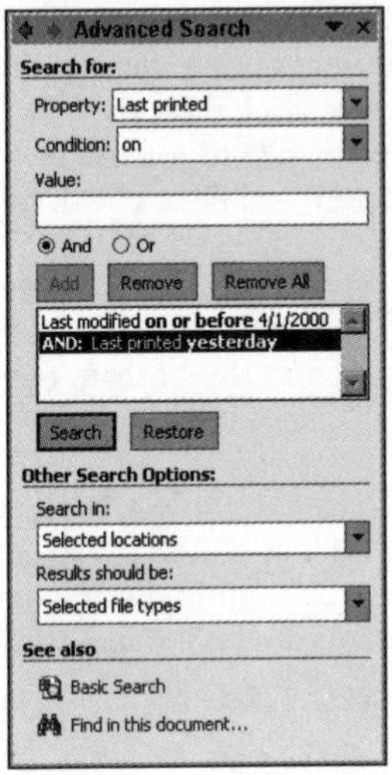

Figure 1-3: Conducting an advanced search.

Fill in the Property, Condition, and Value boxes to describe a search condition, as follows:

- **Property:** In the Property drop-down list, select a property of the file that you know something about. (You enter some file properties by way of the Properties dialog box, as the following section in this chapter explains.) Choose File Name, for example, if you remember all or part of the name of the file you're looking for; choose Last Modified if you know roughly when you last saved the file.
- **Condition:** In the Condition drop-down list, choose a search condition. The options on this list vary depending on the choice that you make in the Property drop-down list.
- **Value:** Type a value or handful of characters to further describe the search condition. What you type in this box also depends on which aspect of the file you're trying to describe. If you choose Last Modified as the property, for example, enter a date in *MM/DD/YY* format.

To search with more than one condition, click the Add button, type another condition, click the And or the Or option, and click the Add button again. Select the And or Or option under these circumstances:

- **And:** For a stringent search in which the file must meet *both* search conditions. It must have the keyword *love,* for example, and have been modified before 4/1/00.

✦ **Or:** For an either/or search in which the file can meet either search condition. It can have the keyword *love*, for example, or have been modified before 4/1/00 for the search to find it.

Click the Search button whenever you're ready to conduct your advanced search.

Entering and Reviewing Information about a File

Office keeps information about your files. You can, for example, find out how long you worked on a file, how many times you saved it, when you created it, where you stored it, and how many words it contains. You can also enter words to help Office find your document if it gets lost.

To get detailed information on any Office file, follow these steps:

1. **With the file open, choose File➪Properties.**

   In some Office programs, the command goes by a slightly different name. In Access, for example, look for the File➪Database Properties command.

2. **Click the tabs to review or make changes to them, as shown in Figure 1-4.**

   The Properties dialog box tabs provide the following functions:

   - **The General tab:** Tells you how long the file is and whether it's an archive, read-only, hidden, or system file.
   - **The Summary tab:** Lists the author, title, and other pertinent information. To make finding the file easier, you can type words in the Category and Keywords boxes. Later, when you search for the file, you can enter the category and keywords you entered here to help with the search.
   - **The Statistics tab:** Tells you when you (or someone else) created the file; who last saved it and when; and, in Microsoft Word, how much work went into it in terms of time, pages, words, and characters.
   - **The Contents tab:** Sketches out the contents of the file. What you see in this tab depends on the Office program in which you're working.
   - **The Custom tab:** Enables you to create other means of keeping statistics about your documents.

3. **Click OK.**

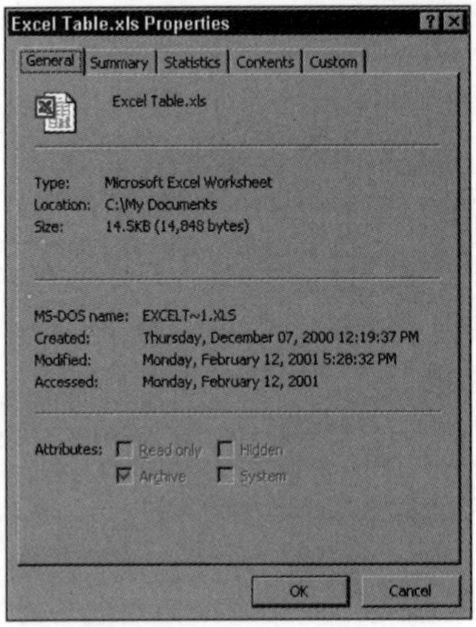

Figure 1-4: A file's properties tell you everything that you need to know about a file.

The fast way to get the statistics on a Word document is to choose Tools➪Word Count. A dialog box appears with the number of words, characters, pages, paragraphs, and lines. And if you're really keen on knowing the number of words, characters, lines, and pages in a Word document (maybe you're being paid by the word and you want to beef up the page count!), choose View➪Toolbars➪Word Count. After the Word Count toolbar appears, you can select options from its drop-down list and find out right away how many words, characters, and so on are in your document.

Chapter 2: Trading Data between Office Files and Programs

In This Chapter

- **Embedding data from one program in another program**
- **Placing an Excel worksheet on a Word page**
- **Using Word headings as the text for a PowerPoint slide presentation**
- **Getting data from Access in a Word table**
- **Sending e-mail messages from Word**
- **Publishing an Access report in Word**

Microsoft favors recycling. You can turn the report you create in Access into a Word document. Headings in a Word document can become grist for a PowerPoint presentation. With a lift of the finger and a click of the mouse, you can put an Excel worksheet right in the middle of a Word file.

This chapter looks at different ways of trading data between programs. You find out how to embed data from one program in another, place Excel worksheets in Word, turn document headings into the text of a PowerPoint presentation, retrieve Access data for a Word table, send e-mail from Word, and change an Access report into a Word document.

Embedding One Kind of File in Another

Embedding an object means placing one type of file inside another. Examples include a media clip inside a Word document and a chart inside an Access worksheet. Microsoft designed Office files to accommodate different kinds of data. Anyone who views the file need not know that the chart, for example, was not created in Access, but in another program.

After you embed an object, you can double-click it to open the program in which you created it. The program appears right away, and you can tinker with the object — the chart, the media clip, or whatever — until it's just right.

To embed an object (don't you hate computer terminology?), follow these steps:

1. **Click at the point in your file where you want to create something that you can't create by using the program that you're currently working in.**

   That's the purpose of embedding — to throw something in a file that the program you're using can't help you with.

2. **Choose Insert⇨Object.**

   The Object dialog box appears, as shown in Figure 2-1. The dialog box offers two ways to place an object in a file:

   - **Create the object from scratch:** On the Create New tab, scroll down the Object Type list and select the kind of object that you want to create. The list shows all the objects that the software on your computer enables you to create. The Result area describes the object that you select.
   - **Get the object from a file you already created:** On the Create from File tab, click the Browse button. In the Browse dialog box that appears, find and select the file that you want to insert and click the Insert button. But you can't necessarily embed all files successfully. If the software that you need for working with the kind of file that you select isn't available on your computer, you can't embed the object.

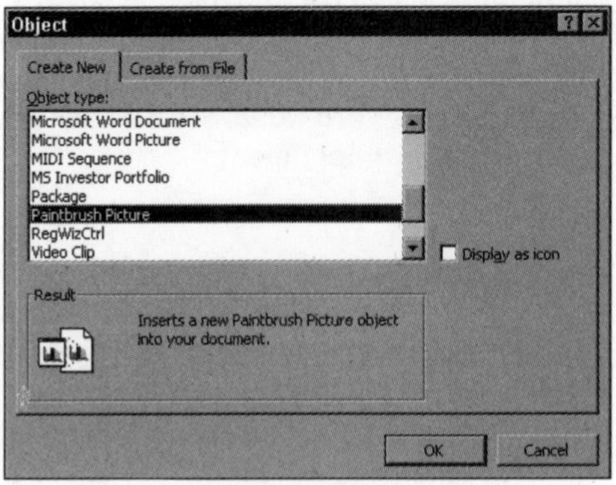

Figure 2-1: The Object dialog box enables you to embed one file inside another.

3. **Click OK.**

   If the software for making the object that you're embedding happens to be installed on your computer, the menus and toolbars that were onscreen a moment ago disappear. In their places appear menus and toolbars from a different program — the one that you need to create or embellish the object you're embedding.

4. **Fiddle with your object until you want to return to the Office program you were in before and then click anywhere outside the object.**

The file you just embedded is an *object*. As such, you can modify it by following any of these instructions:

- **Go back to work on the object:** Double-click the object to open the program in which you made it and get down to business.
- **Change the object's size:** Click the object to select it. Drag a corner selection handle to change its size but keep its proportions; drag a side handle to stretch or shrink it.
- **Move the object:** Move the pointer over the object and, after you see the four-headed arrow, click and start dragging.
- **Delete the object:** If you decide to get rid of the thing, click it once to select it and then press the Delete key.

Creating an Excel Worksheet in a Word Document

Word and Excel are joined at the hip. All you have to do to place an Excel worksheet in a Word document is click the Insert Microsoft Excel Worksheet button on the Standard toolbar in Word. The worksheet is embedded in your Word document (read the previous section in this chapter if you aren't sure what "embedded" means). When you click the worksheet, Excel buttons and tools appear on-screen where Word buttons and tools used to be.

Embedding an Excel worksheet in a Word document is a great way to take advantage of the mathematical functions that Excel offers without leaving Word. After you print the document, the worksheet part of it looks like a Word table.

To place an Excel worksheet in a Word document, follow these steps:

1. **In a Word document, place the cursor where you want the Excel worksheet to go.**
2. **Click the Insert Microsoft Excel Worksheet button on the Standard toobar.**

   A grid appears below the button so that you can choose the number of rows and columns you want.
3. **Move the cursor onto the grid and click to specify a certain number of rows and columns.**

   The bottom of the grid tells you how many rows and columns you get after you click. After you click, an Excel worksheet appears on-screen and you see all the Excel commands and buttons, as shown at the top of Figure 2-2.

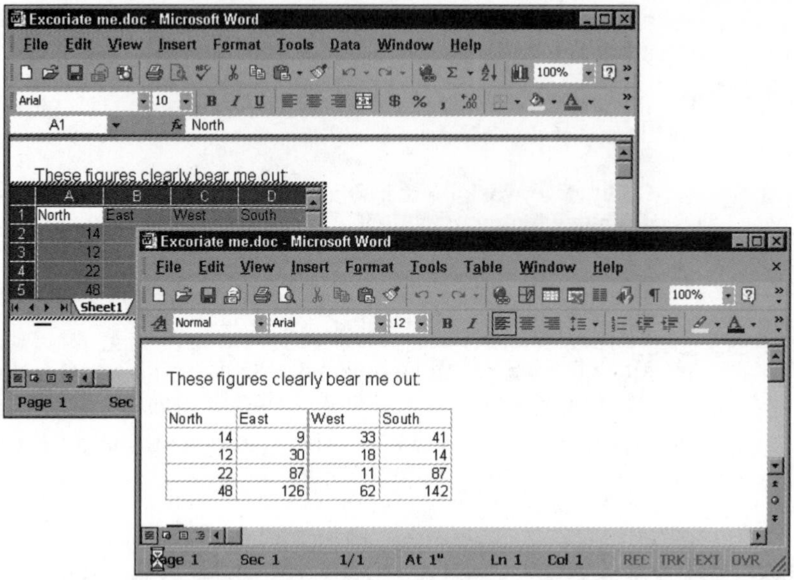

Figure 2-2: Calling on Excel to create a table in Word.

Click outside the Excel worksheet to turn the worksheet into a Word table — your document now looks something like the Word document shown at the bottom of Figure 2-2. Double-click the table when you want to see the worksheet rows and columns again as well as the Excel menus and toolbars. Double-click the table when you want to start working in Excel again.

TIP

Excel offers an AutoFormat command for decorating an entire worksheet. To use this command, however, you must start by clicking the Select All button, the cell in the upper-left corner of the worksheet. (If you don't click that button first, Excel thinks you want to decorate a column or cell.) After you click the Select All button, choose Format⇨AutoFormat and select a worksheet design in the AutoFormat dialog box.

Transferring Headings from a Word Document to Your PowerPoint Text

INTEGRATION

One of the easiest ways to enter text in a PowerPoint presentation is to borrow it from a Word document. Headings serve the same purpose as slide text — they hit the high points and describe which topics are under review. Because headings can serve as PowerPoint text, Office enables you to retrieve text from a Word document and ease it right into PowerPoint.

Before you can use this trick, however, you must assign heading styles to the headings in the Word document, as shown in Figure 2-3. Headings that you assign the Heading 1 style become slide titles in the PowerPoint presentation. Heading 2 styles and beyond go in bulleted lists on the slides. Chapter 9 in Book II explains outlining in Word.

If you have a Word document that can do double-duty as a PowerPoint presentation, follow these steps to use headings from the Word document as text for the PowerPoint slides:

1. **In PowerPoint, switch to Normal View and click the Outline tab (refer to Figure 2-3).**

   You can see the text better after you select the Outline tab. Chapter 1 in Book VI explains how to switch views in a PowerPoint presentation.

2. **Choose Insert⇨Slides from Outline.**

   The Insert Outline dialog box appears.

3. **Locate and select the Word document that you want to get the slide text from.**

4. **Click the Insert button.**

Figure 2-3: Getting the text for a PowerPoint presentation from a Word document.

Stocking a Word Table with Data from Access

As long as you know your way around Access — and not everyone does, because Access is a complicated data-management program — you can grab Access data and plug it straight into a Word table. You can place the telephone list that you keep in Access in a Word table with hardly any trouble at all. What's more, you can link an Access database to a Word table so that, as the database is updated, so is the Word table.

You can query the data that you bring from Access into Word by using tools in Word. But you're better off querying the data in Access first and then bringing it into Word. The Access tools for querying a more sophisticated and easier to use than the Word tools for querying. Besides Access tables, you can bring data from Access queries into Word. Query the data in Access if the data needs querying before it lands in your Word table.

Retrieving the data

To gather data from an Access database and plug it into a Word table, follow these steps:

1. **In Word, choose View⇨Toolbars⇨Database or right-click a toolbar and choose Database to display the Database toolbar.**
2. **Click the Insert Database button on the Database toolbar.**

   The Database dialog box appears.
3. **Click the Get Data button.**

   The Select Data Source dialog box appears.
4. **Find and select the Access file that holds the data that you need and then click the Open button.**

   The Select Table dialog box appears, as shown in Figure 2-4. This dialog box lists tables and queries in the database that you select. Notice that icons designate which files are tables and which are queries.
5. **Click to select the query or table that you need.**
6. **Click OK to return to the Database dialog box.**
7. **Click the Insert Data button in the Database dialog box.**

   The Insert Data dialog box appears.
8. **Click OK to import all the data.**

If you want to update your table as the source data in Access changes, select the Insert Data as Field check box. When you want to update the data, right-click the table and choose Update Field or simply click the table and press F9.

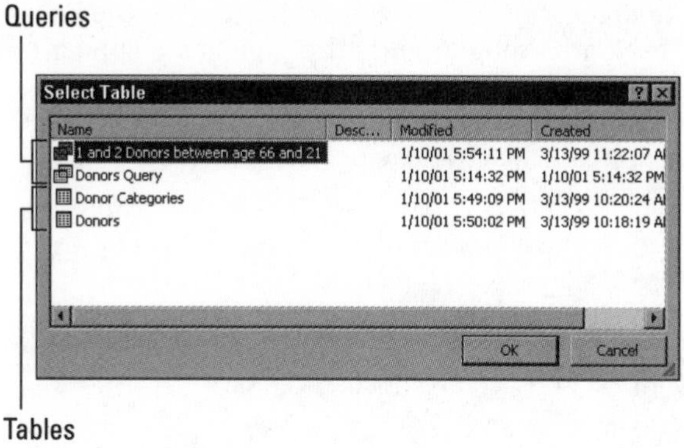

Figure 2-4: Importing data from an Access table or query.

Managing the Word/Access table

Although the data in your table comes from Access, you can treat it as a run-of-the-mill Word table. Format it. Bend it. Spindle it. Or mutate it. Or if you want to take advantage of the buttons on the Database toolbar, more power to you. The Database toolbar offers some nice commands for managing data in a Word/Access table, as the following list describes:

- **Sort the data:** Click the column where the sort is to take place and then click the Sort Ascending or Sort Descending button.
- **Enter a new row:** Click the Add New Record button.
- **Enter data by way of a form:** Click the Data Form button. In the Data Form dialog box that appears, click the Add New button and enter more data. Click the Close button when you have finished entering data.
- **Delete a row:** Click the row that needs deleting and click the Delete Record button.

Sending E-Mail and Files from Word

To add wealth to riches, you can send e-mail from Word without opening Outlook or any other e-mail program. Of course, you must install Outlook first to send e-mail from Word. (These things don't happen by magic, you know.)

By typing e-mail messages in Word, you can take advantage of the spell-checker, text-formatting commands, and other commands that may not be available in the e-mail program that you use.

To send an e-mail message in Word, start by clicking the E-mail button on the Standard toolbar. A toolbar and other amenities appear to help you write and launch an e-mail message (see Figure 2-5). As long as you click the E-mail button first, commands for e-mailing appear on-screen. To make the commands disappear, click to deselect the E-mail button.

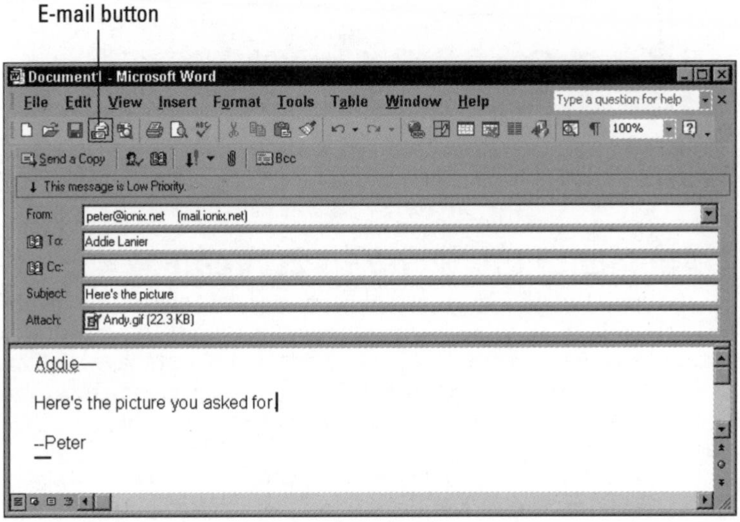

Figure 2-5: Sending e-mail from Word.

After typing your message, click the Send a Copy button. (Odd name for the button, seeing as you're not sending a copy, but an original e-mail message.) You can type e-mail addresses by hand, or you can click any button with an address book icon on it to open your address book and select recipients' names. You get a few other fringe benefits if you send an e-mail in Word. The following list describes all the nifty things that you can do:

- **Send a copy of your message:** Type an e-mail address in the Cc (carbon copy) line to send a copy of the message.
- **Send a blind carbon copy of your message:** Click the Bcc button. A Bcc line appears below the Cc line so that you can type the e-mail address of the person to whom you want to send a blind carbon copy. If you send a copy of a message, the recipient knows that a copy was sent and to whom the copy was sent. But if you send a blind carbon copy, the main recipient is none the wiser.
- **Send a file along with the message:** Click the Attach button. In the Insert Attachment dialog box that appears, find and select the file that you want to send along with your e-mail message. Then click the Attach button again.

- **Prioritize your message:** Open the Set Priority button drop-down list and choose a priority. Special icons mark high- and low-priority messages. But only recipients who use Outlook or Outlook Express to read their e-mail can see the priority icons on your messages.

Turning an Access Report into a Word Document

Access reports are a useful Office tool. Instead of a bunch of figures that are hard to read and interpret, you get a report with labels and headings that help you understand the figures in a database. Access reports are obvious candidates for company reports and other documents where facts and figures are laid bare for all to see. For that reason, Access offers a special command for turning a report into a Word document.

To turn an Access report into a Word document, follow these steps:

1. **In Access, display the report in Print Preview view.**

   To do so, choose View➪Print Preview or open the View button's drop-down list and select Print Preview.

2. **Open the Office Links button's drop-down list and select Publish It with Microsoft Word (see Figure 2-6).**

   Word opens (if it's not open already) and you see your Access report in a Word document. Office lays out the report in Word the same way it does in Access.

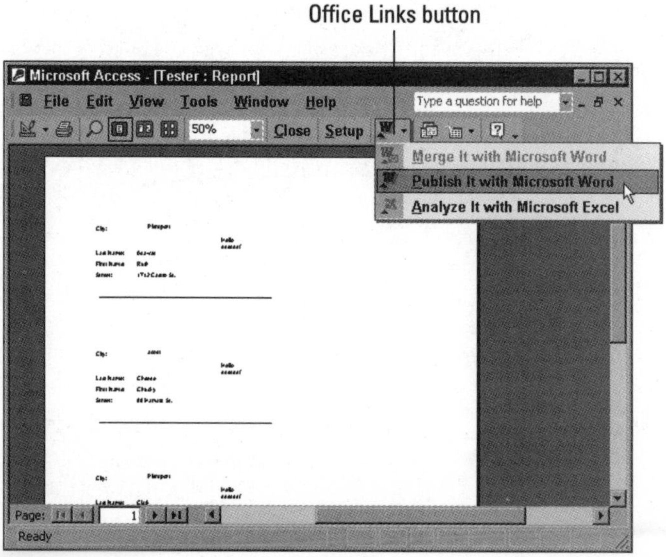

Figure 2-6: Publishing an Access report in Word.

An Access report you create in Word is an RTF (rich-text format) file, not a standard Word document. If you're more comfortable dealing with Word documents than RTF files, however, you can save the file as a Word document: Choose File⇨Save As. In the Save As dialog box that appears, open the Save As Type drop-down list and choose Word Document. Click the Save button.

Chapter 3: Creating Charts with Microsoft Graph

In This Chapter

- **Creating the chart and filling in the datasheet**
- **Altering the appearance of the chart**

When you're working away in Word, Publisher, or PowerPoint, you can create a chart by calling on Microsoft Graph, an auxiliary program that comes with Office.

In this chapter, you find out how to create a chart, how to enter the data from which Microsoft Graph generates the chart, and methods for tinkering with the appearance of charts. What's a report without a good chart or two? Sort of like an emperor without any clothes, don't you think?

TIP

If you're happy creating charts with Excel, however, don't bother with Microsoft Graph. The Excel chart-making tools are superior to Graph's. Refer to Book III for more information about Excel. I'm afraid, however, that you have to use Microsoft Graph to create a chart if you aren't working in Excel.

Entering Data to Create a Chart

The first step in creating a chart is to enter the data from which Microsoft Graph will generate the chart . Don't worry about the chart's appearance at the beginning. Microsoft Graph provides many opportunities for tinkering with a chart's appearance. What's important at the beginning is entering the data correctly. A chart is only as accurate as the numbers from which you generate it.

Click the file at the point where you want the chart to go. To enter the data to create a chart, follow these steps:

1. **Choose Insert➪Picture➪Chart or Insert➪Chart, depending on the Office program you're in.**

   A datasheet with sample data and a sample chart appear, as shown in Figure 3-1. Meanwhile, a new menu bar and toolbars appear on-screen. Welcome to Microsoft Graph!

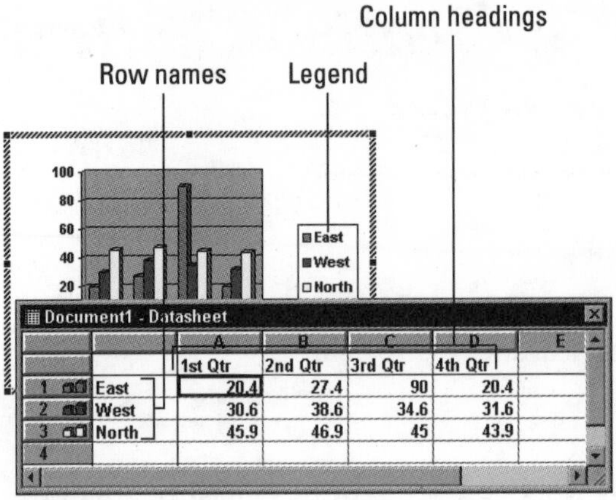

Figure 3-1: Entering the raw data for the chart.

2. **Type the data for the chart in the datasheet.**

   As you type the data, carefully choose row names for the leftmost column and column names for the top row. Those names matter for the *legend* of your chart — the box on the chart that describes what information it's plotting.

3. **Click outside the datasheet and sample graph after you finish typing the data.**

   If you type a number incorrectly, double-click the chart to make the datasheet reappear and retype the number.

REAL WORLD

Entering data in a Word table first

Datasheets can be unwieldy. One way to keep from having to wrestle with the datasheet is to enter the data in a Word table and then copy it to the datasheet.

To use this method, create a table in Word and enter the data there. Then click the table and choose Table⇨Select⇨Table. With the table selected, click the Copy button, press Ctrl+C, or choose Edit⇨Copy.

Back in the datasheet, click the Select All button (the square in the upper-left corner of the datasheet) and press the Delete key to remove the sample data. Then click the first cell in the datasheet (the one in the upper-left corner) and click the Paste button, press Ctrl+V, or choose Edit⇨Paste.

Entering data in a datasheet can be kind of troublesome. Following are some tips to help you along:

- **Deleting sample data:** Highlight the data and click the Delete key. To delete all the data at once, click the first square in the upper-left corner of the data sheet and press the Delete key. (That square is the Select All button.)
- **Entering data:** Click a *cell* — a square on the datasheet that contains information — and start typing.
- **Making a column wider:** Move the pointer to the top of the column until it's over the boundary between columns. After you see the two-headed arrow, click and drag the border. If a row isn't wide enough to show data, you see a scientific notation in the cell instead of a number.
- **Making additional columns and rows:** Right-click a column letter or row number and choose Insert from the shortcut menu that appears.
- **Making the datasheet larger:** Move the pointer to the lower-right corner of the datasheet, wait until you see the two-headed arrow, click, and drag.
- **Formatting numbers:** Select numbers and click a Style button on the Formatting toolbar — Currency Style, Percent Style, or Comma Style. Click the Increase Decimal or Decrease Decimal button to increase or decrease the number of decimal places on a number.

TIP

You can exclude data from a report. To do so, click the column or row that needs excluding and choose Data⇨Exclude Row/Col.

After you create a chart by using Graph, the chart lands in your file in the form of an embedded object. See Chapter 2 of this book for more information about embedded objects — how to move them and change their size.

Tinkering with the Chart's Layout and Appearance

Graph creates a simple bar chart from the data that you enter, but that doesn't mean that you can't create a chart of your own. Graph offers about 40 different charts. What's more, experimenting with chart types is pretty easy.

Click buttons on the Standard toolbar or choose Chart⇨Chart Options to tinker with charts. Choosing Chart⇨Chart Options opens the Chart Options dialog box, as shown in Figure 3-2. As you make choices in this dialog box, the preview window shows precisely what your tinkering does to a chart's appearance. So keep an eye on the Preview window as you go along.

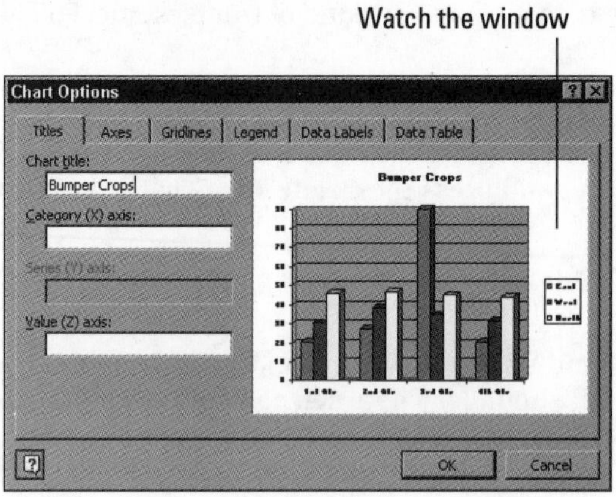

Figure 3-2: The preview window in the Chart Options dialog box shows your chart taking shape.

Besides dragging the datasheet to the side, you can click the View Datasheet button on the Standard toolbar to remove the datasheet and get a better look at your chart.

Choosing a new type of chart

Experiment boldly with chart types until you find the one that presents your data in the best light. You can change chart types easily by using one of the following options:

- **Chart Type button:** Open the Chart Type button's drop-down list and choose a new type of chart, as shown in Figure 3-3.
- **Chart Type dialog box:** Choose Chart➪Chart Type and select one of the many charts in the Chart Type dialog box that appears — area charts, bar charts, spider charts . . . you name it. Make sure that you also visit the Custom Types tab and check out the charts there.

Notice the Press and Hold to View Sample button in the Chart Type dialog box. Do just that — press and hold down that button to get a good look at the chart type you choose before you close the dialog box. As you hold down the button, a preview of your chart appears where the chart types used to be.

Adding the chart title, legend, and data labels

A legend tells you what's what on a chart, but if you don't think it's necessary, you can click the Legend button on the Standard toolbar to hide the legend. For that matter, try choosing Chart➪Chart Options and clicking the Legend tab in the Chart Options dialog box (refer to Figure 3-2). On that tab, you find options for placing the legend in relation to the chart.

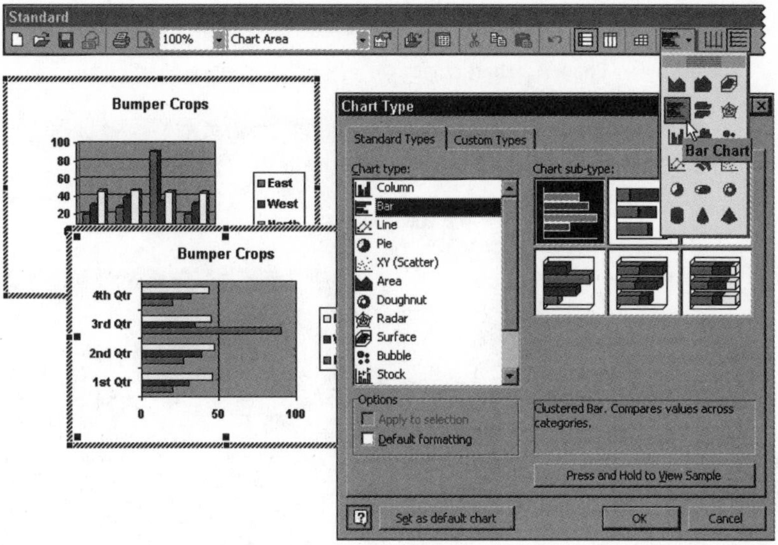

Figure 3-3: Create a new kind of chart by using the Chart Type button or Chart Type dialog box.

The Titles tab of the Chart Options dialog box offers text boxes for entering a chart title and names for the X-axis category and Y-axis value. After deciding on a chart title and axis names, keep your eye on the Preview window to see what your choices mean in real terms.

The Data Labels tab in the Chart Options dialog box enables you to add series names, category names, and value names to the chart. Check it out and keep your eye on the Preview window.

Customizing your chart

Look at a chart carefully and you see that it consists of different areas. (Graph calls them *objects*.) In fact, if you open the Chart Objects drop-down list on the Standard toolbar and make a choice or two, you can see what these areas, or objects, are. Each time that you make a choice, the object you chose is selected in the chart.

After you select an object this way, you can format it and in so doing customize a part of your chart. To format the legend in your chart, for example, choose Legend from the Chart Objects drop-down list (see Figure 3-4). Then, to start formatting, either click the Format button or choose Format⇨Selected Object (or press Ctrl+1). You see the Format dialog box, also shown in Figure 3-4, where you can customize a part of your chart.

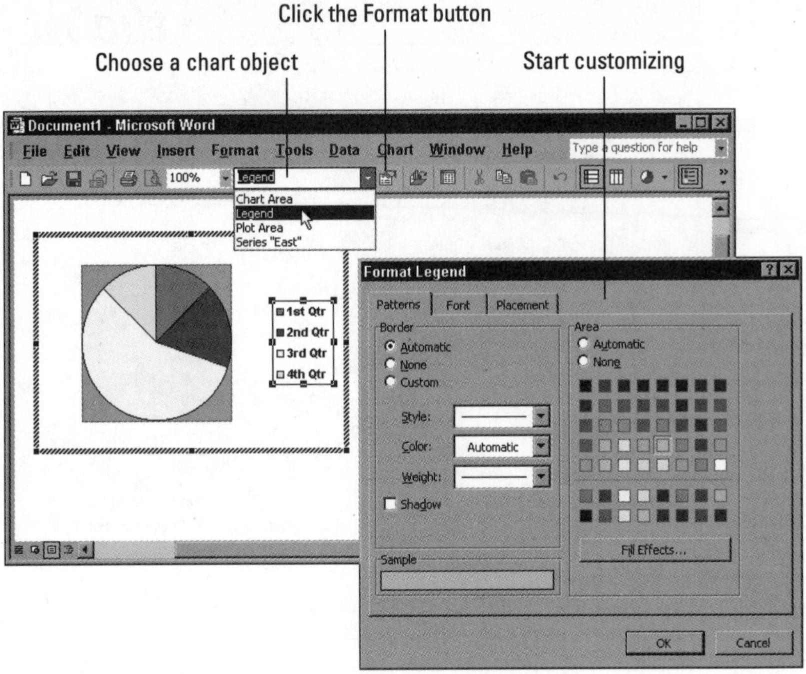

Figure 3-4: Customizing part of a chart.

The fastest way to open the Format dialog box and start customizing is to double-click the part of the chart that you want to customize.

Chapter 4: Managing the Microsoft Clip Organizer

In This Chapter

- **Starting the Microsoft Clip Organizer**
- **Cataloging the media files on your computer**
- **Finding and inserting a media file**
- **Organizing media files**

As computers get faster and better, media — graphics, video clips, and sound — are sure to play a bigger role in computing. Dropping a clip-art image in a Word document won't seem a big deal. Attaching a video clip to an e-mail message is likely to become commonplace. Word-processed files are even going to include sound icons that you can click to hear voice comments, whisperings, and grunts.

Microsoft, well aware that the future is closing in on us, created the Clip Organizer for the newest version of Office. By using the Clip Organizer, you can place graphics, video clips, and sound in files. More important, the Clip Organizer's the place to organize media on your computer so that you can find and make good use of it. This chapter covers ways that you can manage the Microsoft Clip Organizer.

Opening the Microsoft Clip Organizer

Do one of the following to open the Microsoft Clip Organizer:

- ✦ Click the Start button and choose Programs⇨Microsoft Office Tools⇨Microsoft Clip Organizer.
- ✦ Open the Clip Art task pane by choosing Insert⇨Picture⇨Clip Art or clicking the Insert Clip Art button on the Drawing toolbar. At the bottom of the Insert Clip Art task pane, click Clip Organizer.

The Clip Organizer window opens and you see the Collection List and with the Favorites folder selected (see Figure 4-1). You can keep your favorite media files and images in the Favorites folder so that you can find them quickly later on.

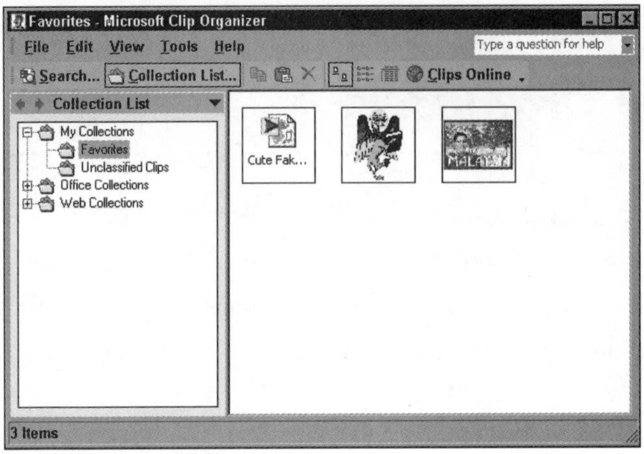

Figure 4-1: The Clip Organizer opens to the Favorites folder.

Although media files appear to be organized into folders in the Clip Organizer, those folders don't really exist on your computer. The folders represent categories, and inside each category you find shortcuts similar to the shortcuts on the Windows desktop that tell your computer where to find the files on your computer. If you select a file in the Clip Organizer, you activate the shortcut, and the program inserts the file from its real location on your computer.

The Collection List classifies media files into the following four folders:

- **My Collections:** Your favorite media files (in the Favorites folder), collections you organize yourself, and the names of folders on your computer where the Clip Organizer found media files during an inventory. (The following section in this chapter describes inventorying.)
- **Office Collections:** Media files you install along with Office.
- **Web Collections:** Files kept on Design Gallery Live, a Web site that Microsoft maintains. To download files from Microsoft, your computer must be connected to the Internet.

Taking Inventory of the Media Files on Your Computer

The first time you open the Clip Organizer, it asks you whether you want to inventory the clip art, sound, and video files on your computer. By inventorying, you enable the Clip Organizer to take note of the clip-art files, sound files, and so on in the C:\Windows folder and its subfolders on your computer. You thereafter make searching for media files easier.

Whether you click Yes or No the first time you're asked about inventorying, you can always do the job by choosing File⇨Add Clips to Gallery⇨Automatically. The Add Clips to Gallery dialog box appears. Click OK to inventory all the files in the C:\Windows folder on your computer. After the Clip Organizer finds a media file on your computer, it places that file in the My Collections folder.

Inserting a Media File by Way of the Clip Organizer

You can insert a media file by way of the Clip Organizer. If you're familiar with inserting images from the Insert Clip Art task pane, you've won half the battle. You already know how to search for media files by keyword. Starting from the Clip Organizer, you can search by keyword for files, or if you happen to know in which folder you can find the file, you can simply go to that folder and retrieve it.

After you locate the file, click the down arrow to open its drop-down list and select Copy, as shown in Figure 4-2. Then click your file at the point where you want the clip-art image, graphic, sound file, or video clip to go, and choose Edit⇨Paste (or press Ctrl+V).

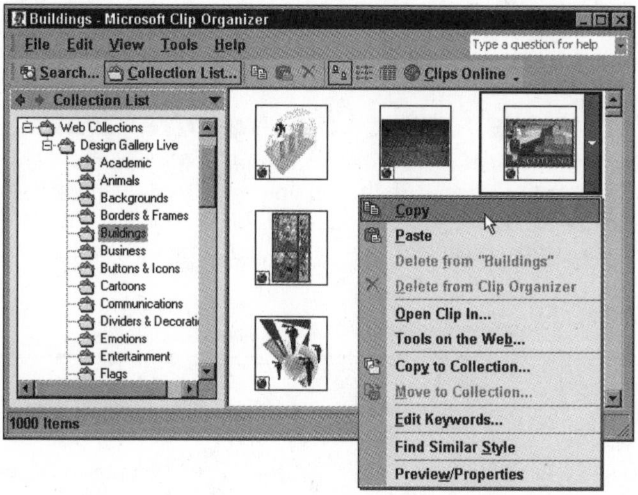

Figure 4-2: Copying a file from the Clip Organizer so that you can paste it in a file.

TIP

Besides searching for clip-art images by way of keywords, you can look for images that exhibit a similar style and perhaps are created by the same artist. To do so, find an example of an Office clip-art image that you like in the Clip Organizer, open the image's drop-down list, and select Find Similar Style. In a moment, clip-art images that look like the image you admire appear in the Clip Organizer window.

Searching by keyword for a media file

To search by keyword for a media file, follow these steps:

1. **Click the Search button in the Clip Organizer (or choose View⇨Search).**

   Search options appear in the Search task pane.

2. **Type a keyword in the Search Text text box that describes what you're looking for.**

3. **Open the Search In drop-down list and select a folder that you want to search in. (Select the Everywhere folder to search throughout the Clip Organizer categories.)**

   The folders in this list are the same ones that you see in the Collection List task pane.

4. **Open the Results Should Be drop-down list and select the type of media you're seeking — clip art, photographs, movies, or sounds.**

   By clicking the plus sign (+) next to a media type, you can look for files of a certain type. To look for JPEG photos, for example, open the Photographs folder and click the check box next to JPEG File Interchange Format.

5. **Click Search.**

   If the Clip Organizer finds what you're looking for, files appear in the window (refer to Figure 4-2). If the Clip Organizer finds no files, the words `No Results Found` appear at the bottom of the Search task pane.

Getting a file from a Clip Organizer folder

Bully for you if you know where a multimedia file you need is located in the Clip Organizer. To locate the file, all you have to do is click the Collection List button (or choose View⇨Collection List) and open the folder where the file resides. After you select the file, its icon appears on the right side of the window.

REAL WORLD

Getting media files from Microsoft

Microsoft has ambitious plans for permitting users of Office to get their clip art, sound files, and video clips from a Microsoft Web site. To see what kind of media Microsoft offers online, choose Tools⇨Tools on the Web. After your machine connects to the Internet, you go directly to a Web page where you can perform the following tasks:

- ✦ Download collections of clip art and other media files to your computer.
- ✦ Trade clip art with other people.
- ✦ Correspond with other Office users.

Organizing Files in the Clip Organizer

The Clip Organizer is a convenient place for storing the media files that you use in your work. But as good as it is, you can make it even better. You can put media files in the Favorites folder, where you can find them quickly. You can even create new folders for storing media files. You can catalog the media files that you keep on your computer in the Clip Organizer. Finally, you can attach your own keywords to media files so that they're easier to find.

Copying a file to the Favorites folder

Suppose that you find a file in the Clip Organizer that looks intriguing. You tell yourself, "Maybe I can use that one someday." In moments like that, copy the file to the Favorites folder. That way, you can find it easily if you do need it. All you need to do is open the Favorites folder and there it is. By contrast, tracking down a media file that you vaguely remember can prove frustrating and often futile.

To copy a file in the Clip Organizer to the Favorites folder, follow these steps:

1. **After you have located the file and it appear on the right side of the Clip Organizer window, open the file's drop-down list and choose Copy to Collection.**

   The Copy to Collection dialog box appears, as shown in Figure 4-3.

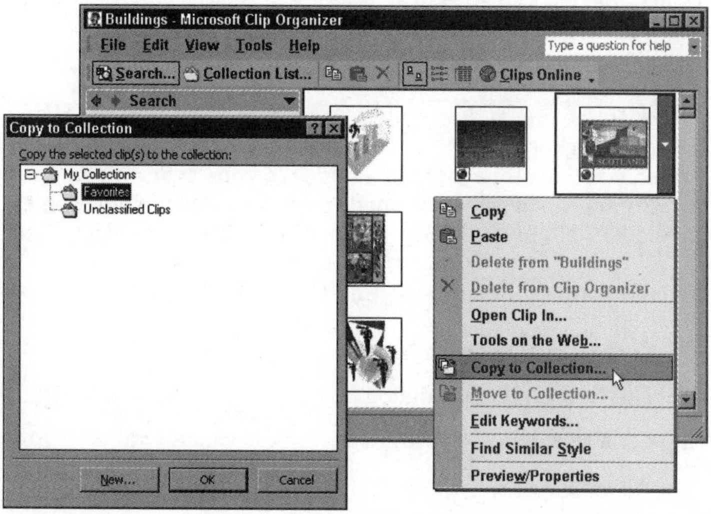

Figure 4-3: Placing a media file in the Favorites folder.

2. **Click to select the Favorites Folder.**

   If necessary, click the plus sign (+) beside the My Collections folder to see the Favorites folder.

3. **Click OK.**

To remove a file from the Favorites folder, open the file's drop-down list and select Delete From Favorites.

Copying more than one file to a folder

You can save time by copying more than one media file at a time to a folder. To copy more than one file at a time, use the standard technique for copying, which I describe at the end of this section if you need a refresher, but select more than one file to start with.

In the Clip Organizer window, click the List button to view a list of file names instead of thumbnail views of files. Then select the files by using one of the following techniques:

- Ctrl+click file names to select a file here or there.
- Shift+click to select files with names that appear next to one another. Click the first file that you want and then Shift+click the last one.
- Press Ctrl+A (or choose Edit➪Select All) to select all the files.

Now follow the standard procedure for copying files: Choose Edit➪Copy to Collection, click to select the folder where you want to copy the files in the Copy to Collection dialog box that appears, and click OK.

Creating your own folder in the Clip Organizer

Besides storing media files you may need in the future in the Favorites folder, you can store them in a folder of your own. You can put photographs in a Photographs folder or music files in a Music folder. You can then find media files simply by going to the folder where you place them.

To create a new folder in the Clip Organizer, follow these steps:

1. **Choose File➪New Collection.**

   The New Collection dialog box appears, as shown in Figure 4-4.

2. **Click to select the folder in which to place your new folder.**

   Clicking My Collections is the best choice, but you can place your new folder wherever you want.

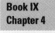

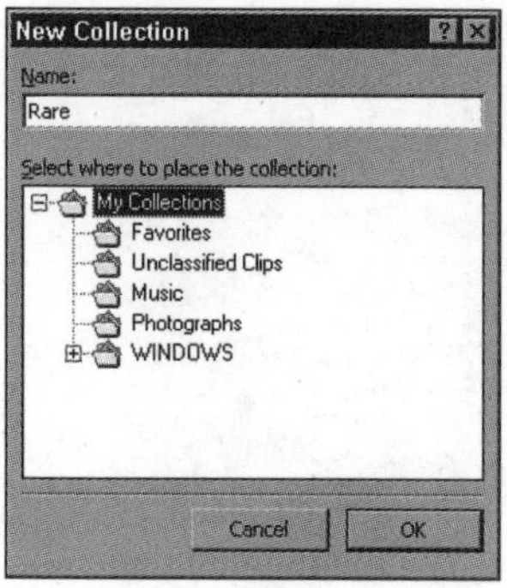

Figure 4-4: Create a new folder for storing media files in the New Collection dialog box.

3. **Type a name for the folder in the Name text box.**
4. **Click OK.**

If you need to rename the folder, click to select it in the Collection List, choose Edit⇨Rename Collection, and type a new name. To remove it, choose Edit⇨Delete from Clip Organizer.

Putting your own media files in the Clip Organizer

As "Taking Inventory of the Media Files on Your Computer" explained near the start of this chapter, the Clip Organizer can scour the C:\Windows folder on your computer for clip art, sound files, and video files and then enter their names in the Clip Organizer. But the Clip Organizer can't inventory all the media files on your computer.

How would you like to enroll media files that you keep on your computer in the Clip Organizer? Remember that the files in the Clip Organizer are merely pointers to the locations of real files on your computer. By putting your own media files in the Gallery, you make finding those files easier. And you can insert them by using the same techniques that you use to insert any media file in the Gallery.

You can store your own files in the Favorites folder or a folder that you create yourself. To put your own media files in the Clip Organizer, follow these steps:

1. **Click the Collection List button, if necessary, to see the Collection List, and click to select the folder where you want to store the media files.**
2. **Choose File⇨Add Clips to Gallery⇨On My Own.**

   The Add Clips to Gallery dialog box appears, as shown in Figure 4-5.

Figure 4-5: Use this dialog box for putting your own stuff in the Clip Organizer.

3. **In the dialog box, select the name of the file or files that you want to store in the Clip Organizer.**

   You can select more than one file by Ctrl+clicking or Shift+clicking.

   If you change your mind about which Clip Organizer folder to put the files in, you can click the Add To button and, in the Import to Collection dialog box, choose a different folder.

4. **Click the Add button.**

To remove a media file from the Organizer, open its drop-down list on the right side of the Organizer window and select Delete from Clip Organizer. Don't worry, removing a file from the Clip Organizer does not delete the file from your hard drive.

Changing the keywords associated with a file

If you've ever searched for a media file by keyword, you know that keywords are associated with files in the Clip Organizer. To find out what a file's keywords are, open its drop-down list and select Edit Keywords. The Keywords dialog box appears (see Figure 4-6), where you can see which keywords are necessary to turn up the file in a keyword search.

Sometimes the keywords aren't very descriptive. In the case of files that you put in the Clip Organizer yourself and files that the Clip Organizer retrieves during an inventory, the keywords can be downright meaningless in that they aren't descriptive and won't turn up the file in a search.

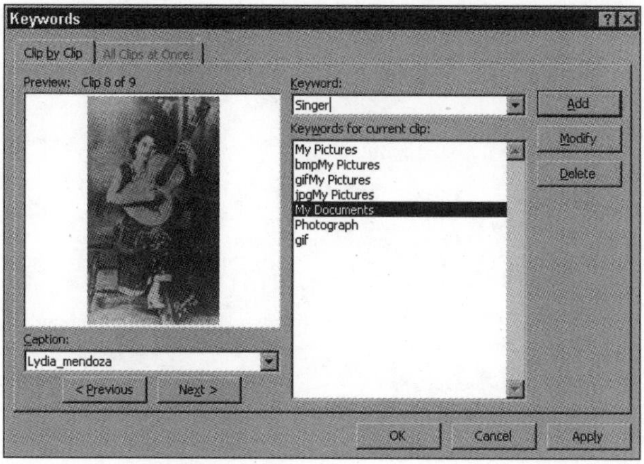

Figure 4-6: This dialog box associates a handful of keywords with each media file.

From the Keywords dialog box, you can change the keywords that Clip Organizer associates with a file and make the file easier to locate in searches. To do so, follow these instructions:

- **To enter a new keyword:** Type a word in the Keyword text box and click the Add button.
- **To remove a keyword:** Click to select the word in the dialog box and click the Delete button.

Click the Apply button after you finish fooling with keywords.

To change the keywords that the Clip Organizer associates with other files in the folder you're working in, click the Previous or Next button in the Keywords dialog box and get to work. You don't need to click OK in the Keywords dialog box and start all over in the Clip Organizer.

Chapter 5: Drawing Lines and Shapes

In This Chapter

- **Drawing shapes and autoshapes**
- **Choosing a look and color for lines**
- **Adding color to a shape**
- **Drawing lines and arrows**
- **Managing objects that overlap**

All the Office programs except Access and Outlook provide drawing tools that you can use to doodle, draw lines, and draw shapes. The drawing tools enable you to add something extra to your files — to make your files a little brighter and a little more attractive. The drawing tools are also a fine way of passing the time on a rainy day. Think of them as an Etch-A-Sketch for adults.

In this chapter, you find out how to use the drawing tools and place the drawings that you make inside files.

Starting from the Drawing Toolbar

You find the drawing tools on the Drawing toolbar, as shown in Figure 5-1. So important is the Drawing toolbar, Microsoft provides a button for displaying it — the Drawing button. Click that button, choose View⇨Toolbars⇨Drawing, or right-click a toolbar and choose Drawing from the shortcut menu to display the Drawing toolbar.

Figure 5-1: The Drawing toolbar.

REAL WORLD

A word about the drawing canvas

As you start drawing a line or shape in Microsoft Word, the drawing canvas appears. The drawing canvas is there to help you place objects such as lines and shapes on the page. Objects inside the drawing canvas are treated the same as one another. Following are a couple of techniques for handling the drawing canvas:

✦ **Drawing without the canvas:** To dispense with the drawing canvas, draw your line or shape outside the canvas. After you finish drawing, the canvas disappears. You can then move your line or shape where you want on the page.

✦ **Shrinking the drawing canvas:** If more than one object is on the drawing canvas, you can click the Fit button on the Drawing Canvas toolbar to make the canvas as large as necessary to take in all objects. If it's not already visible, right-click the drawing canvas and choose Show Drawing Canvas Toolbar from the shortcut menu to see this toolbar.

To create a line or shape, click a button on the Drawing toolbar and start dragging. As you drag, you see an outline of the thing that you're drawing appear on-screen. Release the mouse button after your drawing reaches the right size.

TIP

When drawing a rectangle or oval, press and hold the Shift key as you draw to make a perfect circle or square. Without holding down the Shift key, you get an oval or rectangle.

All lines and shapes, when you click to select them, display drawing handles. Shapes have eight handles, one at each corner and one on each side. Lines have two handles, one on each end. By dragging a handle, you can change the size of a shape or line.

Besides the standard shapes that you can draw by using the Rectangle and the Oval tool, you can draw *autoshapes* — unusual shapes such as polygons and stars. To draw an autoshape, click the AutoShapes button on the Drawing toolbar, choose an option from the pop-up menu, and select the shape that you want to draw from the submenu. Figure 5-2 shows the different submenus and the different autoshapes that you can draw.

TIP

You can format lines and shapes by using the tools on the Drawing toolbar, but you can also format a line or shape by double-clicking it to open the Format dialog box. The Format dialog box offers options for changing the size of lines and shapes, changing their color, and changing their lines.

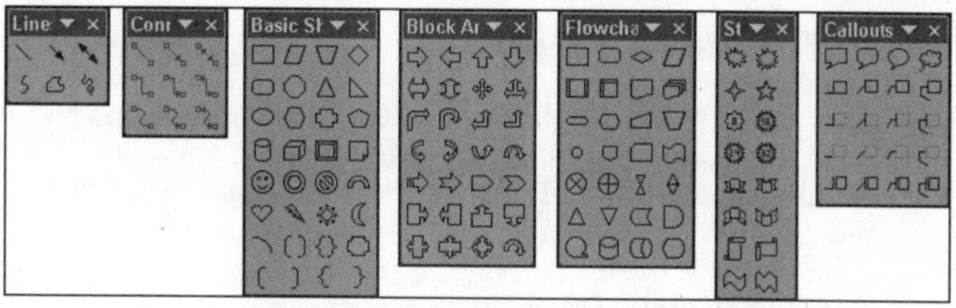

Figure 5-2: The AutoShape submenus.

Choosing Lines, Line Widths, and Line Colors

After you draw a line or shape, you can use tools on the Drawing toolbar to choose a line type, line width, and line color for the drawing (see Figure 5-3). The following list explains how to use those tools:

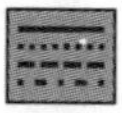

✦ **Choosing a line type:** Click the Dash Style button and choose an option from the drop-down list.

✦ **Choosing a line width:** Click the Line Style button and select an option from the drop-down list. By selecting More Lines, you can open the Format dialog box and choose among many kinds of lines on the Style drop-down list.

✦ **Choosing a line color:** Open the Line Color button's drop-down list and select a color.

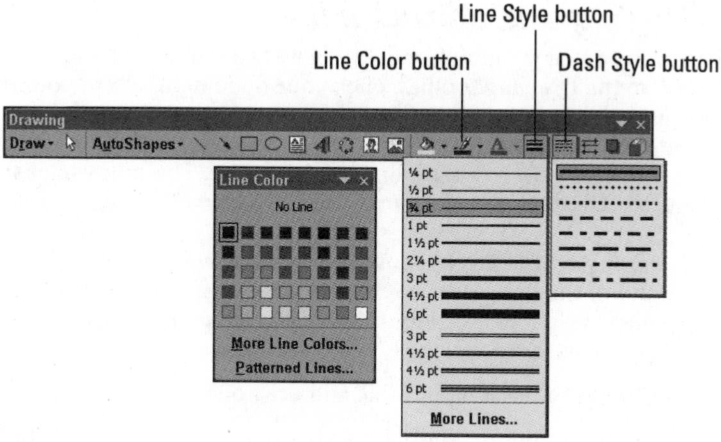

Figure 5-3: Change the type, size, and color of lines by using these buttons on the Drawing toolbar.

Filling a Shape with Color

Filling a shape with color is easy: Select the shape, open the Fill Color button's drop-down list on the Drawing toolbar, and choose a color. If no color suits you, you can choose More Fill Colors or Fill Effects from the drop-down list:

- **More Fill Colors:** Opens the Color dialog box, where you can choose among 256 colors.
- **Fill Effects:** Opens the Fill Effects dialog box, where you can choose a *fill effect,* which is a gradient, texture, or pattern for the shape.

Check out the Shadow Style and 3-D Style tools on the Drawing toolbar, too. By using these tools, you can open a pop-up menu, choose an option, and make a shape cast a shadow or appear in three dimensions.

Drawing Lines and Arrows

Your average user of Office has to draw an arrow now and then to point out, in a PowerPoint presentation or Word document, how well everything is going. In this section, you find out how to draw a line, change its angle, and attach an arrow to the end of a line. You also discover how to draw curves, draw freeform, and draw a closed shape.

Drawing and editing a line

Drawing a line is much like creating a shape or autoshape: Click the Line tool on the Drawing toolbar, click your document where you want the line to begin, and start dragging. The tricky part is getting the line just right. The section "Choosing Lines, Line Widths, and Line Colors," earlier in this chapter, explains how to alter a line's appearance. The following list tells you how to change the angle, length, and position of a line:

- **Changing the angle:** Move the pointer over the selection handle at one end of the line. After you see the double-arrow, click and start dragging the handle. A dotted line shows you what angle your line will have when you release the mouse button (see Figure 5-4).
- **Changing the length:** Click and drag one of the selection handles.
- **Changing the position:** Move the pointer over the middle of line and, after you see the four-headed arrow, click and start dragging the line.

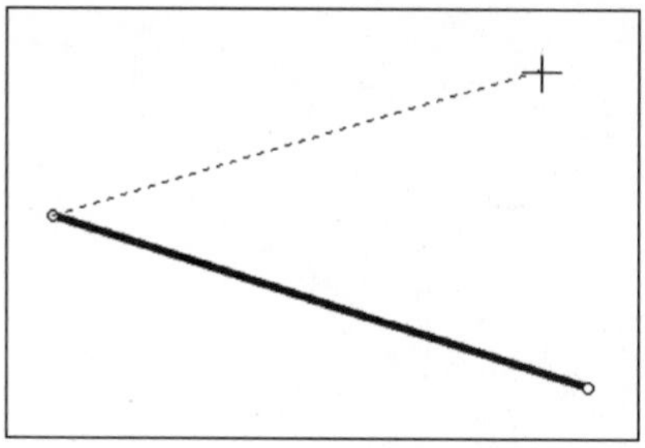

Figure 5-4: Changing the angle of a line.

Attaching an arrow to a line

To draw a line with an arrow, start by using the Arrow tool on the Drawing toolbar. Click and drag to draw the line as you normally do (see the preceding section). You end up with a line with a single arrowhead on it.

The next step is to choose what style arrowhead you want and where you want the arrowhead to go. Select the line, click the Arrow Style button on the Drawing toolbar, and then do one of the following:

- ✦ Choose an arrow from the Arrow Style drop-down list.
- ✦ Choose More Arrows from the Arrow Style drop-down list. The Format AutoShape dialog box opens. In the Arrows area of the dialog box, select a Begin Style and End Style option from a drop-down list box. Choose a Begin Size and End Size option as well.

Drawing curves and arcs

To draw a curve or arc, click the AutoShapes button on the Drawing toolbar, choose Lines from the pop-up menu, and choose Curve from the submenu. Then drag on-screen and click at the point where you want to draw a curve. Each time that you click, you make an *edit point* on the line, as shown in Figure 5-5. Double-click to complete the drawing.

To change the angle of a curve, click to select the drawing, click the Draw button on the Drawing toolbar, and choose Edit Points on the pop-up menu. Edit points appear on the line. Click and drag an edit point to change the angle of a curve.

Suppose that you want to close off a drawing you've made to turn it into a shape, not a line. To close off a line and connect its beginning and end, double-click to end the line as normally and then right-click immediately and choose Close Path from the shortcut menu that appears.

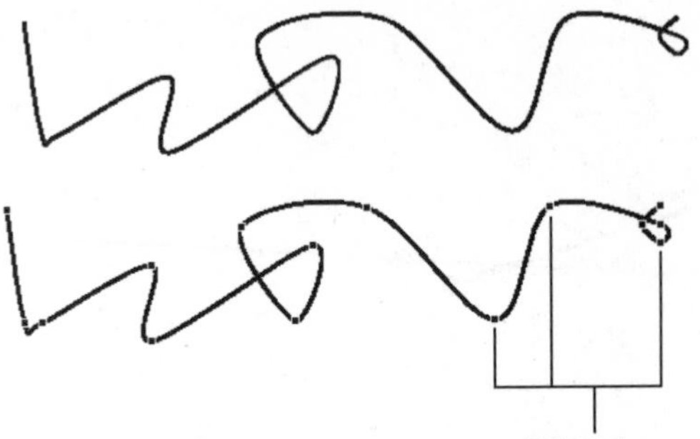

Figure 5-5: To alter a curve, drag its edit point.

Handling Shapes and Lines that Overlap

As you fill a page with lines and shapes, they inevitably overlap. How do you make one line or shape appear in front of the other? How do you move a line or shape to the background?

To handle overlapping lines and shapes, right-click the line or shape that needs to go toward the foreground or background, choose Order from the shortcut menu, and choose one of the following commands from the Order submenu (see Figure 5-6):

- **Bring to Front:** Brings the shape or line to the top of the stack.
- **Send to Back:** Sends the shape or line to the bottom of the stack.
- **Bring Forward:** In a stack of three or more objects, moves the shape or line toward the front but not necessarily to the top.
- **Send Backward:** In a stack of three or more objects, moves the shape or line toward the back but not necessarily to the bottom.

In Microsoft Word documents, objects such as shapes and lines can appear on the foreground layer in front of text or on the background layer behind text. So Word provides the two more Order commands:

- **Bring in Front of Text:** Moves the line or shape from the background layer to the foreground layer, where it obscures the text.
- **Send Behind Text:** Moves the line or shape from the foreground layer to the background layer, where the text obscures it.

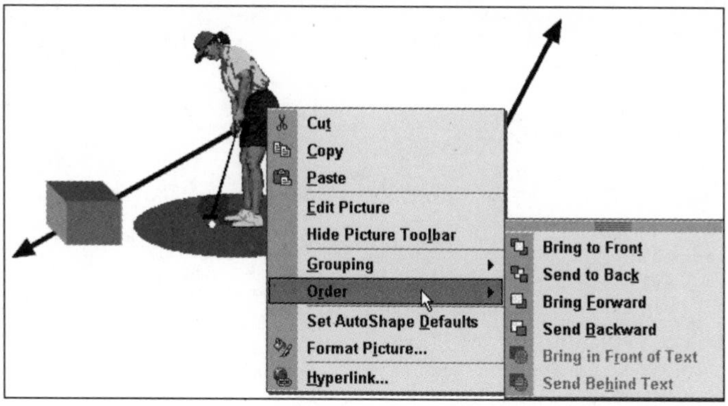

Figure 5-6: Choose an Order command to decide what overlaps what.

Index

A

B

C

D

E

F

H

I

L

M

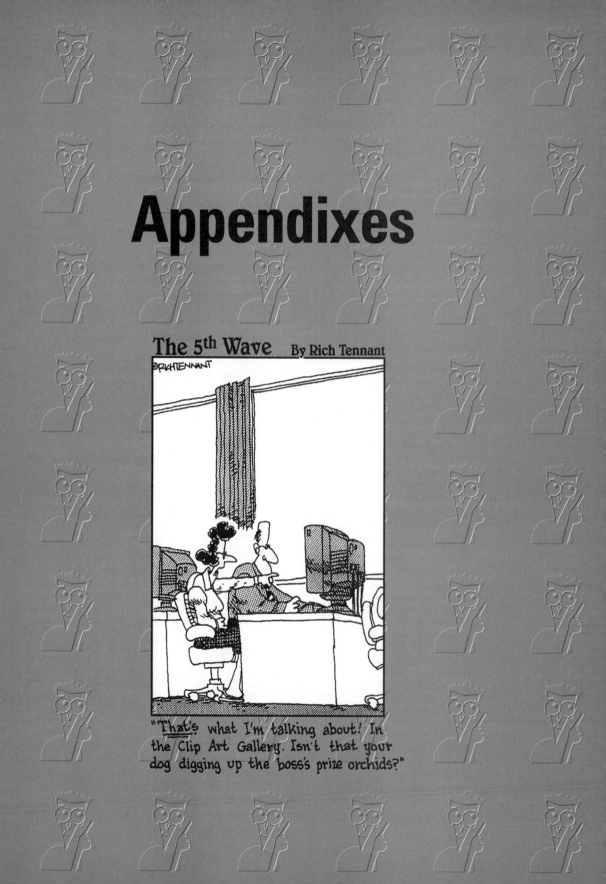

Appendixes

The 5th Wave By Rich Tennant

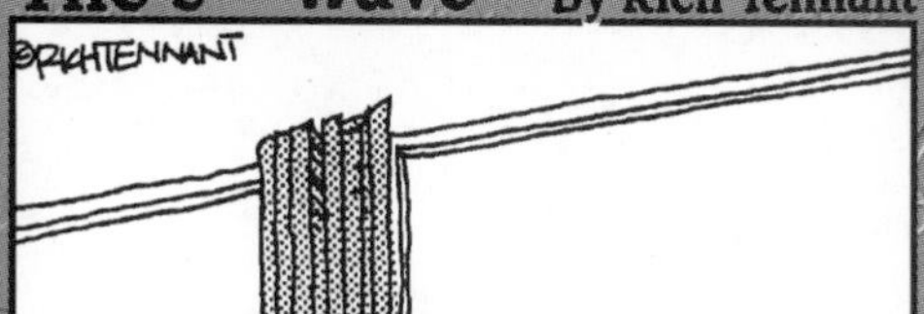

"That's what I'm talking about! In the Clip Art Gallery. Isn't that your dog digging up the boss's prize orchids?"

Contents at a Glance

Appendix A: Starting, Surviving, and Getting Help

In This Appendix

- **Opening an Office application**
- **Mousing your way through Office applications**
- **Understanding cursors and pointers**
- **Utilizing shortcut keys**
- **Using the Office clipboard to cut, copy, and paste**
- **Undoing your mistakes**
- **Getting help**

Office may seem to consist of a bunch of complex and mysterious products (and they certainly can be), but Office is an integrated group that shares many similar ways of doing things. This appendix covers some of the common aspects of Office, from starting an application to finding help if you need it.

Starting an Office Application

Windows almost always gives you more than one way to perform a task, and starting an Office application is no exception. The most popular way to begin a task is to use the Start button in the taskbar. To use the Start button, follow these steps:

1. **Click the Start button on the taskbar. (You find the Start button in the lower-left corner of your screen.)**
2. **Choose Programs on the Start menu that appears.**
3. **Choose your application (such as Microsoft Word, Microsoft PowerPoint, Microsoft Excel, and so on) from the Programs menu.**

Following are some other easy ways to get going.

- ✦ Click the Start button and choose New Office Document. (You find this option at the top of the Start menu.) You see the New Office Document dialog box. Double-click the template representing the application you want to work in, such as Word, Excel, PowerPoint, or Access.
- ✦ Double-click an existing Office file in Windows Explorer or My Computer. Windows starts the application and opens the document that you double-click.
- ✦ Click the Start button and choose Documents. You see a menu with the names of the last 15 files you opened. Click a file name to open a file.

Using the Mouse

Odds are that you can recognize your mouse, even at ten paces. Or perhaps you use a trackball or another pointing device. The important thing is that you have a pointing device and know how to use it. Otherwise, an Office application can be next to impossible to navigate.

Your pointing device controls the cursor and the pointer. (See the section "Cursors and Pointers" later in this appendix.) In general, if an Office application tells you to click something, you want to move the mouse pointer to that thing and then click the left mouse button. Table A-1 shows some common pointing procedures and how to perform them.

Table A-1 Clicking Your Way through Office

Clicking Action	*What It Means or Does*
Click something	Move the pointer to the thing and click the left mouse button.
Double-click something	Move the pointer to the thing and click the left mouse button twice quickly, without moving the pointer even the slightest bit.
Right-click something	Move the pointer to the thing and click the right mouse button.
Click and drag	Move the pointer to the thing and click the left mouse button — but don't release it. Continue to hold the left mouse button and move the mouse without letting go of the button.
Ctrl+click	Press and then hold the Ctrl key as you click the left mouse button.

Cursors and Pointers

Cursors and *pointers* are little symbols that tell you where you are on-screen and what the computer's doing. Office gives you a bunch of different cursors and pointers, but the only ones that you really need to know about I list in Table A-2.

Table A-2	Must-Know Cursors and Pointers	
Cursor/Pointer	*Name*	*What It Does*
	Insertion point	Sits in the text and blinks on and off. (In Word, for example, you find it on the page you're using; in Excel, it's in the Formula bar; and so on.) All the action takes place at the insertion point: After you start typing, text appears at this point, and if you paste something from the Clipboard, what you paste appears at the insertion point.
	I-beam pointer	If you move the pointer into editable text, it turns into the shape of the capital letter *I*. To enter text in a new place, move this I-beam pointer to that location, click to anchor the pointer in that spot, and begin typing.
	Arrow pointer	If you move the pointer over something that you can select — a menu item or a button, for example — it turns into an arrow. Click the mouse to select a menu item or press an on-screen button.
	Busy cursor	If an application is very busy, you see an hourglass on-screen. Twiddle your thumbs until the hourglass disappears, and then (and only then) you can get back to work.
	Link Select cursor	If you move the pointer over a hyperlink, you see the Link Select cursor, which takes the form of a gloved hand. (A *hyperlink* is a link between two documents or a document and a page on the Internet.) Click a hyperlink and you travel to another document or to a Web page.

Shortcut Keys for Doing It Quickly

Next to some commands on menus are Ctrl+key combinations, which are known as *shortcut keys*. If you want to select all the text in a document, for example, you can press Ctrl+A, the shortcut key equivalent of the Edit⇨Select All menu command.

Lots of menu commands have shortcut keys that help you get your work done faster. If you find yourself using a command often, see whether it has a shortcut key and start using the shortcut key to save time. Many menu commands display buttons next to their names that correspond to buttons on the toolbar. So instead of choosing these commands from menus, you can simply click the equivalent button on a toolbar.

Cutting, Copying, and Pasting

As in other Windows-based programs, the Cut, Copy, and Paste commands involve the Clipboard. The Office Clipboard holds the last 24 items you cut or copied. You can copy and collect items from virtually any other program and they remain on the Office Clipboard until you exit all Office programs.

To move or copy data, follow these steps:

1. **Select the data that you want to move or copy.**
2. **Perform one of the following tasks:**
   - **To move:** Choose Edit⇨Cut, click the Cut button, or press Ctrl+X. You can also right-click and choose Cut from the shortcut menu.
   - **To copy:** Choose Edit⇨Copy, click the Copy button, or press Ctrl+C. You can also right-click and choose Copy from the shortcut menu.
3. **Place the cursor at the point in your file where you want to move or copy the data.**
4. **Choose Edit⇨Paste, click the Paste button, press Ctrl+V, or right-click and choose Paste from the shortcut menu to paste the text into your document.**

You can also move or copy data by dragging and dropping. Select the data you want to move or copy, click it, and hold down the mouse button. Then drag it to a new location to move it, or hold down the Ctrl key and drag to copy it.

Data retains its formatting when you move or copy it. Italicized text remains *italicized;* 24-point text is still 24 points high. Suppose, however, that you want the data that you move or copy to look like neighboring text? In that case, click the Paste Options icon, which appears after you paste text (see Figure A-1). Click the icon to open a drop-down list from which you can choose one of the following options (only the first two options are available in some Office applications):

- ✦ **Keep Source Formatting:** The text keeps its original formatting (the default option).
- ✦ **Match Destination Formatting:** The text adopts the formatting of surrounding text.
- ✦ **Keep Text Only:** The text loses all its formatting — its boldfacing, for example, or any italics.
- ✦ **Apply Style or Formatting:** The Style and Formatting task pane opens so that you can choose a different format or a style for the text.

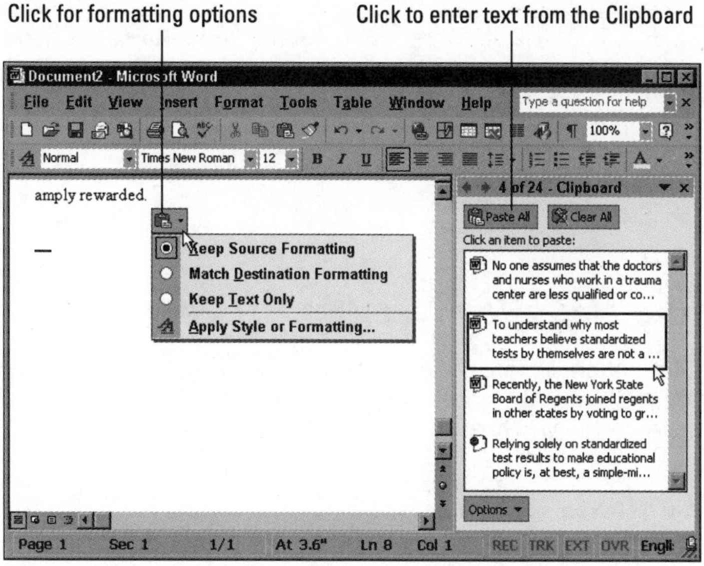

Figure A-1: Office offers many tools for copying and pasting data.

To paste data that you cut or copied some time ago, make use of the Office Clipboard. Place the cursor where you want the data to go and choose Edit⇨Office Clipboard. The Clipboard task pane opens (refer to Figure A-1) and shows you the last 24 items that were cut or copied to the Clipboard. Click an item to copy it into your document. (To remove an item from the Clipboard, click its down arrow to open its menu and choose Delete.)

Undoing Errors

The Undo command is wonderful because it literally undoes your last action in an Office application. Cleared text reappears. Moved text goes back to its original location. Undo tracks all actions since you opened the file you are working on. You can choose the Undo command in the following three ways:

✦ Choose Edit⇨Undo from the menu bar.

✦ Click the Undo button on the Standard toolbar.

✦ Press Ctrl+Z.

In case you're the finicky sort, Office also provides a Redo command, which enables you to redo whatever you undo. You can use the Redo command as follows:

✦ Choose Edit➪Redo from the menu bar.

✦ Click the Redo button on the Standard toolbar.

✦ Press Ctrl+Y.

Getting the Help You Need in Office

Office offers a bunch of different ways to get help, and one or two of them are really useful. Choose your favorite way or mix and match. The following sections tell you how.

Contents and index

The best way to get help is to choose Help➪Microsoft Help or press F1. A Help program opens at the side of your screen (see Figure A-2). It offers the following three tabs for finding the instructions that you need:

✦ **Contents:** A bunch of general topics. Double-click a Book icon, and it opens to more topics, each with a question mark beside its name. Click the question mark beside the topic that interests you, if general topics are your cup of tea.

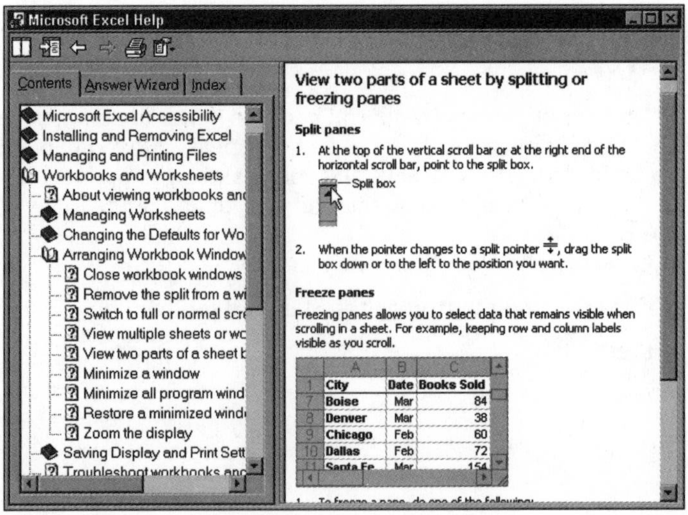

Figure A-2: Microsoft Excel is willing to help.

✦ **Answer Wizard:** Enables you to ask a question. Enter a question in the text boxes and click the Search button to get Help instructions.

✦ **Index:** Type the name of the topic that puzzles you in box 1. An alphabetical list of topics appears in box 2. Either click a keyword in box 2 or type a second topic name in box 1. After you click the Search button, topics that include the keywords you enter or choose appear in box 3. Click a topic in box 3 to read its Help instructions.

TIP

You can address a question to the Answer Wizard without opening the Help program. At the right side of the menu bar is a text box. Type a question there and press the Enter key. A list of questions appears. Click the one to which you need an answer to open the Help program and maybe get that answer.

The Help window is designed so that you can keep it open, read instructions, and continue to work in the program you're in at the same time. You can take advantage of the following buttons in the Help window:

✦ **Untile/Auto Tile:** Untile squeezes the program window into the space to the right of the Help window. Auto Tile, the button's name after you click Untile, enables the Help window to overlap the program window.

✦ **Hide/Show:** Hides or displays the three Help window tabs: Contents, Answer Wizard, and Index.

✦ **Back:** Takes you to the previous Help window.

✦ **Forward:** Returns you to instructions you backed away from earlier when you clicked the Back button.

✦ **Print:** Enables you to print Help window instructions.

✦ **Options:** Displays a drop-down list of options — things that you can do with the Help windows.

Close the Help window by clicking its Close button.

What's this?

Another useful way to get help is to choose Help⇨What's This? or press Shift+F1.The pointer changes into an arrow with a question mark beside it. Click this quizzical cursor on the menu command that mystifies you. That's right — just choose the command as though you really meant to activate it.

You also find a What's This? Help command in dialog boxes. Click the question mark in the upper-right corner of a dialog box and then click a dialog box option. An explanation of the option appears on-screen, as shown in Figure A-3.

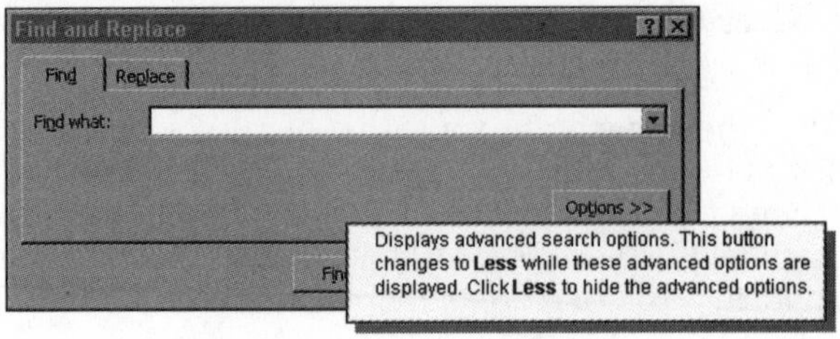

Figure A-3: Getting Help with the What's This? button.

Help from the Internet

Yet another way to seek help is to find it on the Internet. Choose Help⇨Office on the Web to go to the official Microsoft Office Web site, where you can get advice about using each Office product and even submit questions to Microsoft technicians (but don't expect an answer right away). Open your Web browser before you choose this command.

The Office Assistant

In keeping with its goal of making computers as much fun to use as watching Saturday morning cartoons, Microsoft offers the Office Assistant. (If the Office Assistant isn't already on-screen, choose Help⇨Show Office Assistant.) The Office Assistant appears in a corner of the screen along with a bubble caption into which you can type a question (see Figure A-4). Type your question, click Search, and you see a handful of Help topics. By clicking a topic, you can open the Help program and get instructions.

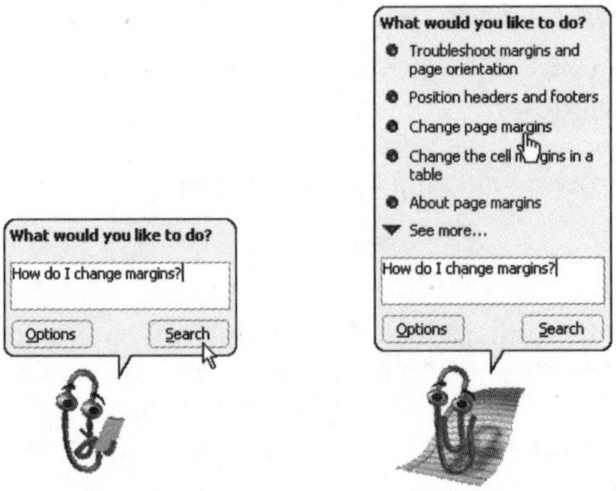

Figure A-4: Getting Help from the Office Assistant.

The Office Assistant provides the following types of Help:

- ✦ It watches you work and tells you if the program offers a more efficient way to perform an operation. A yellow light bulb appears next to the Assistant (or in the Microsoft Help toolbar button) if it has a tip for you. Click the light bulb to read the tip.
- ✦ It provides automatic Help with certain tasks.
- ✦ It responds to natural language questions. Just type your question in the Assistant's text box and click Search.

If you find that the Office Assistant is sometimes too helpful and it gets distracting, customize it to your liking: Click the Options button on the bubble caption. The Office Assistant dialog box appears with the Options tab selected. To turn the Assistant off, deselect the Use the Office Assistant check box. (To turn the Assistant on again, select the Help⇨Show the Office Assistant command.)

To exchange one Office Assistant character for another, follow these steps:

1. **Right-click the Office Assistant and choose Choose Assistant from the shortcut menu.**

   The Gallery tab of the Office Assistant dialog box appears.

2. **Browse the Gallery by clicking Next or Back until you find an Assistant that you like.**

   Figure A-5 shows the animated figures that you can choose from.

3. **Click OK to accept your choice of Office Assistant.**

Figure A-5: Choose among these Office Assistant figures.

Appendix B: Printing an Office Document

In This Appendix

- Previewing before you print
- Choosing some options for your printing
- Printing a document
- Canceling your printing

Printing an Office document can prove as easy as clicking a button or as complicated as going through a bunch of menus and dialog boxes to get what you want. Fortunately, most of the printing chores in Office applications are similar, so you can often go from Excel to Word to Publisher, for example, without missing a beat.

This appendix introduces you to the basics of printing in Office. If you have some special printing considerations for a particular application (such as printing noncontiguous ranges in Excel or something fun like that), make sure that you check out the application's Help files. You can read all about getting Help in Office simply by flipping back to Appendix A.

Previewing What You Print

Before you print a document, do yourself a big favor by *previewing* it. That way, you can catch errors before you send it through the printer and waste 1, 2, 5, or 20 sheets of paper. For that matter, preview your documents from time to time to make sure that you laid them out correctly.

To preview a document, follow these steps:

1. **Open the document you're about to print.**

2. **Choose File⇨Print Preview or click the Print Preview button on the toolbar.**

   A panoramic picture of your document appears on the Preview screen (see Figure B-1).

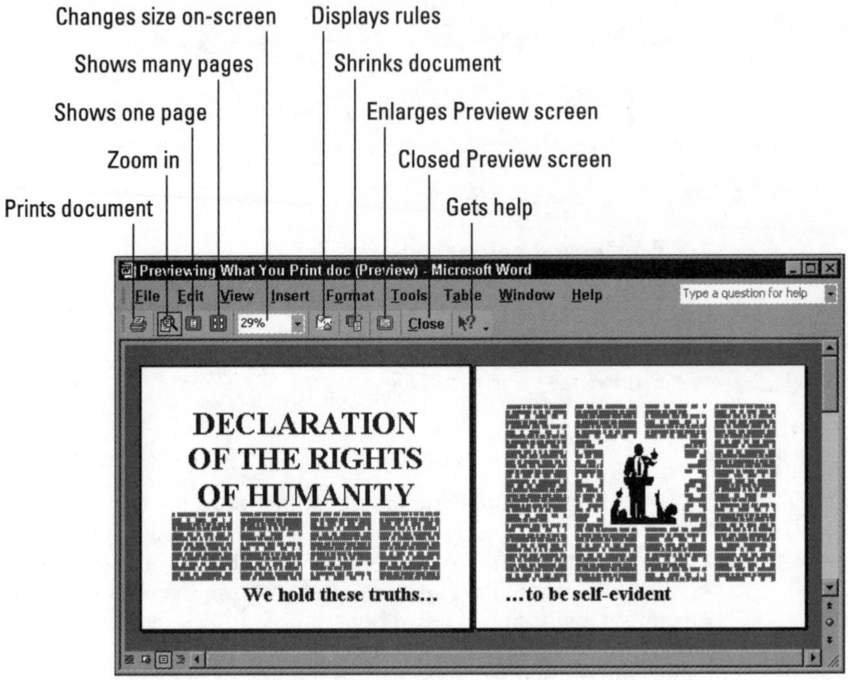

Figure B-1: Previewing a document in Word.

3. **Use these buttons as well as the scroll bar on the Preview screen to get a better look at your document:**

   - Click part of the document to zoom in and examine closely. The pointer, which previously looked like a magnifying glass with a plus sign in it, now displays a minus sign where the plus sign was. Click again to zoom out and get back to the Preview screen. If your pointer doesn't look like a magnifying glass, click the Magnifier button on the Print Preview toolbar.
   - Click the One Page or Multiple Pages button to view one or several pages at once.
   - Click the Zoom Control menu and either enter a percentage in the menu and press the Enter key or choose a different percentage from the menu to see more of a page. You can also click one of the Width settings on the Zoom menu to see a page or pages in different ways.
   - Click the Shrink to Fit button, and your document shrinks a bit if it can. Choose this option if the last page has only a few lines of text and you want to save a piece of paper.
   - The Full Screen button removes the menu bars and ruler so that you can really get the "big picture" of a page.

4. **Click Close if you need to go back to the document and make changes; otherwise, click the Print button.**

Choosing Page Options

You don't need to print exclusively on standard 8.5 x 11 paper; you can print on legal-size paper and other sizes of paper as well. A Word newsletter with an unusual shape really stands out in a crowd and gets people's attention. Or maybe your Excel spreadsheet begs to fit across a big page. You can also sometimes choose the direction in which you want to print on the page (portrait or landscape).

REMEMBER: Office applications share many options, but each program also has unique needs and demands. Make sure that you explore what each program can do for you.

To choose page options, follow these steps:

1. **Choose File⇨Page Setup.**

   The Page Setup dialog box appears.

2. **If you don't see page setup options right away, click the tab where you find the various paper options (generally labeled as Page, Paper, or Printer & Paper depending on the application you're using).**

3. **Pick and choose your paper options, as follows:**

   - Choose a setting from the Size drop-down list (as shown in Access in Figure B-2). If none of the settings suits you, you can choose a size from a drop-down list (as shown in Word in Figure B-3) or perhaps scale your document (in Excel). In Publisher, you can choose your layout and your fold (see Figure B-4).

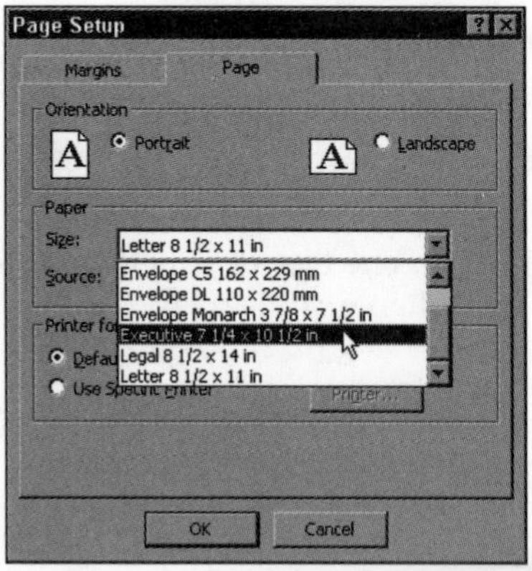

Figure B-2: Access enables you to choose a paper size for printing.

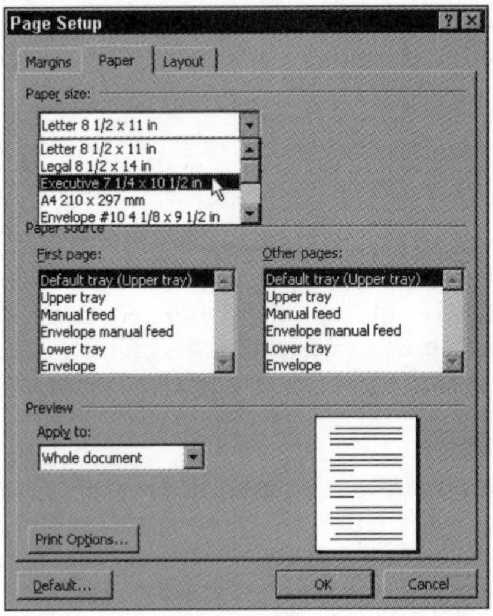

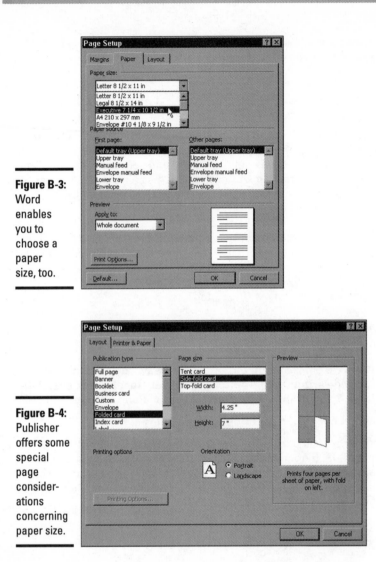

Figure B-3: Word enables you to choose a paper size, too.

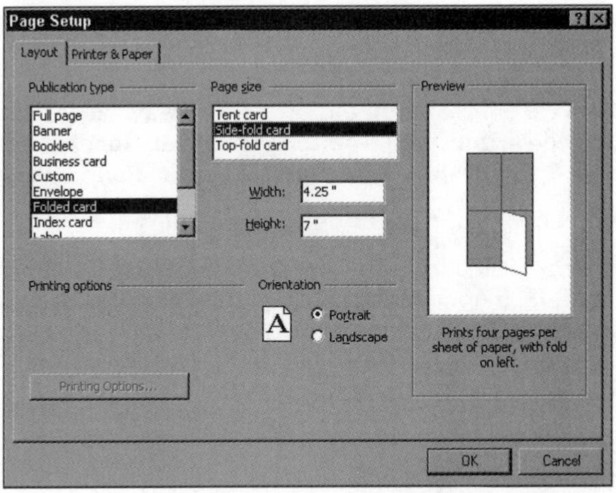

Figure B-4: Publisher offers some special page consider-ations concerning paper size.

- Select either Portrait (tall pages) or Landscape (wide pages) by selecting an option.
- If you keep legal-size paper in one tray of your printer and standard-size paper in another, for example, find a Paper Source drop-down list or tab in the Page Setup dialog box and choose the appropriate setting from the drop-down list.

- Some applications also enable you to adjust your margins from the Page Setup dialog box. (A *margin* is the blank space on the side of the printed page. The wider the margins are, the less space is available for printing.) In Access, for example, you can control all four page margins. Just look for the Margins tab and make your adjustments (see Figure B-5) by either typing a number or using the spinner arrows to choose a number.

4. **Click OK after you finish playing around with your page setup options.**

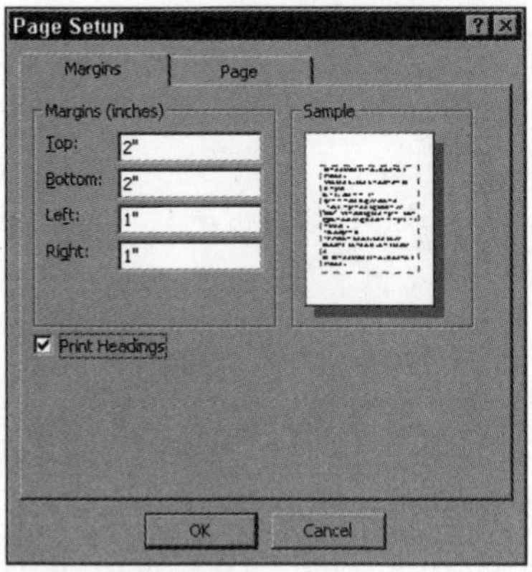

Figure B-5: You can adjust four margins on your page in Access.

Printing a Document

The fastest way to print a document is to click the Print button on the Standard toolbar. Go this route if you want to print the entire thing from start to finish.

To print part of a document, selected text in a document, the entire thing, or even unusual things such as comments and summary text, follow these steps:

1. **Choose File⇨Print (or press Ctrl+P) to open the Print dialog box (see Figure B-6).**
2. **If you don't see your printer name in the Name text box of the Printer section, use the drop-down list to select it.**
3. **Enter the number of copies that you want in a Number of Copies text box.**

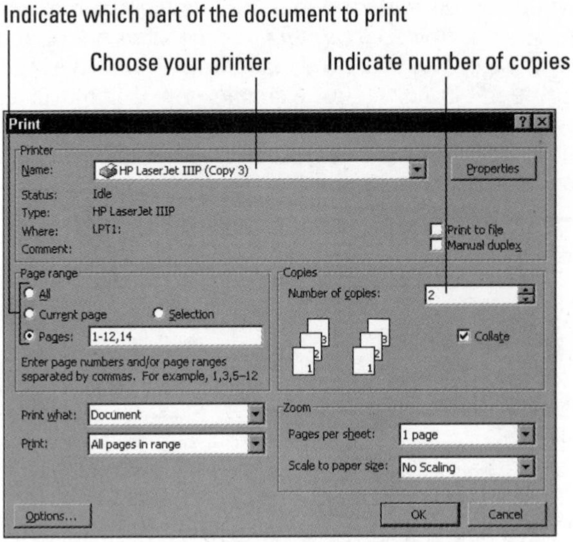

Figure B-6: The Print dialog box in Word.

4. **Tell the application how much of the document to print by looking for a Print Range area in this dialog box and clicking the appropriate radio button (and filling in a range if necessary).**

   Depending on the application, you can indicate possibilities such as all, the current page, the pages that you specify, the portion that's currently selected, and so on.

5. **(Optional) Select the Print to File check box near the top of the dialog box to copy the document to a print file if you plan to take your document to a print shop for printing.**
6. **Click OK.**

A Print dialog box also offers options for collating your print job. If you're printing more than one copy of a document with many pages and you don't want the application to collate copies, deselect the Collate check box. If you print three three-page documents, for example, the pages come out of the printer 111, 222, 333, instead of 123, 123, 123.

Canceling a Print Job

If your printer directly connects to your computer, you get two chances to cancel a print job. The first chance is after you see a small dialog box telling you that your table (or report or whatever) is printing. The dialog box includes a Cancel button that you can click to cancel the print job.

The printer doesn't stop printing immediately, however, and may print out another page or two, but clicking the Cancel button stops the application from sending more information to the printer.

If you want to stop a print job after the dialog box with the Cancel button disappears, you must resort to the fallback method — using the Windows Printer window. If any document is printing in Windows, a small printer appears in the *system tray* in the taskbar. (The tray usually appears at the right end of the taskbar, near the clock.) Double-click that small printer icon to display the Windows Printer window — a window that contains the name of your printer on the title bar and lists current print jobs.

If the printer you use is on a network, you can't always use the Printer window to cancel a print job. You need to identify your network guru (or someone who knows how to cancel print jobs) to find out how to cancel a print job on your network.

To cancel a print job from the Printer window, follow these steps:

1. **Right-click the name of the document that you want to cancel to display the shortcut menu.**
2. **Choose Cancel Printing from the shortcut menu that appears.**

   The printer mercifully stops printing (when it's good and ready).

Index

Symbols & Numbers

A

B

C

Continued

D

E

F

G

H

I

J

K

L

M

N

O

P

Q

Continued

R

S

T

U

V

W

Y

Z

Notes

Notes